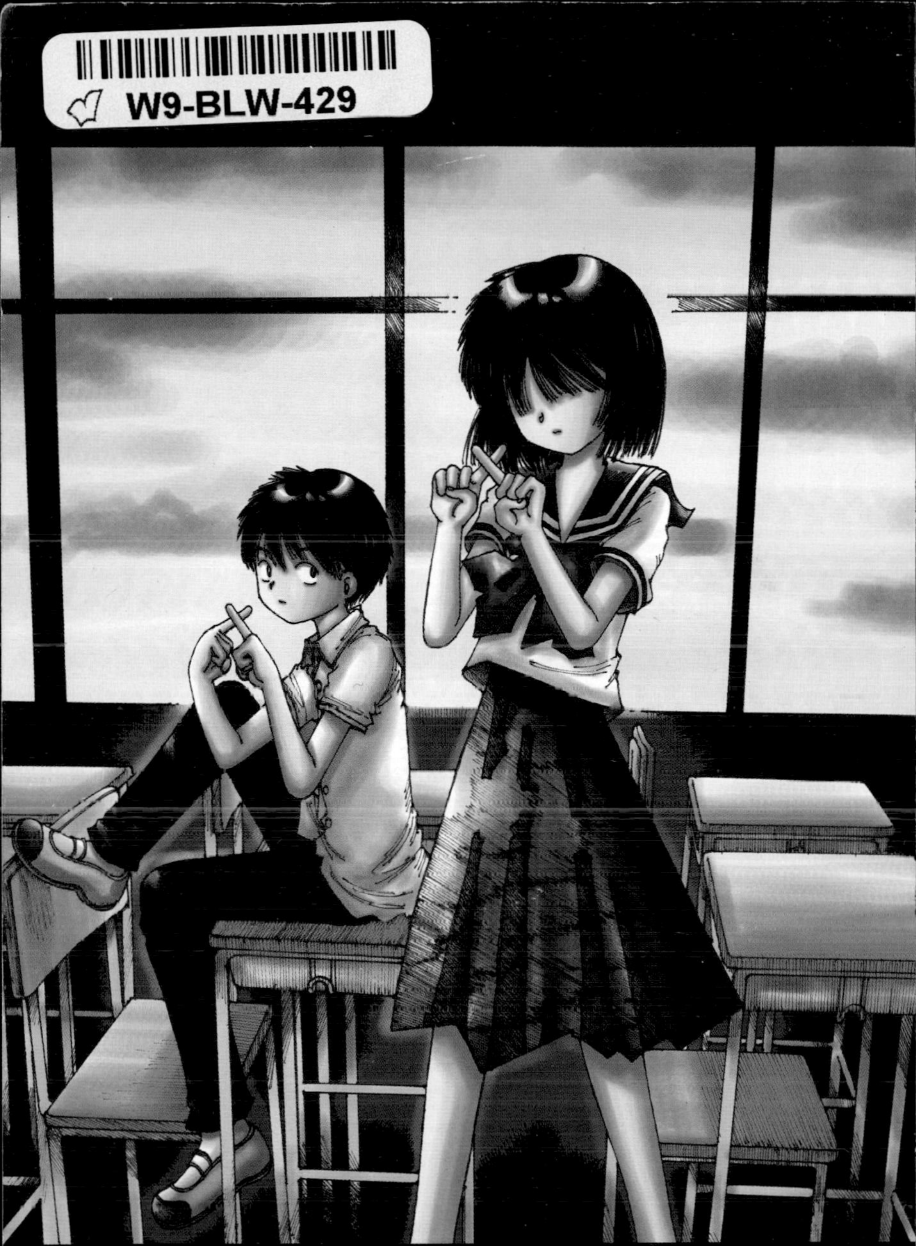

CONTENTS

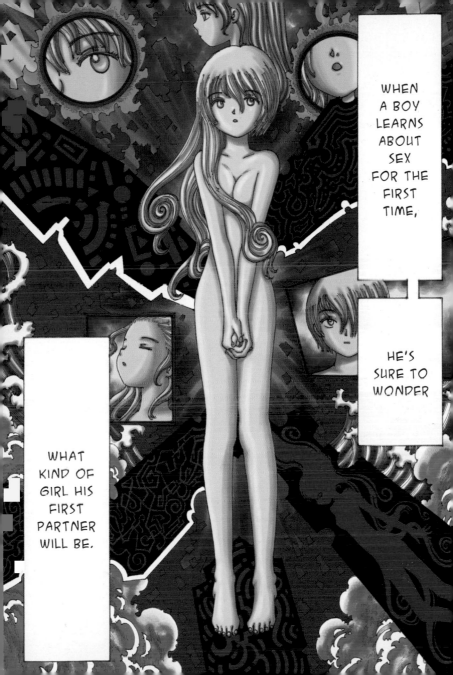

WHEN A BOY LEARNS ABOUT SEX FOR THE FIRST TIME,

HE'S SURE TO WONDER

WHAT KIND OF GIRL HIS FIRST PARTNER WILL BE.

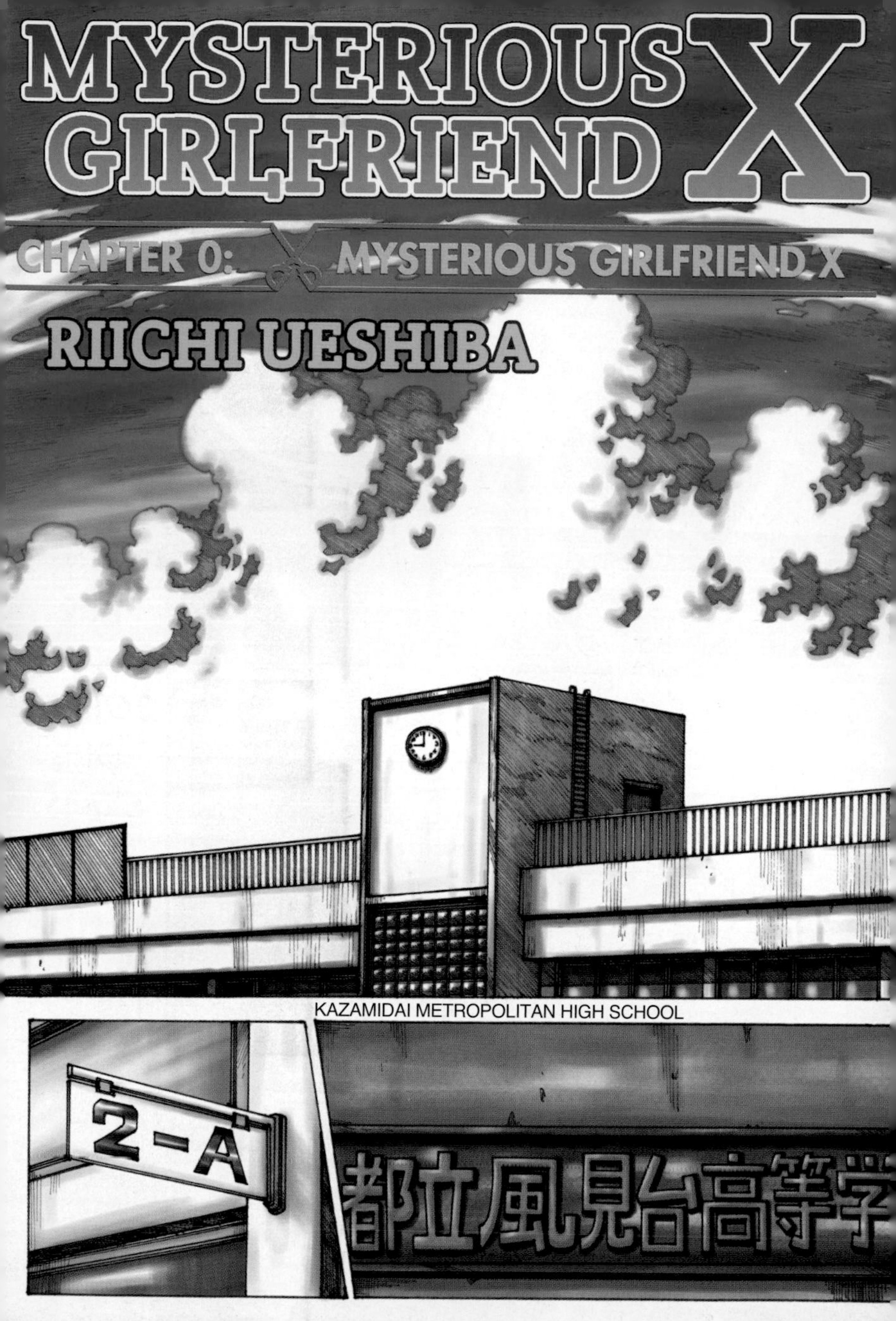
MYSTERIOUS GIRLFRIEND X
CHAPTER 0: MYSTERIOUS GIRLFRIEND X
RIICHI UESHIBA
KAZAMIDAI METROPOLITAN HIGH SCHOOL
都立風見台高等学
2-A

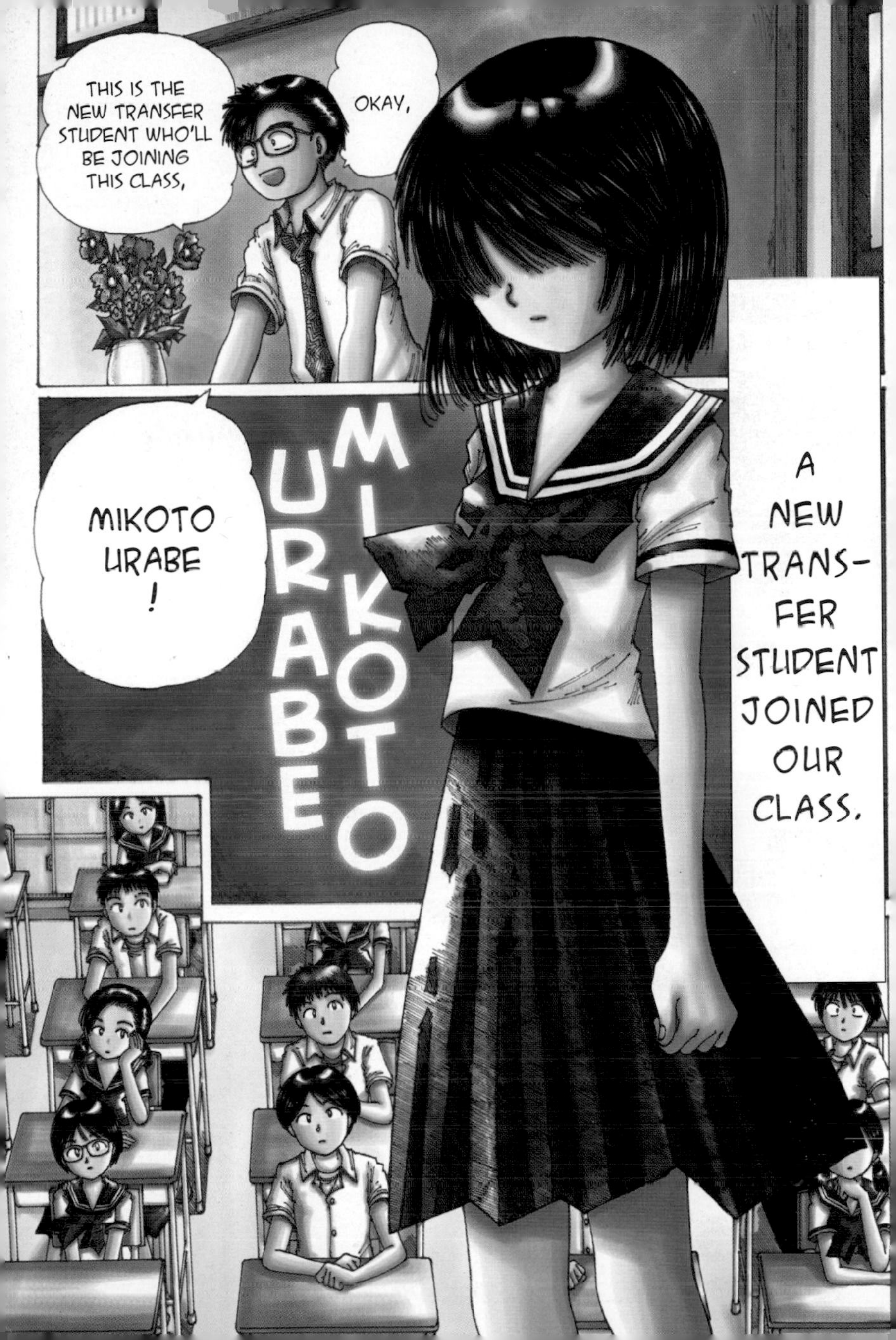
A NEW TRANSFER STUDENT JOINED OUR CLASS.
OKAY,
THIS IS THE NEW TRANSFER STUDENT WHO'LL BE JOINING THIS CLASS,
MIKOTO URABE!
MIKOTO URABE

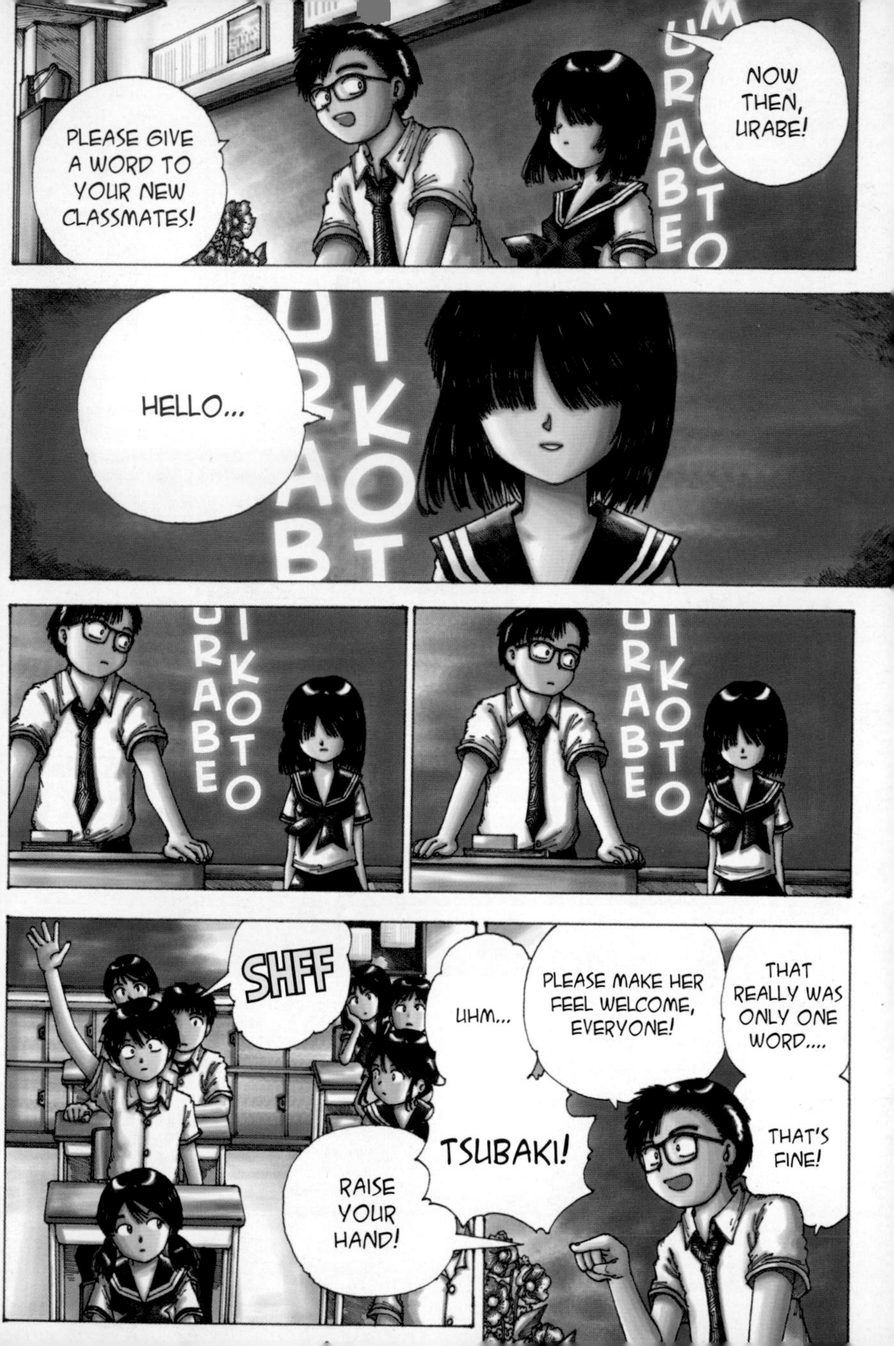
NOW THEN, URABE!
PLEASE GIVE A WORD TO YOUR NEW CLASSMATES!
HELLO...
THAT REALLY WAS ONLY ONE WORD....
THAT'S FINE!
PLEASE MAKE HER FEEL WELCOME, EVERYONE!
UHM...
TSUBAKI!
RAISE YOUR HAND!
SHFF

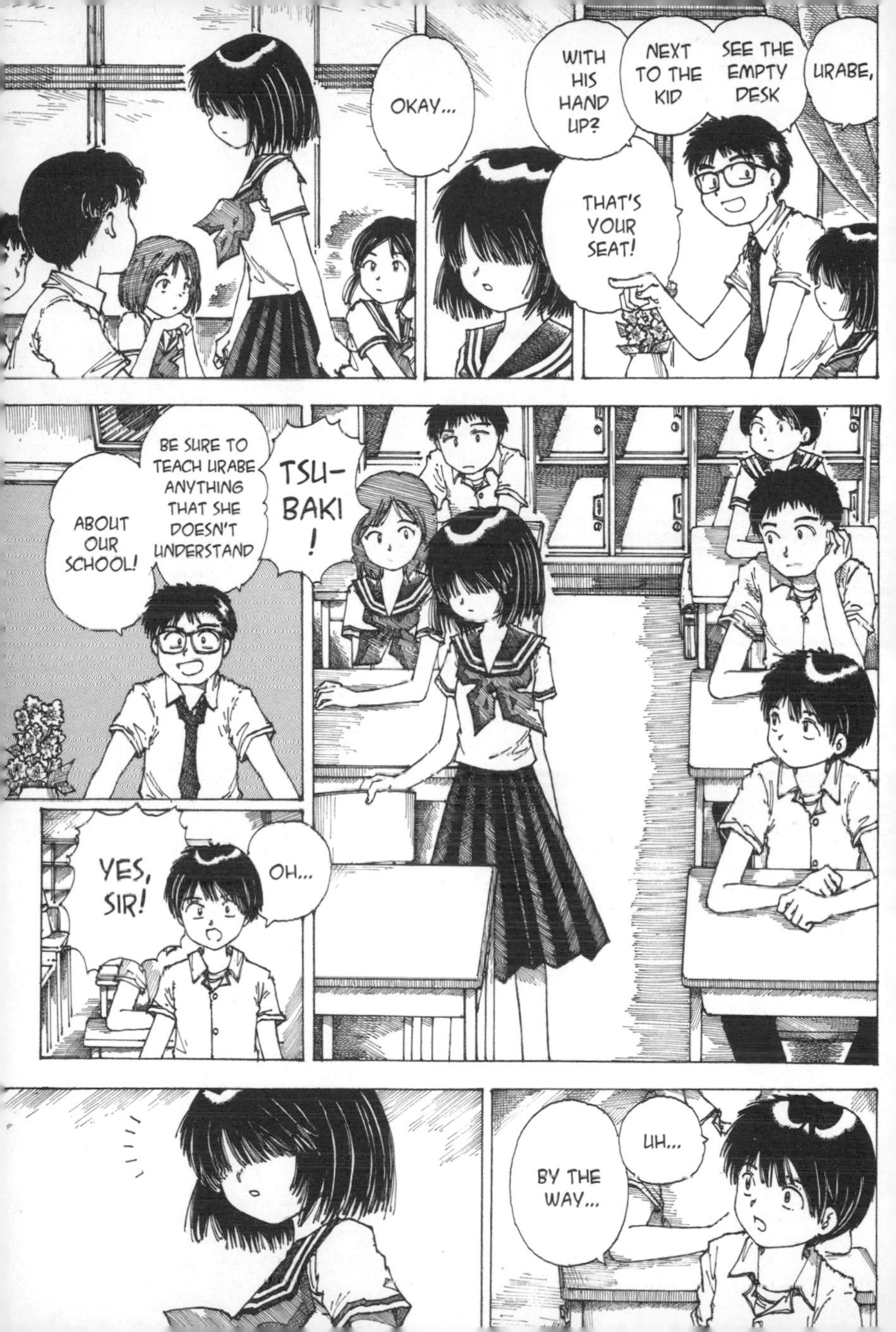
URABE,
SEE THE EMPTY DESK
NEXT TO THE KID
WITH HIS HAND UP?
THAT'S YOUR SEAT!
OKAY...
TSU-BAKI!
BE SURE TO TEACH URABE ANYTHING THAT SHE DOESN'T UNDERSTAND
ABOUT OUR SCHOOL!
OH...
YES, SIR!
UH...
BY THE WAY...

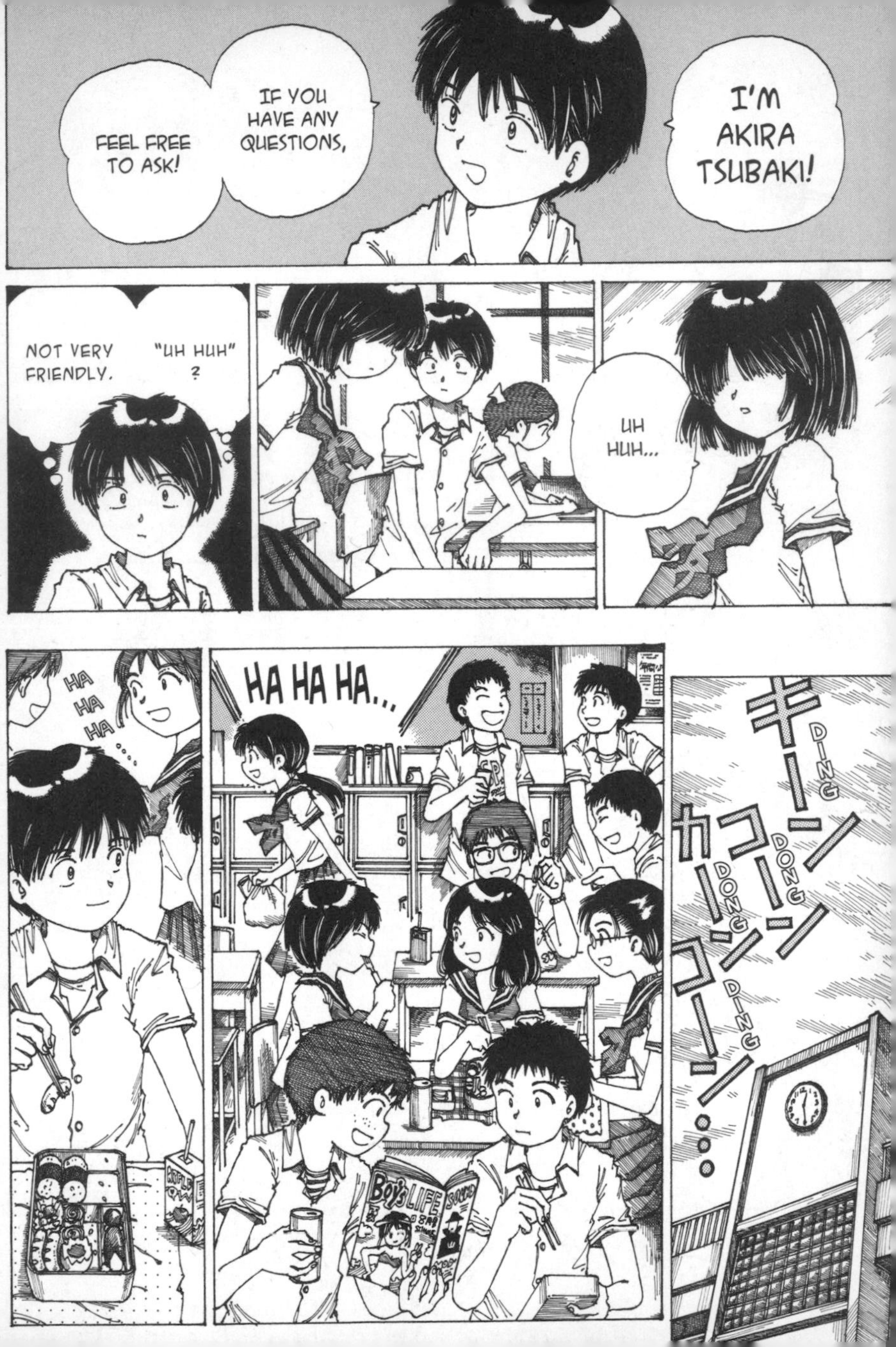
I'M AKIRA TSUBAKI!
IF YOU HAVE ANY QUESTIONS,
FEEL FREE TO ASK!
UH HUH...
"UH HUH" ?
NOT VERY FRIENDLY.
キーンコーン
DING DONG
カーンコーン
DONG DING
HA HA HA...
Boy's LIFE
HA HA HA ...

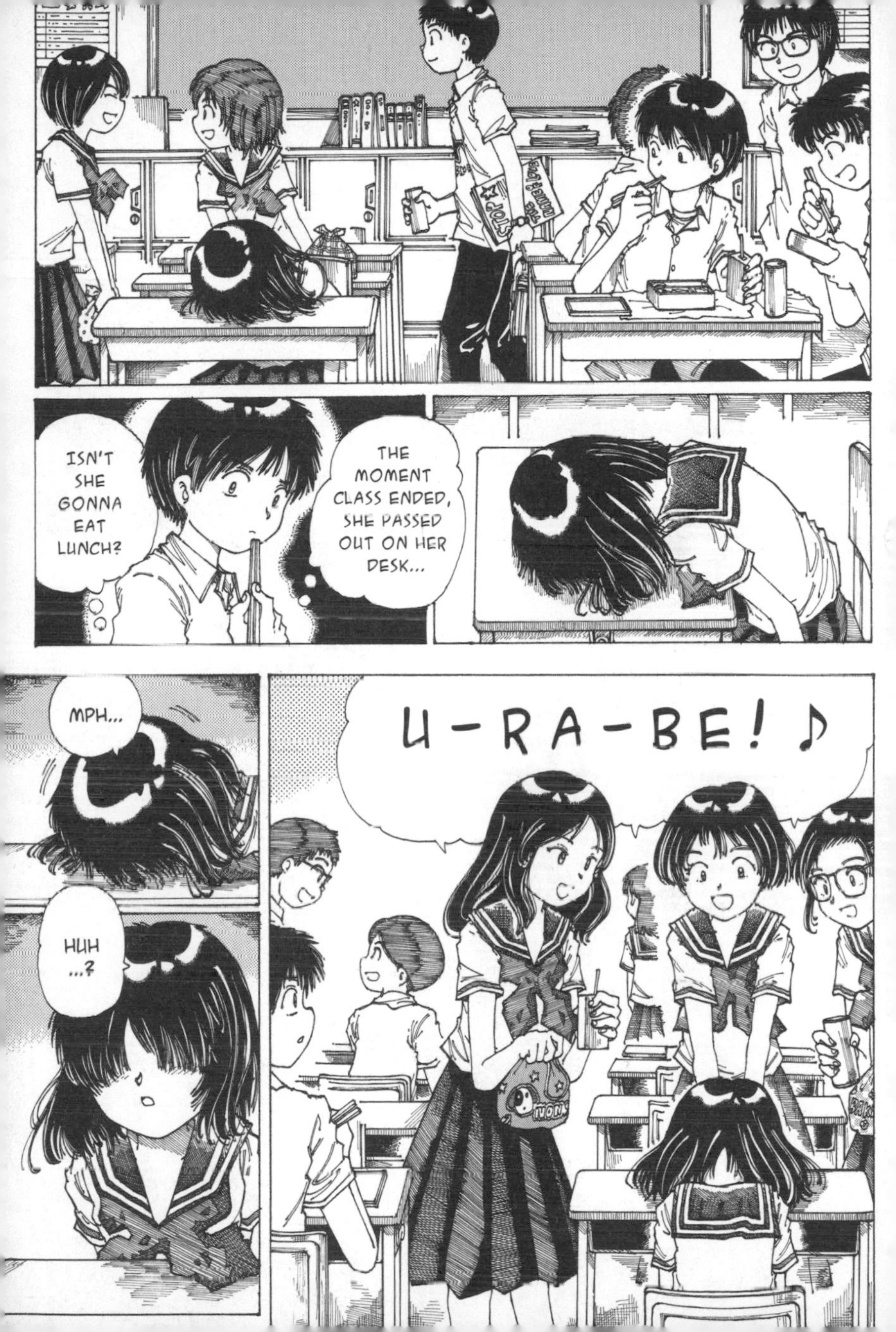
THE MOMENT CLASS ENDED, SHE PASSED OUT ON HER DESK...
ISN'T SHE GONNA EAT LUNCH?
U-RA-BE! ♪
MPH...
HUH ...?

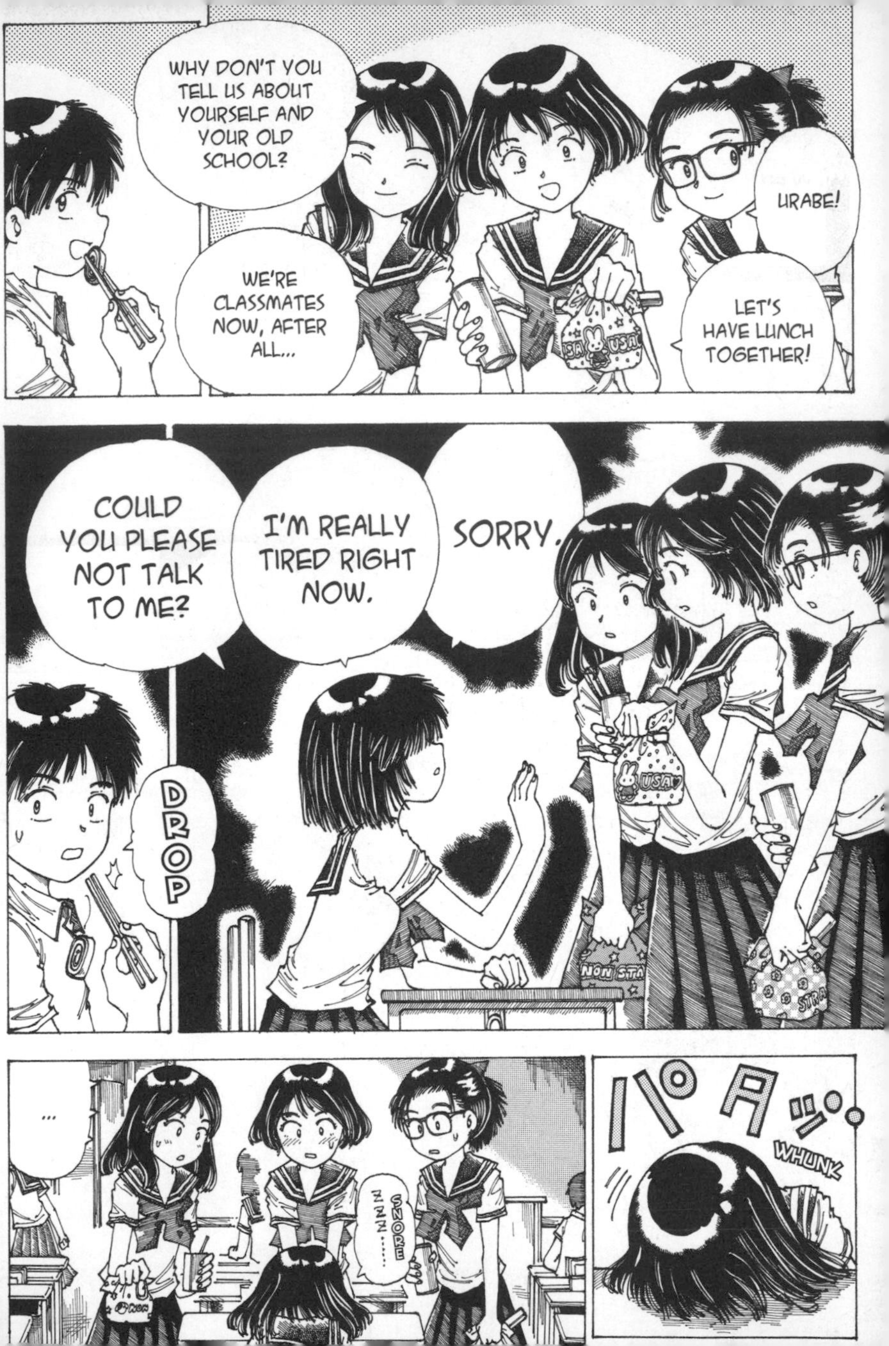
URABE!
LET'S HAVE LUNCH TOGETHER!
WHY DON'T YOU TELL US ABOUT YOURSELF AND YOUR OLD SCHOOL?
WE'RE CLASSMATES NOW, AFTER ALL...
SORRY.
I'M REALLY TIRED RIGHT NOW.
COULD YOU PLEASE NOT TALK TO ME?
DROP
パタッ。
WHUNK
SNORE
ZZZ......
...

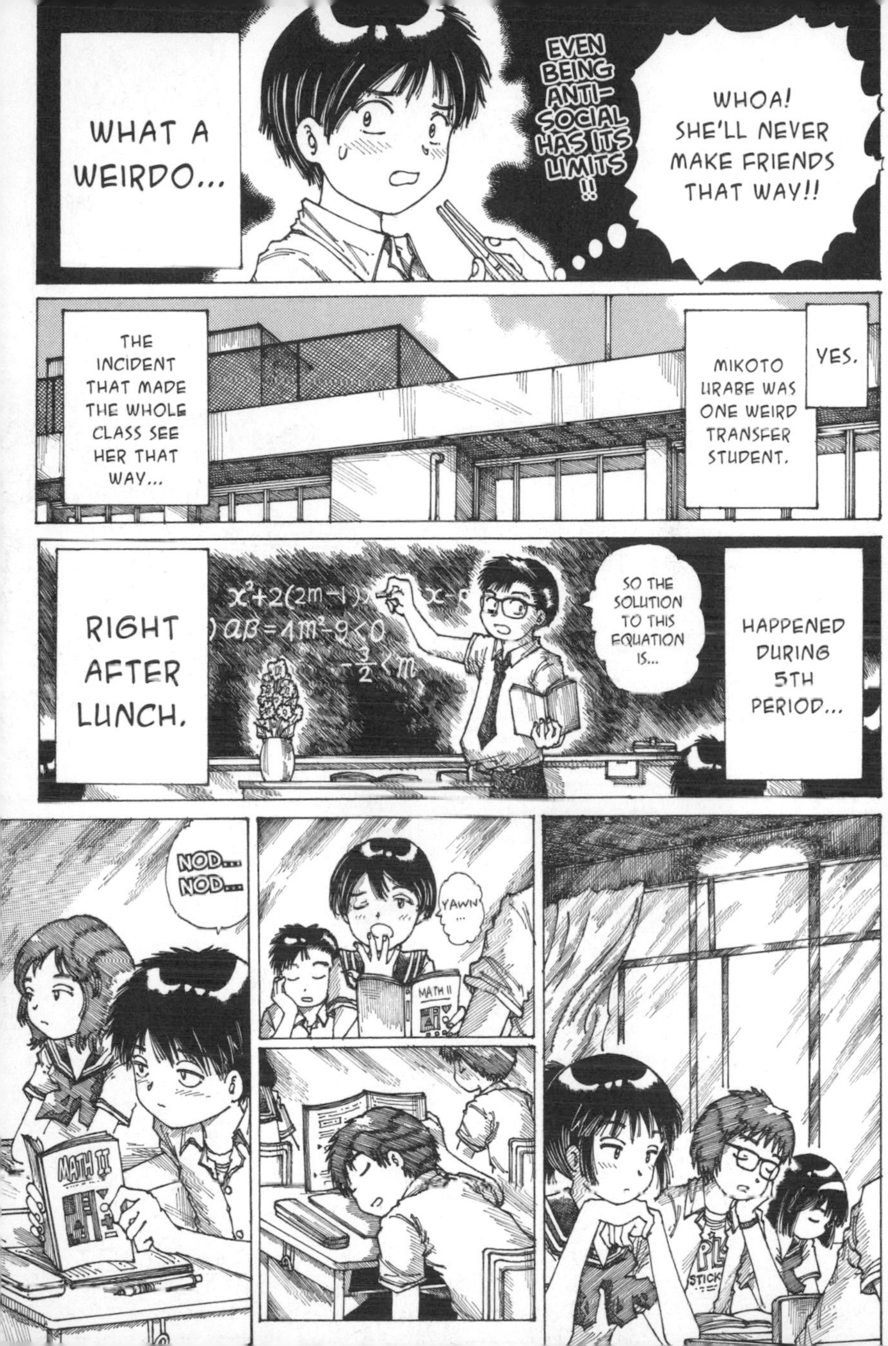
WHOA! SHE'LL NEVER MAKE FRIENDS THAT WAY!!
EVEN BEING ANTI-SOCIAL HAS ITS LIMITS!!
WHAT A WEIRDO...
YES.
MIKOTO URABE WAS ONE WEIRD TRANSFER STUDENT.
THE INCIDENT THAT MADE THE WHOLE CLASS SEE HER THAT WAY...
HAPPENED DURING 5TH PERIOD...
SO THE SOLUTION TO THIS EQUATION IS...
RIGHT AFTER LUNCH.
YAWN...
MATH II
NOD... NOD...
MATH II

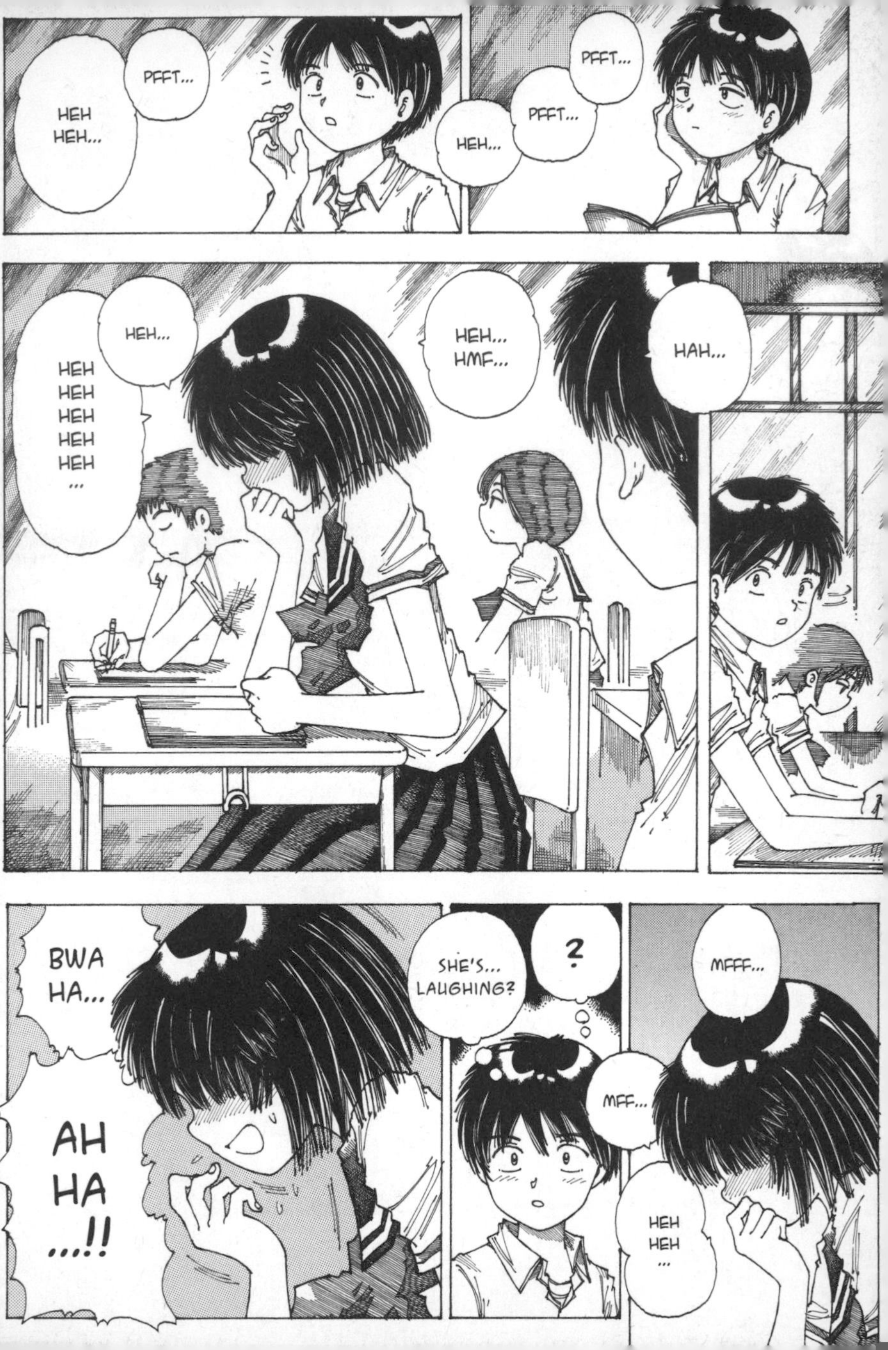
PFFT...
PFFT...
HEH...
PFFT...
HEH HEH...
HAH...
HEH... HMF...
HEH...
HEH HEH HEH HEH HEH ...
MFFF...
MFF...
HEH HEH ...
?
SHE'S... LAUGHING?
BWA HA...
AH HA ...!!

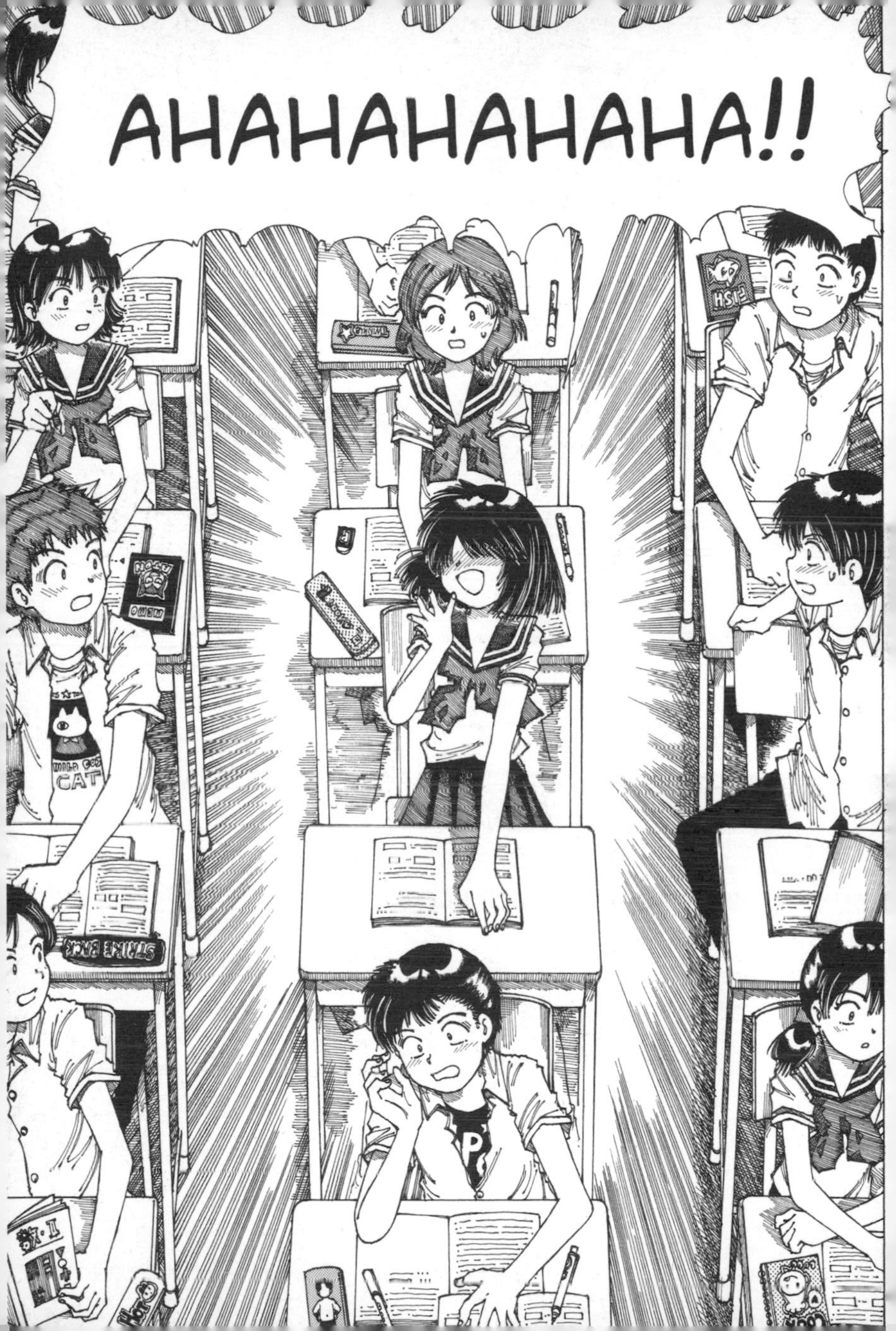
AHAHAHAHAHA!!

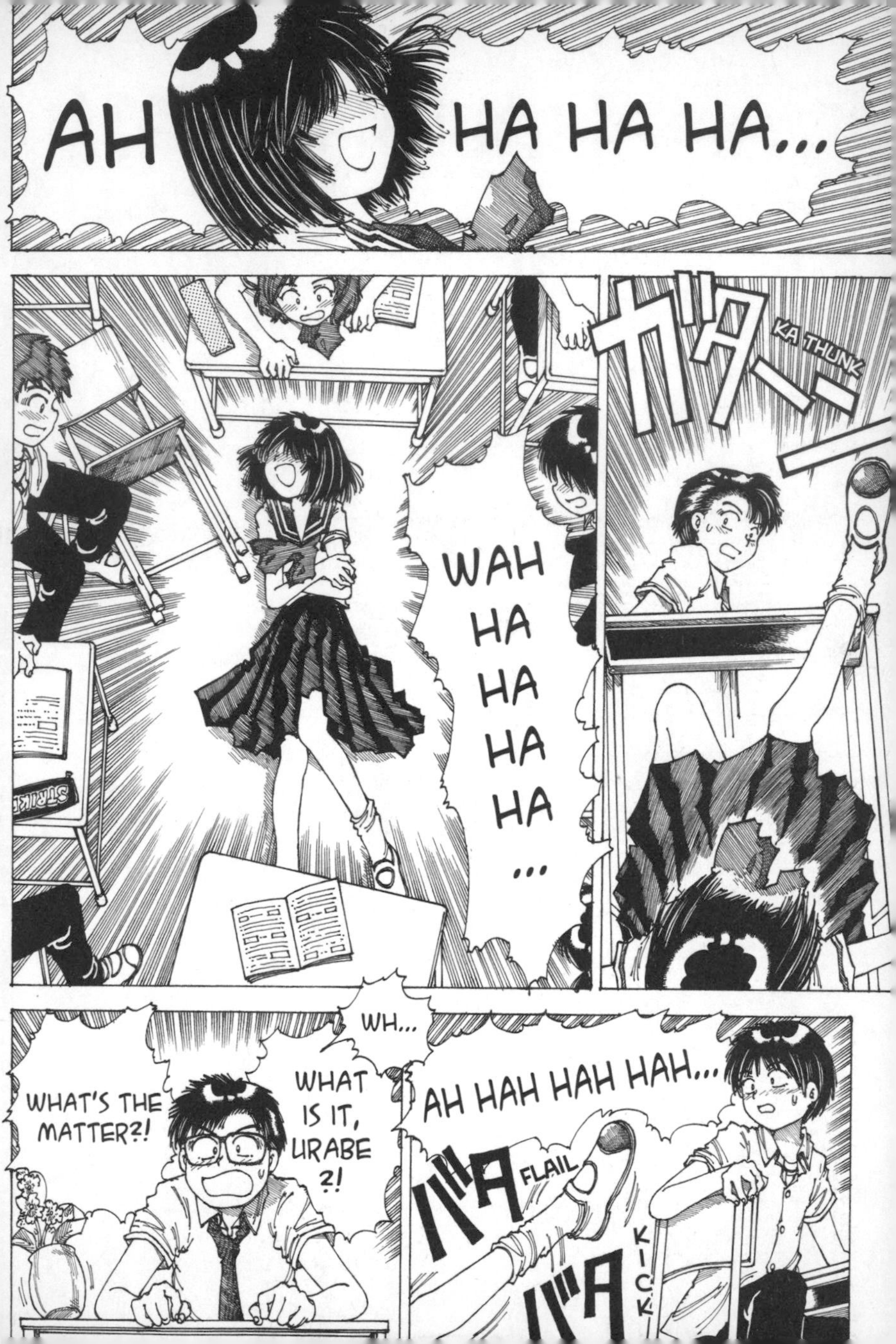
AH HA HA HA HA...
KA THUNK
WAH HA HA HA HA HA ...
AH HAH HAH HAH...
FLAIL
KICK
WH...
WHAT IS IT, URABE?!
WHAT'S THE MATTER?!

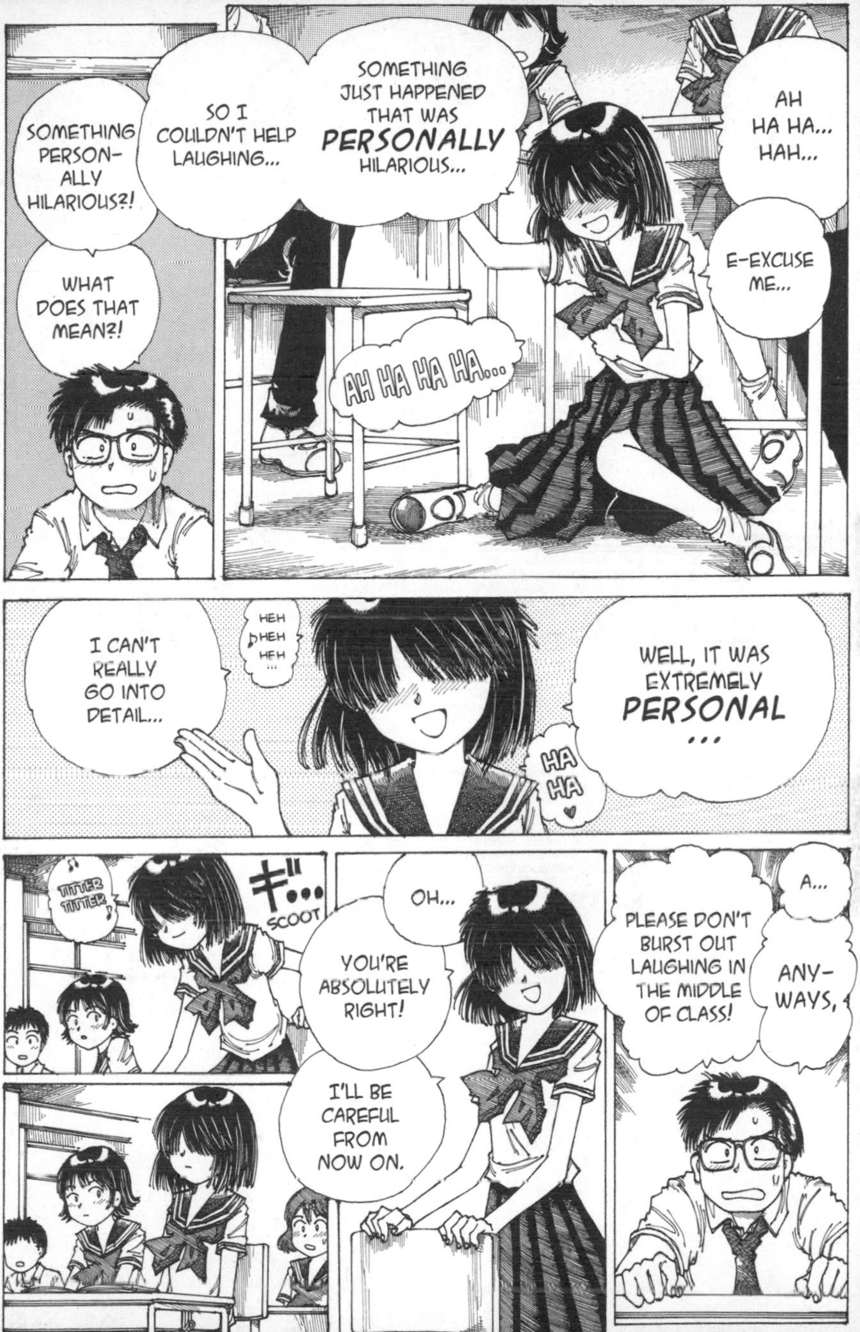
AH HA HA... HAH...
E-EXCUSE ME...
SOMETHING JUST HAPPENED THAT WAS PERSONALLY HILARIOUS...
SO I COULDN'T HELP LAUGHING...
AH HA HA HA...
SOMETHING PERSON-ALLY HILARIOUS?!
WHAT DOES THAT MEAN?!
WELL, IT WAS EXTREMELY PERSONAL ...
HA HA
HEH HEH HEH ...
I CAN'T REALLY GO INTO DETAIL...
A...
ANY-WAYS,
PLEASE DON'T BURST OUT LAUGHING IN THE MIDDLE OF CLASS!
OH...
YOU'RE ABSOLUTELY RIGHT!
I'LL BE CAREFUL FROM NOW ON.
ギ...
SCOOT
TITTER TITTER

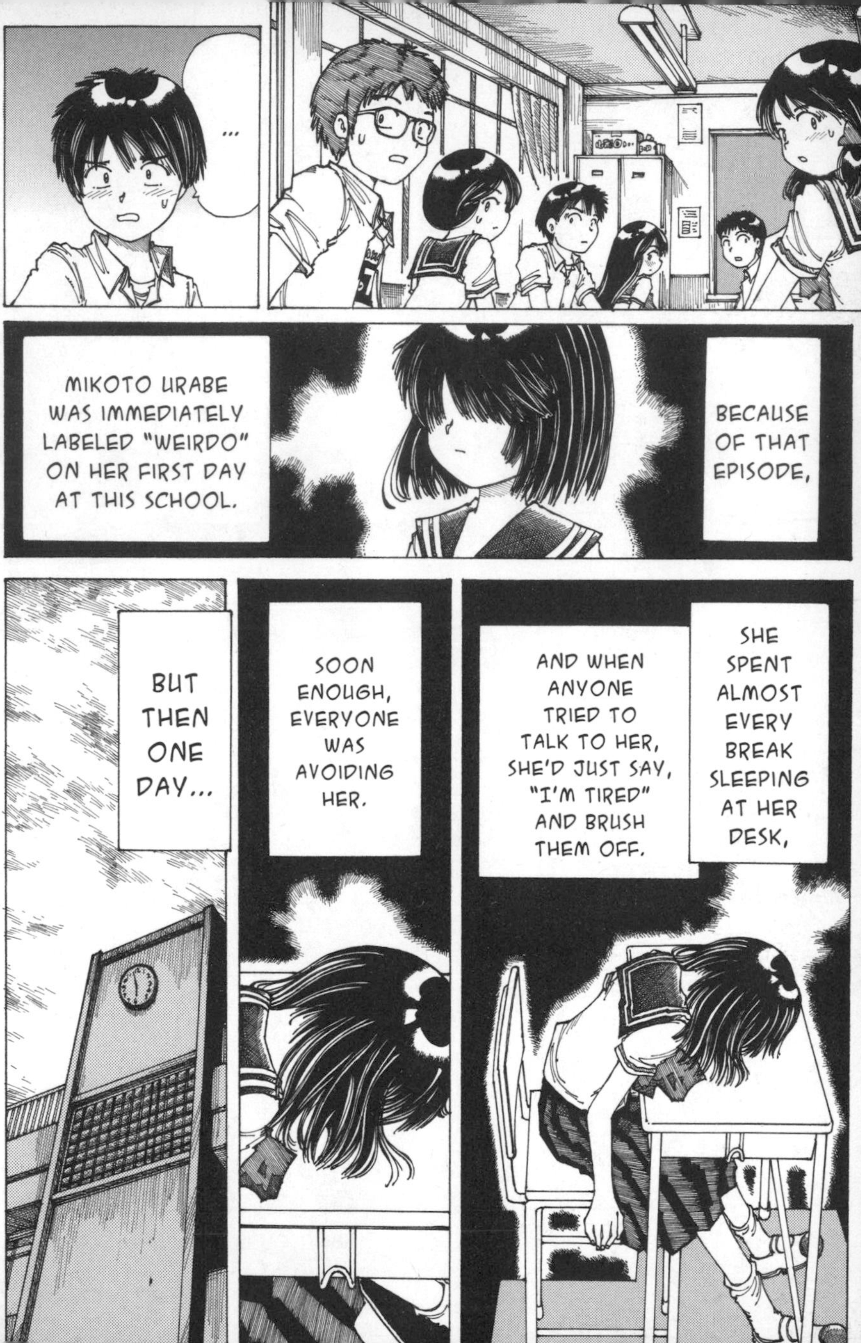
...
BECAUSE OF THAT EPISODE,
MIKOTO URABE WAS IMMEDIATELY LABELED "WEIRDO" ON HER FIRST DAY AT THIS SCHOOL.
SHE SPENT ALMOST EVERY BREAK SLEEPING AT HER DESK,
AND WHEN ANYONE TRIED TO TALK TO HER, SHE'D JUST SAY, "I'M TIRED" AND BRUSH THEM OFF.
SOON ENOUGH, EVERYONE WAS AVOIDING HER.
BUT THEN ONE DAY...

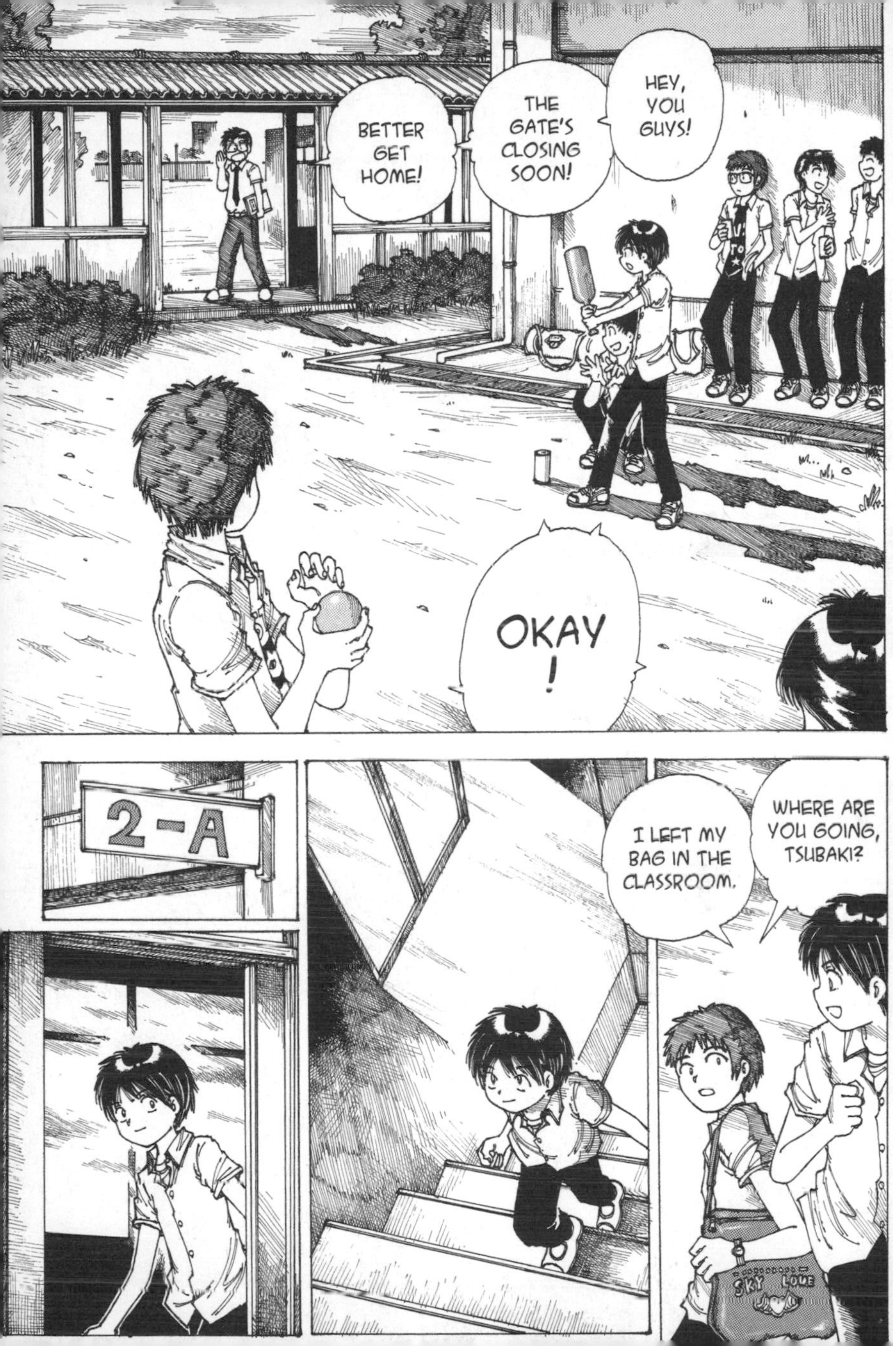
HEY, YOU GUYS!
THE GATE'S CLOSING SOON!
BETTER GET HOME!
OKAY !
WHERE ARE YOU GOING, TSUBAKI?
I LEFT MY BAG IN THE CLASSROOM.
SKY LOVE
2-A

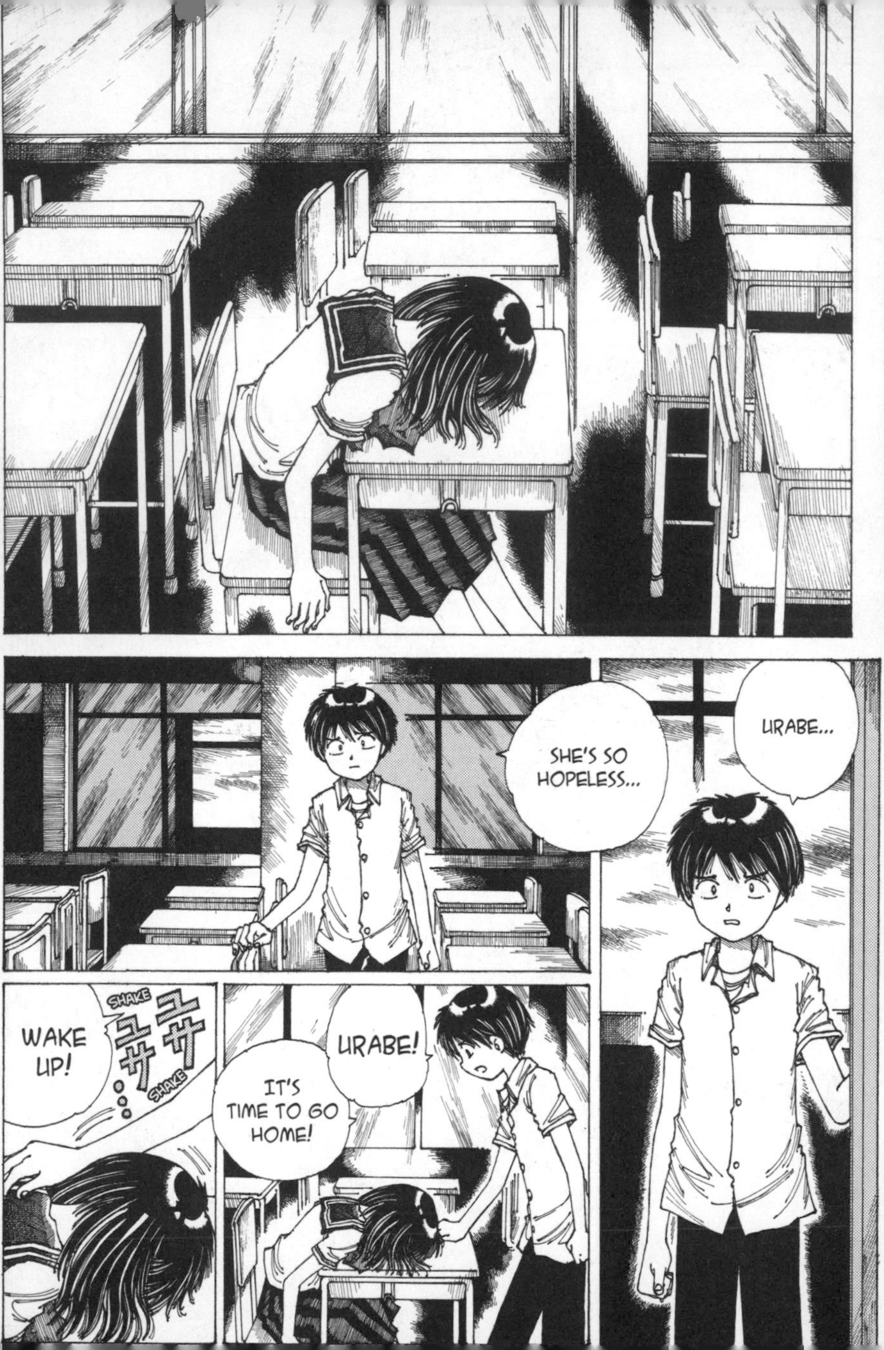
URABE...
SHE'S SO HOPELESS...
URABE!
IT'S TIME TO GO HOME!
ユサユサ
SHAKE
SHAKE
WAKE UP!

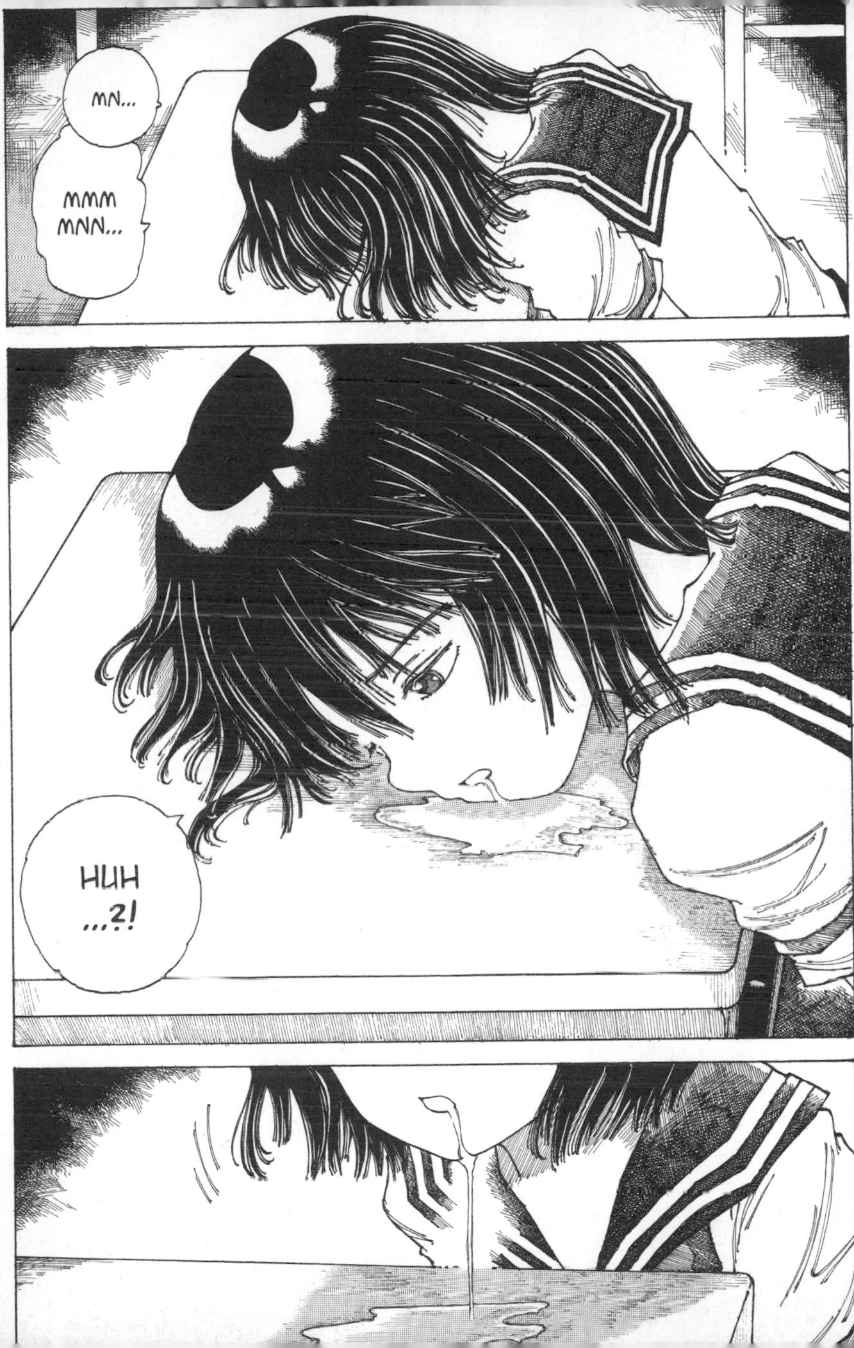
MN...
MMM MNN...
HUH ...?!

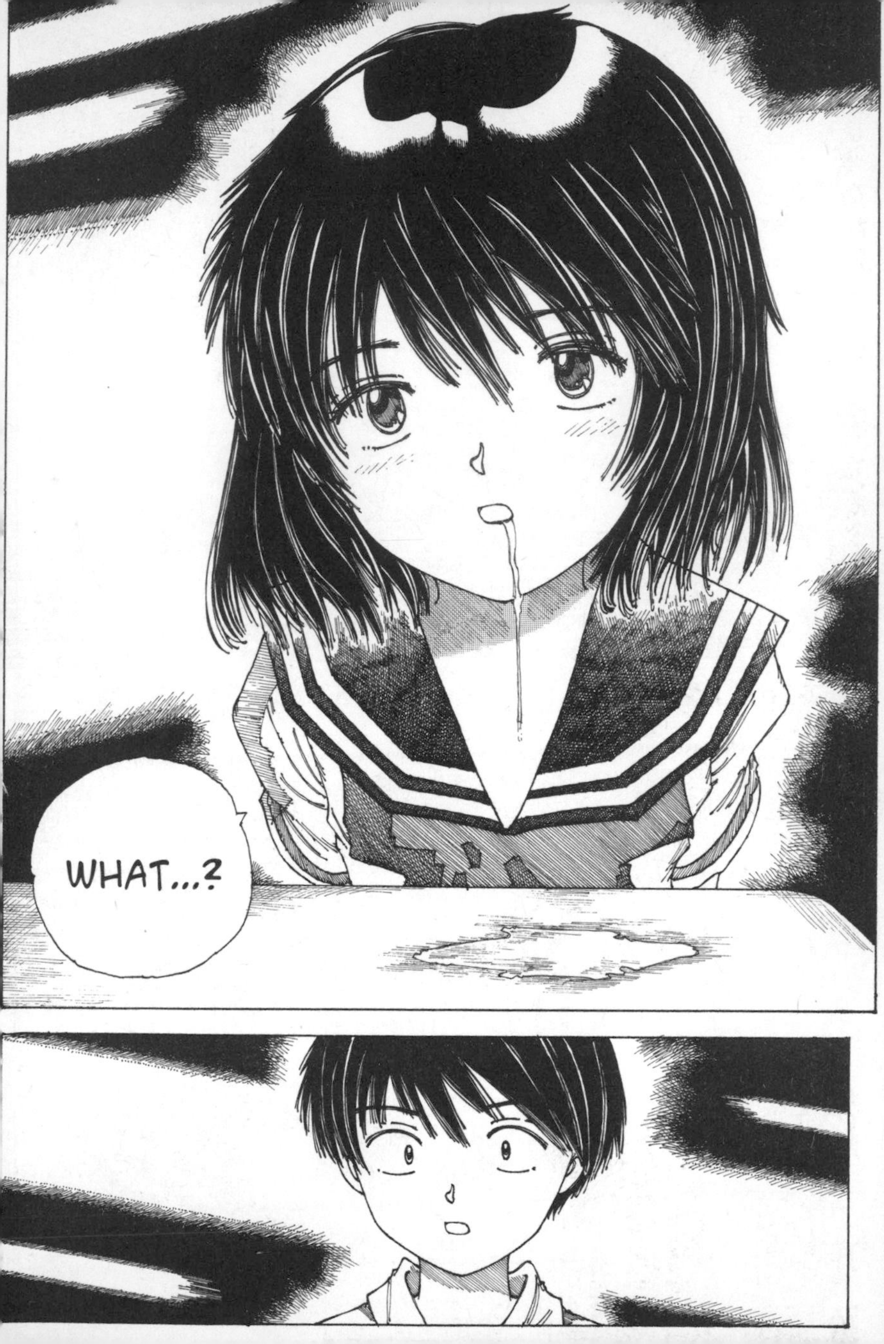
WHAT...?

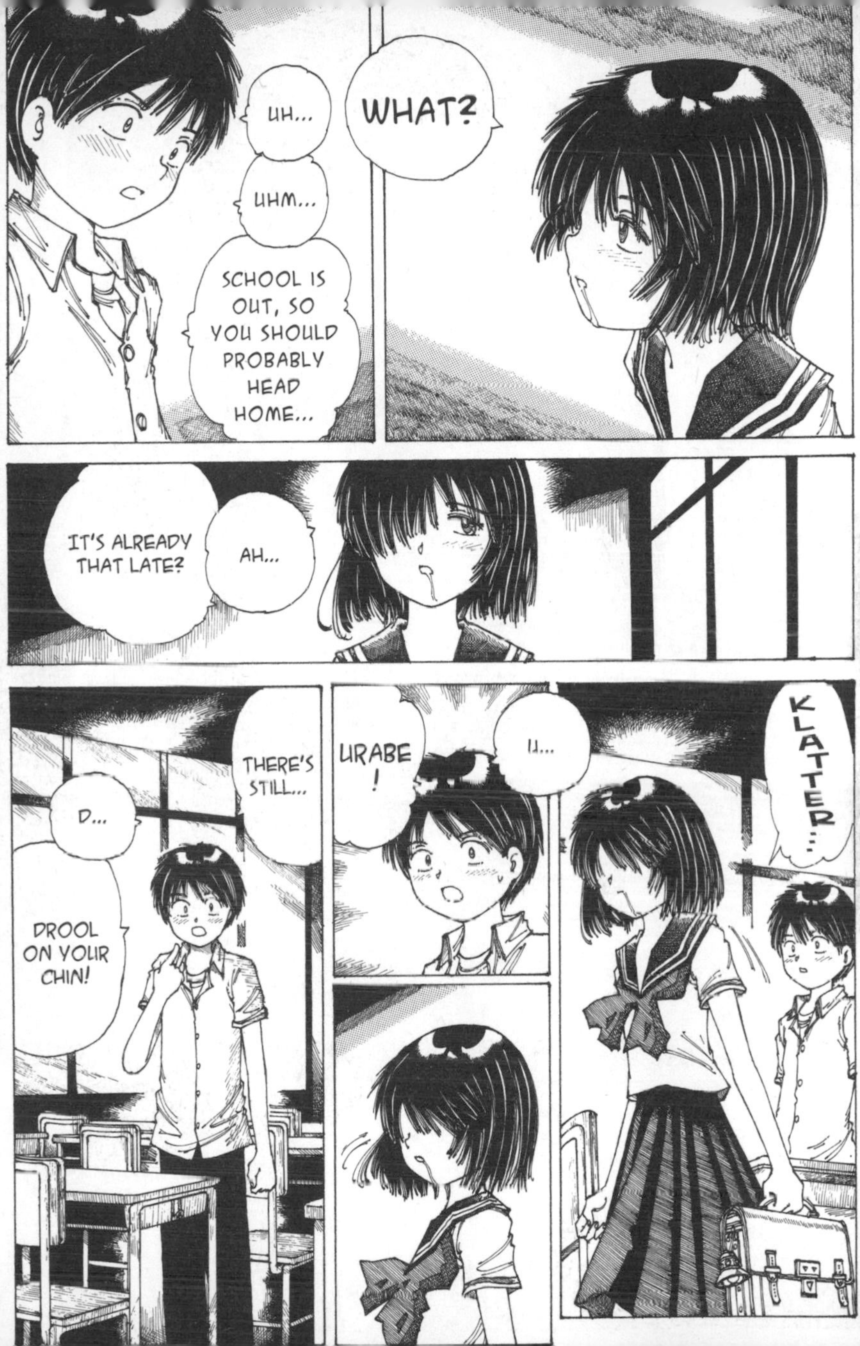
WHAT?
UH...
UHM...
SCHOOL IS OUT, SO YOU SHOULD PROBABLY HEAD HOME...
AH...
IT'S ALREADY THAT LATE?
KLATTER...
U...
URABE!
THERE'S STILL...
D...
DROOL ON YOUR CHIN!

RUB

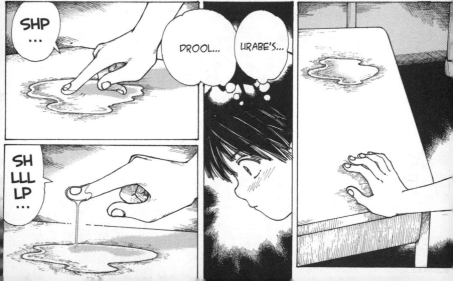

SHP
...

DROOL...

URABE'S...

SH
LLL
LP
...

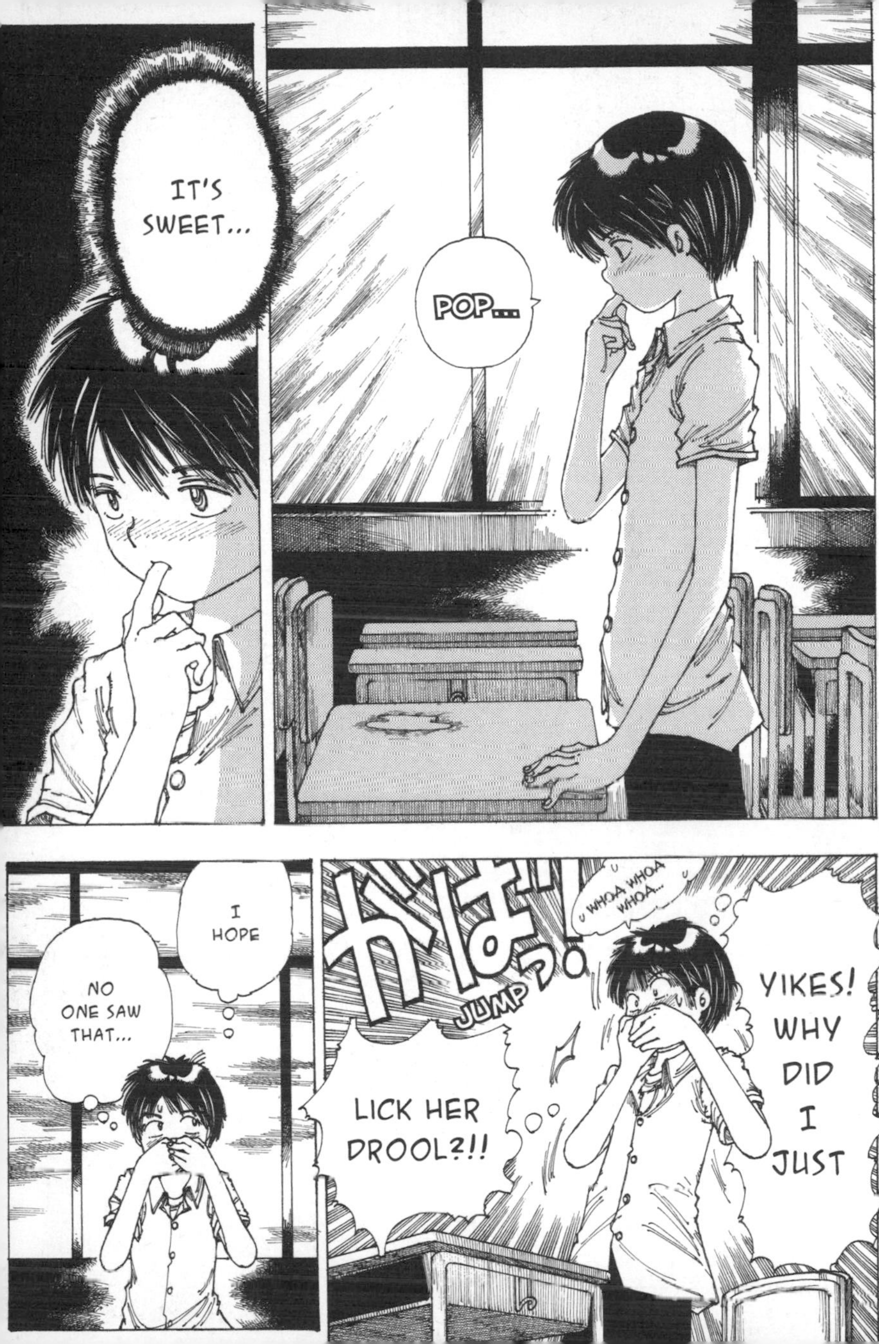
POP...
IT'S SWEET...
かぱっ!
JUMP
WHOA WHOA WHOA...
YIKES! WHY DID I JUST
LICK HER DROOL?!!
I HOPE
NO ONE SAW THAT...

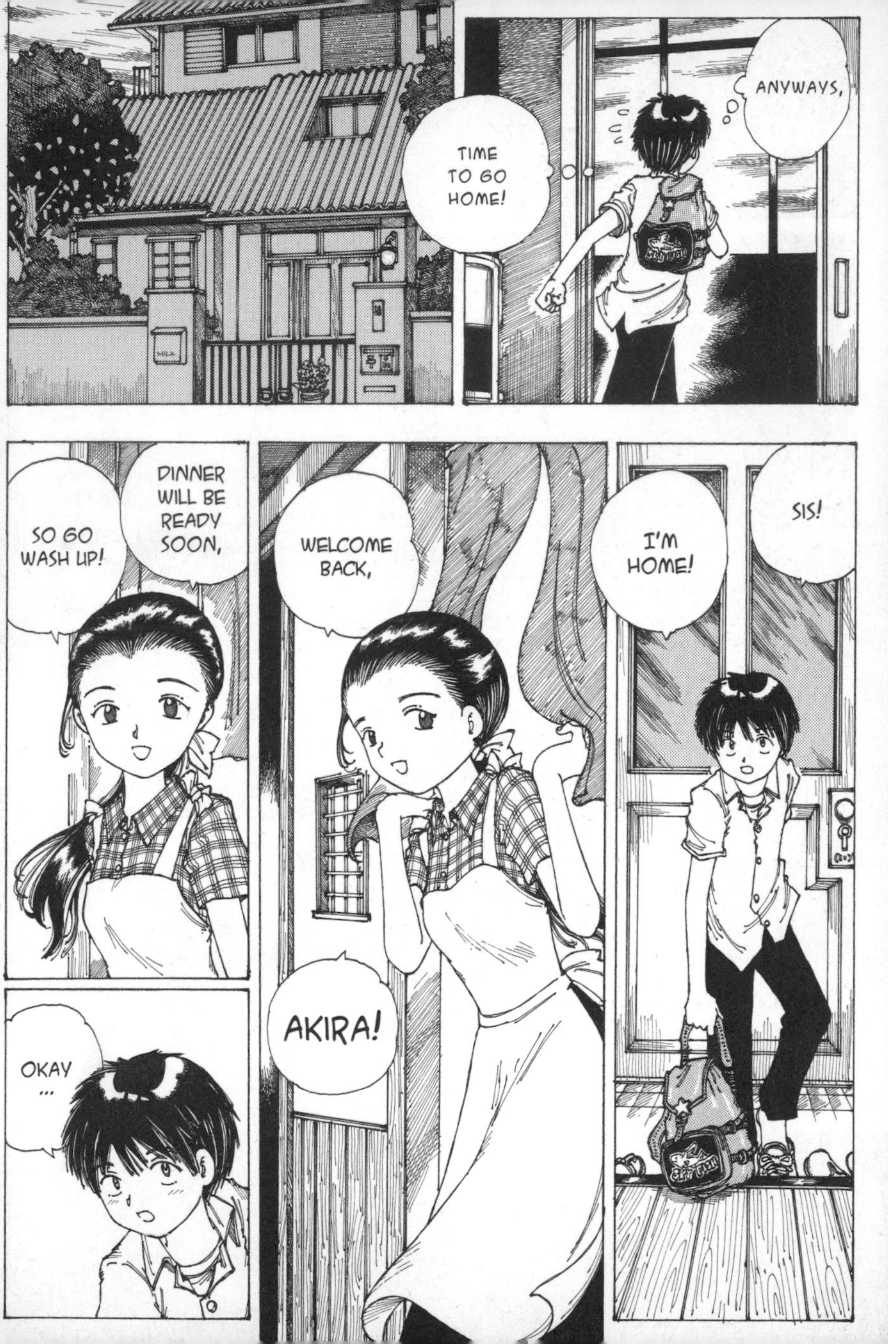
ANYWAYS,
TIME TO GO HOME!
SIS!
I'M HOME!
WELCOME BACK,
AKIRA!
DINNER WILL BE READY SOON,
SO GO WASH UP!
OKAY ...

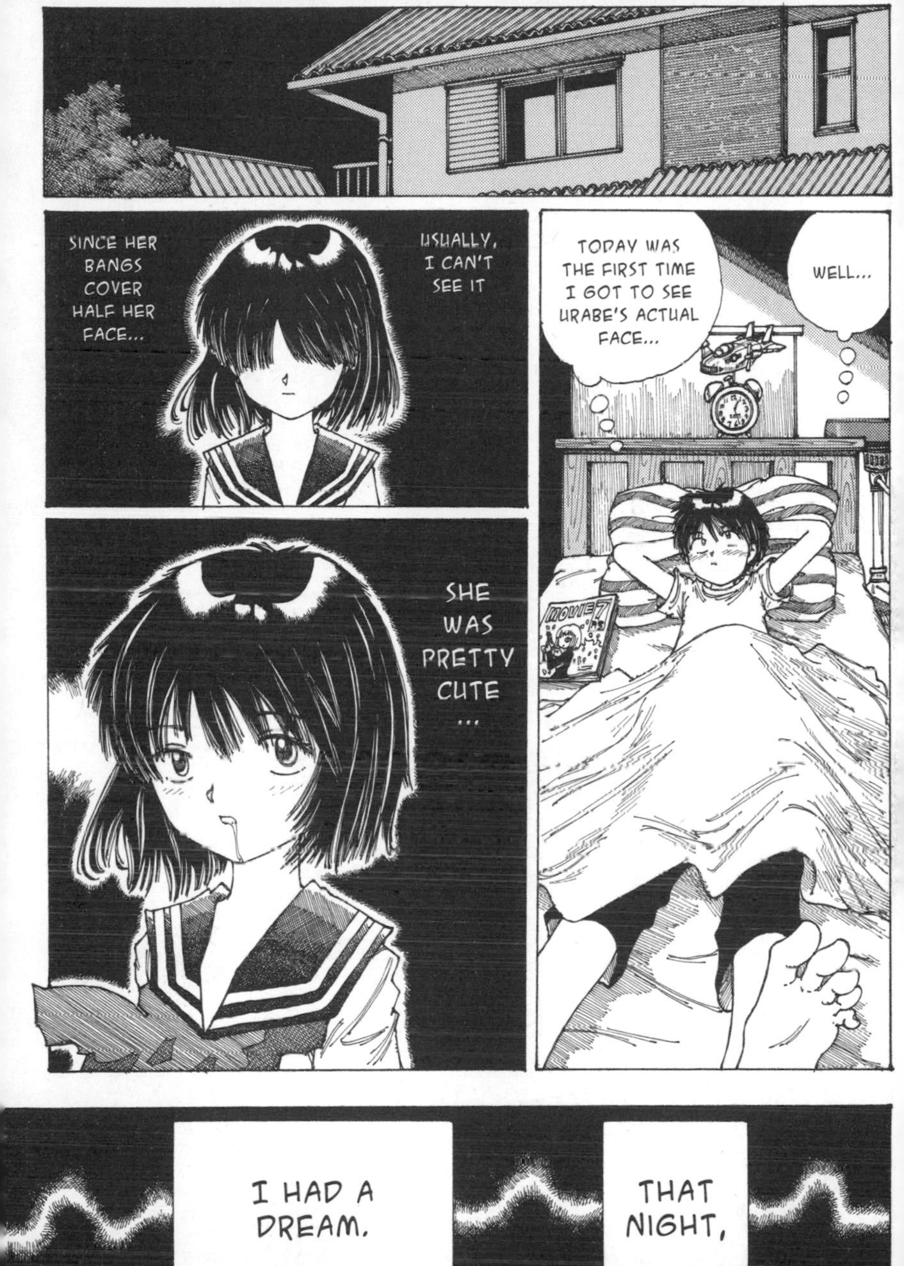
WELL...
TODAY WAS THE FIRST TIME I GOT TO SEE URABE'S ACTUAL FACE...
USUALLY, I CAN'T SEE IT
SINCE HER BANGS COVER HALF HER FACE...
SHE WAS PRETTY CUTE ...
THAT NIGHT,
I HAD A DREAM.

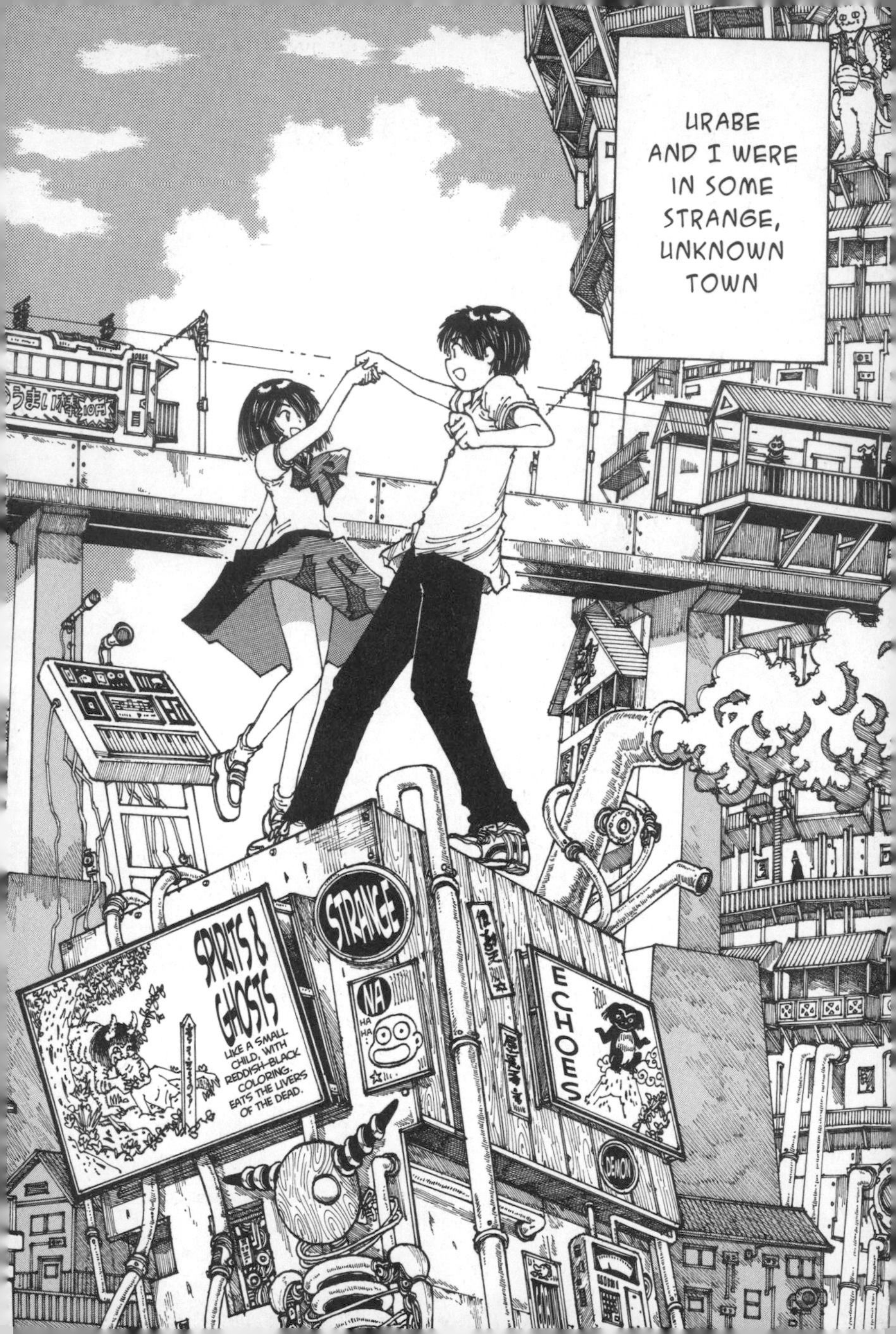
URABE AND I WERE IN SOME STRANGE, UNKNOWN TOWN
SPIRITS & GHOSTS
LIKE A SMALL CHILD, WITH REDDISH-BLACK COLORING. EATS THE LIVERS OF THE DEAD.
STRANGE
NA
HA HA
ECHOES
DEMON

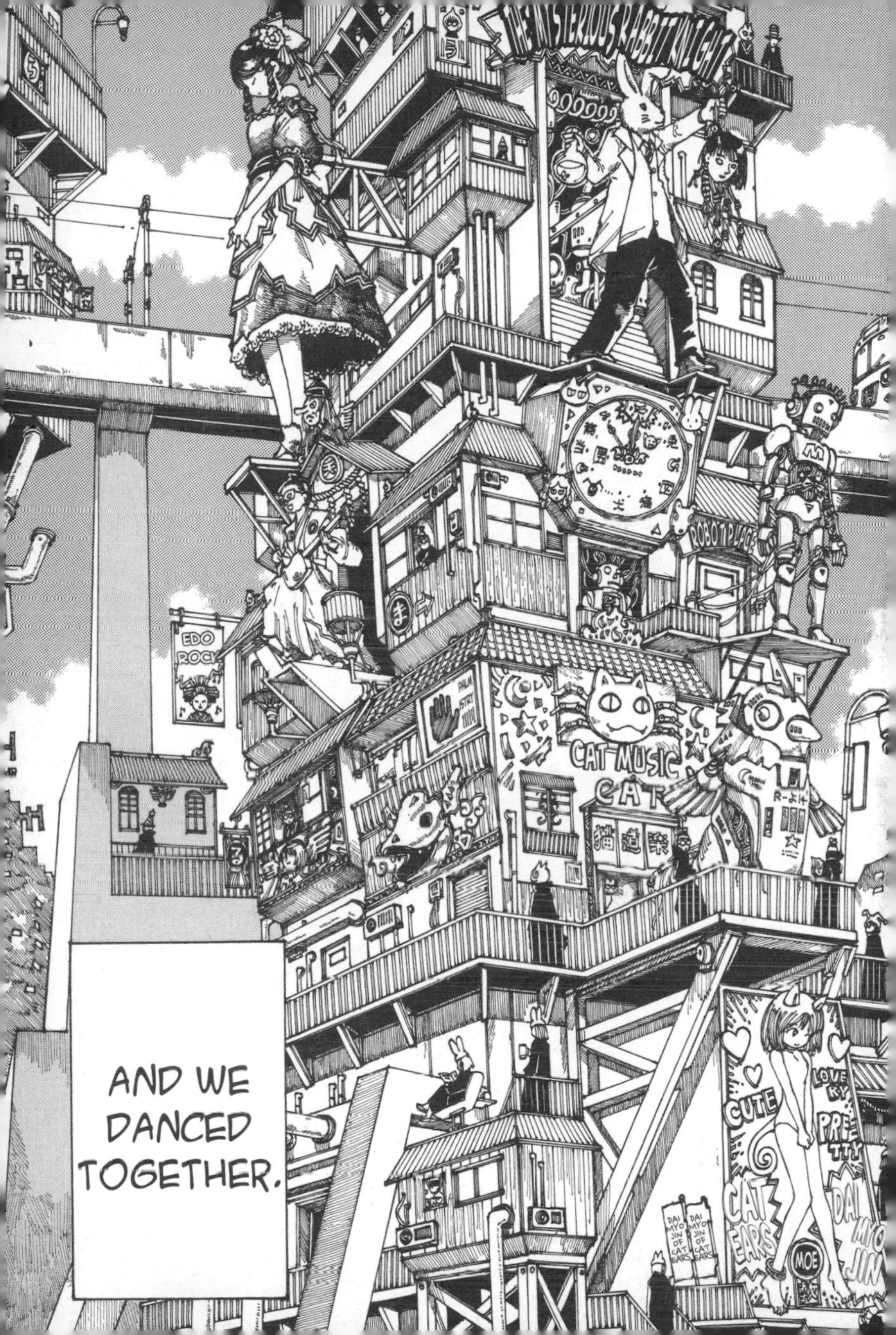
THE MYSTERIOUS RABBIT KNIGHT
ROBOT PLACE
EDO ROCK
CAT MUSIC
CAT
猫道楽
AND WE DANCED TOGETHER.
CUTE
LOVELY
PRETTY
CAT EARS
DAI MYO JIN
MOE
DAI MYO JIN OF CAT EARS
DAI MYO JIN OF CAT EARS

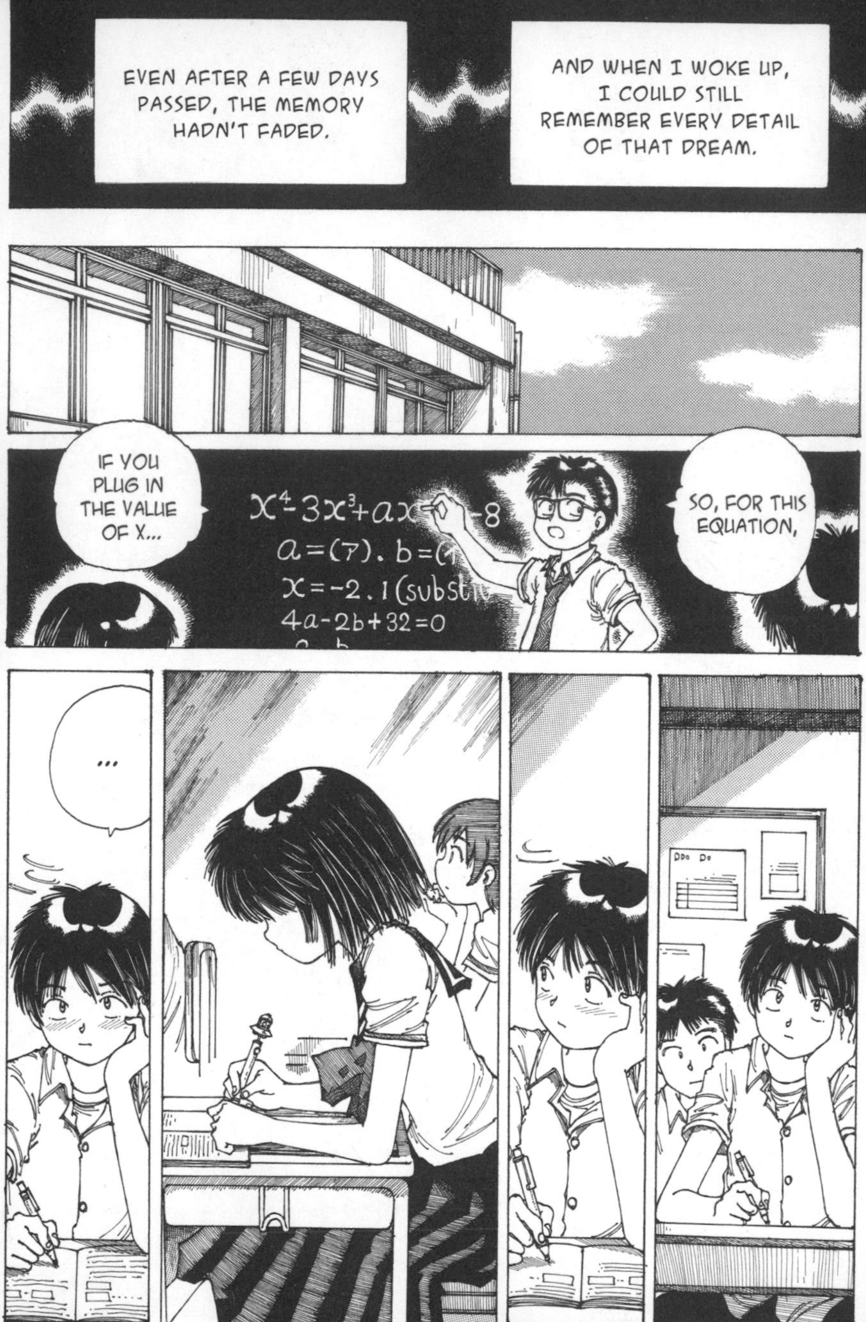
AND WHEN I WOKE UP, I COULD STILL REMEMBER EVERY DETAIL OF THAT DREAM.
EVEN AFTER A FEW DAYS PASSED, THE MEMORY HADN'T FADED.
SO, FOR THIS EQUATION,
4a-2b+32=0
IF YOU PLUG IN THE VALUE OF X...
...

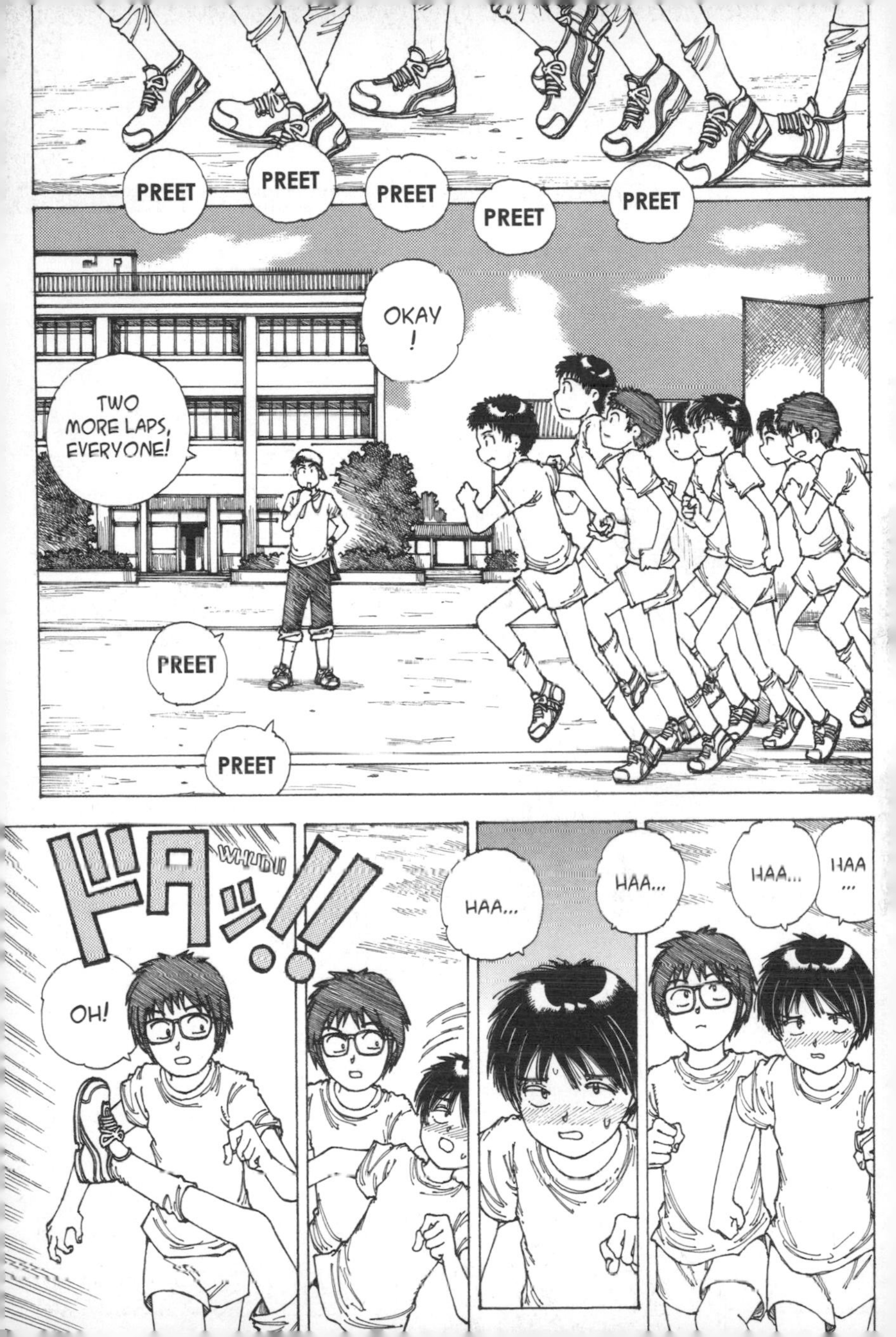
PREET
PREET
PREET
PREET
PREET
OKAY!
TWO MORE LAPS, EVERYONE!
PREET
PREET
HAA ...
HAA...
HAA...
HAA...
ドタッ!!
WHUD!!
OH!

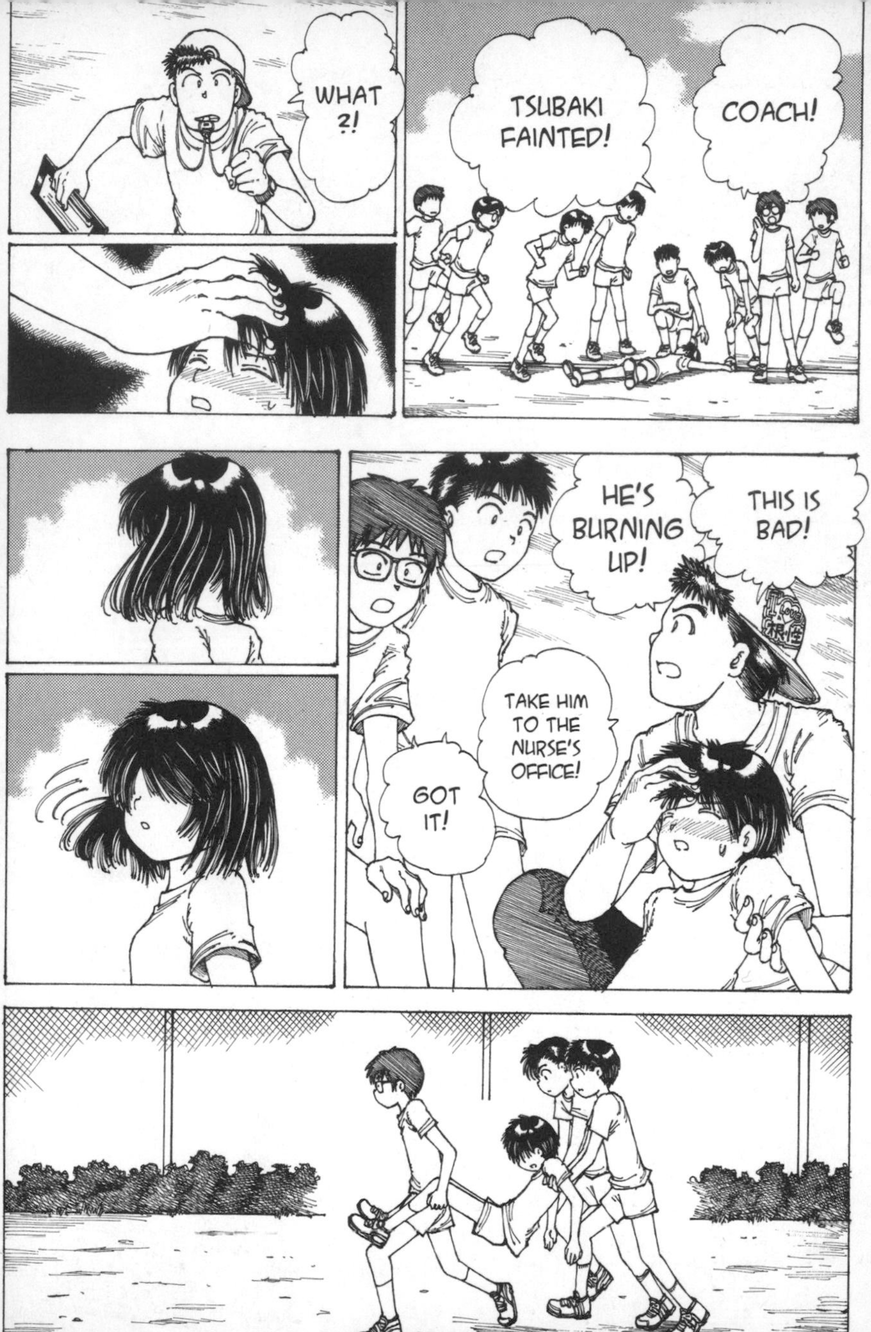
COACH!
TSUBAKI FAINTED!
WHAT ?!
THIS IS BAD!
HE'S BURNING UP!
TAKE HIM TO THE NURSE'S OFFICE!
GOT IT!

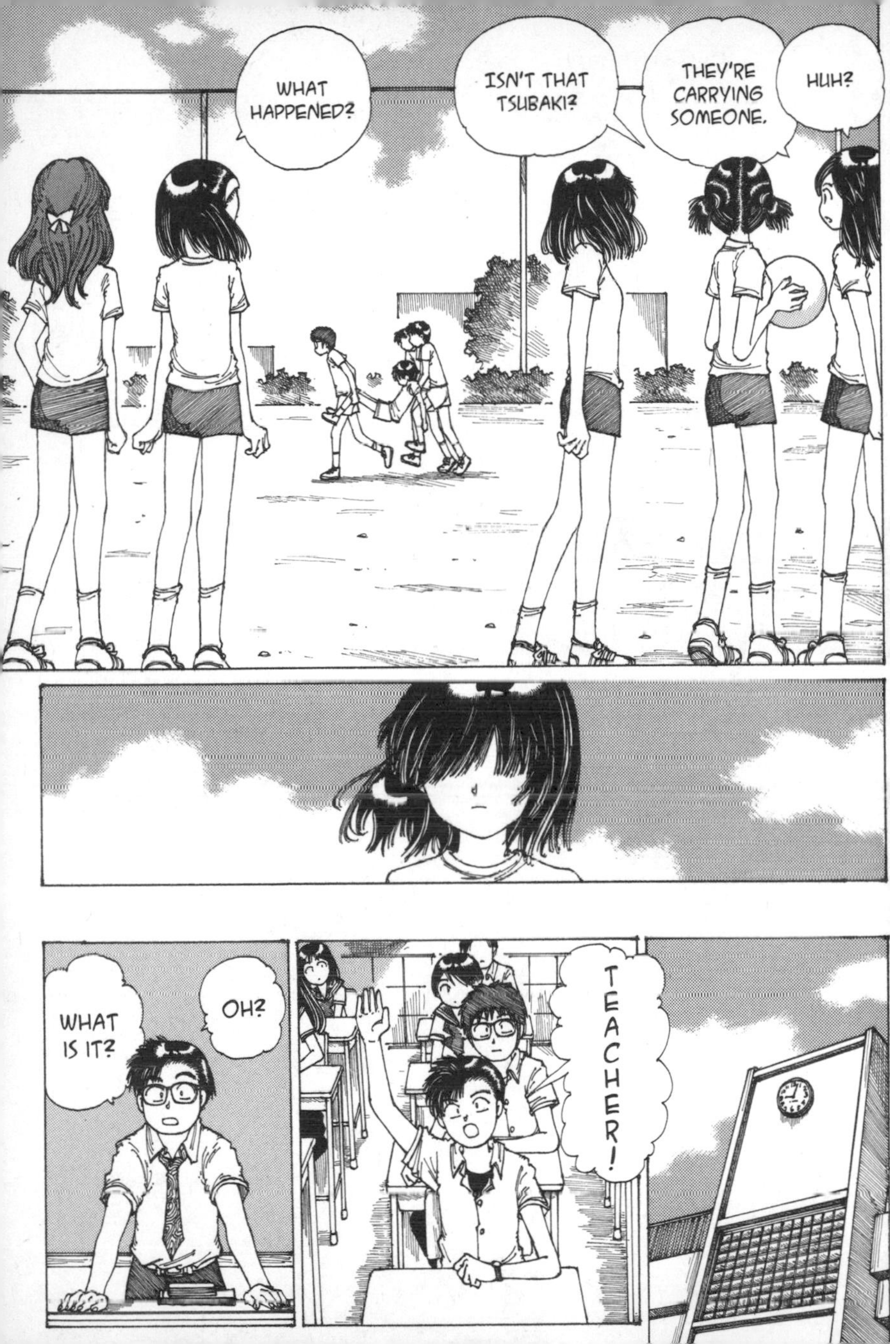
HUH?
THEY'RE CARRYING SOMEONE.
ISN'T THAT TSUBAKI!?
WHAT HAPPENED?
TEACHER!
OH?
WHAT IS IT?

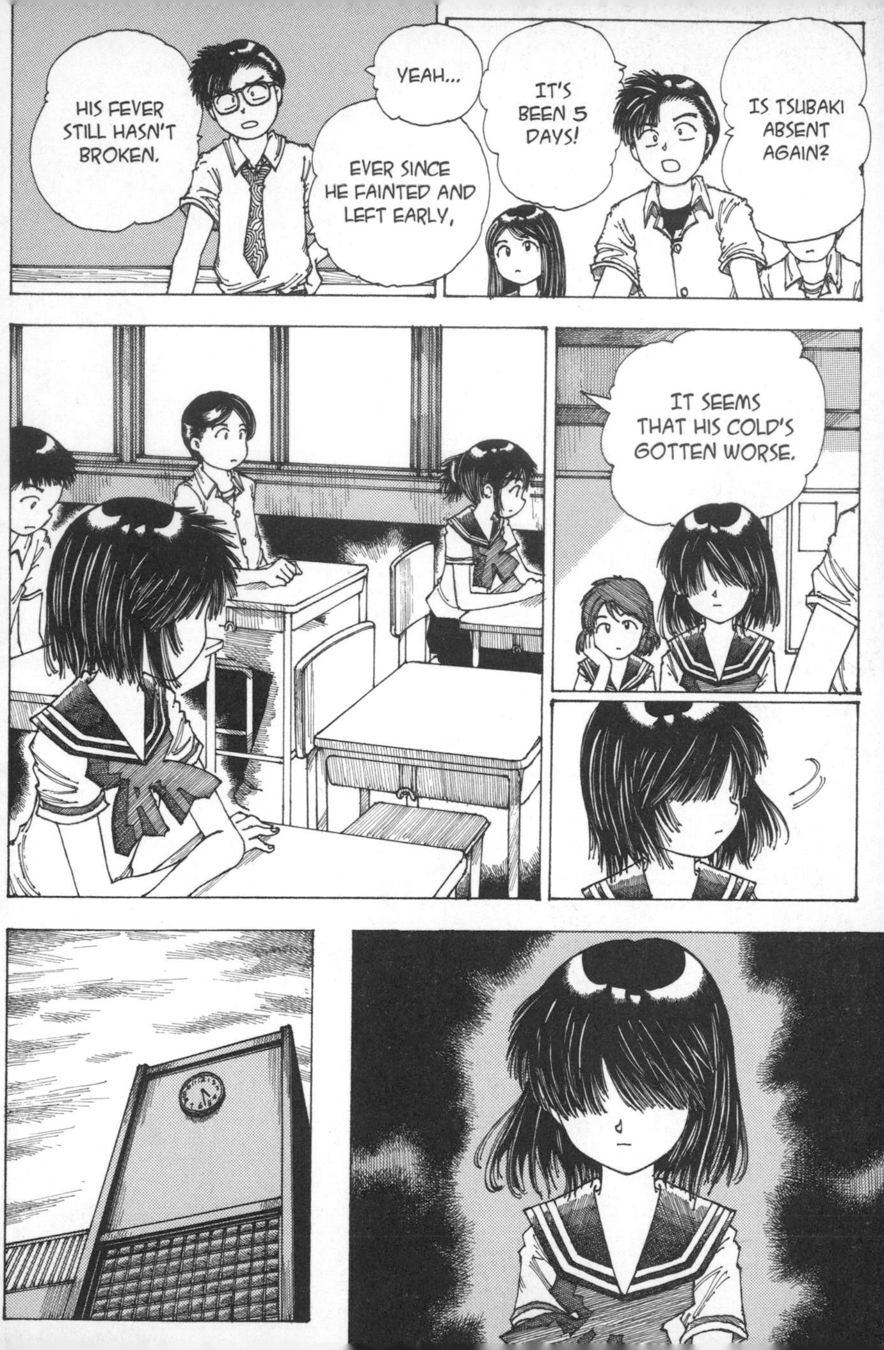
IS TSUBAKI ABSENT AGAIN?
IT'S BEEN 5 DAYS!
YEAH...
EVER SINCE HE FAINTED AND LEFT EARLY,
HIS FEVER STILL HASN'T BROKEN.
IT SEEMS THAT HIS COLD'S GOTTEN WORSE.

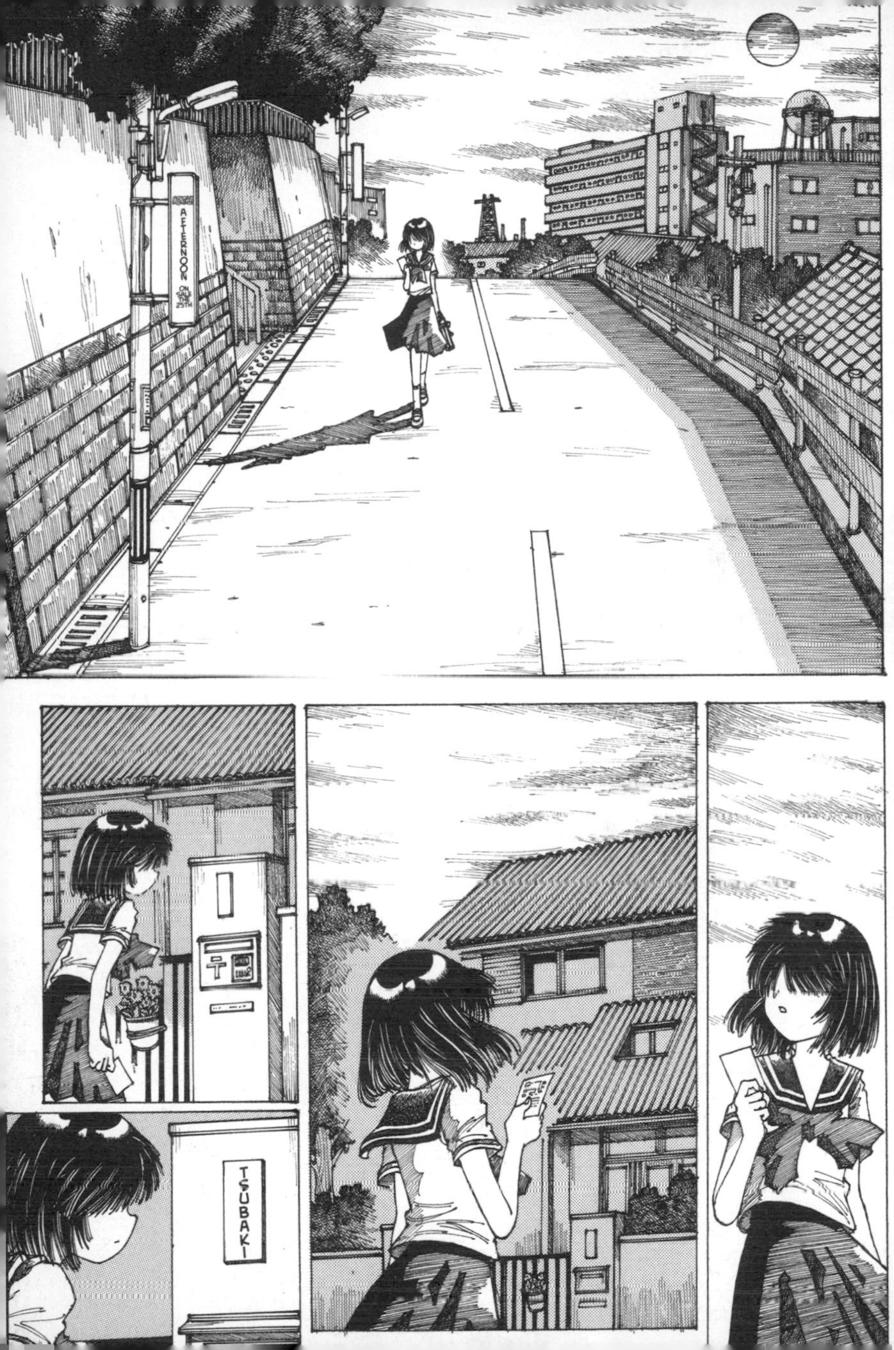
AFTERNOON
ON SALE THE 25TH
TSUBAKI

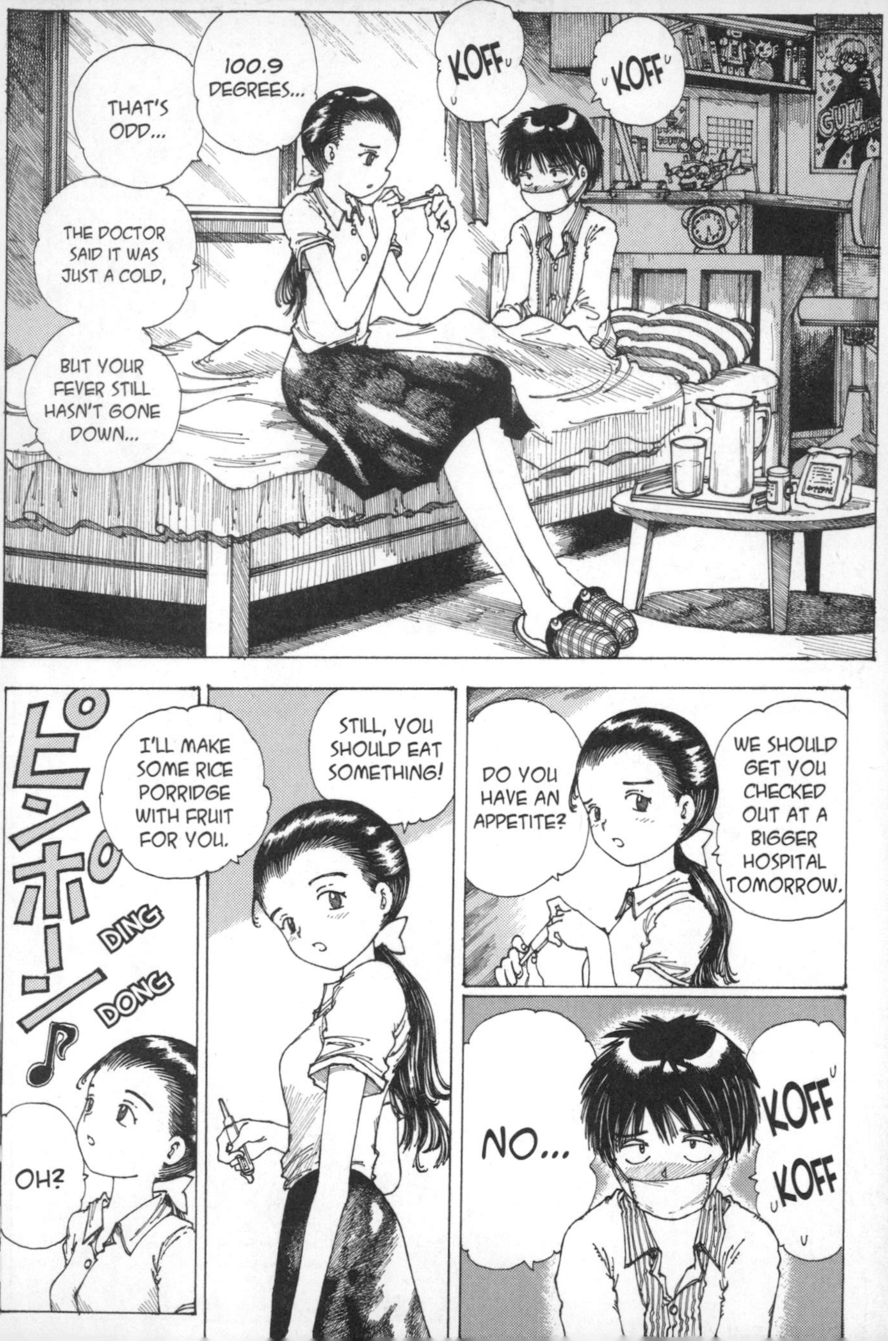
KOFF KOFF
KOFF
100.9 DEGREES...
THAT'S ODD...
THE DOCTOR SAID IT WAS JUST A COLD,
BUT YOUR FEVER STILL HASN'T GONE DOWN...
WE SHOULD GET YOU CHECKED OUT AT A BIGGER HOSPITAL TOMORROW.
DO YOU HAVE AN APPETITE?
KOFF KOFF
NO...
STILL, YOU SHOULD EAT SOMETHING!
I'LL MAKE SOME RICE PORRIDGE WITH FRUIT FOR YOU.
ピンポーン♪
DING DONG
OH?

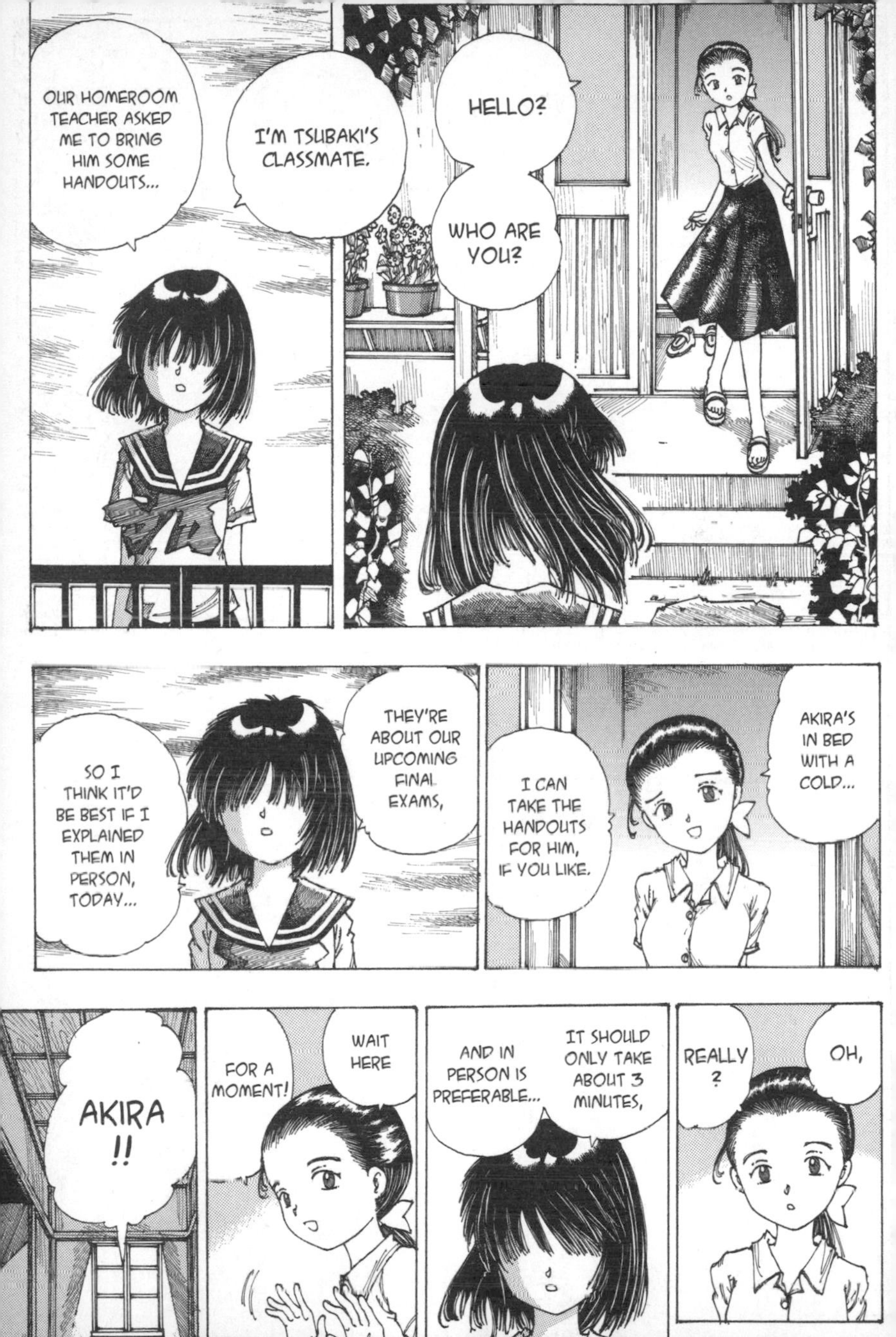
HELLO?
WHO ARE YOU?
I'M TSUBAKI'S CLASSMATE.
OUR HOMEROOM TEACHER ASKED ME TO BRING HIM SOME HANDOUTS...
AKIRA'S IN BED WITH A COLD...
I CAN TAKE THE HANDOUTS FOR HIM, IF YOU LIKE.
THEY'RE ABOUT OUR UPCOMING FINAL EXAMS,
SO I THINK IT'D BE BEST IF I EXPLAINED THEM IN PERSON, TODAY...
OH,
REALLY?
IT SHOULD ONLY TAKE ABOUT 3 MINUTES,
AND IN PERSON IS PREFERABLE...
WAIT HERE
FOR A MOMENT!
AKIRA!!

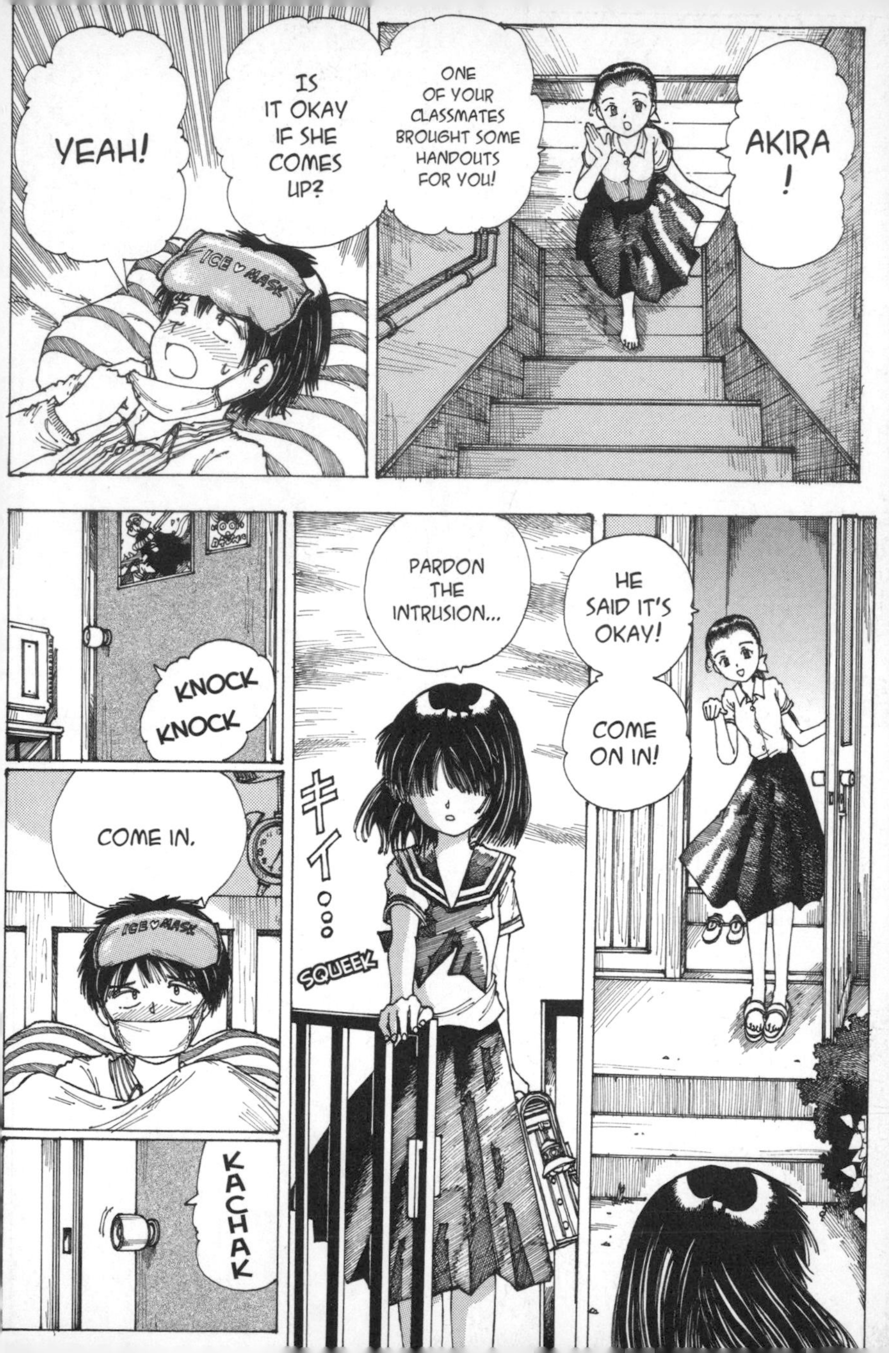
AKIRA!
ONE OF YOUR CLASSMATES BROUGHT SOME HANDOUTS FOR YOU!
IS IT OKAY IF SHE COMES UP?
YEAH!
ICE ♥ MASK
HE SAID IT'S OKAY!
COME ON IN!
PARDON THE INTRUSION...
キイ○○○
SQUEEK
KNOCK KNOCK
COME IN.
ICE ♥ MASK
KACHAK

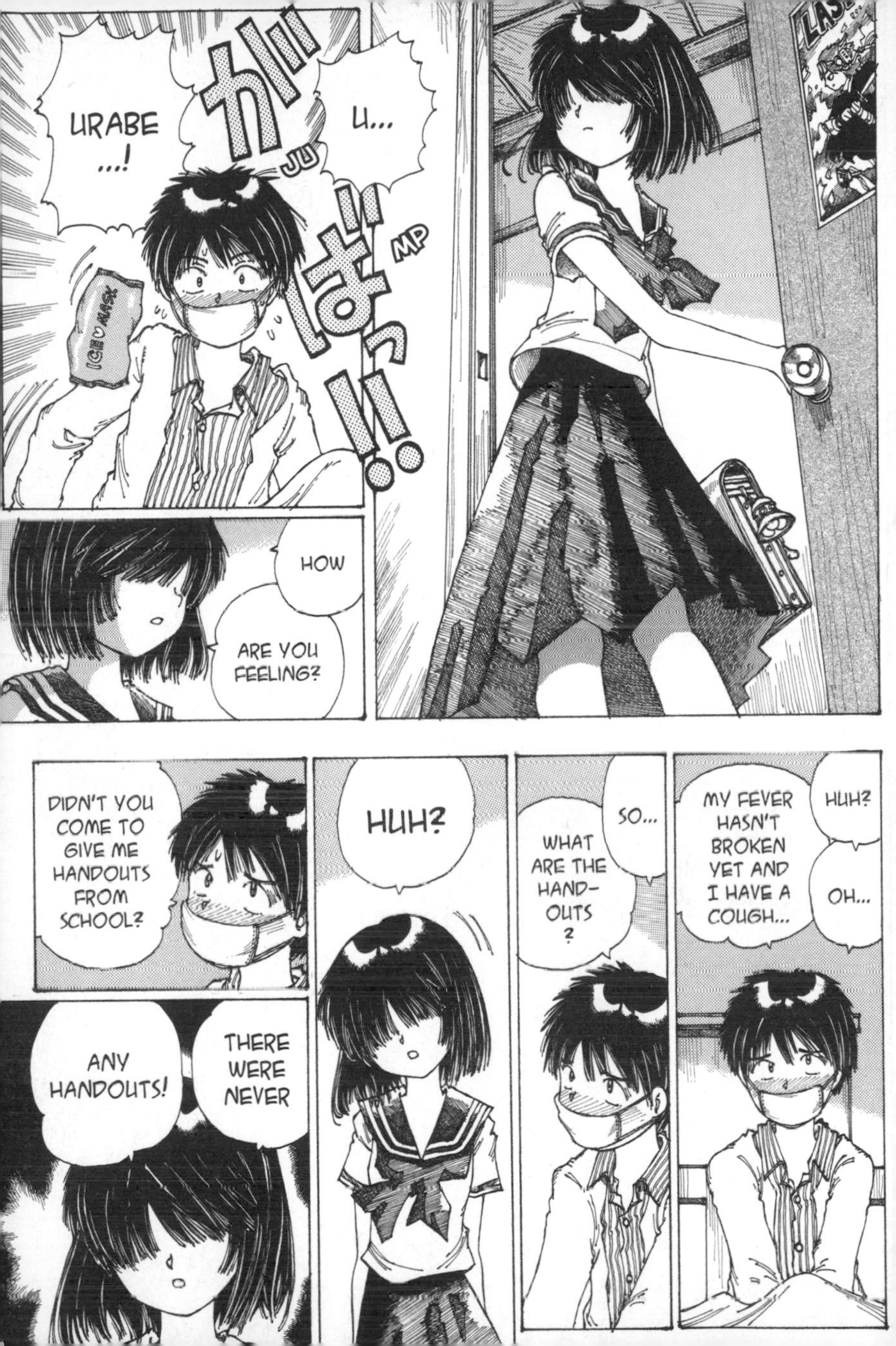
U...
JU
URABE ...!
MP
HOW
ARE YOU FEELING?
HUH?
MY FEVER HASN'T BROKEN YET AND I HAVE A COUGH...
OH...
SO...
WHAT ARE THE HAND-OUTS?
HUH?
DIDN'T YOU COME TO GIVE ME HANDOUTS FROM SCHOOL?
THERE WERE NEVER
ANY HANDOUTS!

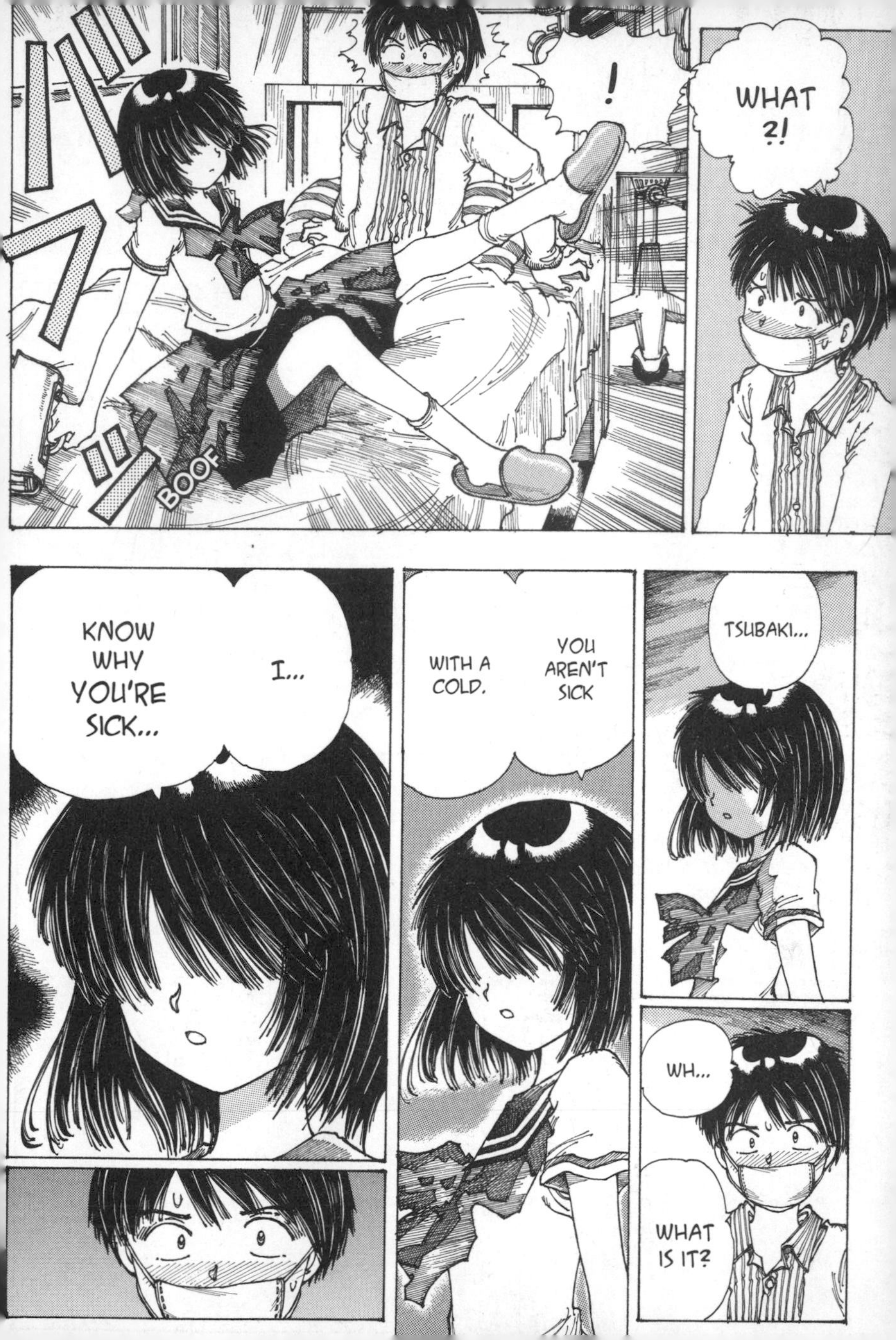
WHAT ?!
!
BOOF
TSUBAKI...
WH...
WHAT IS IT?
YOU AREN'T SICK
WITH A COLD.
I...
KNOW WHY YOU'RE SICK...

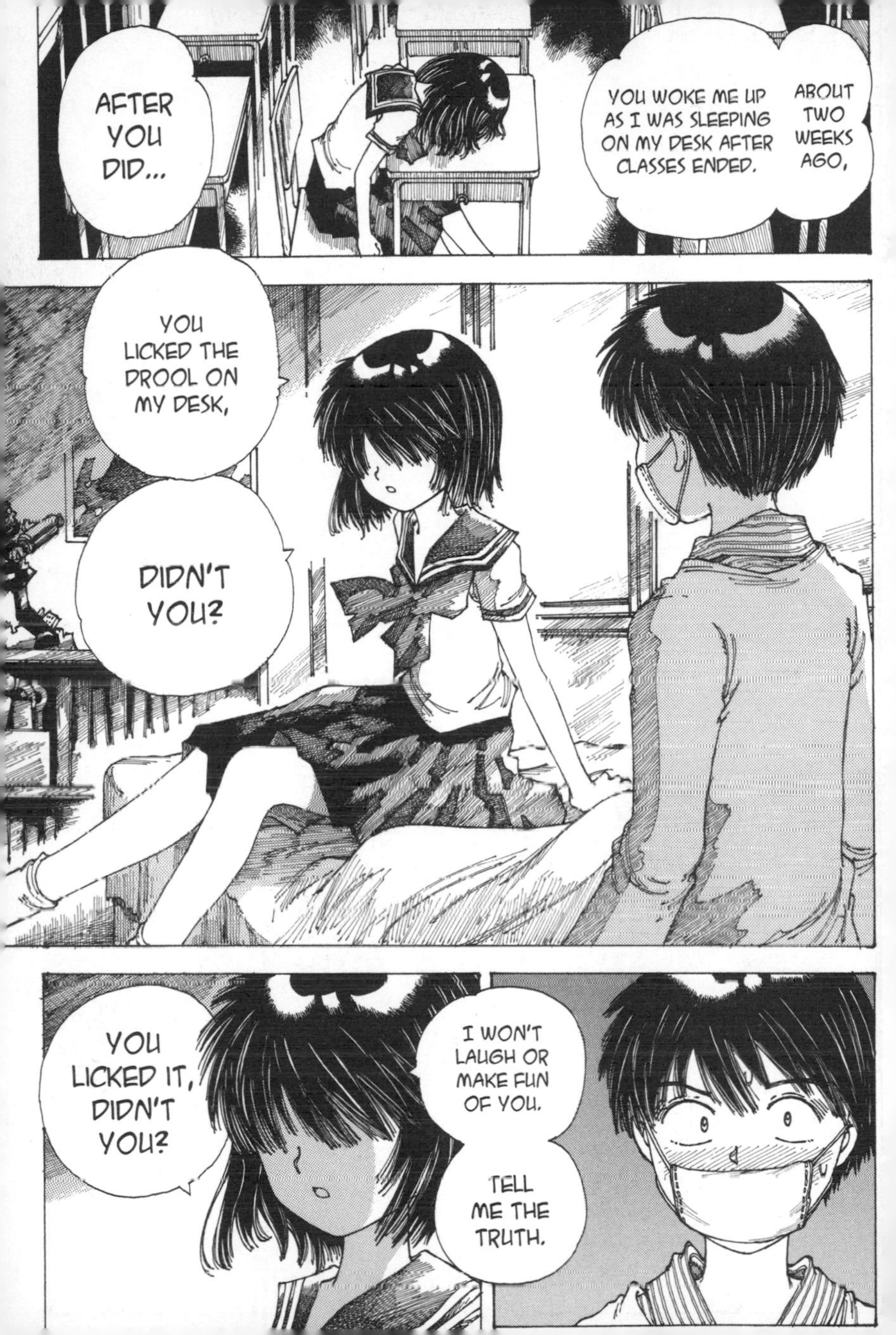
ABOUT TWO WEEKS AGO,
YOU WOKE ME UP AS I WAS SLEEPING ON MY DESK AFTER CLASSES ENDED.
AFTER YOU DID...
YOU LICKED THE DROOL ON MY DESK,
DIDN'T YOU?
I WON'T LAUGH OR MAKE FUN OF YOU.
TELL ME THE TRUTH.
YOU LICKED IT, DIDN'T YOU?

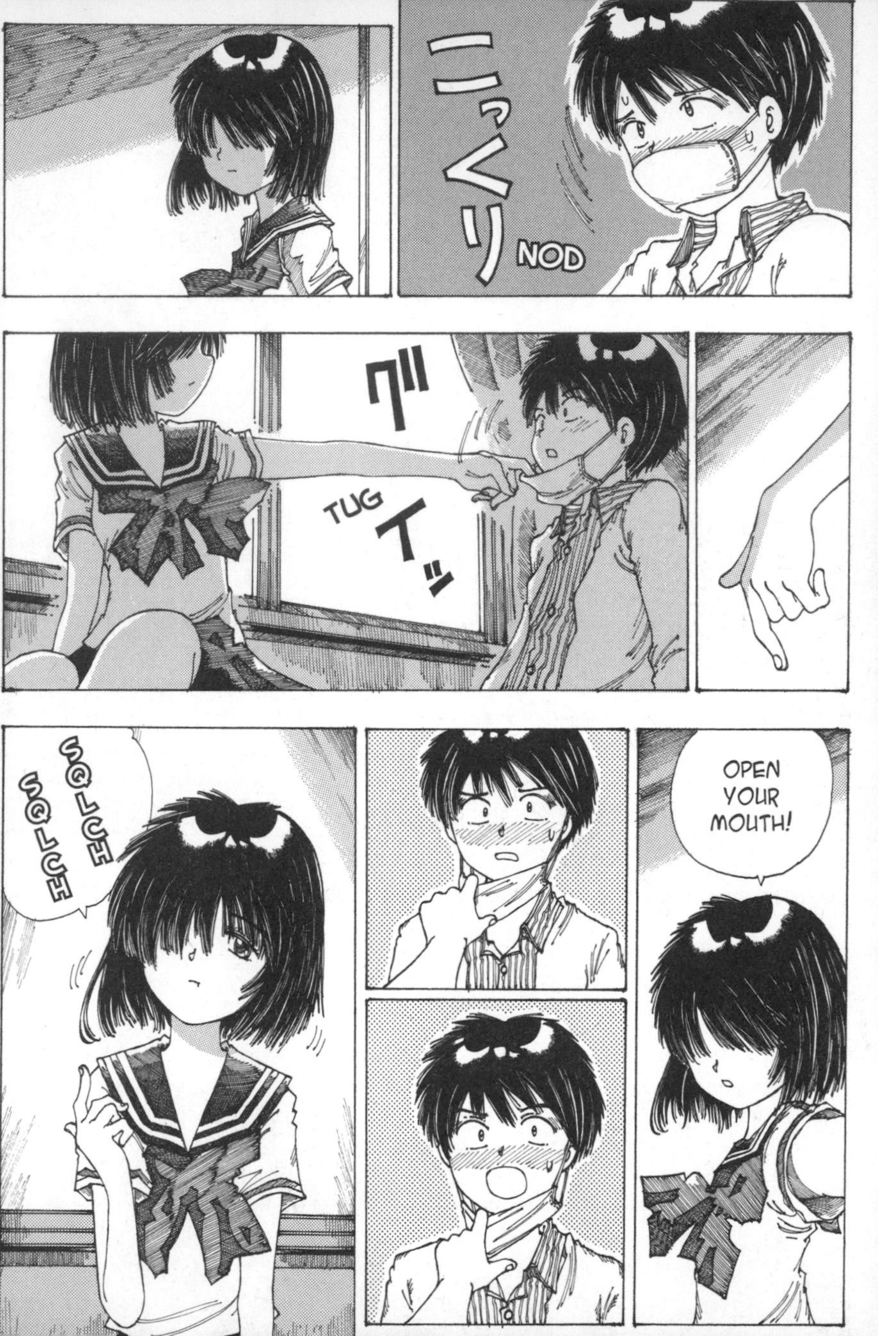
こっくり
NOD
グイッ
TUG
OPEN YOUR MOUTH!
S@LCH S@LCH

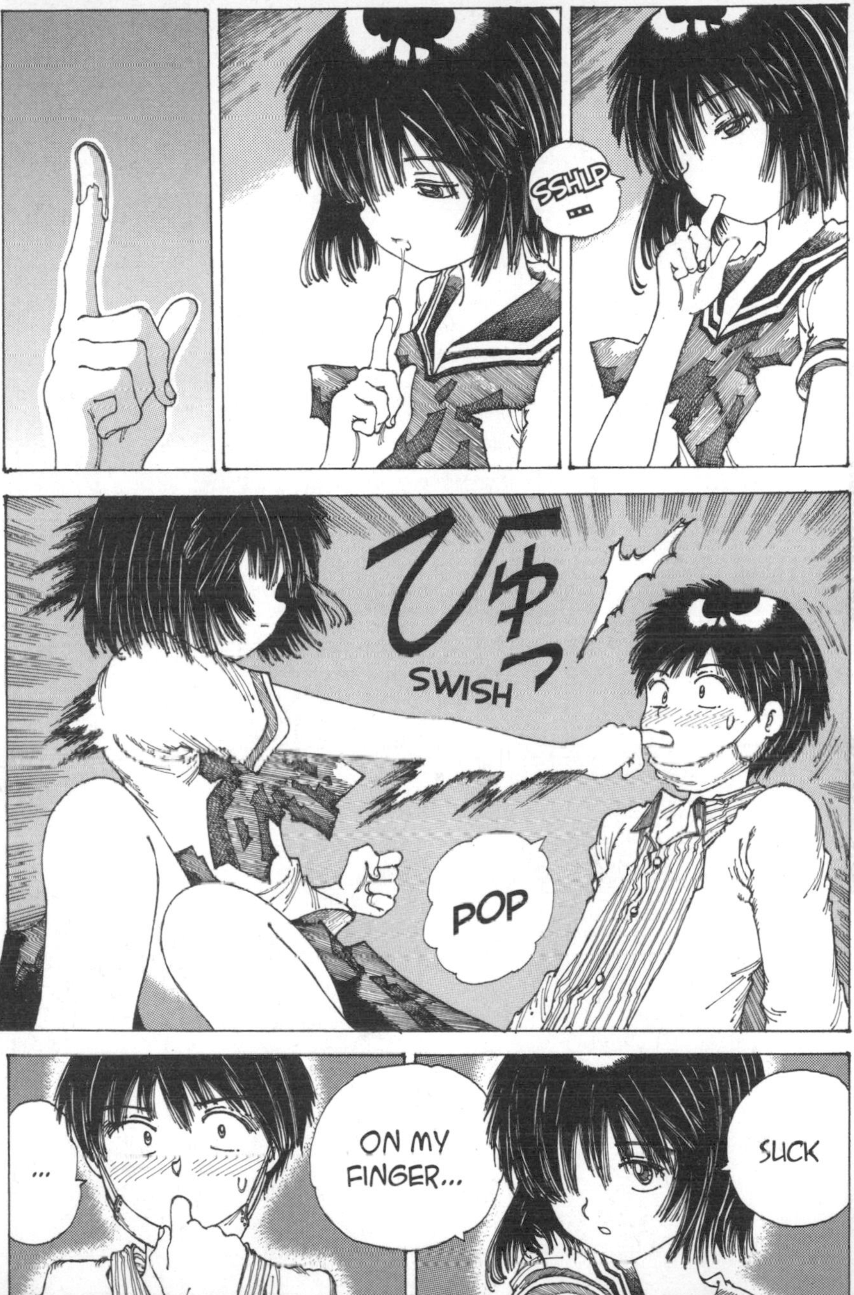
SSHLP
...
ひゅっ
SWISH
POP
SUCK
ON MY FINGER...
...

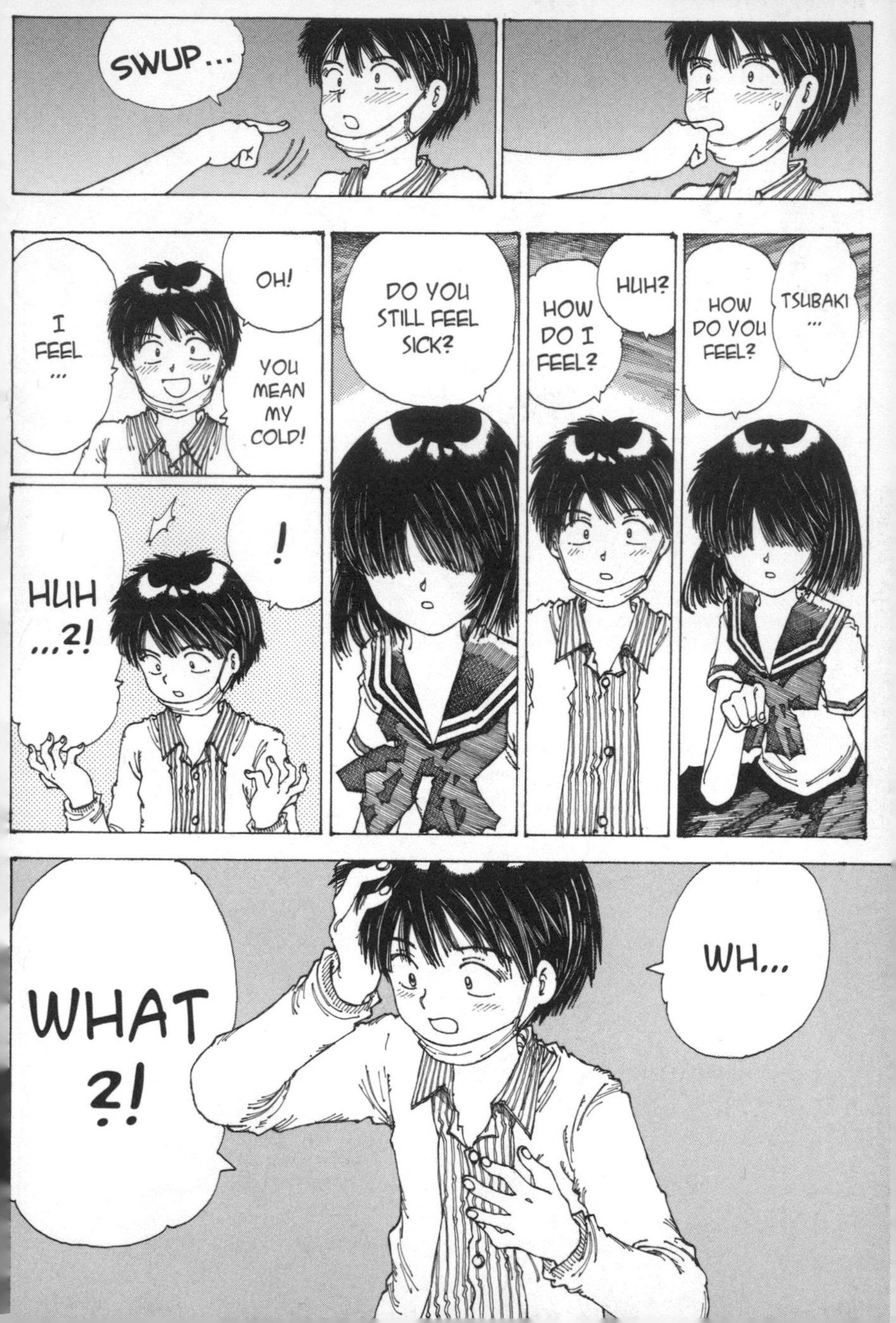
SWUP...
TSUBAKI ...
HOW DO YOU FEEL?
HUH?
HOW DO I FEEL?
DO YOU STILL FEEL SICK?
OH!
YOU MEAN MY COLD!
I FEEL ...
!
HUH ...?!
WH...
WHAT ?!

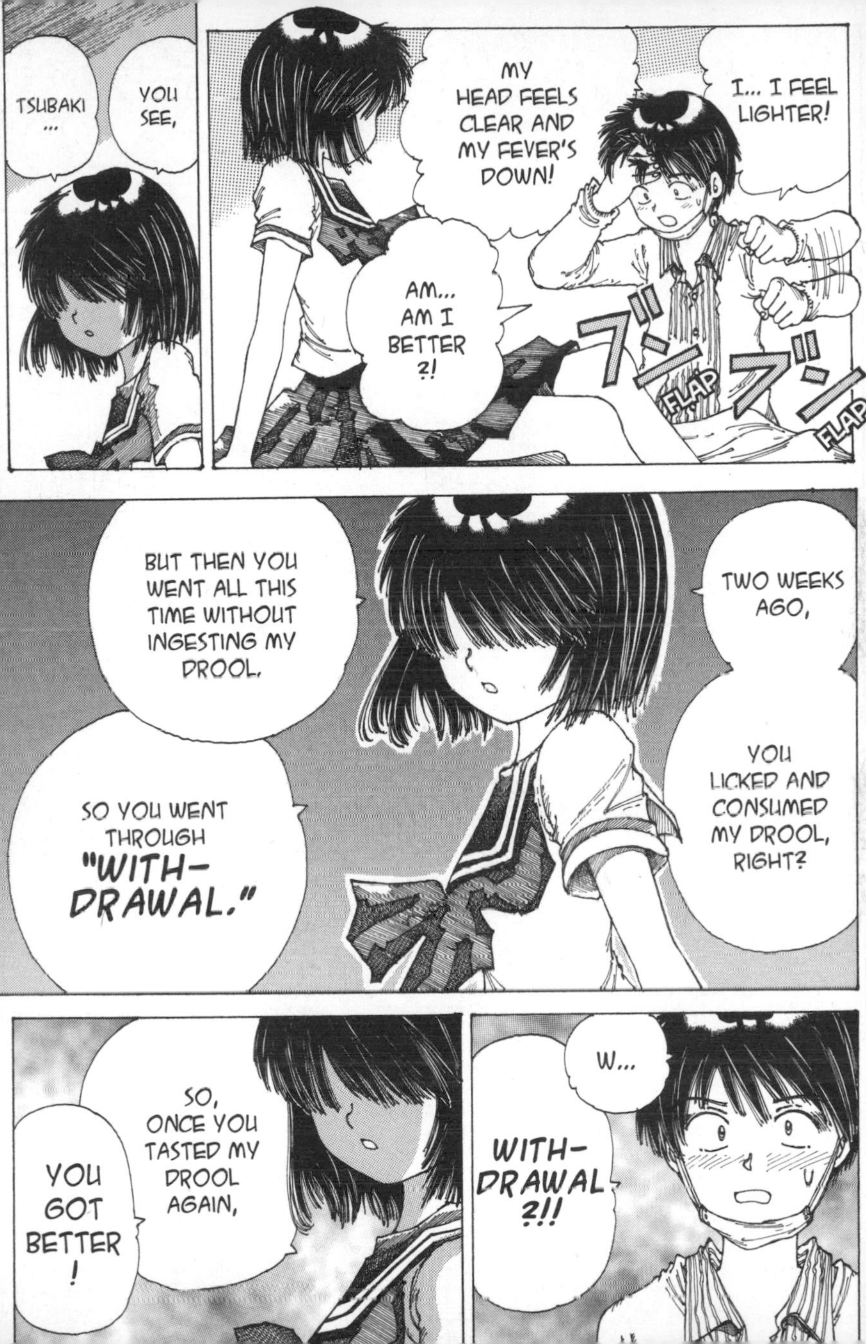
I... I FEEL LIGHTER!
MY HEAD FEELS CLEAR AND MY FEVER'S DOWN!
AM... AM I BETTER ?!
ブン FLAP
ブン FLAP
YOU SEE,
TSUBAKI ...
TWO WEEKS AGO,
YOU LICKED AND CONSUMED MY DROOL, RIGHT?
BUT THEN YOU WENT ALL THIS TIME WITHOUT INGESTING MY DROOL.
SO YOU WENT THROUGH "WITH-DRAWAL."
W...
WITH-DRAWAL ?!!
SO, ONCE YOU TASTED MY DROOL AGAIN,
YOU GOT BETTER !

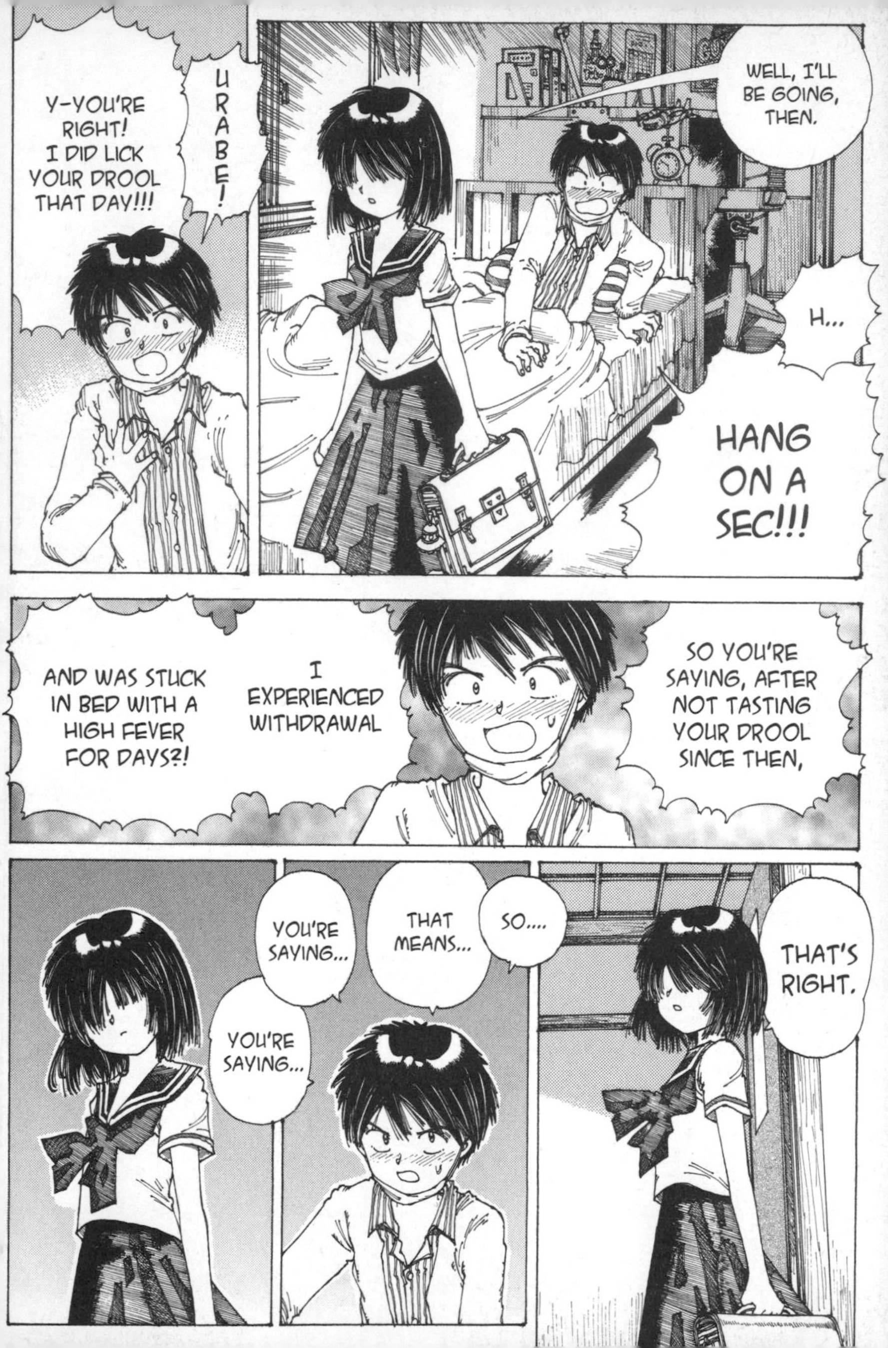
WELL, I'LL BE GOING, THEN.
H...
HANG ON A SEC!!!
URABE!
Y-YOU'RE RIGHT! I DID LICK YOUR DROOL THAT DAY!!!
SO YOU'RE SAYING, AFTER NOT TASTING YOUR DROOL SINCE THEN,
I EXPERIENCED WITHDRAWAL
AND WAS STUCK IN BED WITH A HIGH FEVER FOR DAYS?!
THAT'S RIGHT.
SO....
THAT MEANS...
YOU'RE SAYING...
YOU'RE SAYING...

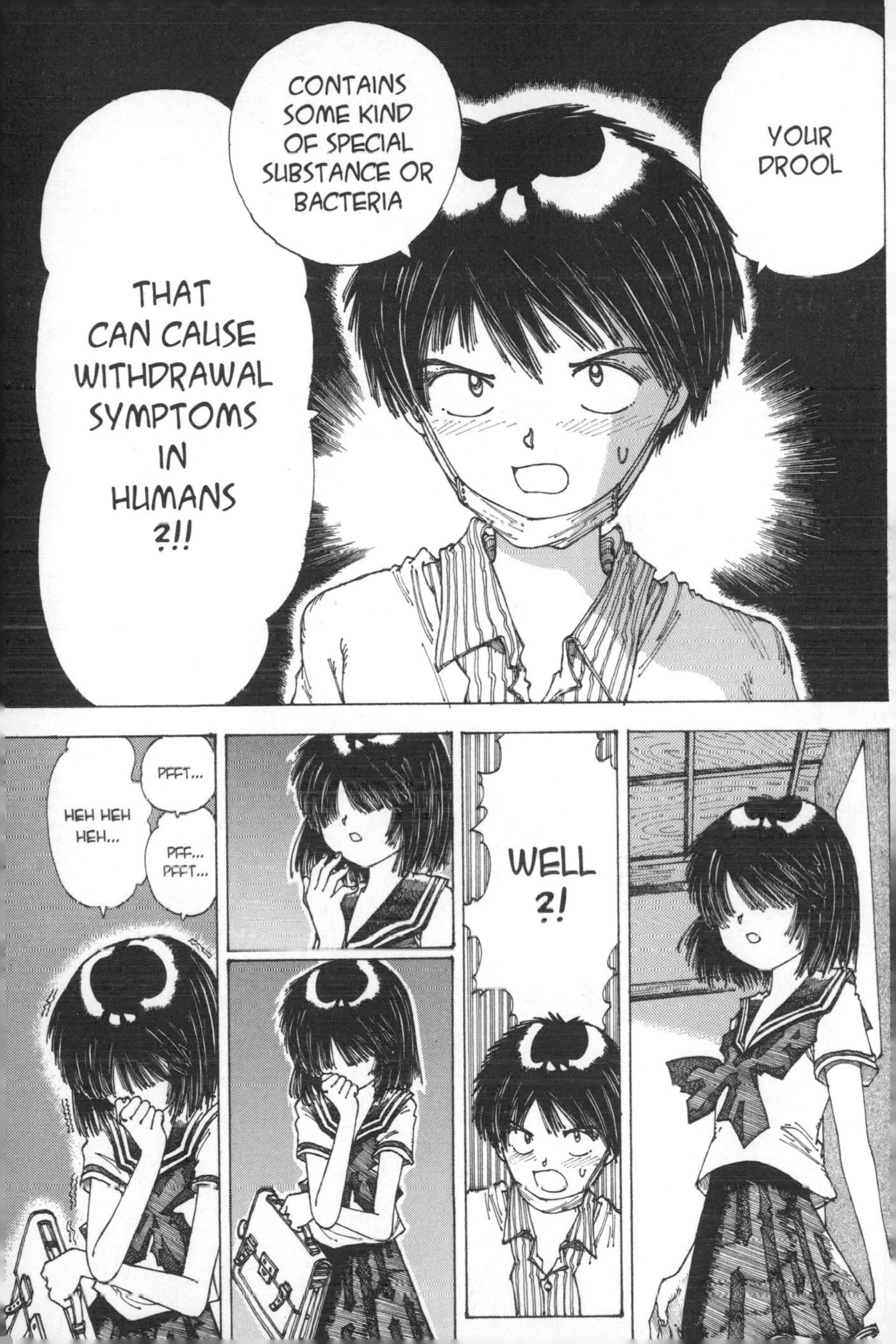
YOUR DROOL
CONTAINS SOME KIND OF SPECIAL SUBSTANCE OR BACTERIA
THAT CAN CAUSE WITHDRAWAL SYMPTOMS IN HUMANS ?!!
WELL ?!
PFFT...
PFF... PFFT...
HEH HEH HEH...

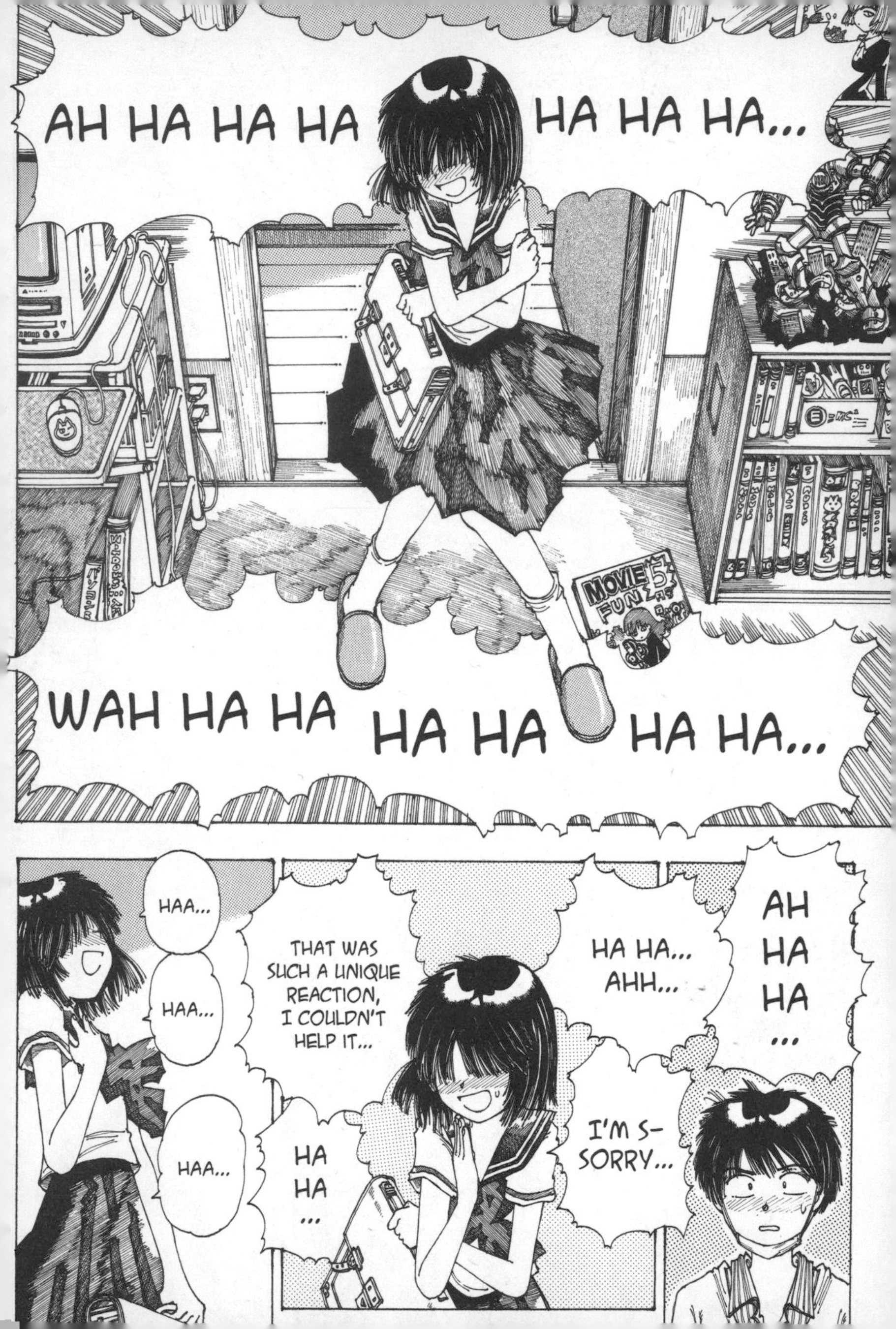
AH HA HA HA HA HA HA...
WAH HA HA HA HA HA HA...
AH HA HA ...
HA HA... AHH...
THAT WAS SUCH A UNIQUE REACTION, I COULDN'T HELP IT...
I'M S-SORRY...
HA HA ...
HAA...
HAA...
HAA...

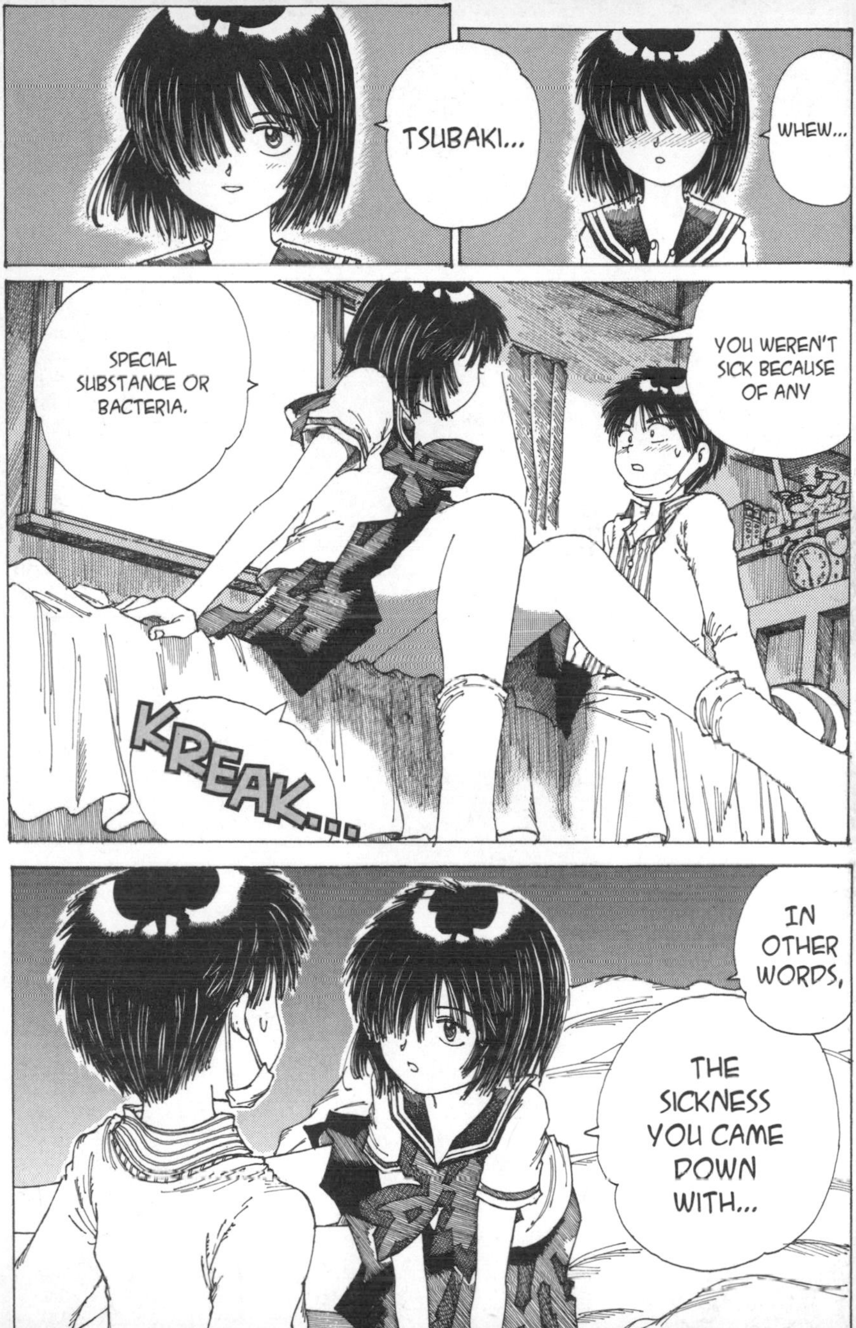
WHEW...
TSUBAKI...
YOU WEREN'T SICK BECAUSE OF ANY
SPECIAL SUBSTANCE OR BACTERIA.
KREAK...
IN OTHER WORDS,
THE SICKNESS YOU CAME DOWN WITH...

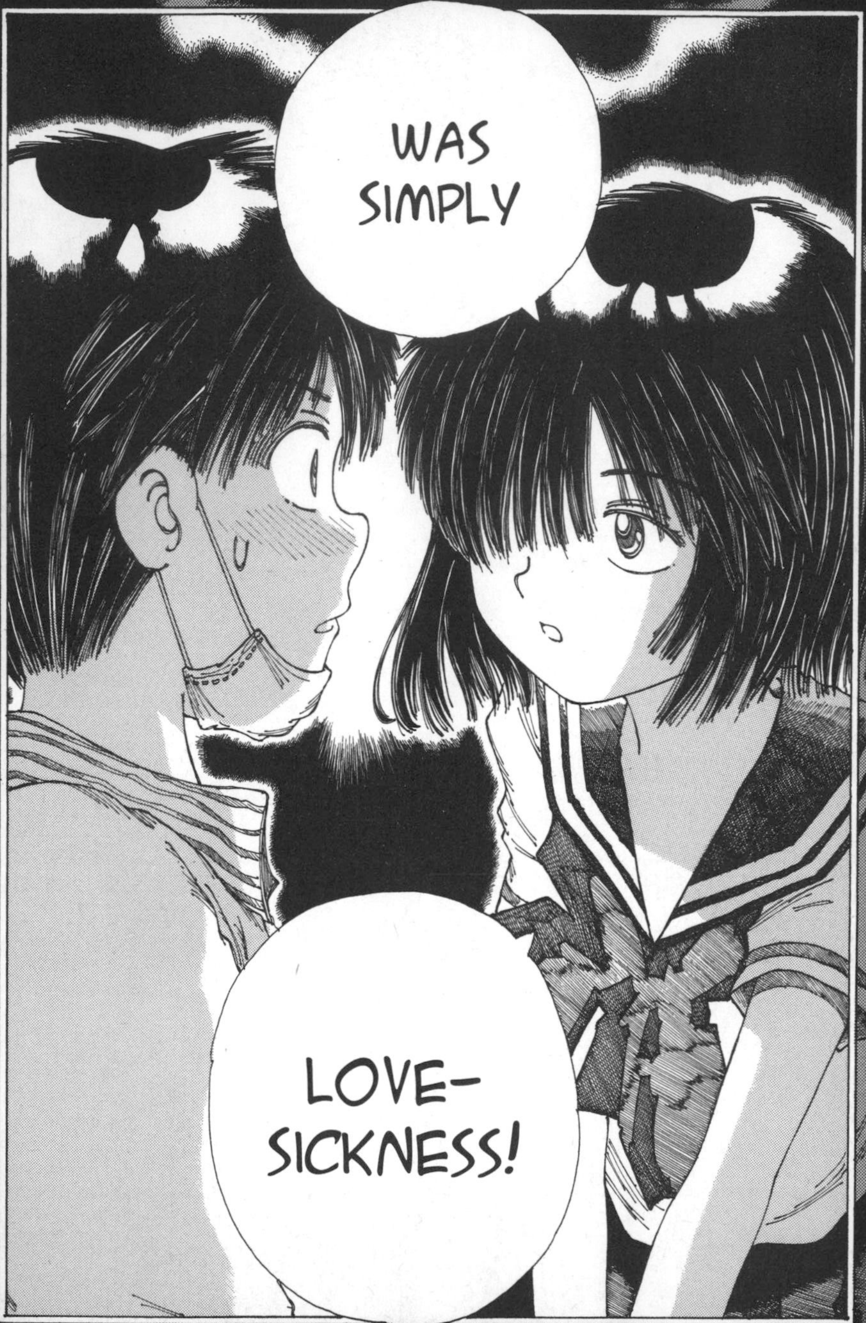
WAS SIMPLY
LOVE-SICKNESS!

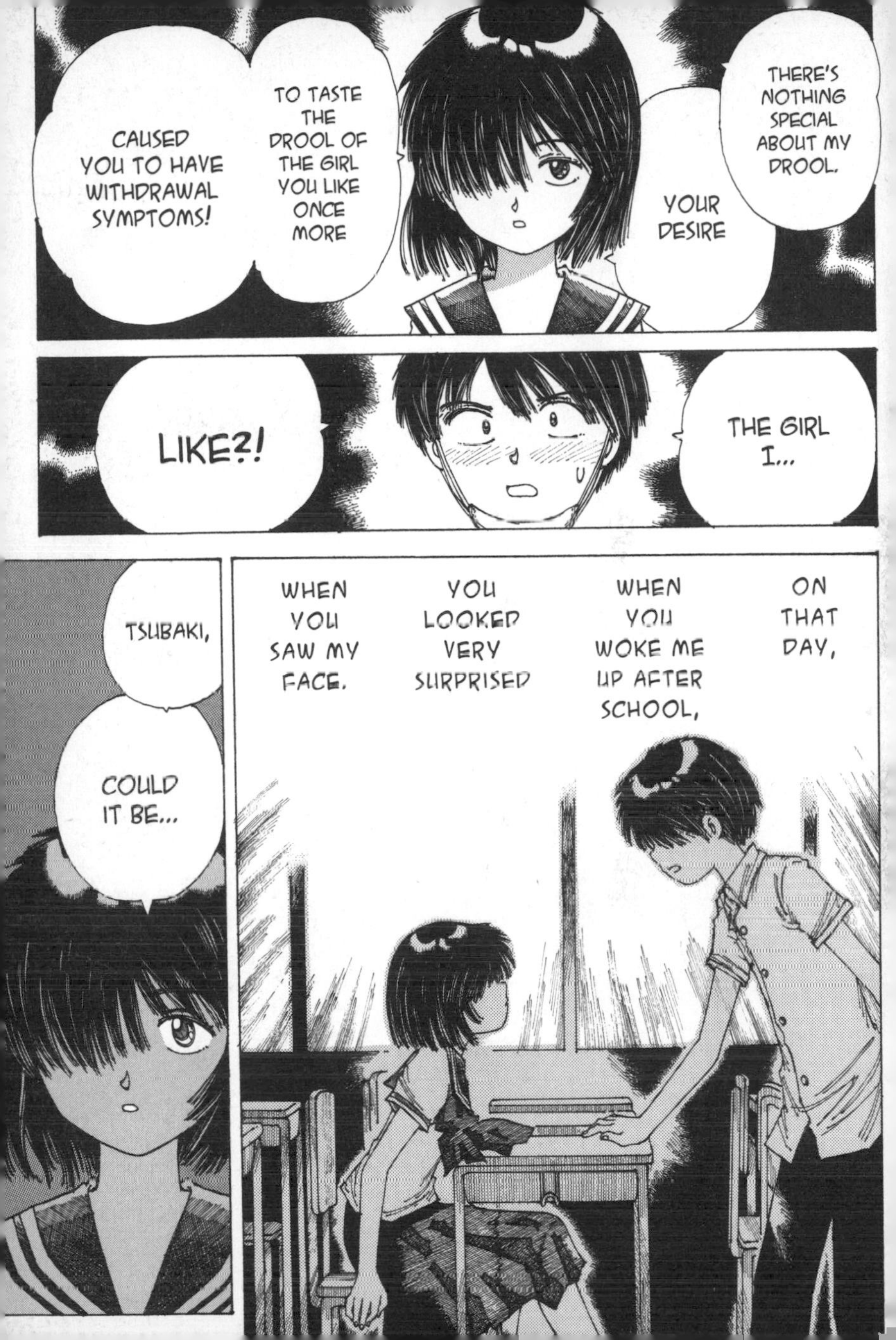
THERE'S NOTHING SPECIAL ABOUT MY DROOL.
YOUR DESIRE
TO TASTE THE DROOL OF THE GIRL YOU LIKE ONCE MORE
CAUSED YOU TO HAVE WITHDRAWAL SYMPTOMS!
THE GIRL I...
LIKE?!
ON THAT DAY,
WHEN YOU WOKE ME UP AFTER SCHOOL,
YOU LOOKED VERY SURPRISED
WHEN YOU SAW MY FACE.
TSUBAKI,
COULD IT BE...

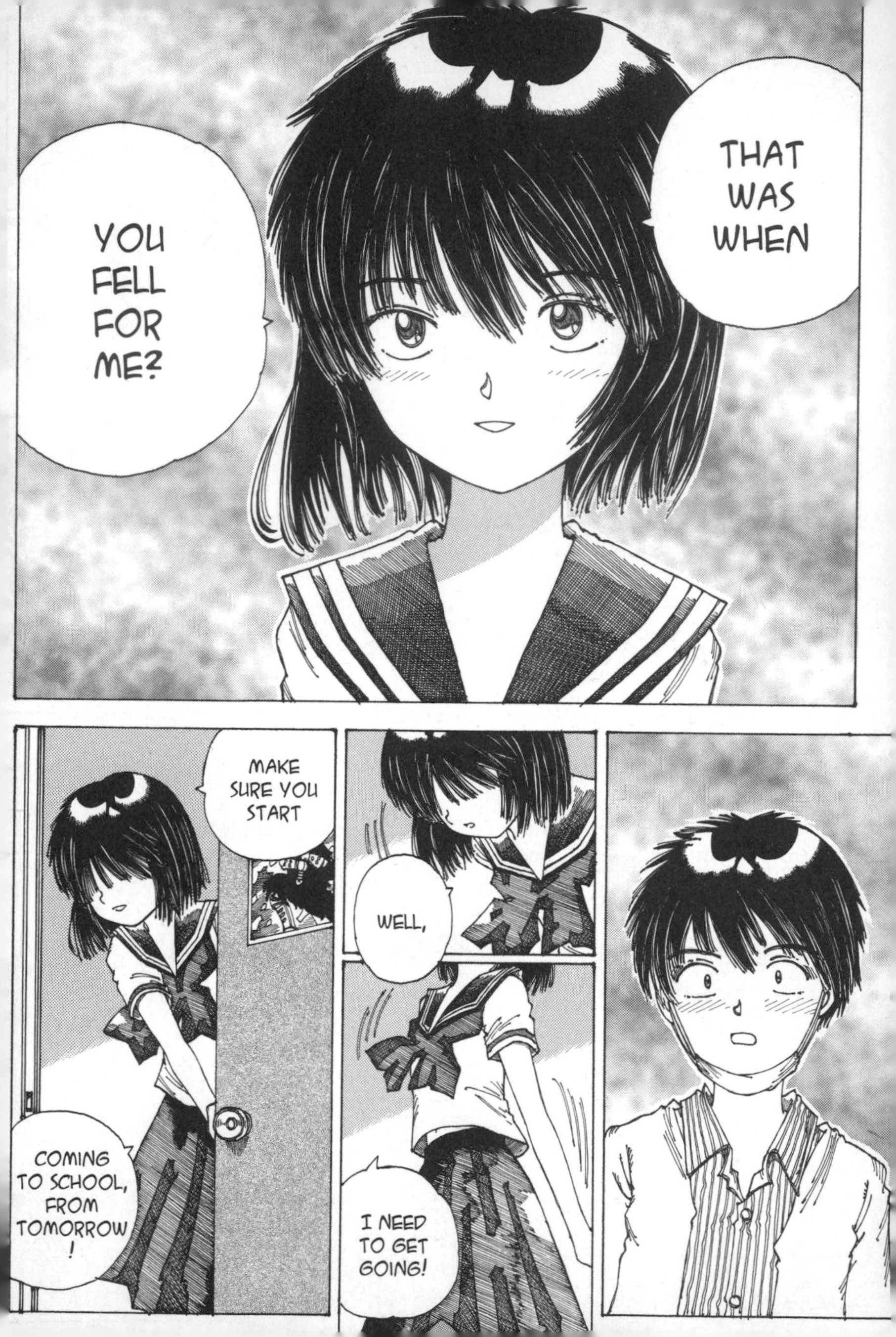
THAT WAS WHEN
YOU FELL FOR ME?
WELL,
I NEED TO GET GOING!
MAKE SURE YOU START
COMING TO SCHOOL, FROM TOMORROW!

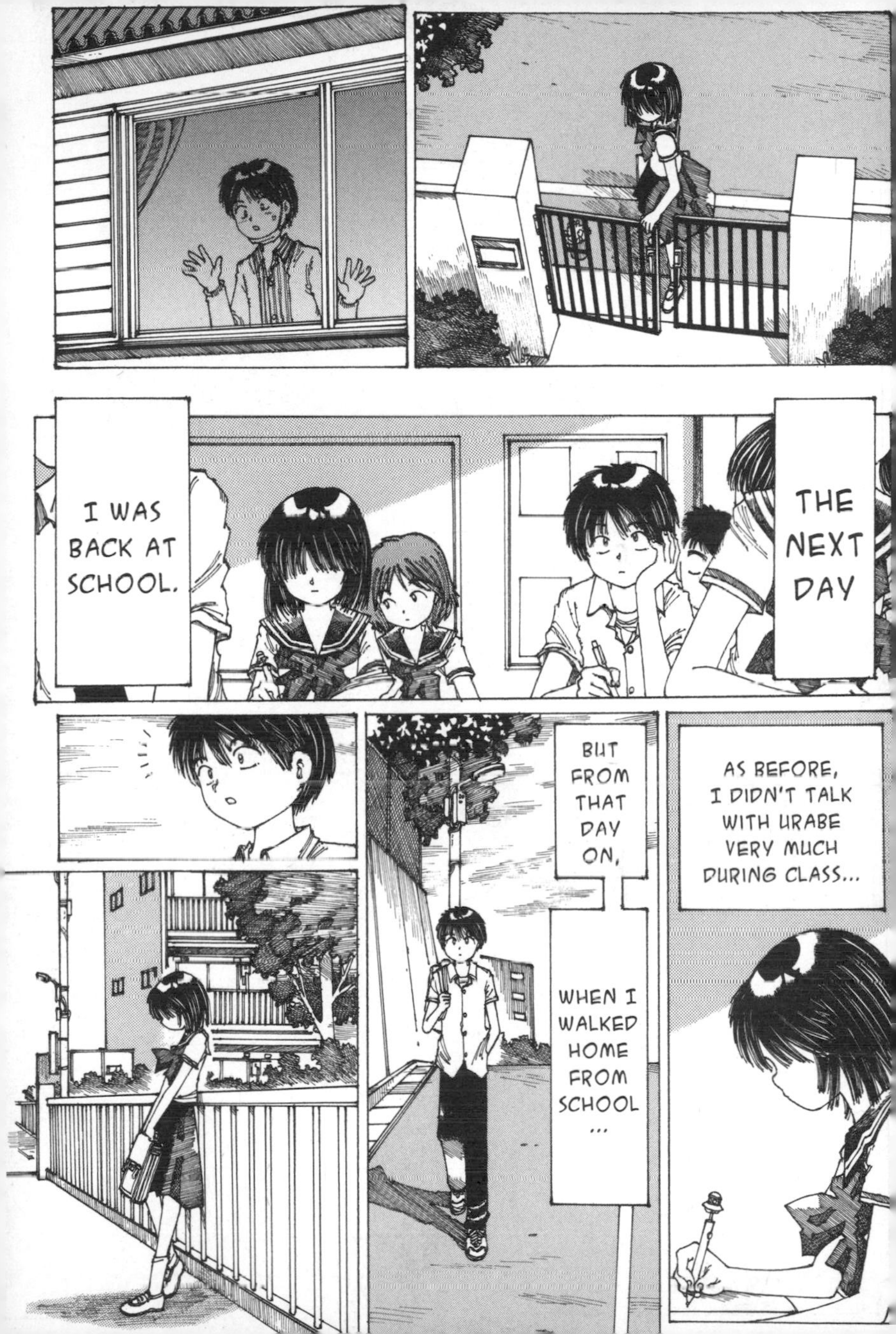
THE NEXT DAY
I WAS BACK AT SCHOOL.
AS BEFORE, I DIDN'T TALK WITH URABE VERY MUCH DURING CLASS...
BUT FROM THAT DAY ON,
WHEN I WALKED HOME FROM SCHOOL ...

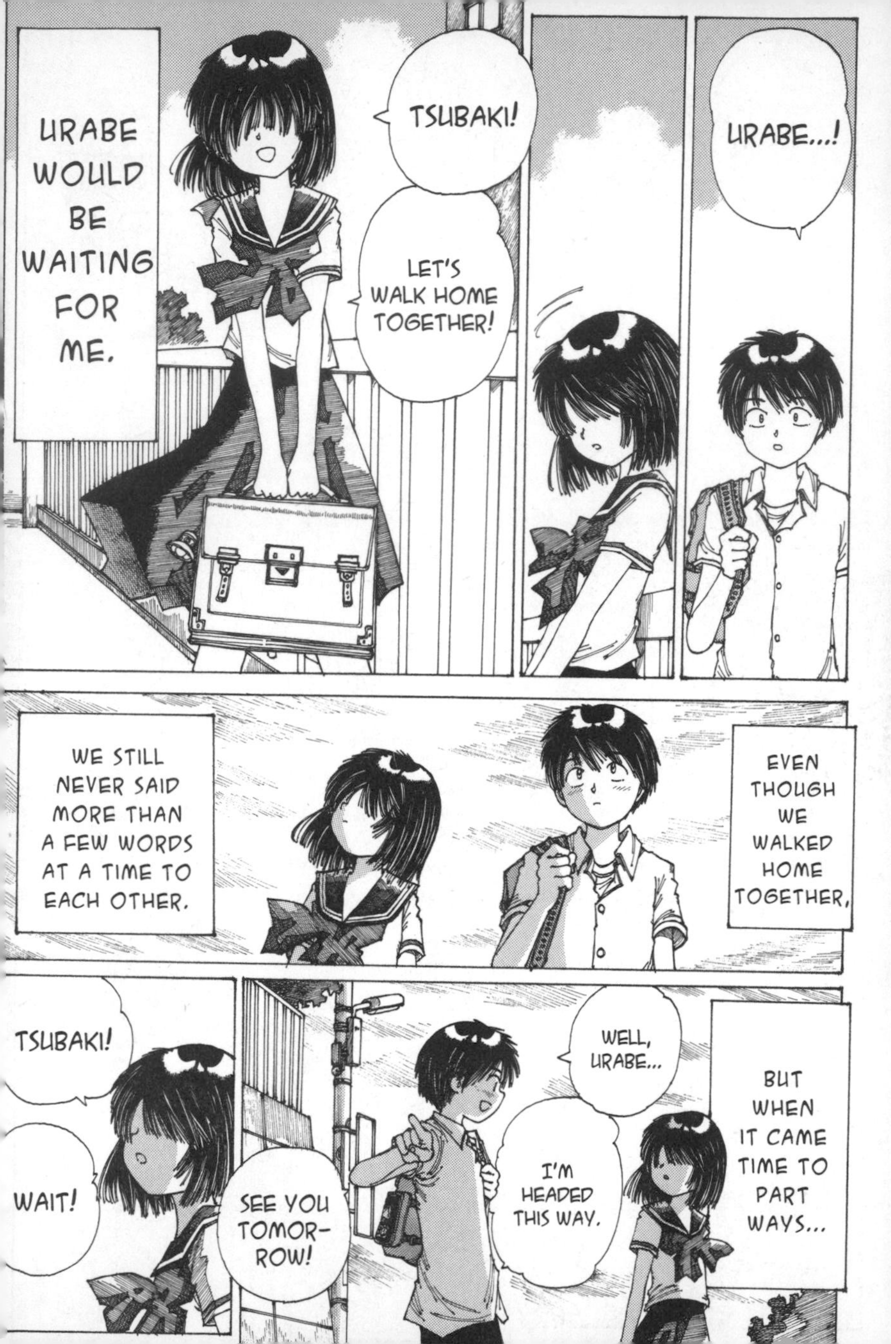
URABE...!
TSUBAKI!
LET'S WALK HOME TOGETHER!
URABE WOULD BE WAITING FOR ME.
EVEN THOUGH WE WALKED HOME TOGETHER,
WE STILL NEVER SAID MORE THAN A FEW WORDS AT A TIME TO EACH OTHER.
BUT WHEN IT CAME TIME TO PART WAYS...
WELL, URABE...
I'M HEADED THIS WAY.
SEE YOU TOMOR-ROW!
TSUBAKI!
WAIT!

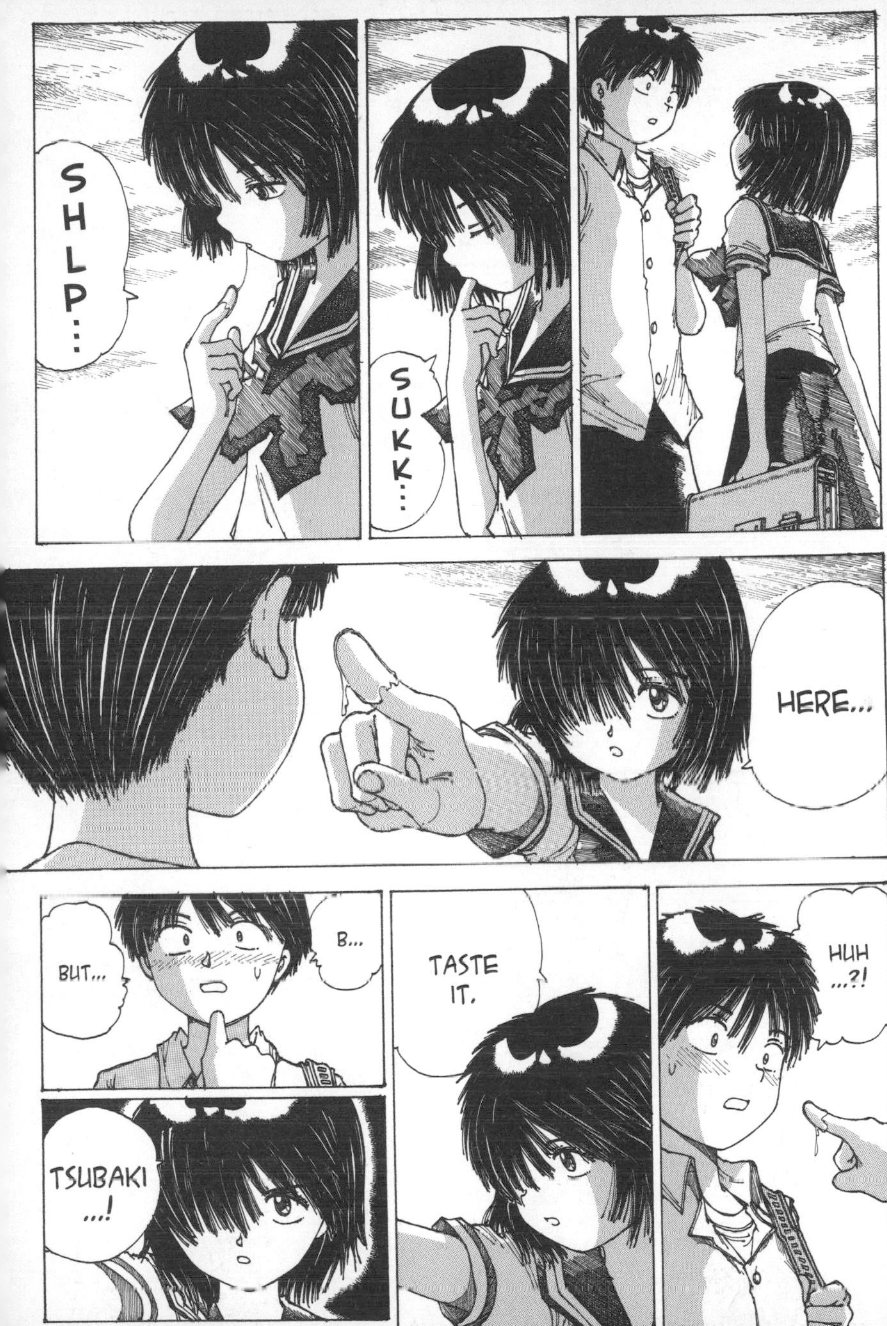
SUKK...
SHLP...
HERE...
HUH ...?!
TASTE IT.
B...
BUT...
TSUBAKI ...!

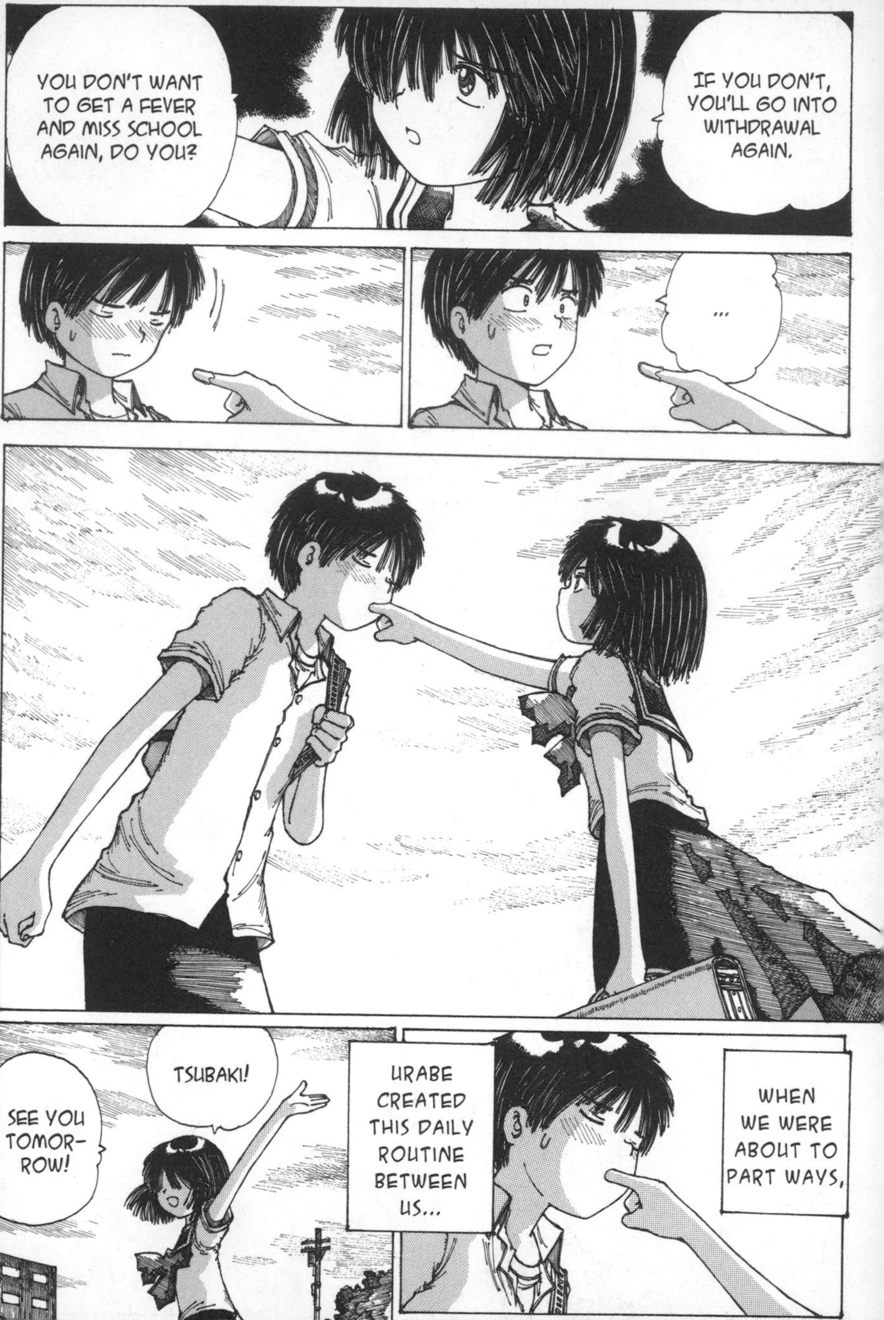
IF YOU DON'T, YOU'LL GO INTO WITHDRAWAL AGAIN.
YOU DON'T WANT TO GET A FEVER AND MISS SCHOOL AGAIN, DO YOU?
...
WHEN WE WERE ABOUT TO PART WAYS,
URABE CREATED THIS DAILY ROUTINE BETWEEN US...
TSUBAKI!
SEE YOU TOMOR-ROW!

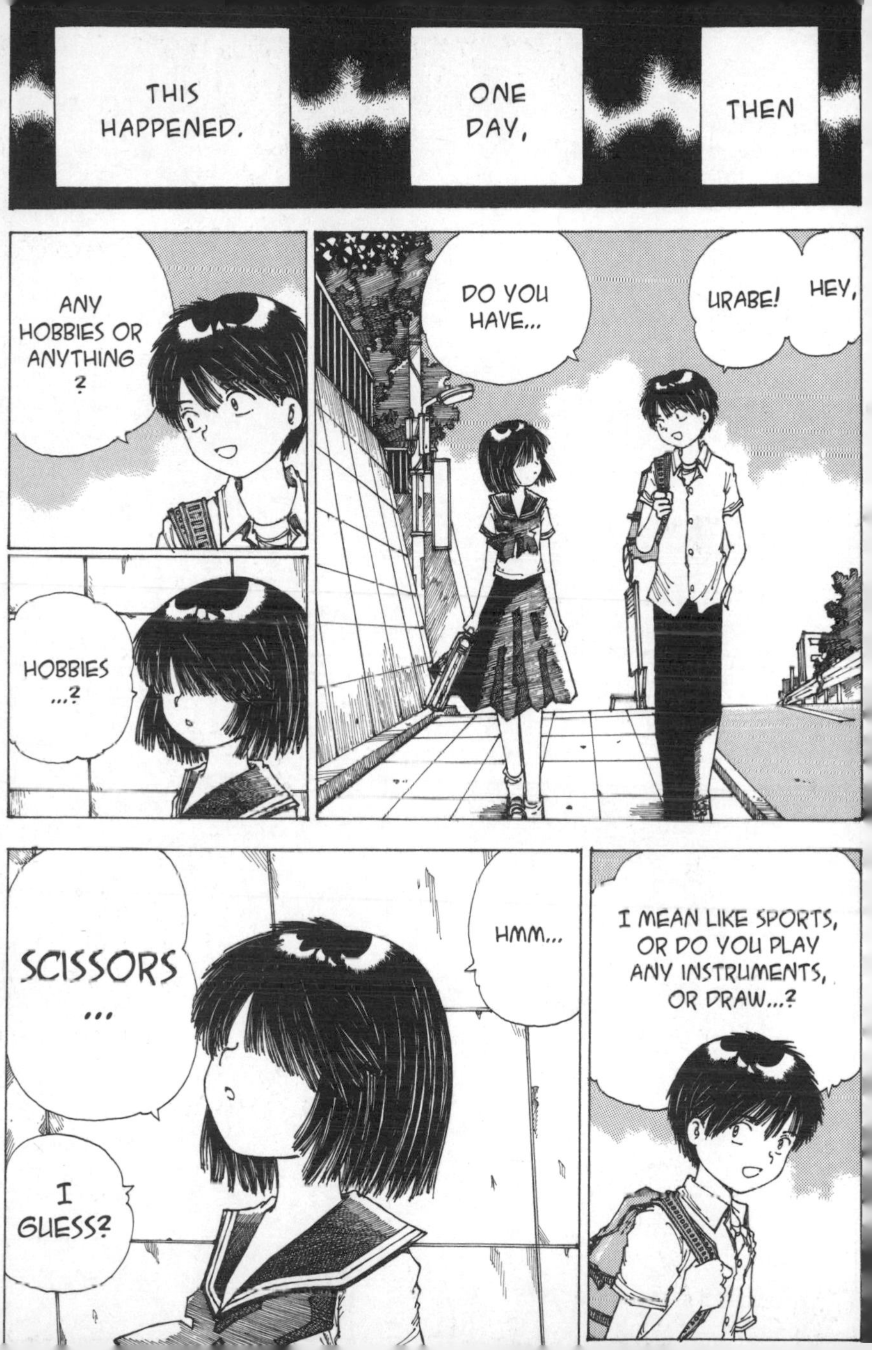
THEN
ONE DAY,
THIS HAPPENED.
HEY, URABE!
DO YOU HAVE...
ANY HOBBIES OR ANYTHING?
HOBBIES ...?
I MEAN LIKE SPORTS, OR DO YOU PLAY ANY INSTRUMENTS, OR DRAW...?
HMM...
SCISSORS ...
I GUESS?

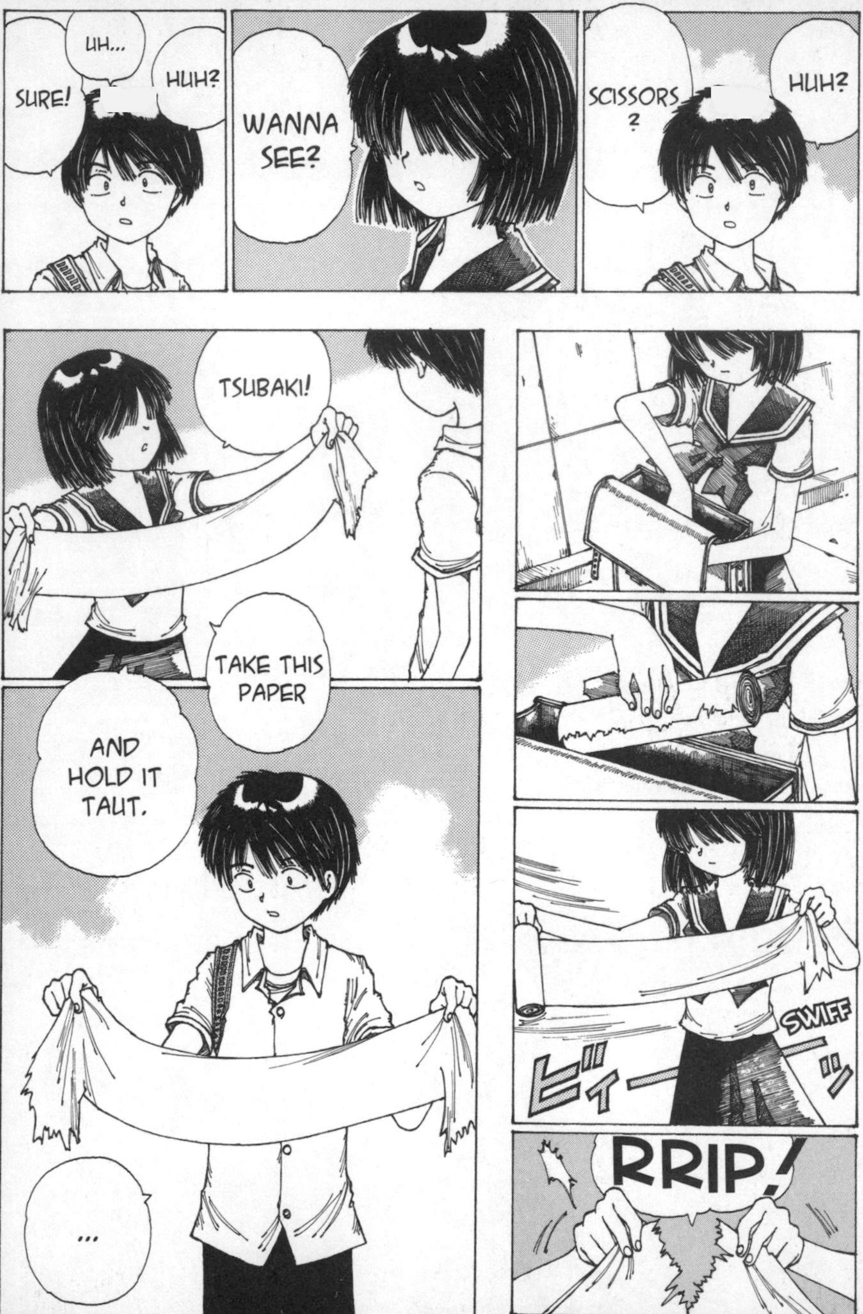
HUH?
SCISSORS ?
WANNA SEE?
HUH?
UH...
SURE!
SWIFF
ビィーッ
RRIP!
TSUBAKI!
TAKE THIS PAPER
AND HOLD IT TAUT.
...

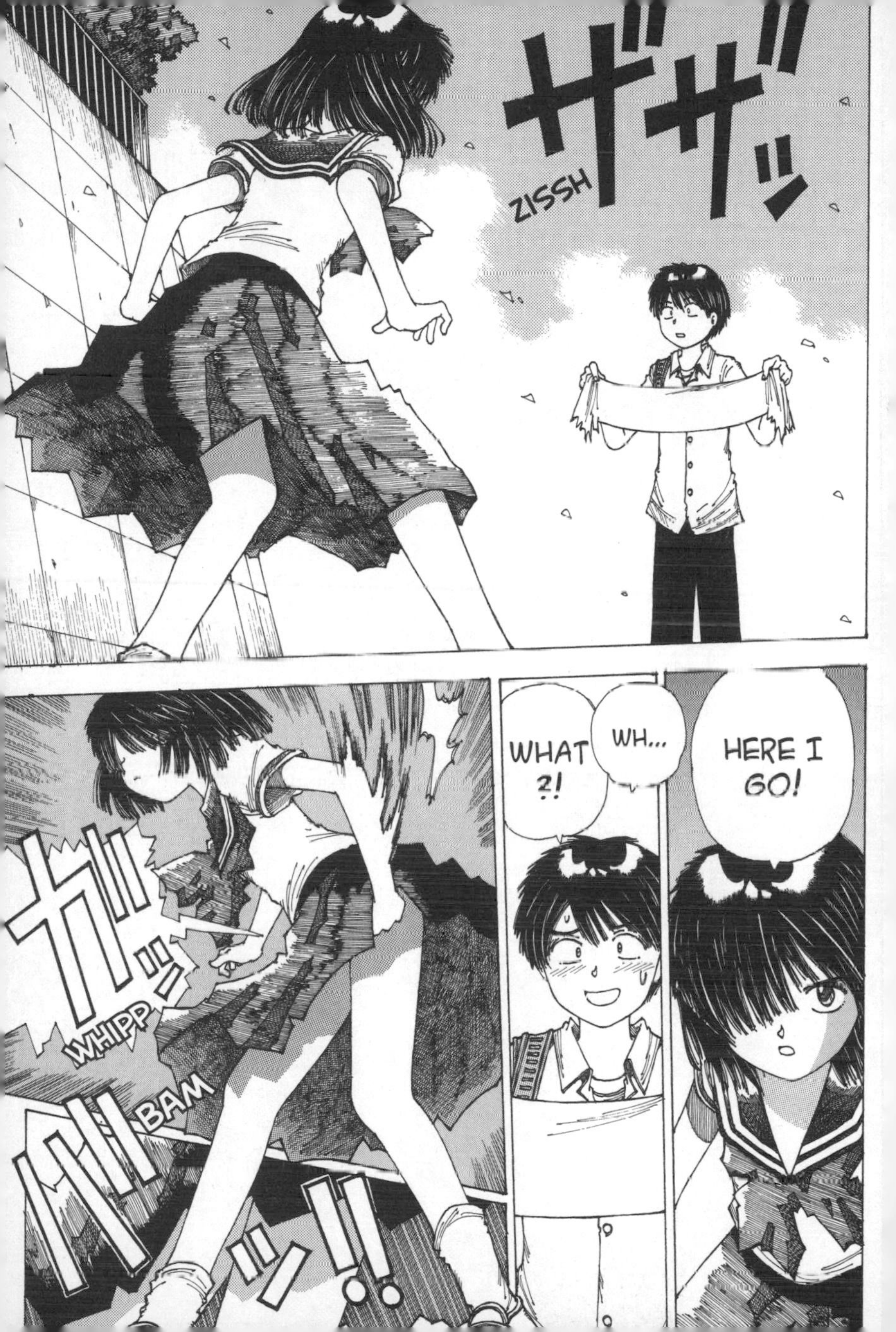
ザザッ
ZISSH
HERE I GO!
WH...
WHAT ?!
WHIPP
BAM

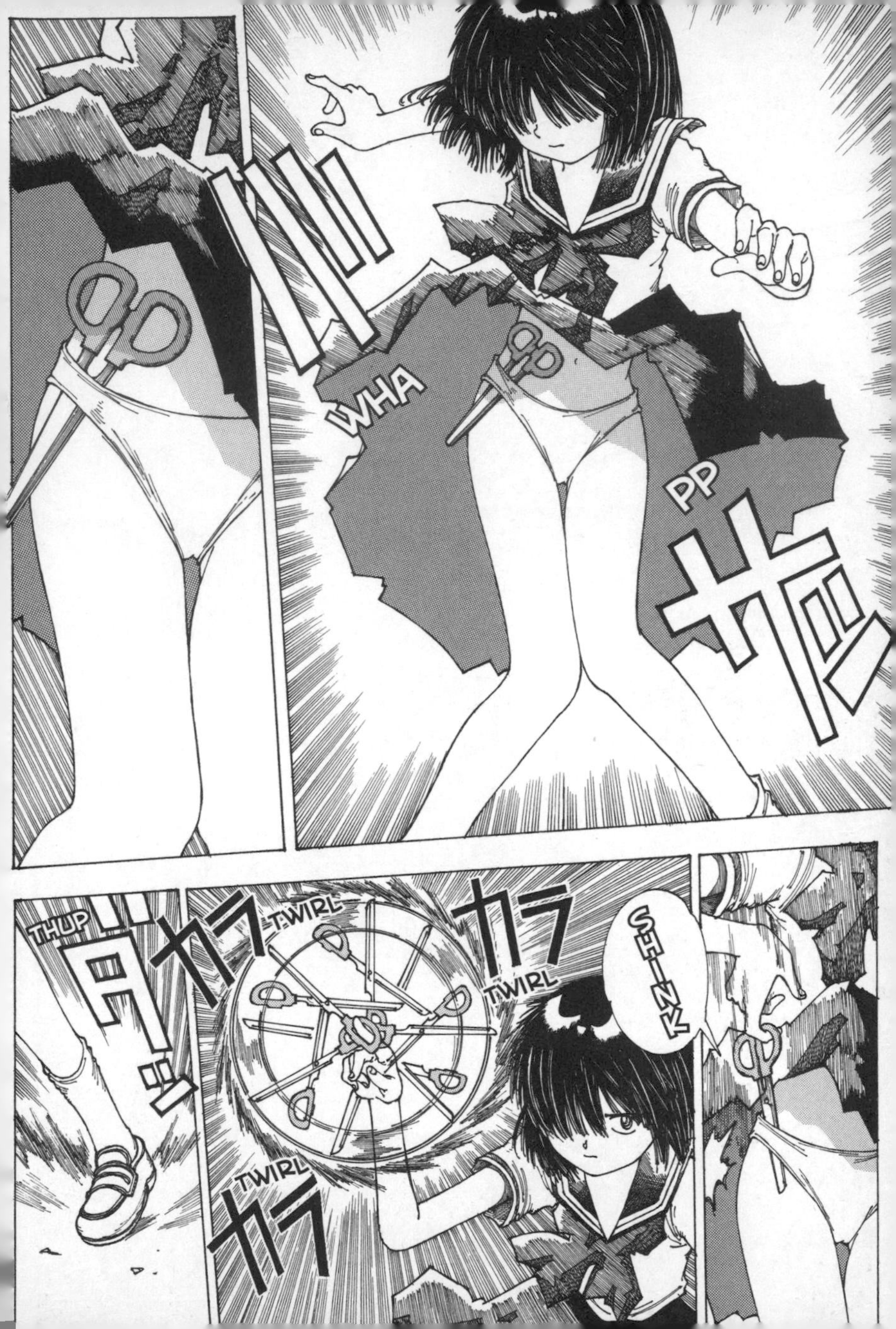
WHA
PP
SHINK
カラ
TWIRL
カラ
TWIRL
カラ
TWIRL
THUP

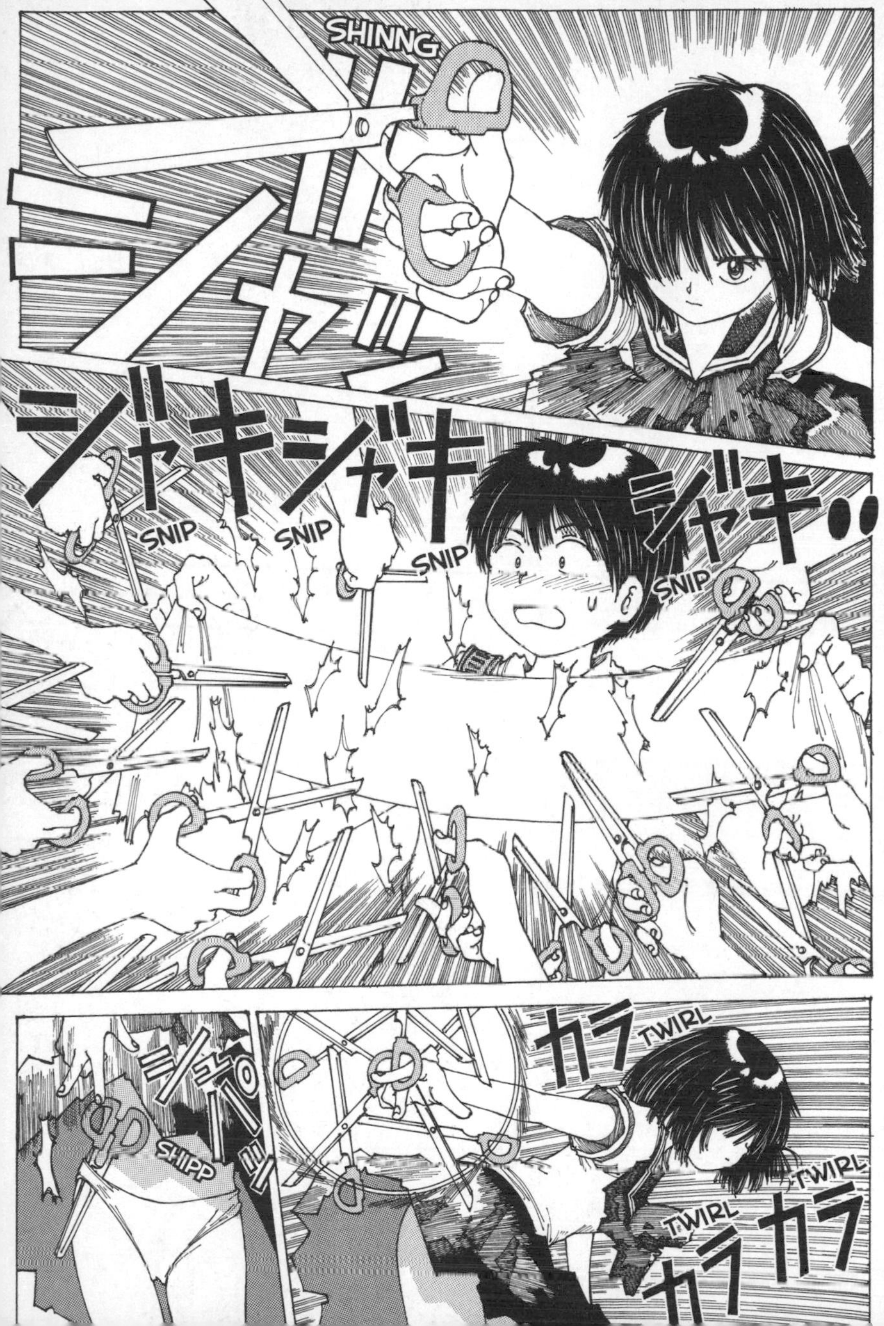
SHINNG
シャキシャキ
SNIP
SNIP
SNIP
シャキ‥
SNIP
カラ
TWIRL
TWIRL
TWIRL
カラカラ
SHIPP

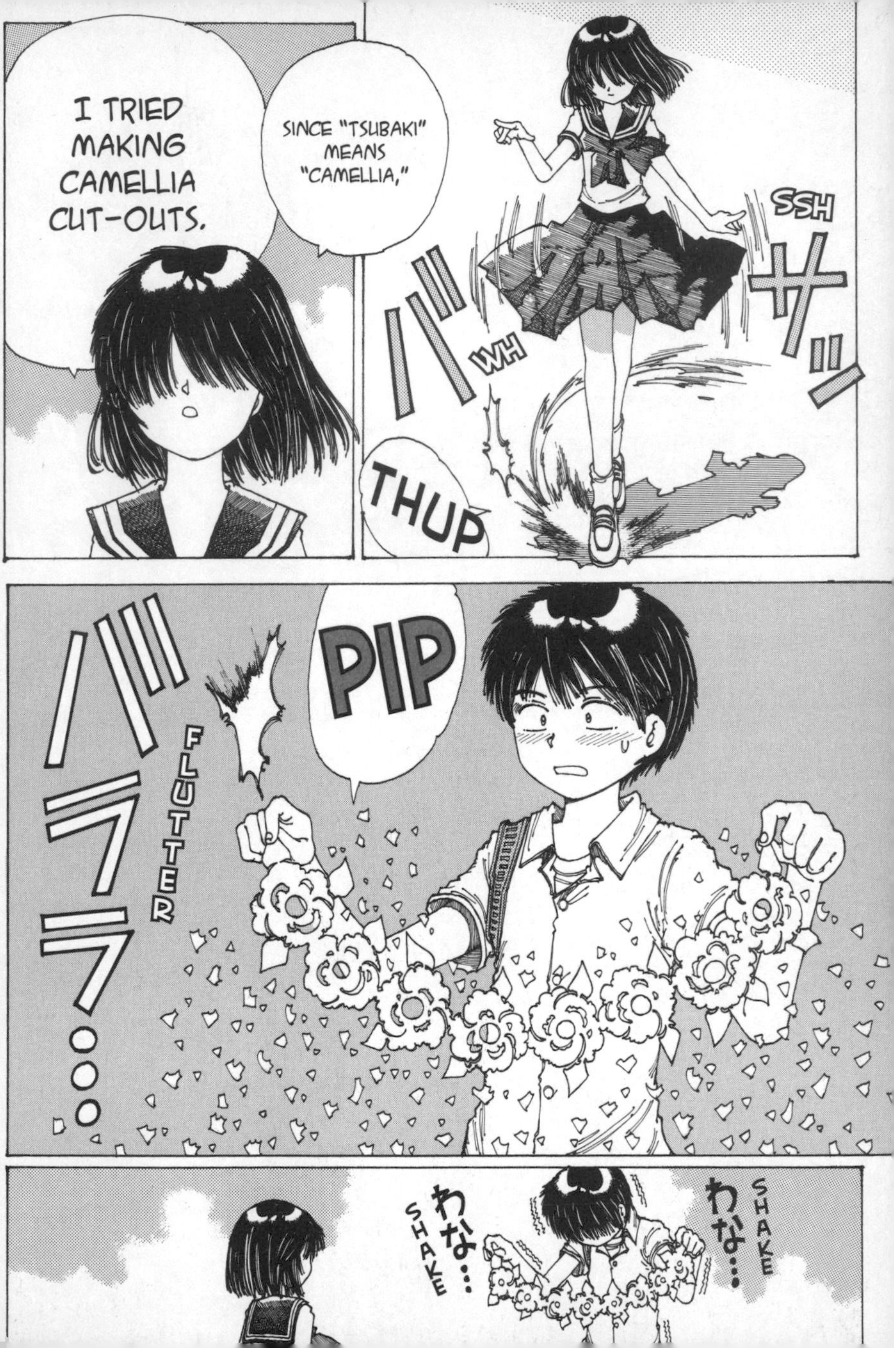
サッ
SSH
バッ
WH
THUP
SINCE "TSUBAKI" MEANS "CAMELLIA,"
I TRIED MAKING CAMELLIA CUT-OUTS.
PIP
バラララ…
FLUTTER
わな…
SHAKE
わな…
SHAKE

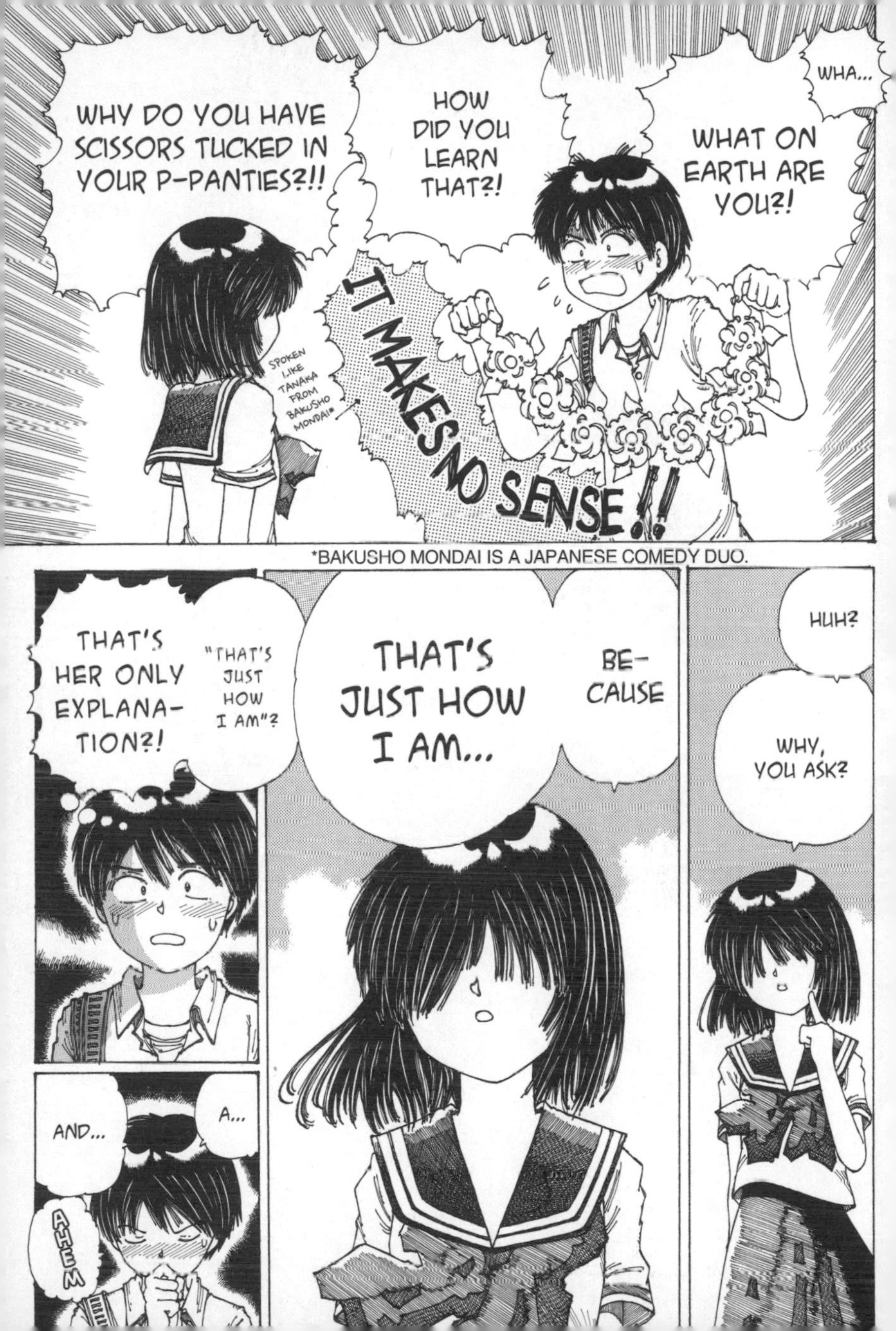
WHA...
WHAT ON EARTH ARE YOU?!
HOW DID YOU LEARN THAT?!
WHY DO YOU HAVE SCISSORS TUCKED IN YOUR P-PANTIES?!!
IT MAKES NO SENSE!!
SPOKEN LIKE TANAKA FROM BAKUSHO MONDAI*
*BAKUSHO MONDAI IS A JAPANESE COMEDY DUO.
HUH?
WHY, YOU ASK?
BE- CAUSE
THAT'S JUST HOW I AM...
"THAT'S JUST HOW I AM"?
THAT'S HER ONLY EXPLANATION?!
A...
AND...
AHEM

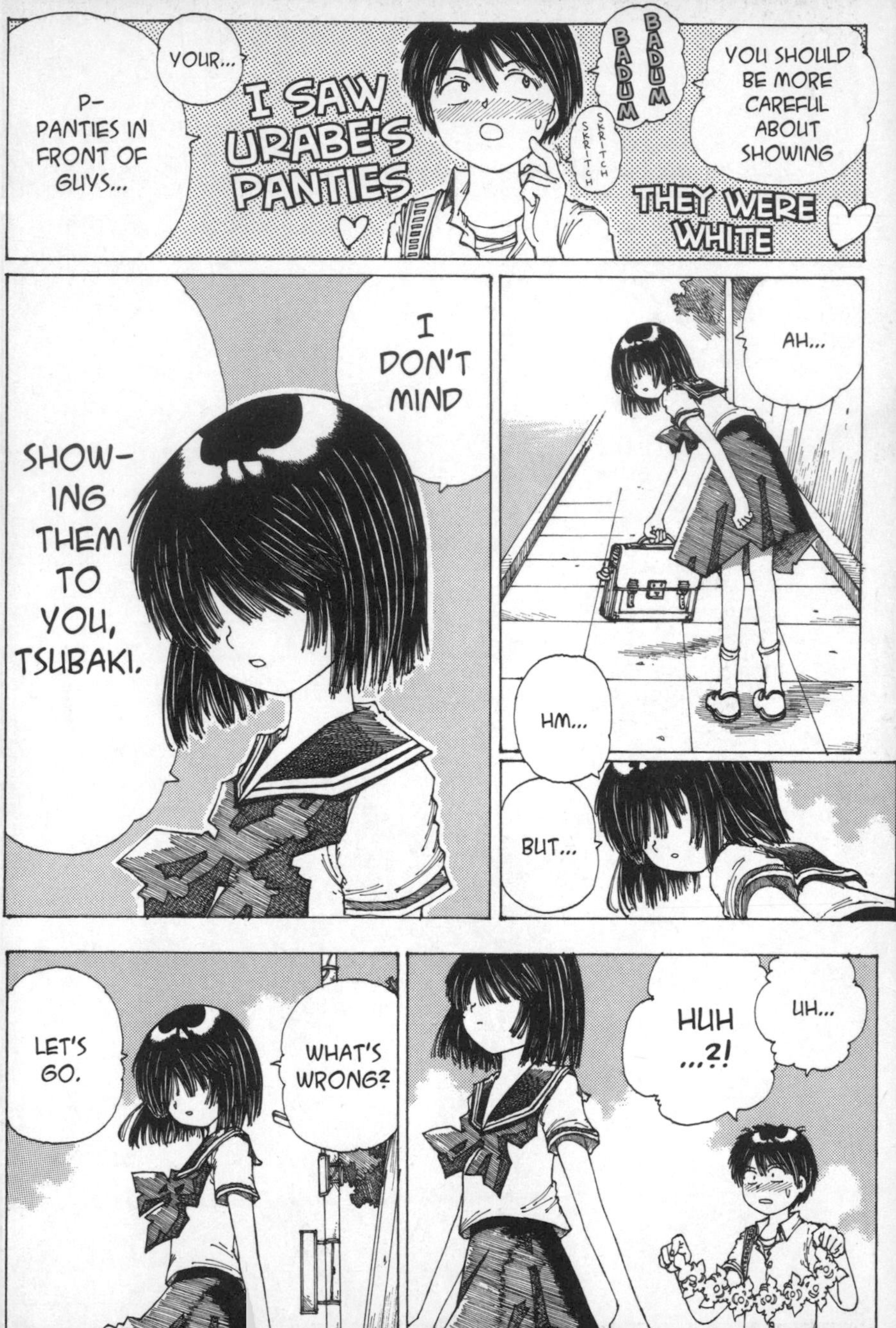
YOU SHOULD BE MORE CAREFUL ABOUT SHOWING
THEY WERE WHITE
BADUM BADUM
SKRITCH SKRITCH
I SAW URABE'S PANTIES
YOUR...
P-PANTIES IN FRONT OF GUYS...
AH...
HM...
BUT...
I DON'T MIND
SHOWING THEM TO YOU, TSUBAKI.
UH...
HUH ...?!
WHAT'S WRONG?
LET'S GO.

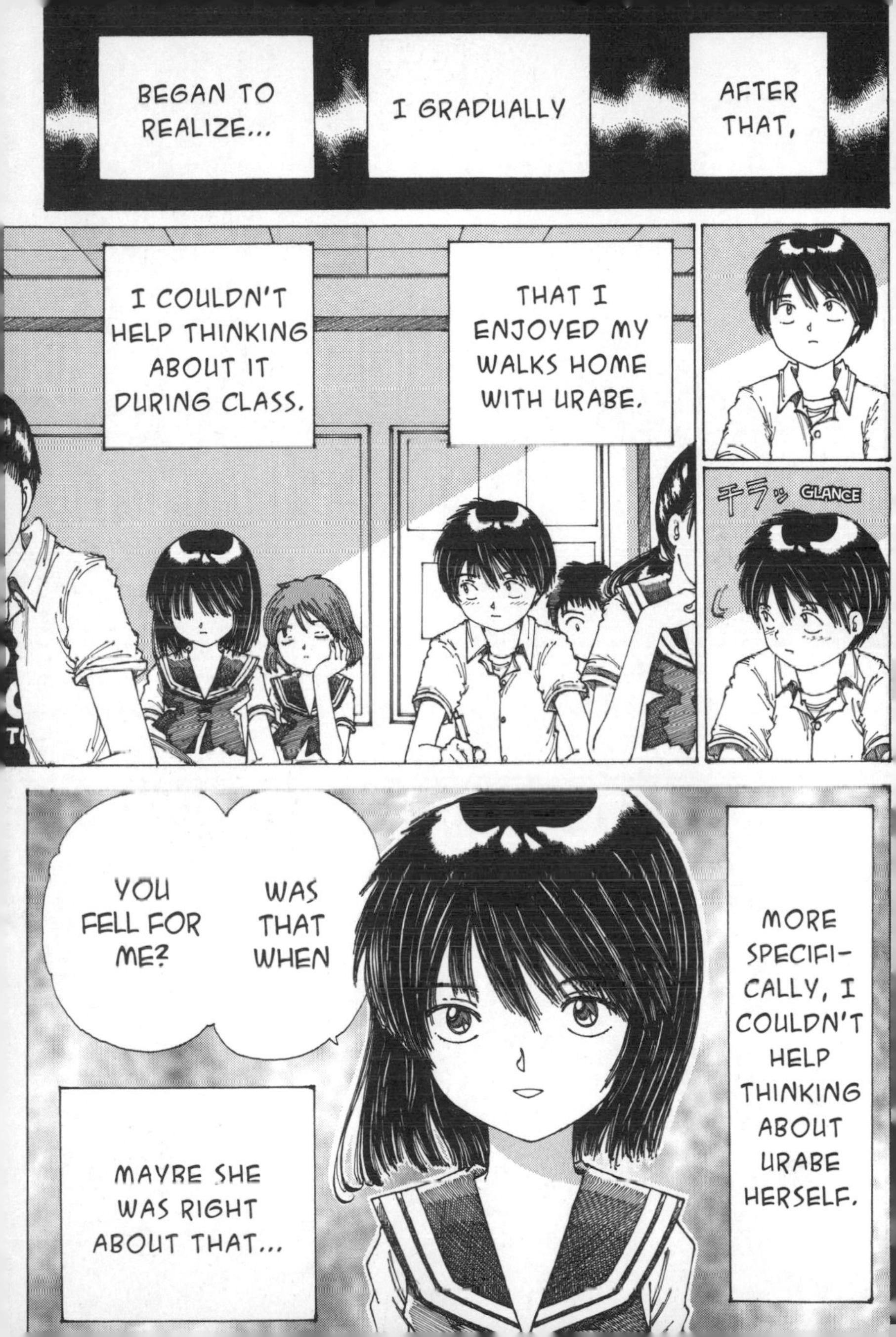
AFTER THAT,
I GRADUALLY
BEGAN TO REALIZE...
チラッ GLANCE
THAT I ENJOYED MY WALKS HOME WITH URABE.
I COULDN'T HELP THINKING ABOUT IT DURING CLASS.
MORE SPECIFI- CALLY, I COULDN'T HELP THINKING ABOUT URABE HERSELF.
WAS THAT WHEN YOU FELL FOR ME?
MAYBE SHE WAS RIGHT ABOUT THAT...

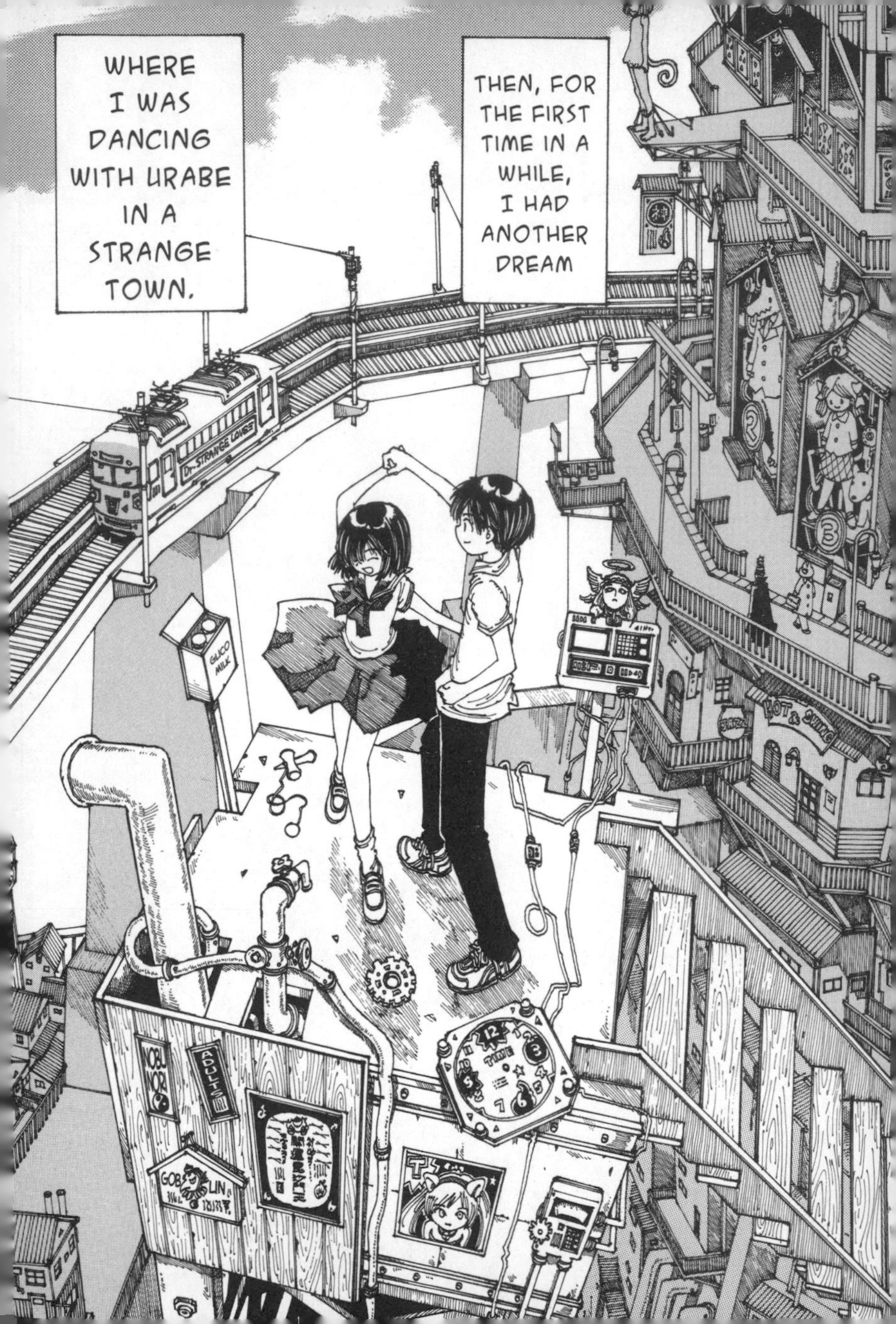
THEN, FOR THE FIRST TIME IN A WHILE, I HAD ANOTHER DREAM
WHERE I WAS DANCING WITH URABE IN A STRANGE TOWN.
HOT & SWING
JAZZ
GLICO MILK
NOBU NORI
ADULTS
TIME
GOB LIN

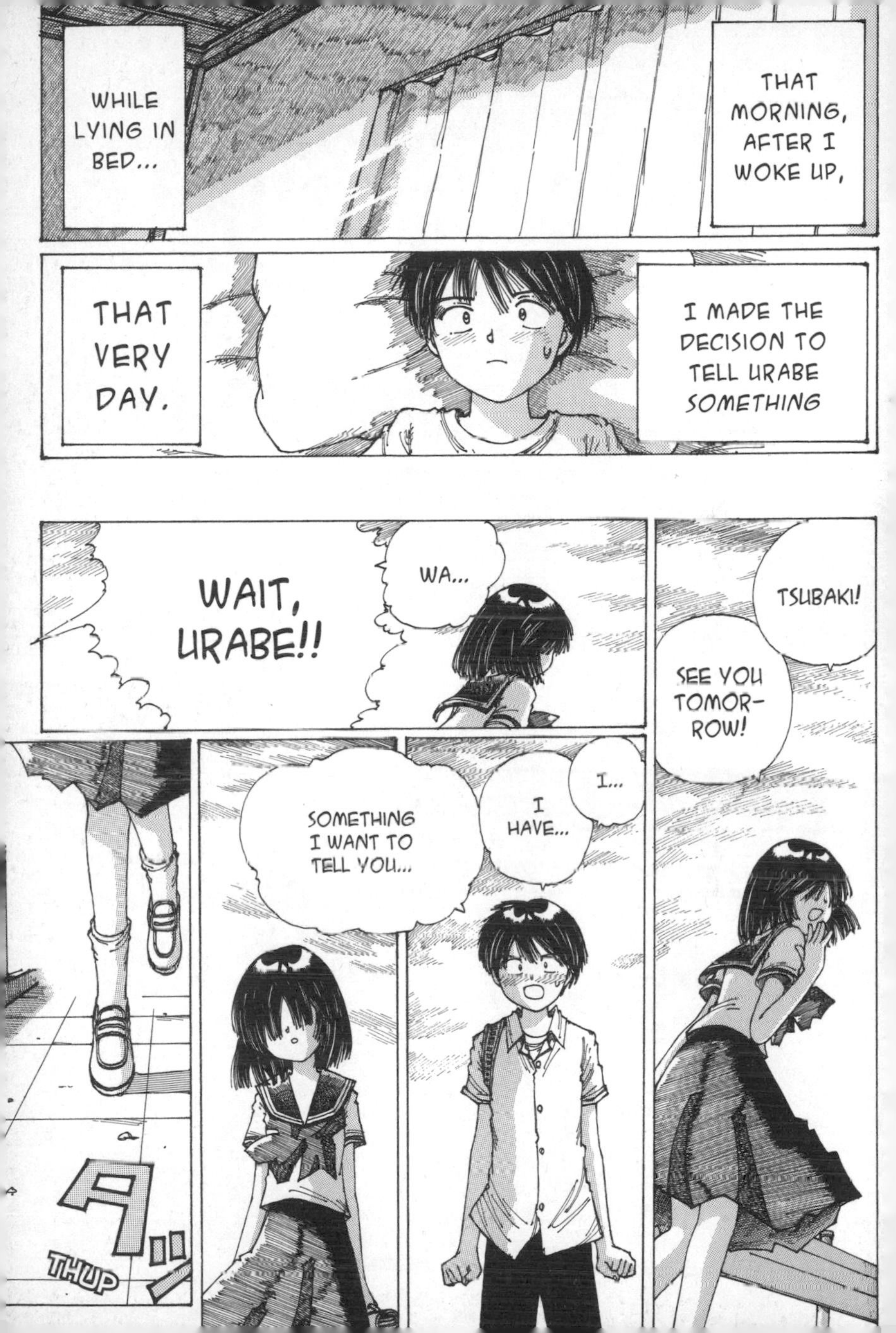
THAT MORNING, AFTER I WOKE UP,
WHILE LYING IN BED...
I MADE THE DECISION TO TELL URABE SOMETHING
THAT VERY DAY.
TSUBAKI!
SEE YOU TOMORROW!
WA...
WAIT, URABE!!
I...
I HAVE...
SOMETHING I WANT TO TELL YOU...
THUP

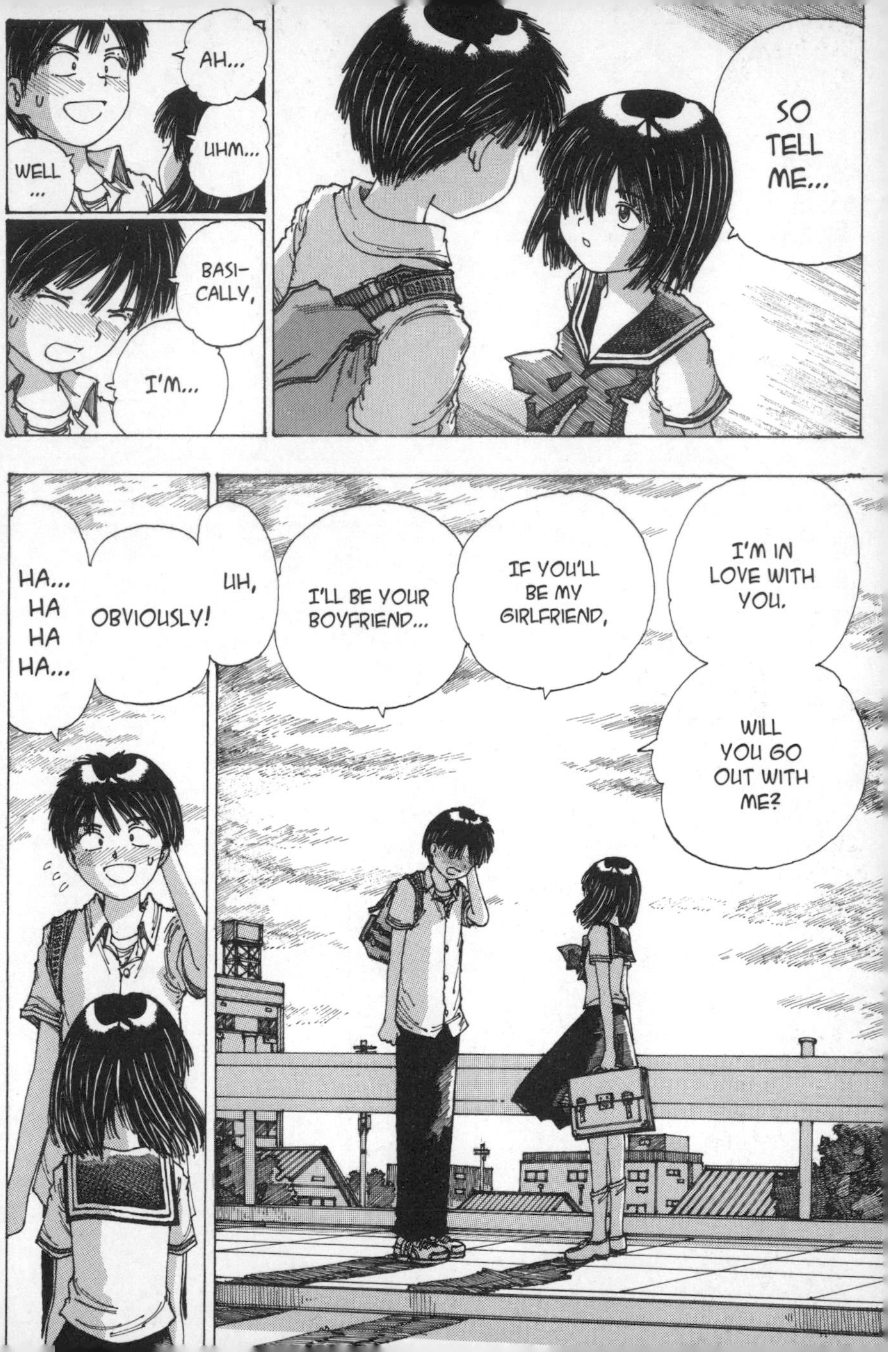
SO TELL ME...
AH...
UHM...
WELL ...
BASI-CALLY,
I'M...
I'M IN LOVE WITH YOU.
WILL YOU GO OUT WITH ME?
IF YOU'LL BE MY GIRLFRIEND,
I'LL BE YOUR BOYFRIEND...
UH, OBVIOUSLY!
HA... HA HA HA...

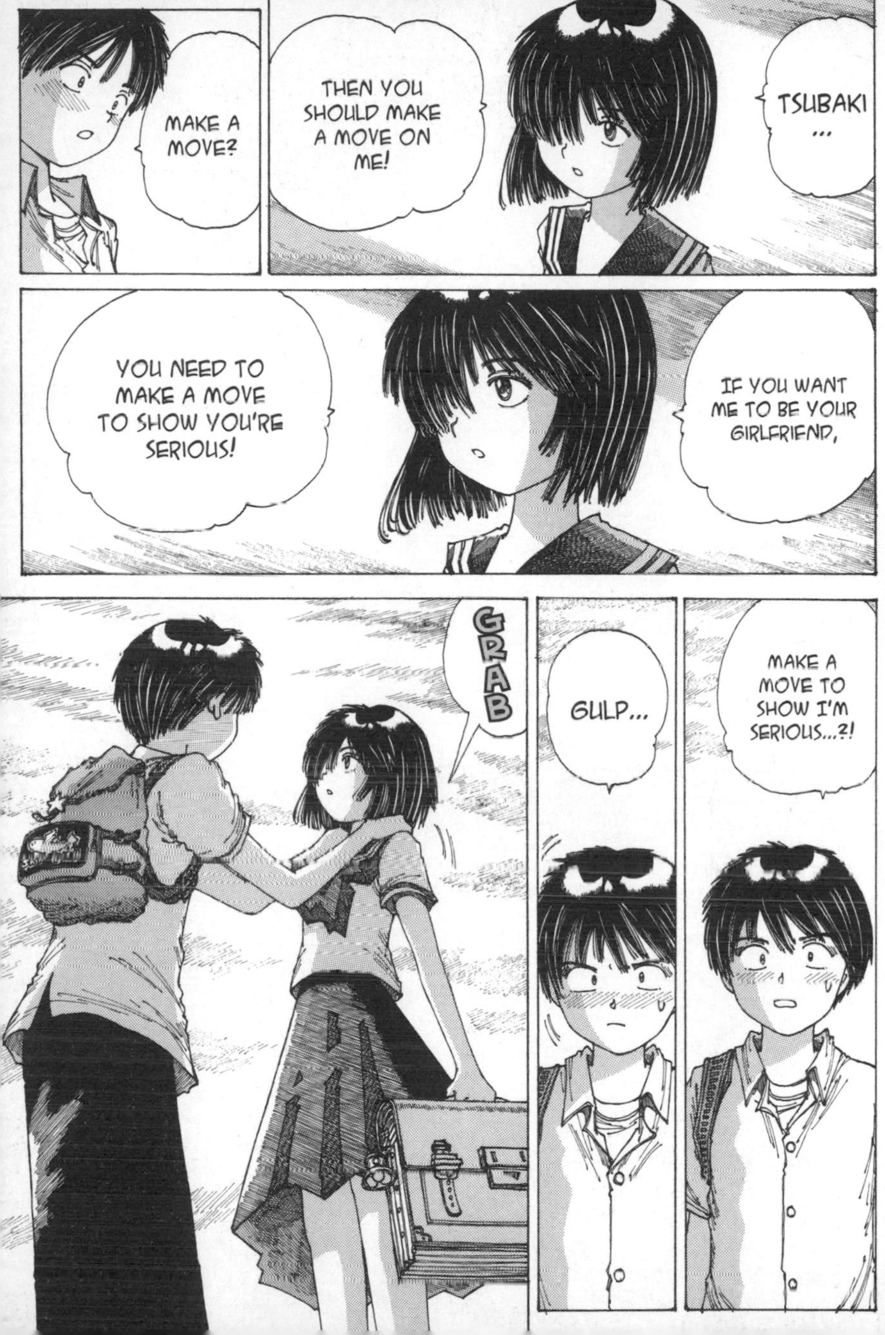
TSUBAKI ...
THEN YOU SHOULD MAKE A MOVE ON ME!
MAKE A MOVE?
IF YOU WANT ME TO BE YOUR GIRLFRIEND,
YOU NEED TO MAKE A MOVE TO SHOW YOU'RE SERIOUS!
MAKE A MOVE TO SHOW I'M SERIOUS...?!
GULP...
GRAB

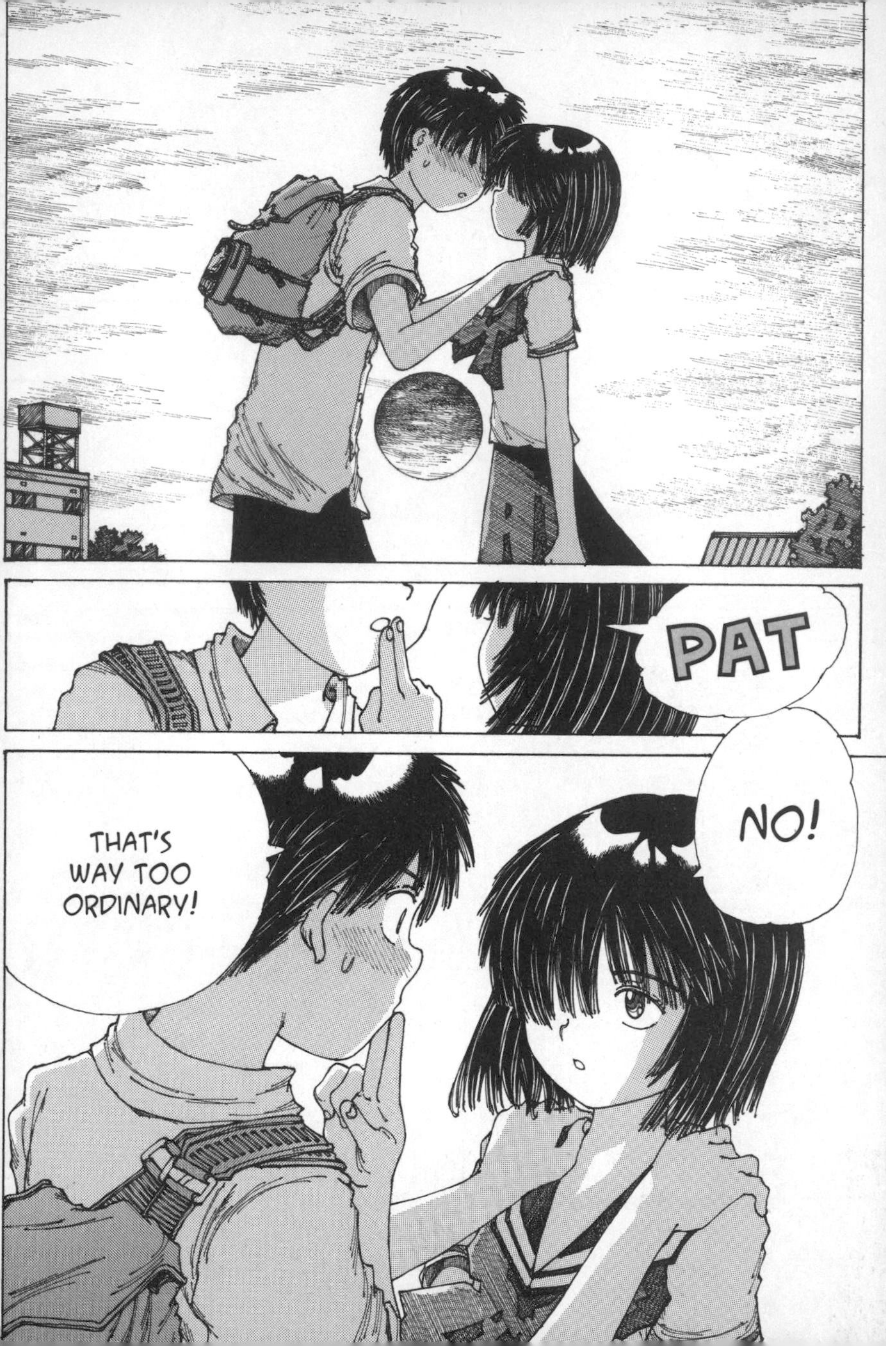
PAT
NO!
THAT'S WAY TOO ORDINARY!

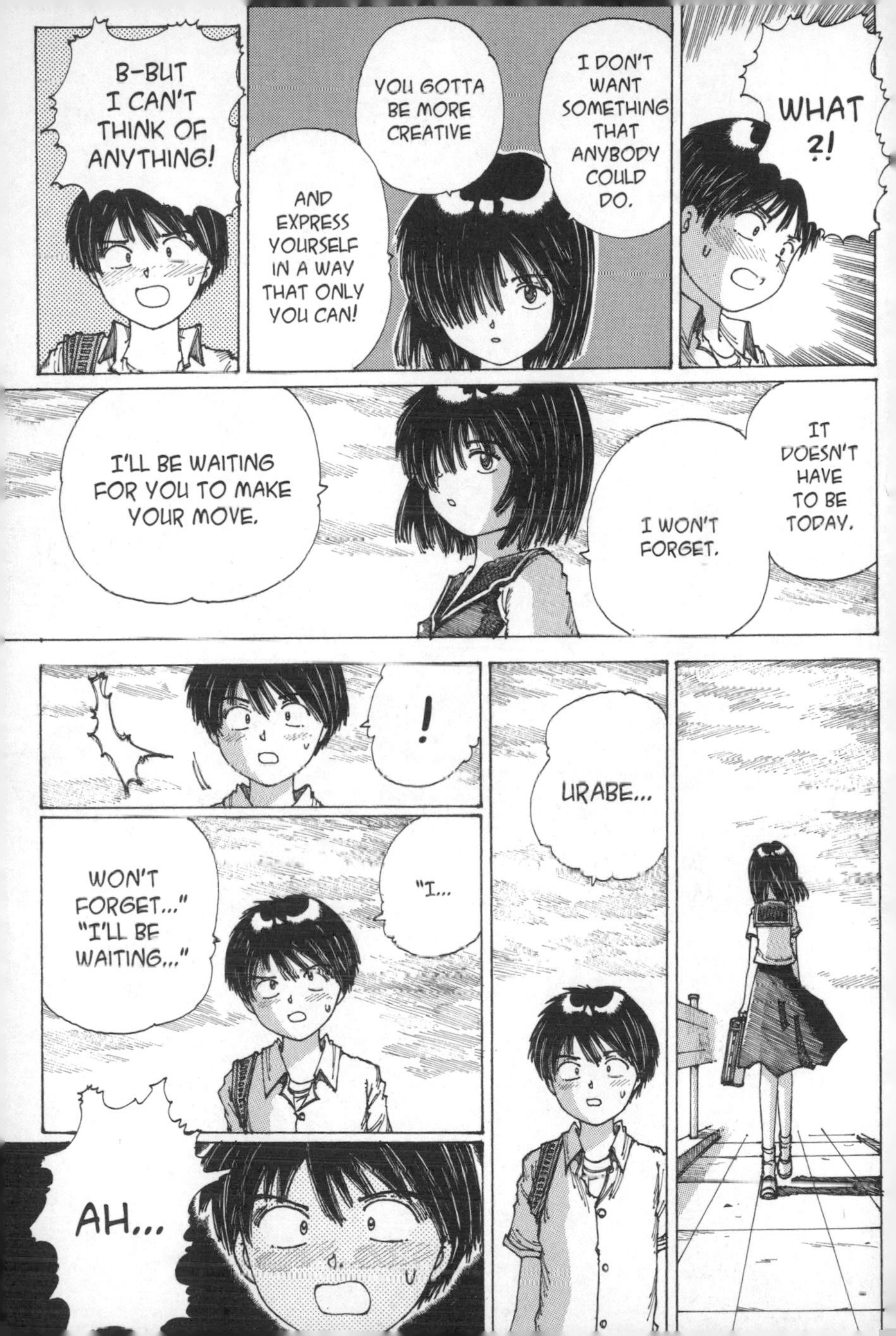
WHAT ?!
I DON'T WANT SOMETHING THAT ANYBODY COULD DO.
YOU GOTTA BE MORE CREATIVE
AND EXPRESS YOURSELF IN A WAY THAT ONLY YOU CAN!
B-BUT I CAN'T THINK OF ANYTHING!
IT DOESN'T HAVE TO BE TODAY.
I WON'T FORGET.
I'LL BE WAITING FOR YOU TO MAKE YOUR MOVE.
URABE...
!
"I...
WON'T FORGET..." "I'LL BE WAITING..."
AH...

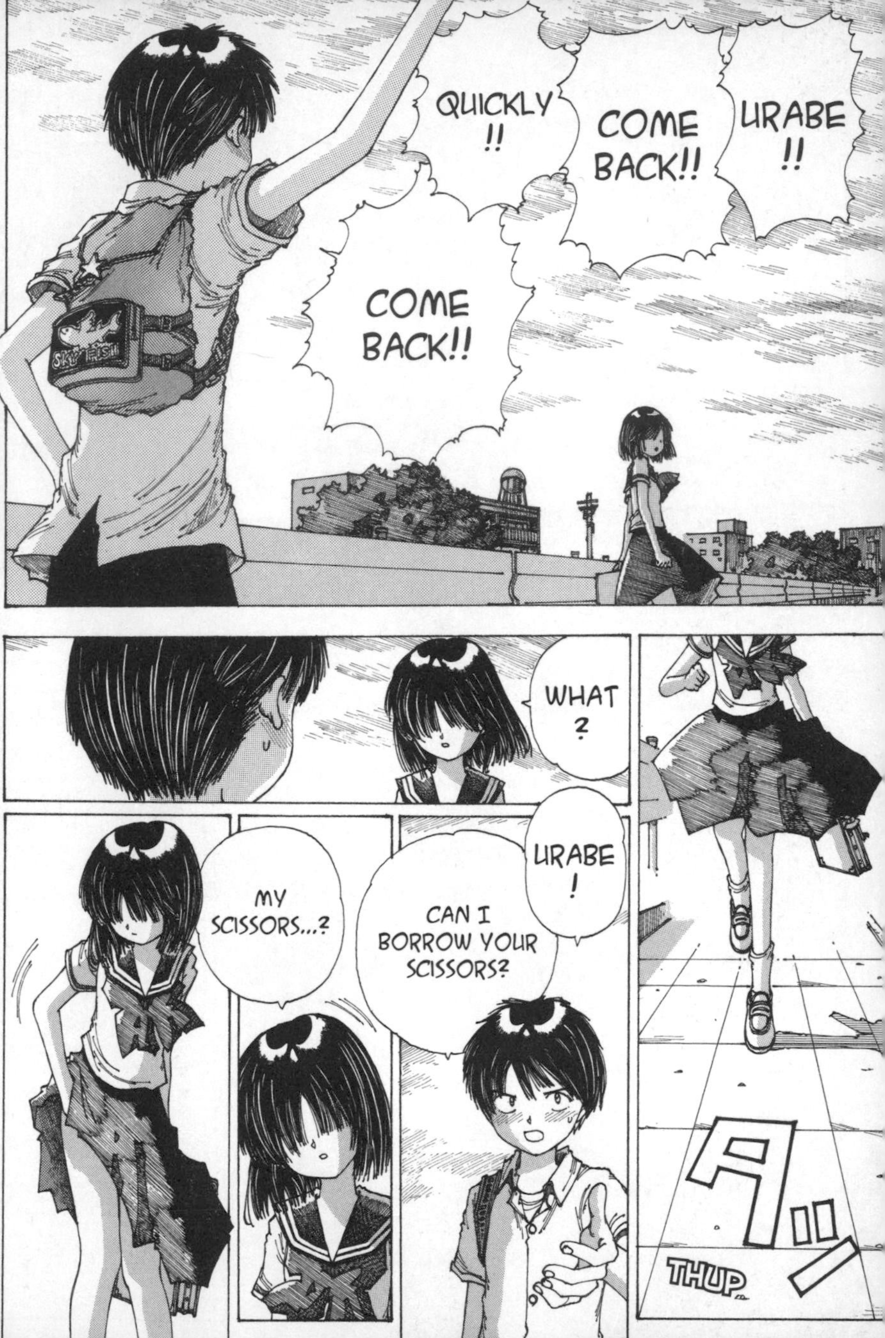
URABE !!
COME BACK!!
QUICKLY !!
COME BACK!!
THUP
WHAT ?
URABE !
CAN I BORROW YOUR SCISSORS?
MY SCISSORS...?

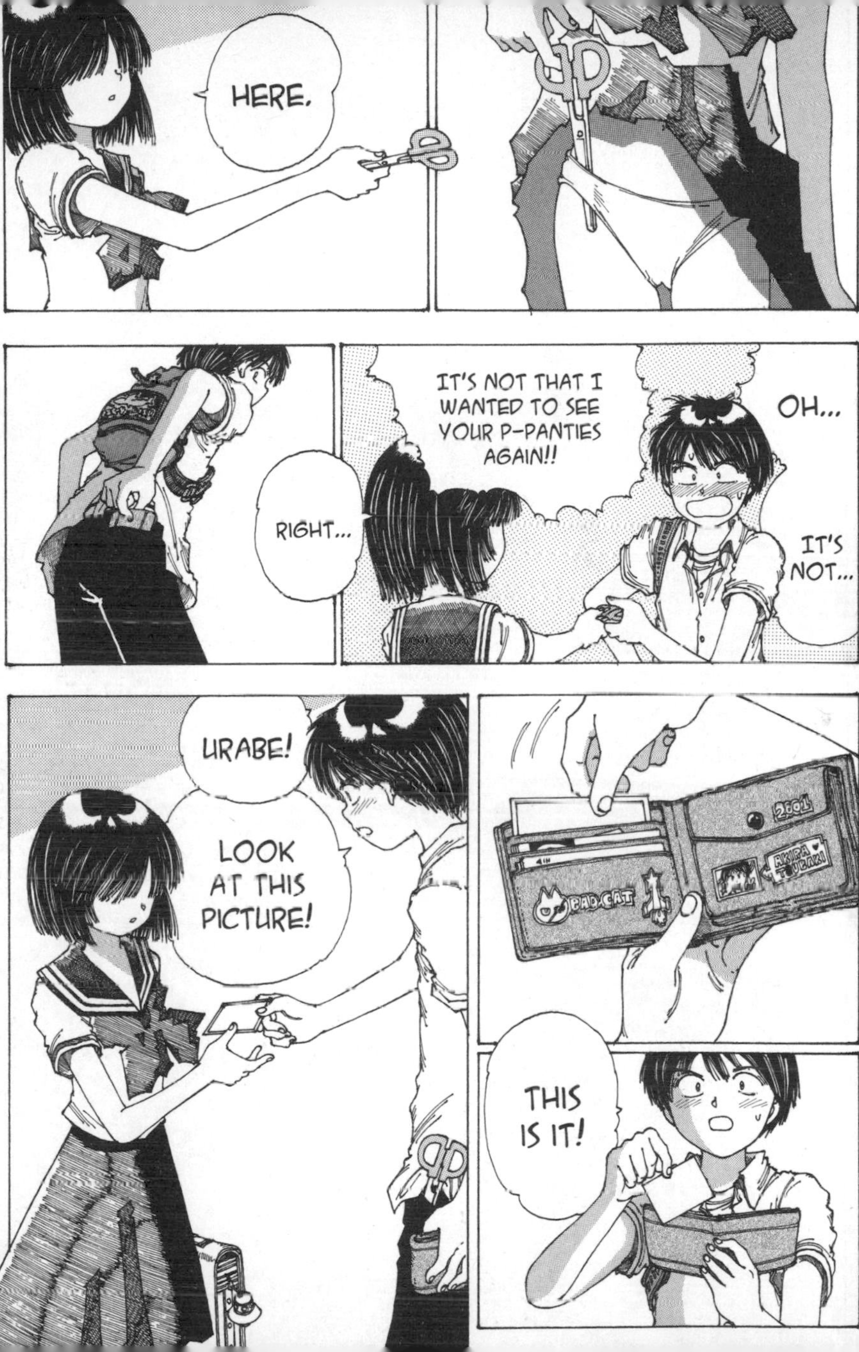
HERE.
OH...
IT'S NOT...
IT'S NOT THAT I WANTED TO SEE YOUR P-PANTIES AGAIN!!
RIGHT...
THIS IS IT!
URABE!
LOOK AT THIS PICTURE!

CUTE, ISN'T SHE?

WHAT IS

THIS?

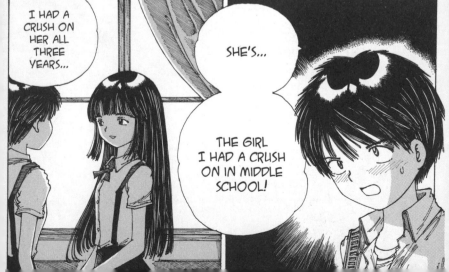

I HAD A CRUSH ON HER ALL THREE YEARS...

SHE'S...

THE GIRL I HAD A CRUSH ON IN MIDDLE SCHOOL!

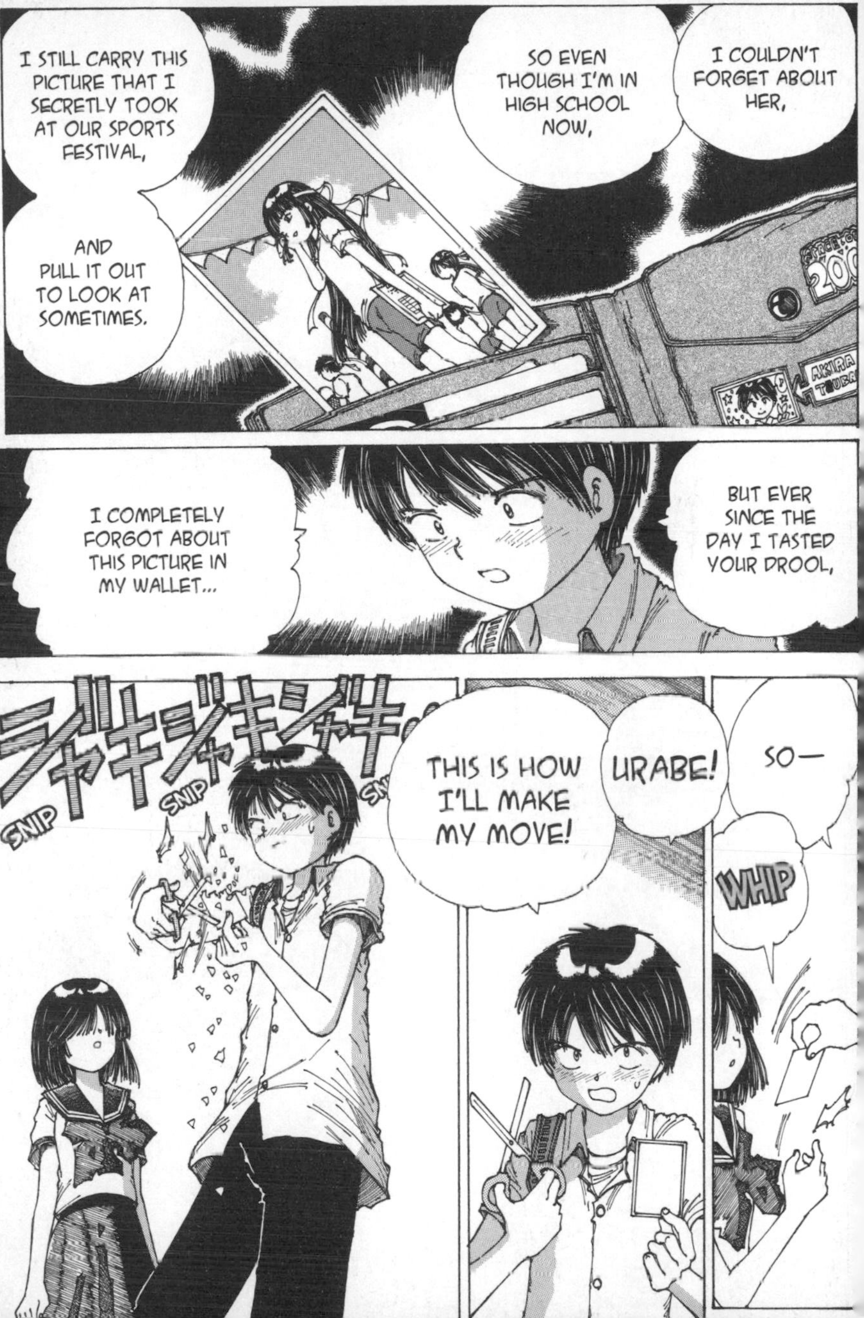
I COULDN'T FORGET ABOUT HER,
SO EVEN THOUGH I'M IN HIGH SCHOOL NOW,
I STILL CARRY THIS PICTURE THAT I SECRETLY TOOK AT OUR SPORTS FESTIVAL,
AND PULL IT OUT TO LOOK AT SOMETIMES.
BUT EVER SINCE THE DAY I TASTED YOUR DROOL,
I COMPLETELY FORGOT ABOUT THIS PICTURE IN MY WALLET...
SO—
WHIP
URABE!
THIS IS HOW I'LL MAKE MY MOVE!
シャキジャキジャキ…
SNIP
SNIP

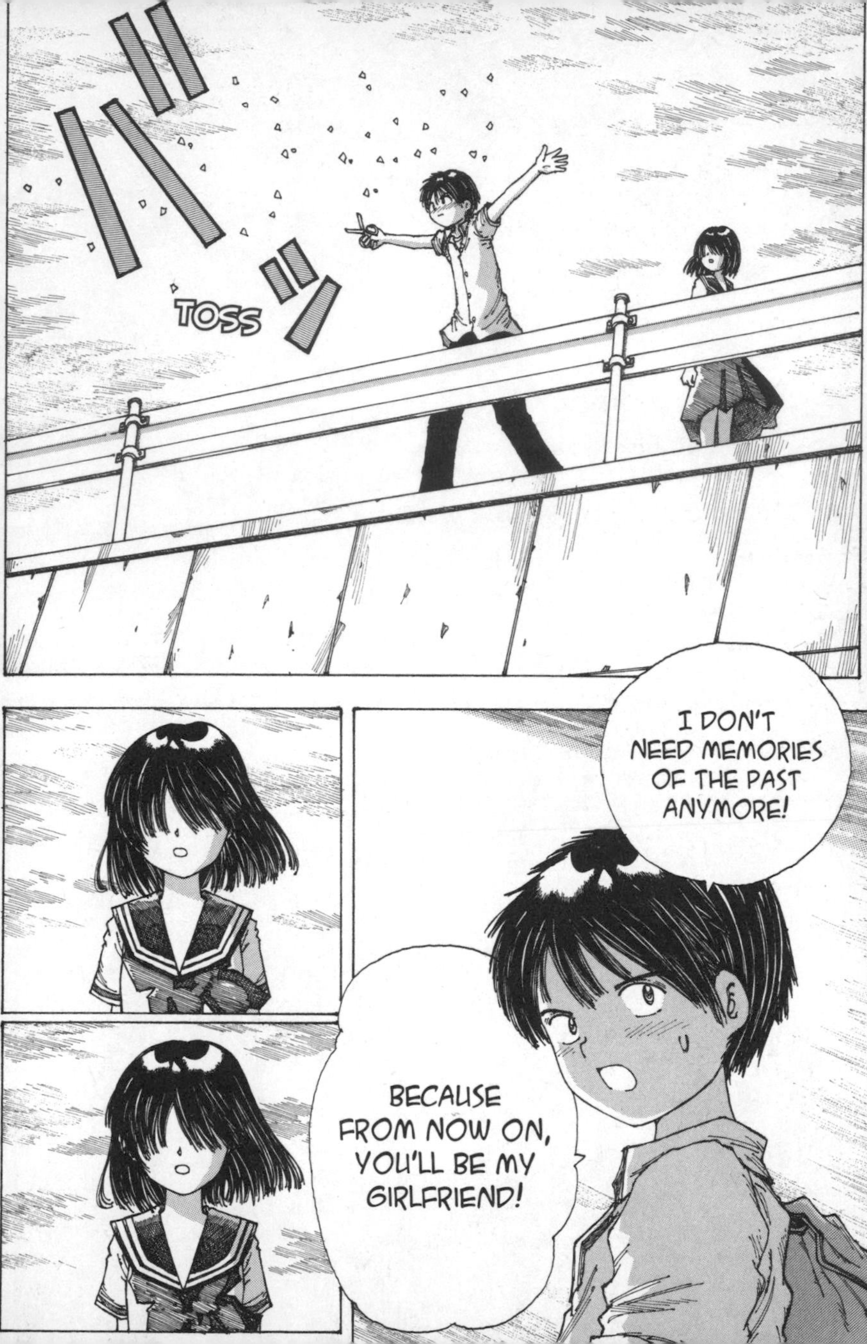
TOSS
I DON'T NEED MEMORIES OF THE PAST ANYMORE!
BECAUSE FROM NOW ON, YOU'LL BE MY GIRLFRIEND!

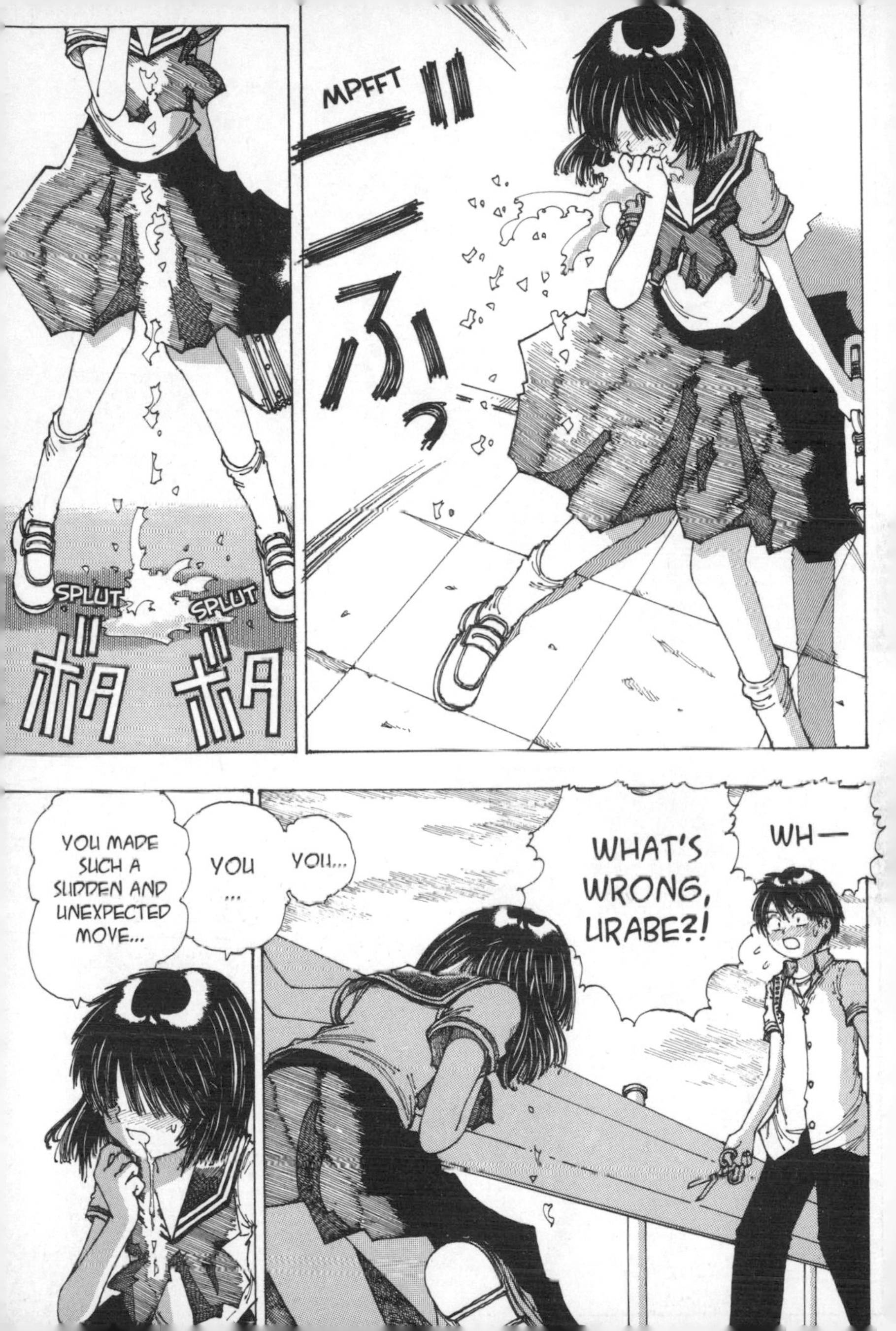
MPFFT
ふっ
SPLUT
SPLUT
ボタボタ
WH—
WHAT'S WRONG, URABE?!
YOU...
YOU ...
YOU MADE SUCH A SUDDEN AND UNEXPECTED MOVE...

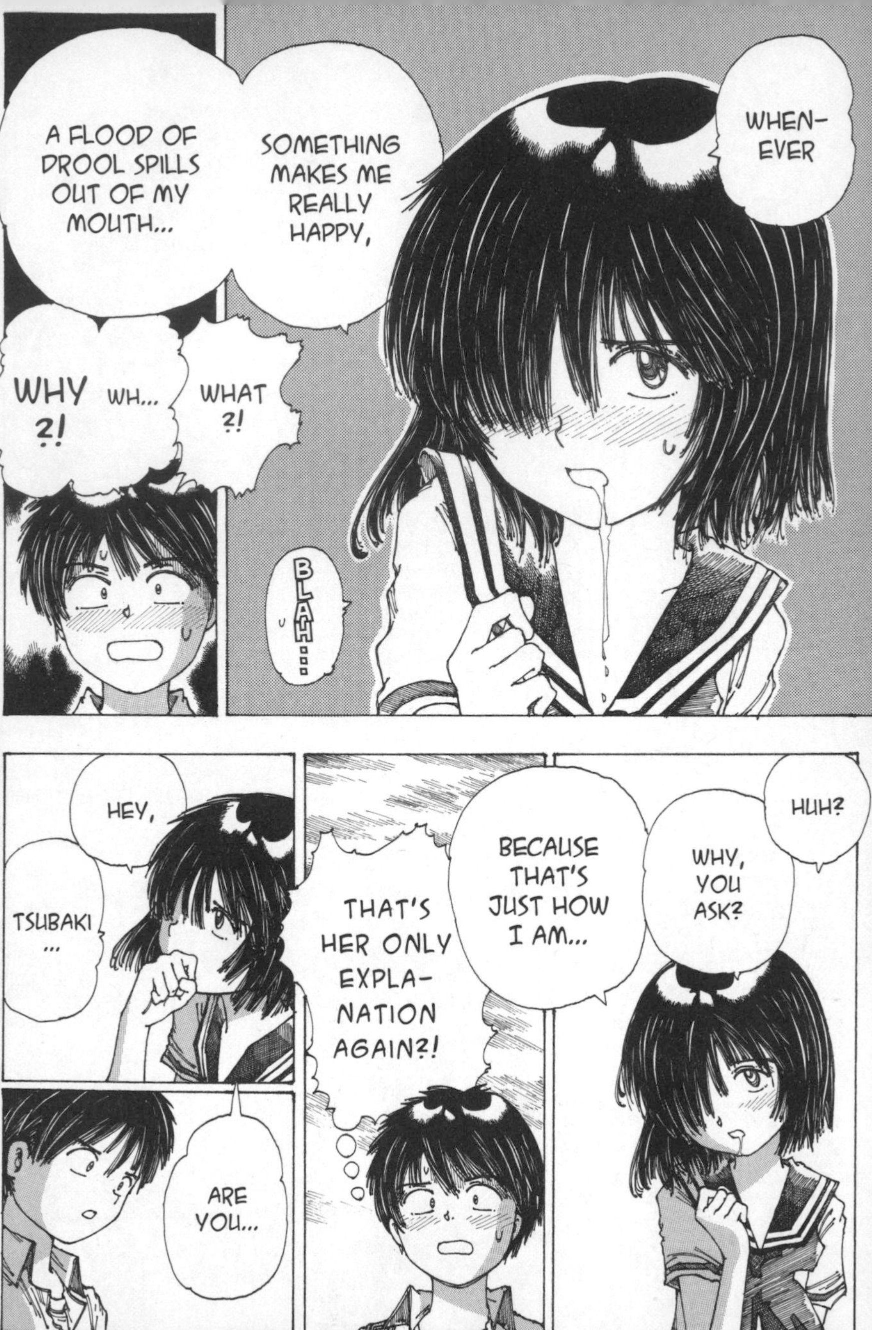
WHEN-EVER
SOMETHING MAKES ME REALLY HAPPY,
A FLOOD OF DROOL SPILLS OUT OF MY MOUTH...
BLAH...
WHAT?!
WH...
WHY?!
HUH?
WHY, YOU ASK?
BECAUSE THAT'S JUST HOW I AM...
THAT'S HER ONLY EXPLA-NATION AGAIN?!
HEY,
TSUBAKI...
ARE YOU...

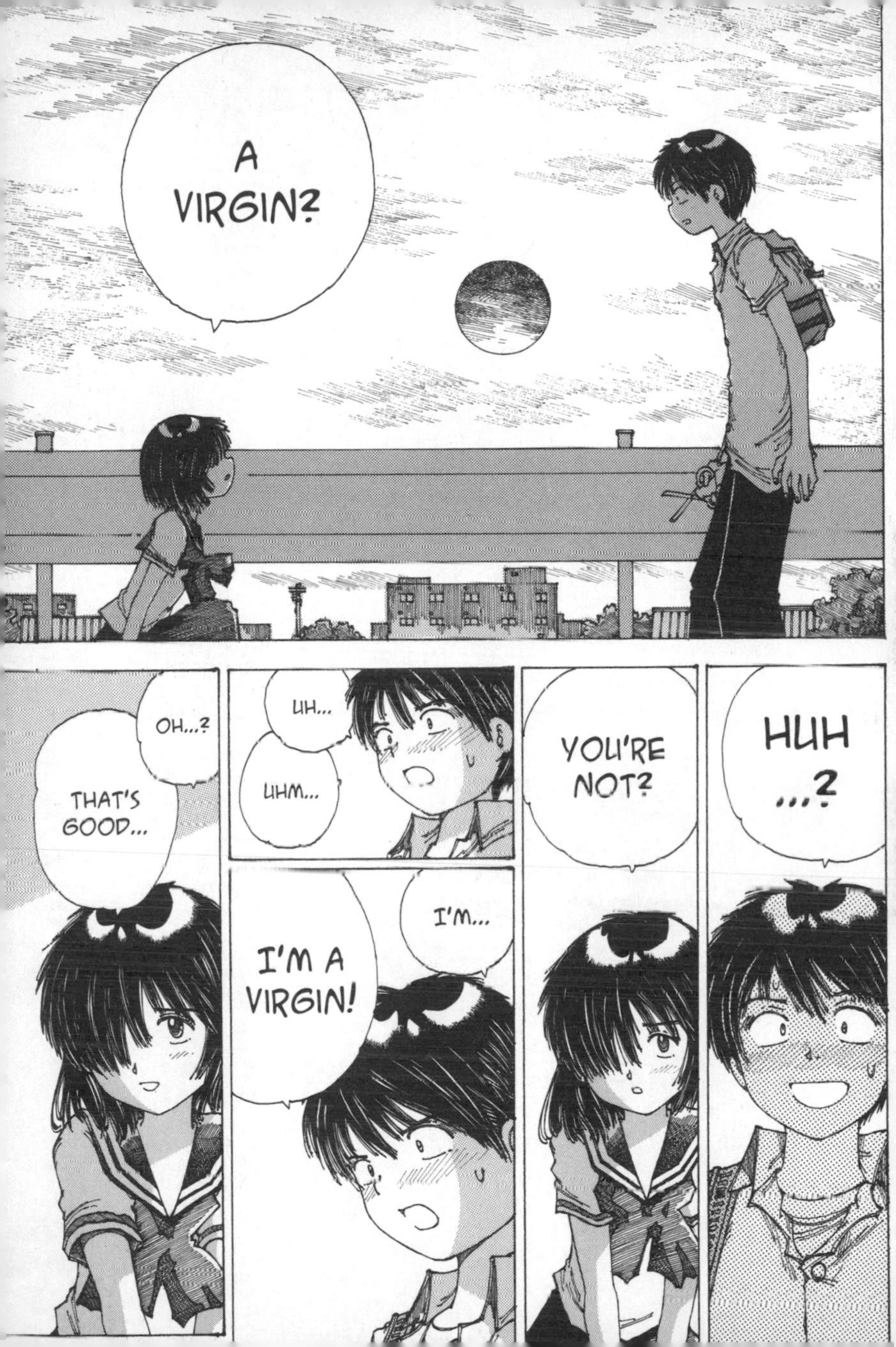
A VIRGIN?
HUH ...?
YOU'RE NOT?
UH...
UHM...
I'M...
I'M A VIRGIN!
OH...?
THAT'S GOOD...

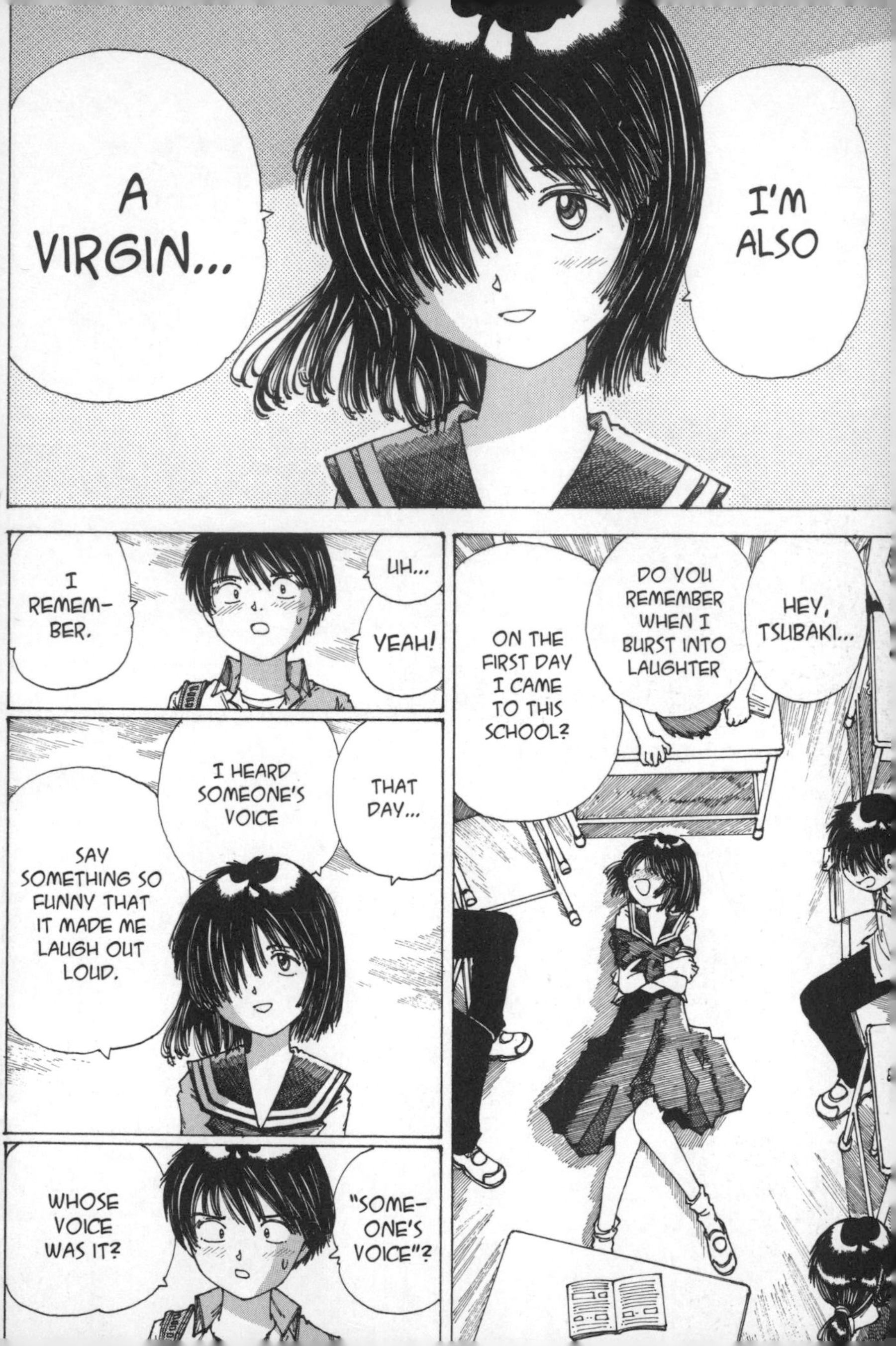
I'M ALSO
A VIRGIN...
HEY, TSUBAKI...
DO YOU REMEMBER WHEN I BURST INTO LAUGHTER
ON THE FIRST DAY I CAME TO THIS SCHOOL?
UH...
YEAH!
I REMEM-BER.
THAT DAY...
I HEARD SOMEONE'S VOICE
SAY SOMETHING SO FUNNY THAT IT MADE ME LAUGH OUT LOUD.
"SOME-ONE'S VOICE"?
WHOSE VOICE WAS IT?

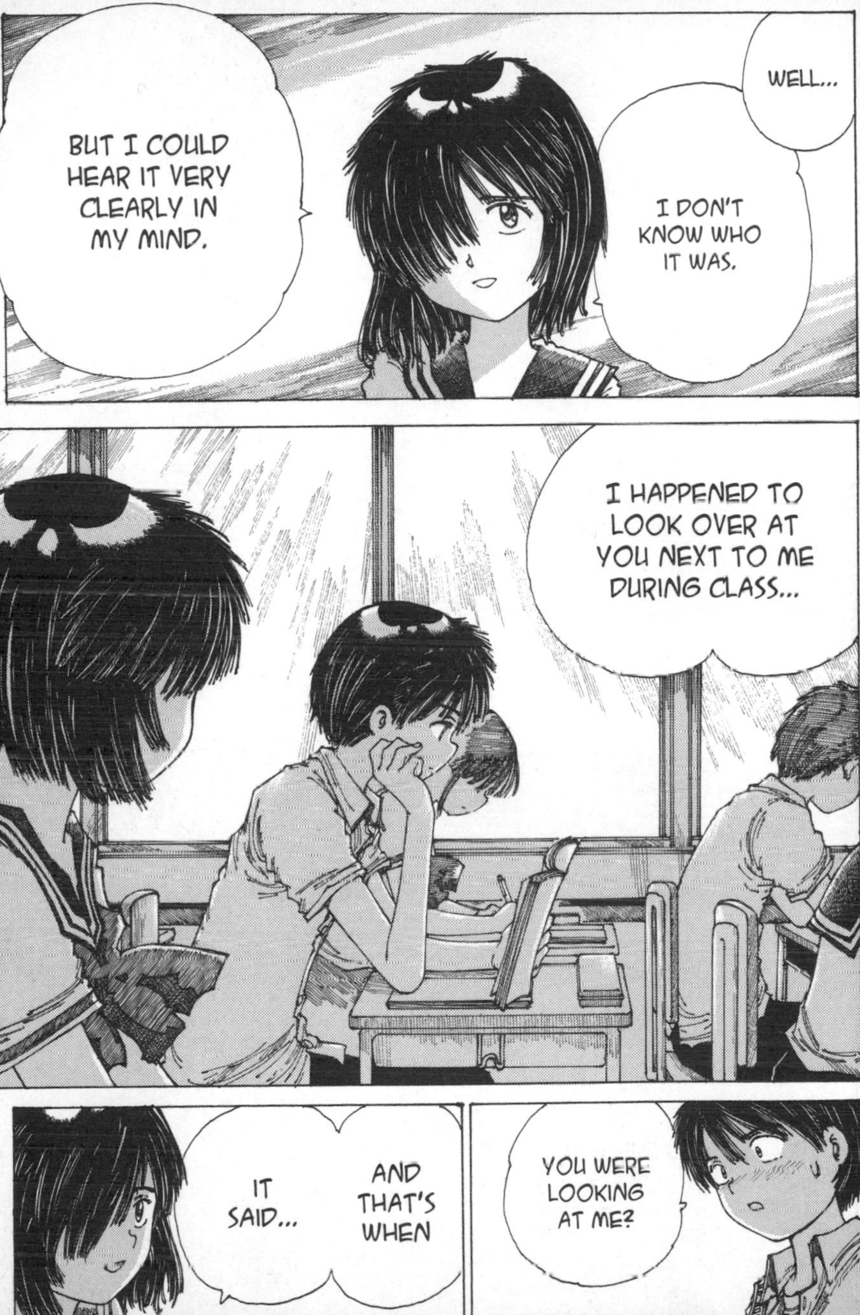
WELL...
I DON'T KNOW WHO IT WAS.
BUT I COULD HEAR IT VERY CLEARLY IN MY MIND.
I HAPPENED TO LOOK OVER AT YOU NEXT TO ME DURING CLASS...
YOU WERE LOOKING AT ME?
AND THAT'S WHEN
IT SAID...

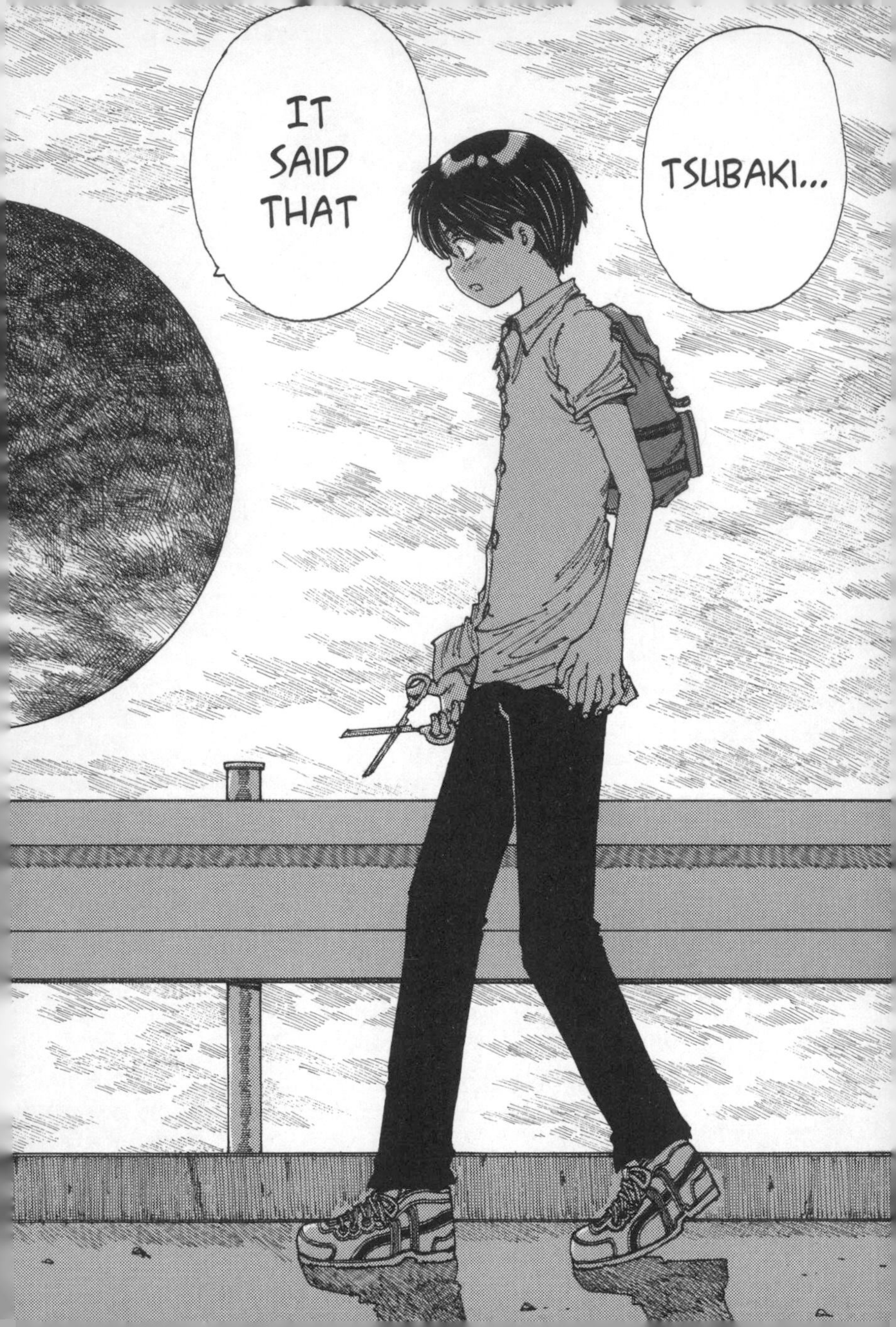
TSUBAKI...
IT SAID THAT

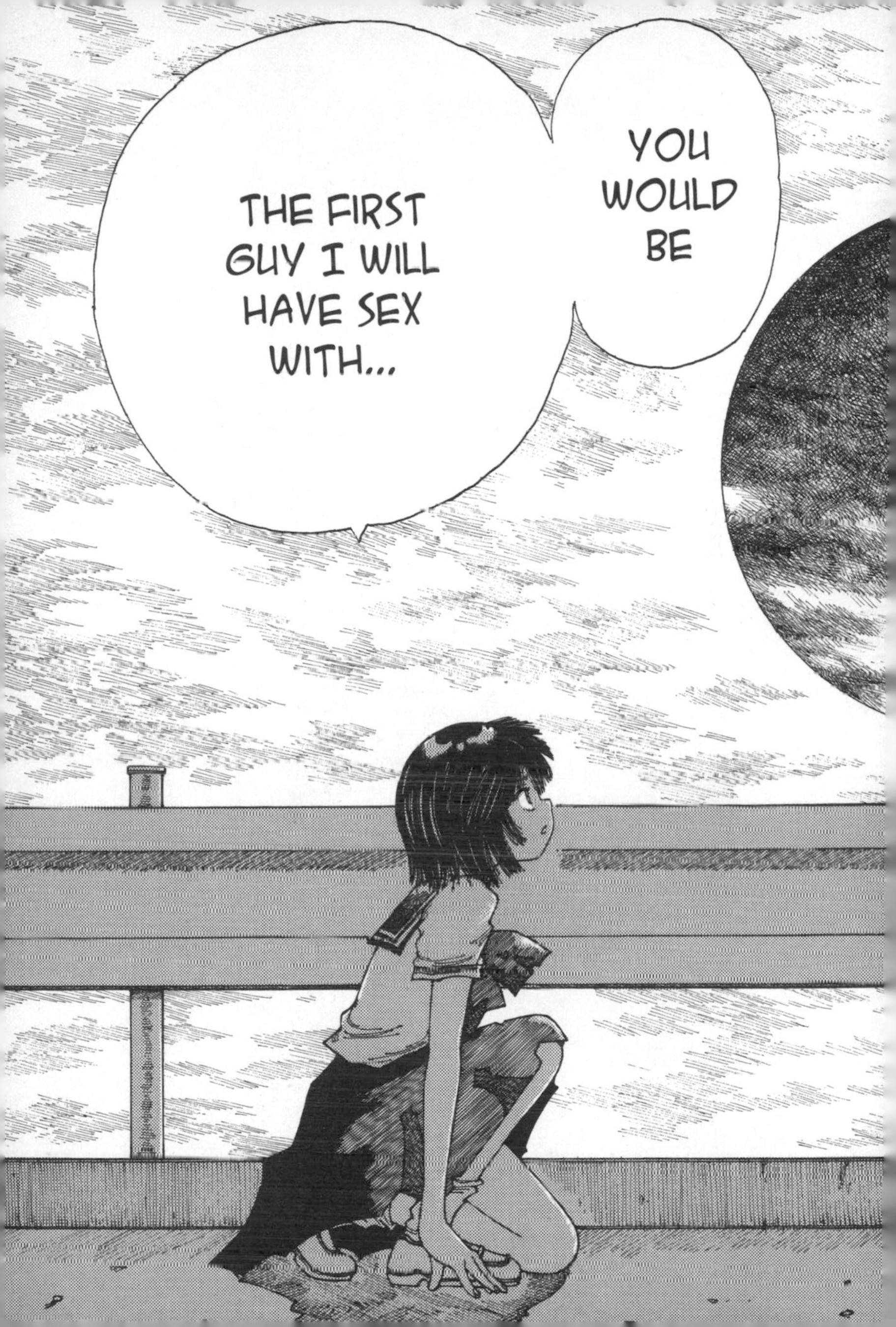
YOU WOULD BE
THE FIRST GUY I WILL HAVE SEX WITH...

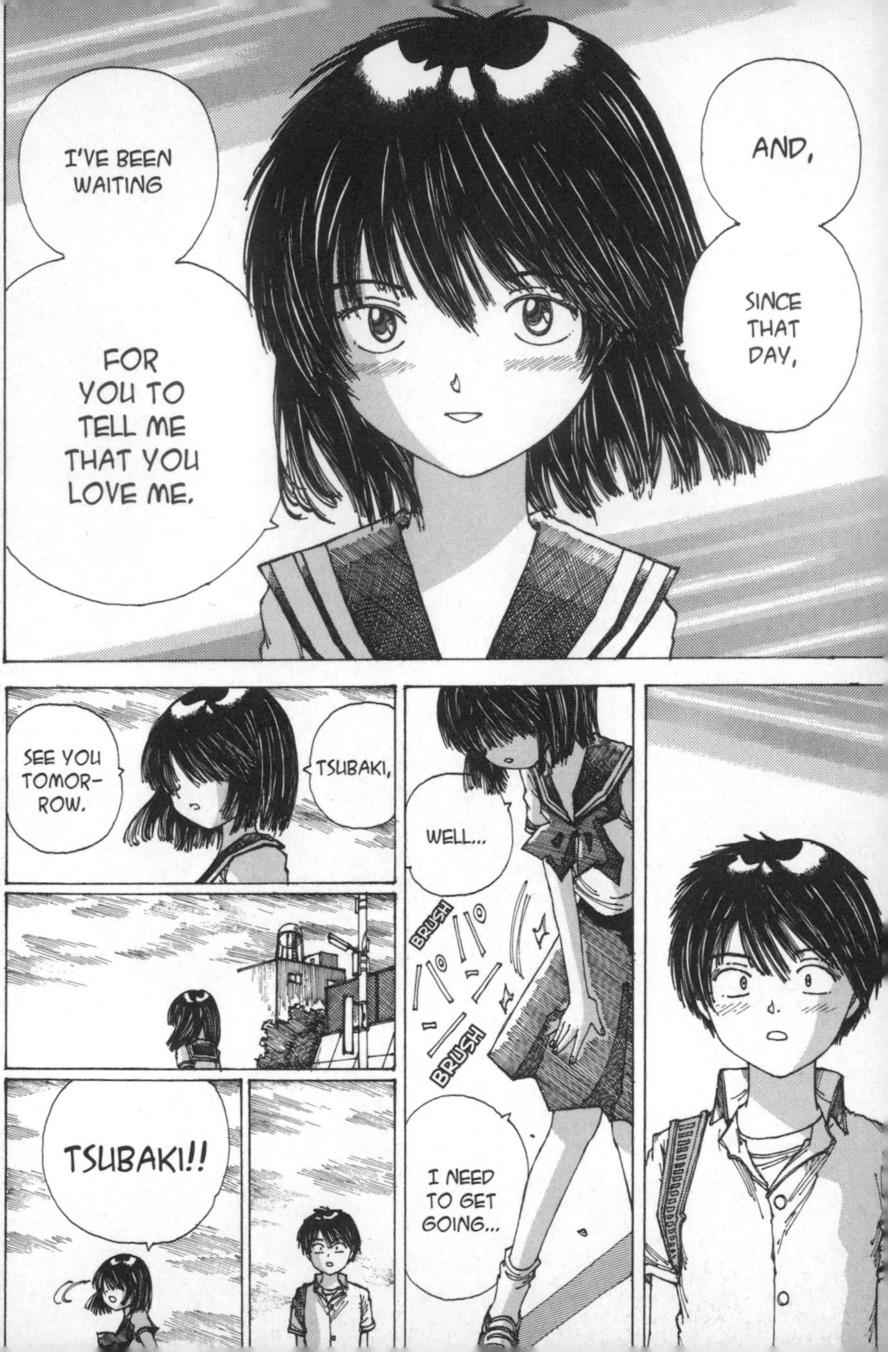
AND,
SINCE THAT DAY,
I'VE BEEN WAITING
FOR YOU TO TELL ME THAT YOU LOVE ME.
WELL...
BRUSH
BRUSH
I NEED TO GET GOING...
TSUBAKI,
SEE YOU TOMOR-ROW.
TSUBAKI!!

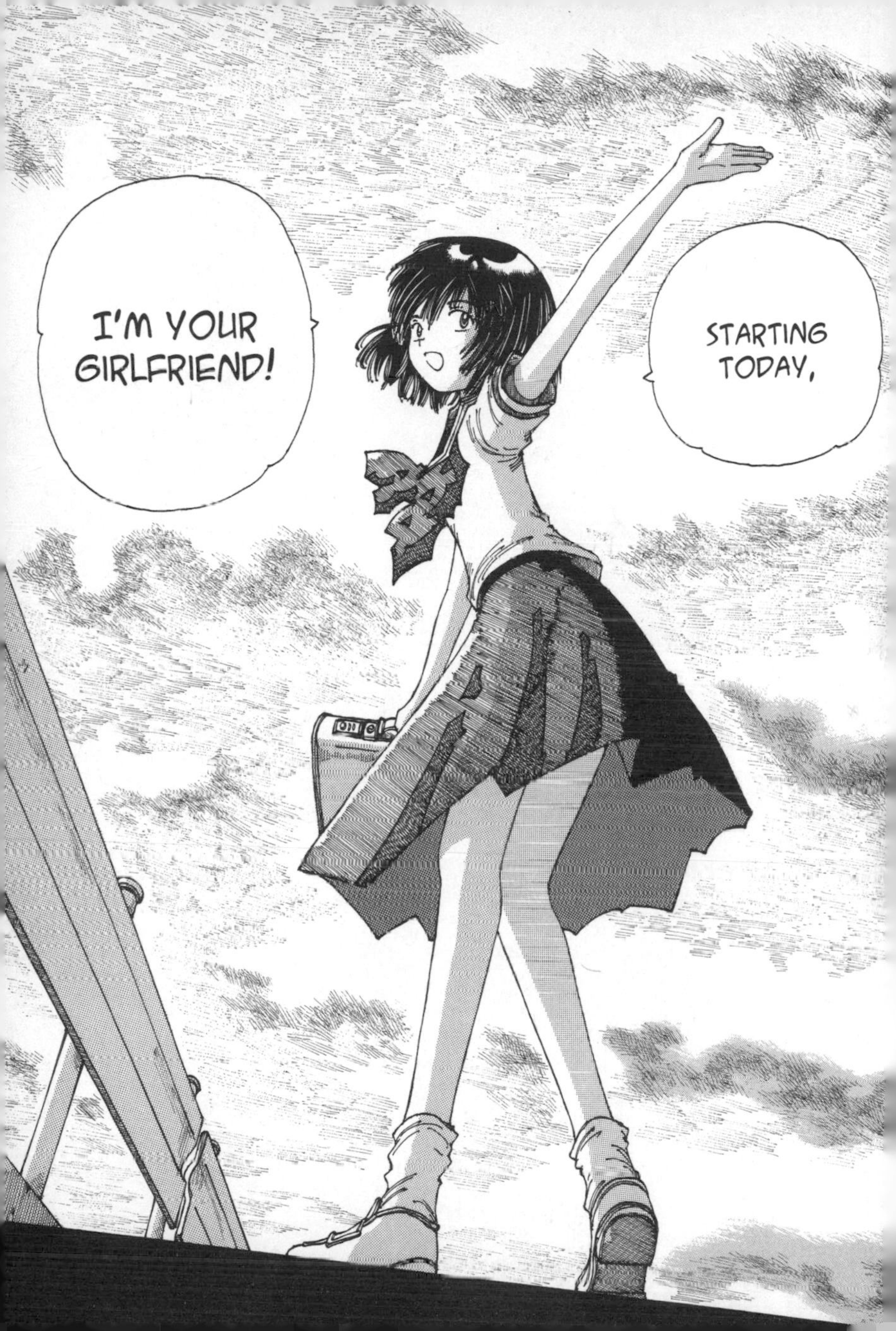
STARTING TODAY,
I'M YOUR GIRLFRIEND!

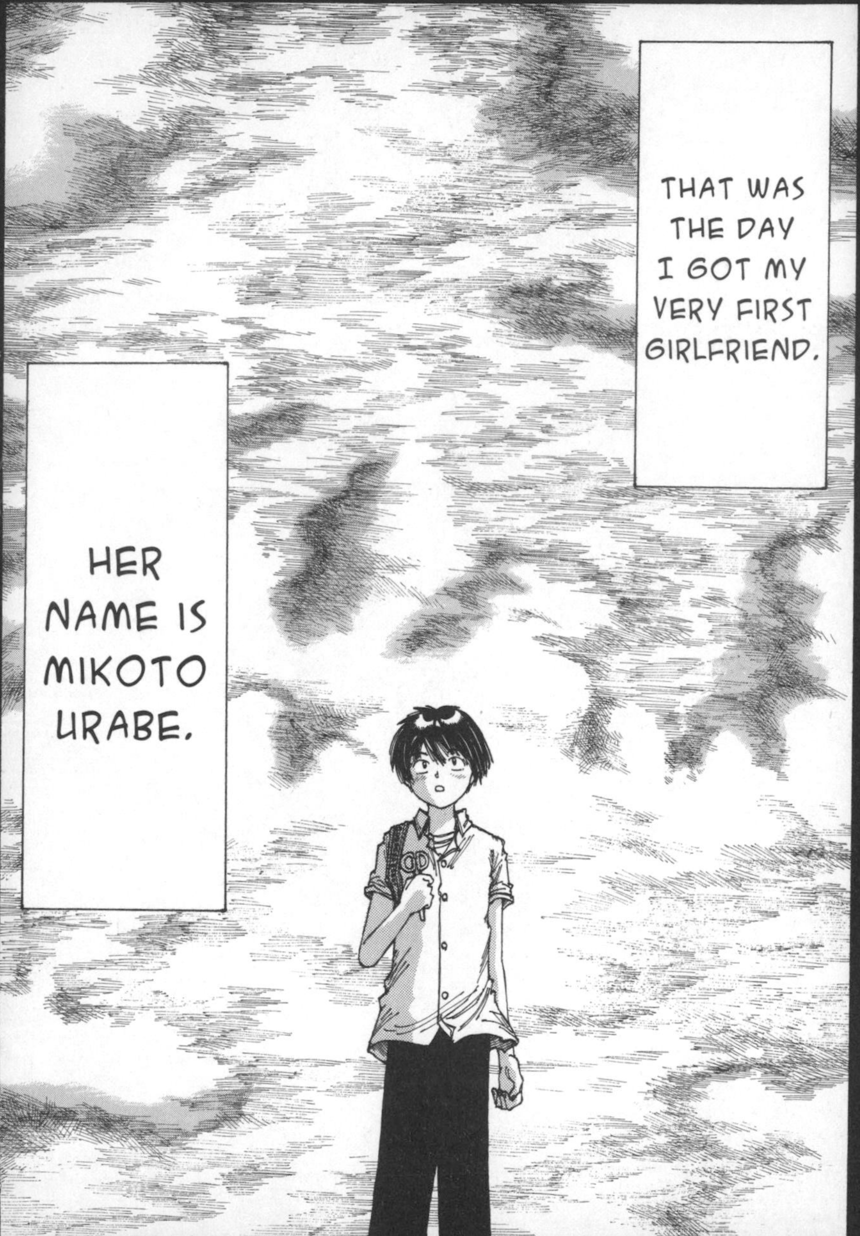
THAT WAS THE DAY I GOT MY VERY FIRST GIRLFRIEND.
HER NAME IS MIKOTO URABE.

END OF CHAPTER 0

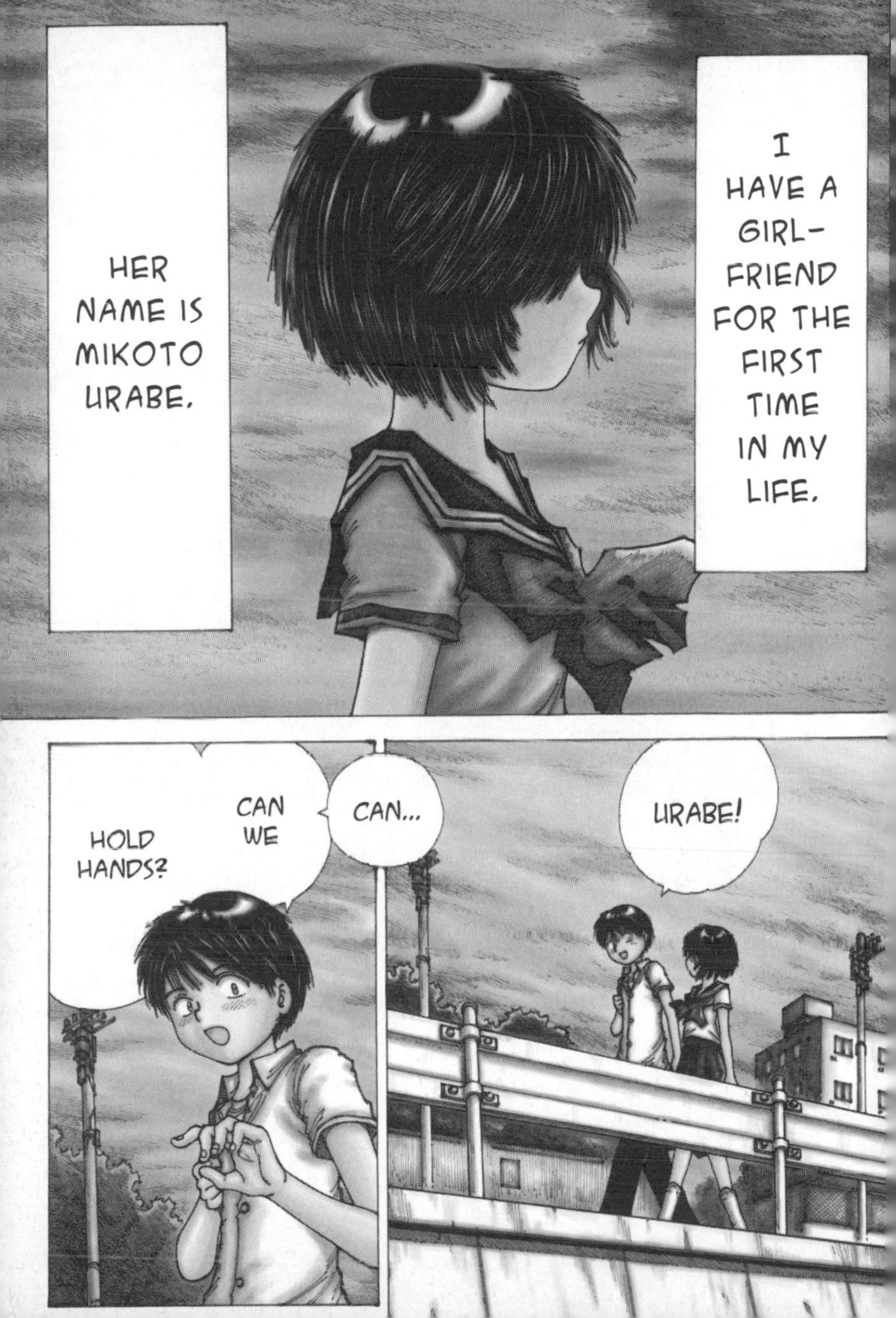
I HAVE A GIRL-FRIEND FOR THE FIRST TIME IN MY LIFE.
HER NAME IS MIKOTO URABE.
URABE!
CAN...
CAN WE HOLD HANDS?

CHAPTER 1: MYSTERIOUS BOND

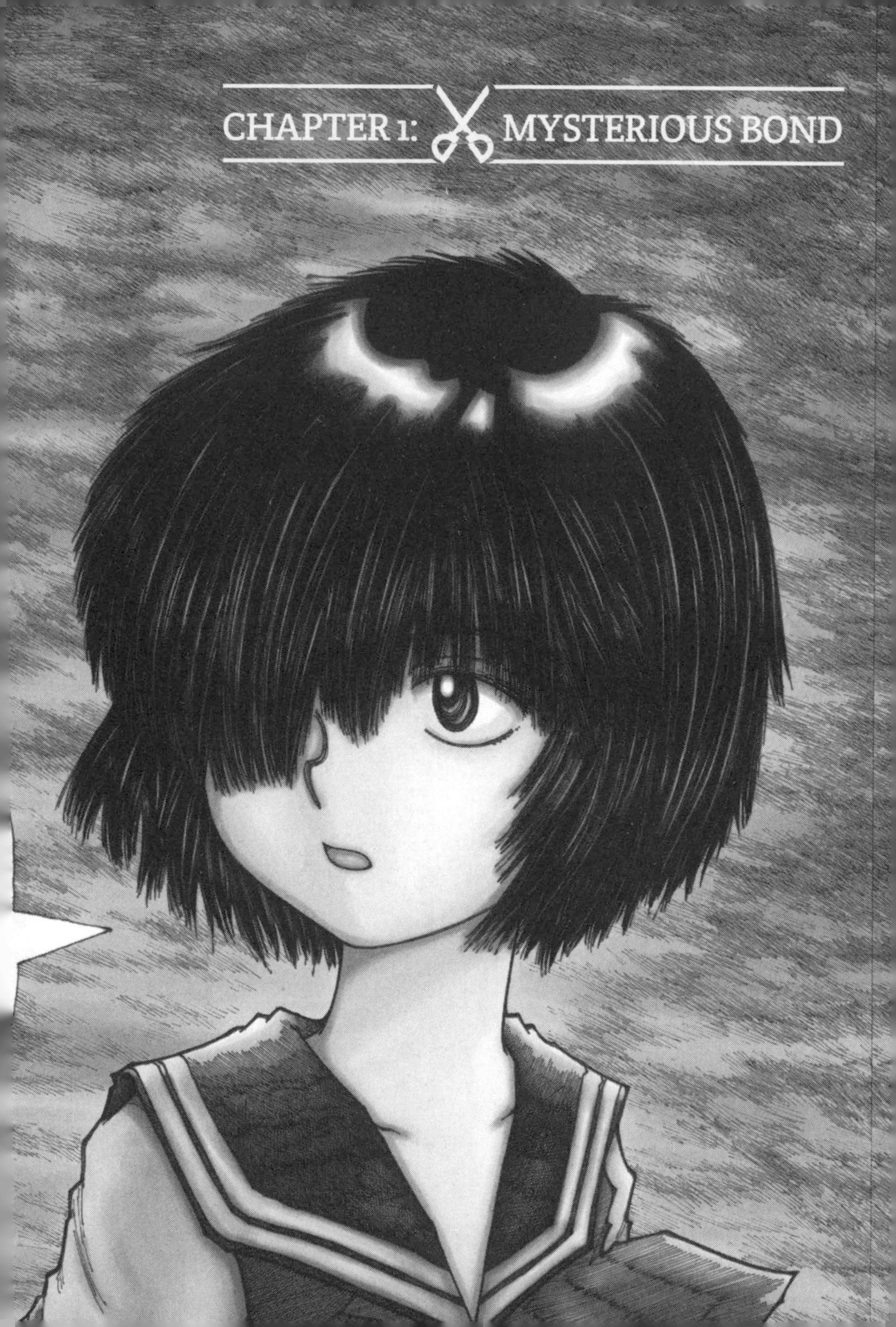

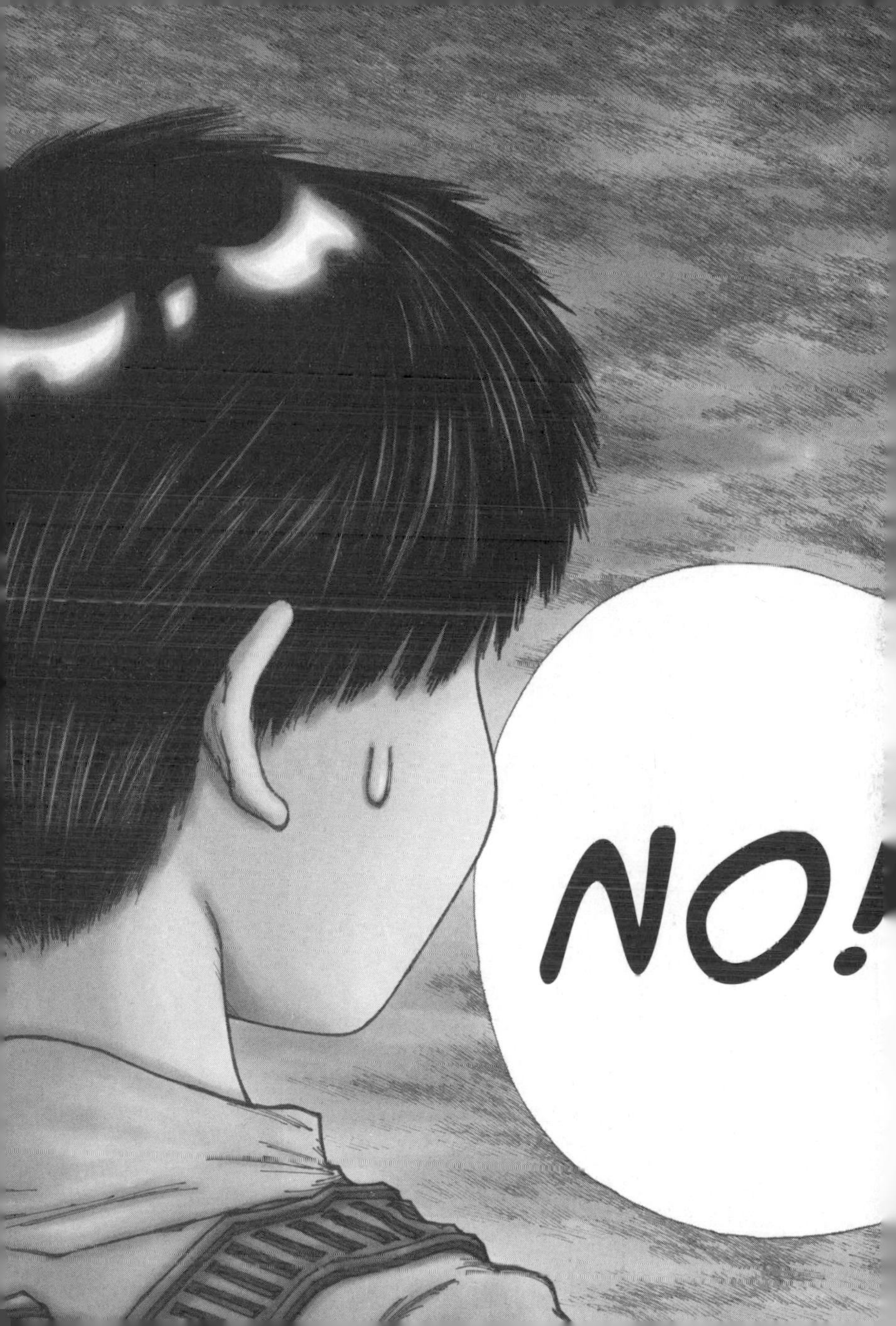
NO!

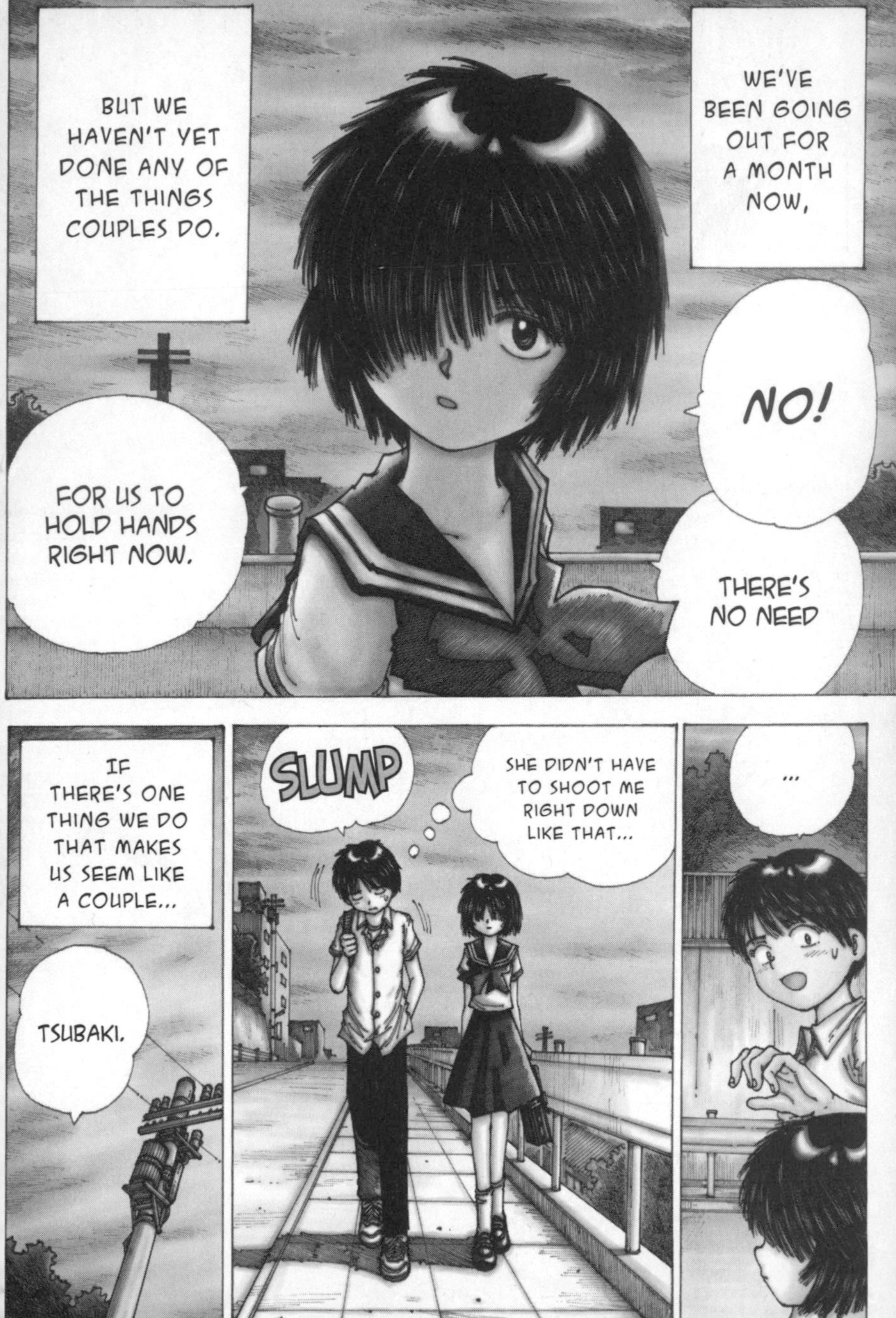
WE'VE BEEN GOING OUT FOR A MONTH NOW,
BUT WE HAVEN'T YET DONE ANY OF THE THINGS COUPLES DO.
NO!
THERE'S NO NEED
FOR US TO HOLD HANDS RIGHT NOW.
...
SHE DIDN'T HAVE TO SHOOT ME RIGHT DOWN LIKE THAT...
SLUMP
IF THERE'S ONE THING WE DO THAT MAKES US SEEM LIKE A COUPLE...
TSUBAKI.

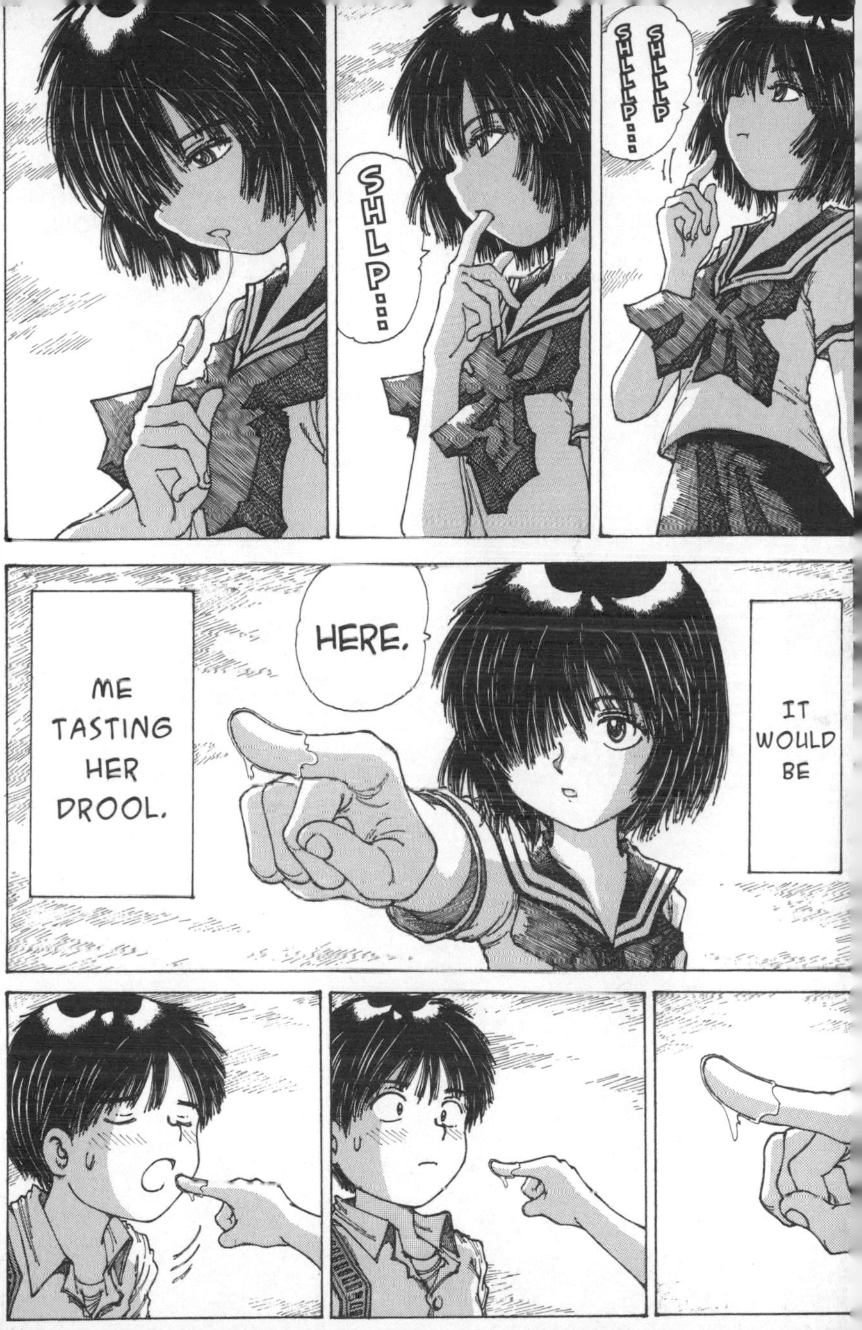
SHLLP
SHLLP...
SHLP...
IT WOULD BE
HERE.
ME TASTING HER DROOL.

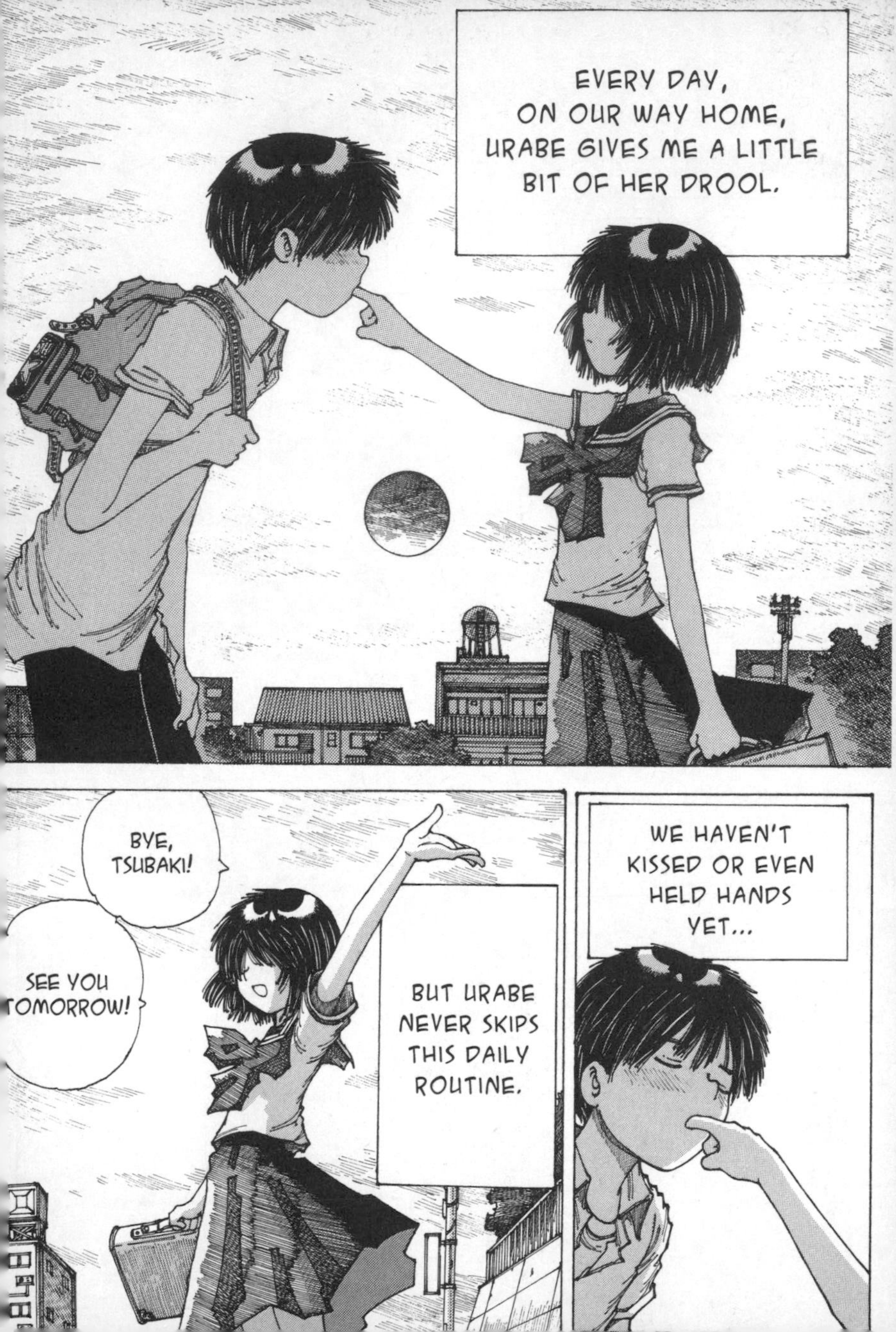
EVERY DAY, ON OUR WAY HOME, URABE GIVES ME A LITTLE BIT OF HER DROOL.
WE HAVEN'T KISSED OR EVEN HELD HANDS YET...
BYE, TSUBAKI!
SEE YOU TOMORROW!
BUT URABE NEVER SKIPS THIS DAILY ROUTINE.

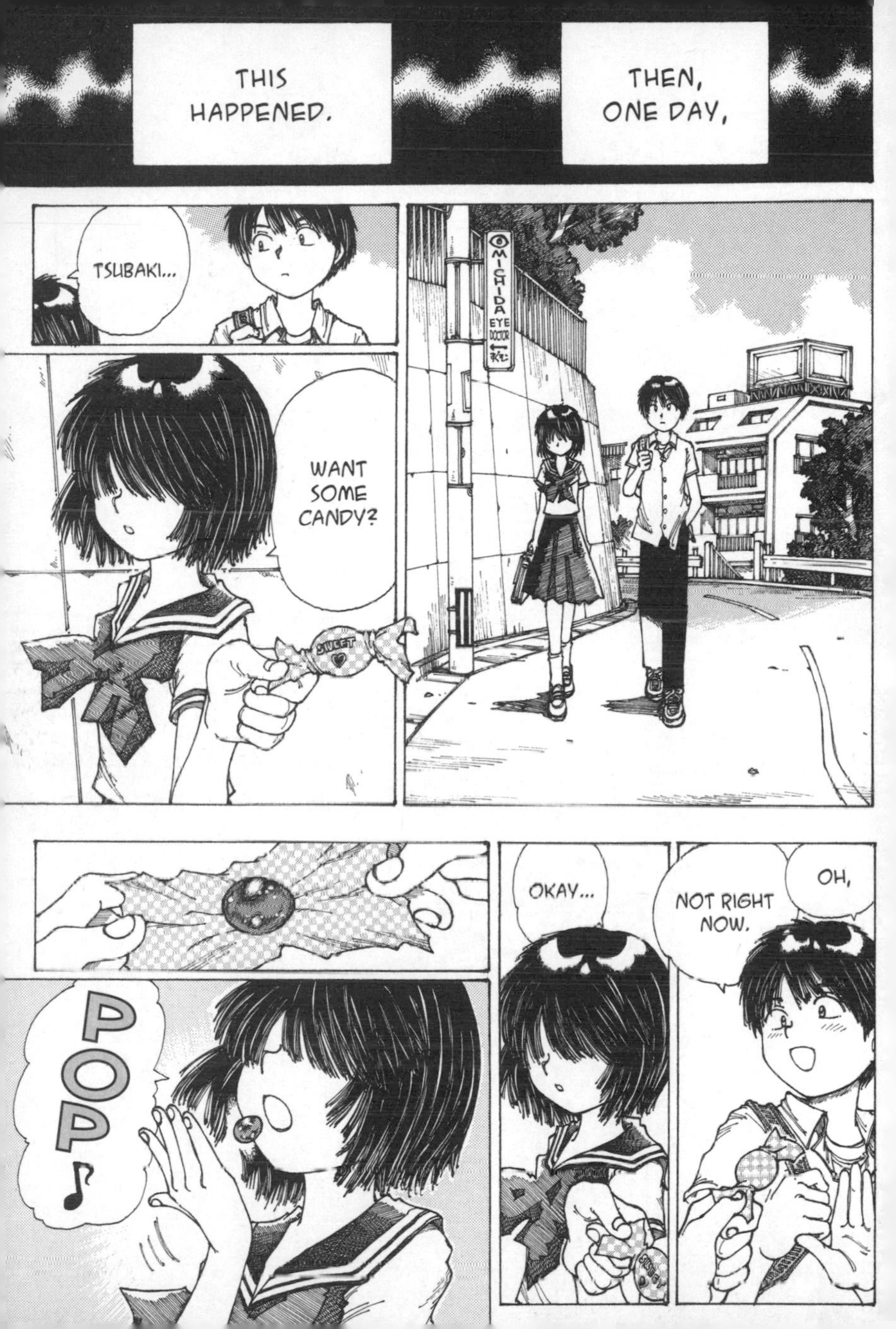
THEN, ONE DAY,
THIS HAPPENED.
MICHIDA EYE DOCTOR
TSUBAKI...
WANT SOME CANDY?
SWEET
OH,
NOT RIGHT NOW.
OKAY...
POP POP♪

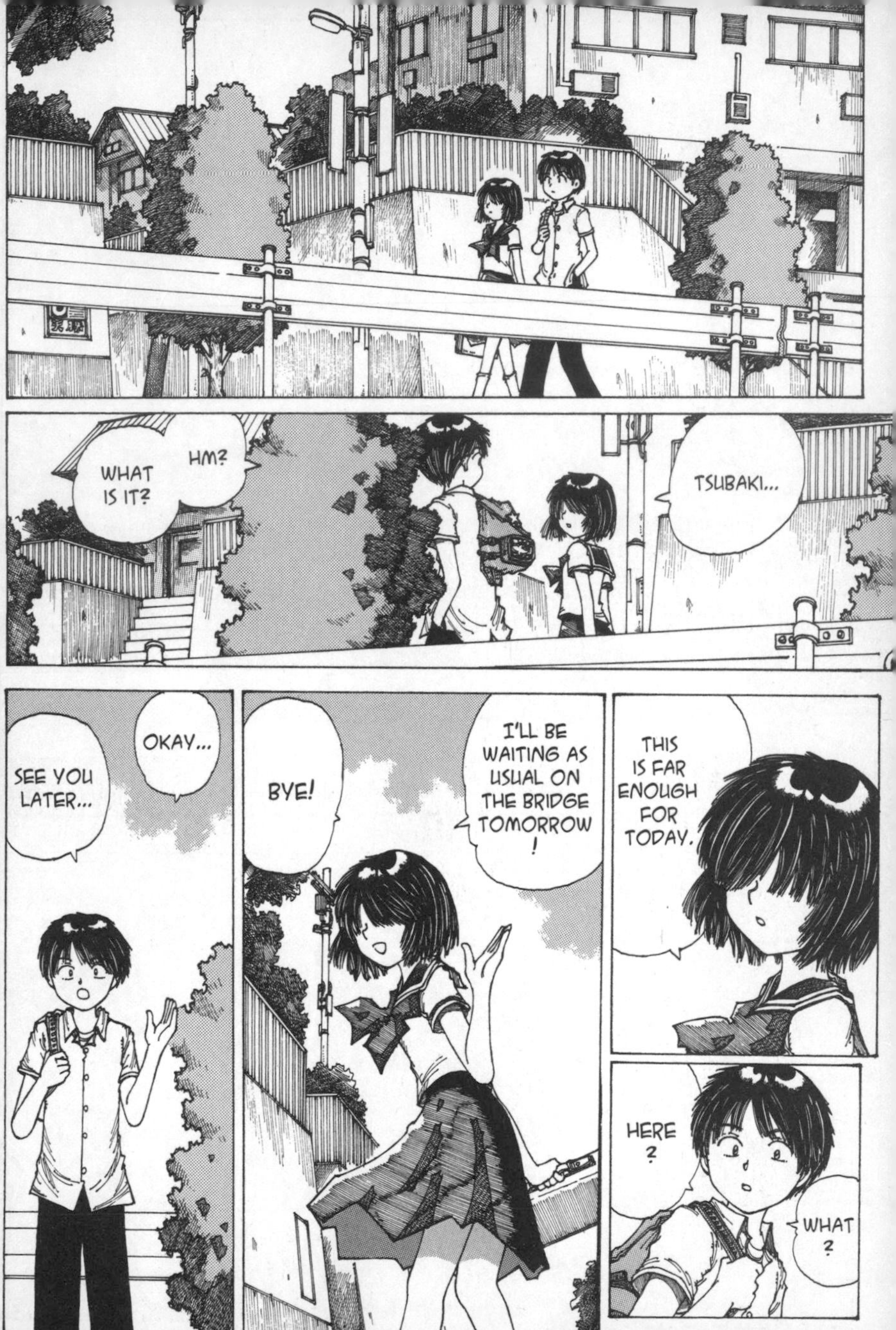
TSUBAKI...
HM? WHAT IS IT?
THIS IS FAR ENOUGH FOR TODAY.
WHAT?
HERE?
I'LL BE WAITING AS USUAL ON THE BRIDGE TOMORROW!
BYE!
OKAY...
SEE YOU LATER...

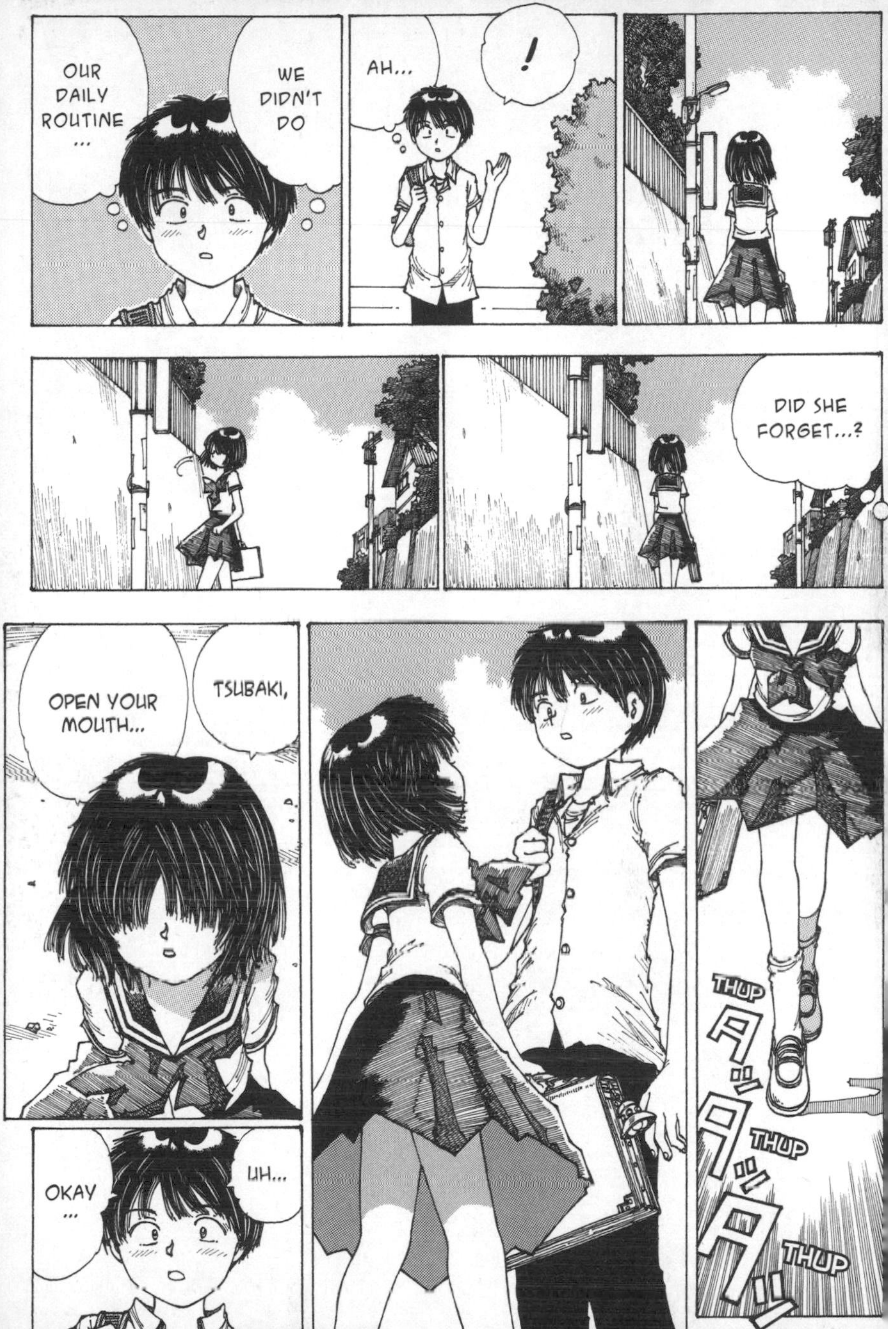
!
AH...
WE DIDN'T DO
OUR DAILY ROUTINE ...
DID SHE FORGET...?
THUP
THUP
THUP
TSUBAKI,
OPEN YOUR MOUTH...
UH...
OKAY ...

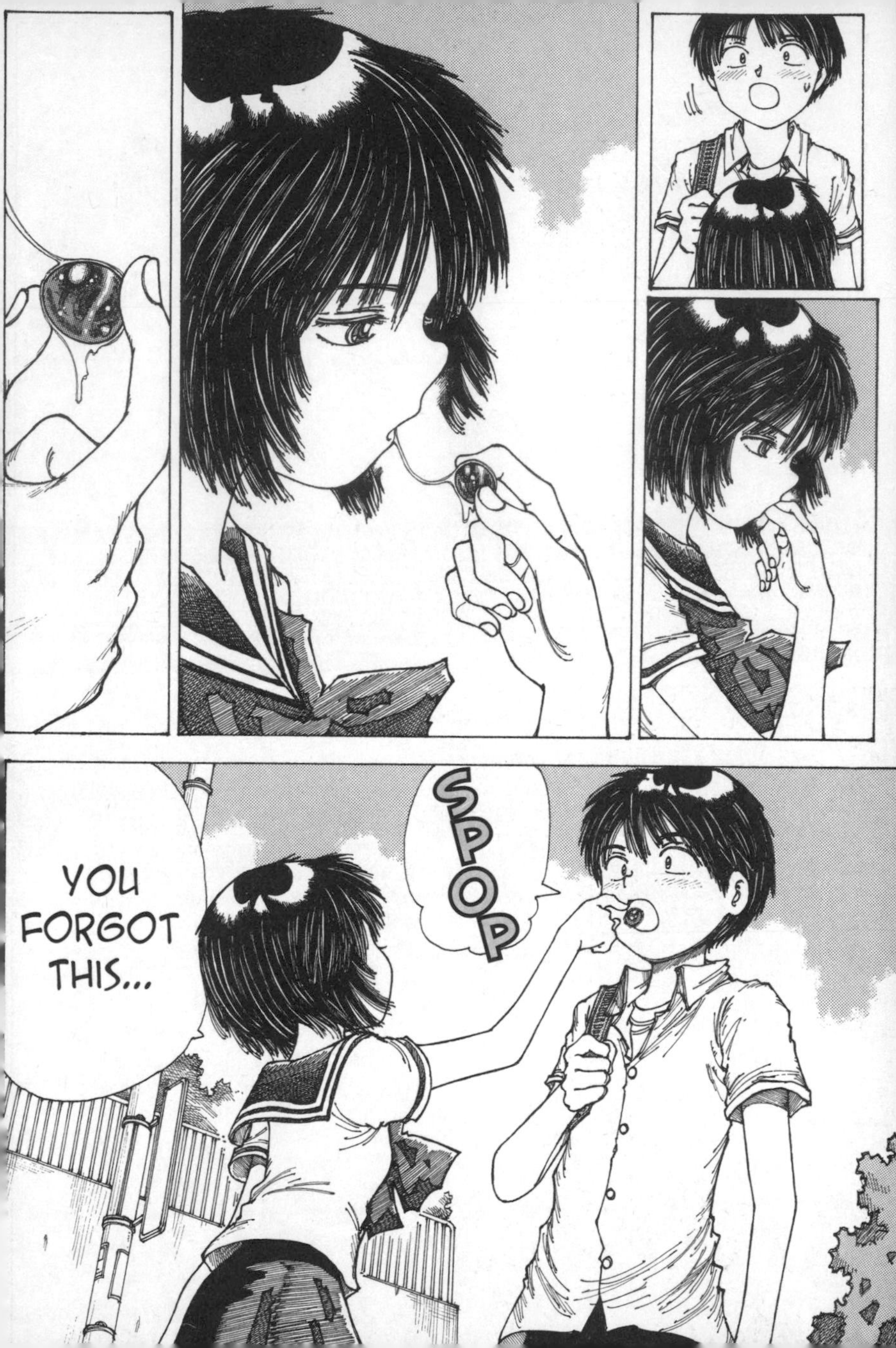
SPOP
YOU FORGOT THIS...

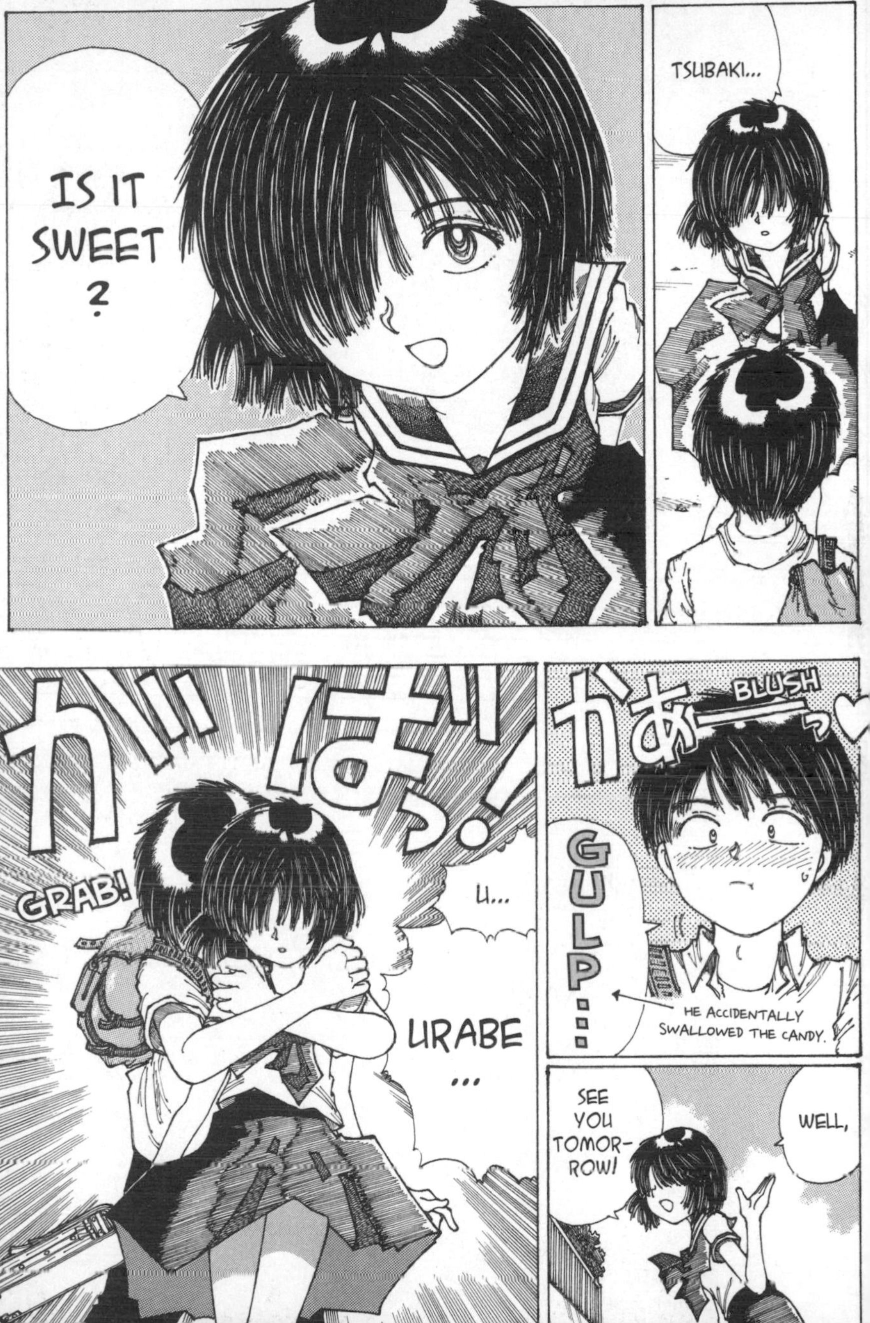
TSUBAKI...
IS IT SWEET?
がぁーっ
BLUSH
GULP...
HE ACCIDENTALLY SWALLOWED THE CANDY.
WELL,
SEE YOU TOMORROW!
がばっ!
GRAB!
U...
URABE...

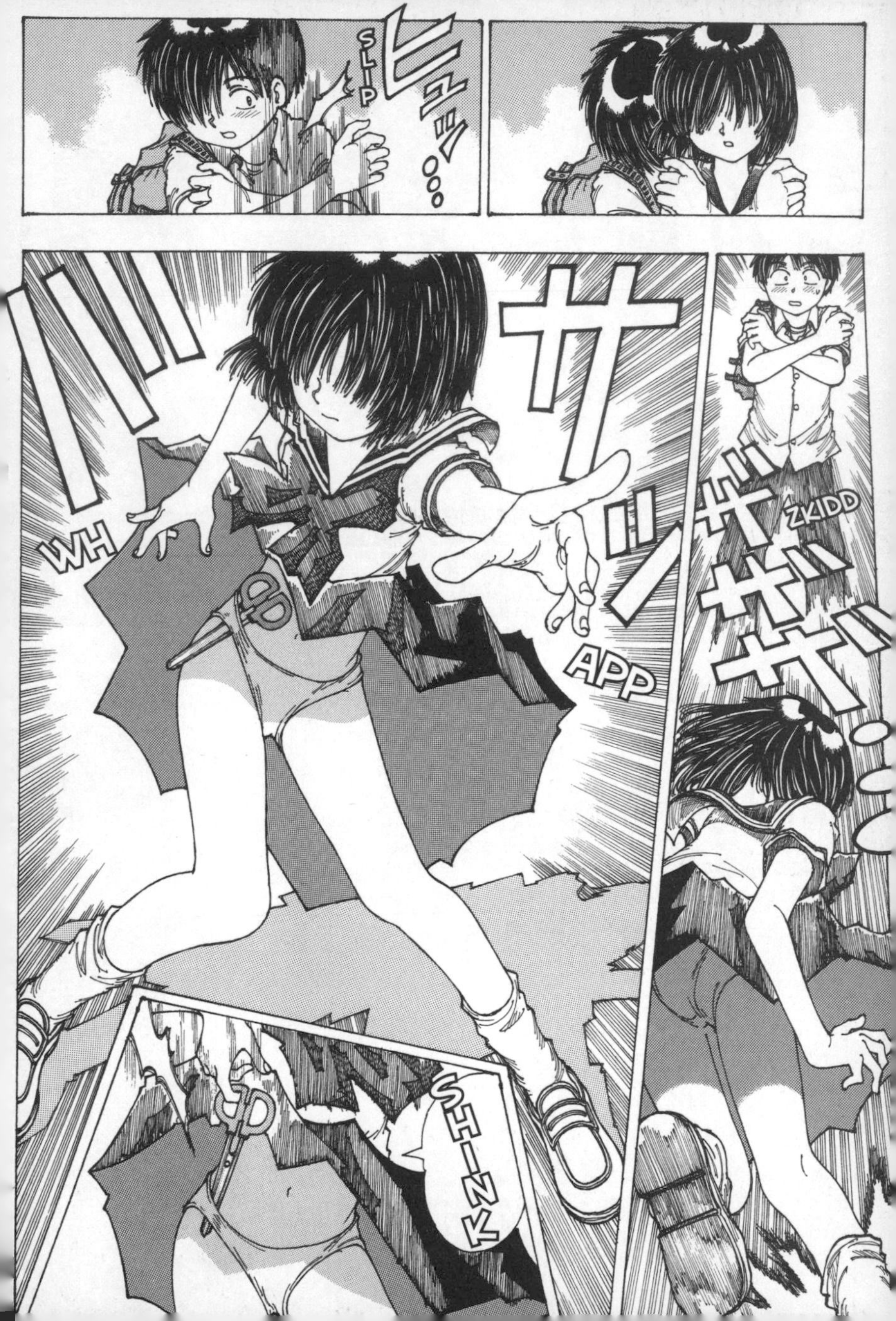
ヒュッ。。。
SLIP
ザッ
ザザザ
ZKIDD
サッ
APP
WH
SHINK

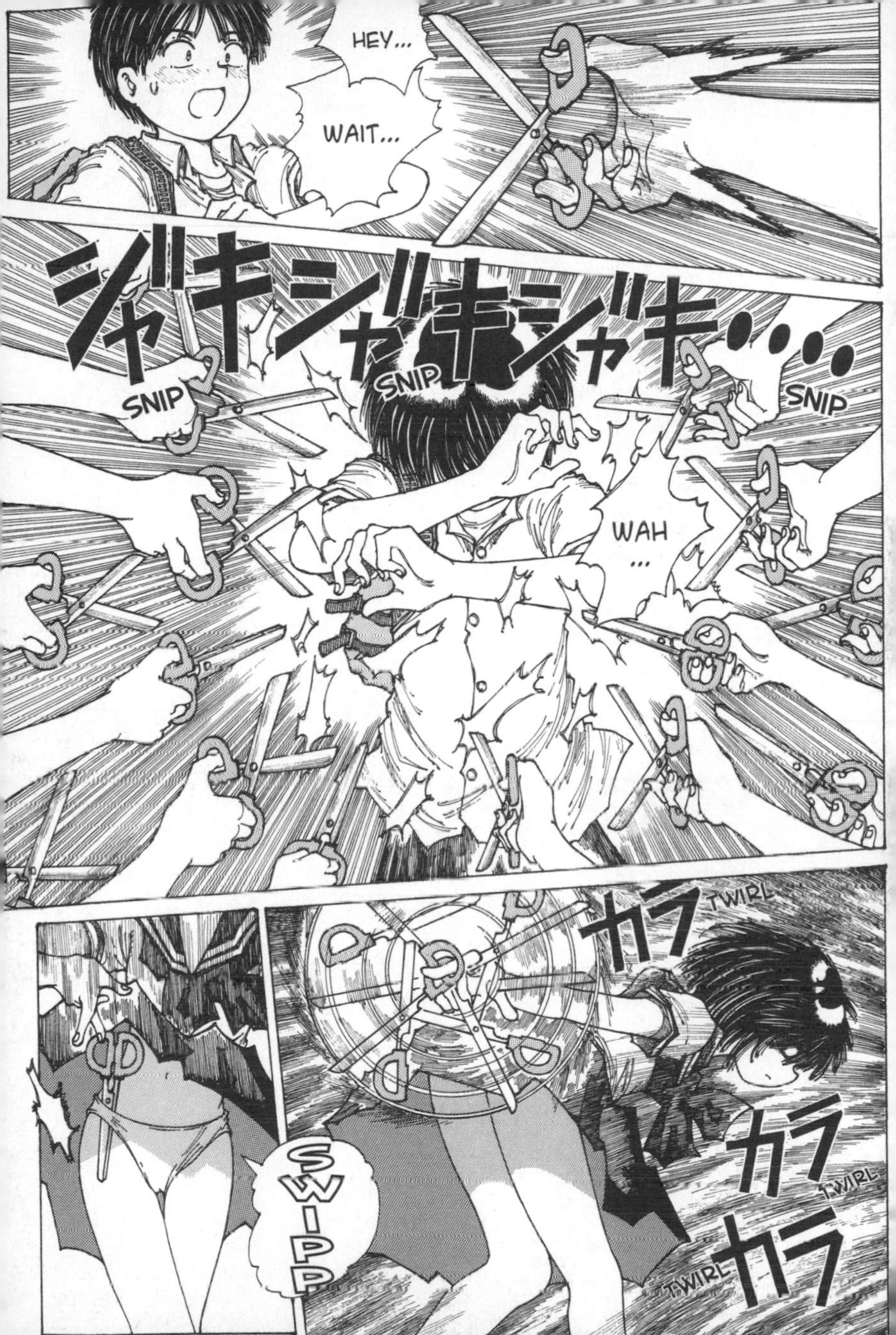
HEY...
WAIT...
ジャキジャキジャキ…
SNIP
SNIP
SNIP
WAH ...
カラ
TWIRL
カラ
TWIRL
カラ
TWIRL
SWIPP

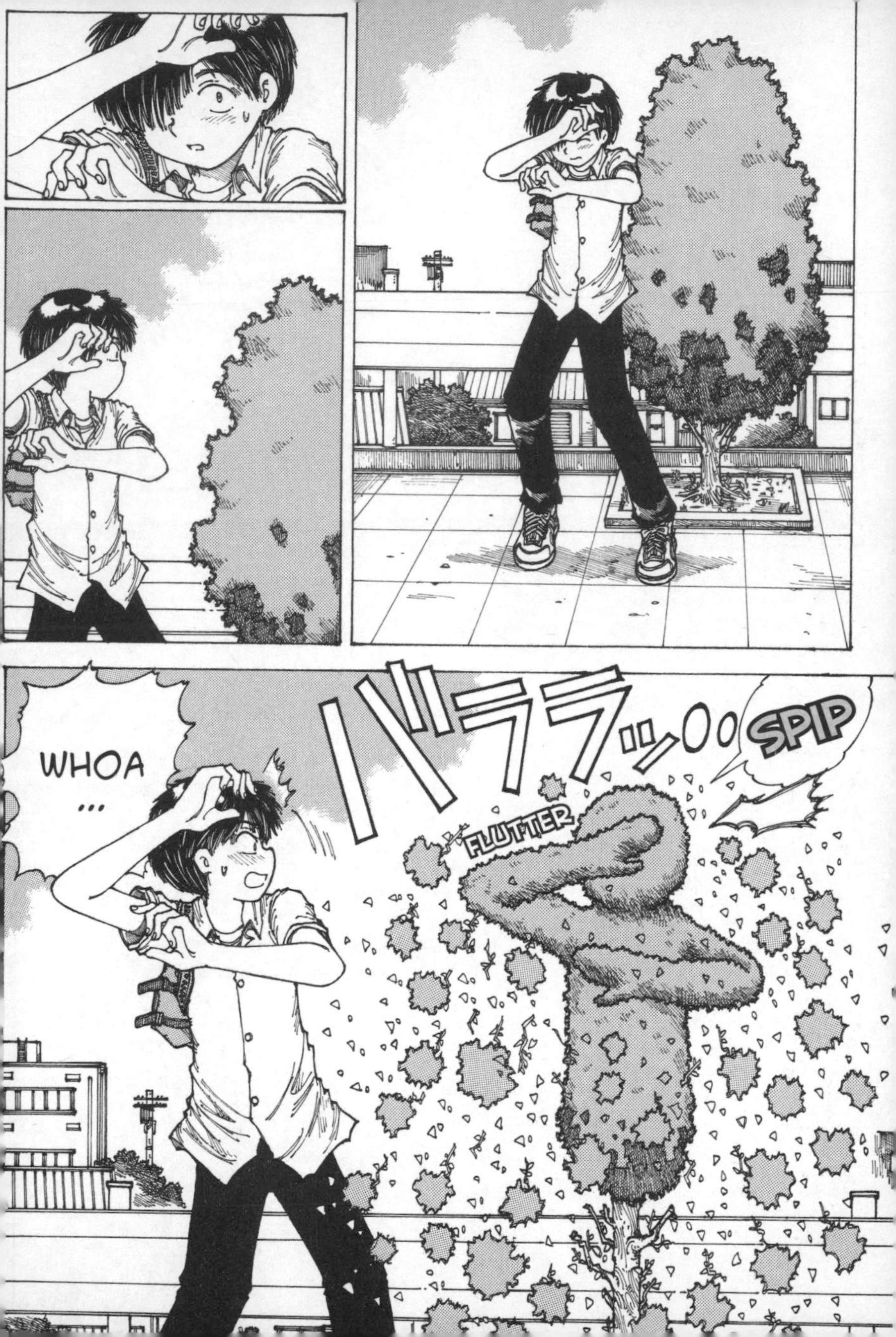

SPIP
バラララッ
FLUTTER
WHOA ...

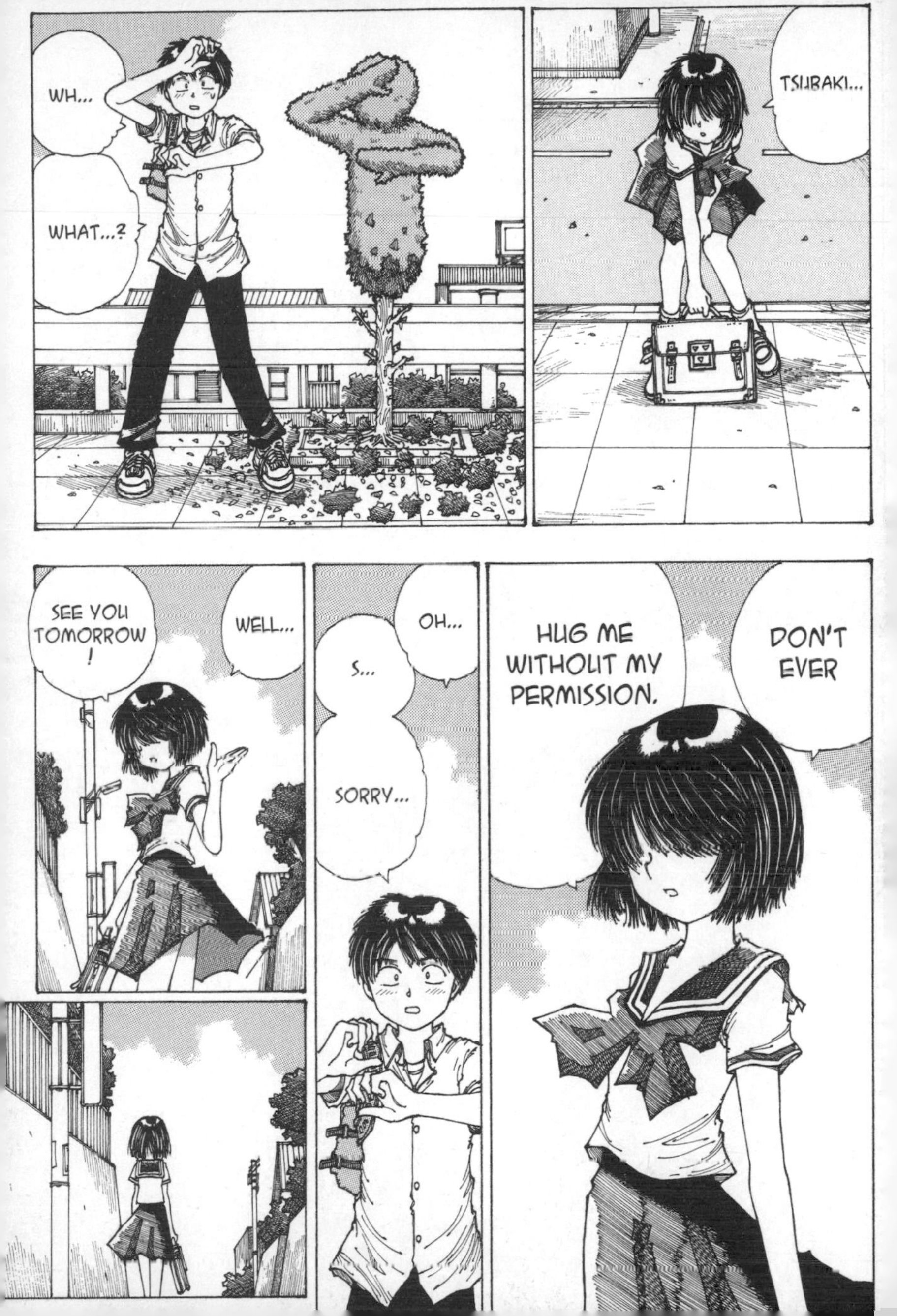
TSUBAKI...
WH...
WHAT...?
DON'T EVER
HUG ME WITHOUT MY PERMISSION.
OH...
S...
SORRY...
WELL...
SEE YOU TOMORROW!

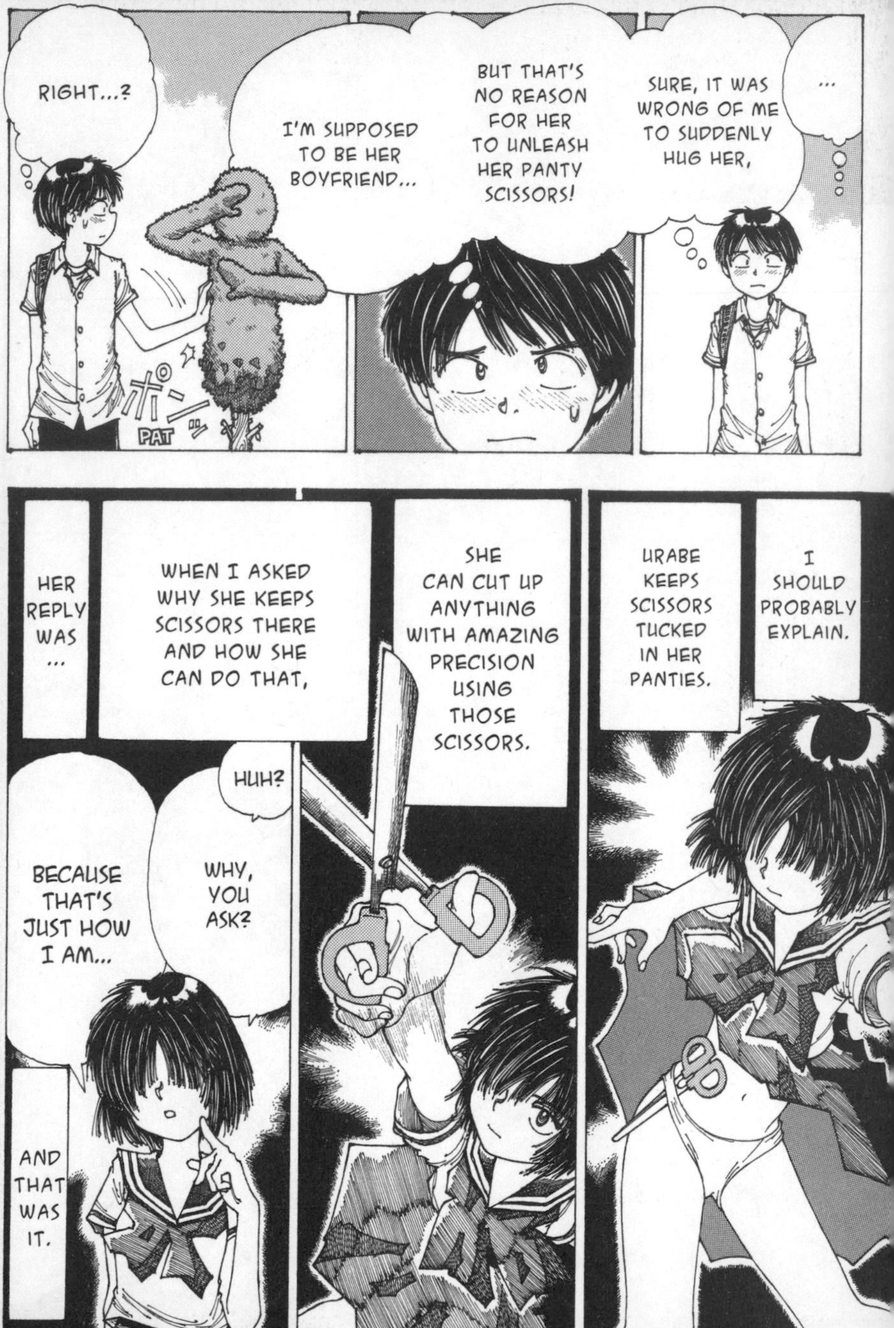
...
SURE, IT WAS WRONG OF ME TO SUDDENLY HUG HER,
BUT THAT'S NO REASON FOR HER TO UNLEASH HER PANTY SCISSORS!
I'M SUPPOSED TO BE HER BOYFRIEND...
RIGHT...?
ポンッ
PAT
I SHOULD PROBABLY EXPLAIN.
URABE KEEPS SCISSORS TUCKED IN HER PANTIES.
SHE CAN CUT UP ANYTHING WITH AMAZING PRECISION USING THOSE SCISSORS.
WHEN I ASKED WHY SHE KEEPS SCISSORS THERE AND HOW SHE CAN DO THAT,
HER REPLY WAS ...
HUH?
WHY, YOU ASK?
BECAUSE THAT'S JUST HOW I AM...
AND THAT WAS IT.

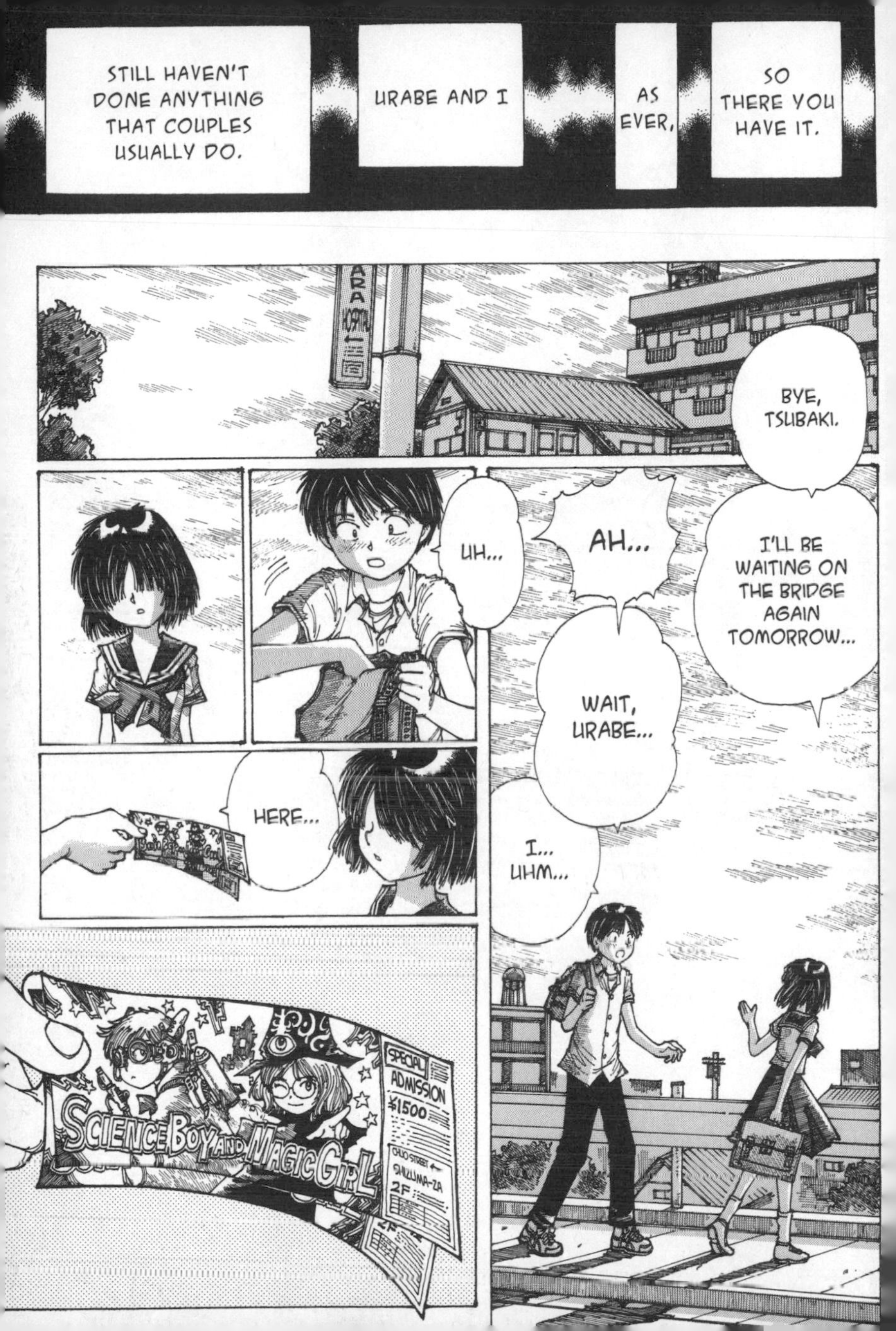
SO THERE YOU HAVE IT.
AS EVER,
URABE AND I
STILL HAVEN'T DONE ANYTHING THAT COUPLES USUALLY DO.
BYE, TSUBAKI.
I'LL BE WAITING ON THE BRIDGE AGAIN TOMORROW...
AH...
WAIT, URABE...
I... UHM...
UH...
HERE...
SCIENCE BOY AND MAGIC GIRL
SPECIAL ADMISSION ¥1500
CHUO STREET ←
SHIZUMA-ZA 2F

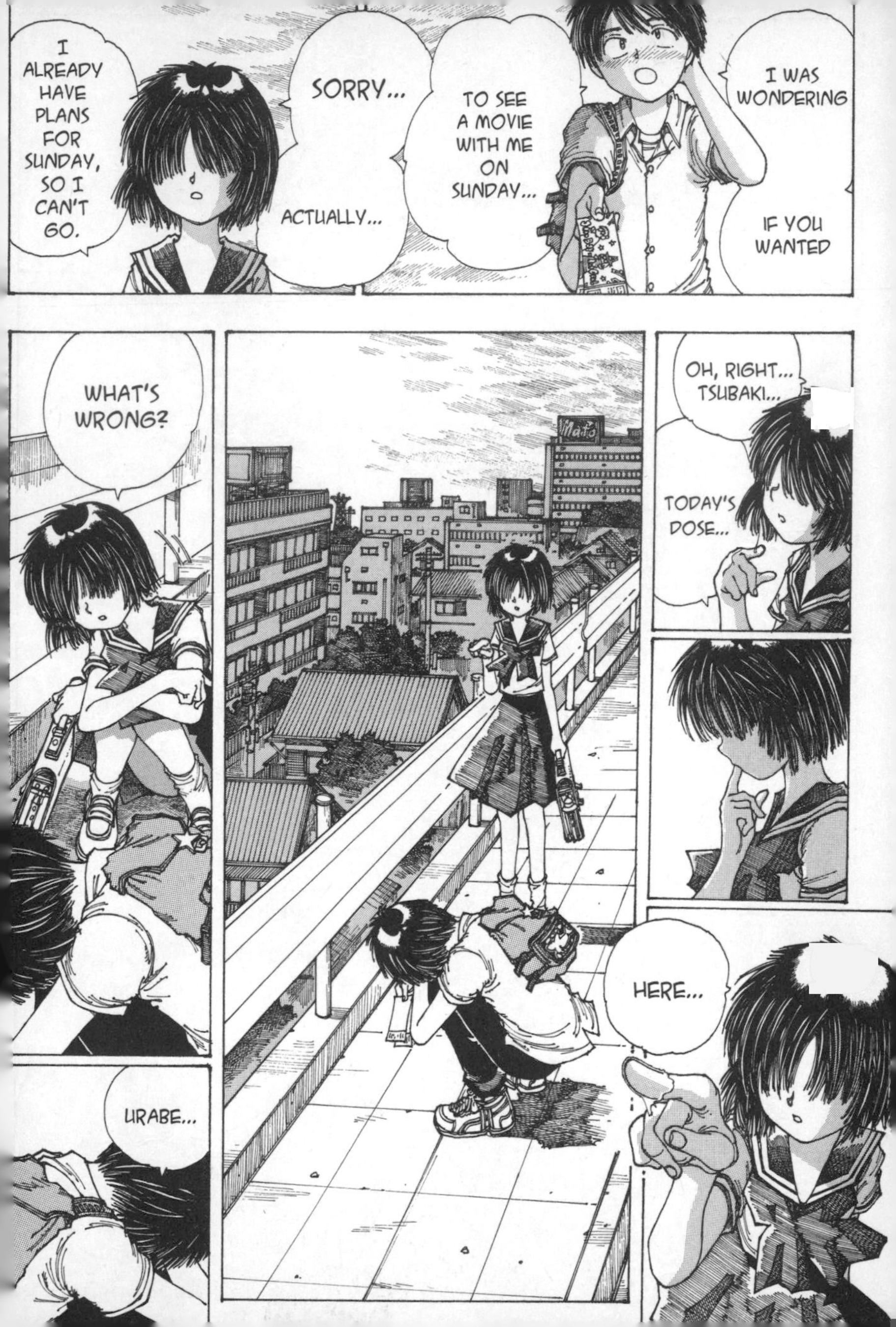
I WAS WONDERING
IF YOU WANTED
TO SEE A MOVIE WITH ME ON SUNDAY...
SORRY...
ACTUALLY...
I ALREADY HAVE PLANS FOR SUNDAY, SO I CAN'T GO.
OH, RIGHT... TSUBAKI...
TODAY'S DOSE...
HERE...
WHAT'S WRONG?
URABE...

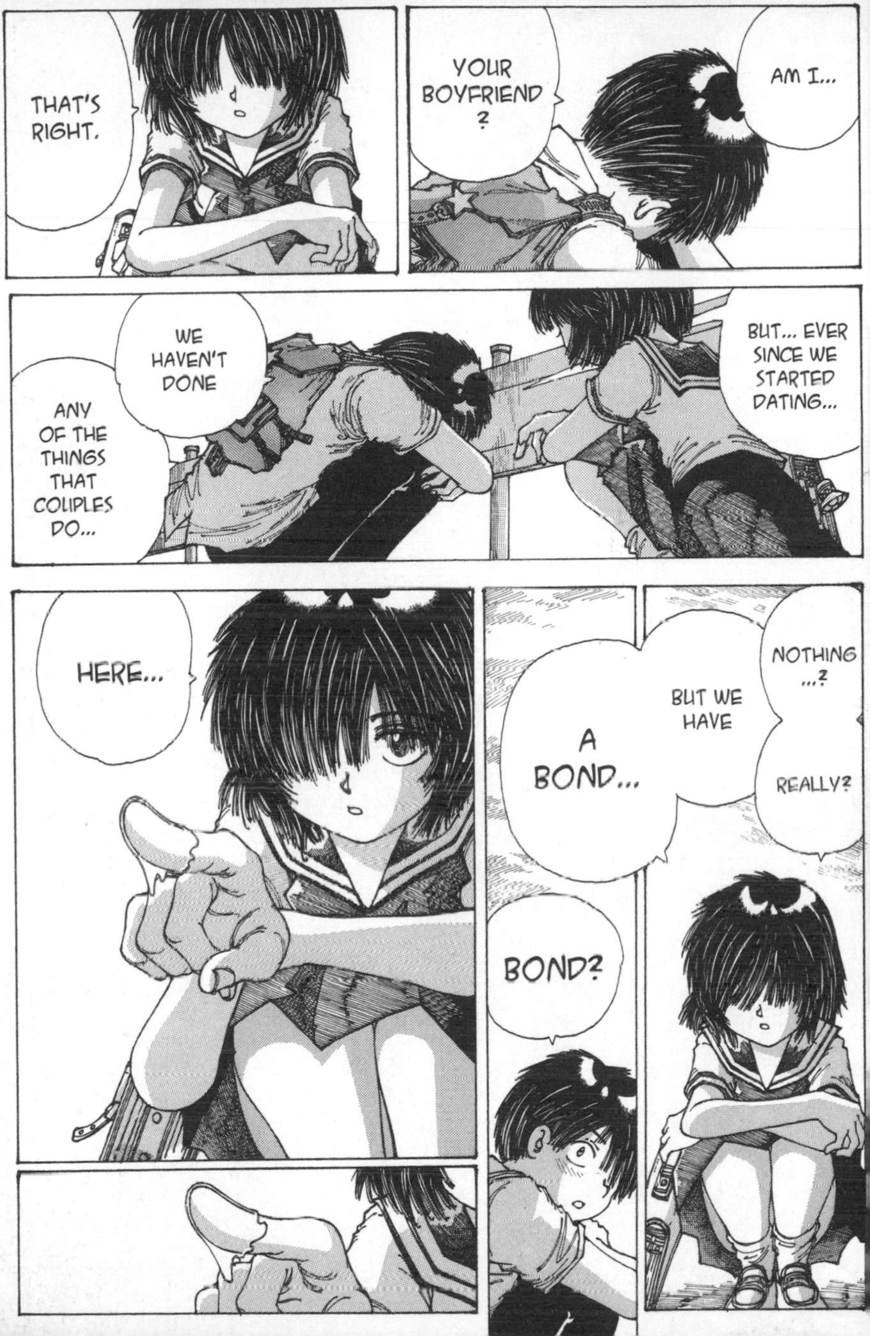
AM I...
YOUR BOYFRIEND?
THAT'S RIGHT.
BUT... EVER SINCE WE STARTED DATING...
WE HAVEN'T DONE
ANY OF THE THINGS THAT COUPLES DO...
NOTHING...?
REALLY?
BUT WE HAVE
A BOND...
BOND?
HERE...

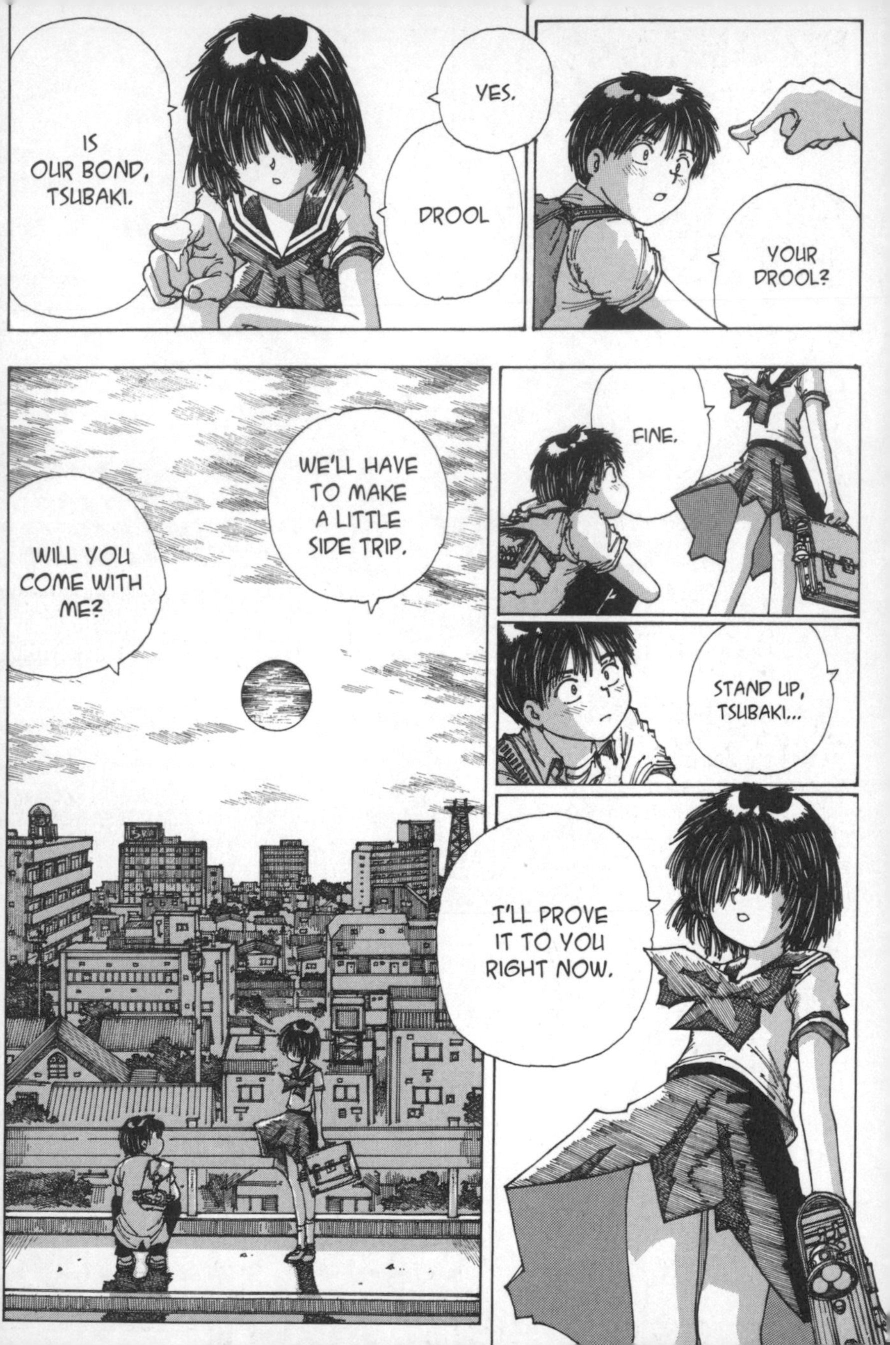
YOUR DROOL?
YES.
DROOL
IS OUR BOND, TSUBAKI.
FINE.
STAND UP, TSUBAKI...
I'LL PROVE IT TO YOU RIGHT NOW.
WE'LL HAVE TO MAKE A LITTLE SIDE TRIP.
WILL YOU COME WITH ME?

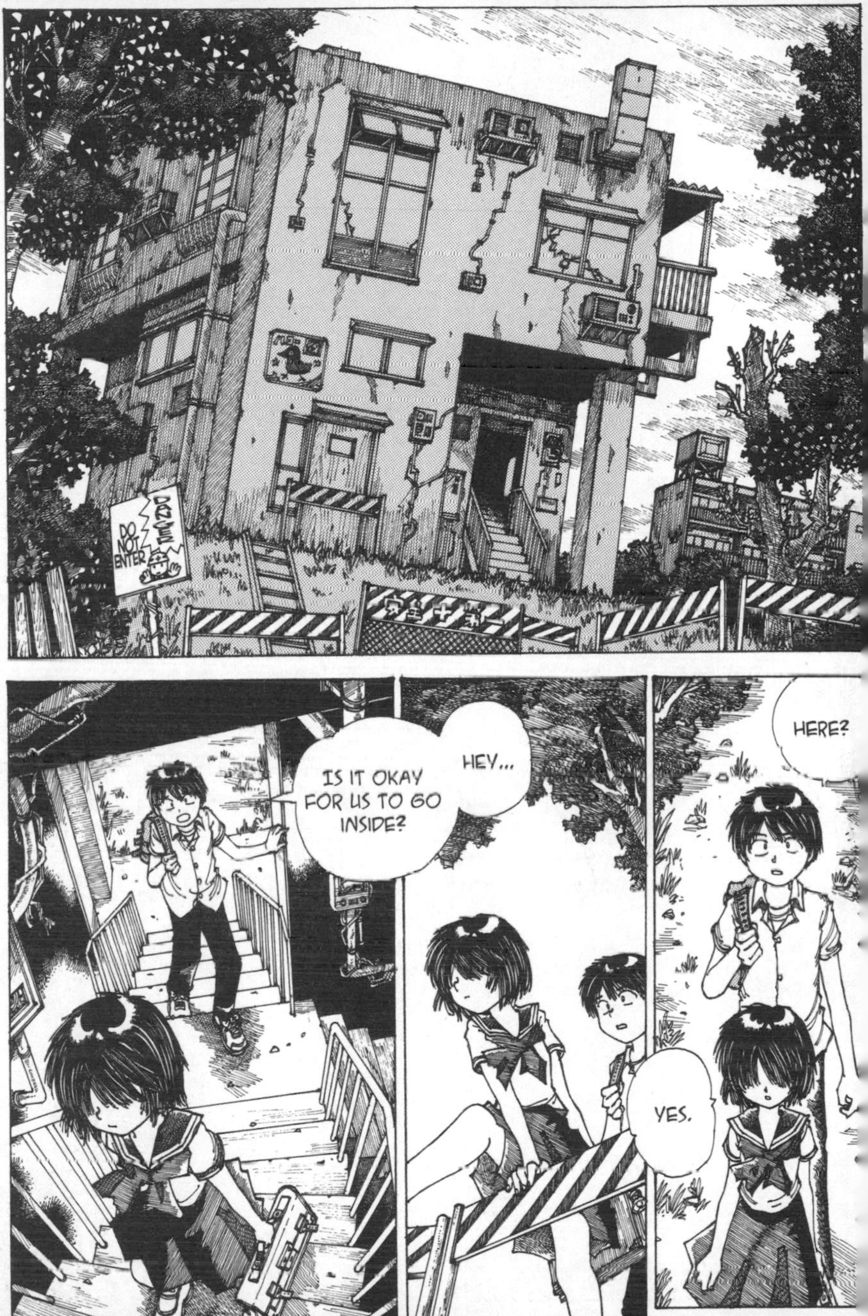
DANGER
DO NOT ENTER
HERE?
HEY...
YES.
IS IT OKAY FOR US TO GO INSIDE?

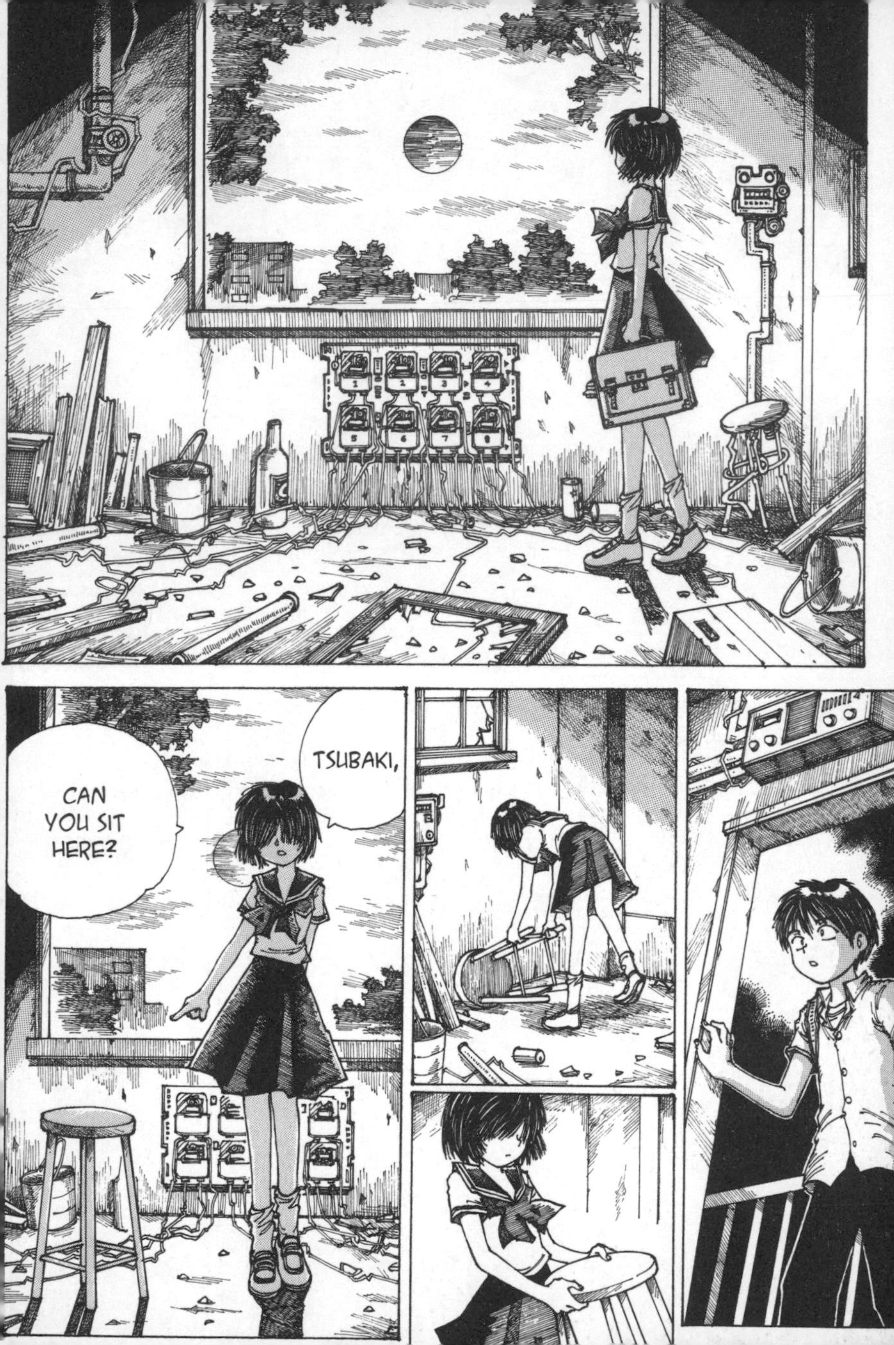
TSUBAKI,
CAN YOU SIT HERE?

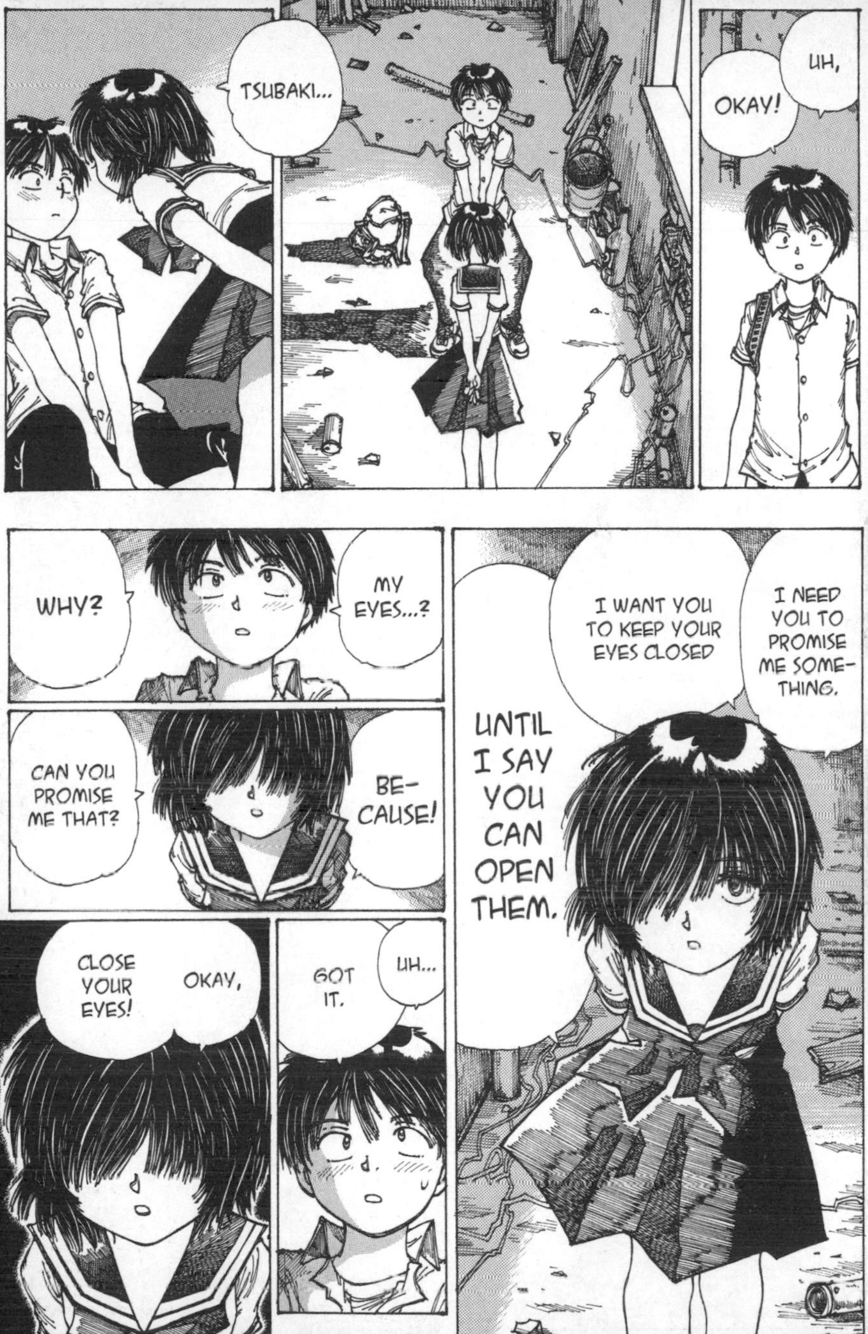
UH,
OKAY!
TSUBAKI...
I NEED YOU TO PROMISE ME SOME-THING.
I WANT YOU TO KEEP YOUR EYES CLOSED
UNTIL I SAY YOU CAN OPEN THEM.
MY EYES...?
WHY?
BE-CAUSE!
CAN YOU PROMISE ME THAT?
UH...
GOT IT.
OKAY,
CLOSE YOUR EYES!

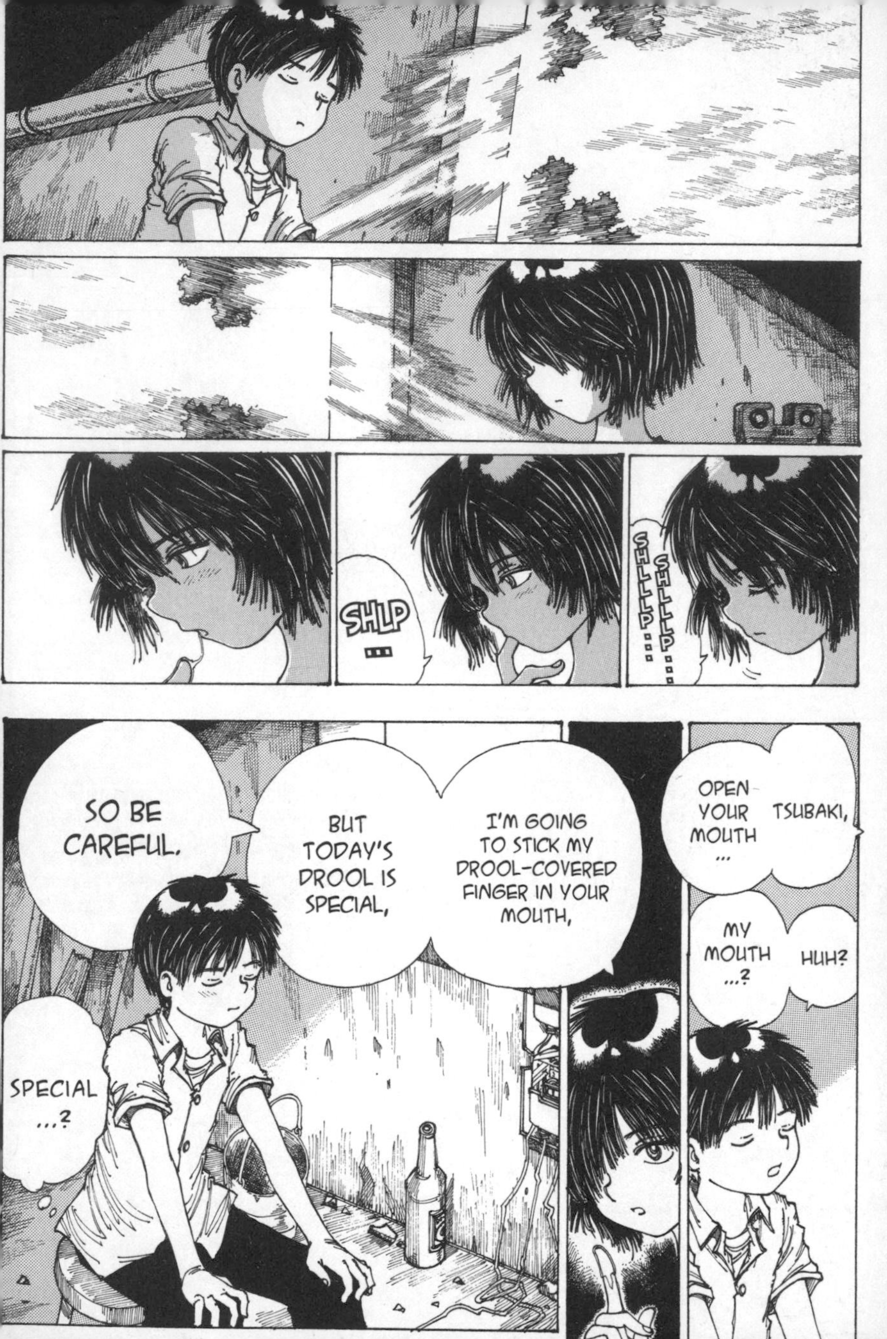
SHLLP...
SHLLP...
SHLP ...
TSUBAKI,
OPEN YOUR MOUTH ...
HUH?
MY MOUTH ...?
I'M GOING TO STICK MY DROOL-COVERED FINGER IN YOUR MOUTH,
BUT TODAY'S DROOL IS SPECIAL,
SO BE CAREFUL.
SPECIAL ...?

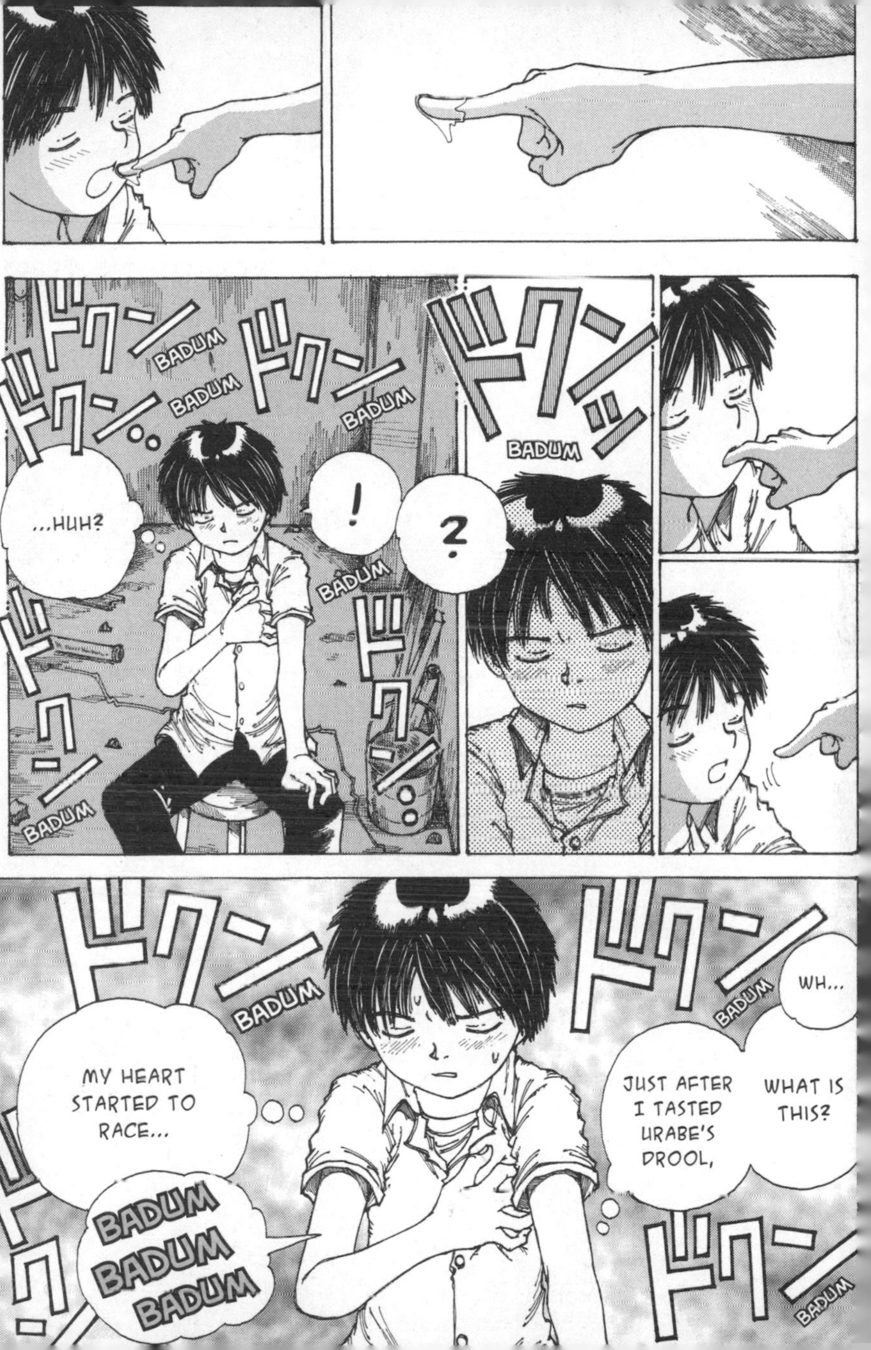

ドクンッ
BADUM
?
ドクーン
BADUM
!
ドクーン
BADUM
BADUM
ドクーン…
...HUH?
ドクーン…
BADUM
ドクーン
BADUM
ドクーン
BADUM
WH...
WHAT IS THIS?
JUST AFTER I TASTED URABE'S DROOL,
MY HEART STARTED TO RACE...
ドクーン
BADUM
ドクーン
BADUM BADUM BADUM
ドクーン
BADUM

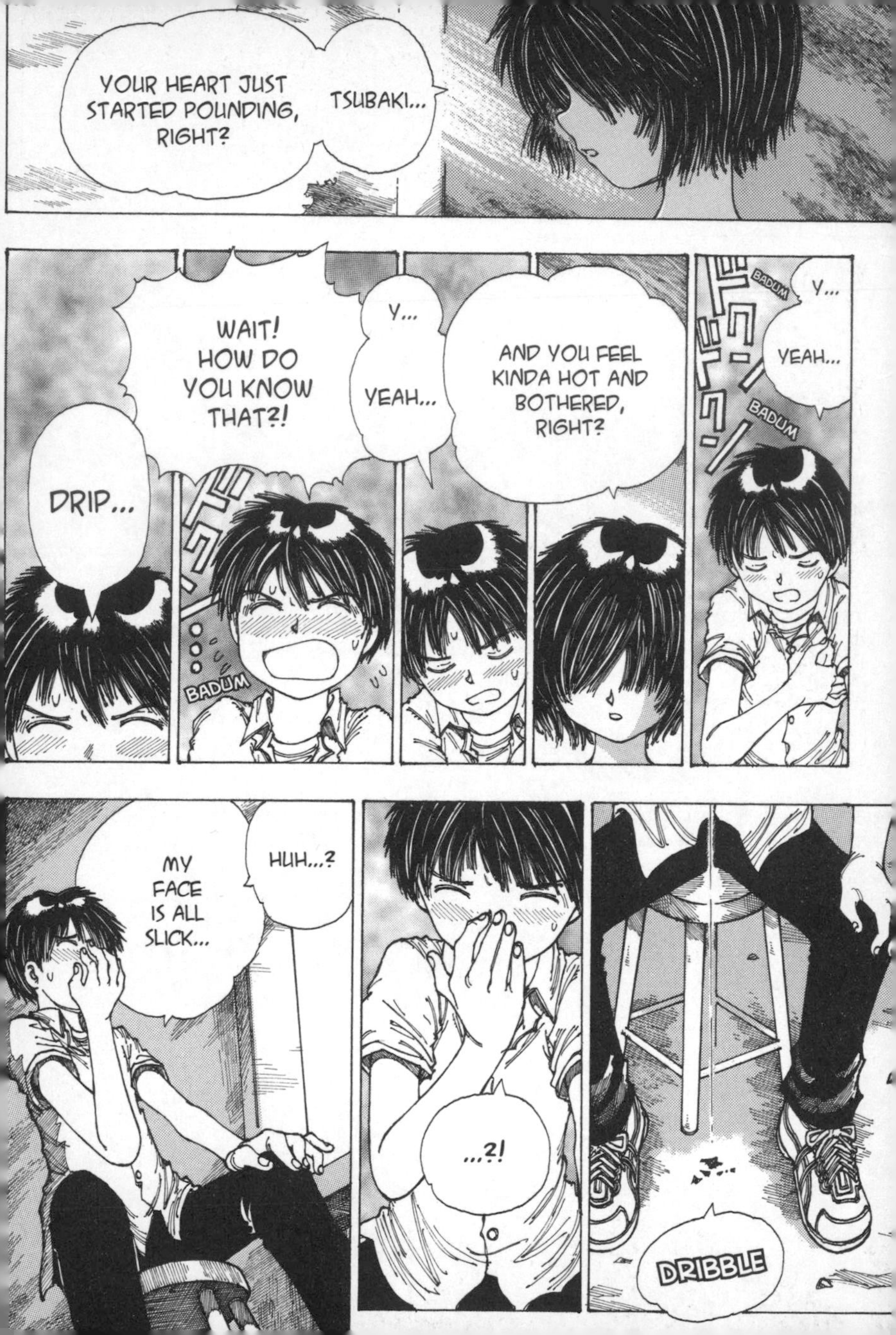
TSUBAKI...
YOUR HEART JUST STARTED POUNDING, RIGHT?
BADUM
Y...
YEAH...
BADUM
AND YOU FEEL KINDA HOT AND BOTHERED, RIGHT?
Y...
YEAH...
WAIT! HOW DO YOU KNOW THAT?!
BADUM
DRIP...
DRIBBLE
...?!
HUH...?
MY FACE IS ALL SLICK...

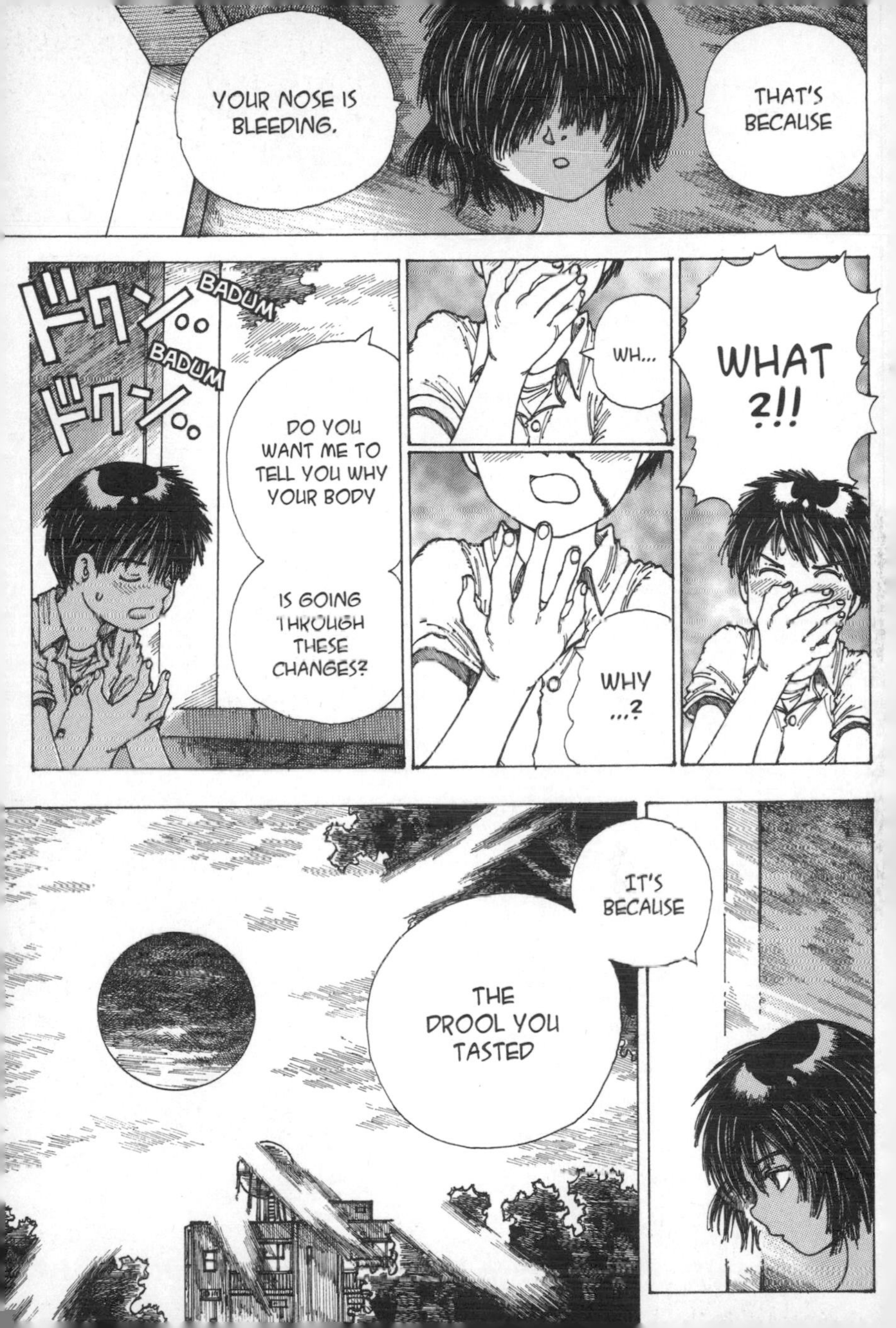
THAT'S BECAUSE
YOUR NOSE IS BLEEDING.
WHAT ?!!
WH...
WHY ...?
DO YOU WANT ME TO TELL YOU WHY YOUR BODY
IS GOING THROUGH THESE CHANGES?
ドクン。。
BADUM
ドクン。。
BADUM
IT'S BECAUSE
THE DROOL YOU TASTED

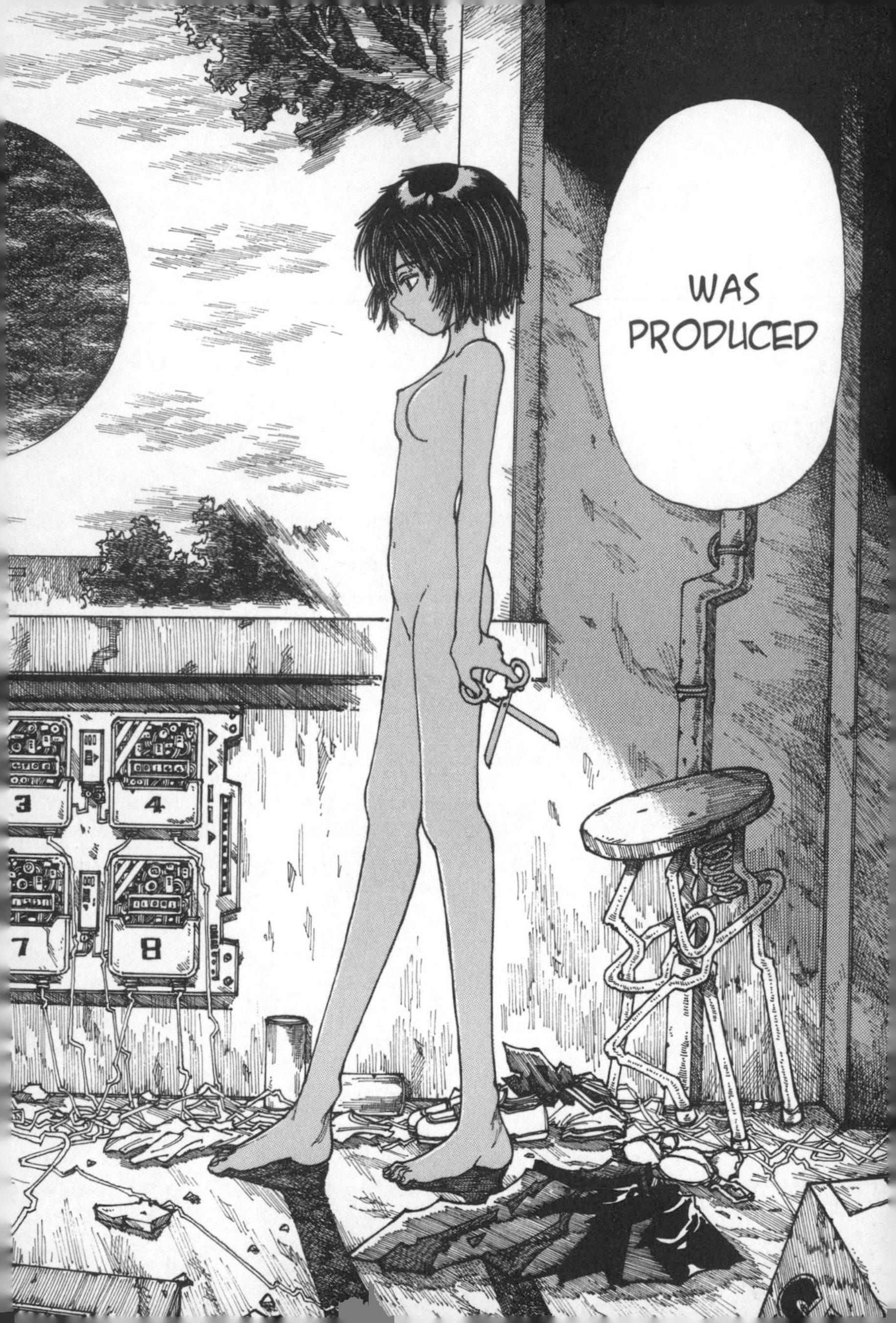
WAS PRODUCED
3
4
7
8

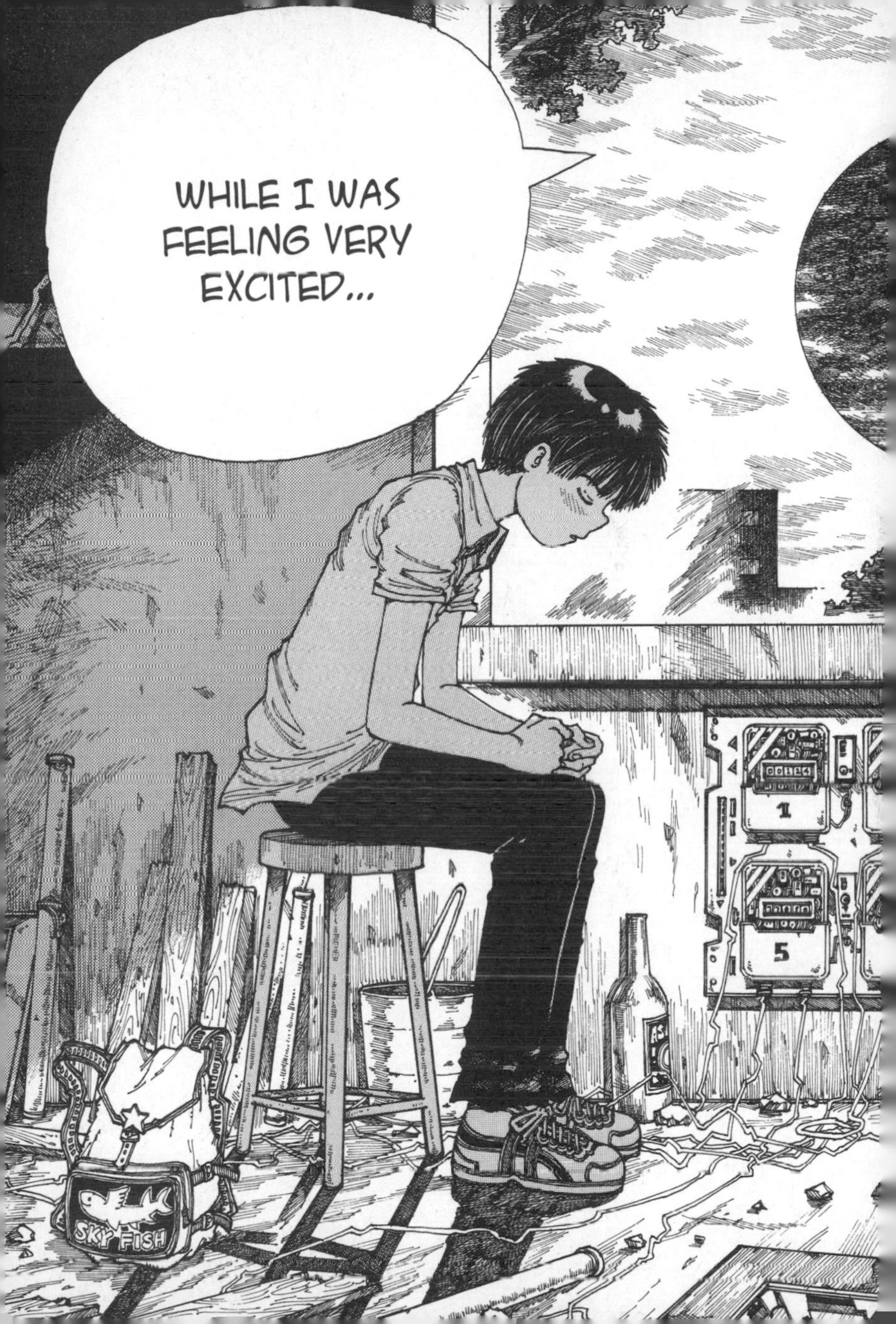
WHILE I WAS FEELING VERY EXCITED...
SKY FISH

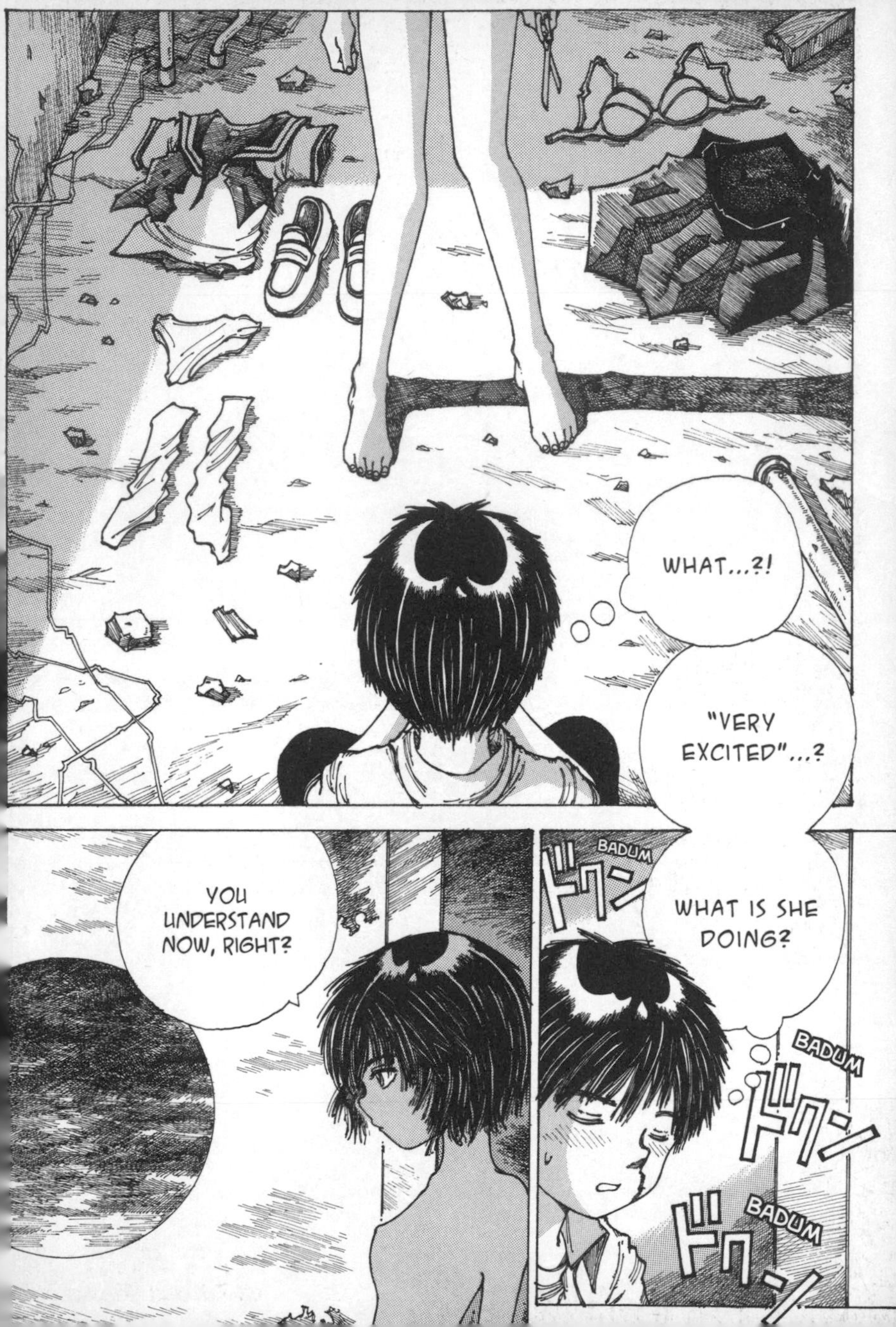
WHAT...?!
"VERY EXCITED"...?
BADUM
ドクーン
WHAT IS SHE DOING?
BADUM
ドクーン
BADUM
ドクーン
YOU UNDERSTAND NOW, RIGHT?

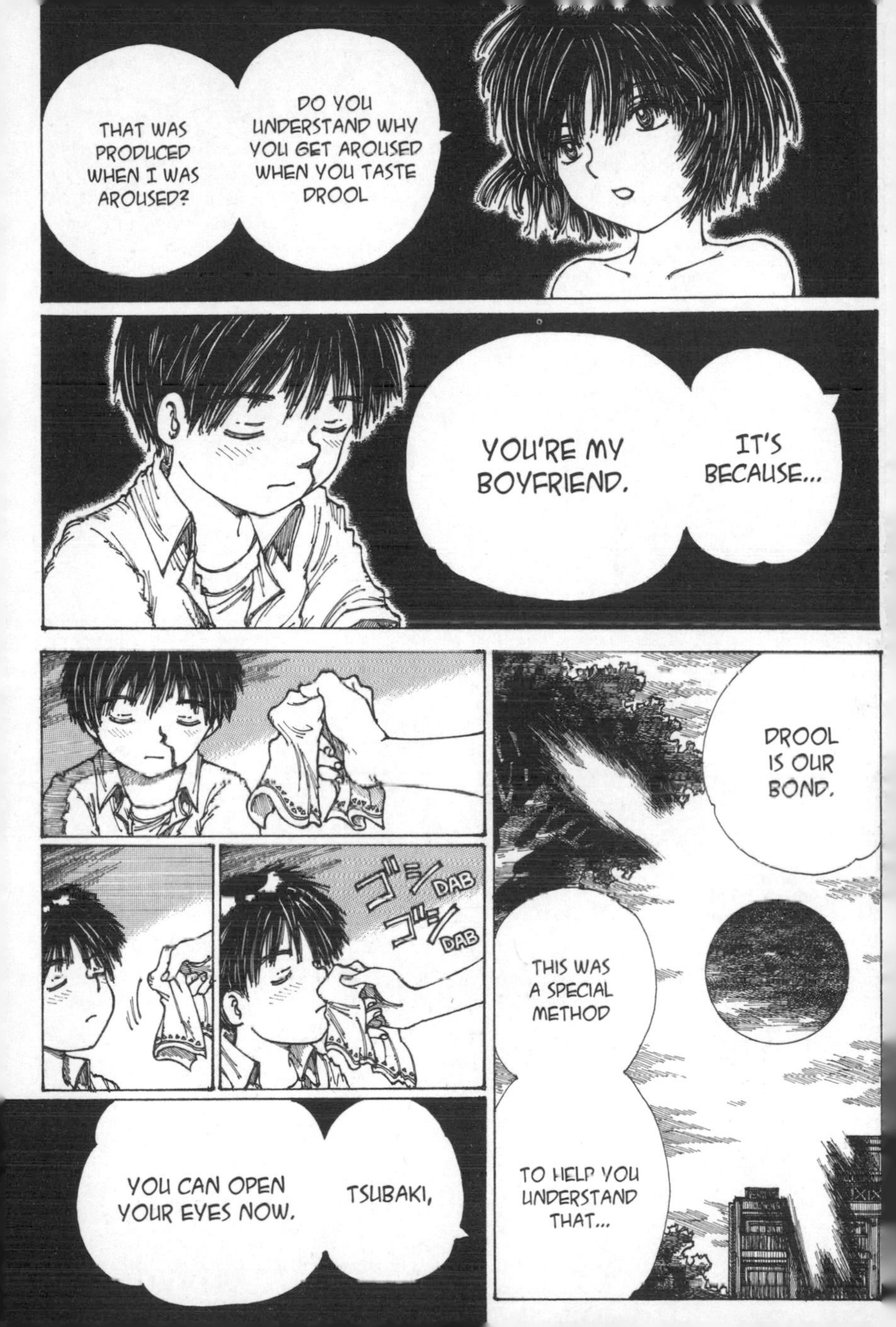
DO YOU UNDERSTAND WHY YOU GET AROUSED WHEN YOU TASTE DROOL
THAT WAS PRODUCED WHEN I WAS AROUSED?
IT'S BECAUSE...
YOU'RE MY BOYFRIEND.
DROOL IS OUR BOND.
THIS WAS A SPECIAL METHOD
TO HELP YOU UNDERSTAND THAT...
ゴシ DAB
ゴシ DAB
TSUBAKI,
YOU CAN OPEN YOUR EYES NOW.

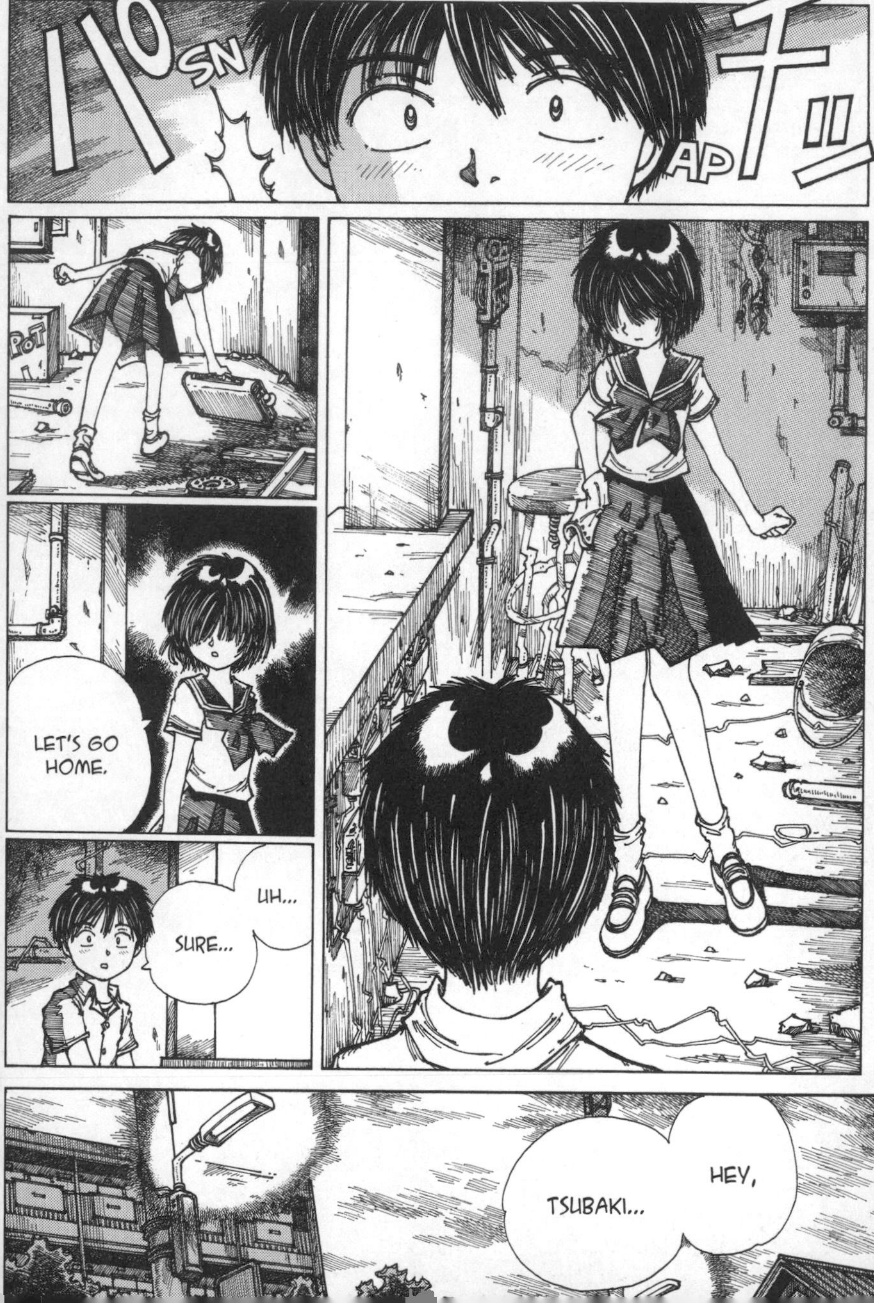
パ
SN
AP
チッ
LET'S GO HOME.
UH... SURE...
HEY, TSUBAKI...

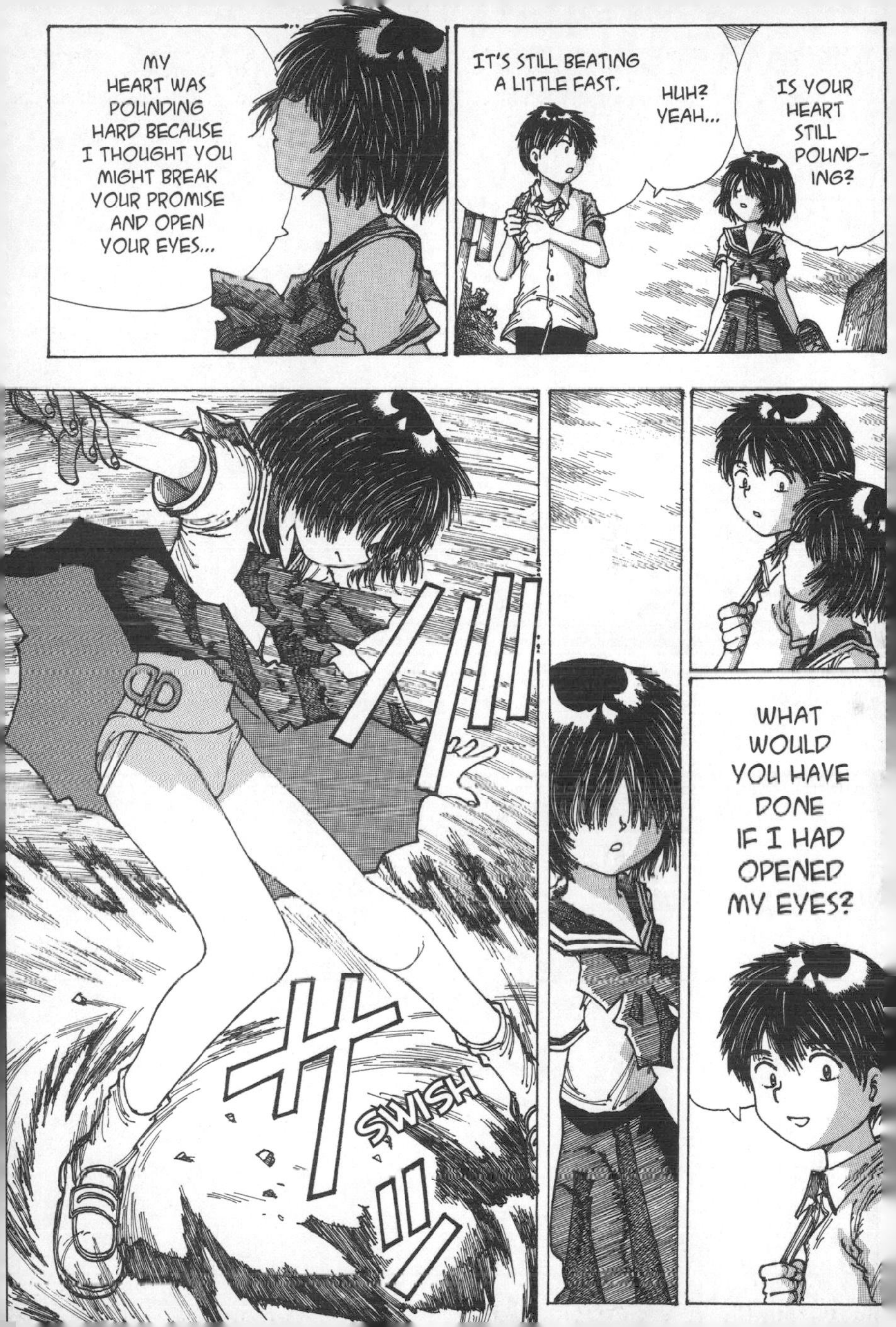
IS YOUR HEART STILL POUND-ING?
HUH? YEAH...
IT'S STILL BEATING A LITTLE FAST.
MY HEART WAS POUNDING HARD BECAUSE I THOUGHT YOU MIGHT BREAK YOUR PROMISE AND OPEN YOUR EYES...
WHAT WOULD YOU HAVE DONE IF I HAD OPENED MY EYES?
SWISH

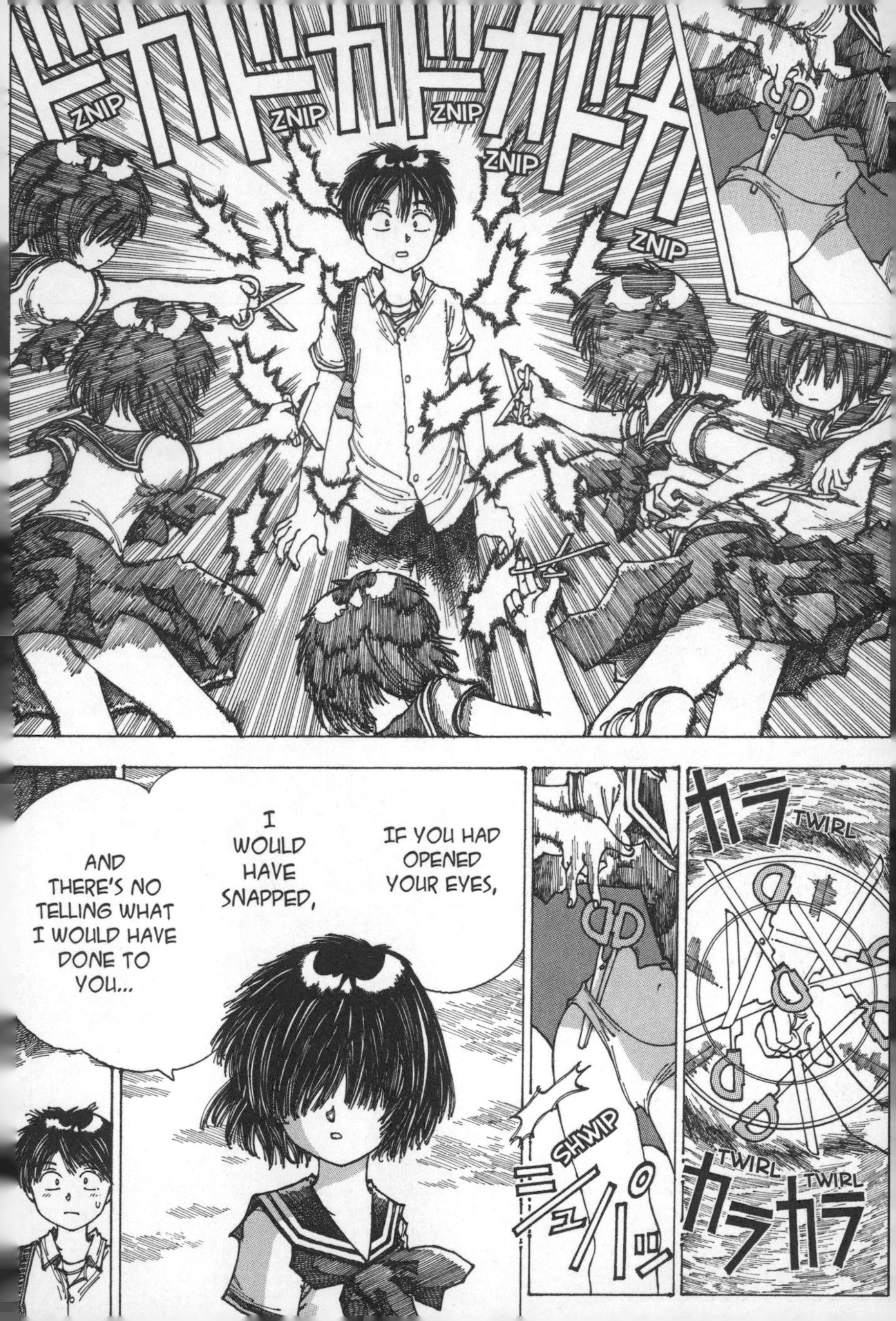
ZNIP
ZNIP
ZNIP
ZNIP
ZNIP
カラ
TWIRL
TWIRL
TWIRL
カラカラ
SHWIP
シュパッ
IF YOU HAD OPENED YOUR EYES,
I WOULD HAVE SNAPPED,
AND THERE'S NO TELLING WHAT I WOULD HAVE DONE TO YOU...

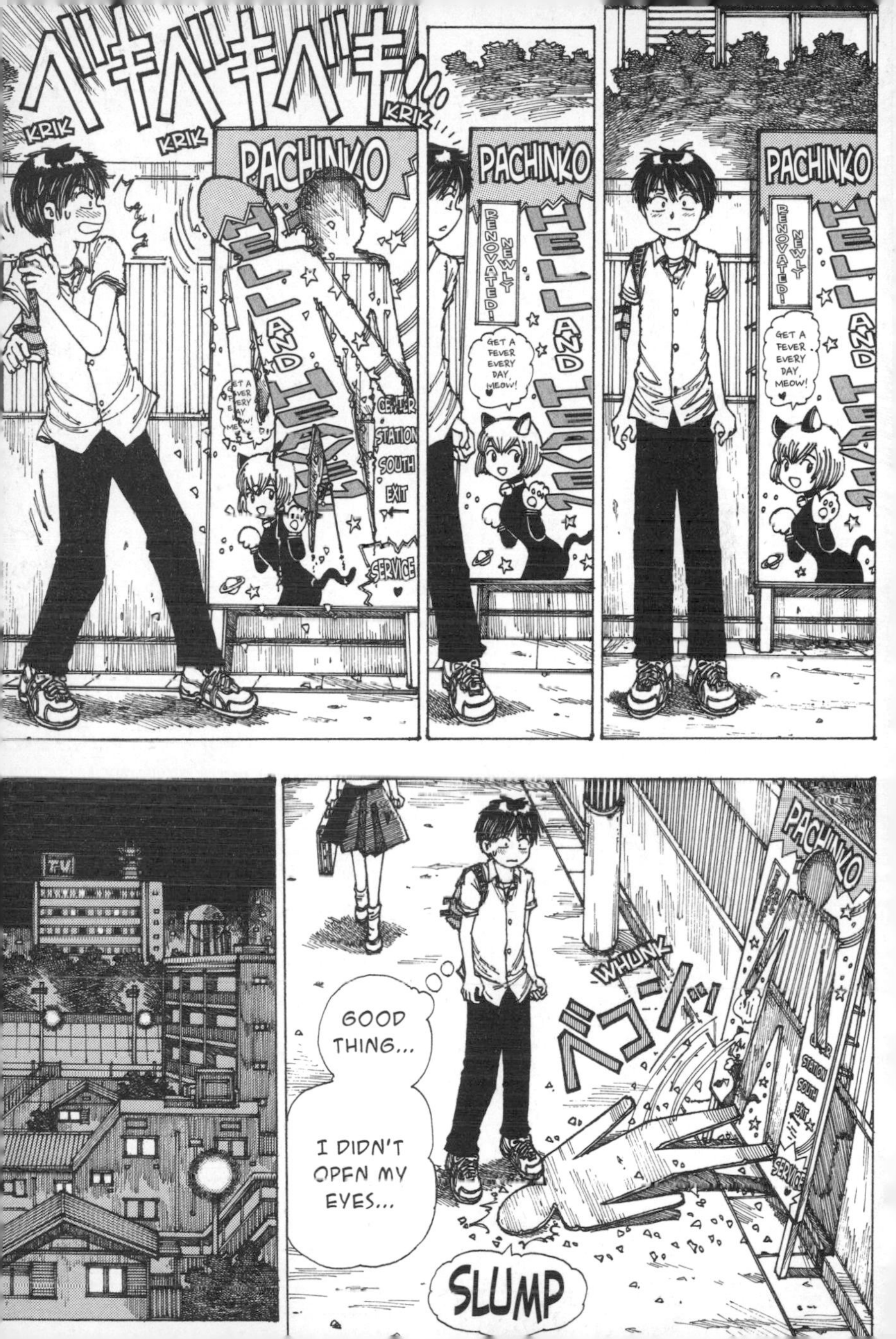
PACHINKO
NEWLY RENOVATED!
GET A FEVER EVERY DAY, MEOW!
PACHINKO
NEWLY RENOVATED!
GET A FEVER EVERY DAY, MEOW!
ベキベキベキ...
KRIK
KRIK
KRIK
PACHINKO
CENTER STATION SOUTH EXIT
SERVICE
GOOD THING...
I DIDN'T OPEN MY EYES...
PACHINKO
WHUNK
ベコン
STATION SOUTH EXIT
SERVICE
SLUMP
TV

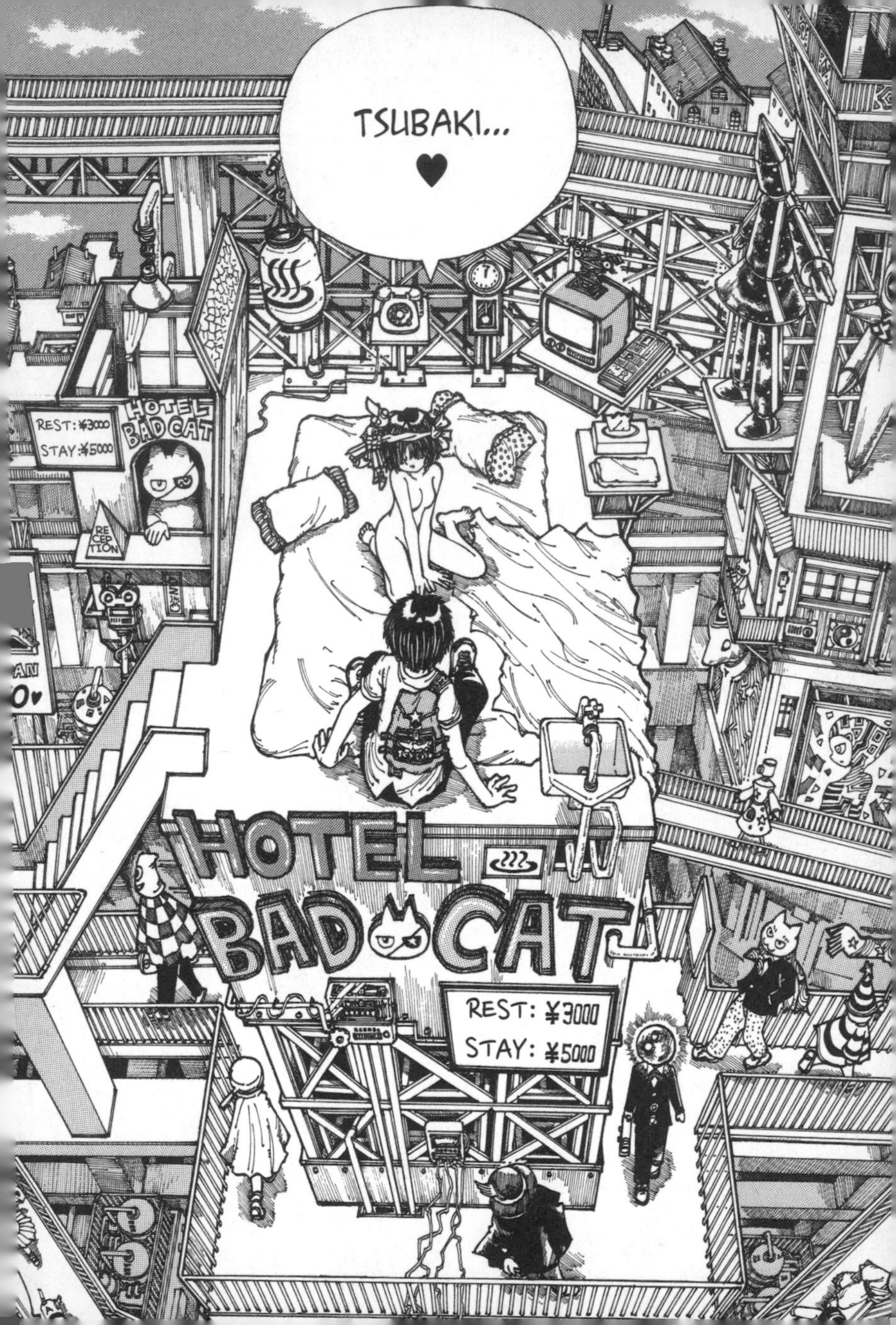
TSUBAKI... ♥
HOTEL BAD CAT
REST: ¥3000
STAY: ¥5000
RECEPTION
HOTEL BAD CAT
REST: ¥3000
STAY: ¥5000

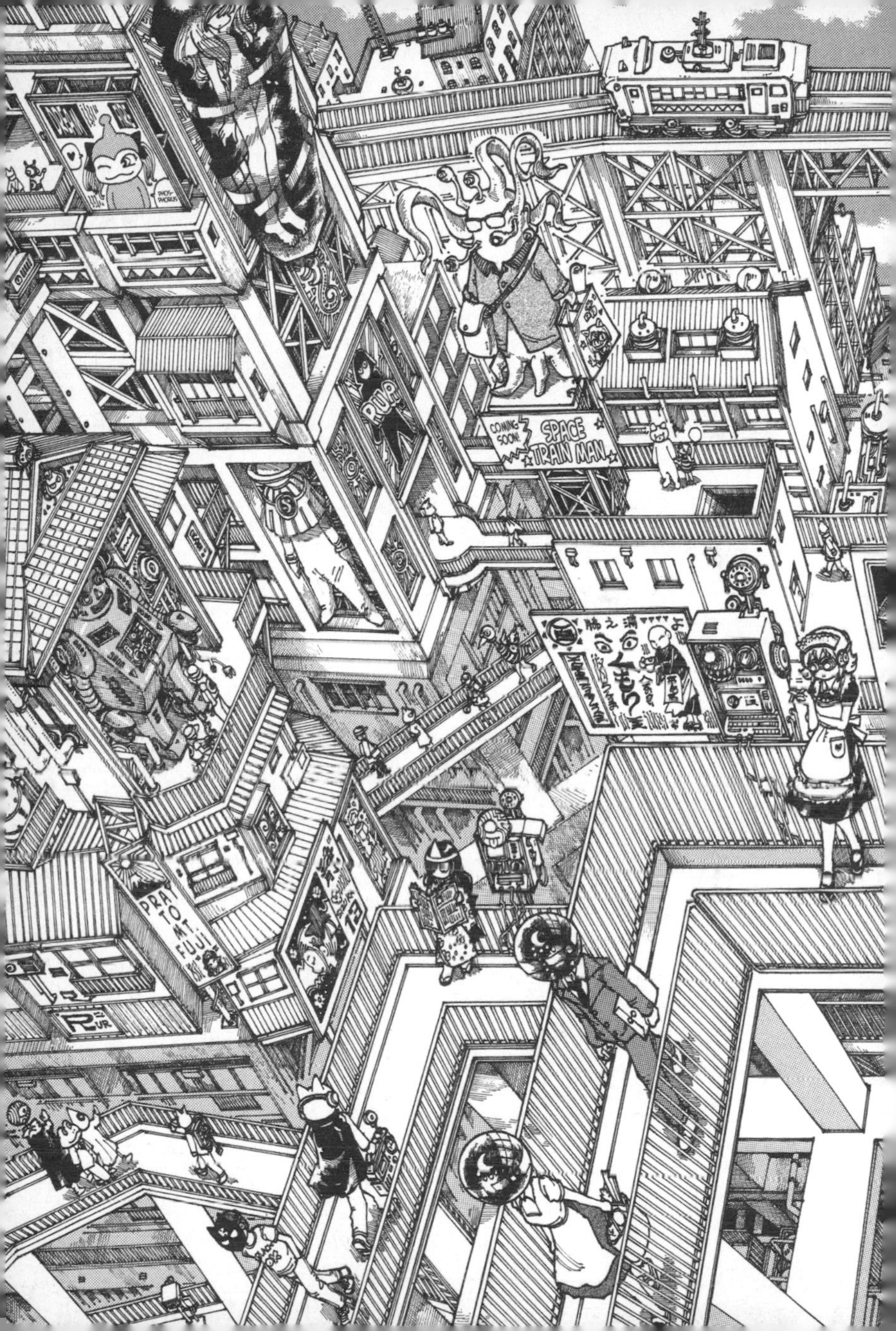

PHOS-
PHORUS
COMING SOON!
SPACE TRAIN MAN
PRAY TO MT. FUJI

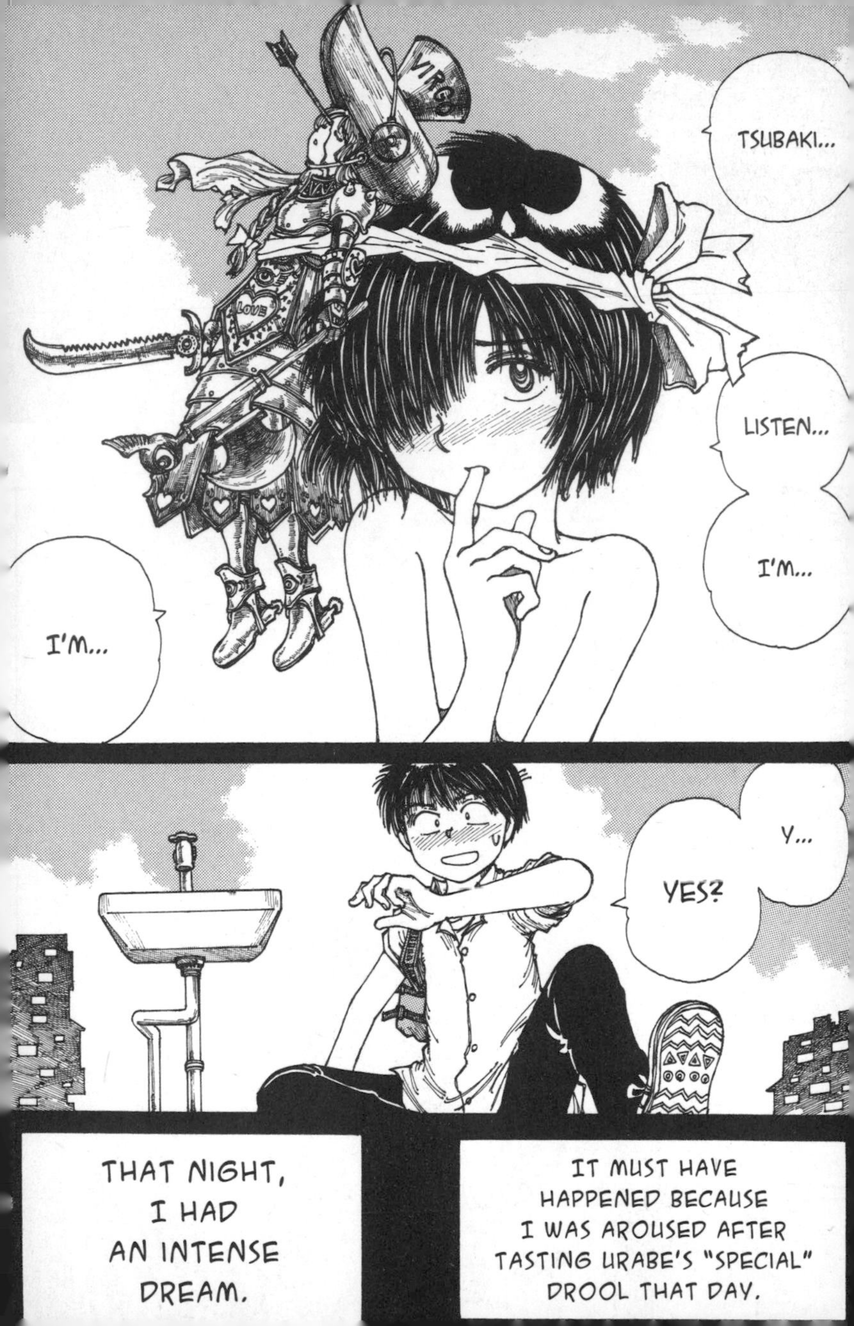
TSUBAKI...
LISTEN...
I'M...
I'M...
Y...
YES?
THAT NIGHT, I HAD AN INTENSE DREAM.
IT MUST HAVE HAPPENED BECAUSE I WAS AROUSED AFTER TASTING URABE'S "SPECIAL" DROOL THAT DAY.

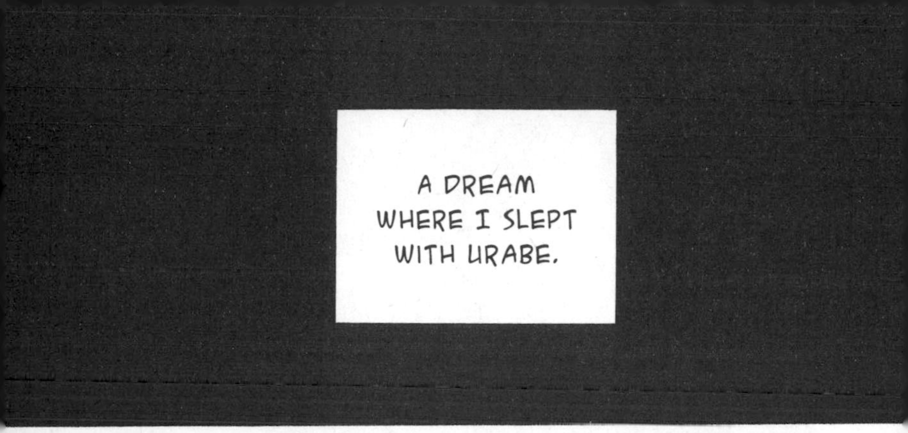
A DREAM
WHERE I SLEPT
WITH URABE.

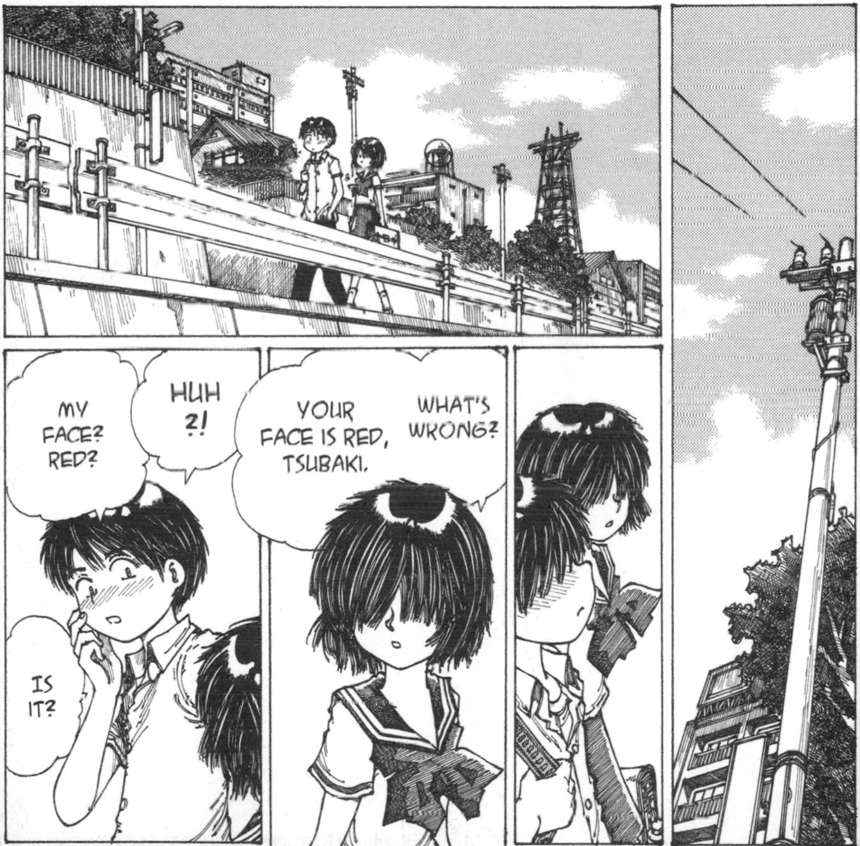
WHAT'S WRONG?
YOUR FACE IS RED, TSUBAKI.
HUH ?!
MY FACE? RED?
IS IT?

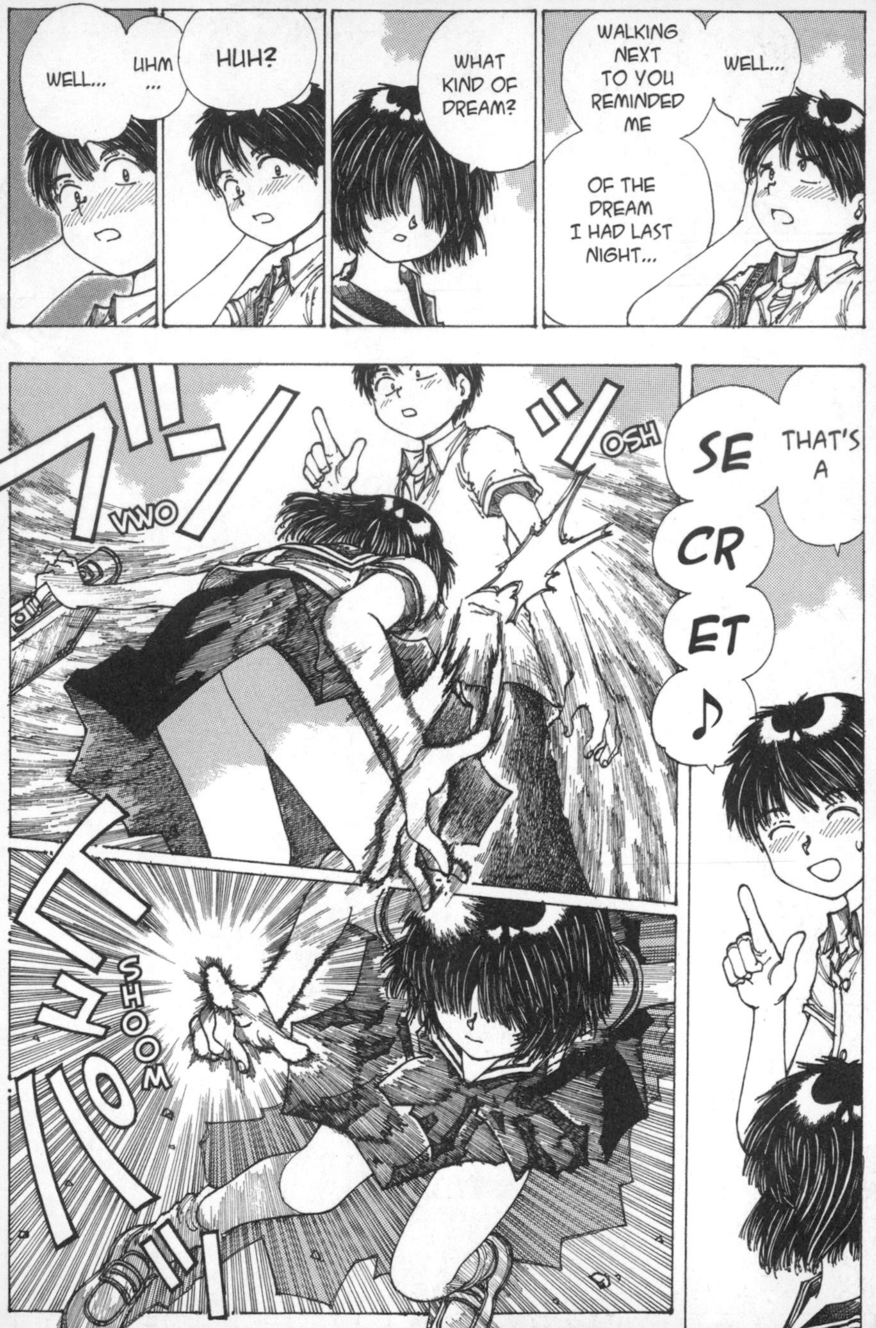
WELL...
WALKING NEXT TO YOU REMINDED ME
OF THE DREAM I HAD LAST NIGHT...
WHAT KIND OF DREAM?
HUH?
WELL... UHM ...
THAT'S A
SE CR ET ♪
OSH
VWO
SHOOM

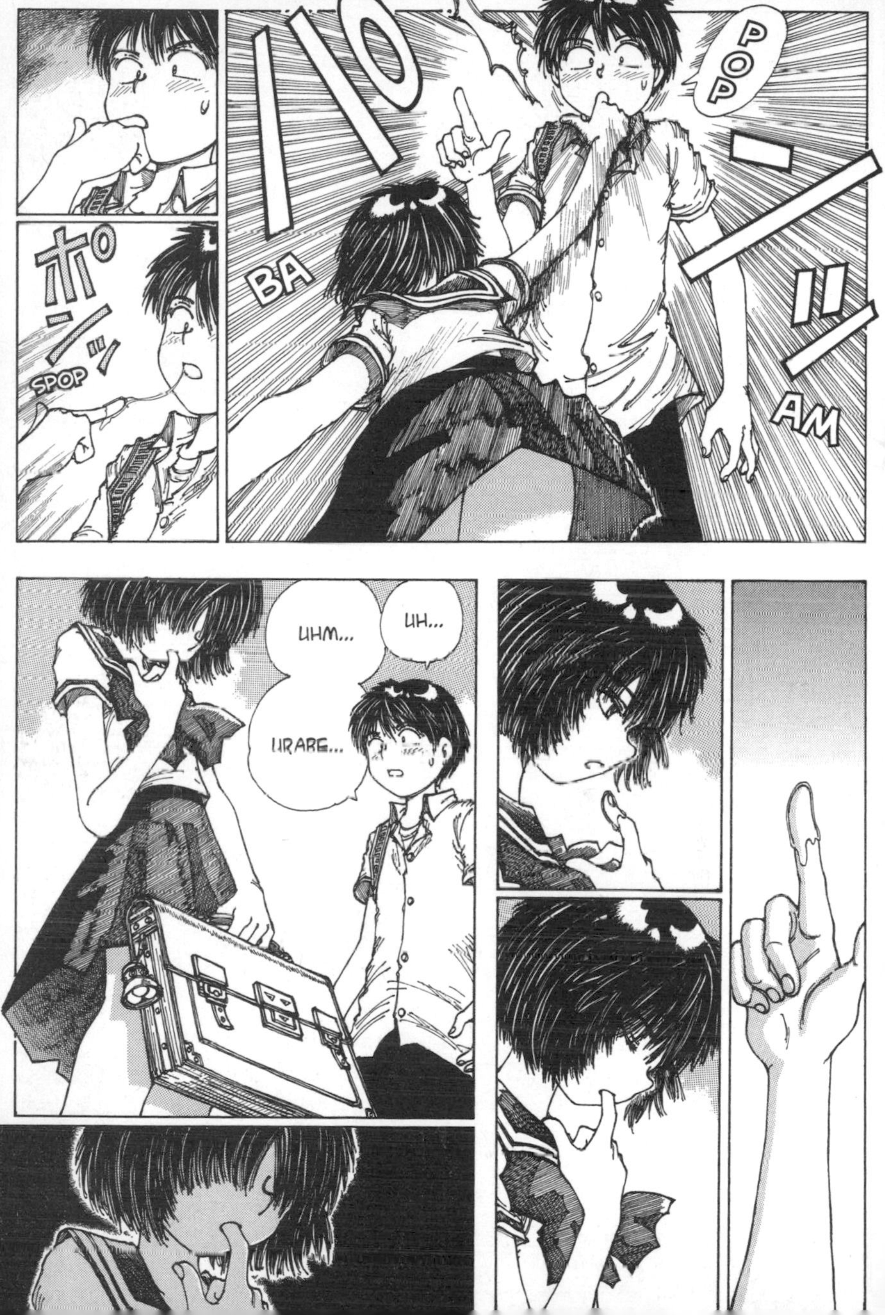
POP
BA
AM
ポンッ
SPOP
UH...
UHM...
URARE...

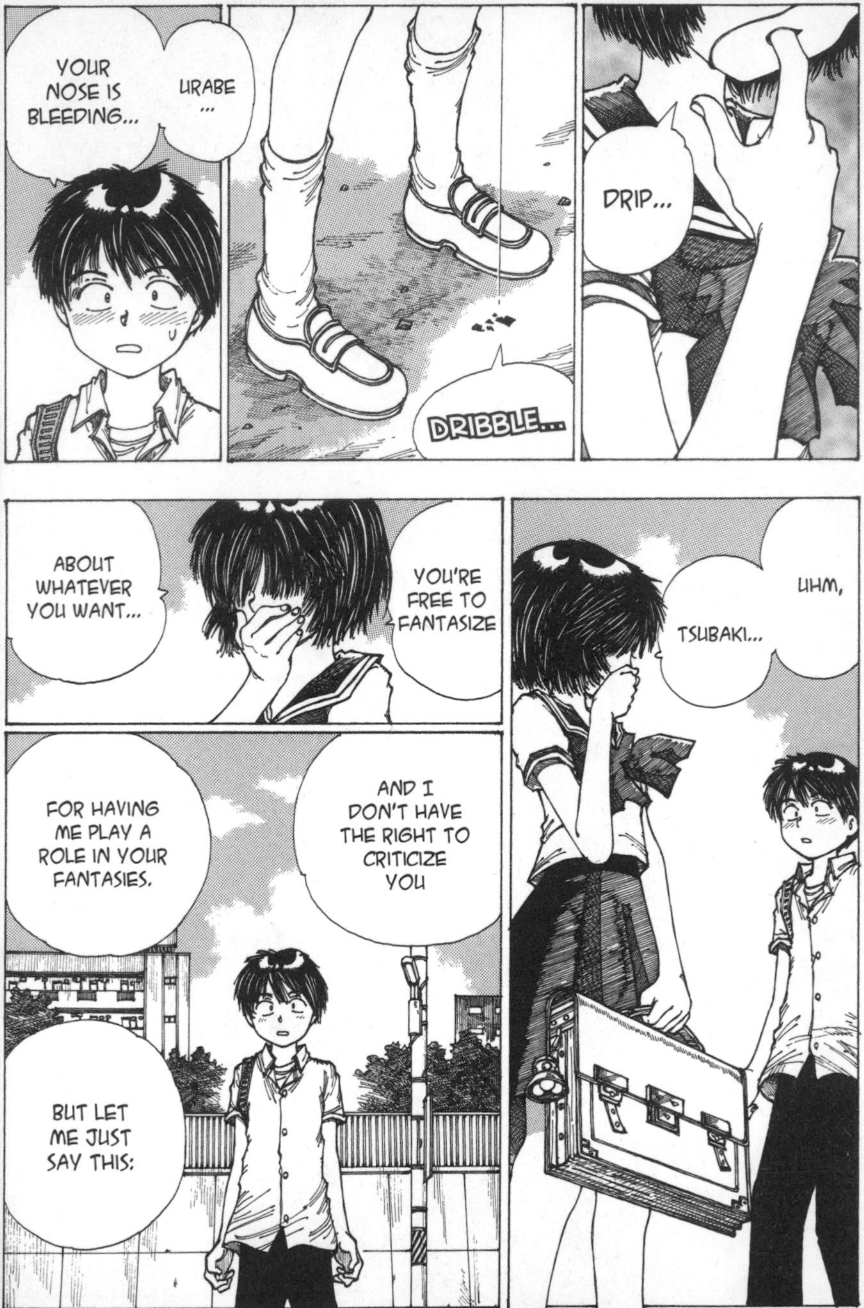
DRIP...
DRIBBLE...
URABE ...
YOUR NOSE IS BLEEDING...
UHM,
TSUBAKI...
YOU'RE FREE TO FANTASIZE
ABOUT WHATEVER YOU WANT...
AND I DON'T HAVE THE RIGHT TO CRITICIZE YOU
FOR HAVING ME PLAY A ROLE IN YOUR FANTASIES.
BUT LET ME JUST SAY THIS:

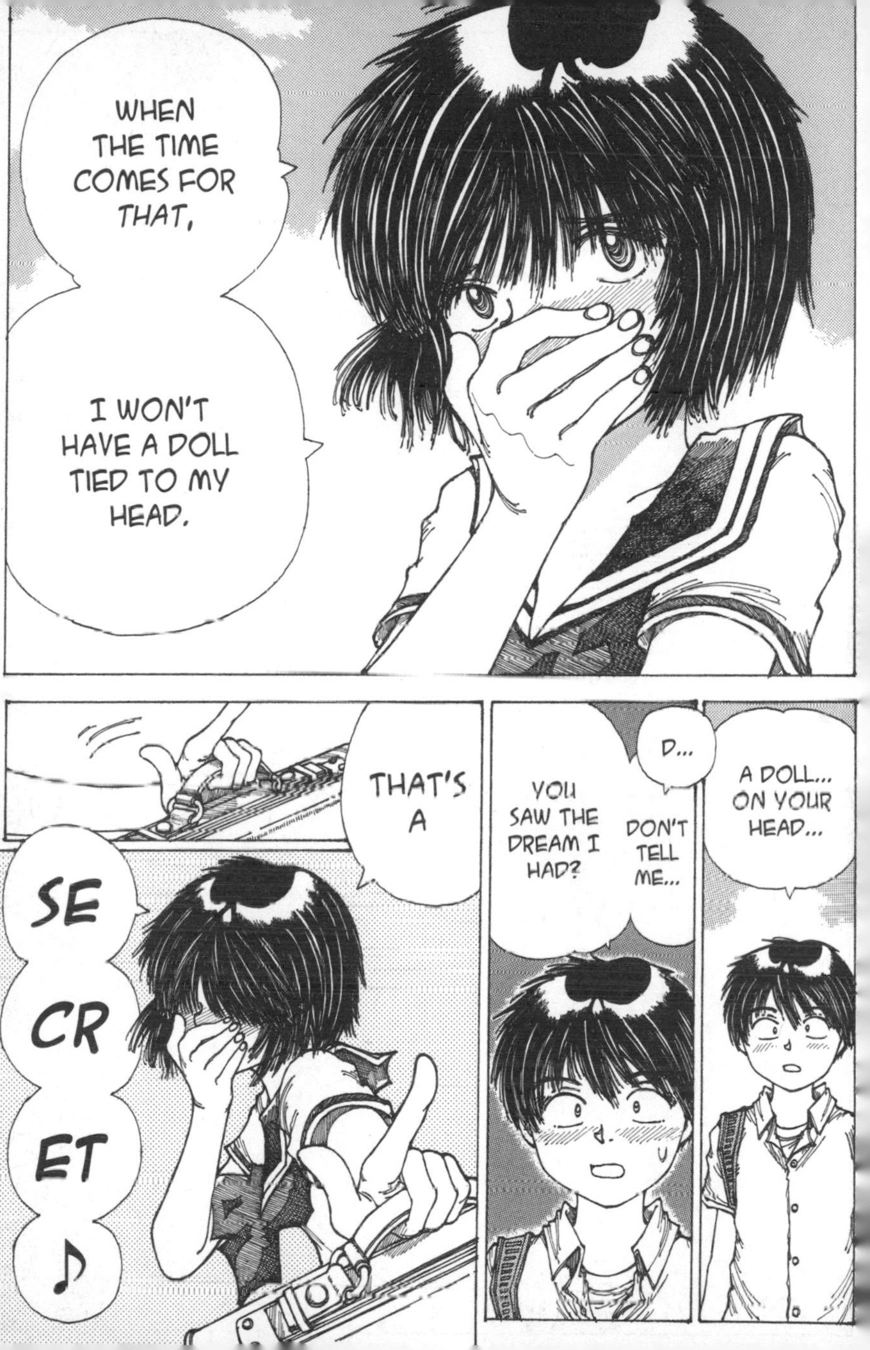

WHEN THE TIME COMES FOR THAT,
I WON'T HAVE A DOLL TIED TO MY HEAD.
A DOLL... ON YOUR HEAD...
D...
DON'T TELL ME...
YOU SAW THE DREAM I HAD?
THAT'S A
SE CR ET ♪

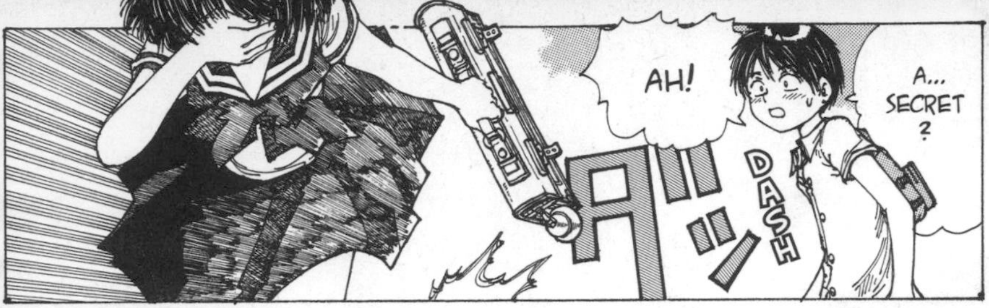
A... SECRET ?
DASH
AH!

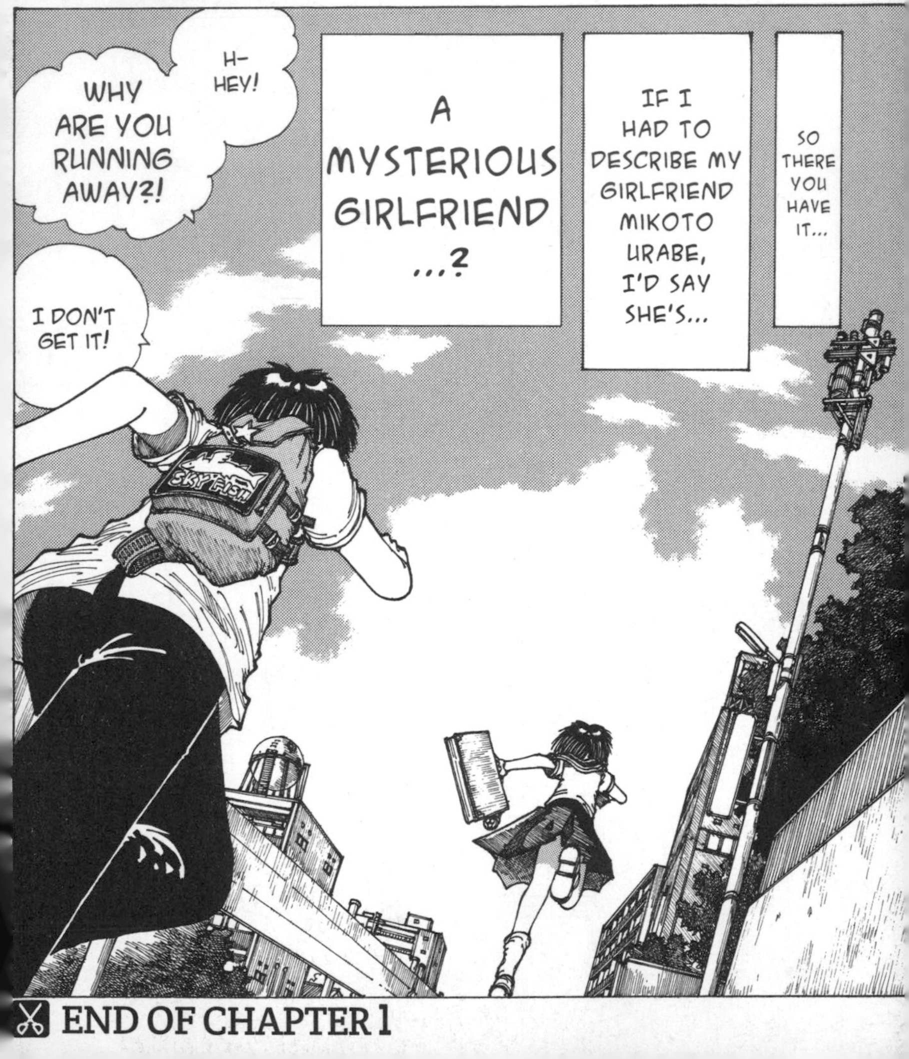
SO THERE YOU HAVE IT...
IF I HAD TO DESCRIBE MY GIRLFRIEND MIKOTO URABE, I'D SAY SHE'S...
A MYSTERIOUS GIRLFRIEND ...?
H- HEY!
WHY ARE YOU RUNNING AWAY?!
I DON'T GET IT!
SKY FISH

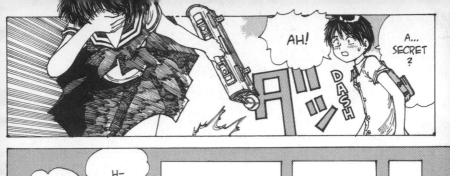

END OF CHAPTER 1

CHAPTER 2: MYSTERIOUS PICTURE

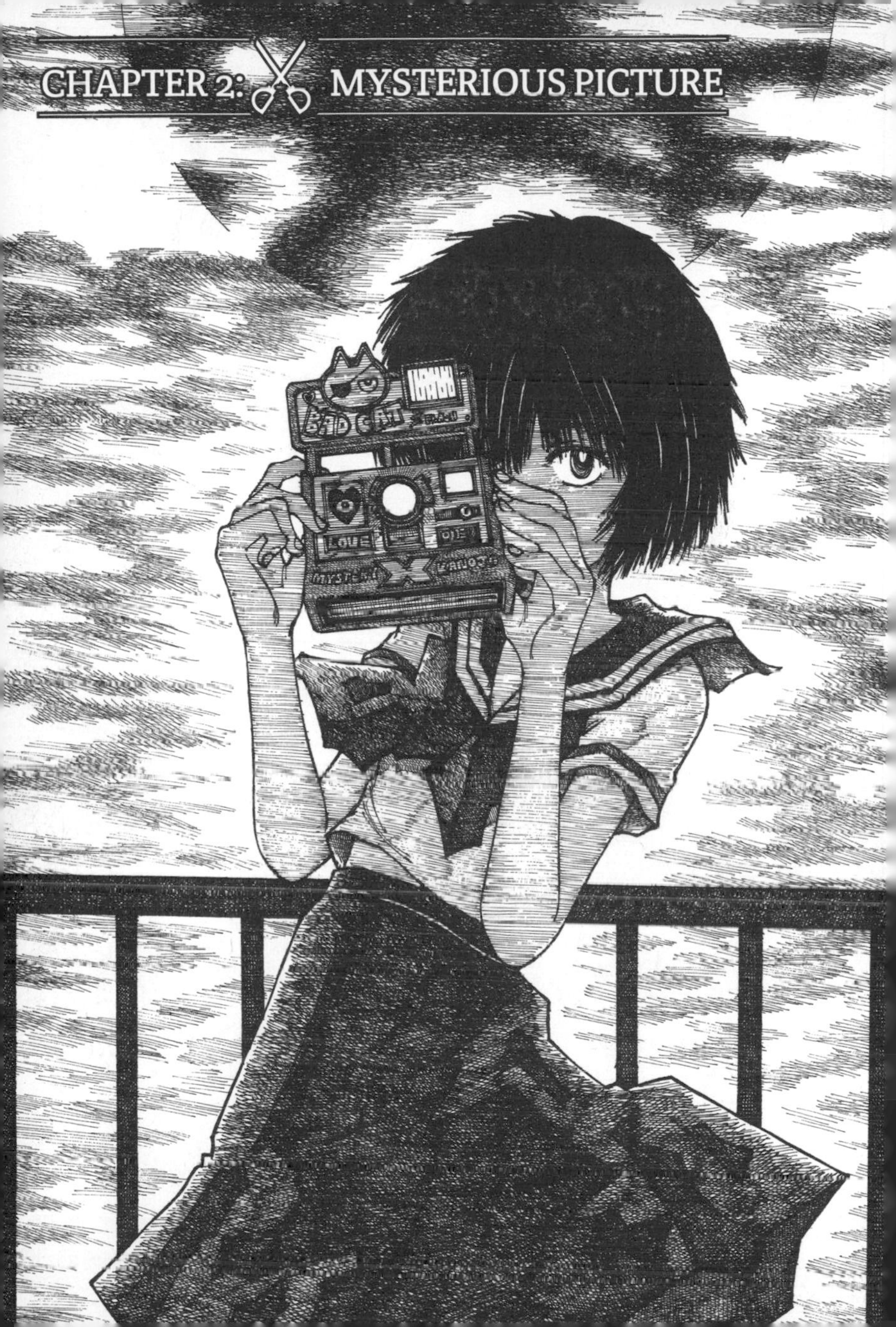

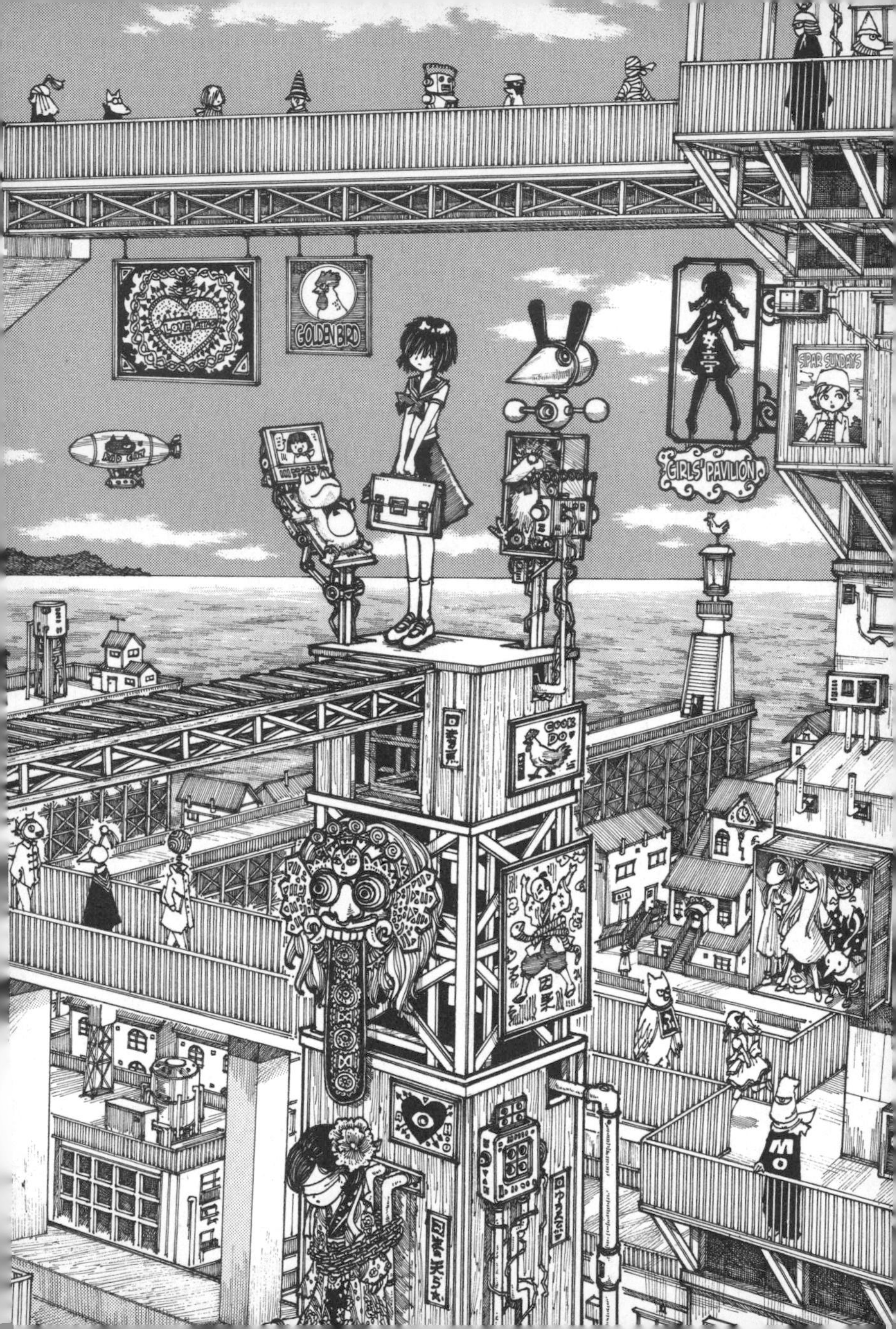
LOVE
GOLDEN BIRD
少女亭
SIPAR SUNDAYS
GIRLS' PAVILION
COOK DO
MO

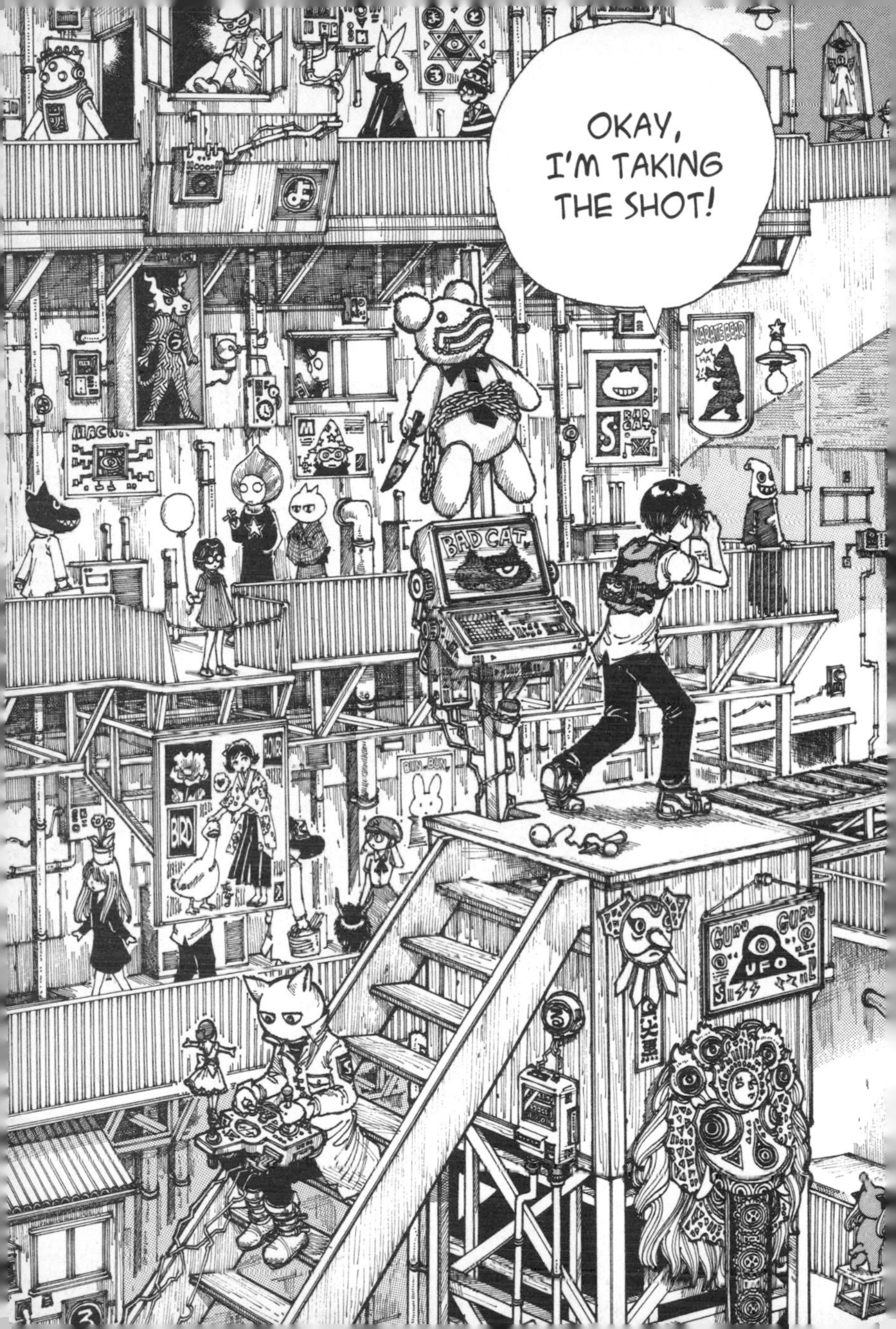
OKAY, I'M TAKING THE SHOT!
KARATE BEAR
BAD CAT
BAD CAT
BUN BUN
BIRD
GURU GURU
UFO

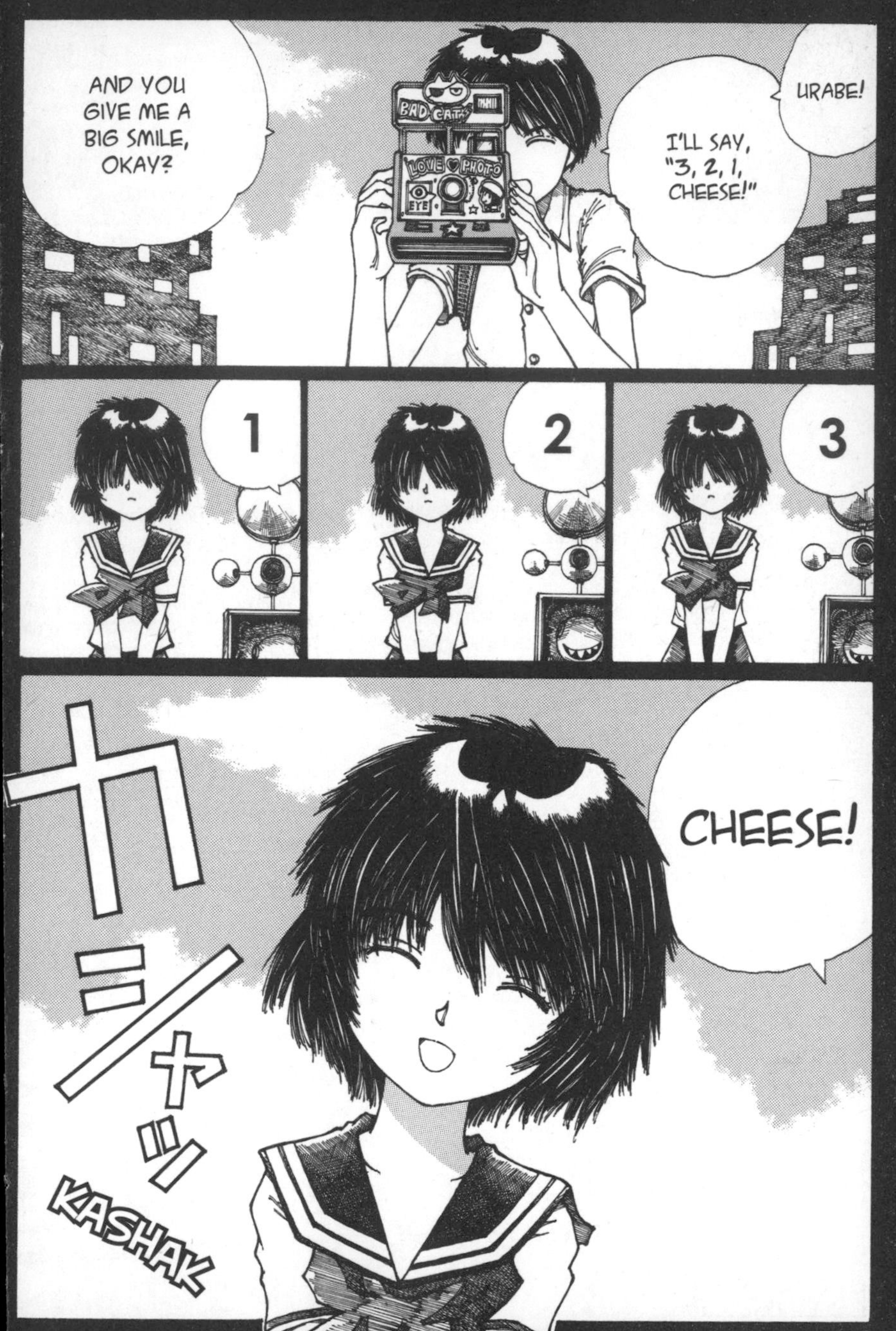

URABE!
I'LL SAY, "3, 2, 1, CHEESE!"
AND YOU GIVE ME A BIG SMILE, OKAY?
3
2
1
CHEESE!
KASHAK

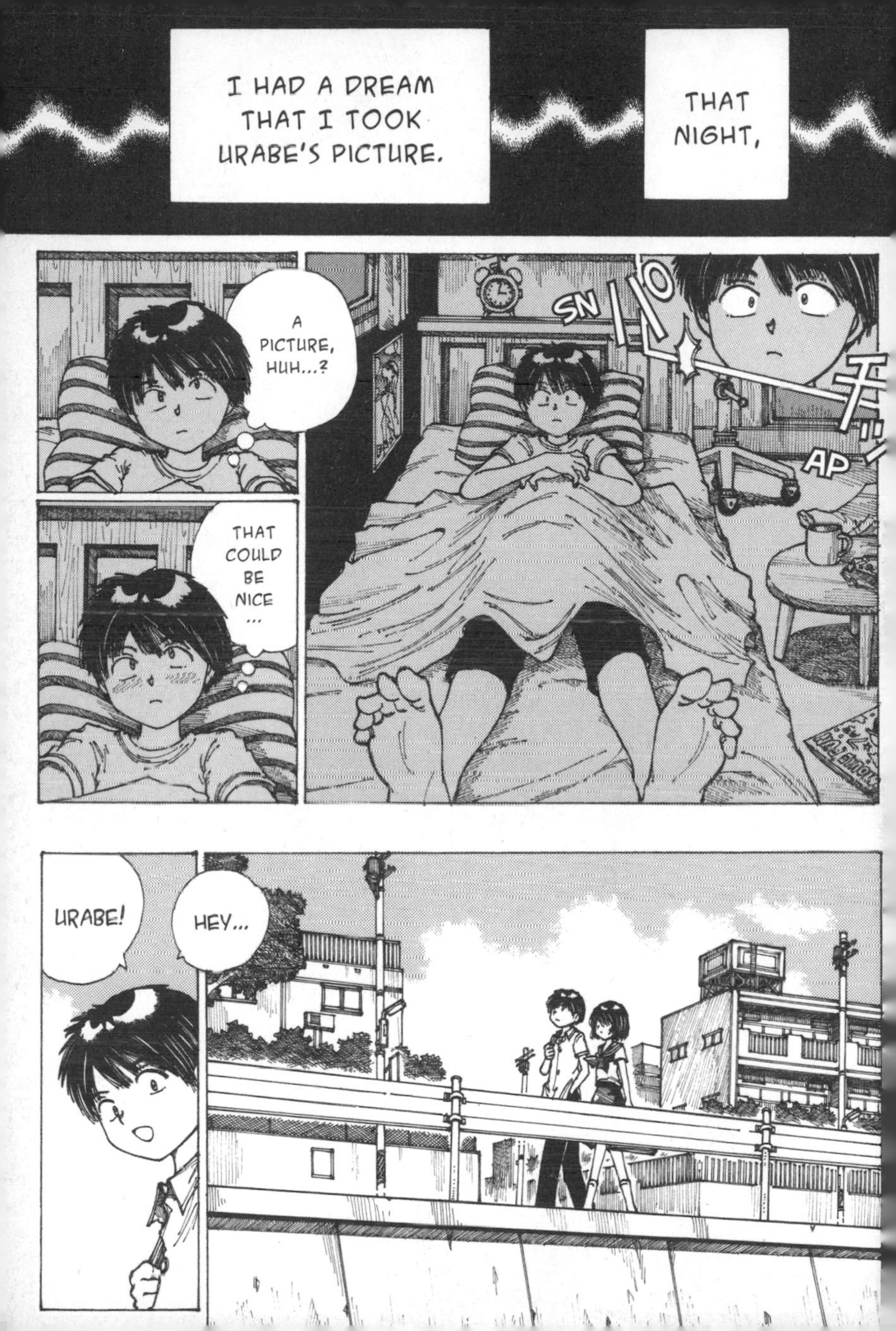
THAT NIGHT,
I HAD A DREAM THAT I TOOK URABE'S PICTURE.
SN
AP
A PICTURE, HUH...?
THAT COULD BE NICE...
HEY...
URABE!

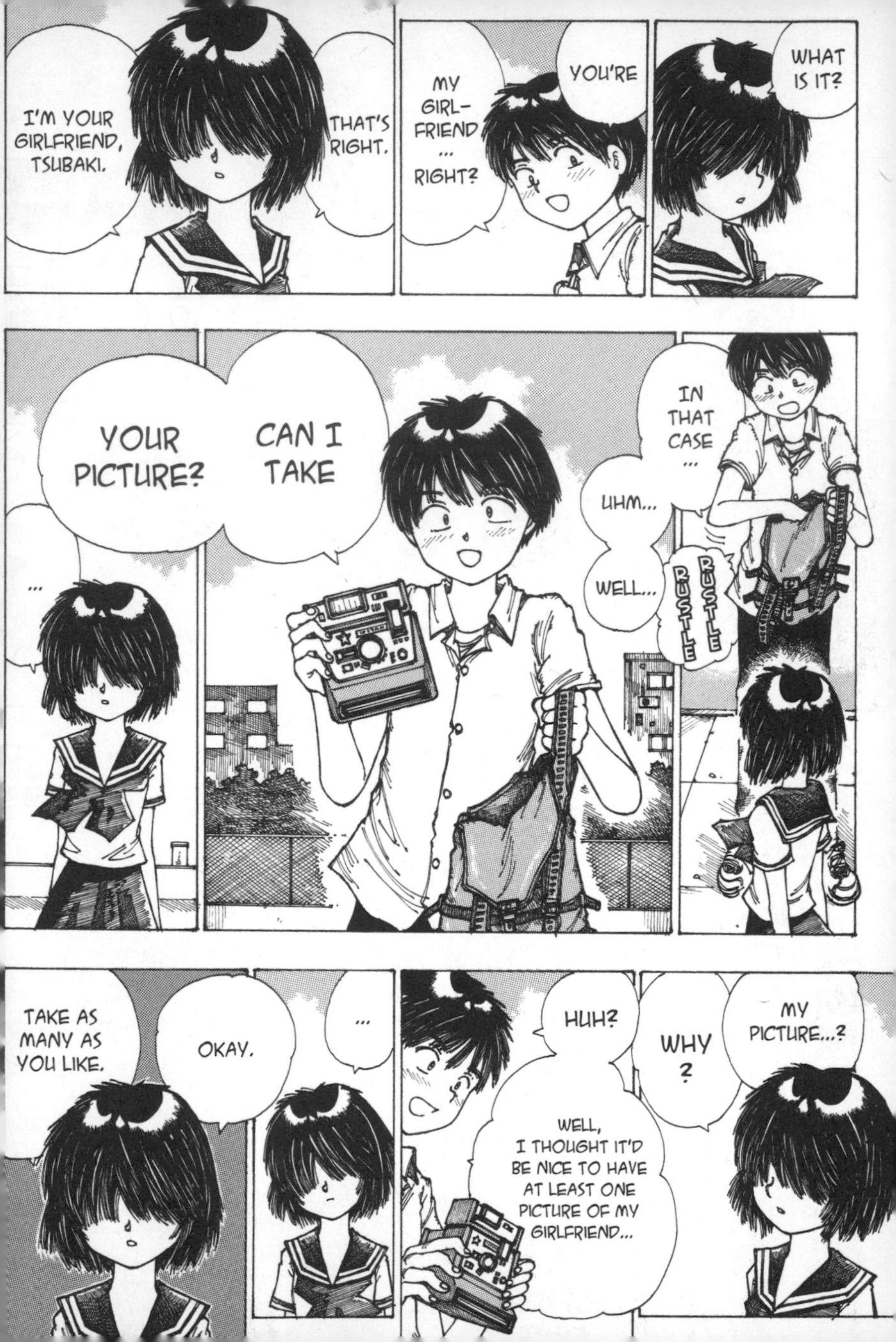
WHAT IS IT?
YOU'RE
MY GIRLFRIEND ... RIGHT?
THAT'S RIGHT.
I'M YOUR GIRLFRIEND, TSUBAKI.
IN THAT CASE ...
UHM...
WELL...
RUSTLE RUSTLE
CAN I TAKE
YOUR PICTURE?
...
MY PICTURE...?
WHY ?
HUH?
WELL, I THOUGHT IT'D BE NICE TO HAVE AT LEAST ONE PICTURE OF MY GIRLFRIEND...
...
OKAY.
TAKE AS MANY AS YOU LIKE.

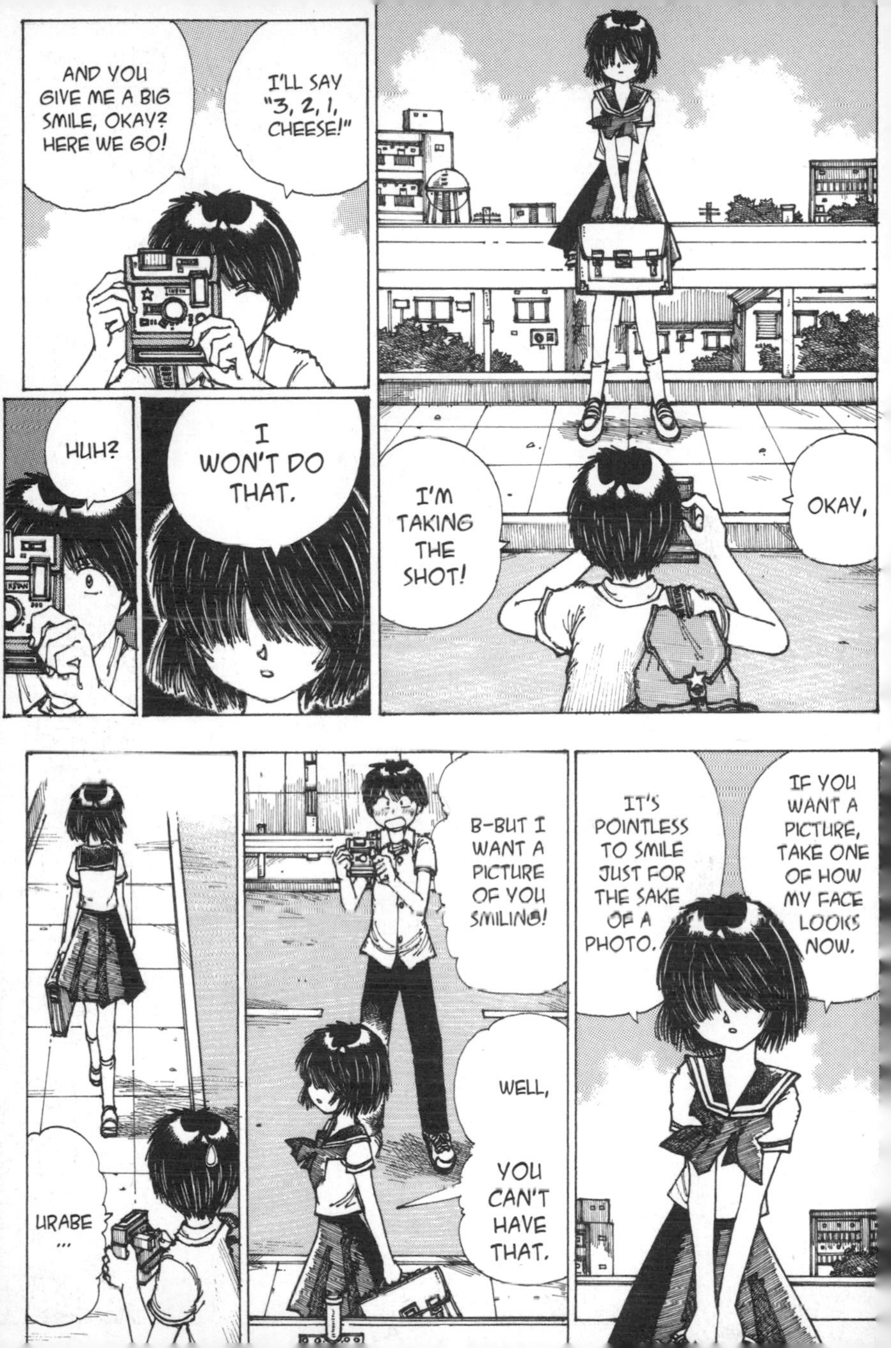
OKAY,
I'M TAKING THE SHOT!
I'LL SAY "3, 2, 1, CHEESE!"
AND YOU GIVE ME A BIG SMILE, OKAY? HERE WE GO!
I WON'T DO THAT.
HUH?
IF YOU WANT A PICTURE, TAKE ONE OF HOW MY FACE LOOKS NOW.
IT'S POINTLESS TO SMILE JUST FOR THE SAKE OF A PHOTO.
B-BUT I WANT A PICTURE OF YOU SMILING!
WELL,
YOU CAN'T HAVE THAT.
URABE ...

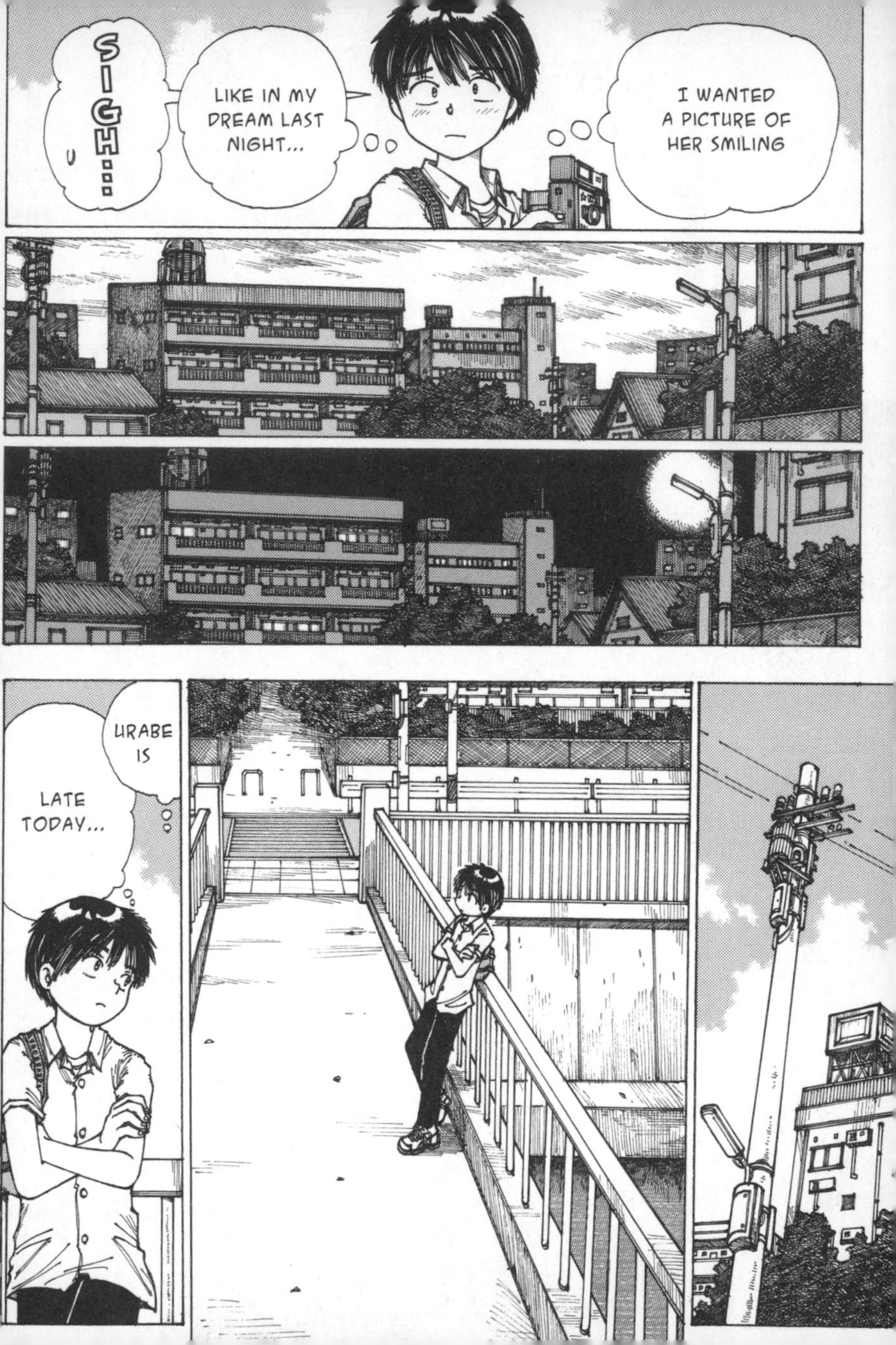
I WANTED A PICTURE OF HER SMILING
LIKE IN MY DREAM LAST NIGHT...
SIGH...
URABE IS
LATE TODAY...

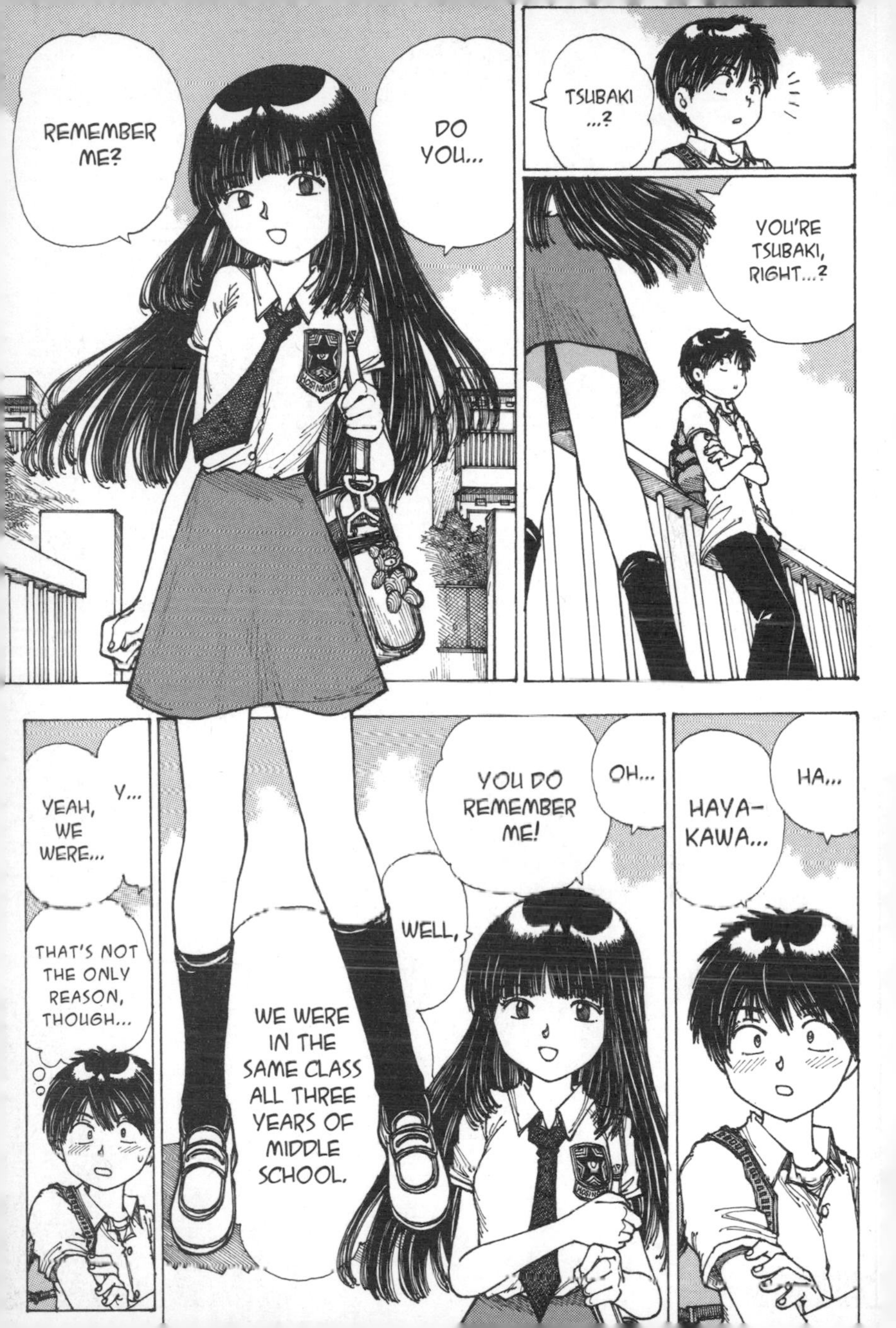
TSUBAKI ...?
YOU'RE TSUBAKI, RIGHT...?
DO YOU...
REMEMBER ME?
HA...
HAYA-KAWA...
OH...
YOU DO REMEMBER ME!
WELL,
WE WERE IN THE SAME CLASS ALL THREE YEARS OF MIDDLE SCHOOL.
Y...
YEAH, WE WERE...
THAT'S NOT THE ONLY REASON, THOUGH...

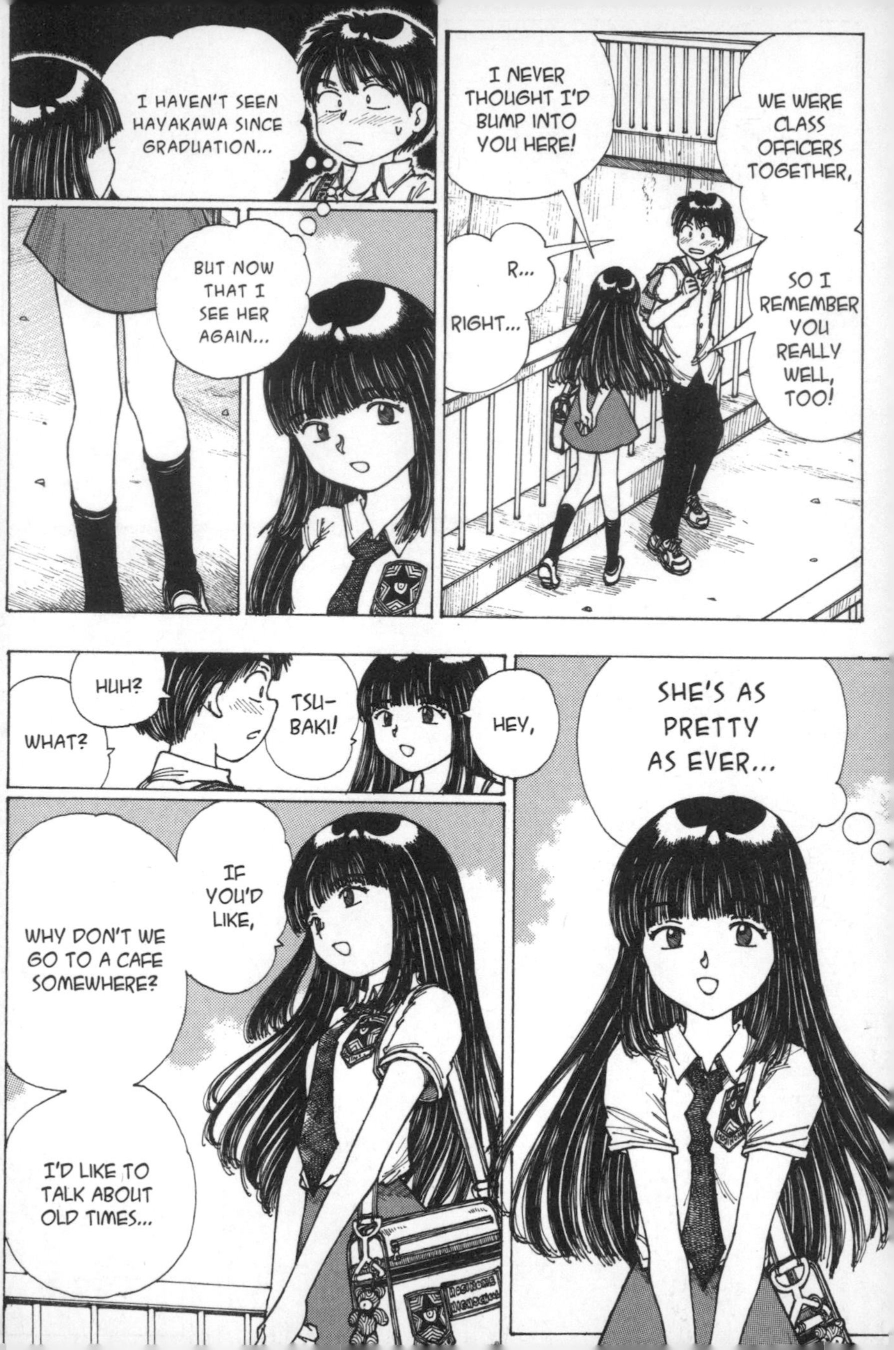
WE WERE CLASS OFFICERS TOGETHER,
SO I REMEMBER YOU REALLY WELL, TOO!
I NEVER THOUGHT I'D BUMP INTO YOU HERE!
R... RIGHT...
I HAVEN'T SEEN HAYAKAWA SINCE GRADUATION...
BUT NOW THAT I SEE HER AGAIN...
SHE'S AS PRETTY AS EVER...
HEY,
TSU-BAKI!
HUH? WHAT?
IF YOU'D LIKE,
WHY DON'T WE GO TO A CAFE SOMEWHERE?
I'D LIKE TO TALK ABOUT OLD TIMES...

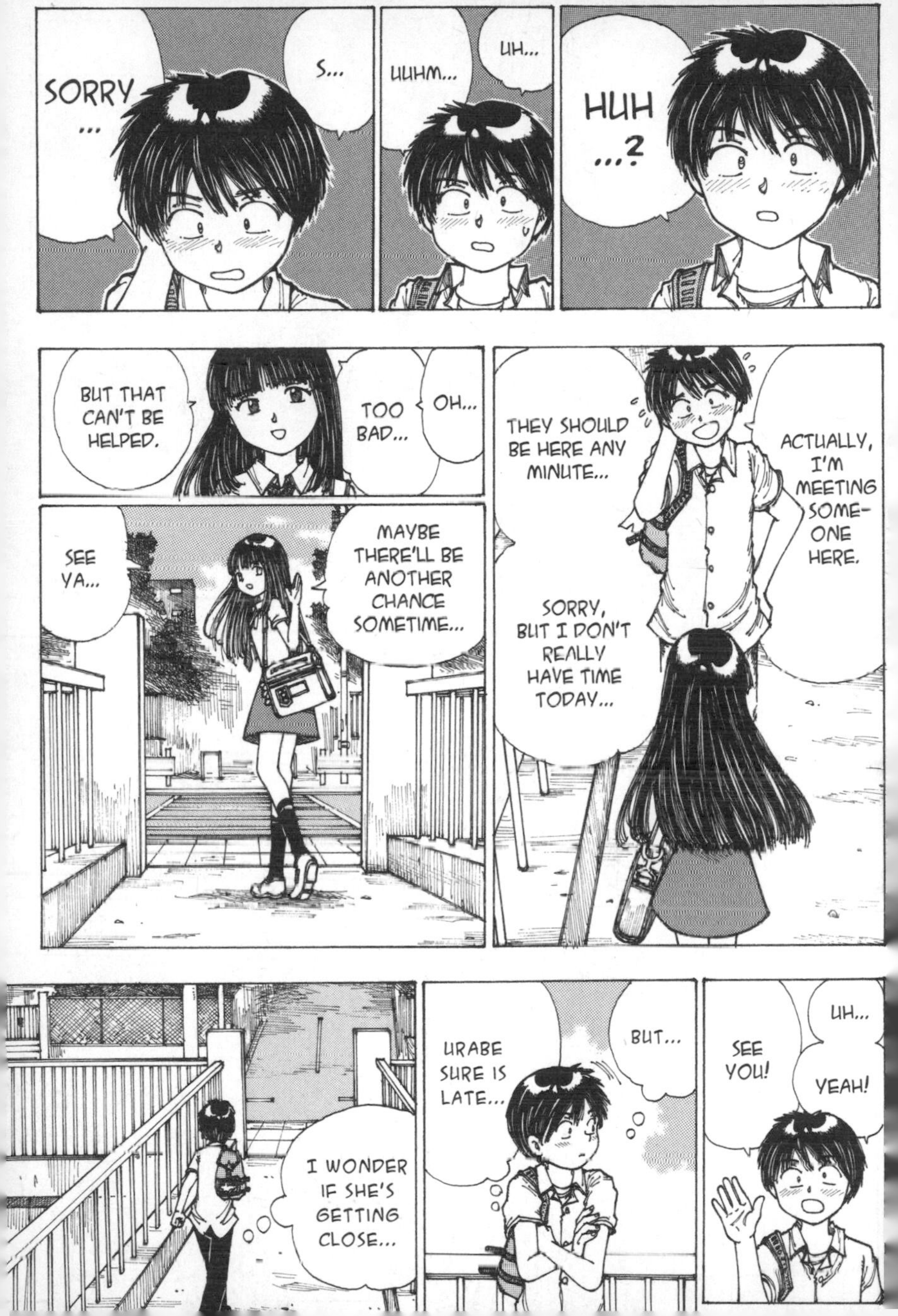
HUH ...?
UH...
UUHM...
S...
SORRY ...
ACTUALLY, I'M MEETING SOME-ONE HERE.
THEY SHOULD BE HERE ANY MINUTE...
SORRY, BUT I DON'T REALLY HAVE TIME TODAY...
OH...
TOO BAD...
BUT THAT CAN'T BE HELPED.
MAYBE THERE'LL BE ANOTHER CHANCE SOMETIME...
SEE YA...
UH...
SEE YOU!
YEAH!
BUT...
URABE SURE IS LATE...
I WONDER IF SHE'S GETTING CLOSE...

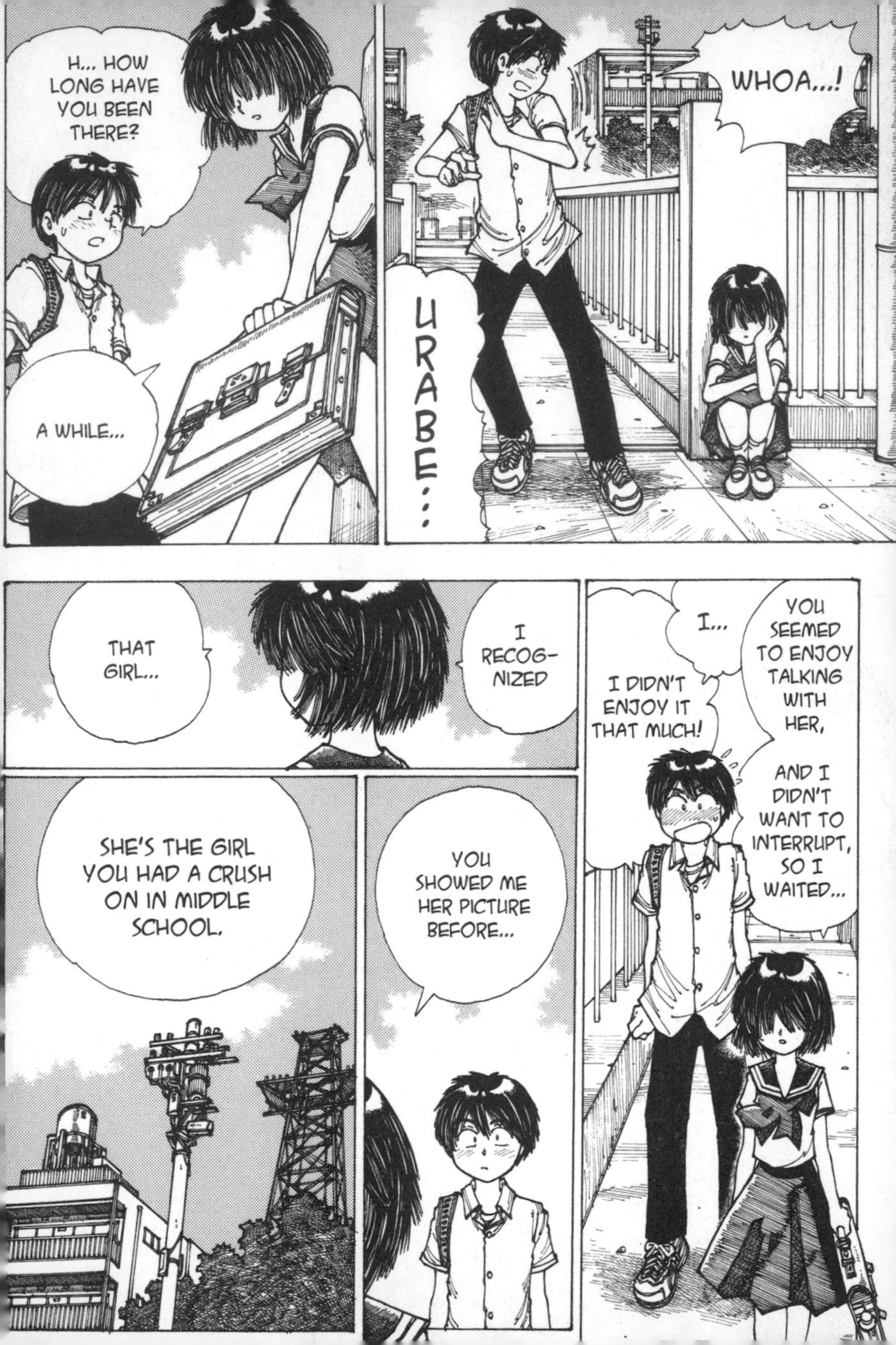
WHOA...!
URABE...
H... HOW LONG HAVE YOU BEEN THERE?
A WHILE...
YOU SEEMED TO ENJOY TALKING WITH HER,
AND I DIDN'T WANT TO INTERRUPT, SO I WAITED...
I...
I DIDN'T ENJOY IT THAT MUCH!
I RECOG-NIZED
THAT GIRL...
YOU SHOWED ME HER PICTURE BEFORE...
SHE'S THE GIRL YOU HAD A CRUSH ON IN MIDDLE SCHOOL.

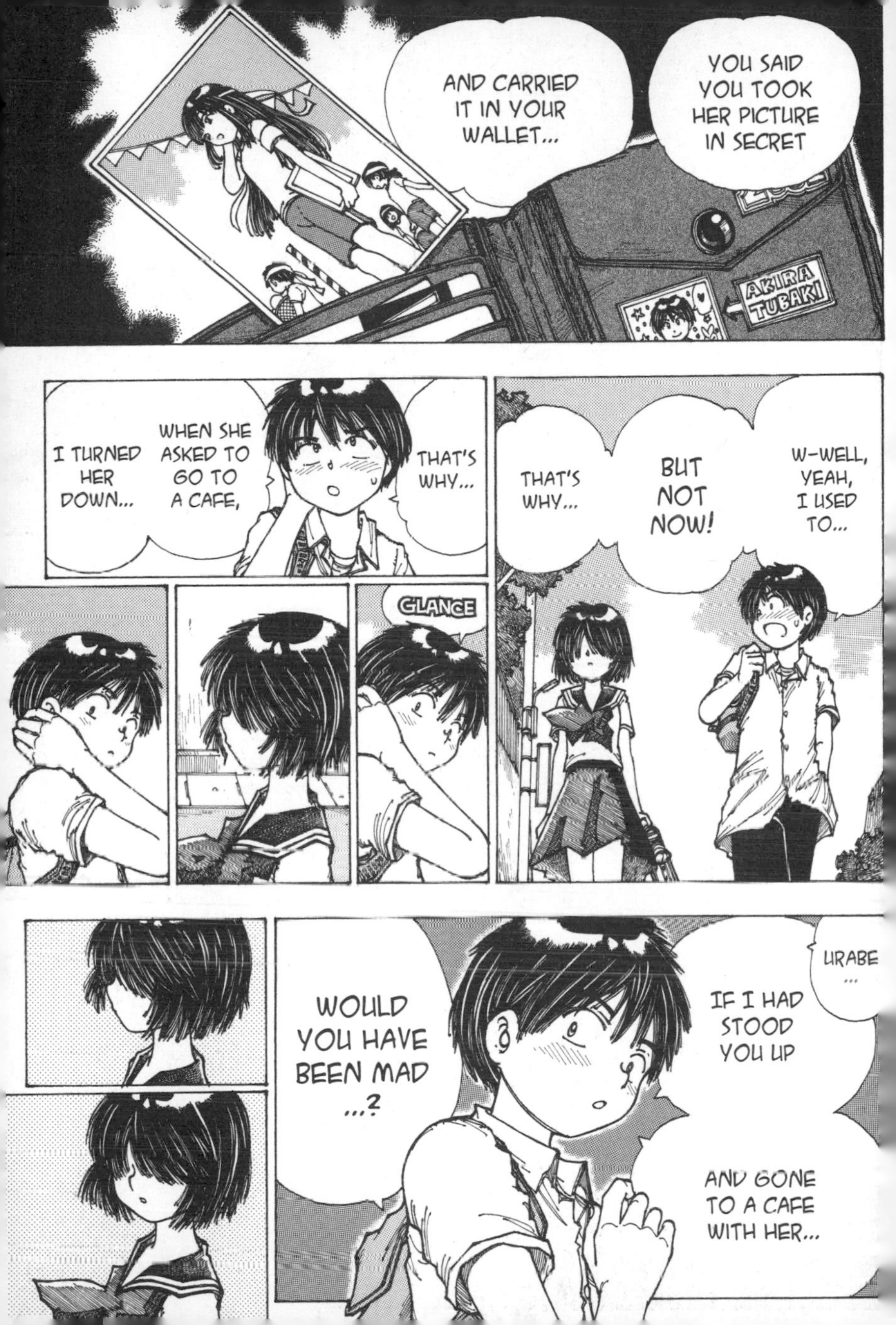
YOU SAID YOU TOOK HER PICTURE IN SECRET
AND CARRIED IT IN YOUR WALLET...
AKIRA TUBAKI
W-WELL, YEAH, I USED TO...
BUT NOT NOW!
THAT'S WHY...
THAT'S WHY...
WHEN SHE ASKED TO GO TO A CAFE,
I TURNED HER DOWN...
GLANCE
URABE ...
IF I HAD STOOD YOU UP
AND GONE TO A CAFE WITH HER...
WOULD YOU HAVE BEEN MAD ...?

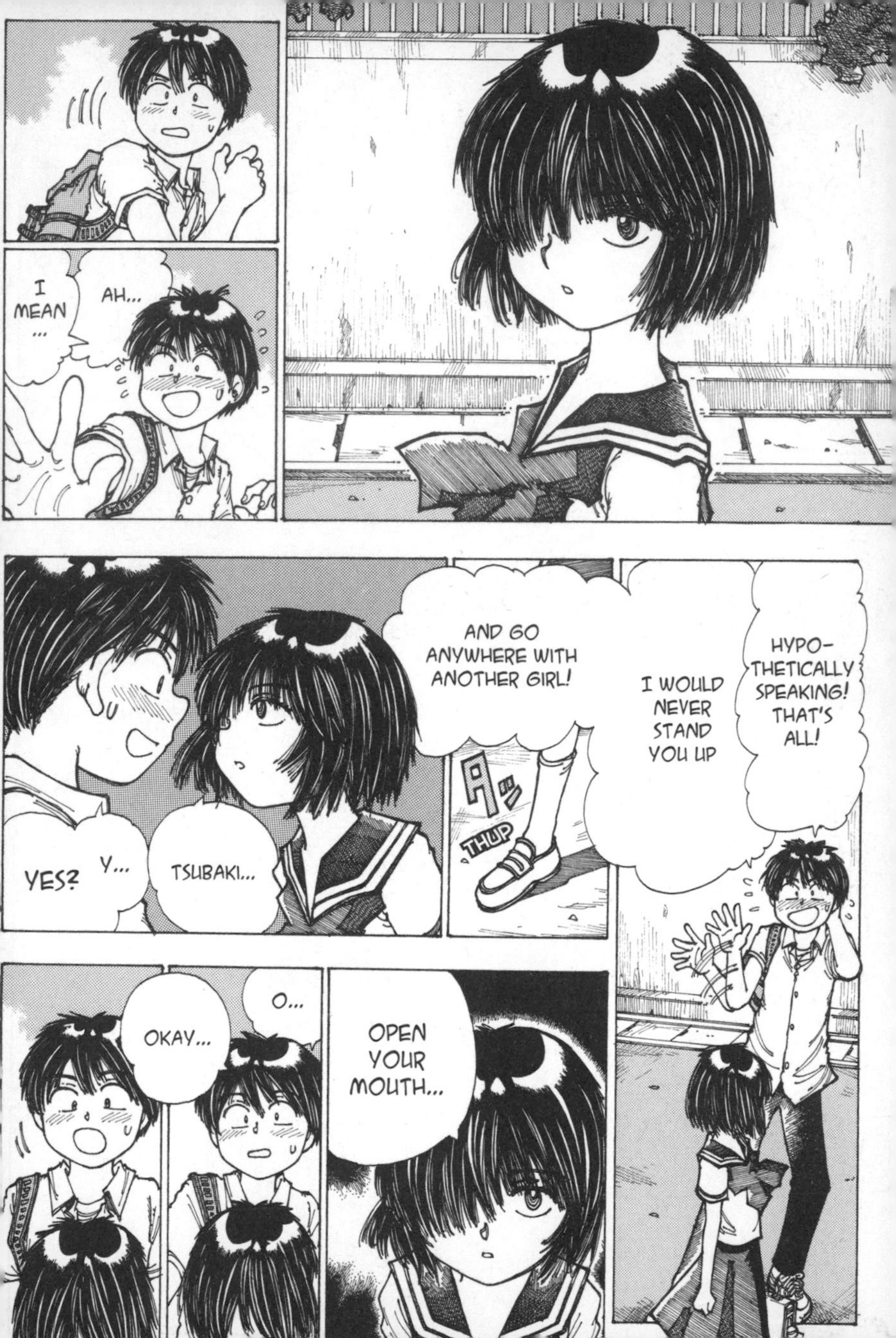
AH...
I MEAN...
HYPO-THETICALLY SPEAKING! THAT'S ALL!
I WOULD NEVER STAND YOU UP
AND GO ANYWHERE WITH ANOTHER GIRL!
THUP
TSUBAKI...
Y...
YES?
OPEN YOUR MOUTH...
O...
OKAY...

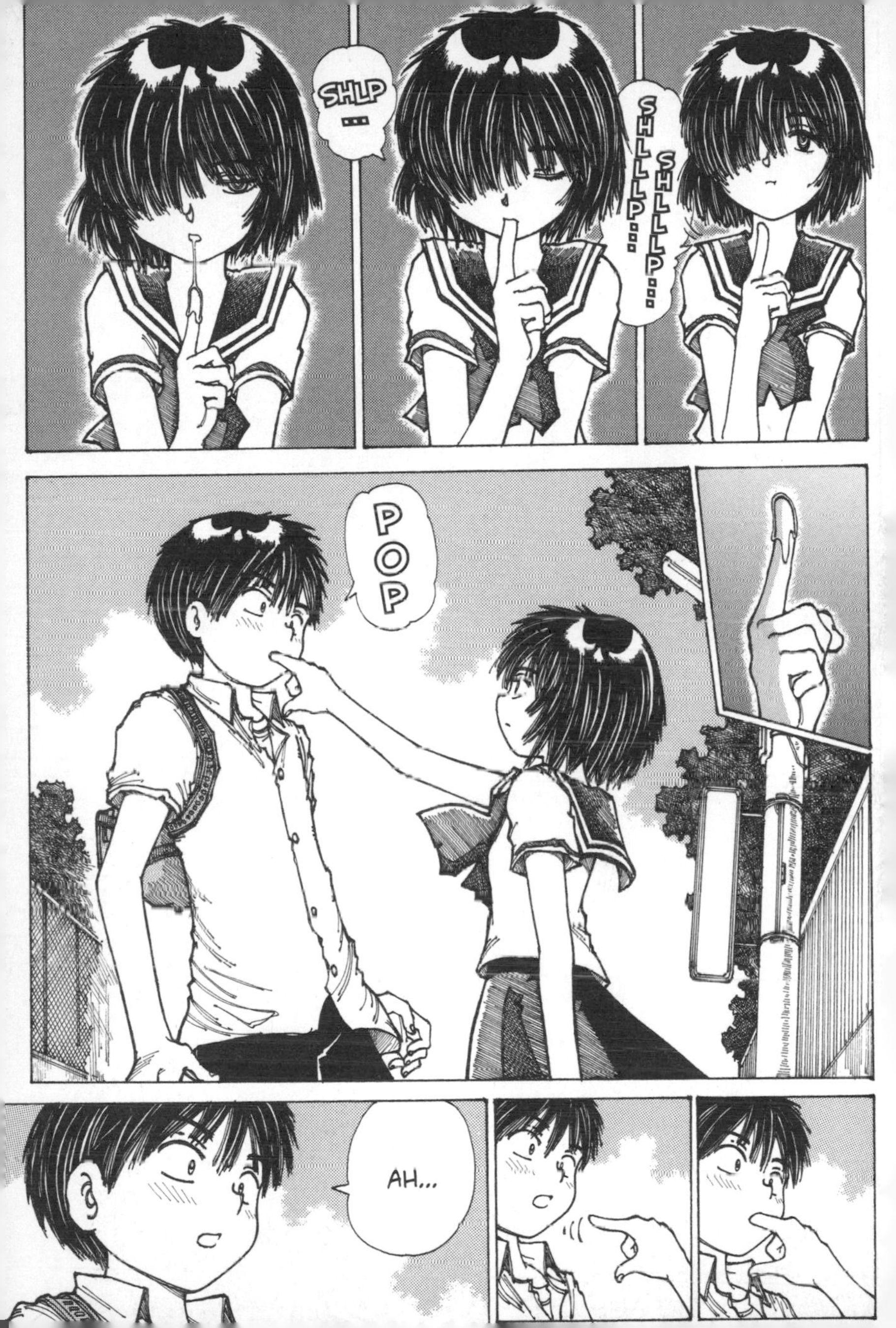
SHLLLP...
SHLLLP...
SHLP ...
POP
AH...

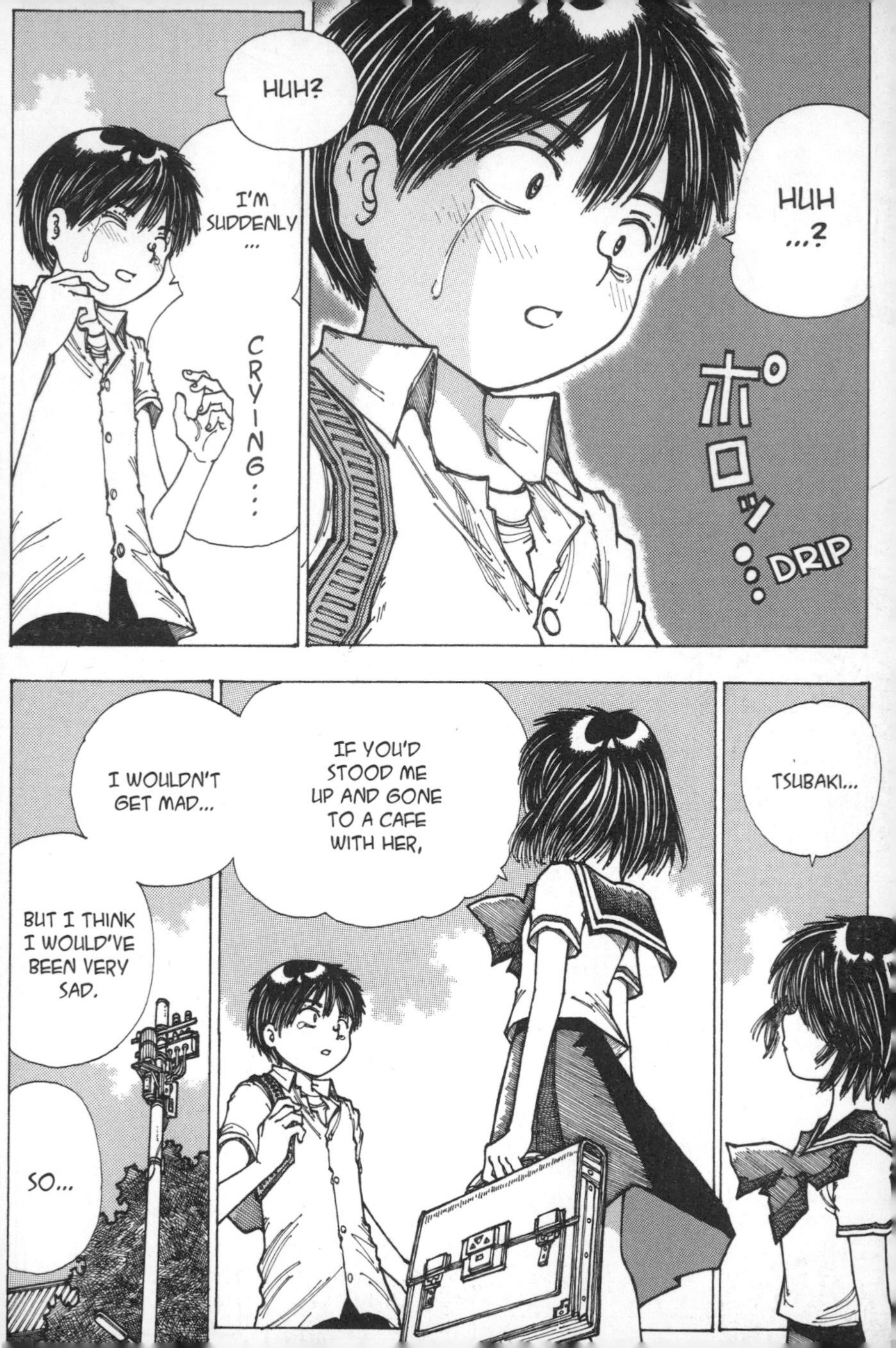
HUH ...?
ポロッ...
DRIP
HUH?
I'M SUDDENLY ... CRYING...
TSUBAKI...
IF YOU'D STOOD ME UP AND GONE TO A CAFE WITH HER,
I WOULDN'T GET MAD...
BUT I THINK I WOULD'VE BEEN VERY SAD.
SO...

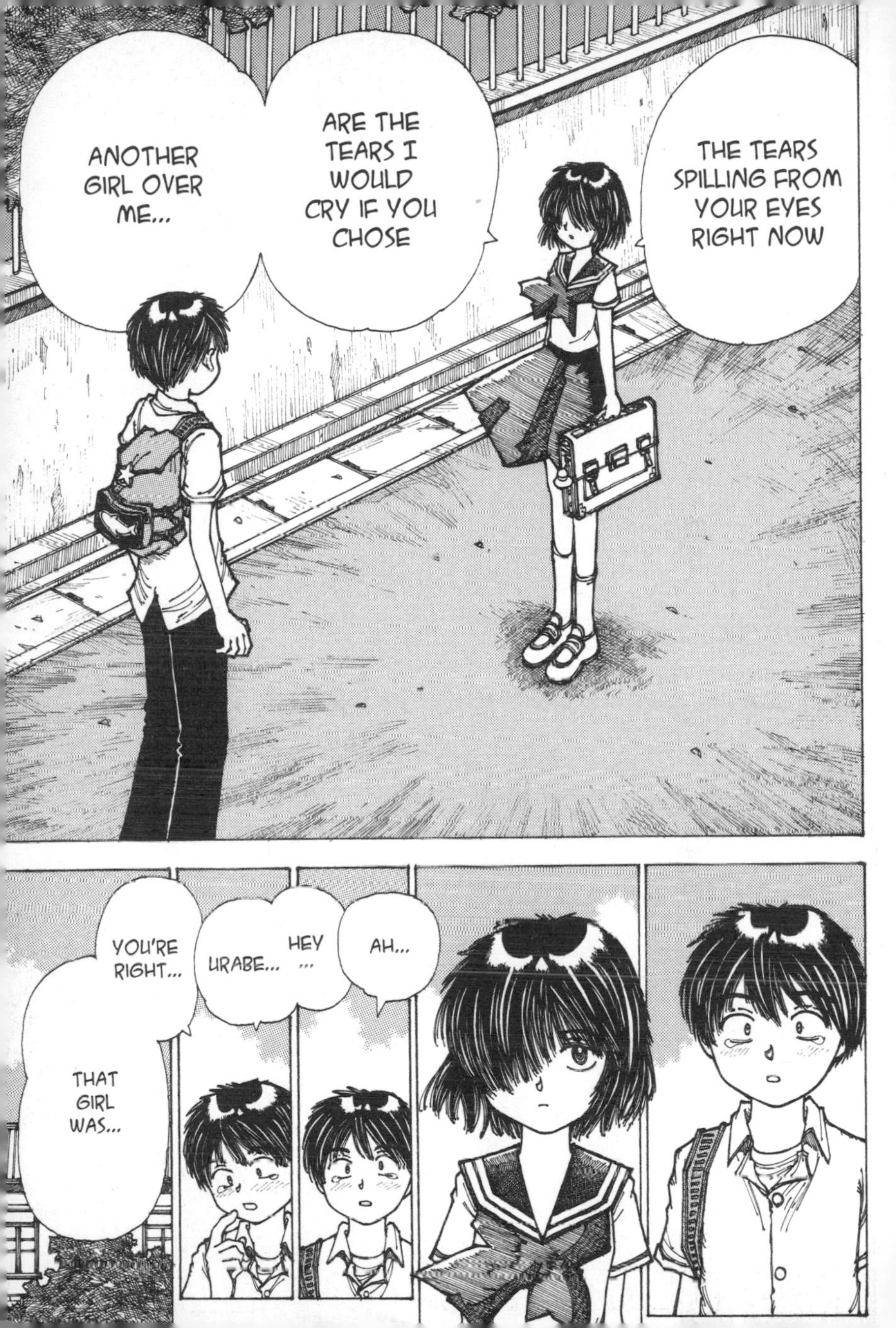
THE TEARS SPILLING FROM YOUR EYES RIGHT NOW
ARE THE TEARS I WOULD CRY IF YOU CHOSE
ANOTHER GIRL OVER ME...
AH...
HEY ...
URABE...
YOU'RE RIGHT...
THAT GIRL WAS...

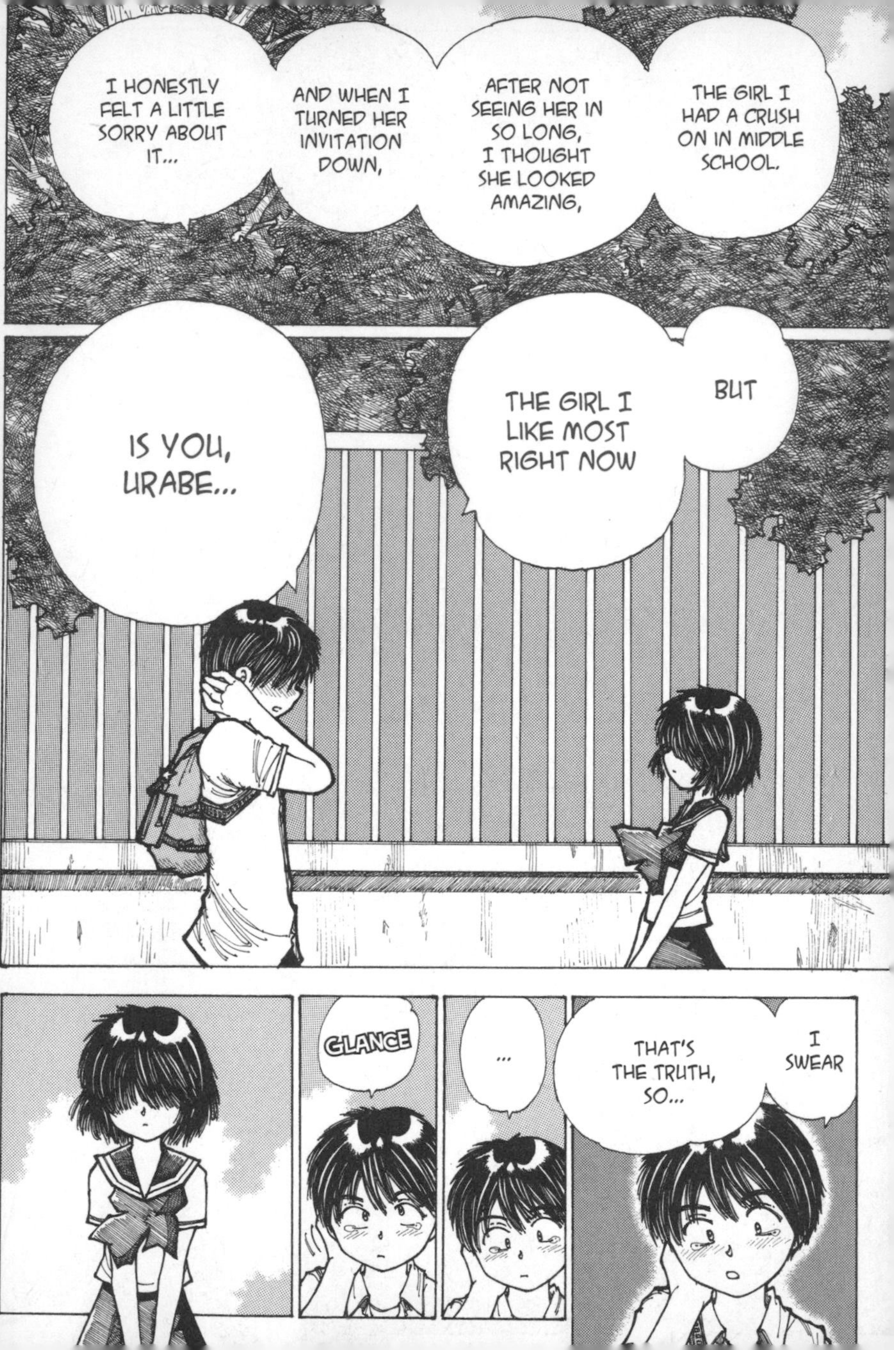
THE GIRL I HAD A CRUSH ON IN MIDDLE SCHOOL.
AFTER NOT SEEING HER IN SO LONG, I THOUGHT SHE LOOKED AMAZING,
AND WHEN I TURNED HER INVITATION DOWN,
I HONESTLY FELT A LITTLE SORRY ABOUT IT...
BUT
THE GIRL I LIKE MOST RIGHT NOW
IS YOU, URABE...
I SWEAR
THAT'S THE TRUTH, SO...
...
GLANCE

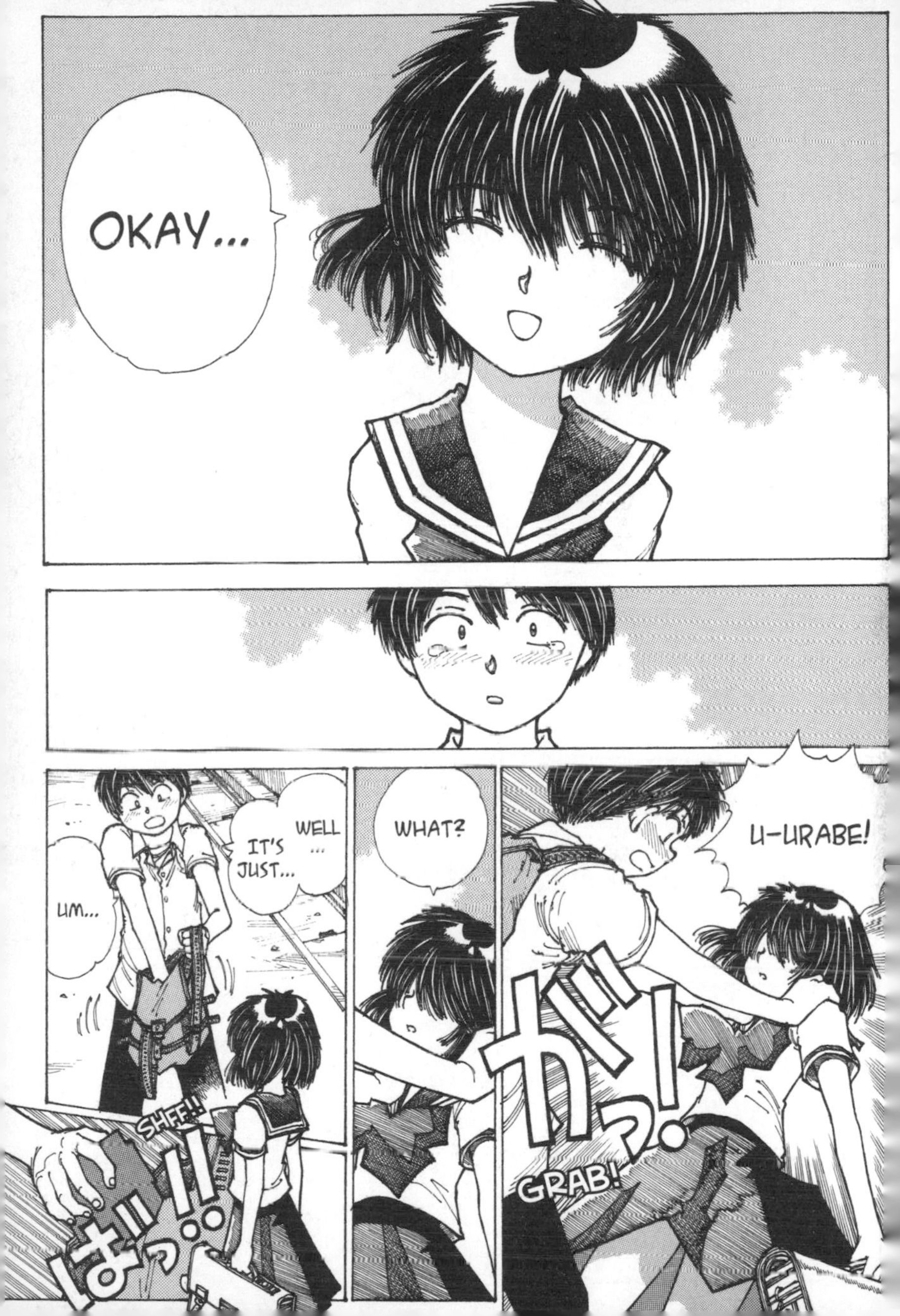
OKAY...
U-URABE!
がっ!
GRAB!
WHAT?
WELL ...
IT'S JUST...
UM...
SHFF!!
ばっ!!

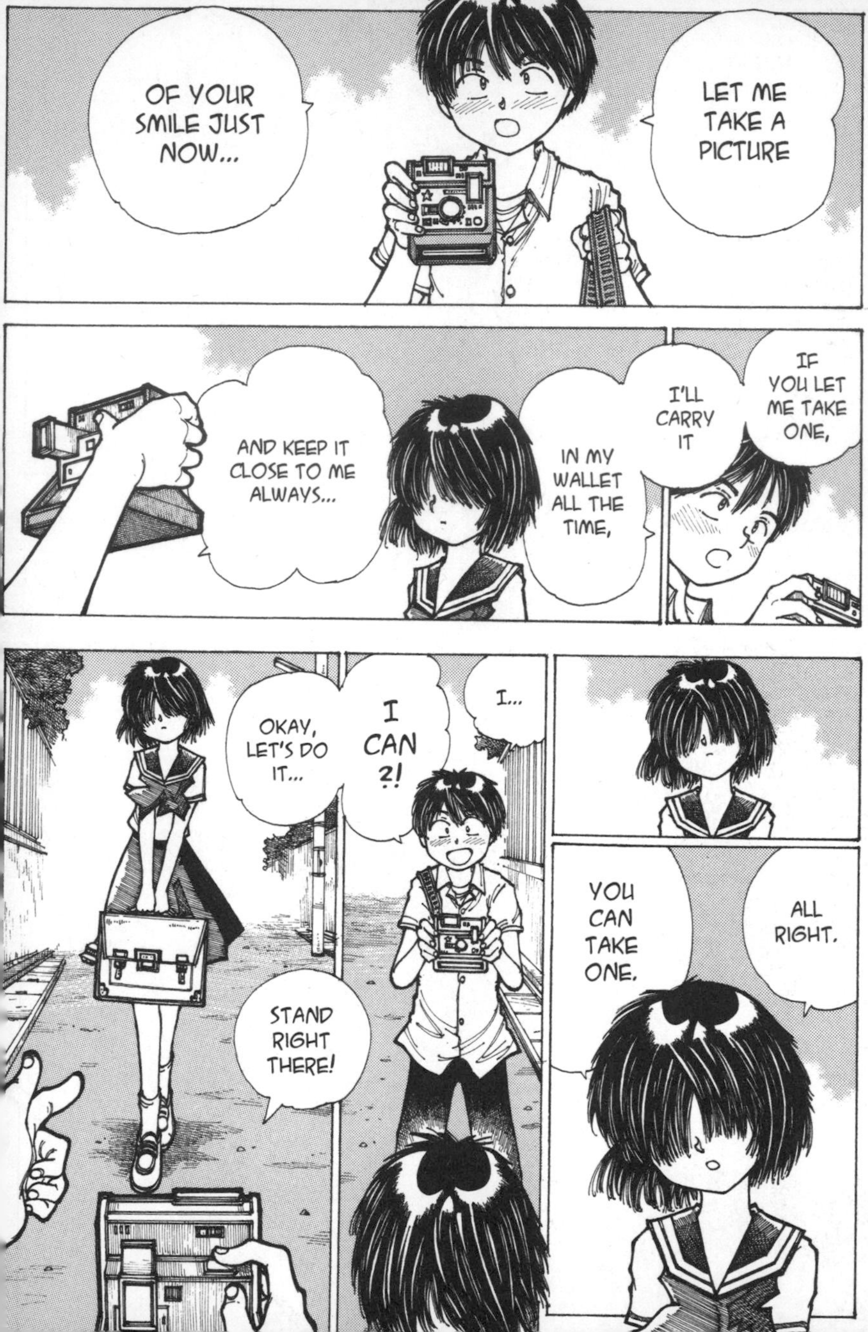
LET ME TAKE A PICTURE
OF YOUR SMILE JUST NOW...
IF YOU LET ME TAKE ONE,
I'LL CARRY IT
IN MY WALLET ALL THE TIME,
AND KEEP IT CLOSE TO ME ALWAYS...
ALL RIGHT.
YOU CAN TAKE ONE.
I...
I CAN ?!
OKAY, LET'S DO IT...
STAND RIGHT THERE!

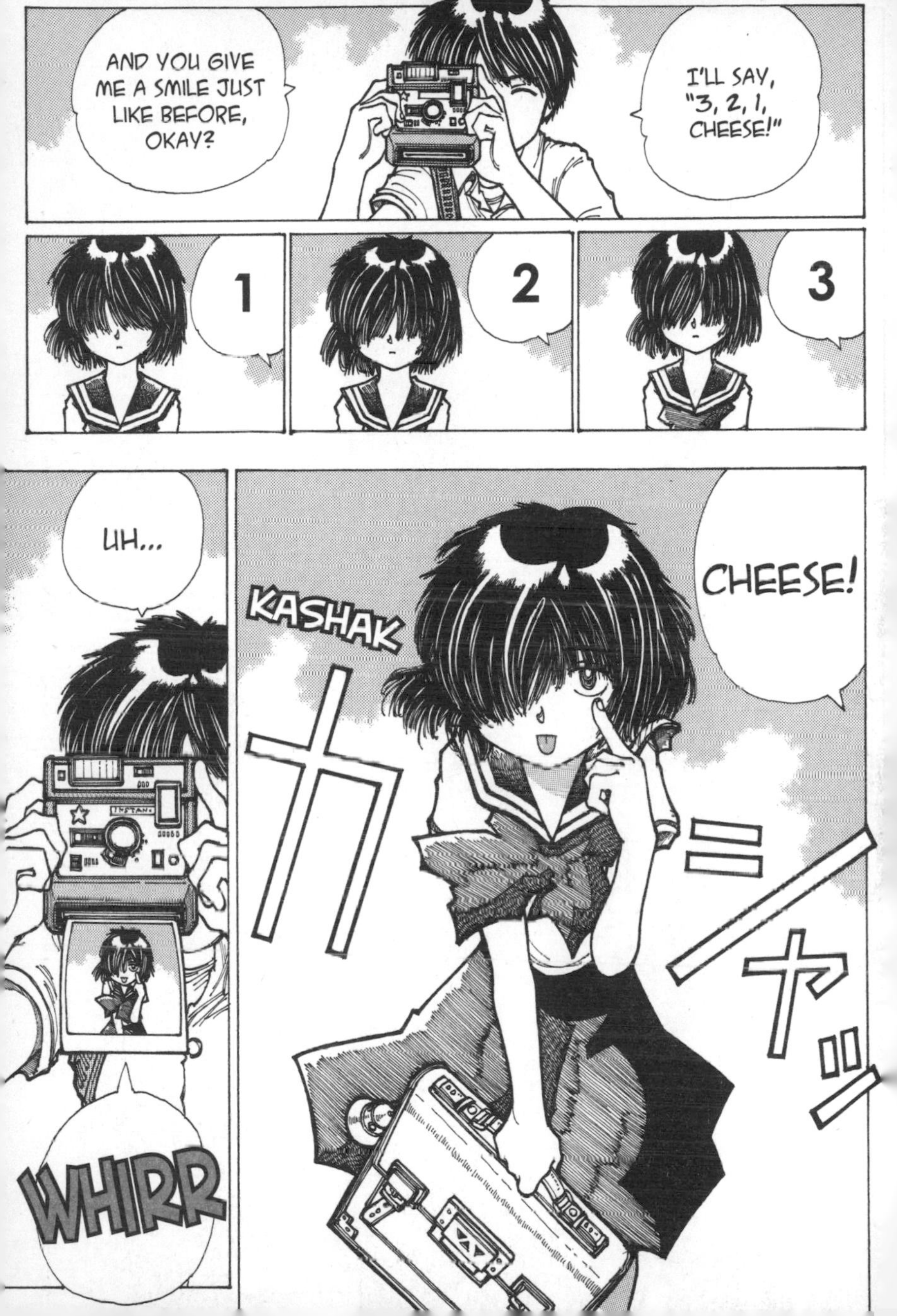

I'LL SAY, "3, 2, 1, CHEESE!"
AND YOU GIVE ME A SMILE JUST LIKE BEFORE, OKAY?
3
2
1
CHEESE!
KASHAK
カシャッ
UH...
WHIRR

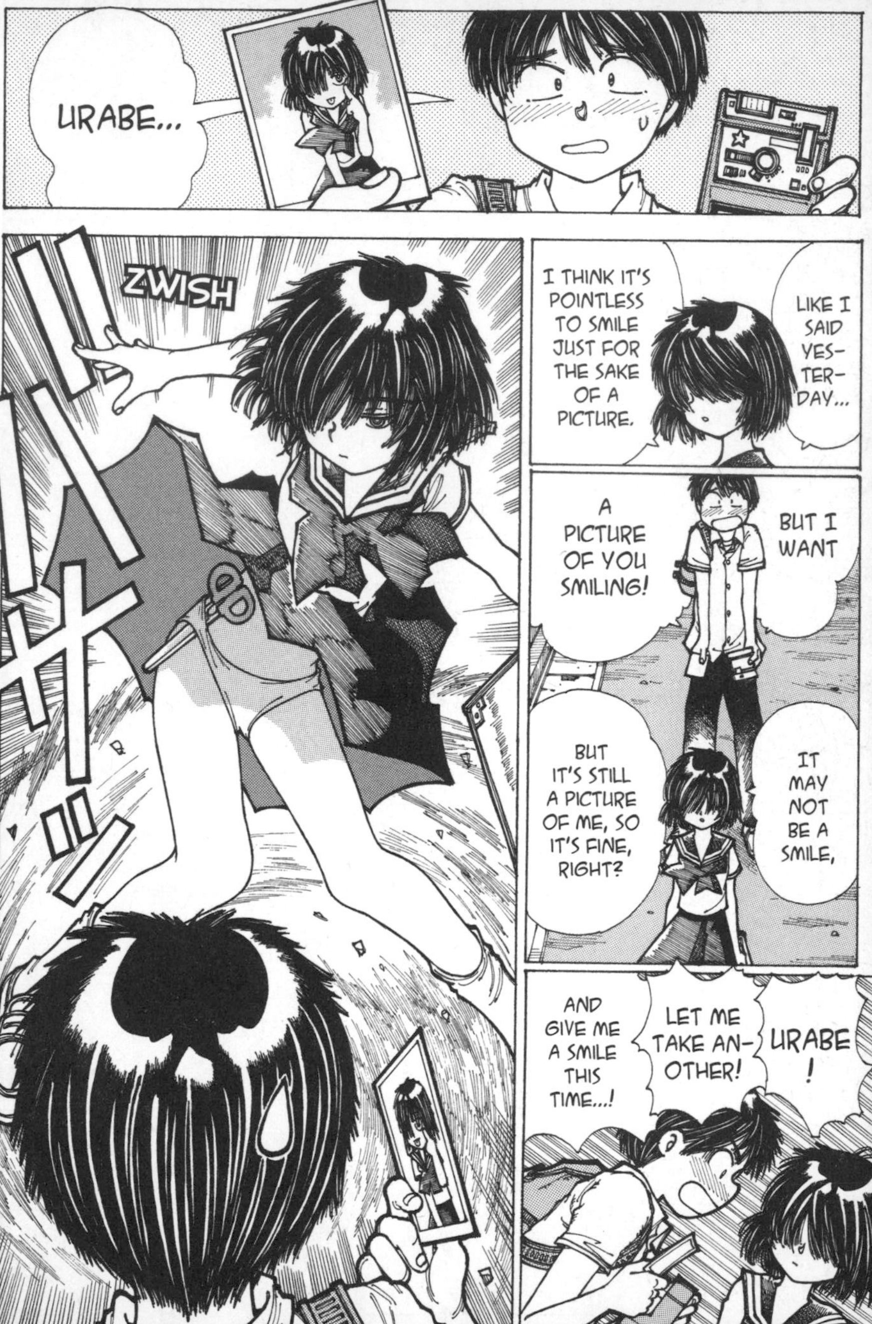
URABE...
LIKE I SAID YES-TERDAY...
I THINK IT'S POINTLESS TO SMILE JUST FOR THE SAKE OF A PICTURE.
BUT I WANT
A PICTURE OF YOU SMILING!
IT MAY NOT BE A SMILE,
BUT IT'S STILL A PICTURE OF ME, SO IT'S FINE, RIGHT?
URABE!
LET ME TAKE AN-OTHER!
AND GIVE ME A SMILE THIS TIME...!
ZWISH

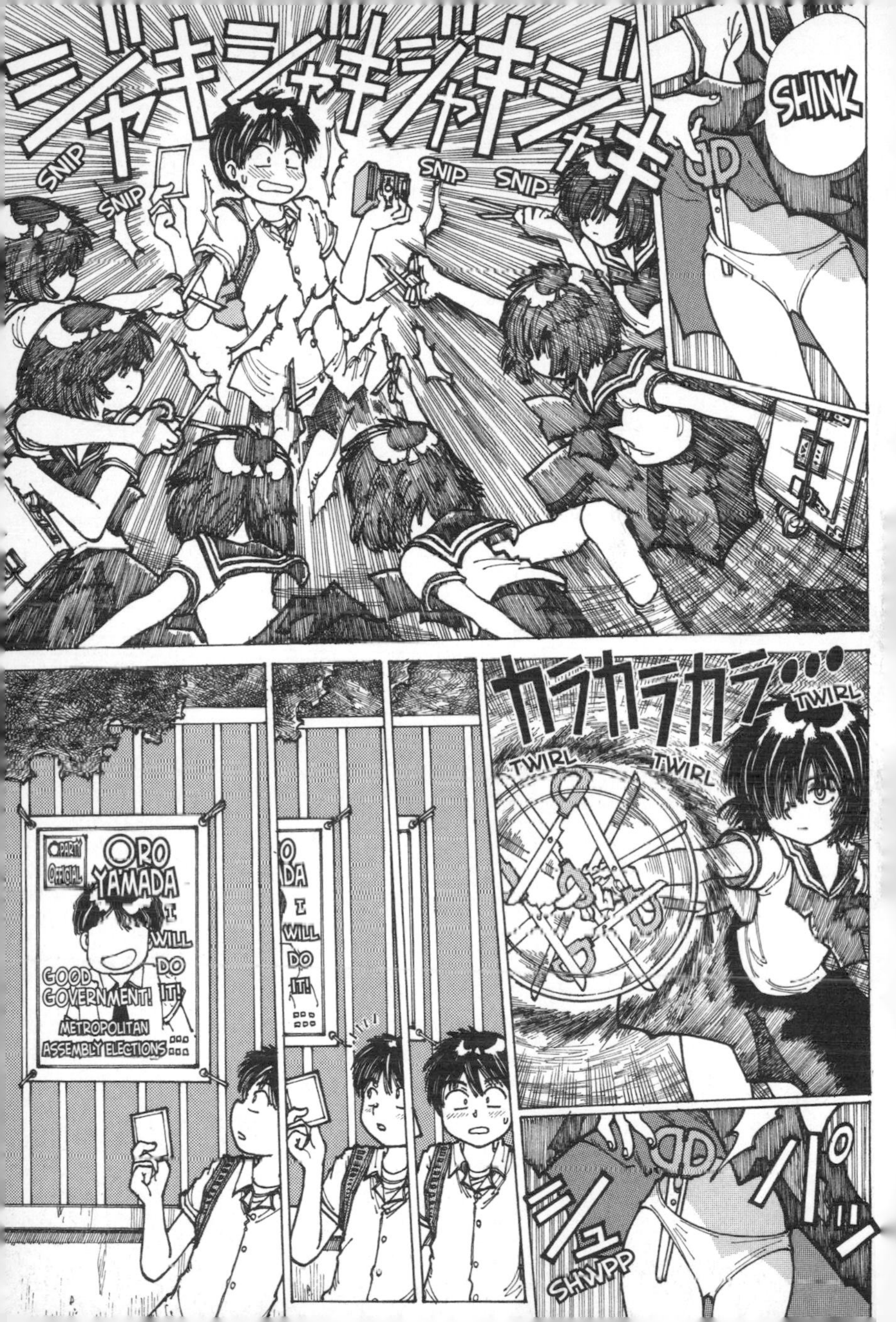
SHINK
ジャキジャキジャキジャキ
SNIP
SNIP
SNIP
SNIP
カラカラカラ…
TWIRL
TWIRL
TWIRL
シュパッ
SHWPP
PARTY OFFICIAL
ORO YAMADA
I WILL DO IT!
GOOD GOVERNMENT!
METROPOLITAN ASSEMBLY ELECTIONS...
I WILL DO IT!
...

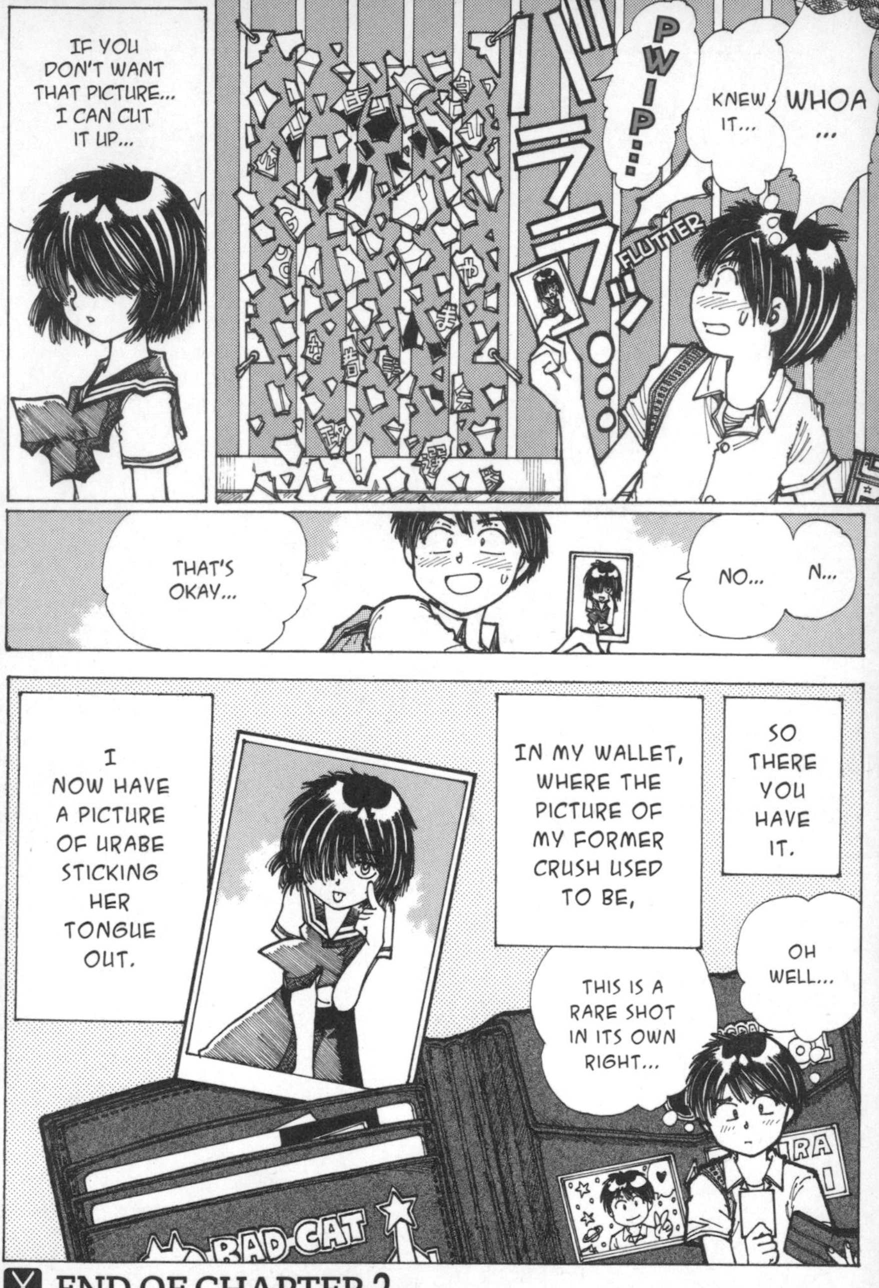
WHOA...
KNEW IT...
PWIP...
バララッ
FLUTTER
IF YOU DON'T WANT THAT PICTURE... I CAN CUT IT UP...
N...
NO...
THAT'S OKAY...
SO THERE YOU HAVE IT.
IN MY WALLET, WHERE THE PICTURE OF MY FORMER CRUSH USED TO BE,
I NOW HAVE A PICTURE OF URABE STICKING HER TONGUE OUT.
OH WELL...
THIS IS A RARE SHOT IN ITS OWN RIGHT...
BAD CAT

END OF CHAPTER 2

CHAPTER 3: MYSTERIOUS TEST TUBE

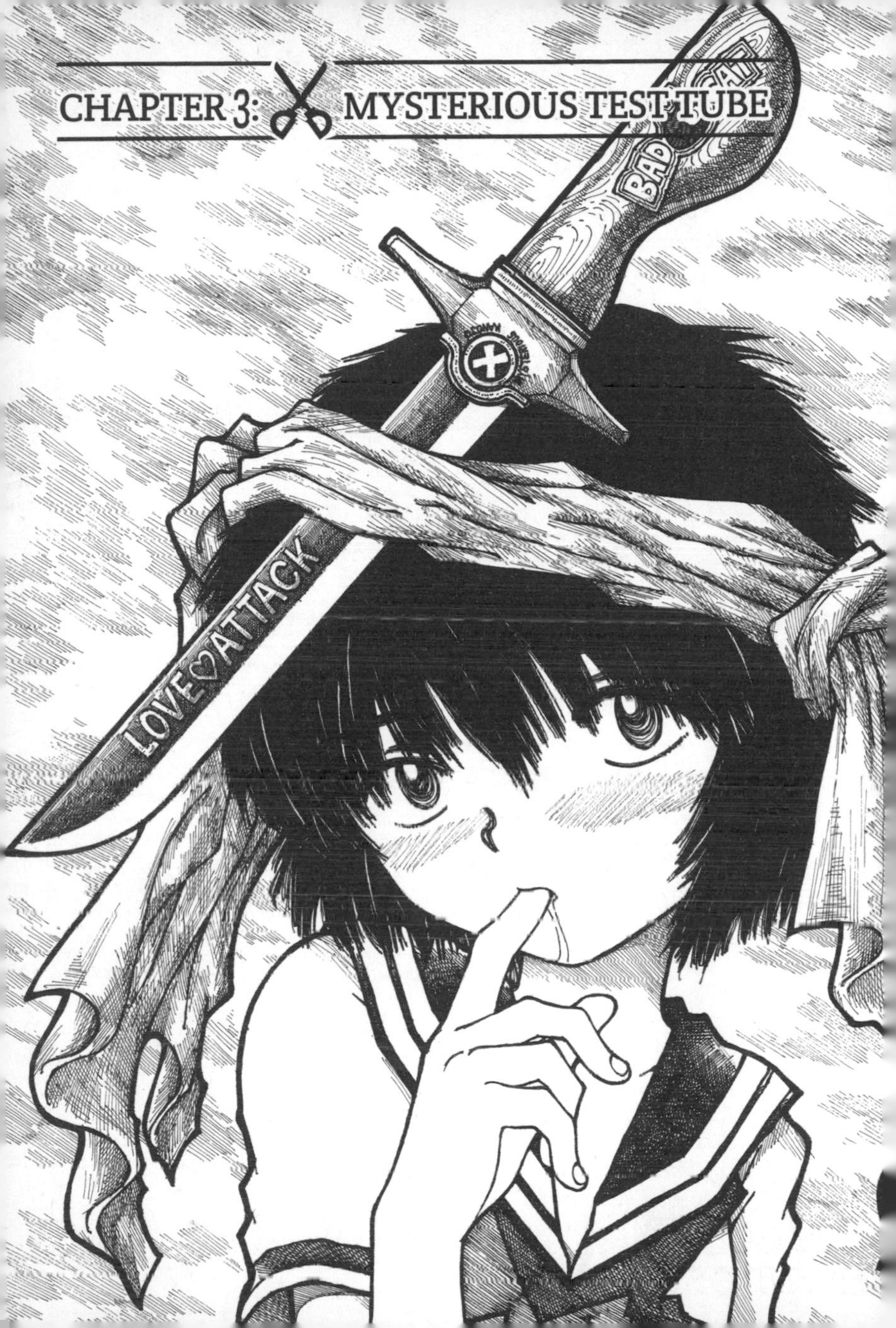
BAD
LOVE♡ATTACK

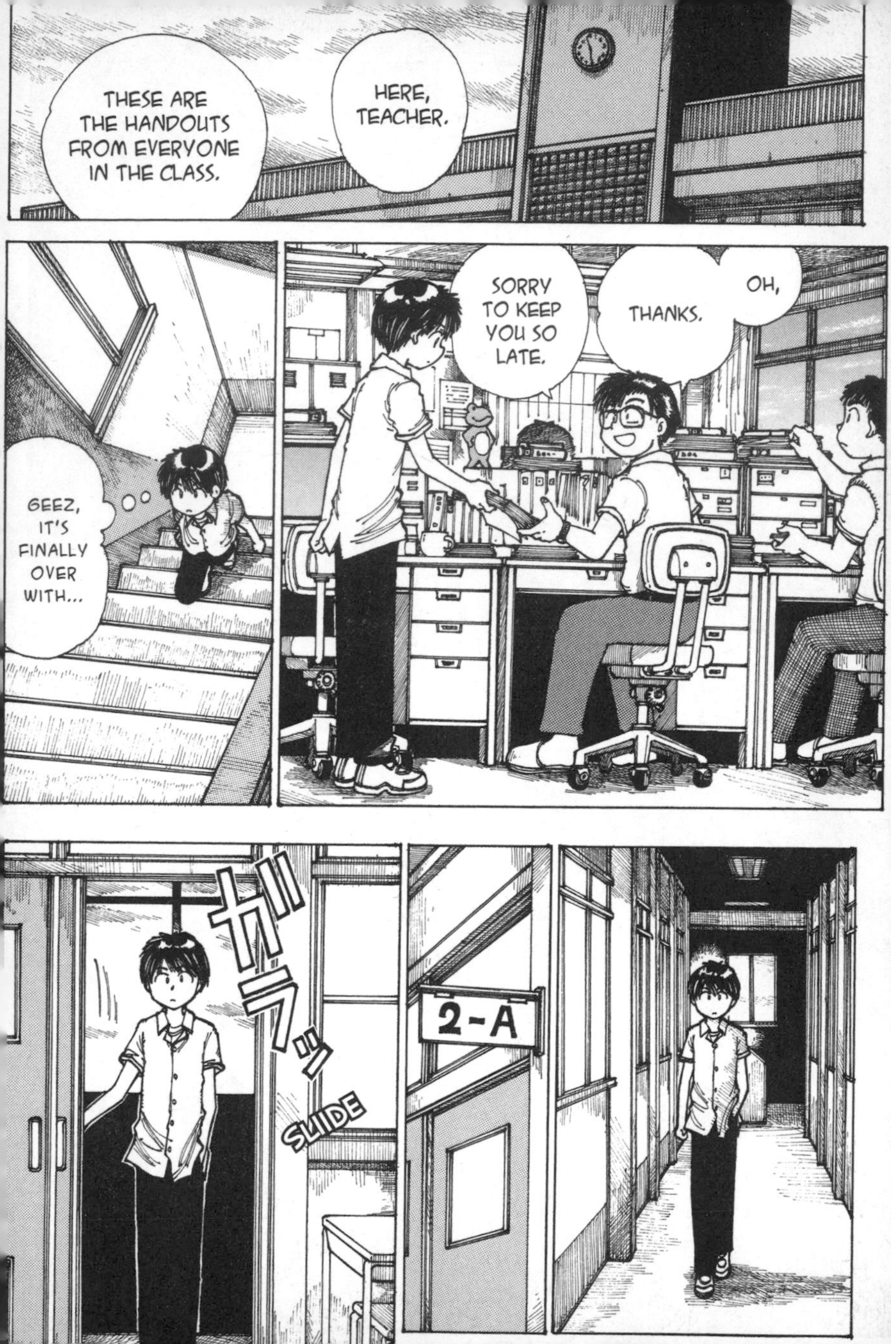
HERE, TEACHER.
THESE ARE THE HANDOUTS FROM EVERYONE IN THE CLASS.
OH, THANKS.
SORRY TO KEEP YOU SO LATE.
GEEZ, IT'S FINALLY OVER WITH...
2-A
ガラッ
SLIDE

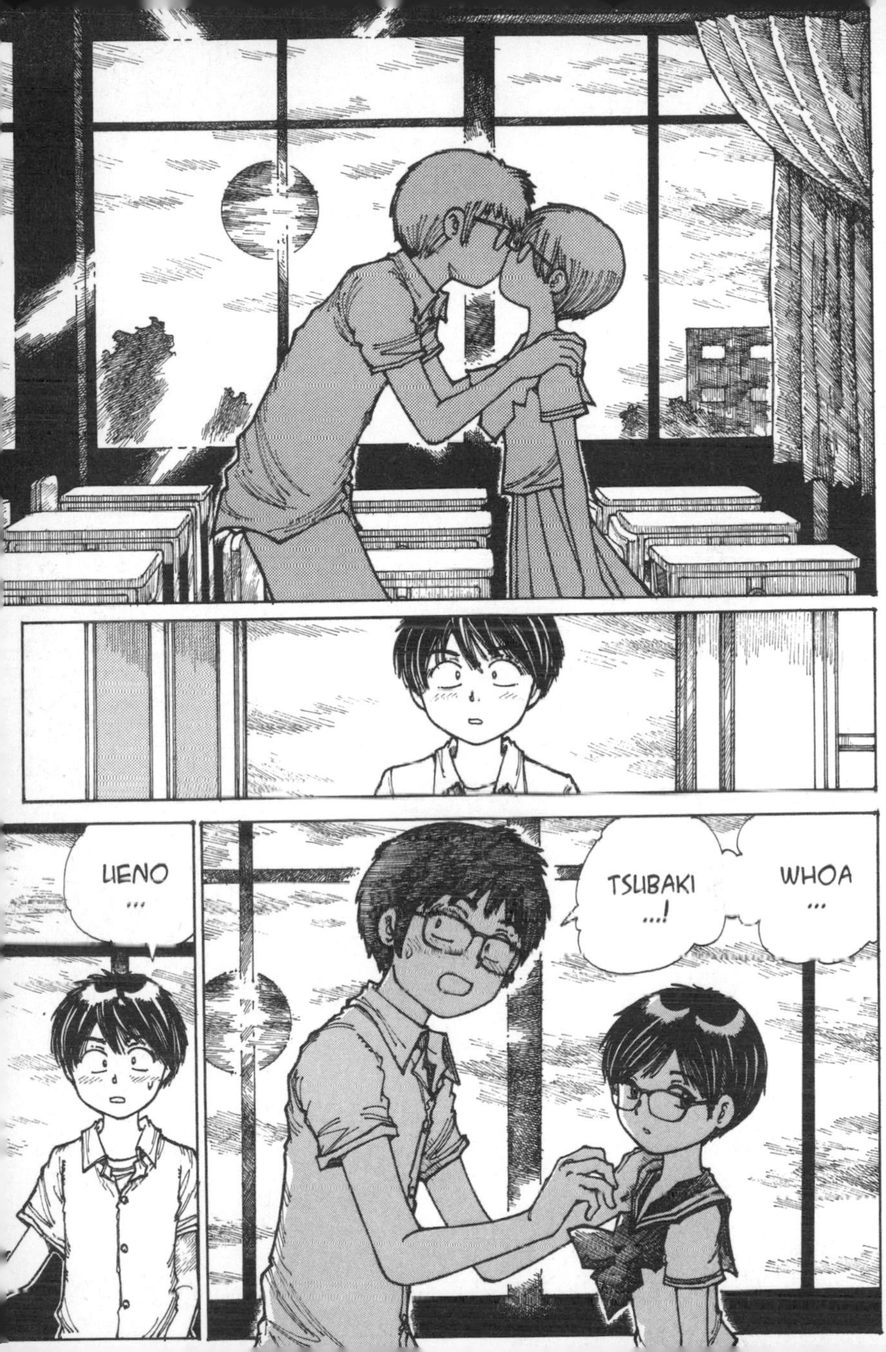
WHOA ...
TSUBAKI ...!
UENO ...

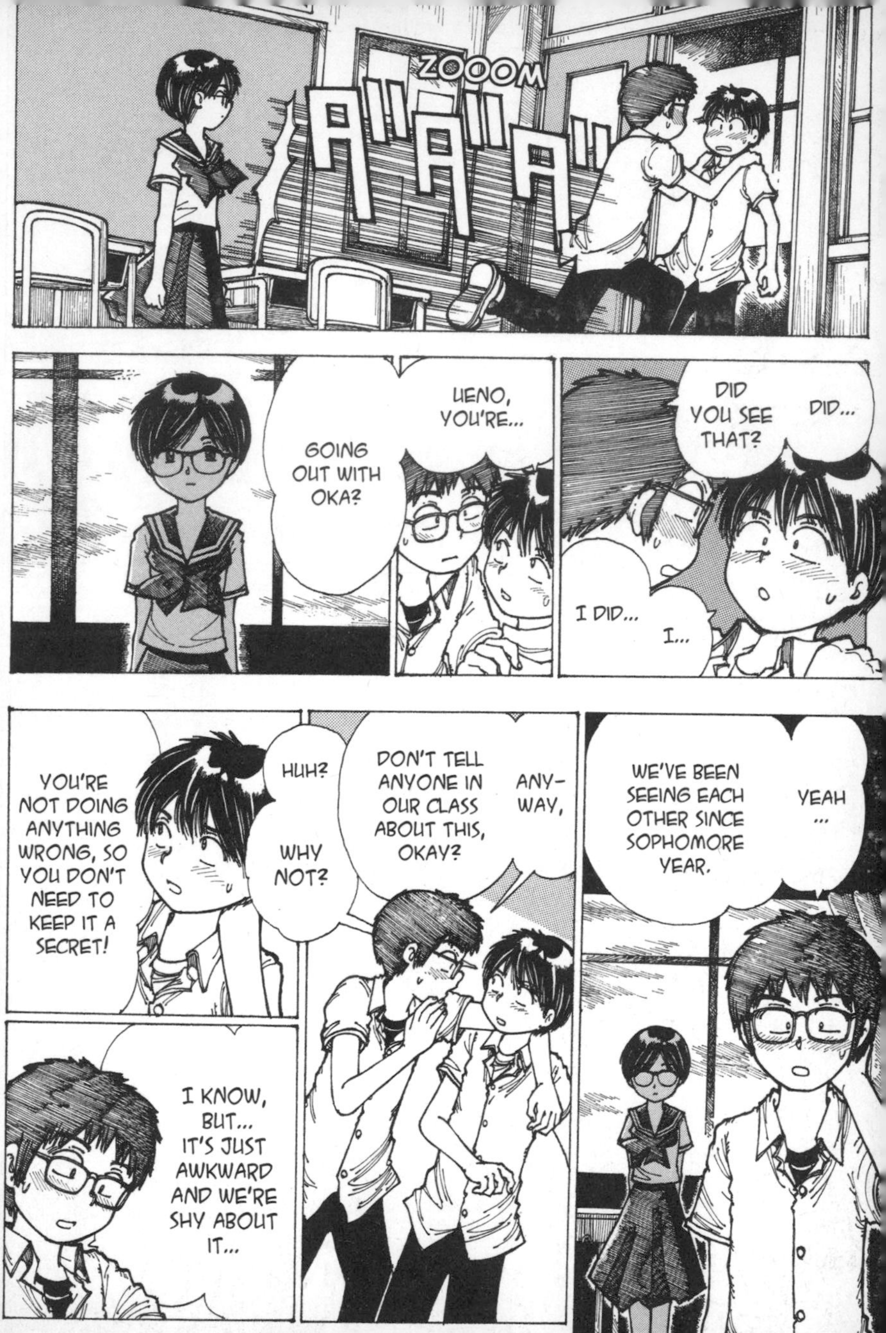
ZOOOM
DID...
DID YOU SEE THAT?
I DID...
I...
UENO, YOU'RE...
GOING OUT WITH OKA?
YEAH...
WE'VE BEEN SEEING EACH OTHER SINCE SOPHOMORE YEAR.
ANY-WAY,
DON'T TELL ANYONE IN OUR CLASS ABOUT THIS, OKAY?
HUH?
WHY NOT?
YOU'RE NOT DOING ANYTHING WRONG, SO YOU DON'T NEED TO KEEP IT A SECRET!
I KNOW, BUT... IT'S JUST AWKWARD AND WE'RE SHY ABOUT IT...

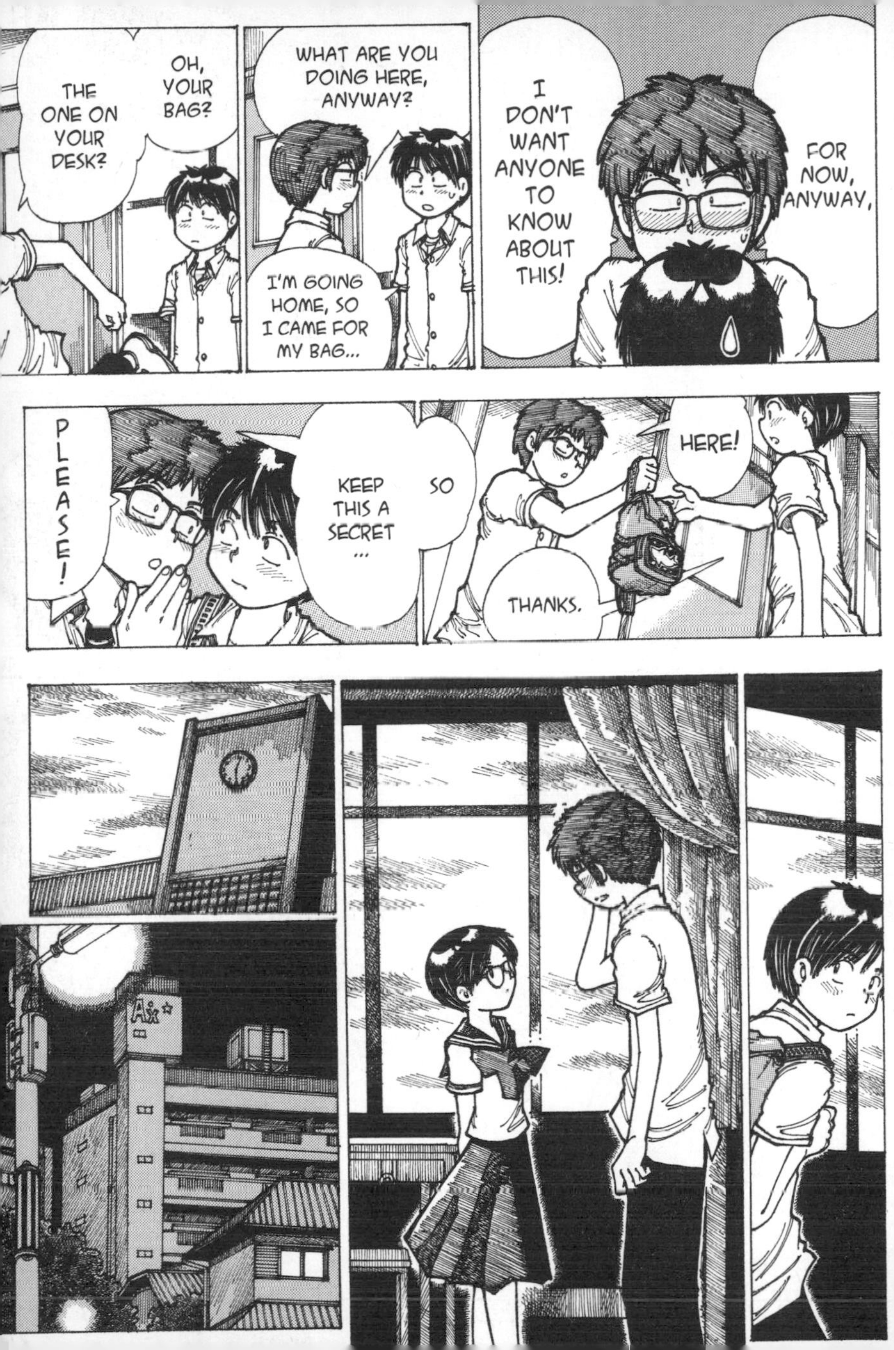
FOR NOW, ANYWAY,
I DON'T WANT ANYONE TO KNOW ABOUT THIS!
WHAT ARE YOU DOING HERE, ANYWAY?
I'M GOING HOME, SO I CAME FOR MY BAG...
OH, YOUR BAG?
THE ONE ON YOUR DESK?
HERE!
THANKS.
SO
KEEP THIS A SECRET ...
PLEASE!

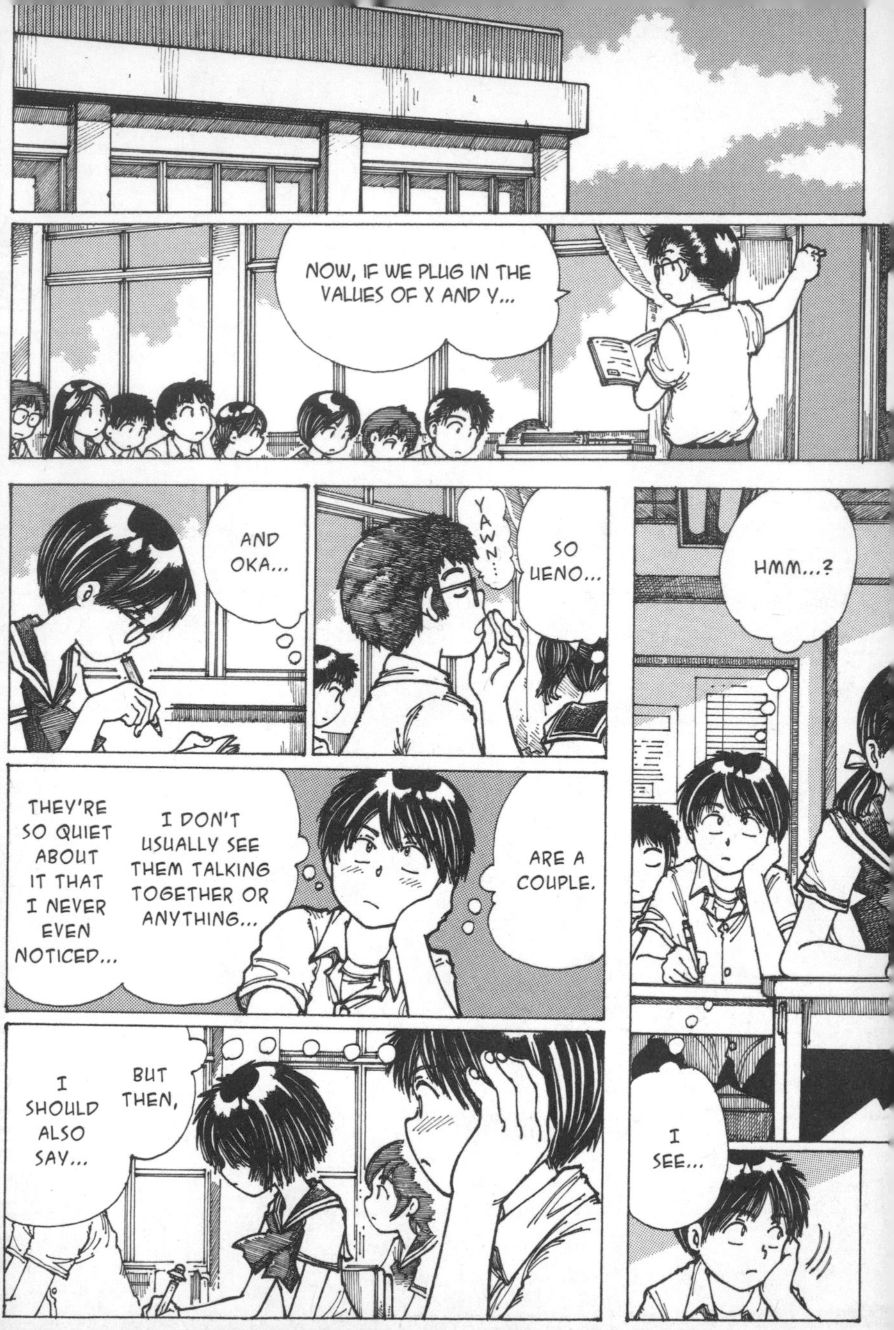
NOW, IF WE PLUG IN THE VALUES OF X AND Y...
HMM...?
SO UENO...
YAWN...
AND OKA...
ARE A COUPLE.
I DON'T USUALLY SEE THEM TALKING TOGETHER OR ANYTHING...
THEY'RE SO QUIET ABOUT IT THAT I NEVER EVEN NOTICED...
I SEE...
BUT THEN,
I SHOULD ALSO SAY...

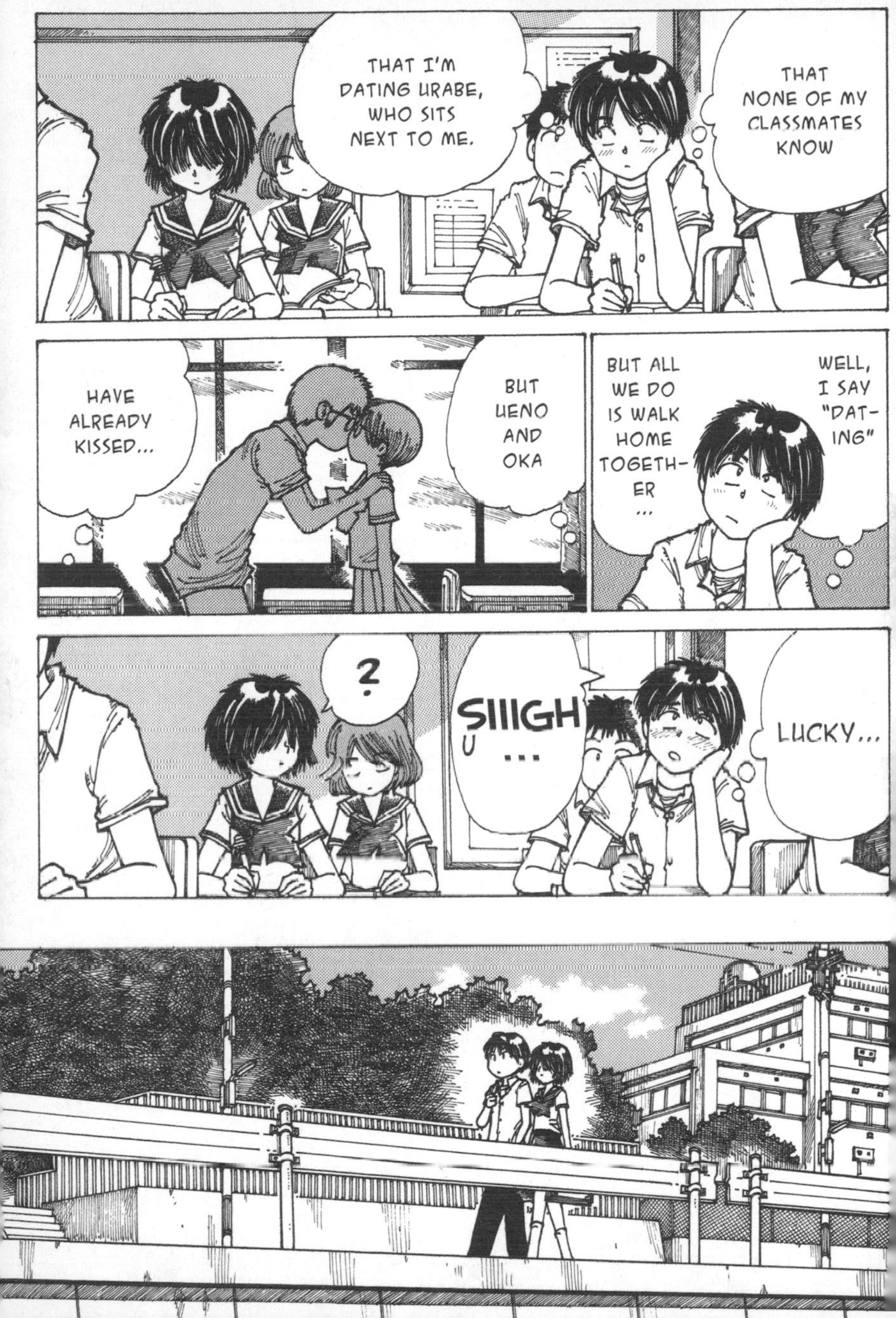
THAT NONE OF MY CLASSMATES KNOW
THAT I'M DATING URABE, WHO SITS NEXT TO ME.
WELL, I SAY "DAT-ING"
BUT ALL WE DO IS WALK HOME TOGETH-ER ...
BUT UENO AND OKA
HAVE ALREADY KISSED...
LUCKY...
SIIIGH
U ...
?

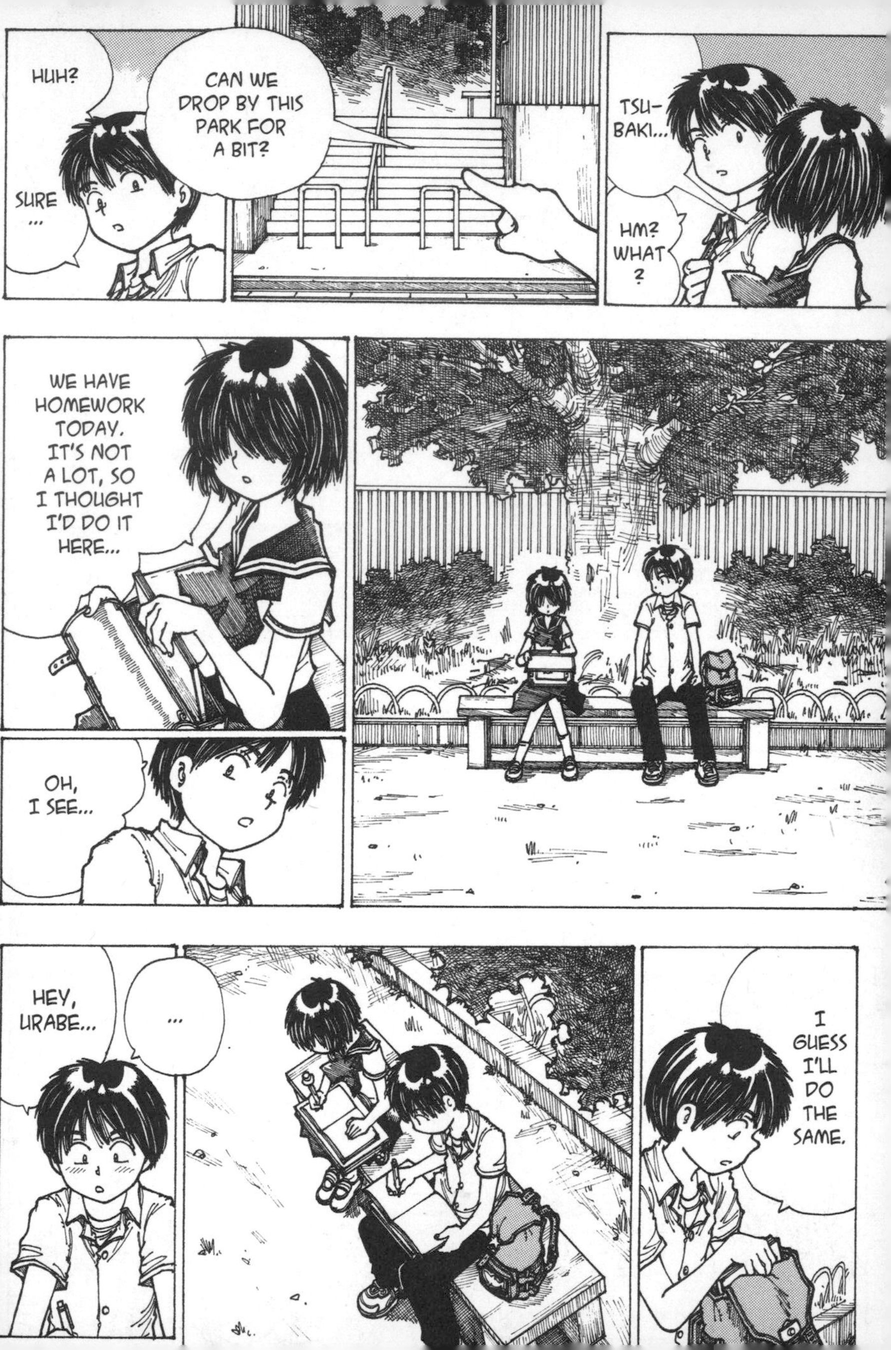

TSU-BAKI...
HM? WHAT?
CAN WE DROP BY THIS PARK FOR A BIT?
HUH?
SURE ...
WE HAVE HOMEWORK TODAY. IT'S NOT A LOT, SO I THOUGHT I'D DO IT HERE...
OH, I SEE...
I GUESS I'LL DO THE SAME.
...
HEY, URABE...

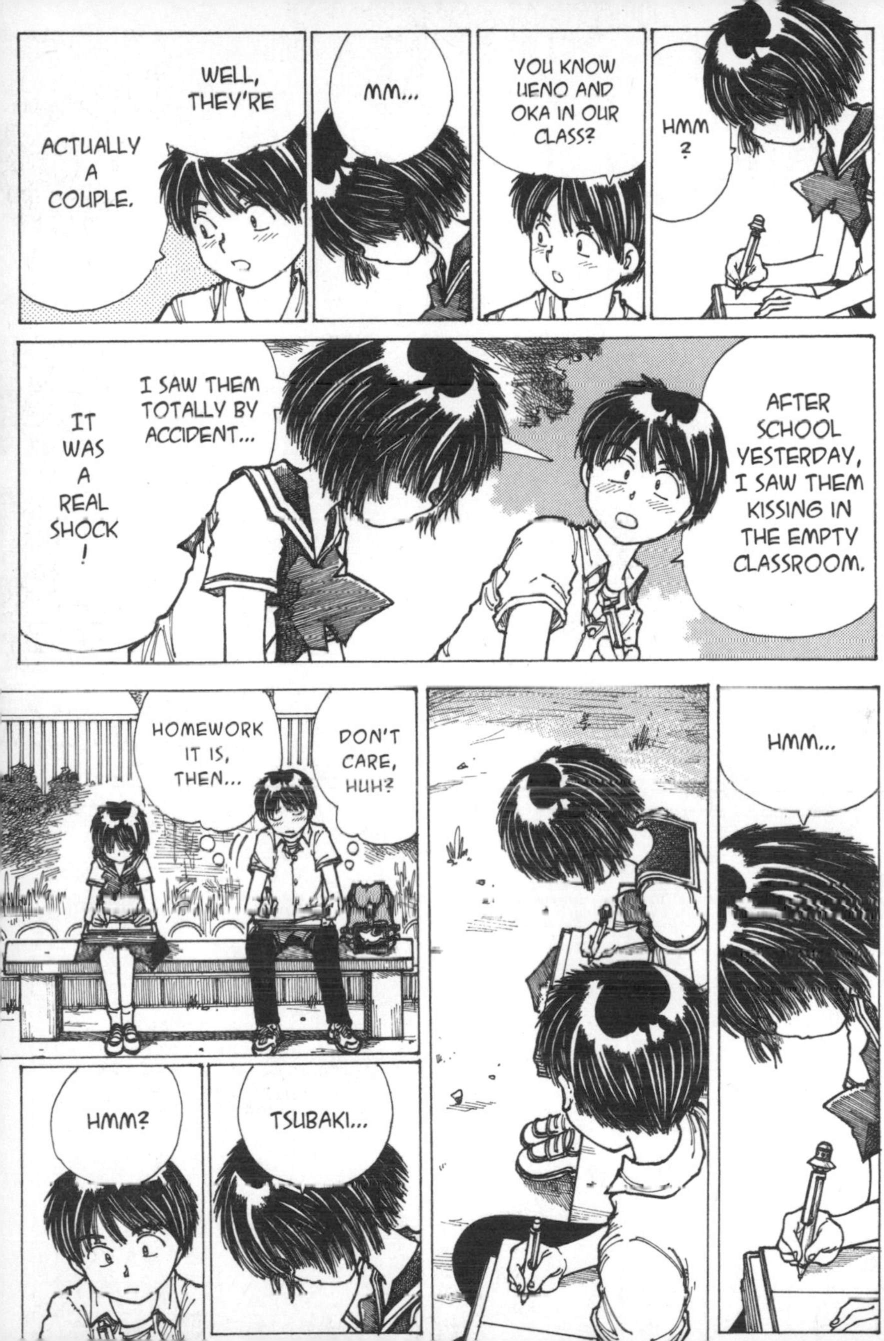
HMM ?
YOU KNOW UENO AND OKA IN OUR CLASS?
MM...
WELL, THEY'RE
ACTUALLY A COUPLE.
AFTER SCHOOL YESTERDAY, I SAW THEM KISSING IN THE EMPTY CLASSROOM.
I SAW THEM TOTALLY BY ACCIDENT...
IT WAS A REAL SHOCK!
HMM...
DON'T CARE, HUH?
HOMEWORK IT IS, THEN...
TSUBAKI...
HMM?

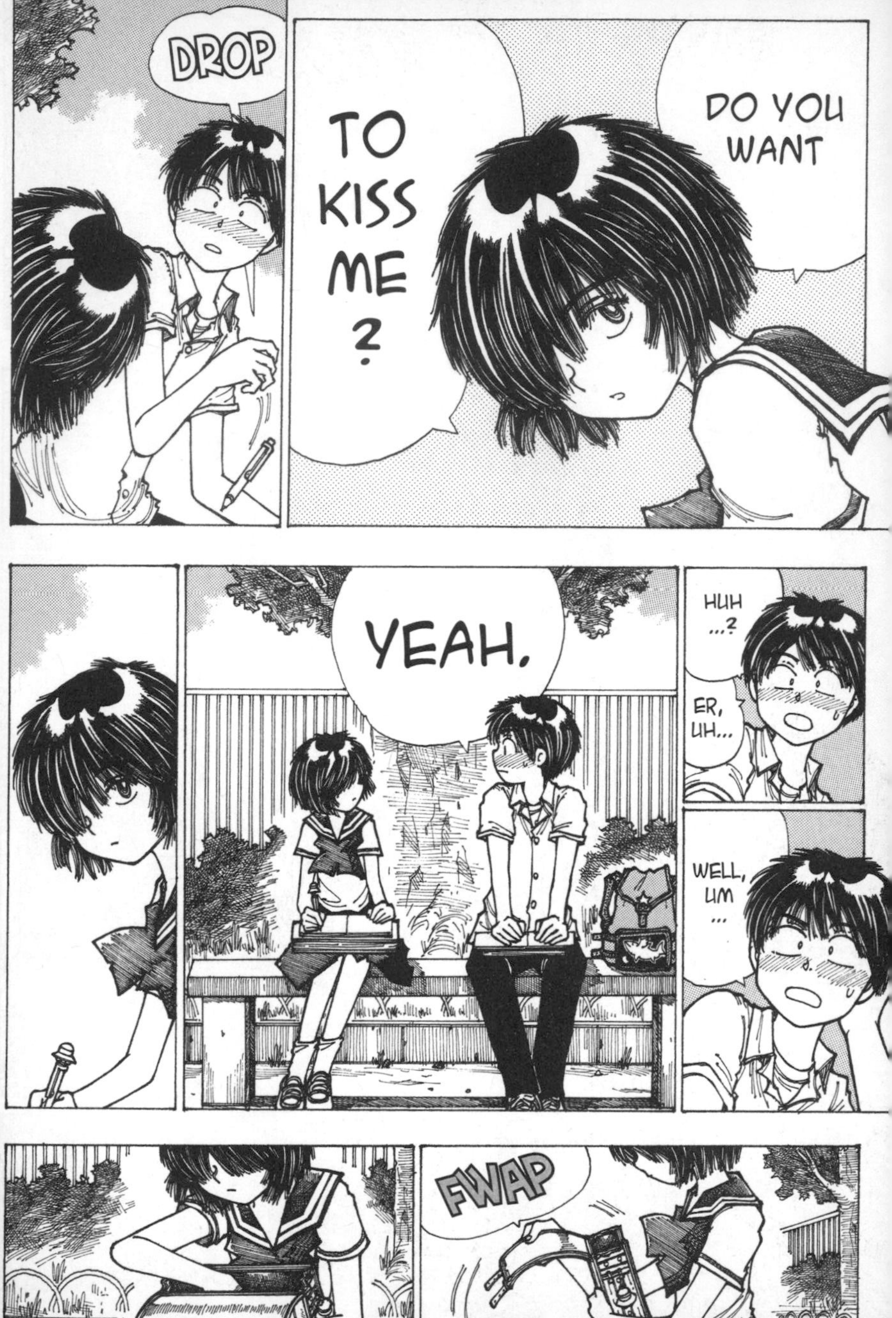
DO YOU WANT
TO KISS ME?
DROP
HUH ...?
ER, UH...
WELL, UM ...
YEAH.
FWAP

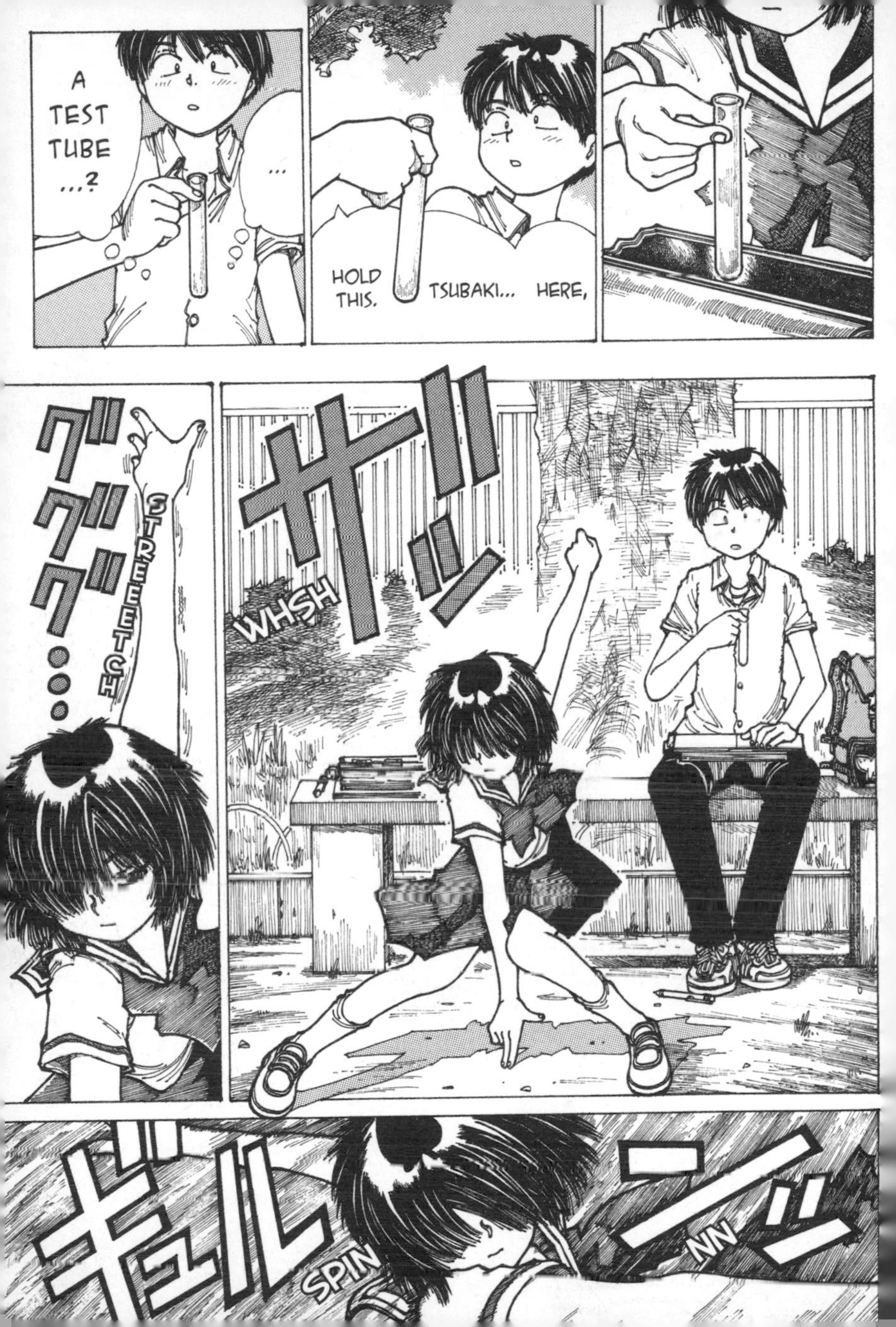
HERE,
TSUBAKI...
HOLD THIS.
...
A TEST TUBE ...?
サッ
WHSH
グググ…
STREEETCH
ギュルーン
SPIN
NN

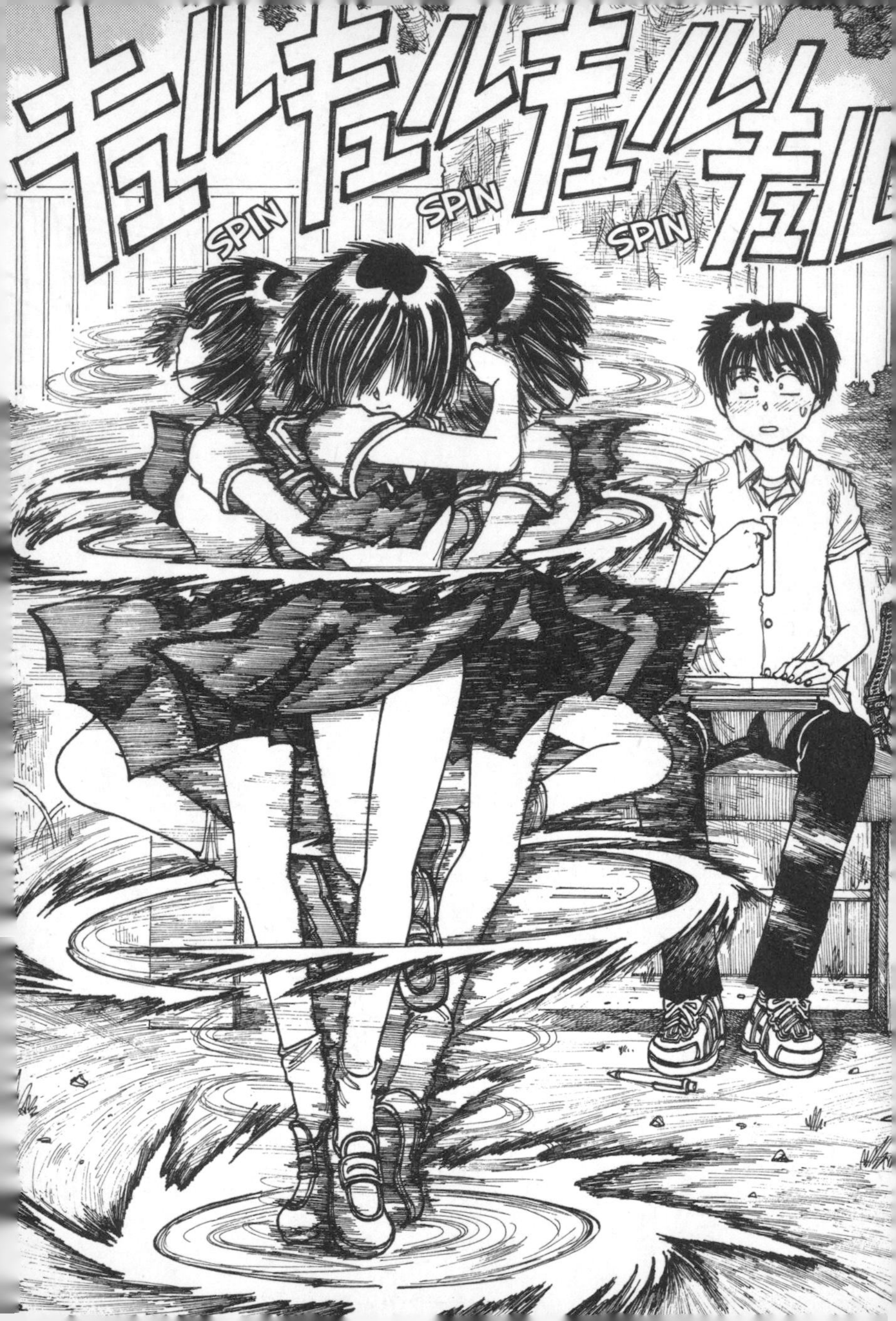
キュルキュルキュルキュル
SPIN
SPIN
SPIN

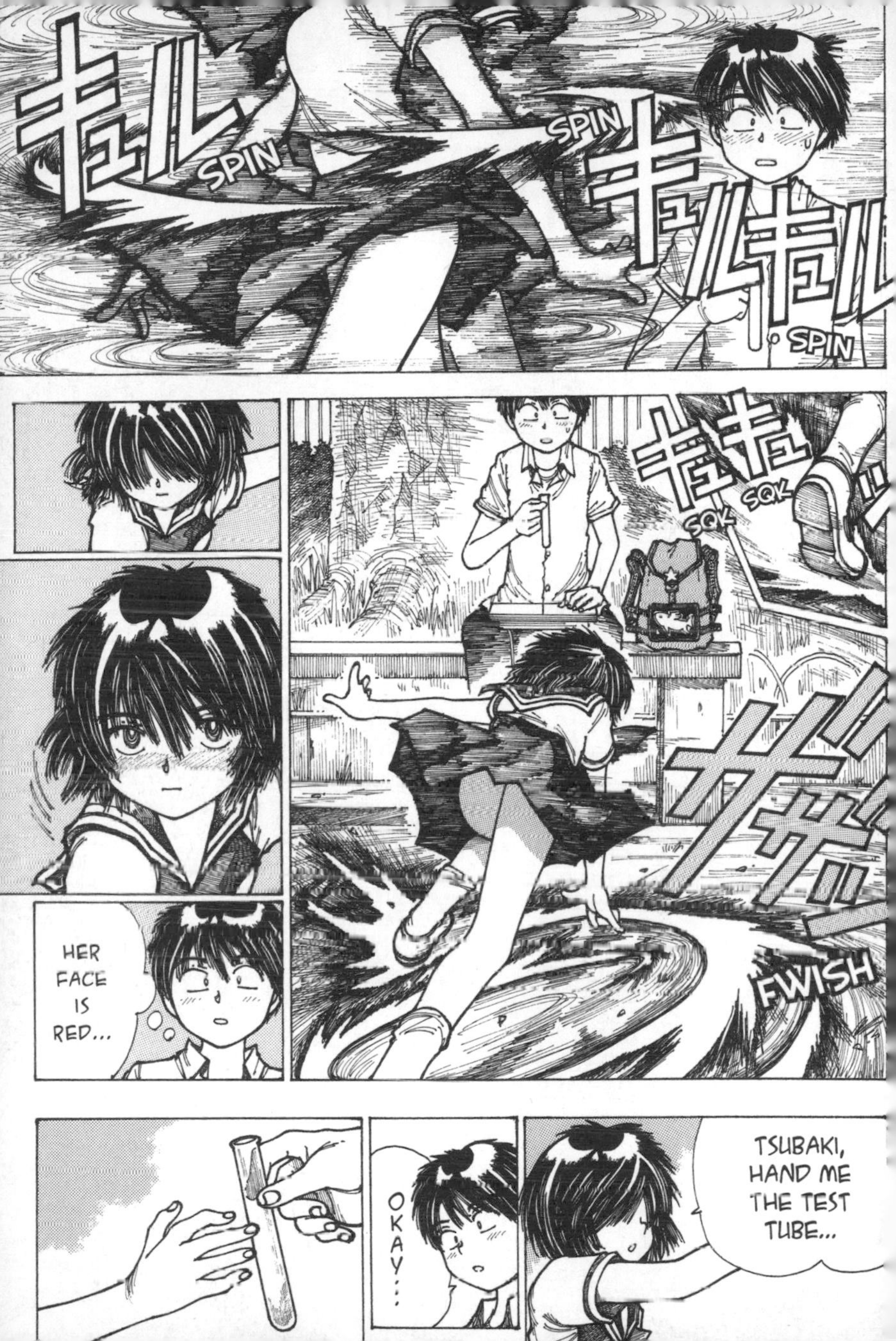
キュルキュル
SPIN
SPIN
キュル
SPIN
キュキュ
SQK SQK
FWISH
HER FACE IS RED...
TSUBAKI, HAND ME THE TEST TUBE...
OKAY...

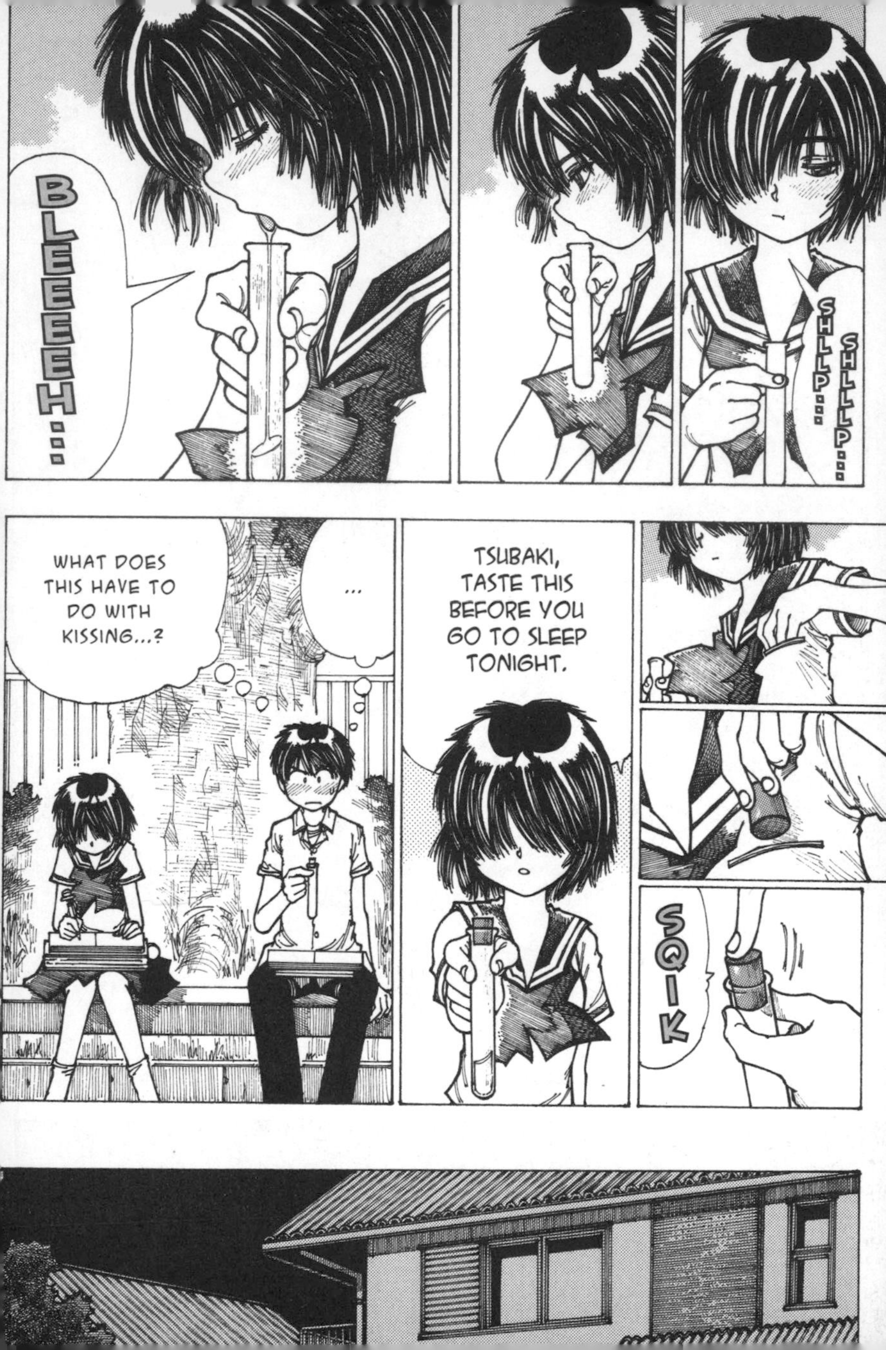
SHLLP... SHLLP...
BLEEEEH...
SQIK
TSUBAKI, TASTE THIS BEFORE YOU GO TO SLEEP TONIGHT.
...
WHAT DOES THIS HAVE TO DO WITH KISSING...?

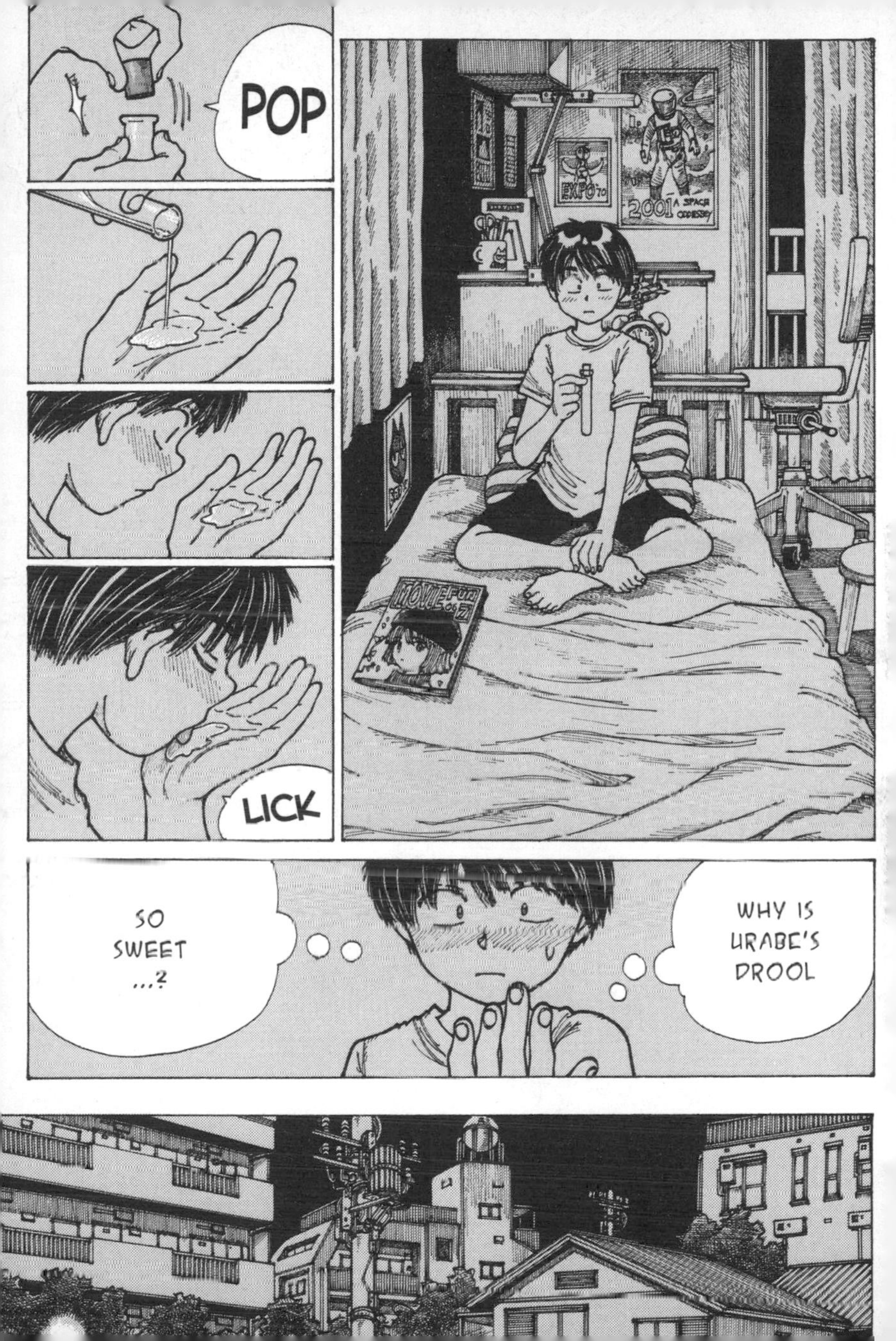
POP
LICK
WHY IS URABE'S DROOL
SO SWEET ...?

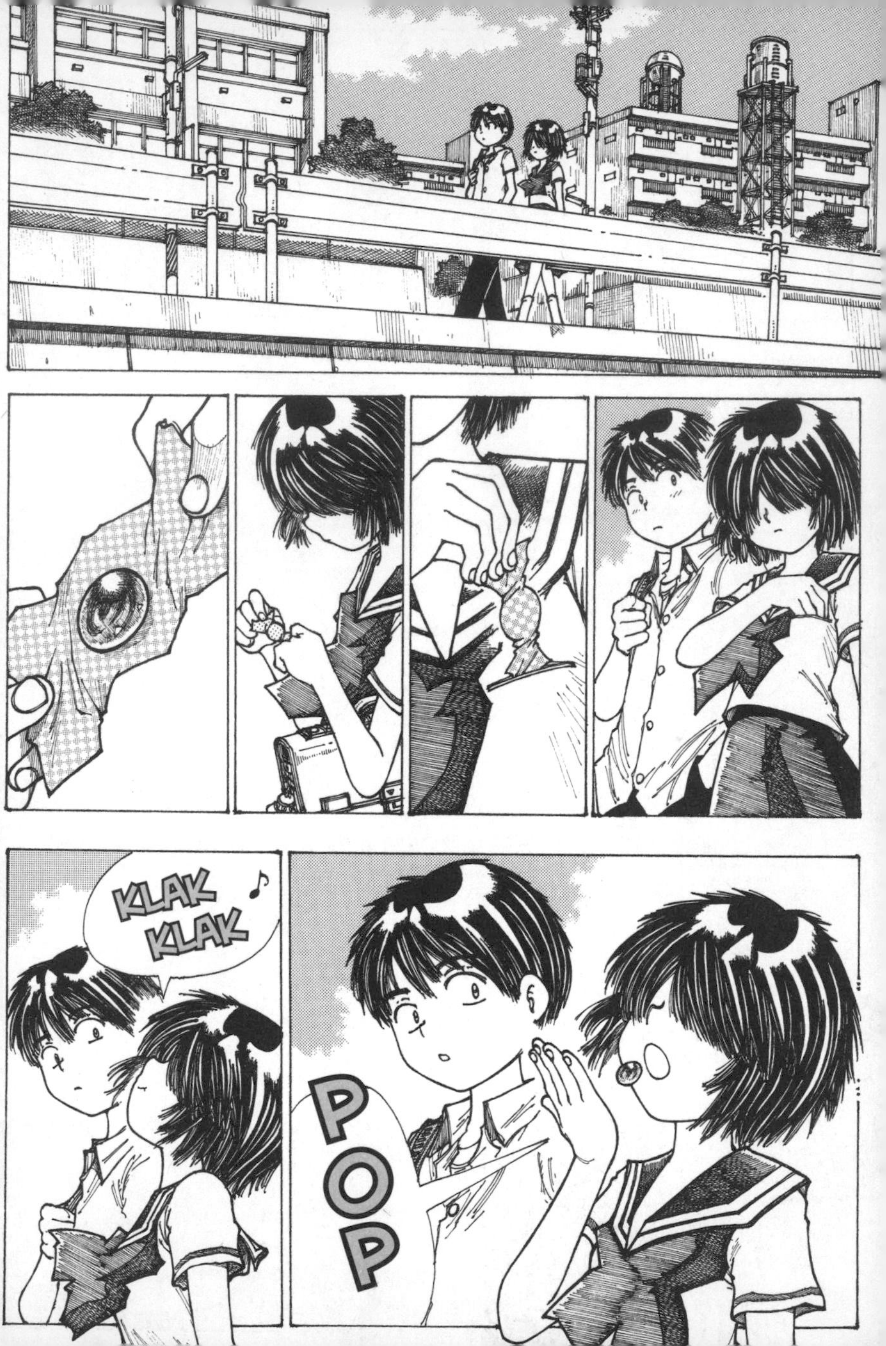
KLAK KLAK ♪
POP

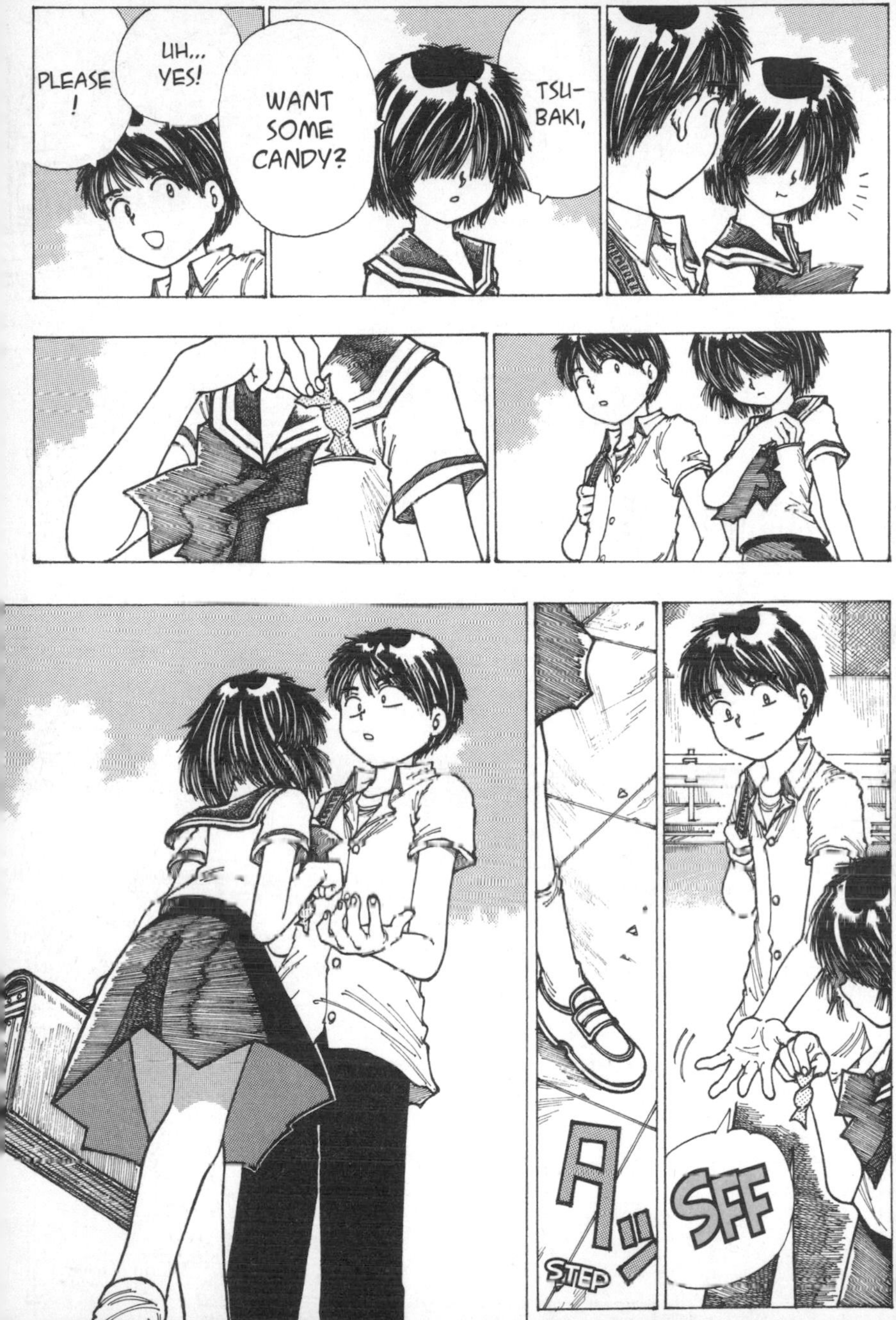

TSU-BAKI,
WANT SOME CANDY?
UH... YES!
PLEASE!
SFF
STEP

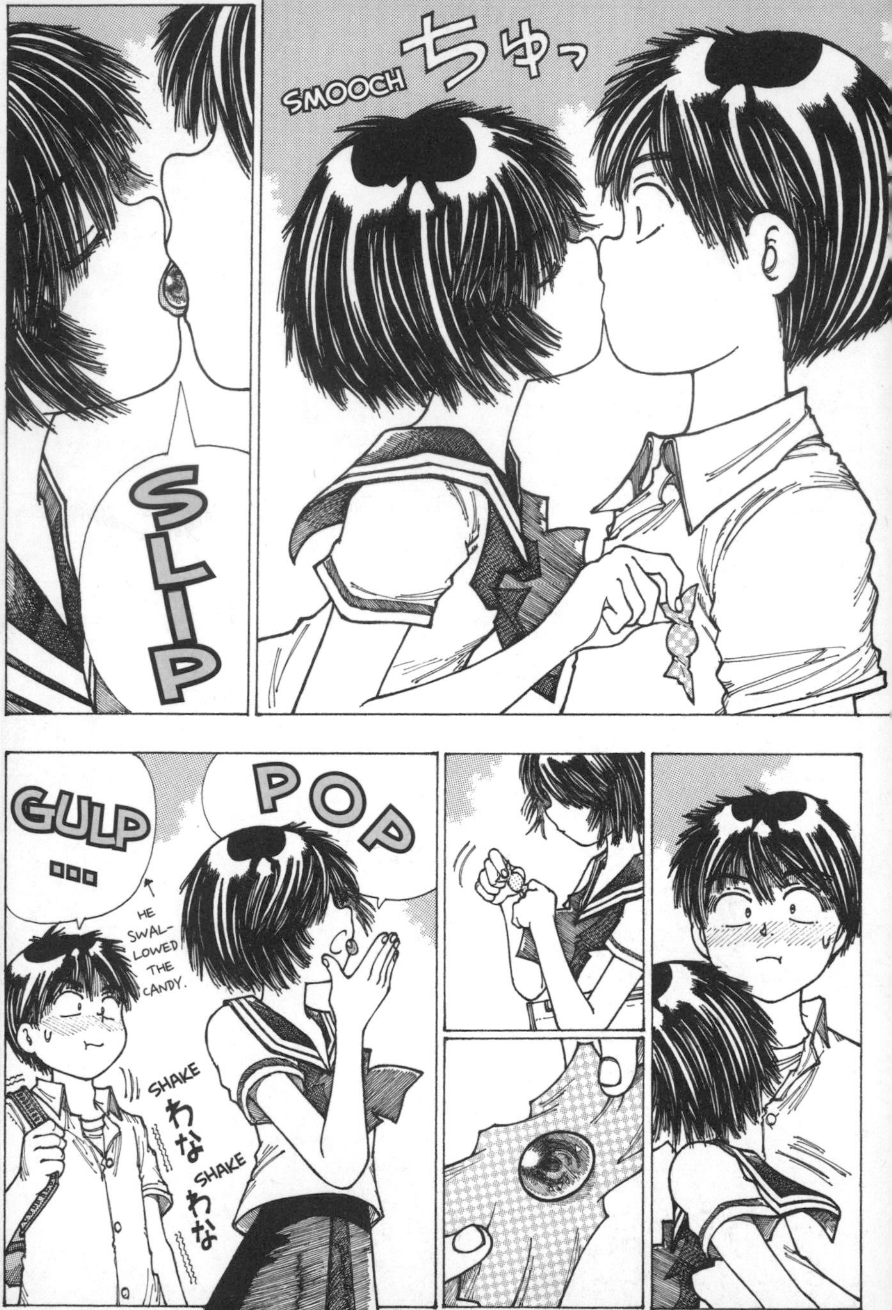
SMOOCH
ちゅっ
SLIP
POP
GULP ...
HE SWALLOWED THE CANDY.
SHAKE わな
SHAKE わな

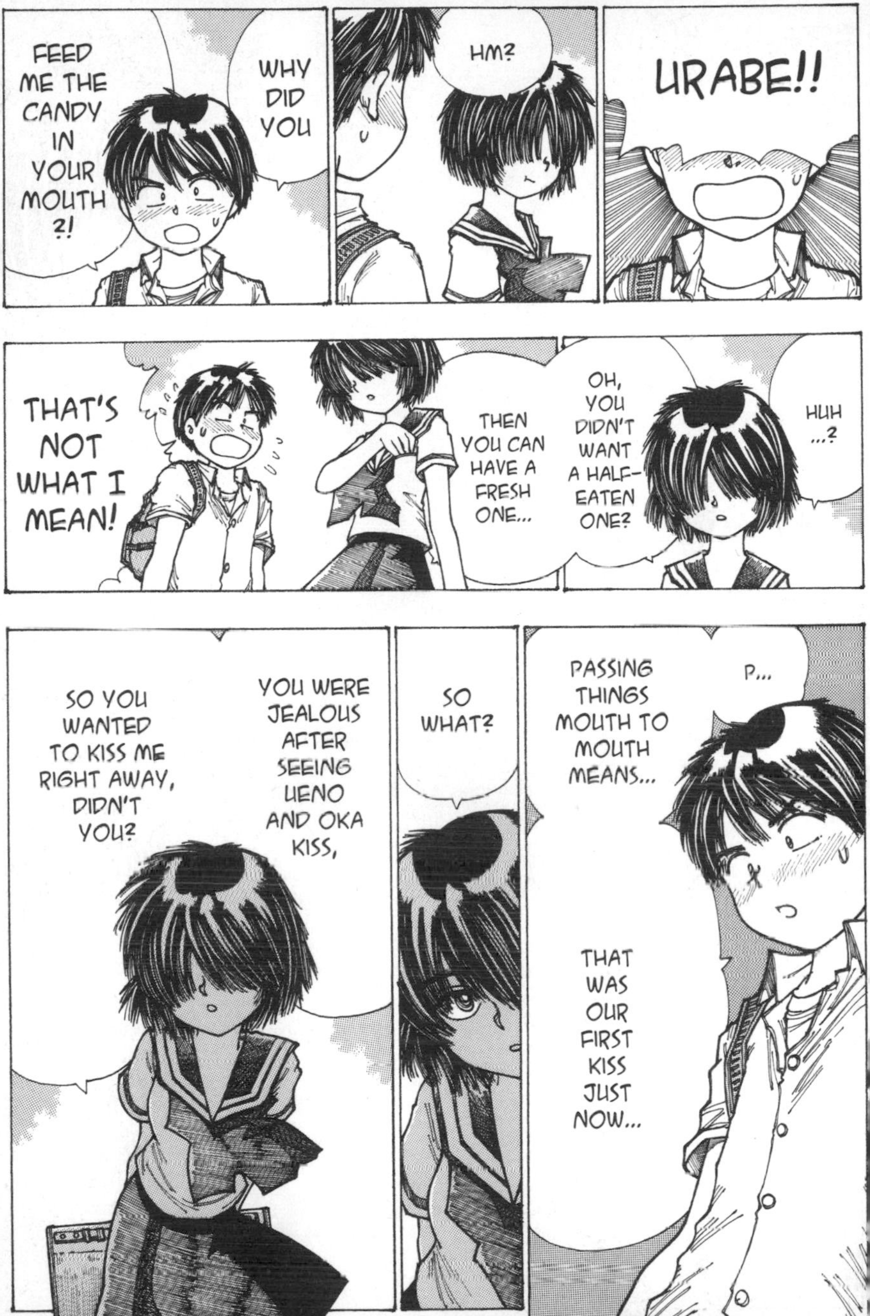
URABE!!
HM?
WHY DID YOU
FEED ME THE CANDY IN YOUR MOUTH ?!
HUH ...?
OH, YOU DIDN'T WANT A HALF-EATEN ONE?
THEN YOU CAN HAVE A FRESH ONE...
THAT'S NOT WHAT I MEAN!
P...
PASSING THINGS MOUTH TO MOUTH MEANS...
THAT WAS OUR FIRST KISS JUST NOW...
SO WHAT?
YOU WERE JEALOUS AFTER SEEING UENO AND OKA KISS,
SO YOU WANTED TO KISS ME RIGHT AWAY, DIDN'T YOU?

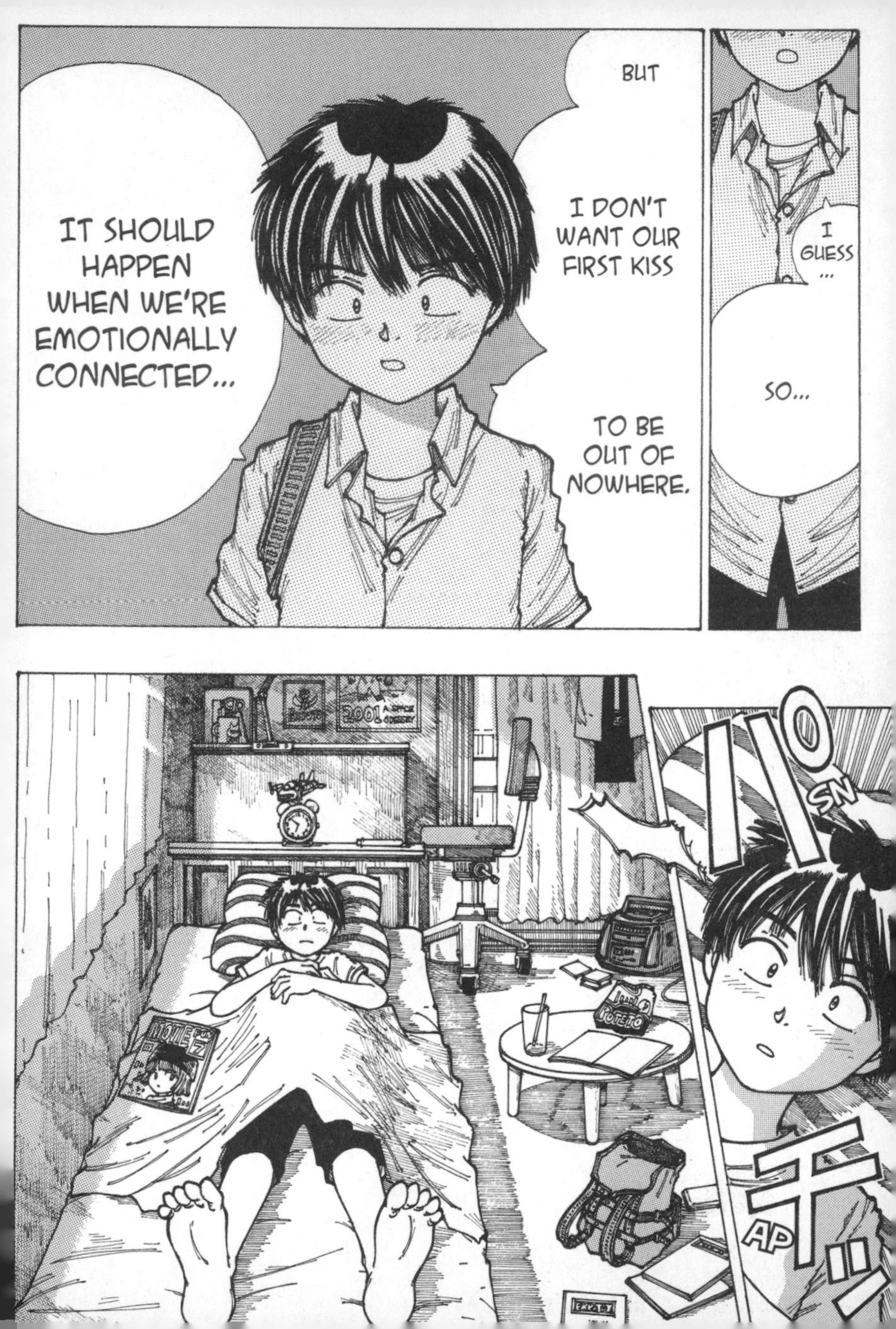
I GUESS ...
SO...
BUT
I DON'T WANT OUR FIRST KISS
TO BE OUT OF NOWHERE.
IT SHOULD HAPPEN WHEN WE'RE EMOTIONALLY CONNECTED...
SNAP
POTETO

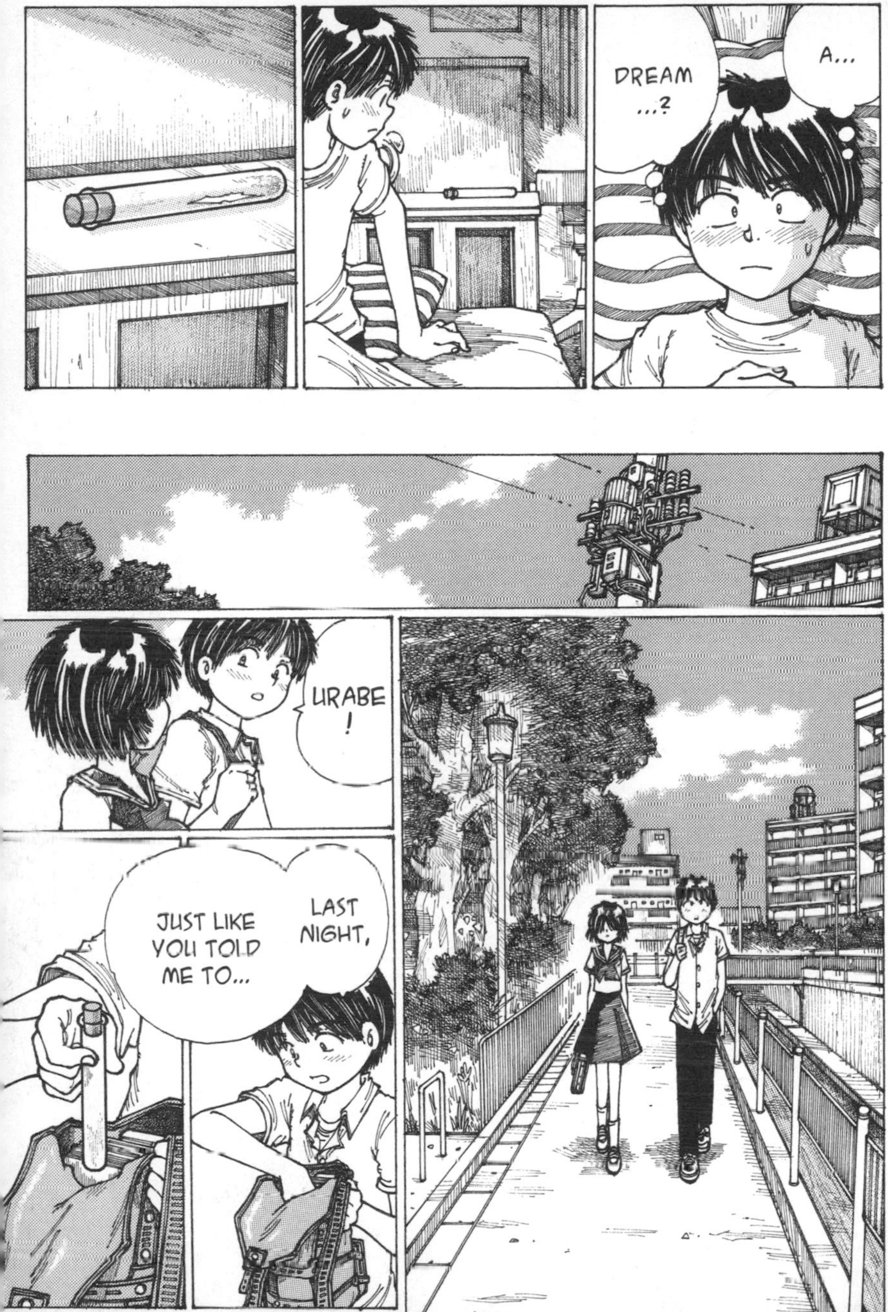
A...
DREAM ...?
URABE!
LAST NIGHT,
JUST LIKE YOU TOLD ME TO...

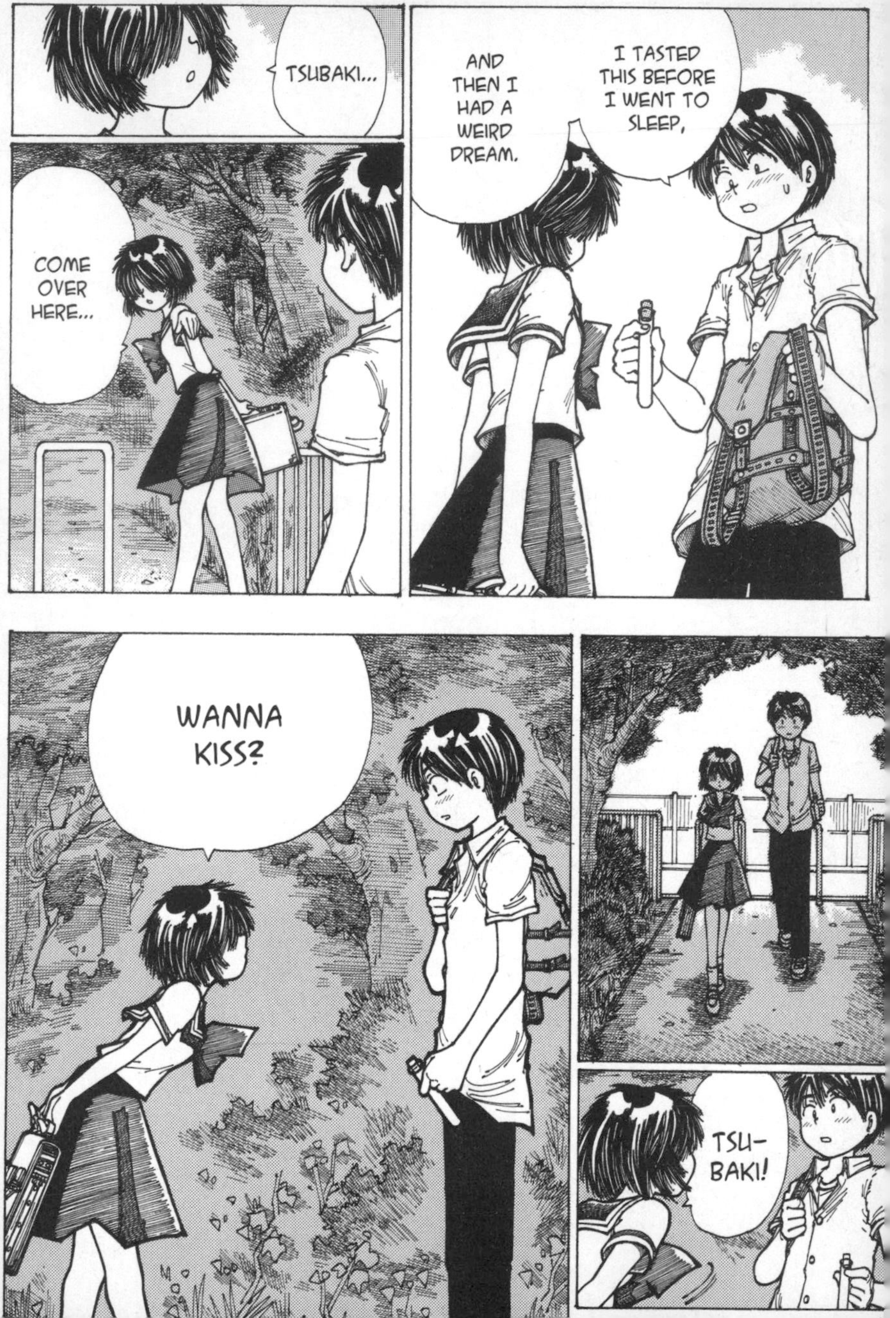
I TASTED THIS BEFORE I WENT TO SLEEP,
AND THEN I HAD A WEIRD DREAM.
TSUBAKI...
COME OVER HERE...
TSU-BAKI!
WANNA KISS?

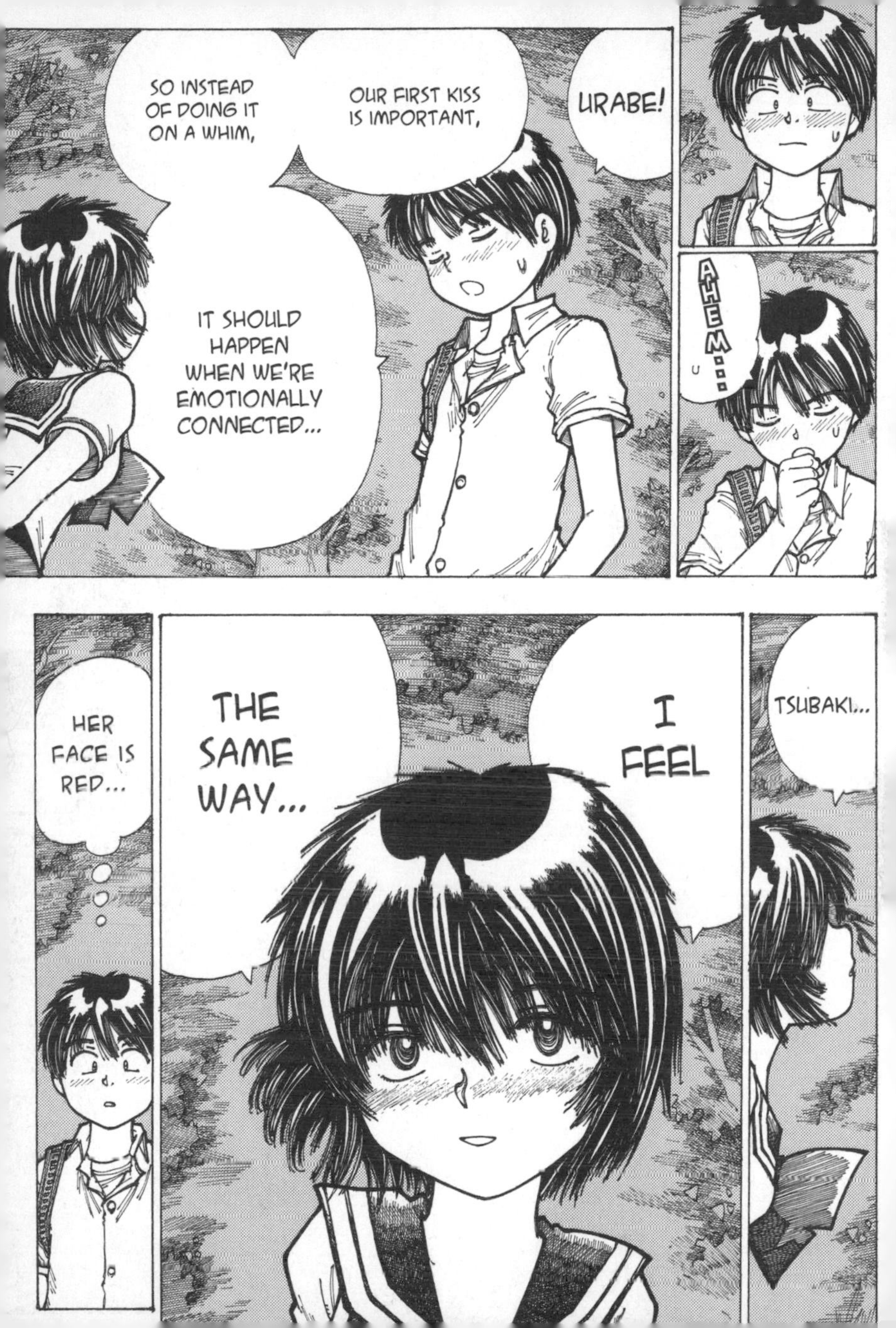
AHEM...
URABE!
OUR FIRST KISS IS IMPORTANT,
SO INSTEAD OF DOING IT ON A WHIM,
IT SHOULD HAPPEN WHEN WE'RE EMOTIONALLY CONNECTED...
TSUBAKI...
I FEEL
THE SAME WAY...
HER FACE IS RED...

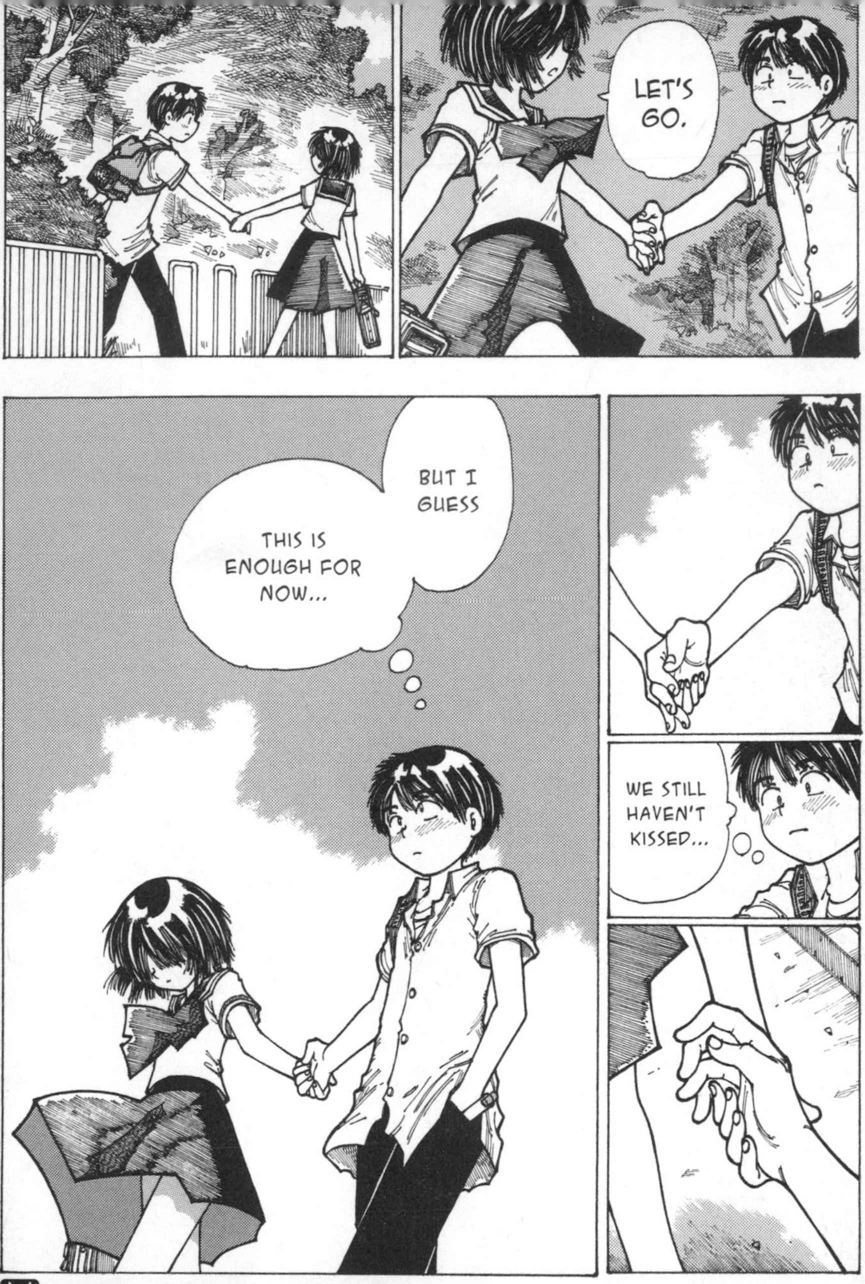
LET'S GO.
WE STILL HAVEN'T KISSED...
BUT I GUESS
THIS IS ENOUGH FOR NOW...

END OF CHAPTER 3

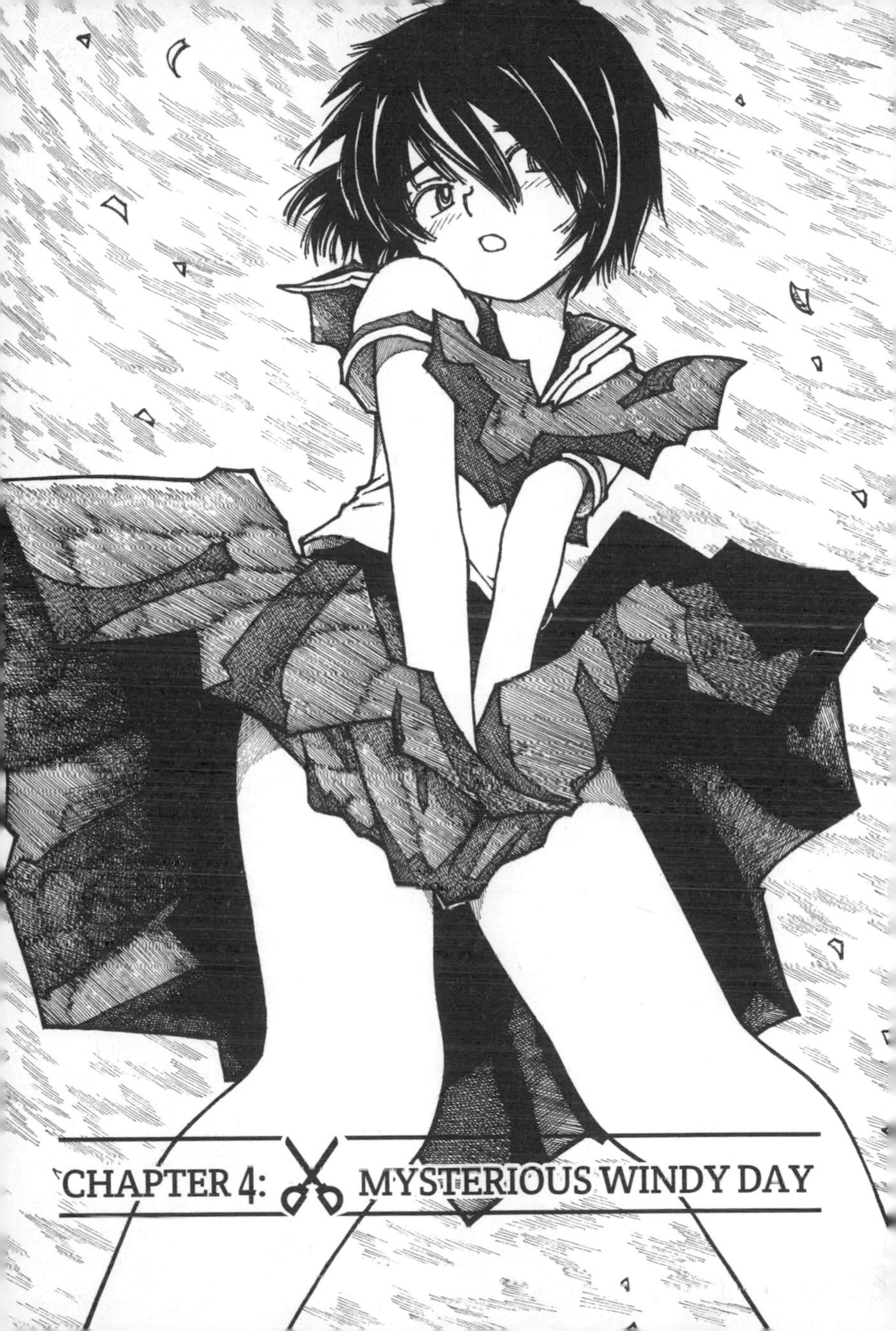

CHAPTER 4: MYSTERIOUS WINDY DAY

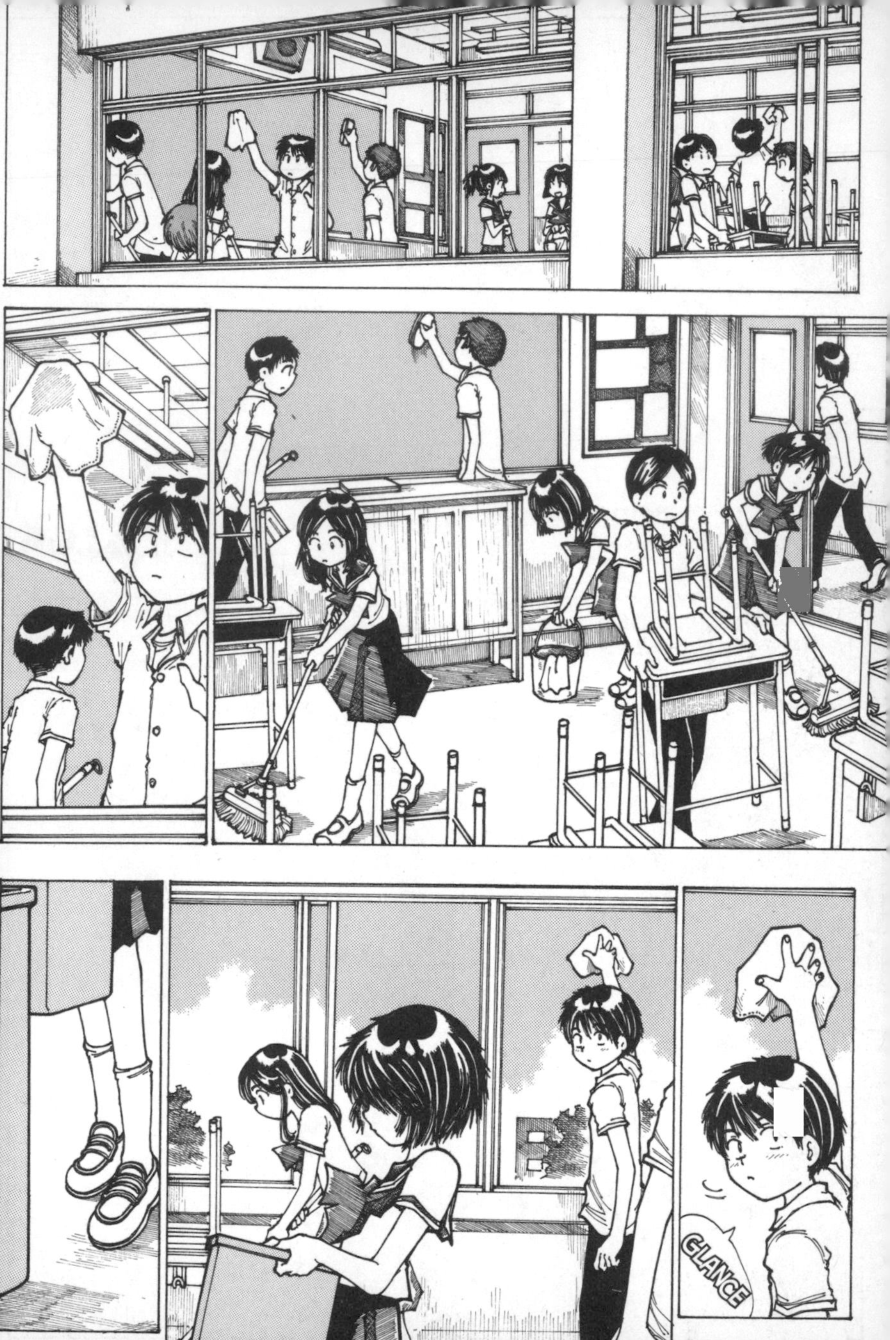
GLANCE

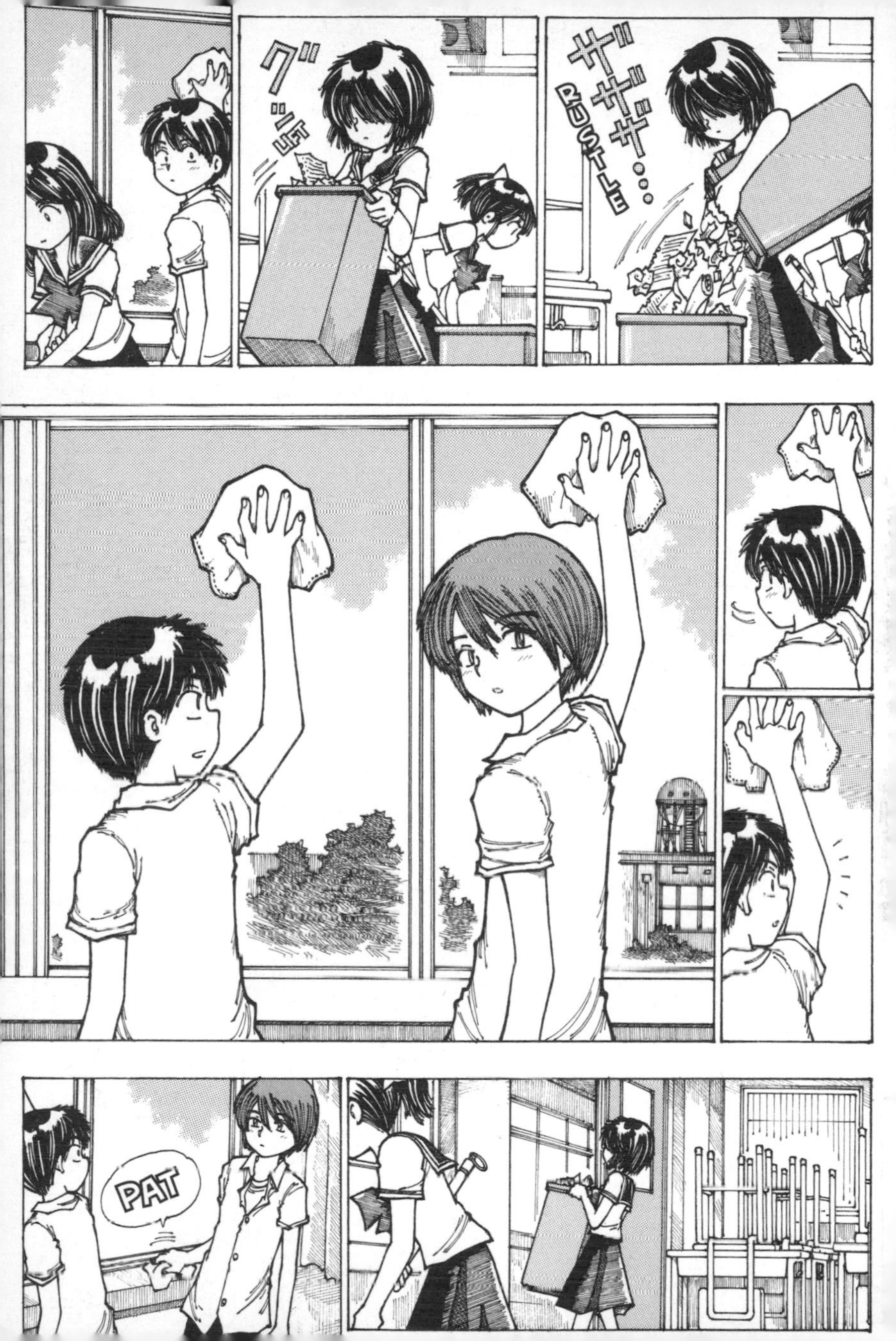
ザザザ…
RUSTLE
グ゛ーッ
LIFT
PAT

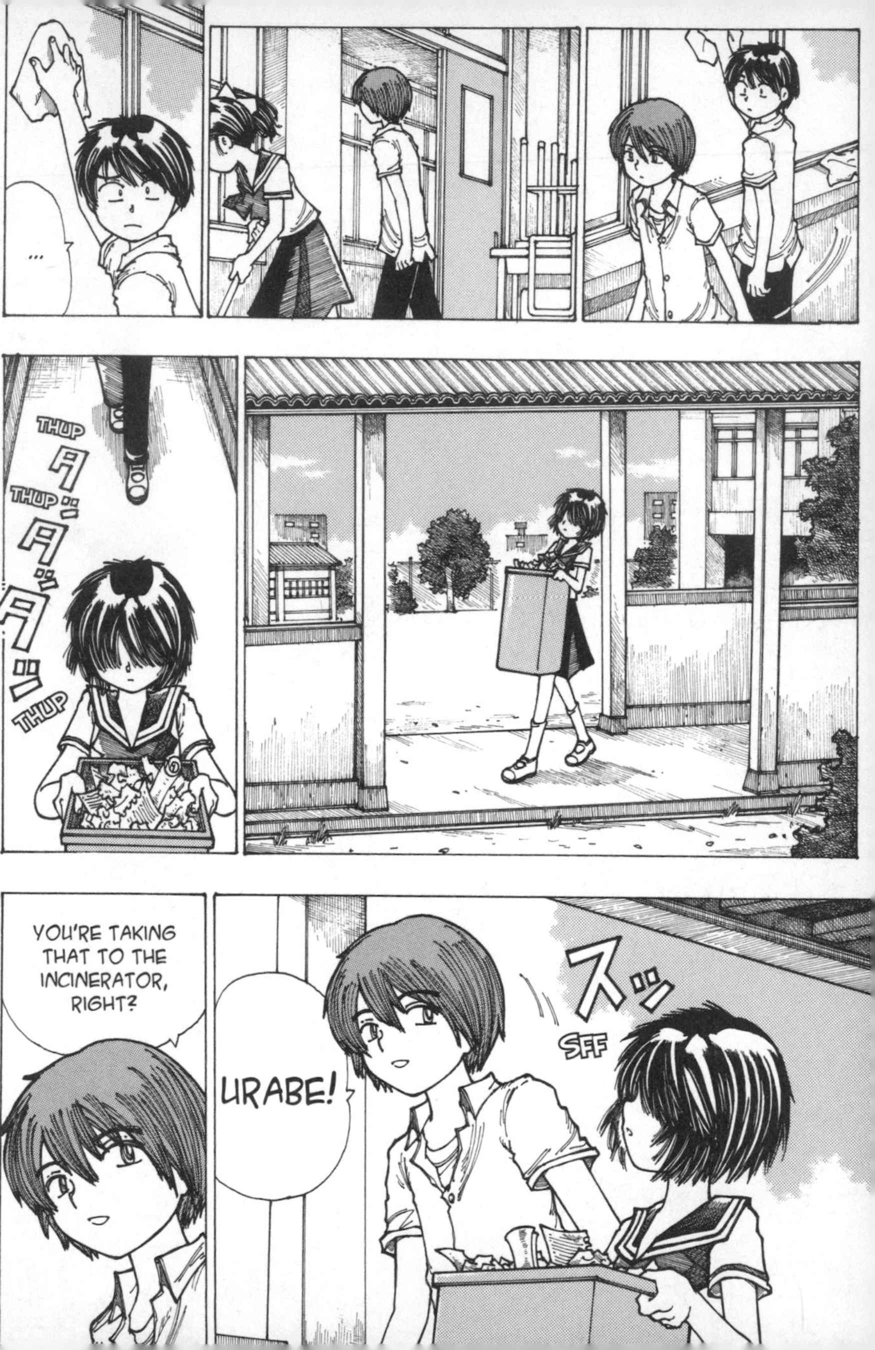

...
THUP
タ
THUP
ダ
ダッ
THUP
スッ
SFF
URABE!
YOU'RE TAKING THAT TO THE INCINERATOR, RIGHT?

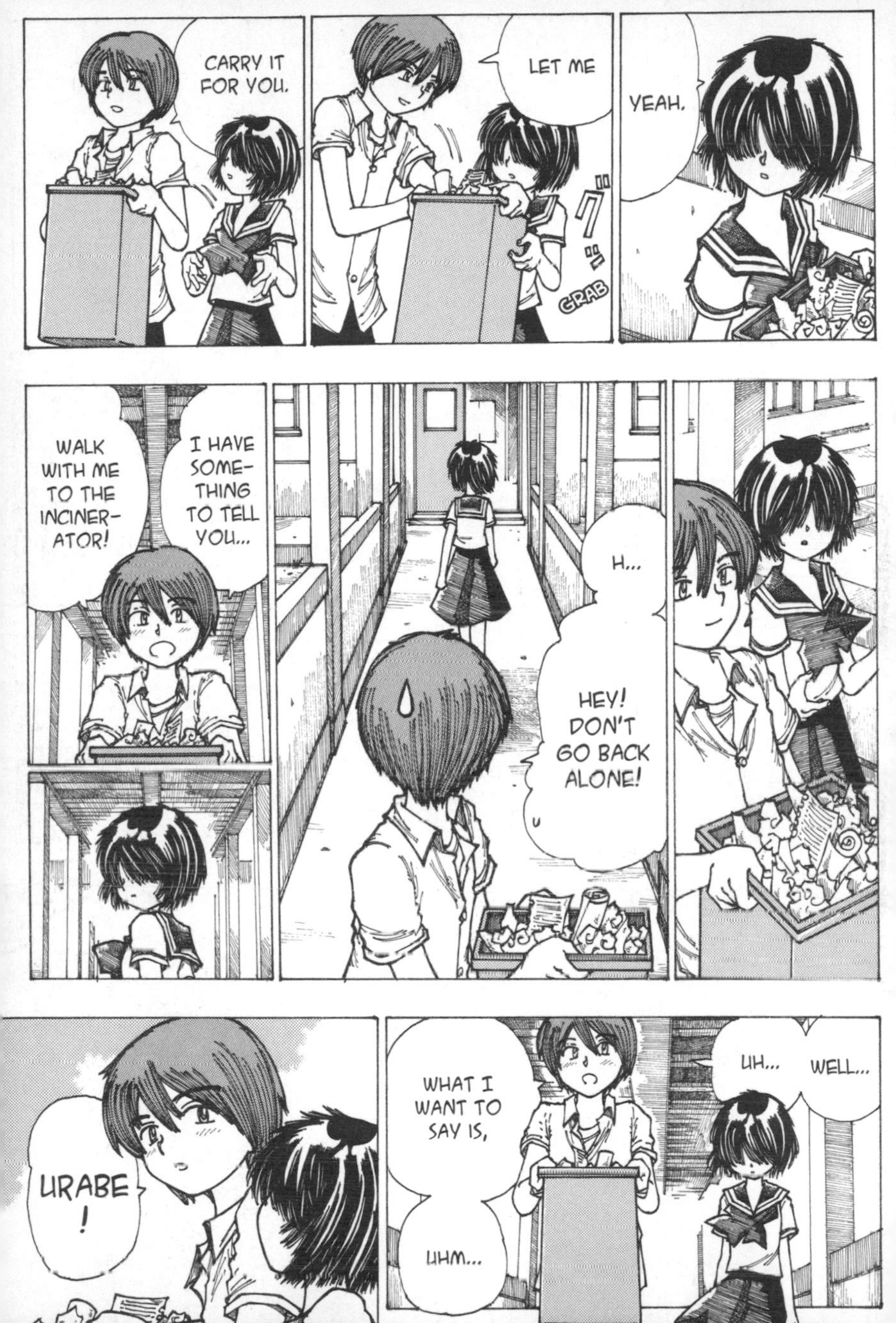
YEAH.
LET ME
GRAB
CARRY IT FOR YOU.
H...
HEY! DON'T GO BACK ALONE!
I HAVE SOME-THING TO TELL YOU...
WALK WITH ME TO THE INCINER-ATOR!
UH...
WELL...
WHAT I WANT TO SAY IS,
UHM...
URABE!

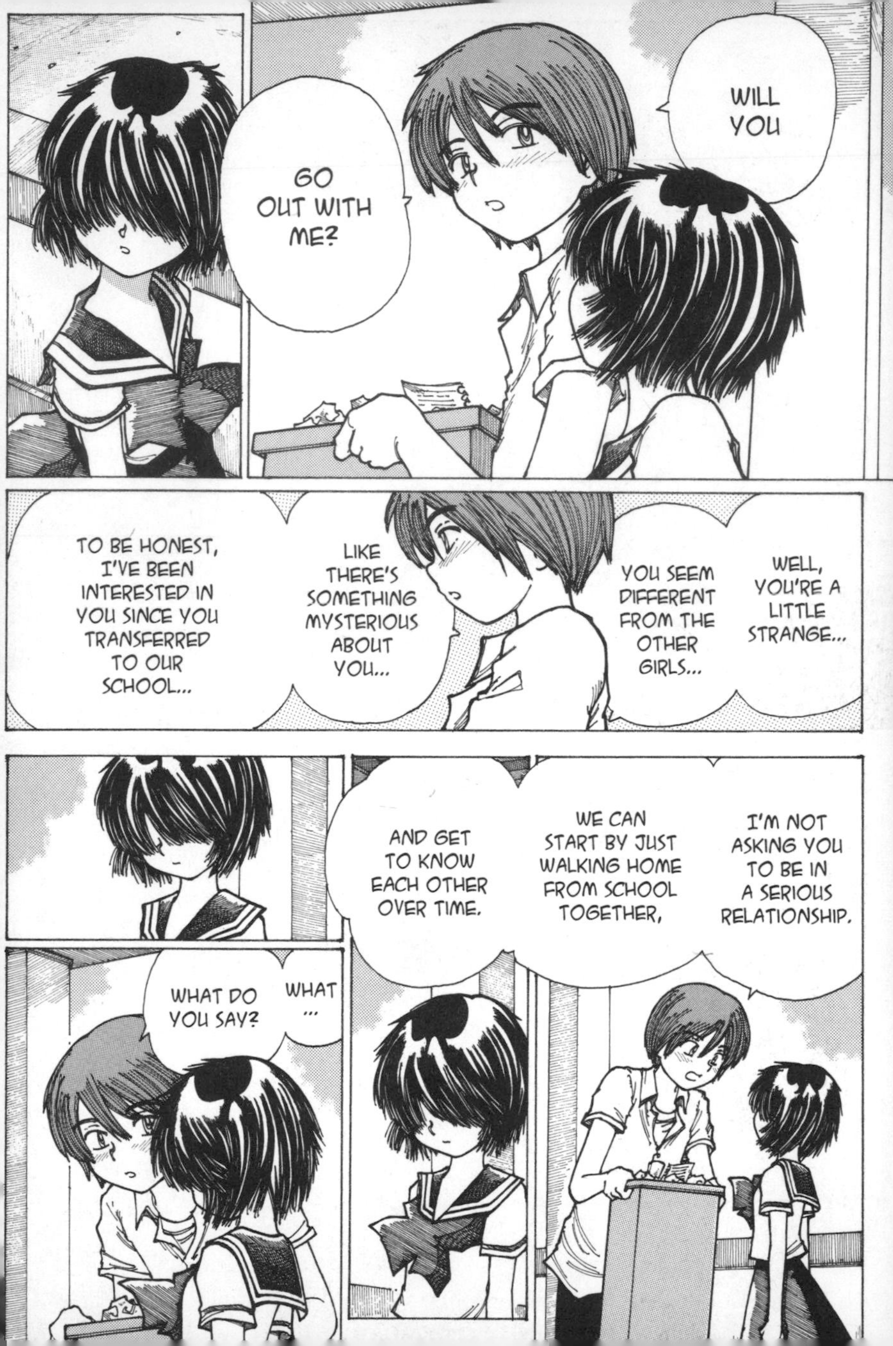
WILL YOU
GO OUT WITH ME?
WELL, YOU'RE A LITTLE STRANGE...
YOU SEEM DIFFERENT FROM THE OTHER GIRLS...
LIKE THERE'S SOMETHING MYSTERIOUS ABOUT YOU...
TO BE HONEST, I'VE BEEN INTERESTED IN YOU SINCE YOU TRANSFERRED TO OUR SCHOOL...
I'M NOT ASKING YOU TO BE IN A SERIOUS RELATIONSHIP.
WE CAN START BY JUST WALKING HOME FROM SCHOOL TOGETHER,
AND GET TO KNOW EACH OTHER OVER TIME.
WHAT ...
WHAT DO YOU SAY?

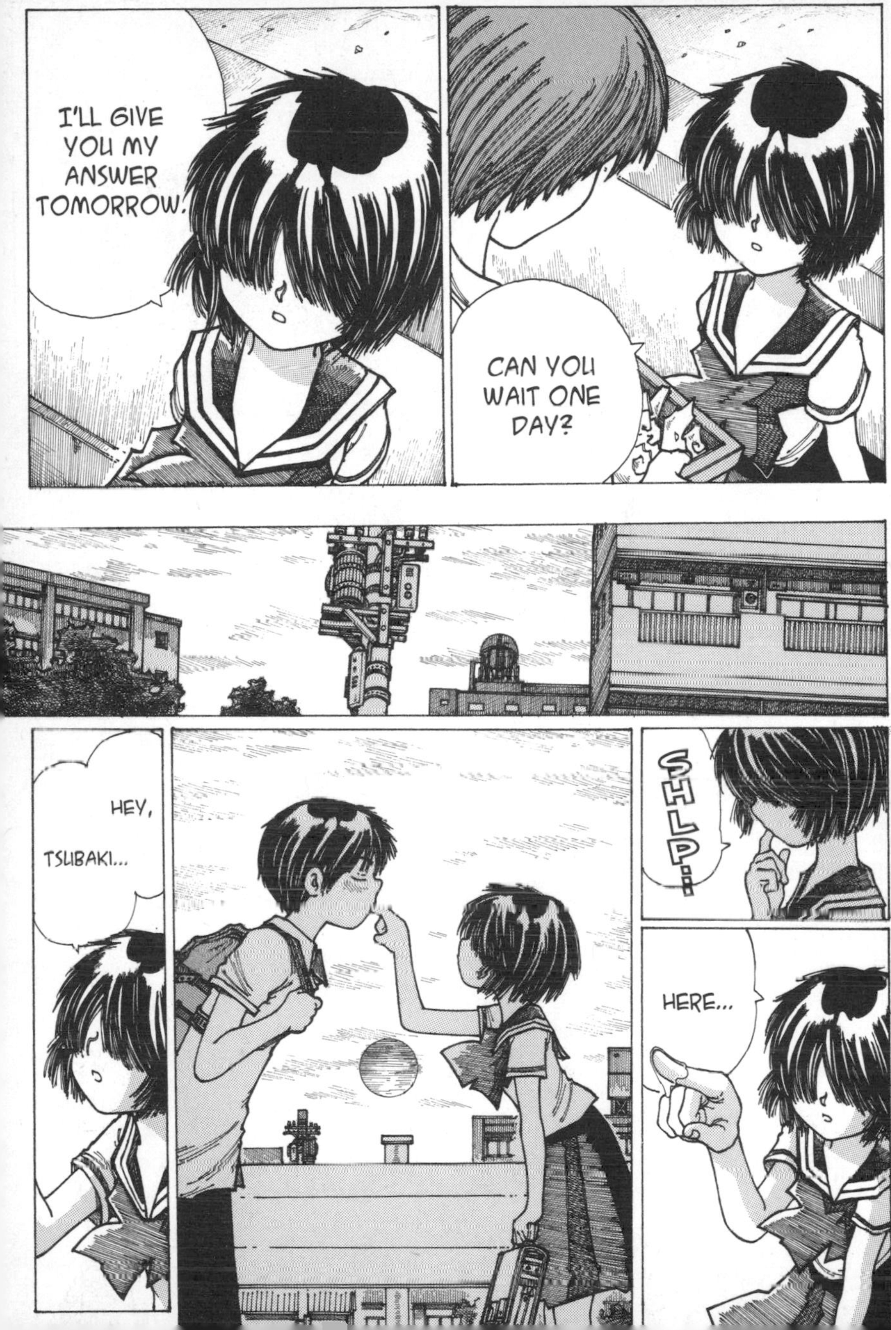
CAN YOU WAIT ONE DAY?
I'LL GIVE YOU MY ANSWER TOMORROW.
SHLP!
HERE...
HEY,
TSUBAKI...

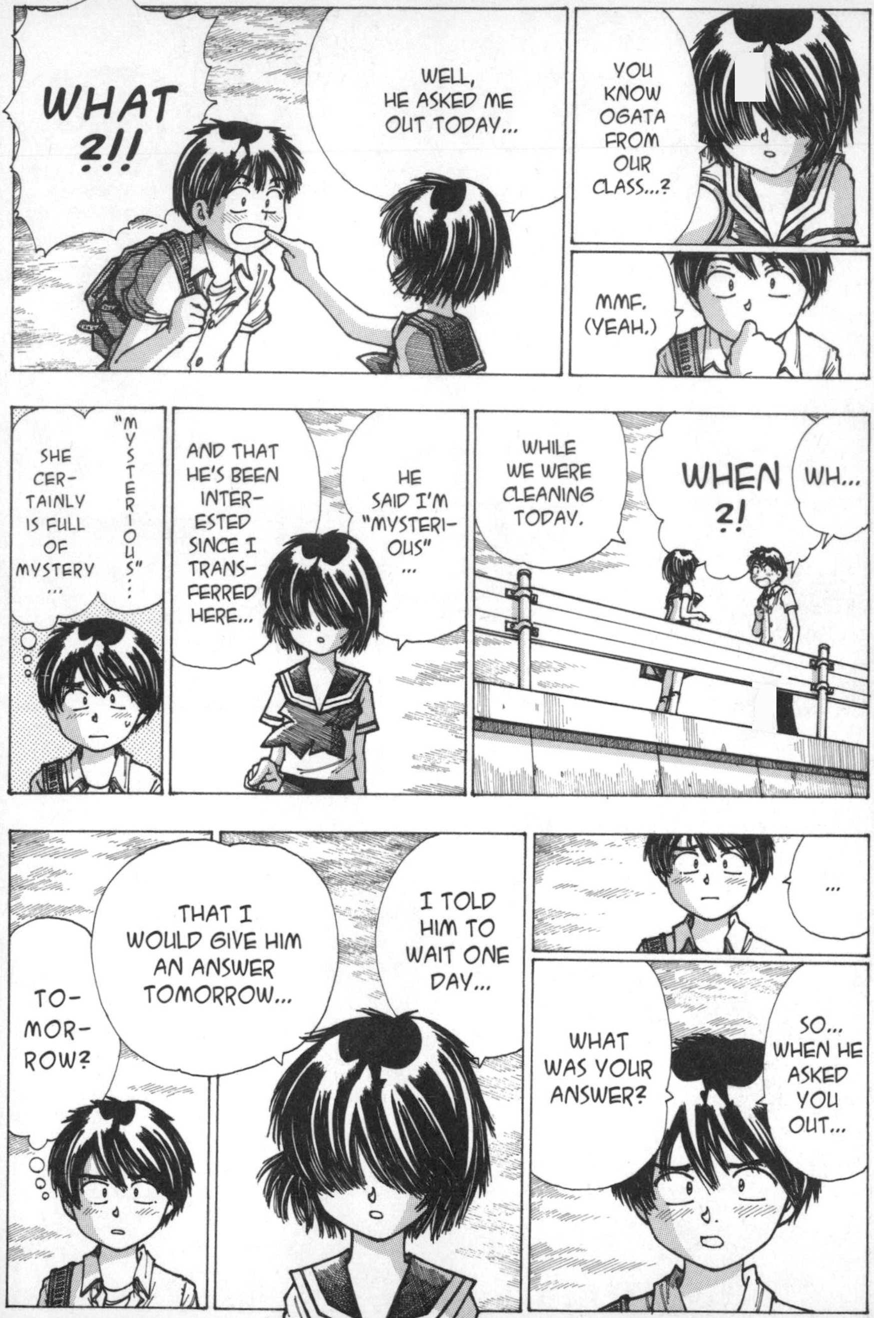
YOU KNOW OGATA FROM OUR CLASS...?
MMF. (YEAH.)
WELL, HE ASKED ME OUT TODAY...
WHAT ?!!
WH...
WHEN ?!
WHILE WE WERE CLEANING TODAY.
HE SAID I'M "MYSTERIOUS"...
AND THAT HE'S BEEN INTERESTED SINCE I TRANSFERRED HERE...
"MYSTERIOUS"...
SHE CERTAINLY IS FULL OF MYSTERY...
...
SO... WHEN HE ASKED YOU OUT...
WHAT WAS YOUR ANSWER?
I TOLD HIM TO WAIT ONE DAY...
THAT I WOULD GIVE HIM AN ANSWER TOMORROW...
TOMORROW?

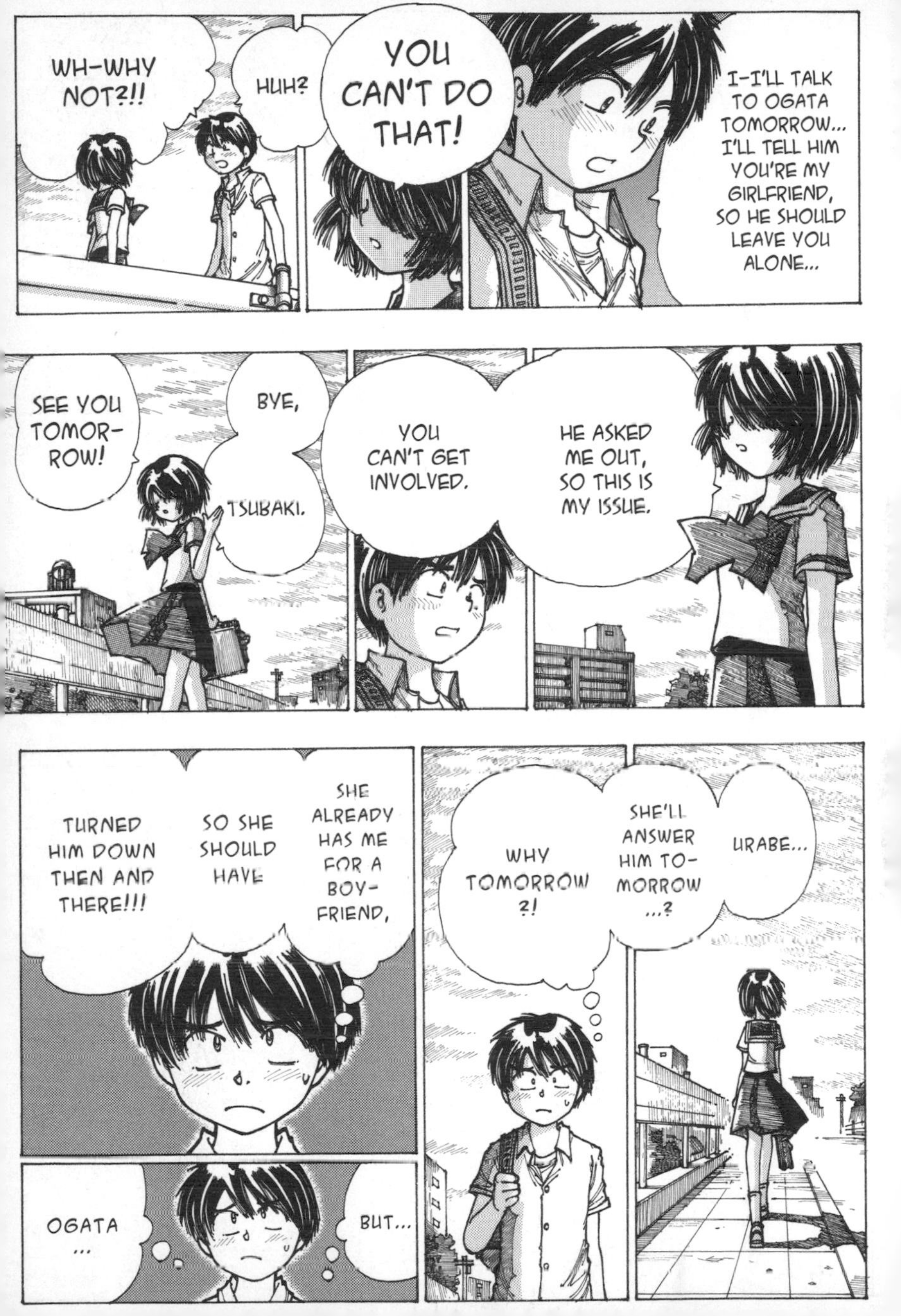
I-I'LL TALK TO OGATA TOMORROW... I'LL TELL HIM YOU'RE MY GIRLFRIEND, SO HE SHOULD LEAVE YOU ALONE...
YOU CAN'T DO THAT!
HUH?
WH-WHY NOT?!!
HE ASKED ME OUT, SO THIS IS MY ISSUE.
YOU CAN'T GET INVOLVED.
BYE,
TSUBAKI.
SEE YOU TOMORROW!
URABE...
SHE'LL ANSWER HIM TOMORROW...?
WHY TOMORROW?!
SHE ALREADY HAS ME FOR A BOYFRIEND,
SO SHE SHOULD HAVE
TURNED HIM DOWN THEN AND THERE!!!
BUT...
OGATA...

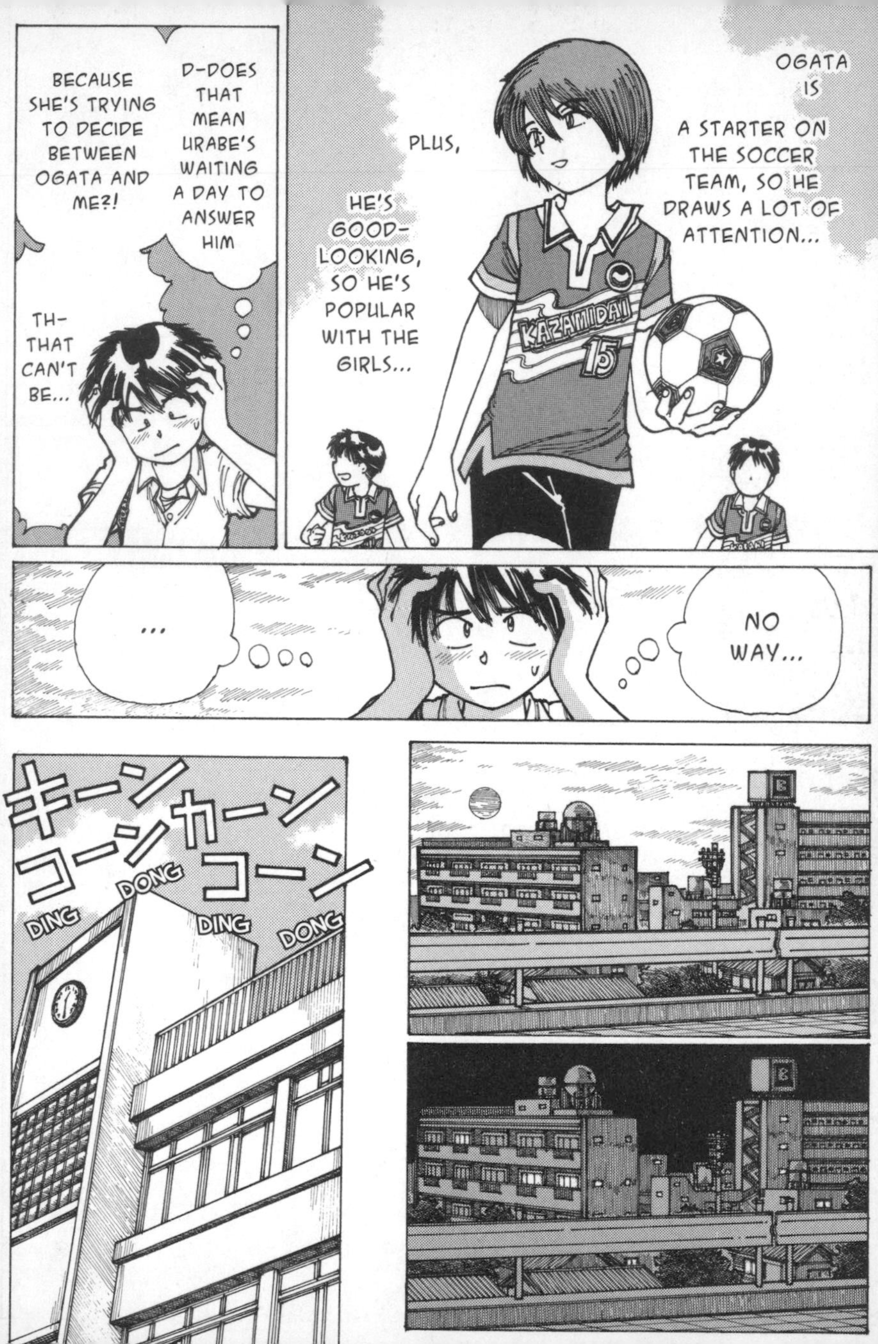
OGATA IS
A STARTER ON THE SOCCER TEAM, SO HE DRAWS A LOT OF ATTENTION...
PLUS,
HE'S GOOD-LOOKING, SO HE'S POPULAR WITH THE GIRLS...
KAZAMIDAI 15
D-DOES THAT MEAN URABE'S WAITING A DAY TO ANSWER HIM
BECAUSE SHE'S TRYING TO DECIDE BETWEEN OGATA AND ME?!
TH-THAT CAN'T BE...
NO WAY...
...
キーンコーンカーンコーン
DING DONG DING DONG

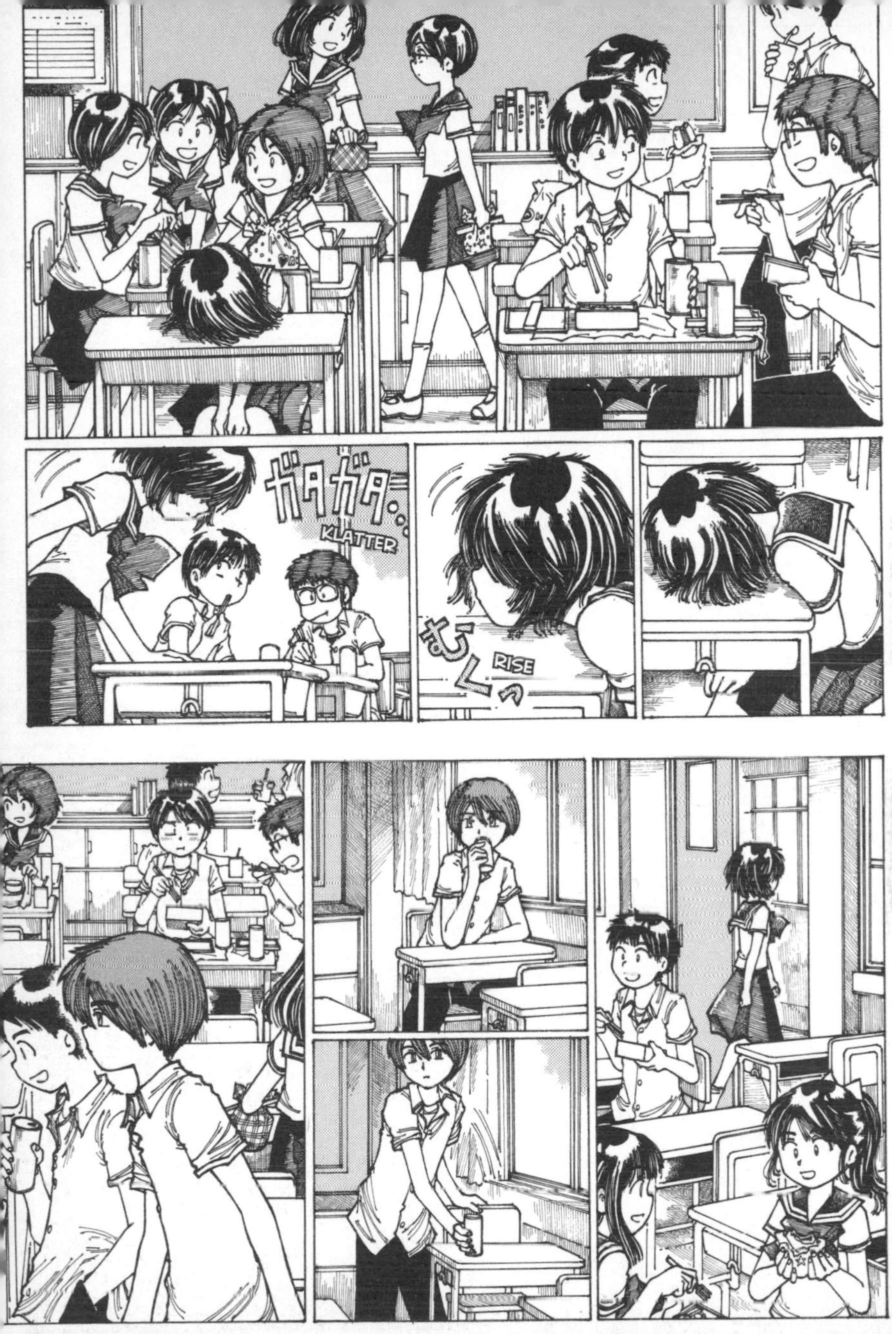
むくっ
RISE
ガタガタ
KLATTER

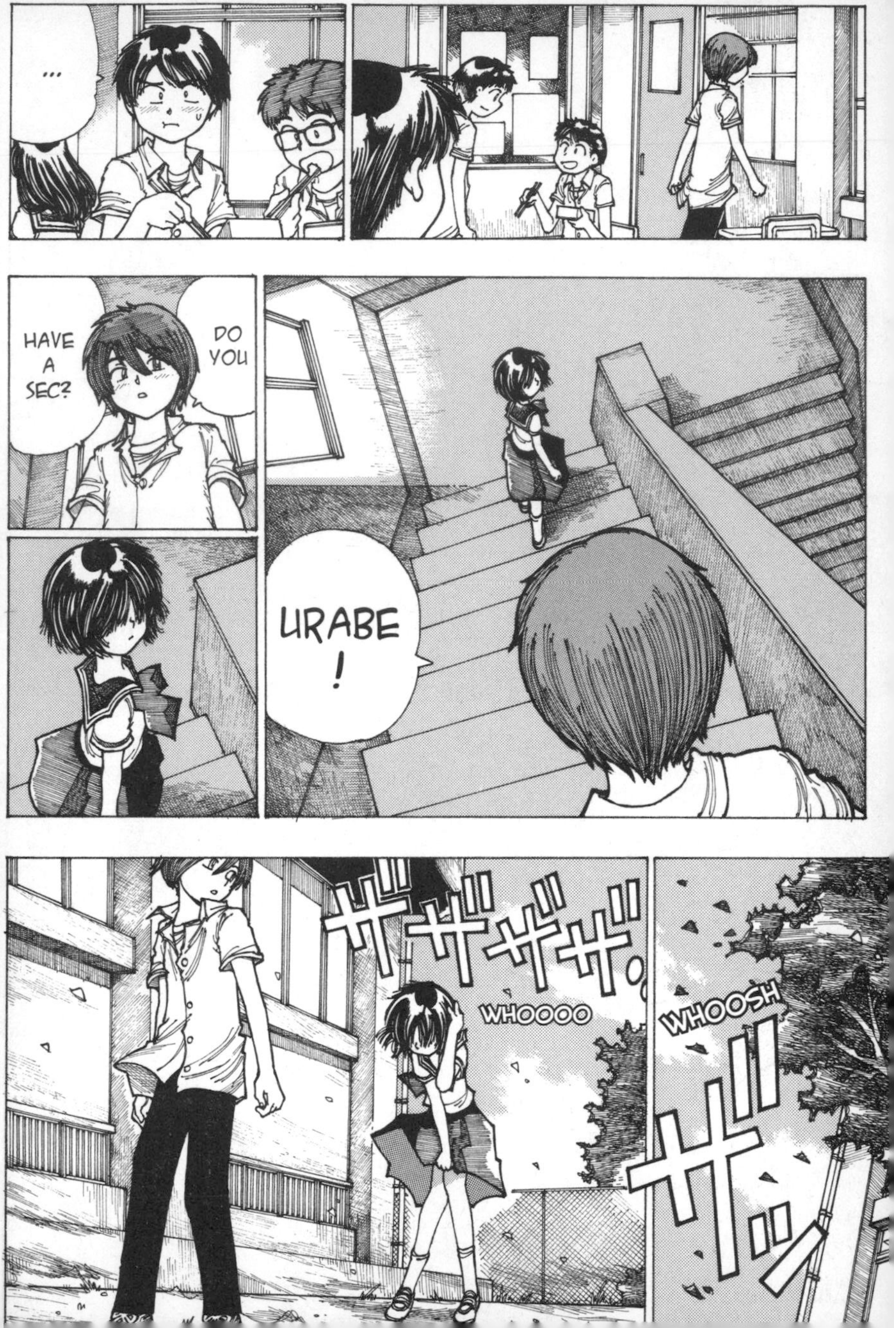
...
URABE
!
DO YOU
HAVE A SEC?
WHOOSH
ザッ
ザザザザ。
WHOOOO

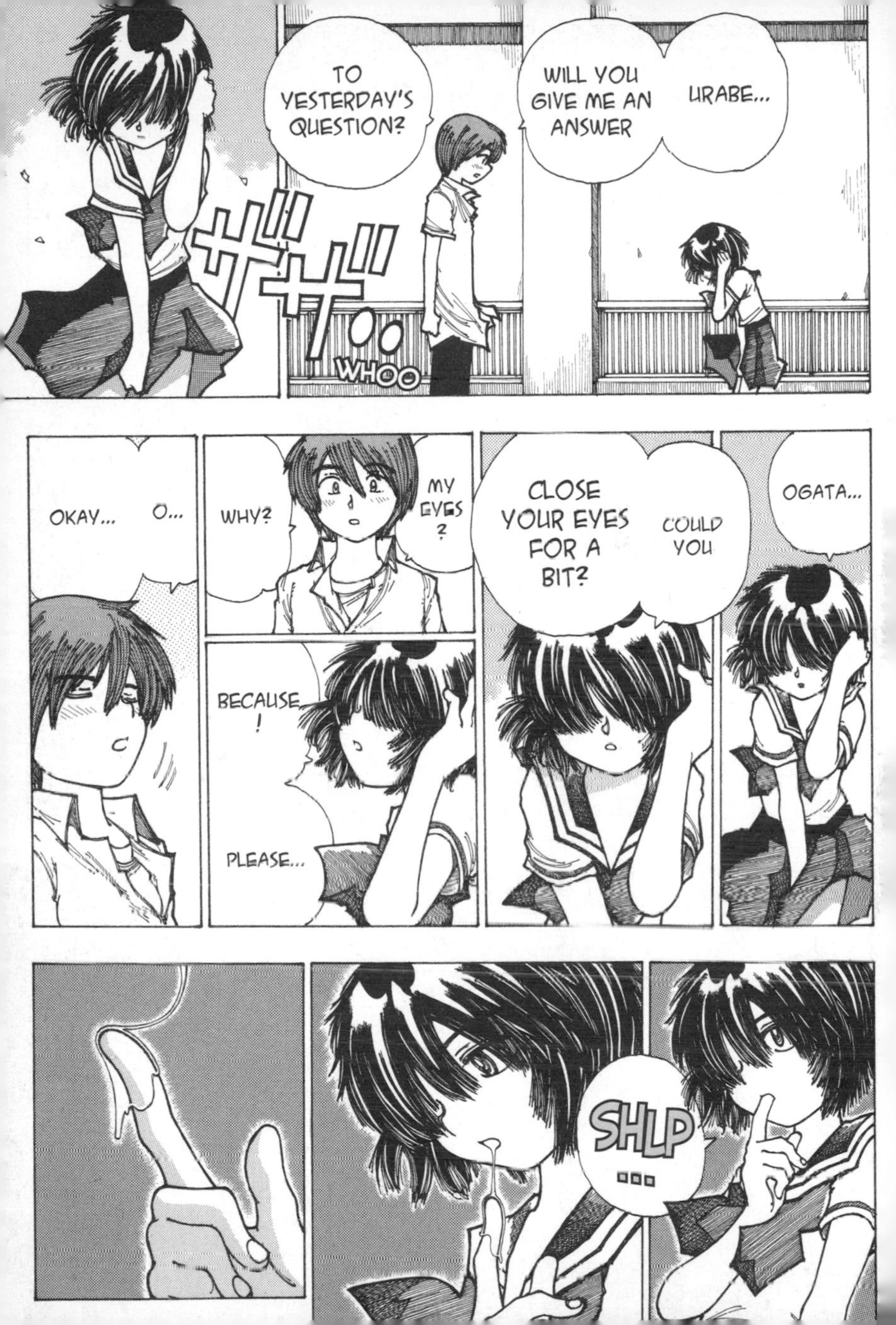
URABE...
WILL YOU GIVE ME AN ANSWER
TO YESTERDAY'S QUESTION?
WHOO
OGATA...
COULD YOU
CLOSE YOUR EYES FOR A BIT?
MY EYES?
WHY?
BECAUSE!
PLEASE...
O...
OKAY...
...
SHLP

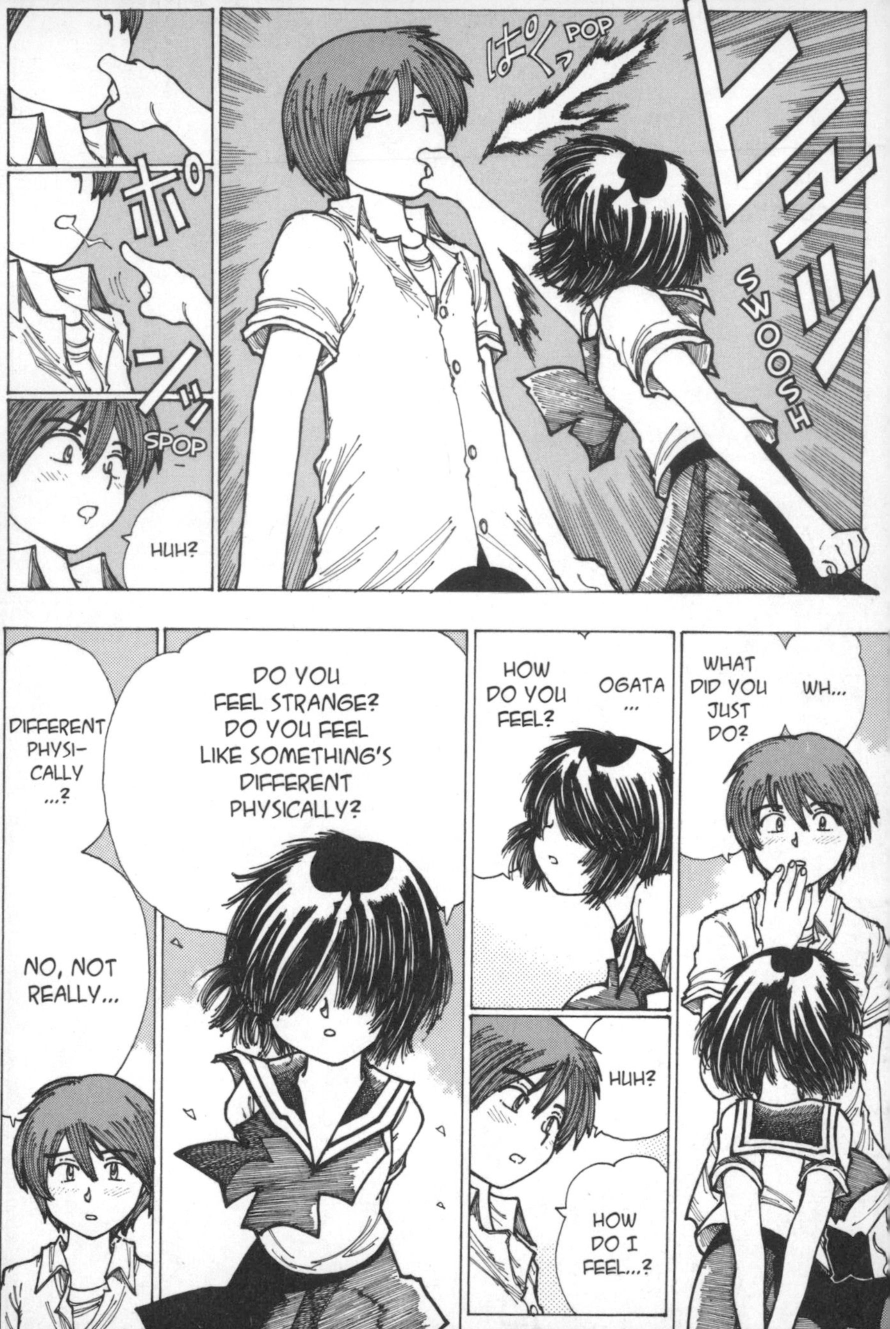

POP
SWOOSH
SPOP
HUH?
WH...
WHAT DID YOU JUST DO?
OGATA...
HOW DO YOU FEEL?
HUH?
HOW DO I FEEL...?
DO YOU FEEL STRANGE? DO YOU FEEL LIKE SOMETHING'S DIFFERENT PHYSICALLY?
DIFFERENT PHYSICALLY...?
NO, NOT REALLY...

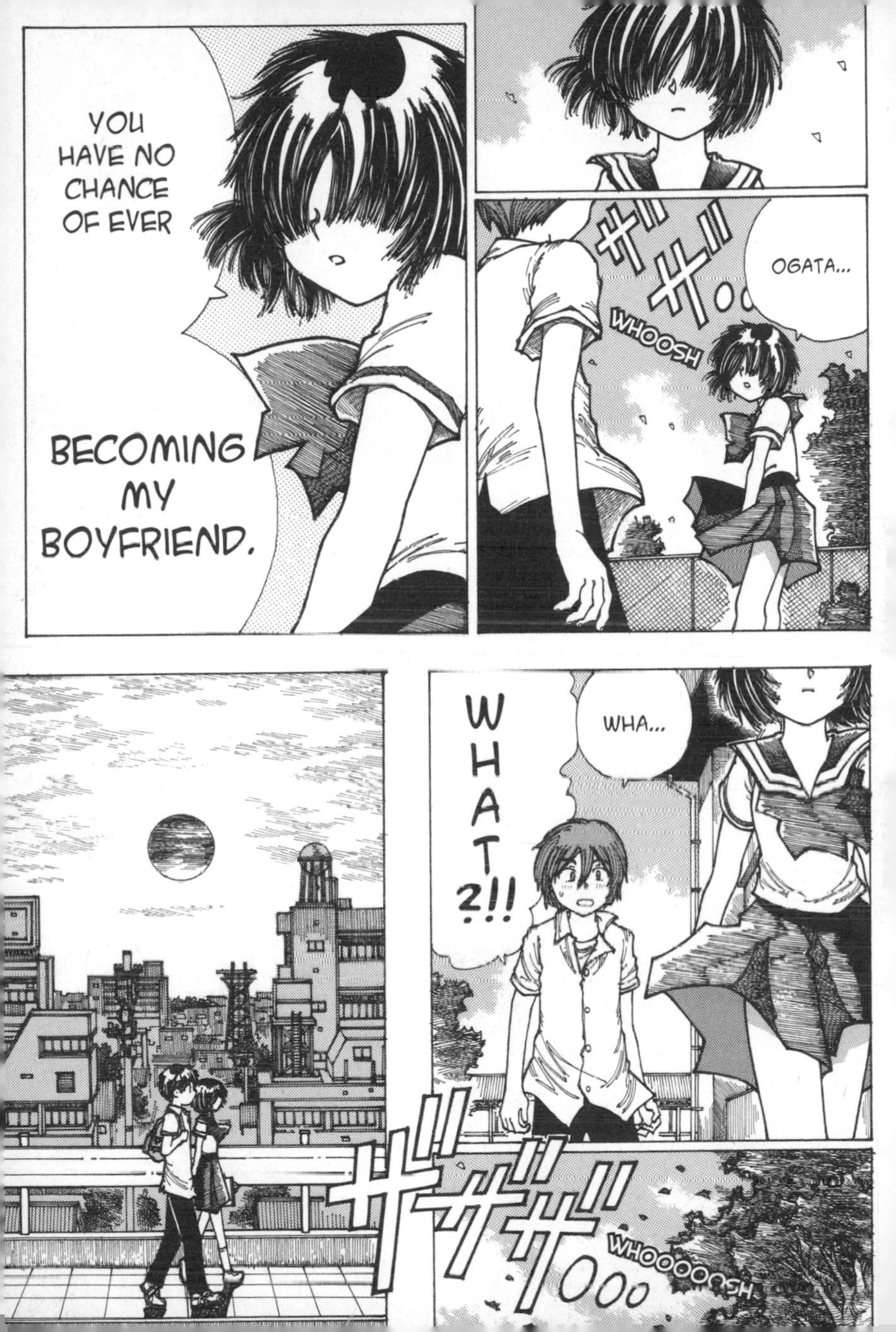
OGATA...
WHOOSH
YOU HAVE NO CHANCE OF EVER
BECOMING MY BOYFRIEND.
WHA...
WHAT?!!
WHOOOOOOSH

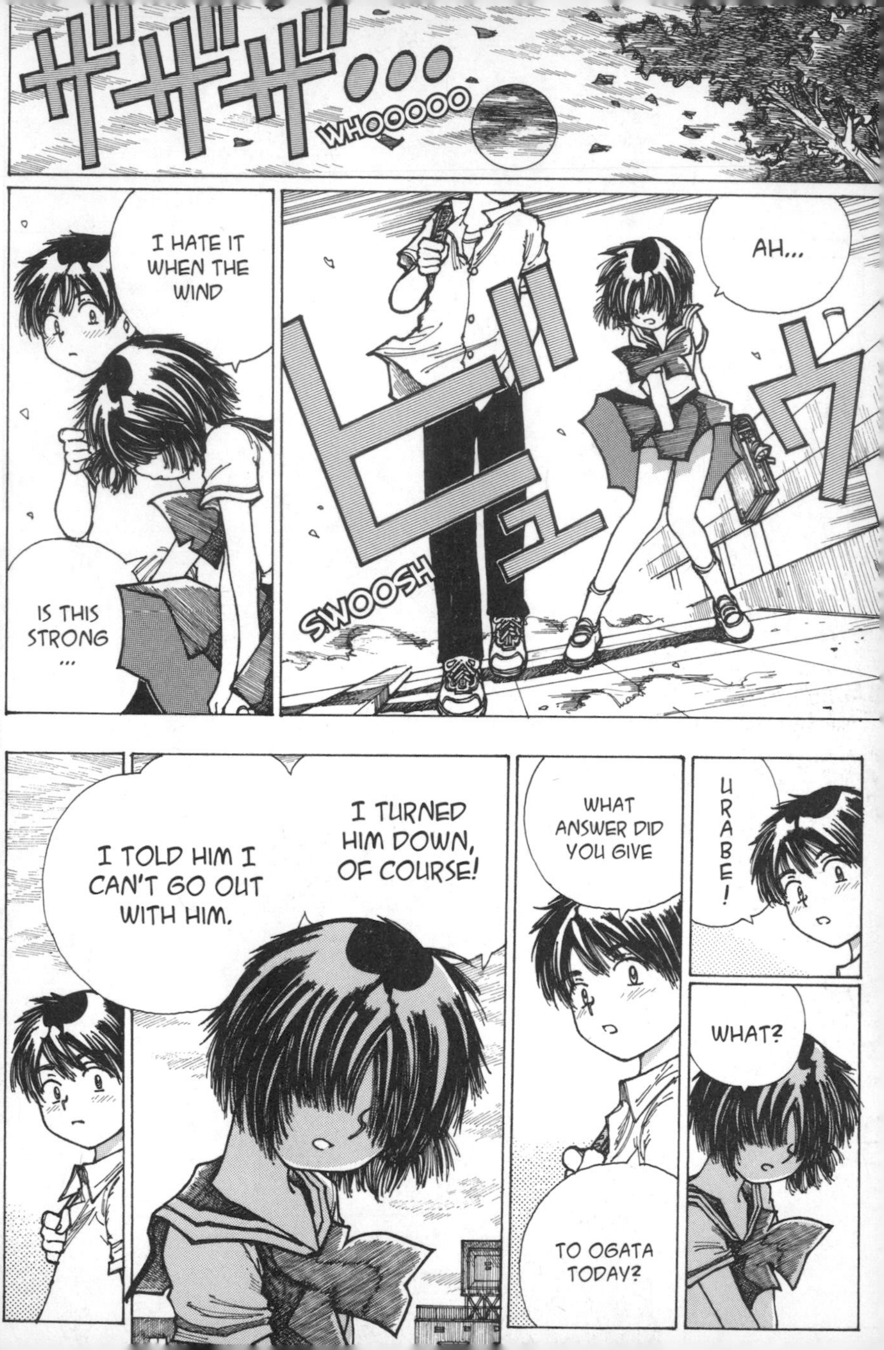
ザザザ○○○
WHOOOOO
AH...
ビュウ
SWOOSH
I HATE IT WHEN THE WIND
IS THIS STRONG ...
URABE!
WHAT?
WHAT ANSWER DID YOU GIVE
TO OGATA TODAY?
I TURNED HIM DOWN, OF COURSE!
I TOLD HIM I CAN'T GO OUT WITH HIM.

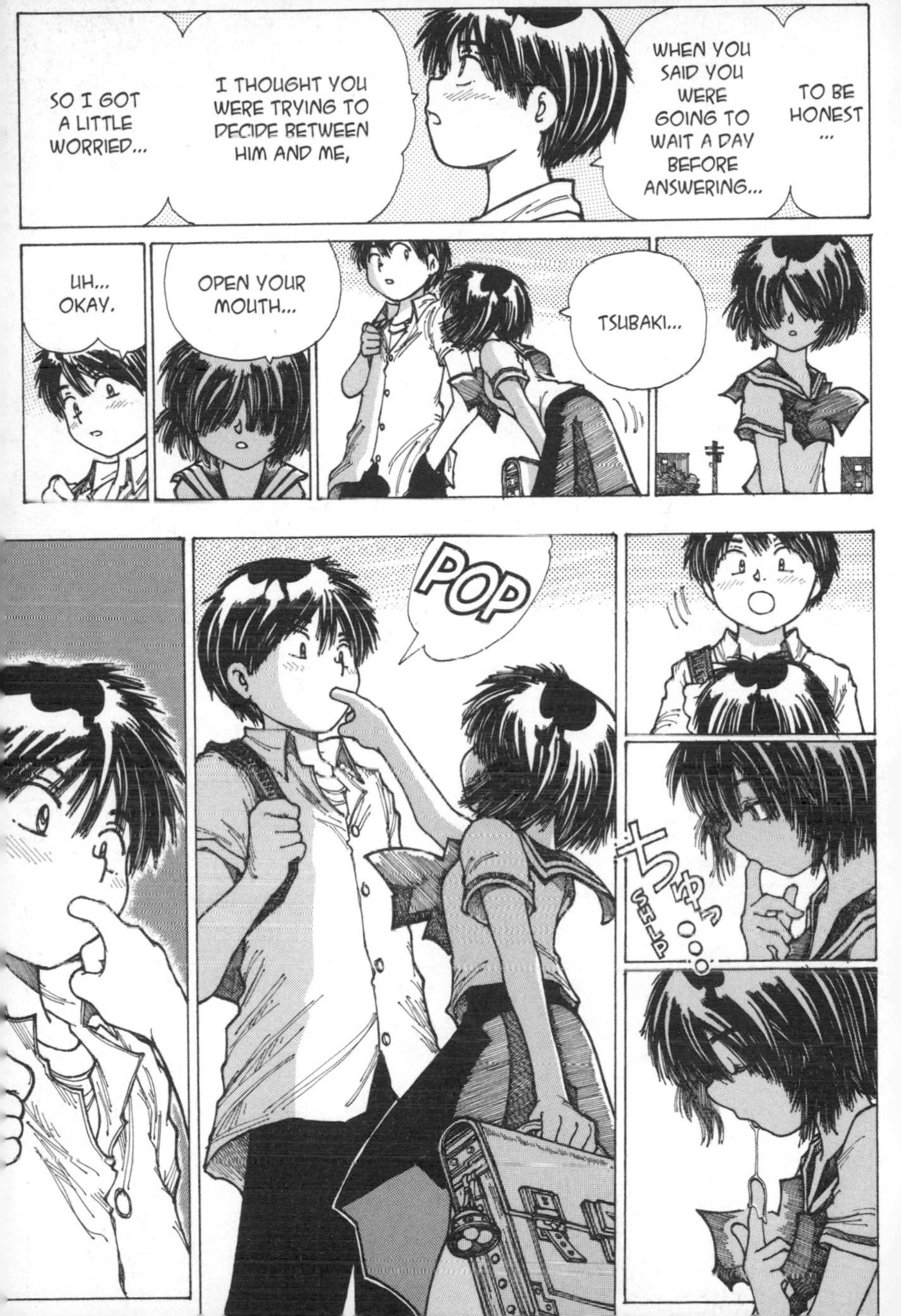
TO BE HONEST ...
WHEN YOU SAID YOU WERE GOING TO WAIT A DAY BEFORE ANSWERING...
I THOUGHT YOU WERE TRYING TO DECIDE BETWEEN HIM AND ME,
SO I GOT A LITTLE WORRIED...
TSUBAKI...
OPEN YOUR MOUTH...
UH... OKAY.
ちゅっ
SHLP
POP

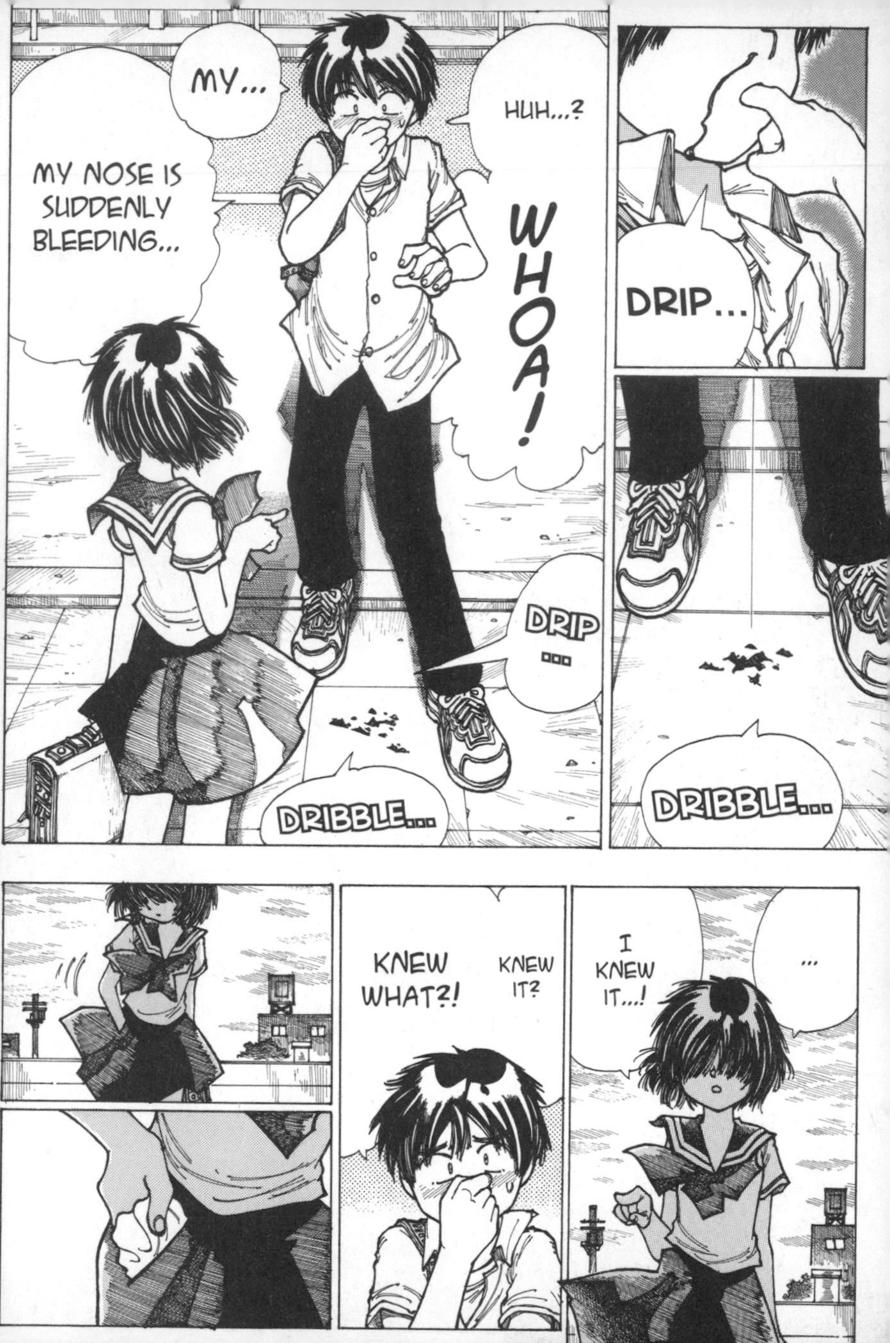
DRIP...
DRIBBLE...
HUH...?
WHOA!
MY...
MY NOSE IS SUDDENLY BLEEDING...
DRIP ...
DRIBBLE...
...
I KNEW IT...!
KNEW IT?
KNEW WHAT?!

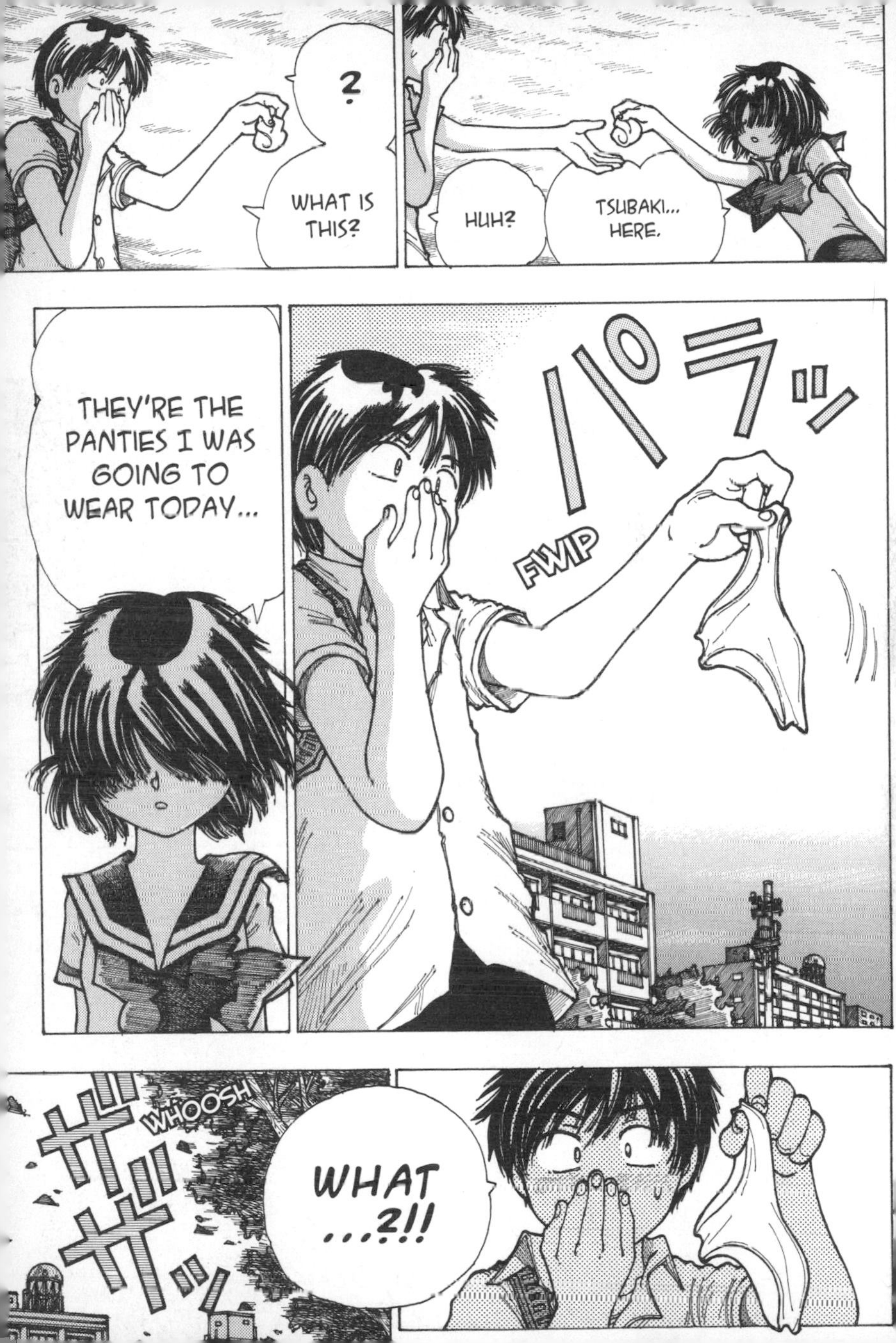
TSUBAKI... HERE.
HUH?
?
WHAT IS THIS?
パラッ
FWIP
THEY'RE THE PANTIES I WAS GOING TO WEAR TODAY...
WHAT ...?!!
ザザッ
WHOOSH

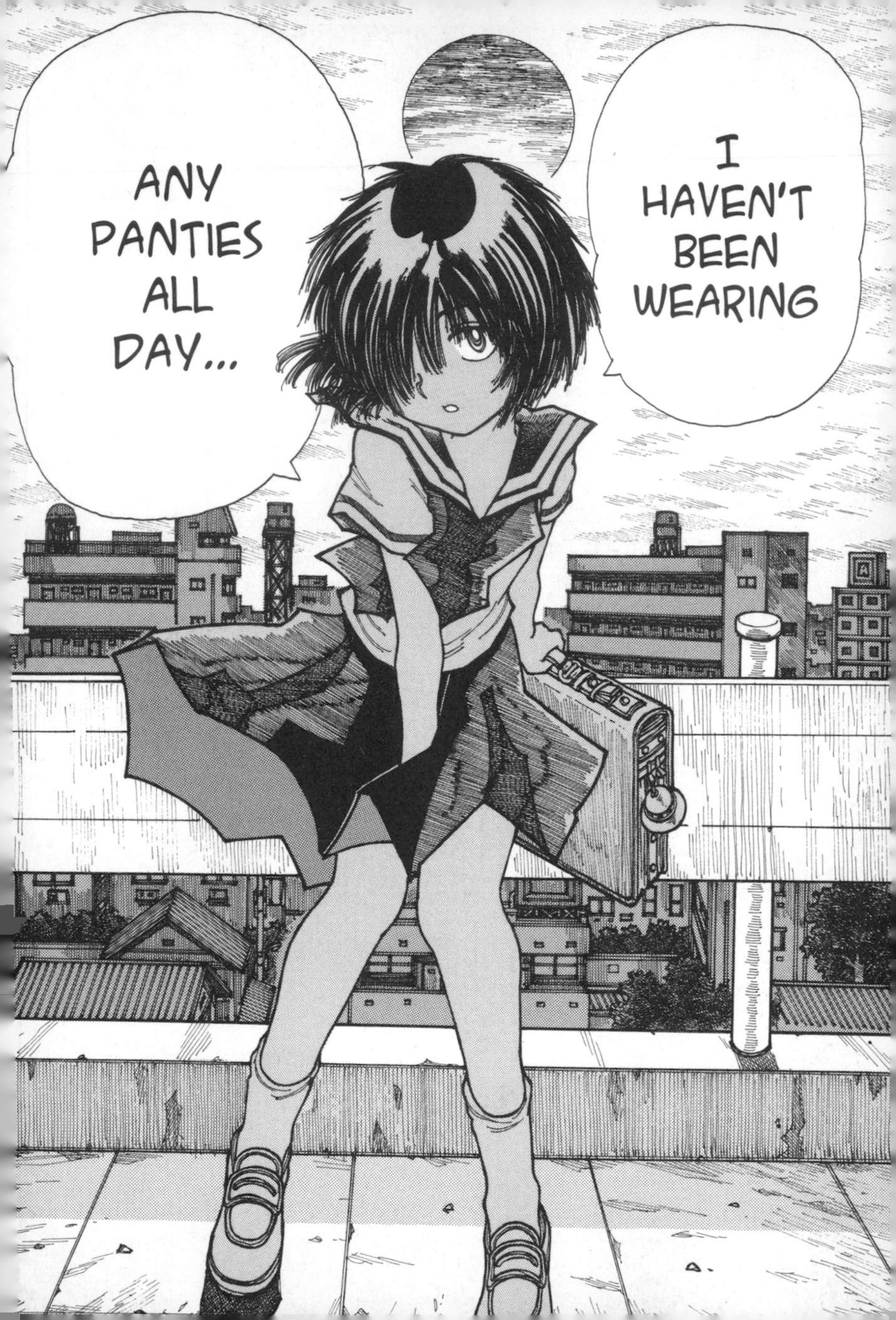
I HAVEN'T BEEN WEARING
ANY PANTIES ALL DAY...

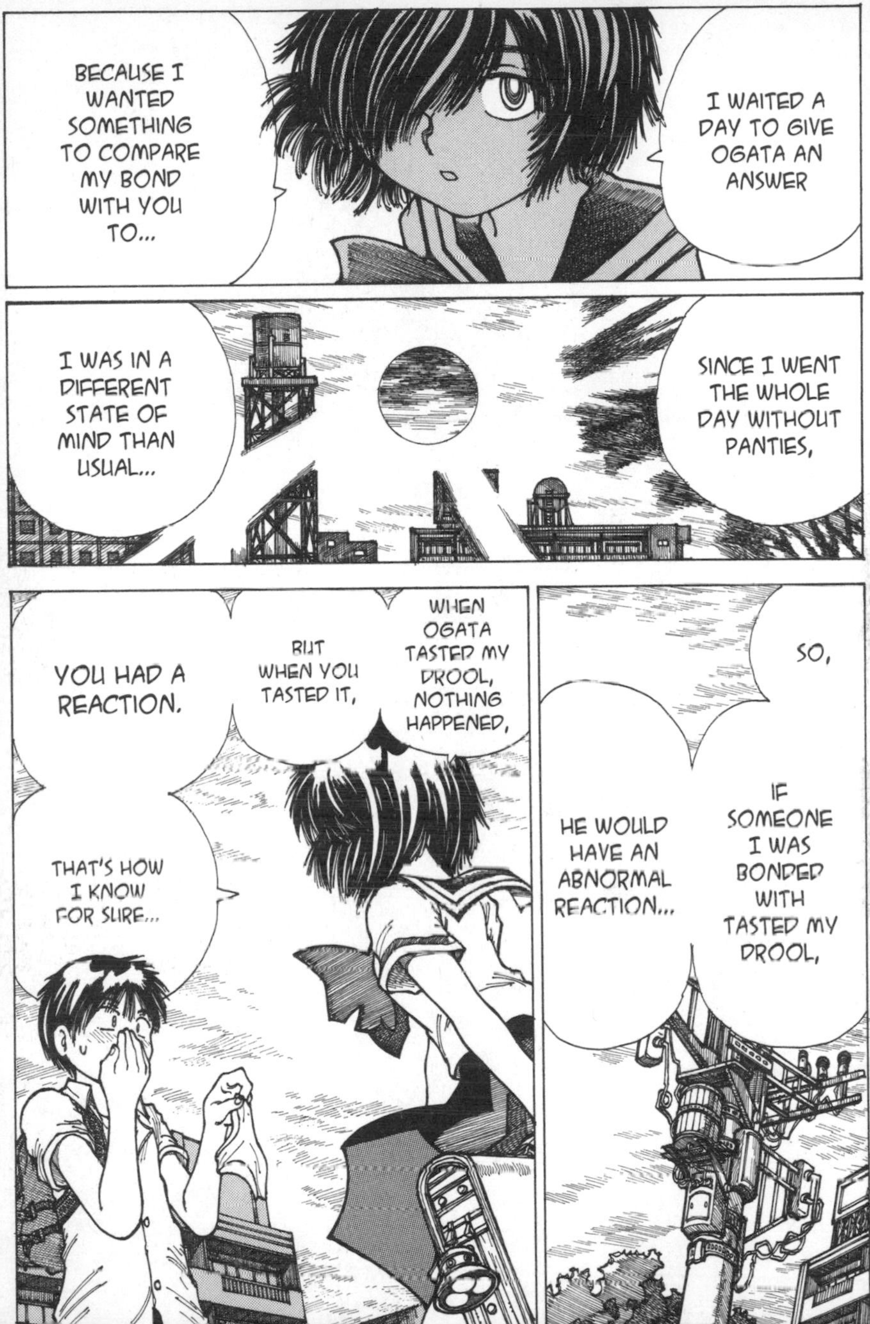
I WAITED A DAY TO GIVE OGATA AN ANSWER
BECAUSE I WANTED SOMETHING TO COMPARE MY BOND WITH YOU TO...
SINCE I WENT THE WHOLE DAY WITHOUT PANTIES,
I WAS IN A DIFFERENT STATE OF MIND THAN USUAL...
SO,
IF SOMEONE I WAS BONDED WITH TASTED MY DROOL,
HE WOULD HAVE AN ABNORMAL REACTION...
WHEN OGATA TASTED MY DROOL, NOTHING HAPPENED,
BUT WHEN YOU TASTED IT,
YOU HAD A REACTION.
THAT'S HOW I KNOW FOR SURE...

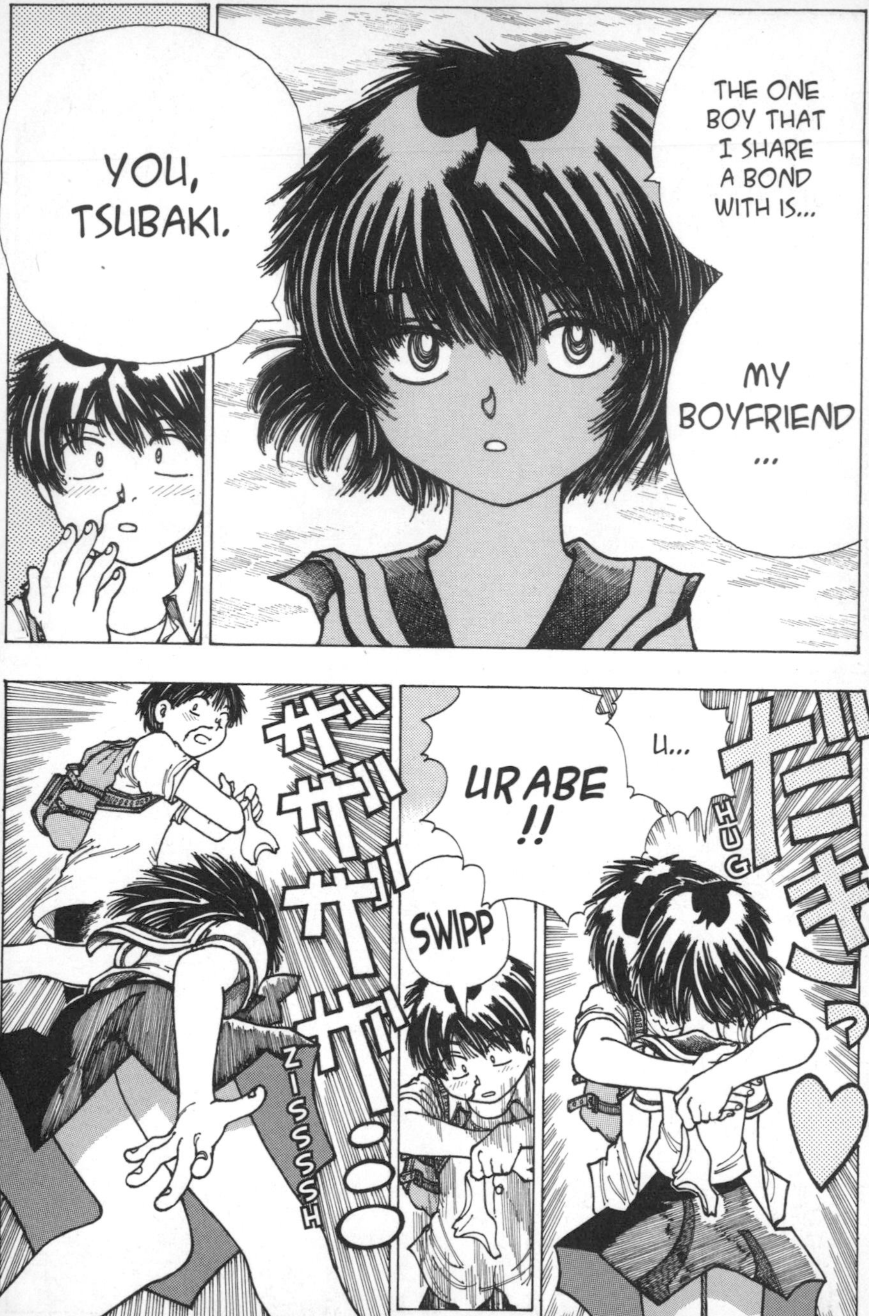
THE ONE BOY THAT I SHARE A BOND WITH IS...
MY BOYFRIEND ...
YOU, TSUBAKI.
U...
HUG
URABE !!
SWIPP
ZISSSSSH

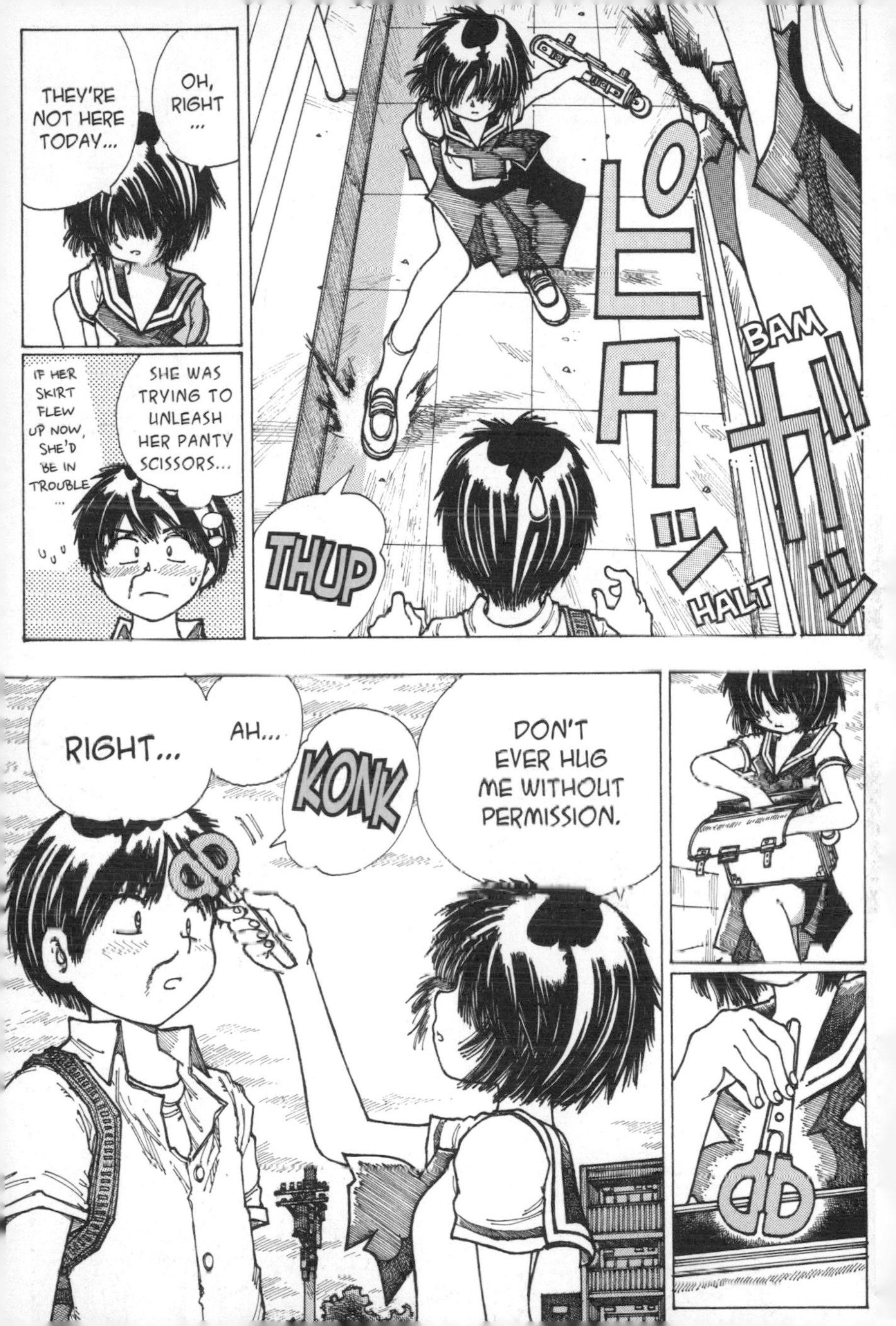
BAM
HALT
THUP
OH, RIGHT ...
THEY'RE NOT HERE TODAY...
SHE WAS TRYING TO UNLEASH HER PANTY SCISSORS...
IF HER SKIRT FLEW UP NOW, SHE'D BE IN TROUBLE ...
DON'T EVER HUG ME WITHOUT PERMISSION.
KONK
AH...
RIGHT...

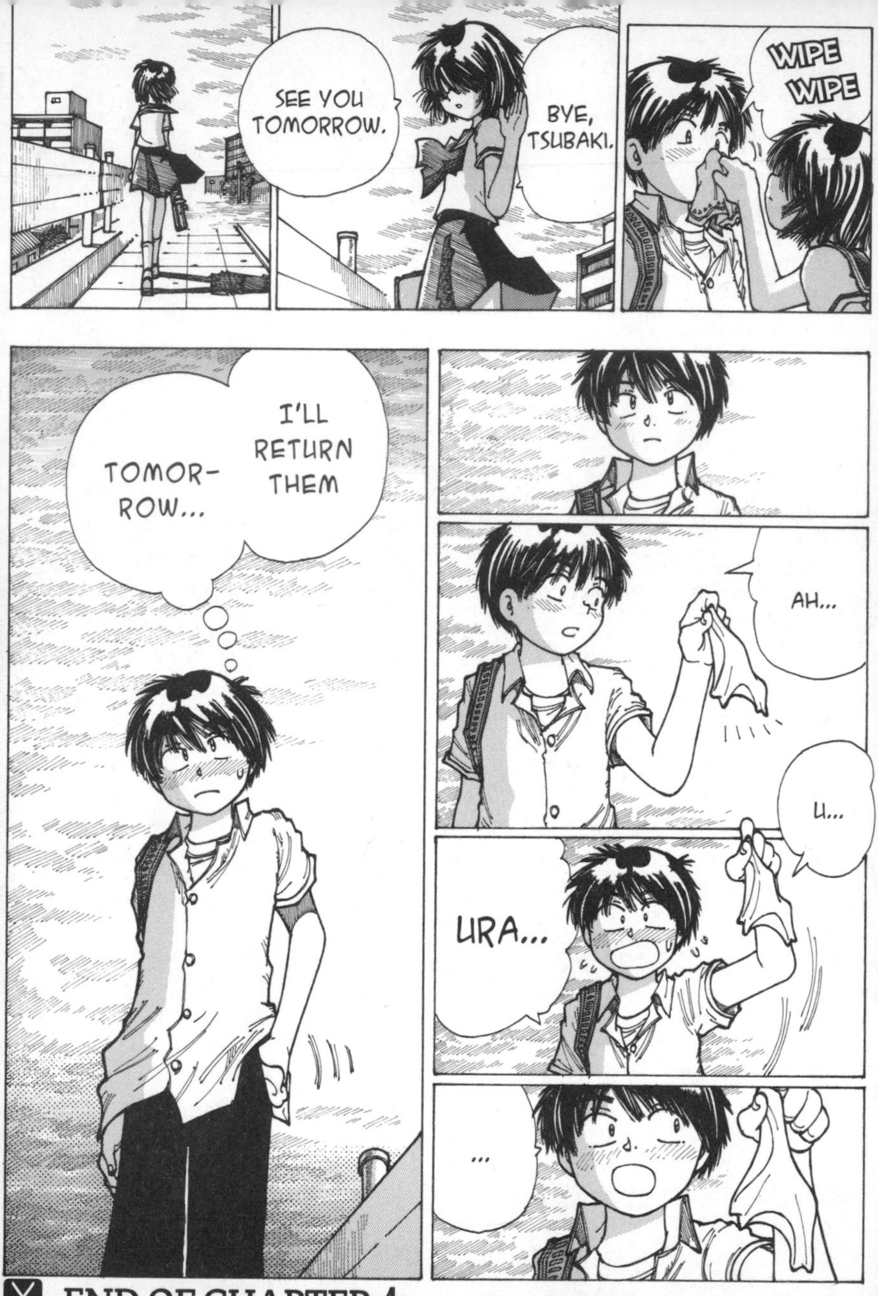
WIPE WIPE
BYE, TSUBAKI.
SEE YOU TOMORROW.
AH...
U...
URA...
...
I'LL RETURN THEM
TOMOR-ROW...

END OF CHAPTER 4

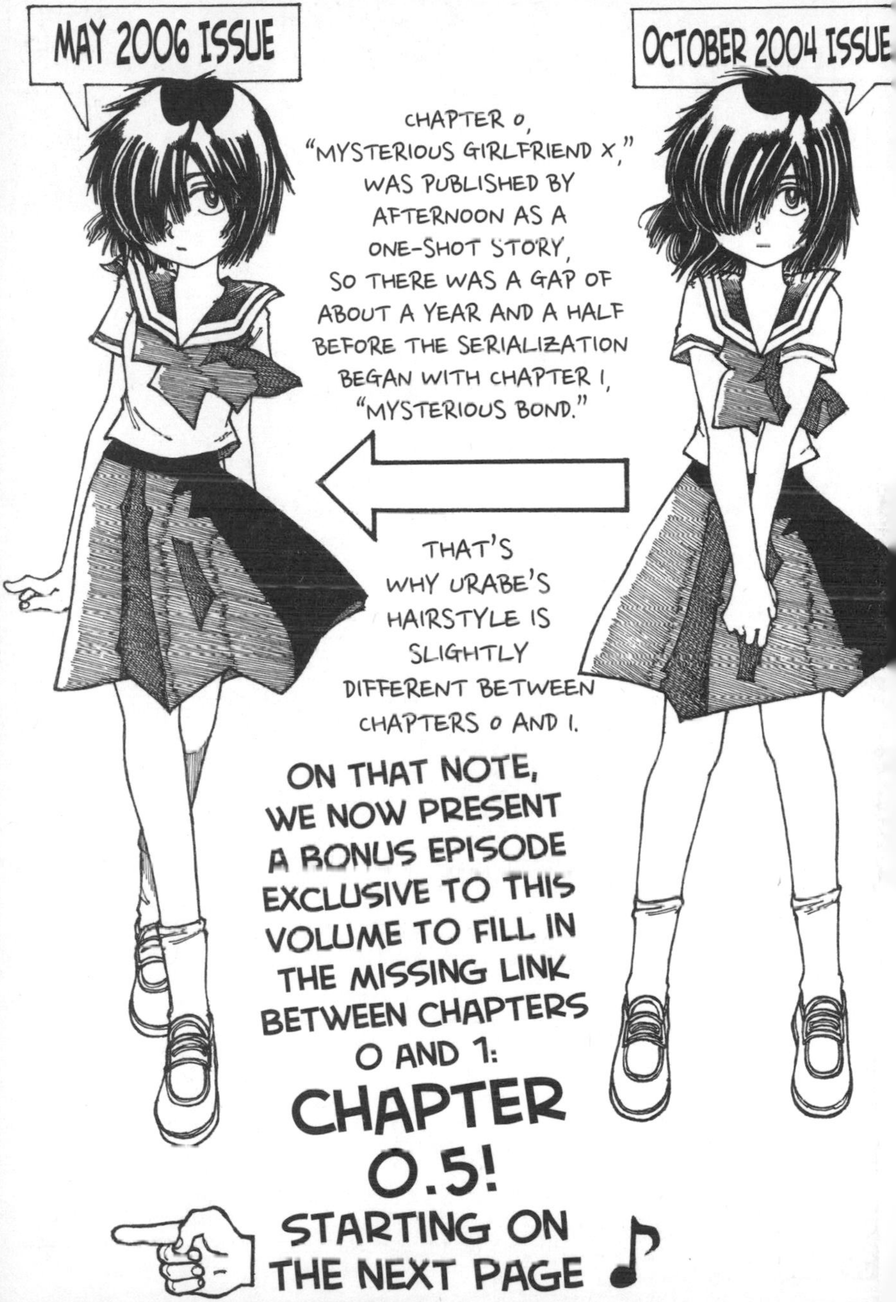
OCTOBER 2004 ISSUE
MAY 2006 ISSUE
CHAPTER 0, "MYSTERIOUS GIRLFRIEND X," WAS PUBLISHED BY AFTERNOON AS A ONE-SHOT STORY, SO THERE WAS A GAP OF ABOUT A YEAR AND A HALF BEFORE THE SERIALIZATION BEGAN WITH CHAPTER 1, "MYSTERIOUS BOND."
THAT'S WHY URABE'S HAIRSTYLE IS SLIGHTLY DIFFERENT BETWEEN CHAPTERS 0 AND 1.
ON THAT NOTE, WE NOW PRESENT A BONUS EPISODE EXCLUSIVE TO THIS VOLUME TO FILL IN THE MISSING LINK BETWEEN CHAPTERS 0 AND 1:
CHAPTER 0.5!
STARTING ON THE NEXT PAGE ♪

AN "UNIDENTIFIABLE ROMANCE" COMIC SURROUNDED IN MYSTERY

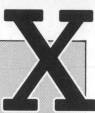

MYSTERIOUS GIRLFRIEND X

RIICHI UESHIBA

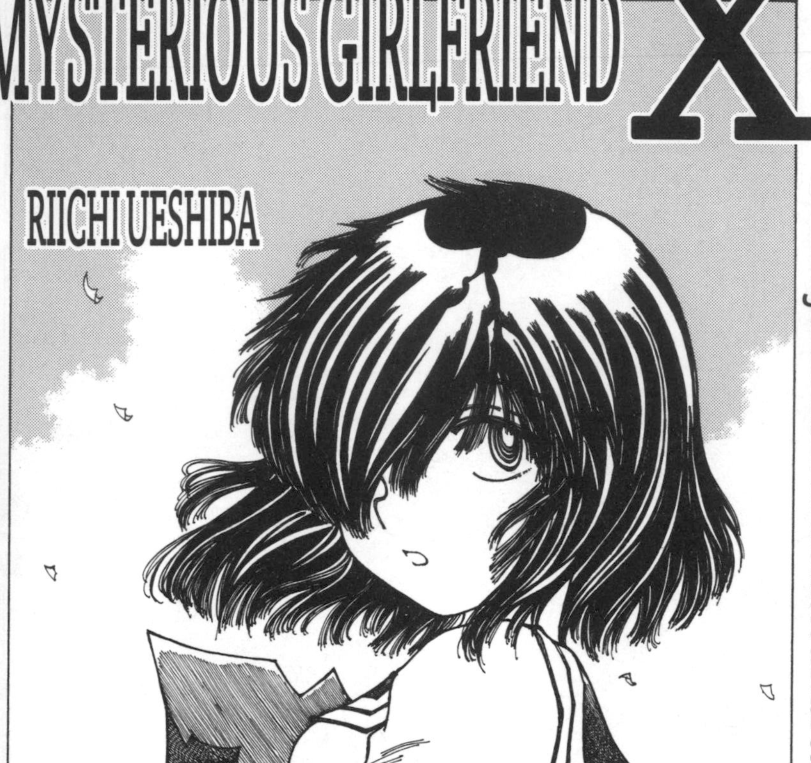
CHAPTER 0.5:
MYSTERIOUS HAIRCUT

The first girlfriend. Even the most trivial conversation feels new and fresh.

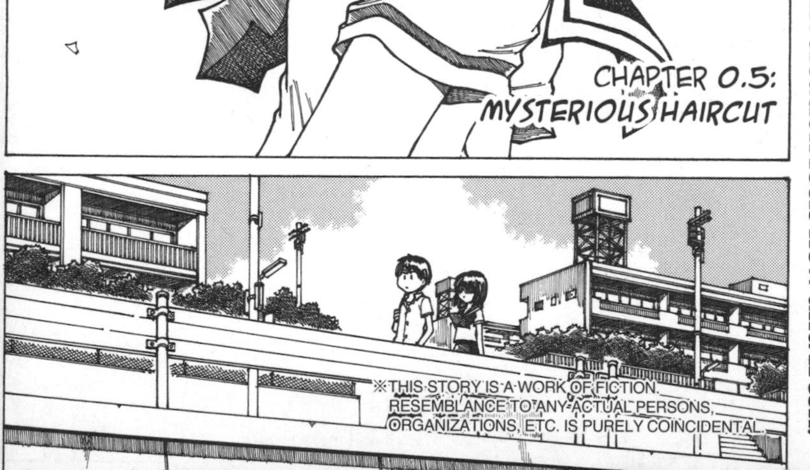
※THIS STORY IS A WORK OF FICTION.
RESEMBLANCE TO ANY ACTUAL PERSONS,
ORGANIZATIONS, ETC. IS PURELY COINCIDENTAL.

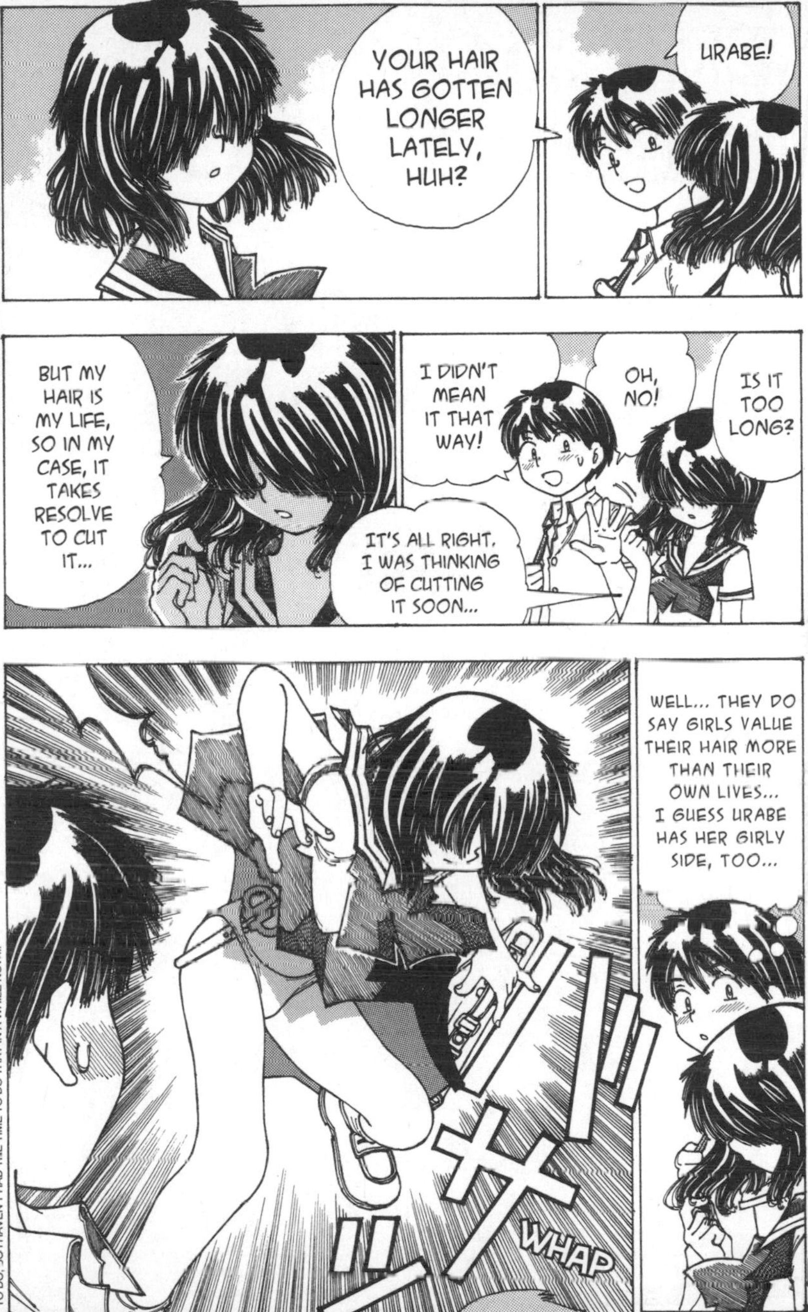
URABE!
YOUR HAIR HAS GOTTEN LONGER LATELY, HUH?
IS IT TOO LONG?
OH, NO!
I DIDN'T MEAN IT THAT WAY!
IT'S ALL RIGHT. I WAS THINKING OF CUTTING IT SOON...
BUT MY HAIR IS MY LIFE, SO IN MY CASE, IT TAKES RESOLVE TO CUT IT...
WELL... THEY DO SAY GIRLS VALUE THEIR HAIR MORE THAN THEIR OWN LIVES... I GUESS URABE HAS HER GIRLY SIDE, TOO...
WHAP

The Latest from the Author

Riichi Ueshiba

RECENTLY, I'VE BEEN GETTING INTO ALL 26 VOLUMES OF "HISTORY OF JAPAN" AND ALL 16 VOLUMES OF "HISTORY OF THE WORLD," PUBLISHED BY CHUOKORON-SHA. GOING TO THE LIBRARY IN THE MORNING WHEN IT'S DESERTED AND GAZING AT THE BOOKSHELVES, PONDERING WHETHER TO READ UP ON THE FRENCH REVOLUTION OR THE NANBOKUCHO WAR, MAKES ME FEEL HAPPY. OF COURSE EVEN AFTER I FINISHED WORKING ON THIS VOLUME, I HAD A LOT OF OTHER WORK TO DO, SO I HAVEN'T HAD THE TIME TO DO THAT IN A WHILE NOW...

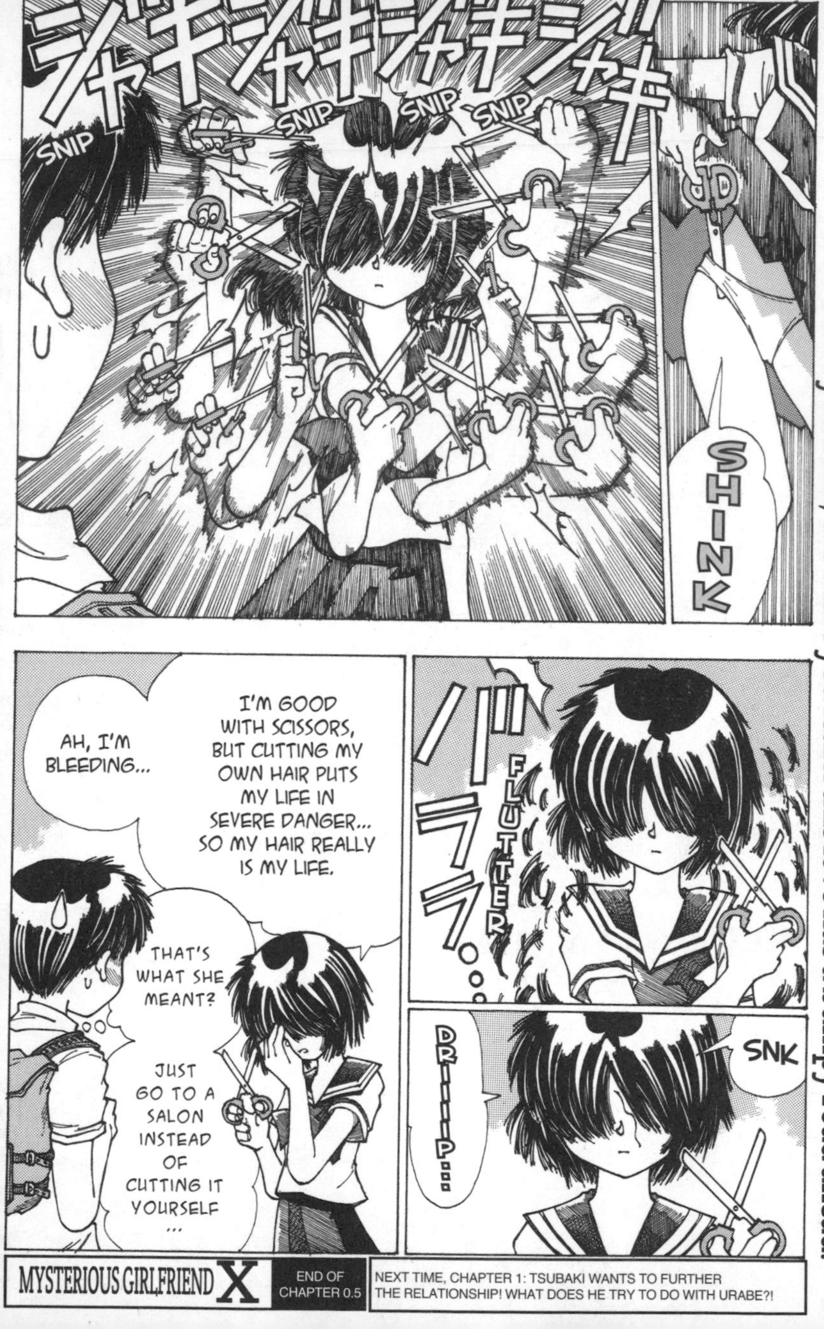
SNIP
SNIP
SNIP
SNIP
SHINK
FLUTTER
SNK
DRIIIIP...
I'M GOOD WITH SCISSORS, BUT CUTTING MY OWN HAIR PUTS MY LIFE IN SEVERE DANGER... SO MY HAIR REALLY IS MY LIFE.
AH, I'M BLEEDING...
THAT'S WHAT SHE MEANT?
JUST GO TO A SALON INSTEAD OF CUTTING IT YOURSELF ...

The more you read, the more you learn this love has a bumpy road ahead!

MYSTERIOUS GIRLFRIEND X | END OF CHAPTER 0.5 | NEXT TIME, CHAPTER 1: TSUBAKI WANTS TO FURTHER THE RELATIONSHIP! WHAT DOES HE TRY TO DO WITH URABE?!

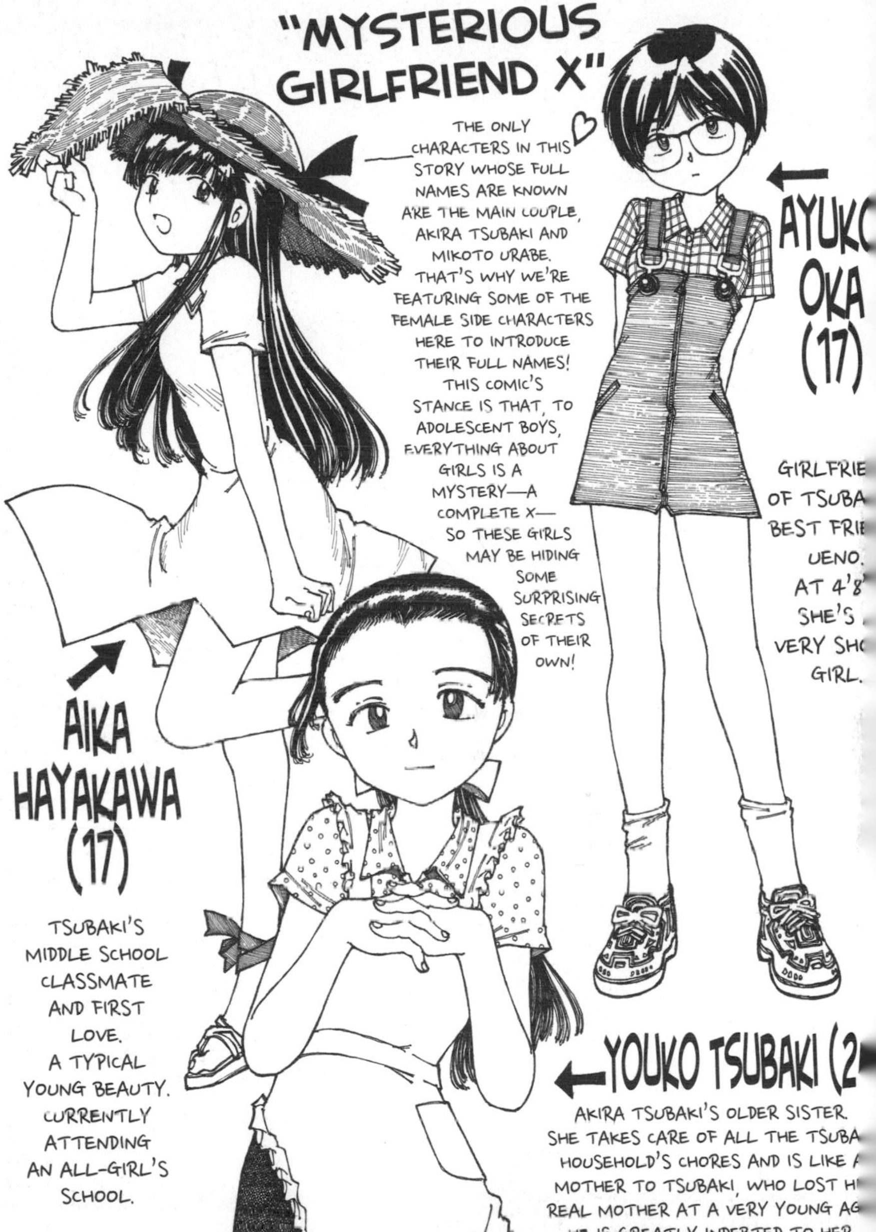
"MYSTERIOUS GIRLFRIEND X"
THE ONLY CHARACTERS IN THIS STORY WHOSE FULL NAMES ARE KNOWN ARE THE MAIN COUPLE, AKIRA TSUBAKI AND MIKOTO URABE. THAT'S WHY WE'RE FEATURING SOME OF THE FEMALE SIDE CHARACTERS HERE TO INTRODUCE THEIR FULL NAMES! THIS COMIC'S STANCE IS THAT, TO ADOLESCENT BOYS, EVERYTHING ABOUT GIRLS IS A MYSTERY—A COMPLETE X—SO THESE GIRLS MAY BE HIDING SOME SURPRISING SECRETS OF THEIR OWN!
AYUK
OKA
(17)
GIRLFRIE
OF TSUBA
BEST FRIE
UENO.
AT 4'8
SHE'S
VERY SH
GIRL.
AIKA HAYAKAWA (17)
TSUBAKI'S MIDDLE SCHOOL CLASSMATE AND FIRST LOVE. A TYPICAL YOUNG BEAUTY. CURRENTLY ATTENDING AN ALL-GIRL'S SCHOOL.
YOUKO TSUBAKI (2
AKIRA TSUBAKI'S OLDER SISTER.
SHE TAKES CARE OF ALL THE TSUBA
HOUSEHOLD'S CHORES AND IS LIKE
MOTHER TO TSUBAKI, WHO LOST H
REAL MOTHER AT A VERY YOUNG AG
HE IS GREATLY INDEBTED TO HER.

MYSTERIOUS GIRLFRIEND X

Characters

Akira Tsubaki (17)

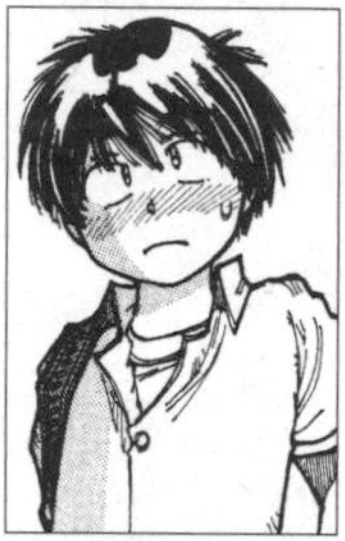

The protagonist of the story. His bizarre relationship with Urabe began after he licked her drool one day. He is as interested in girls as any boy his age, but Urabe takes the lead in their relationship and Tsubaki can't seem to initiate any progress between them.

Mikoto Urabe (17)

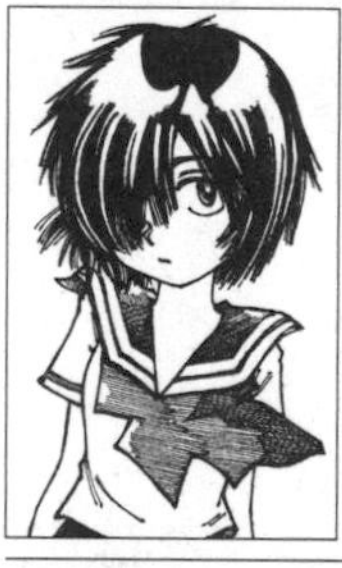

A transfer student who joined Tsubaki's class. She can convey her own feelings through her drool, as well as pick up on Tsubaki's feelings through his. She's antisocial and everything she says and does is mysterious, but her ideas about love are very pure. Her hobby is using scissors, which she can use to cut up anything.

Ayuko Oka (17)

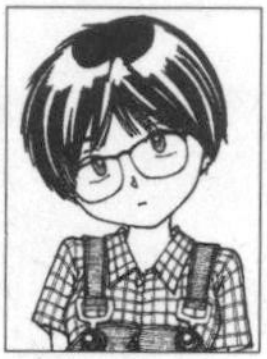

At 4'8", she's very small, but her figure is well-developed and quite gorgeous. Tsubaki spotted her kissing Ueno in the classroom after school, but she's not too bothered by it.

Ueno (17)

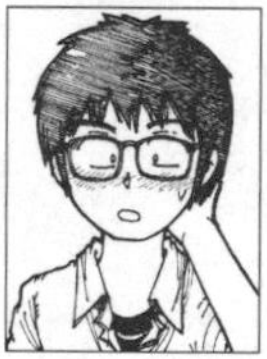

Tsubaki's best friend. He's been going out with their classmate, Oka, since they were sophomores. Ueno's fond way of talking about Oka frequently influences Tsubaki's ideas about relationships.

Youko Tsubaki (24)

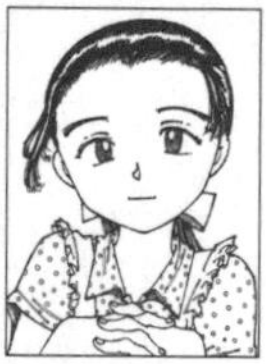

Akira's sister, seven years his senior. She handles all the housework in place of their mother, who died when they were young. Akira is highly indebted to her.

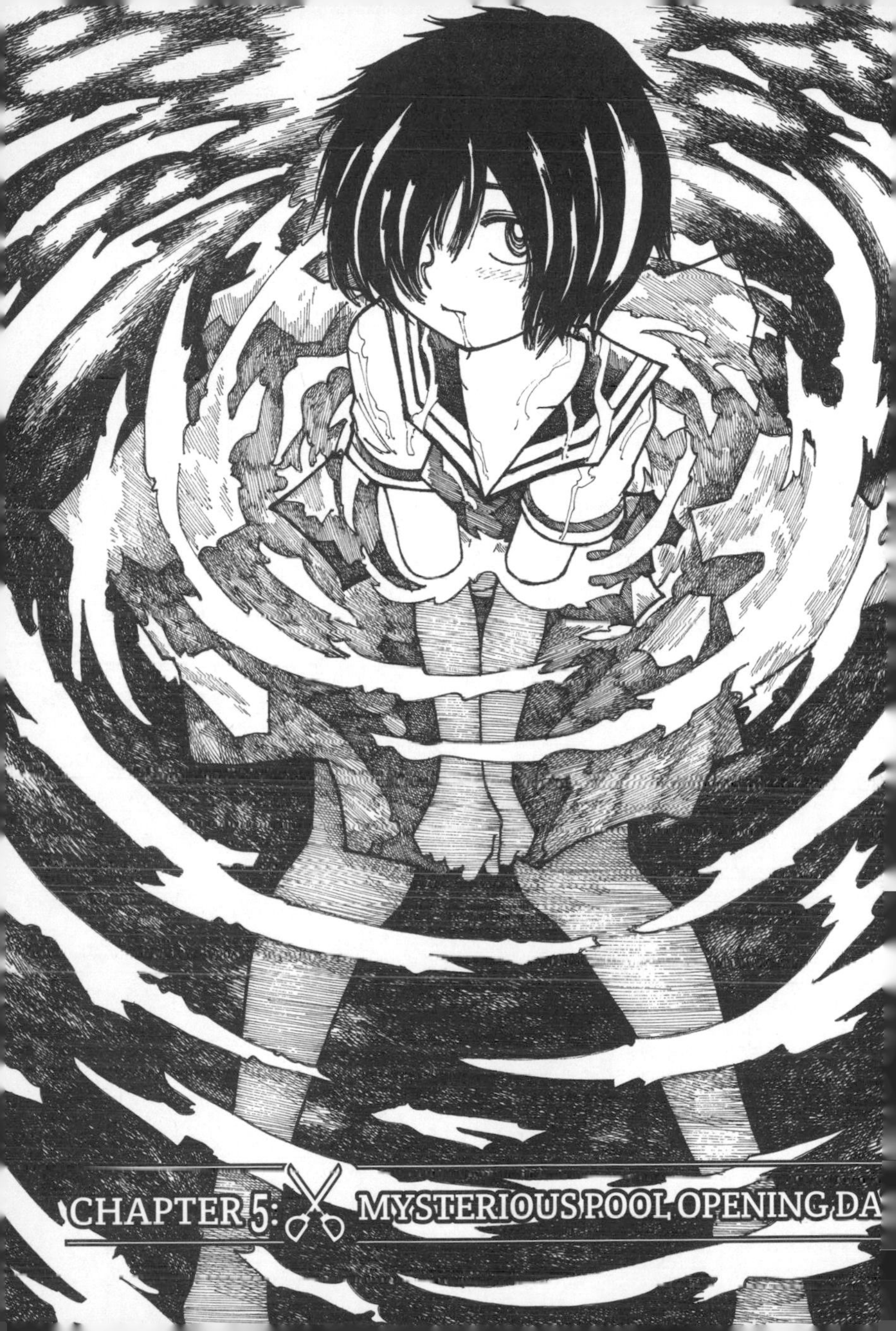
CHAPTER 5: MYSTERIOUS POOL OPENING DA

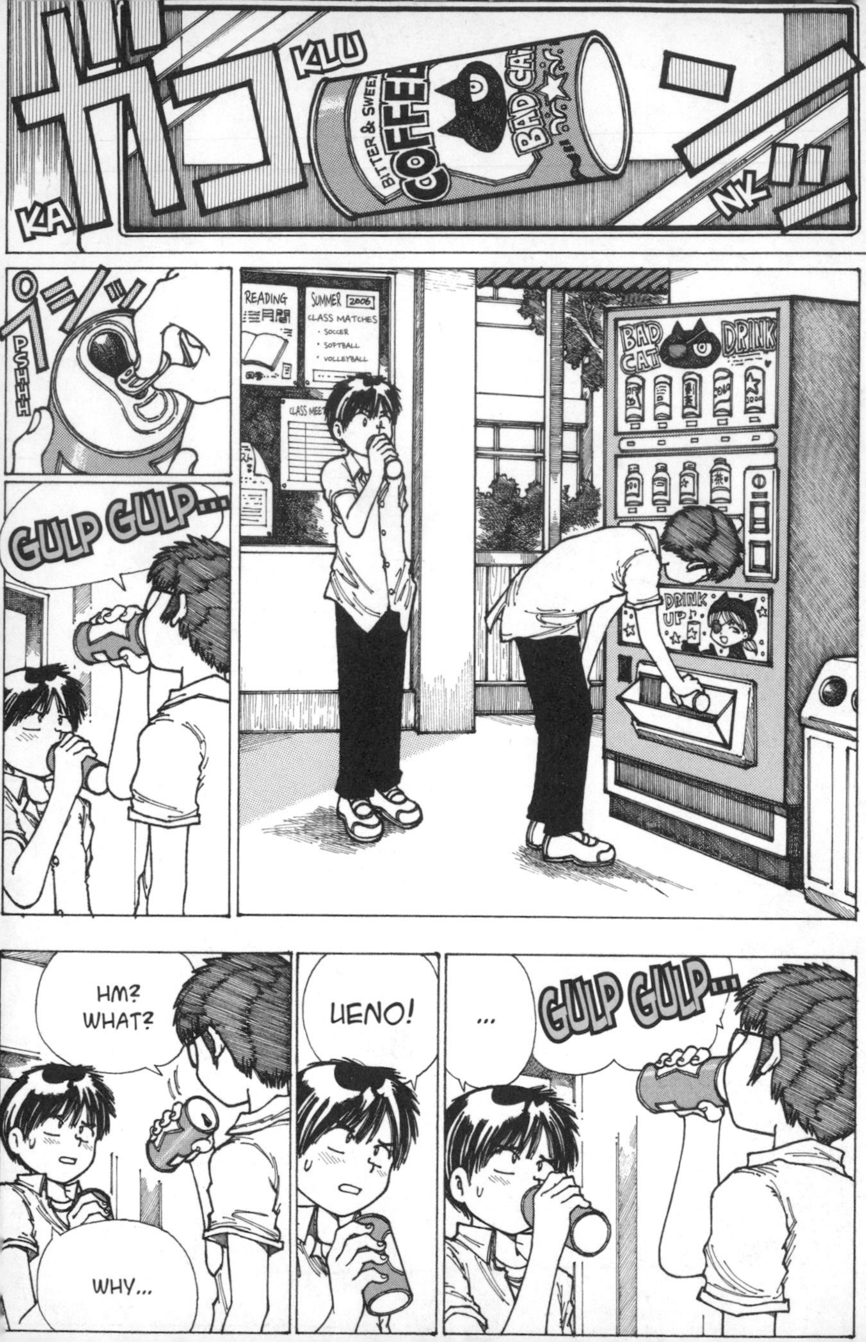
KA
KLU
NK
BITTER & SWEET
COFFEE
BAD CAT
READING
SUMMER 2006
CLASS MATCHES
• SOCCER
• SOFTBALL
• VOLLEYBALL
BAD CAT DRINK
DRINK UP
PSHHH
GULP GULP...
GULP GULP...
...
UENO!
HM? WHAT?
WHY...

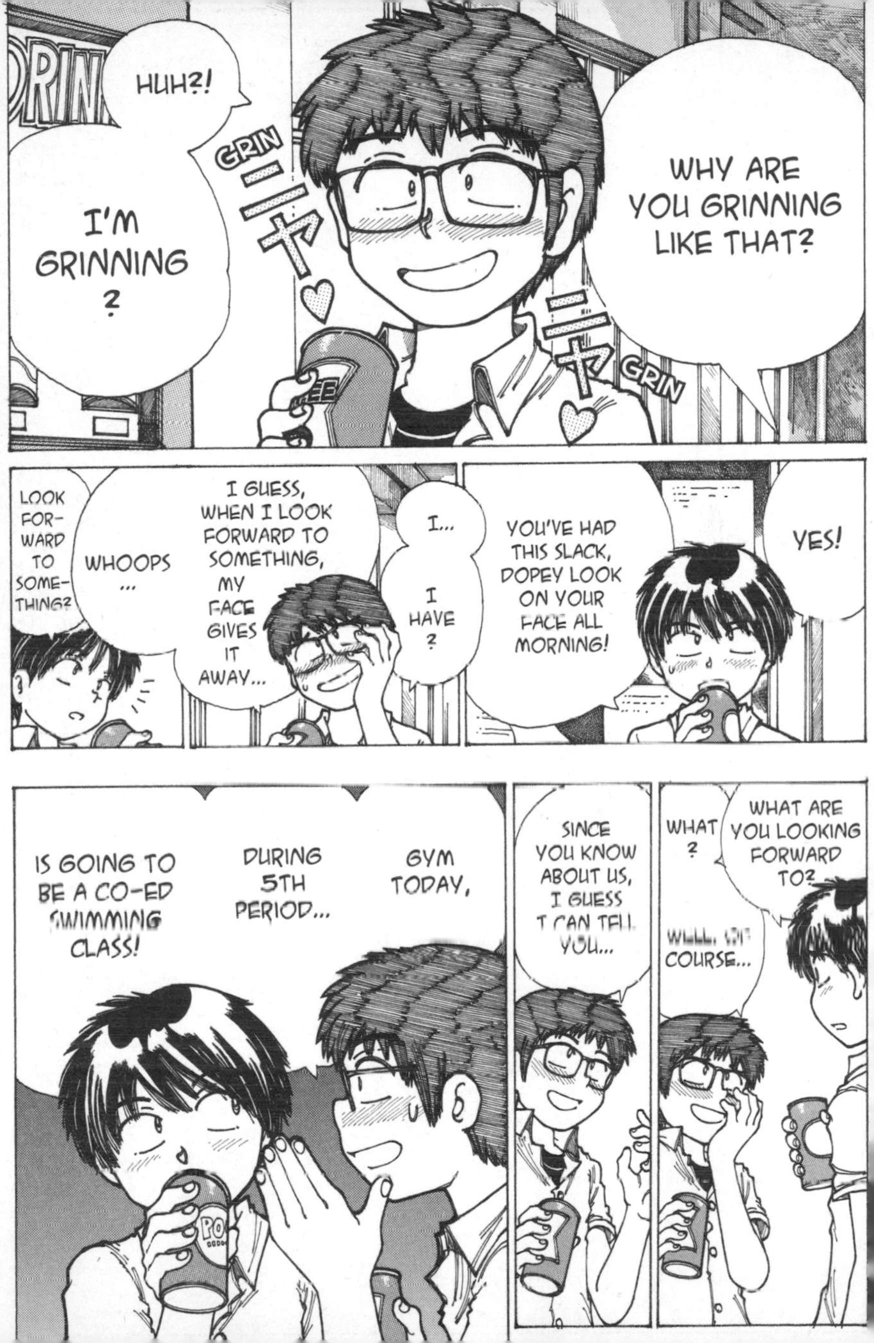
WHY ARE YOU GRINNING LIKE THAT?
GRIN
GRIN
HUH?!
I'M GRINNING?
YES!
YOU'VE HAD THIS SLACK, DOPEY LOOK ON YOUR FACE ALL MORNING!
I... I HAVE?
I GUESS, WHEN I LOOK FORWARD TO SOMETHING, MY FACE GIVES IT AWAY...
WHOOPS...
LOOK FOR-WARD TO SOME-THING?
WHAT ARE YOU LOOKING FORWARD TO?
WHAT?
WELL, OF COURSE...
SINCE YOU KNOW ABOUT US, I GUESS I CAN TELL YOU...
GYM TODAY,
DURING 5TH PERIOD...
IS GOING TO BE A CO-ED SWIMMING CLASS!

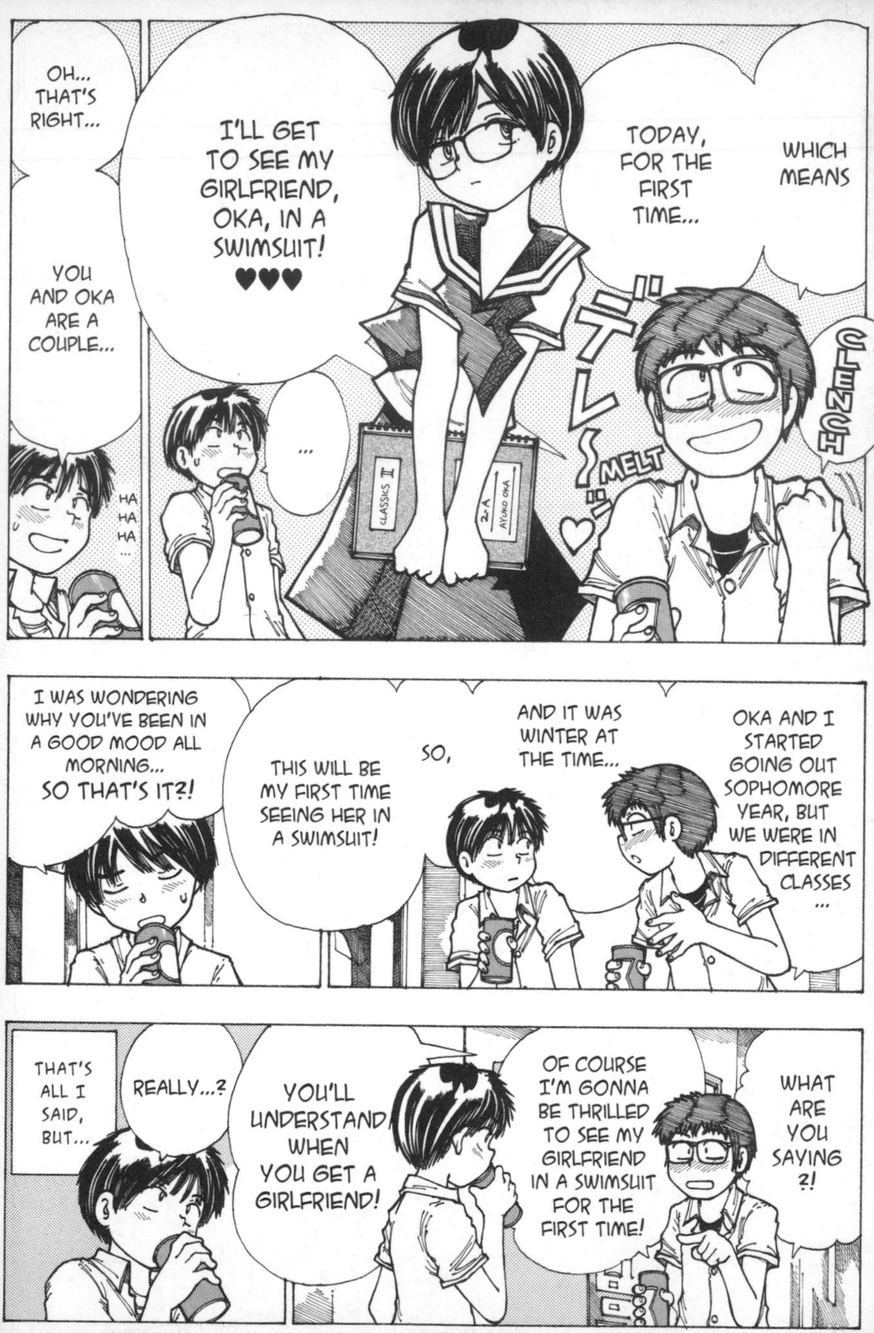
WHICH MEANS
TODAY, FOR THE FIRST TIME...
CLENCH
MELT
I'LL GET TO SEE MY GIRLFRIEND, OKA, IN A SWIMSUIT! ♥♥♥
CLASSICS II
2-A AYUKO OKA
...
OH... THAT'S RIGHT...
YOU AND OKA ARE A COUPLE...
HA HA HA ...
OKA AND I STARTED GOING OUT SOPHOMORE YEAR, BUT WE WERE IN DIFFERENT CLASSES ...
AND IT WAS WINTER AT THE TIME...
SO,
THIS WILL BE MY FIRST TIME SEEING HER IN A SWIMSUIT!
I WAS WONDERING WHY YOU'VE BEEN IN A GOOD MOOD ALL MORNING... SO THAT'S IT?!
WHAT ARE YOU SAYING ?!
OF COURSE I'M GONNA BE THRILLED TO SEE MY GIRLFRIEND IN A SWIMSUIT FOR THE FIRST TIME!
YOU'LL UNDERSTAND WHEN YOU GET A GIRLFRIEND!
REALLY...?
THAT'S ALL I SAID, BUT...

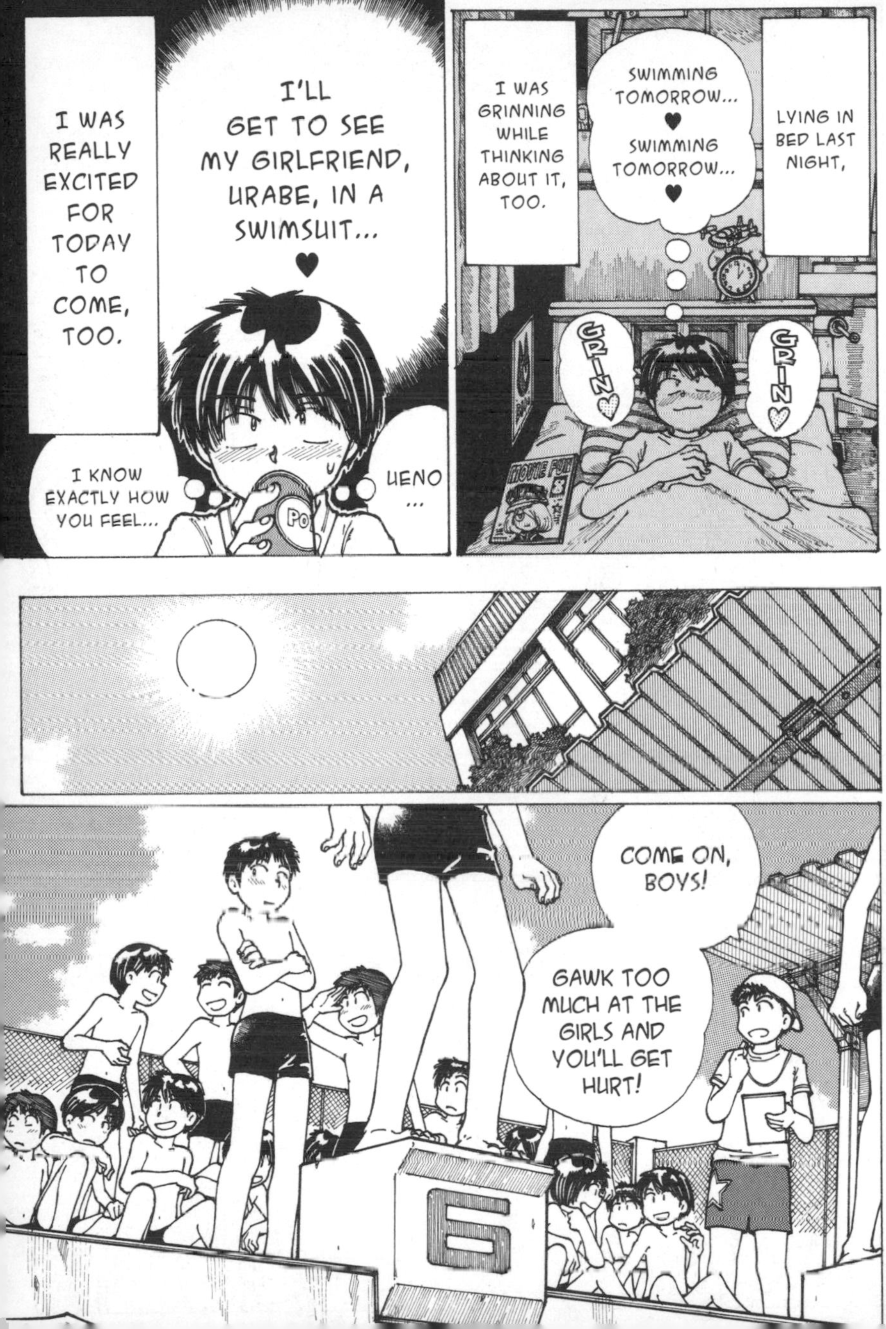
LYING IN BED LAST NIGHT,
SWIMMING TOMORROW... ♥ SWIMMING TOMORROW... ♥
I WAS GRINNING WHILE THINKING ABOUT IT, TOO.
GRIN♥
GRIN♥
I WAS REALLY EXCITED FOR TODAY TO COME, TOO.
I'LL GET TO SEE MY GIRLFRIEND, URABE, IN A SWIMSUIT... ♥
UENO ...
I KNOW EXACTLY HOW YOU FEEL...
COME ON, BOYS!
GAWK TOO MUCH AT THE GIRLS AND YOU'LL GET HURT!

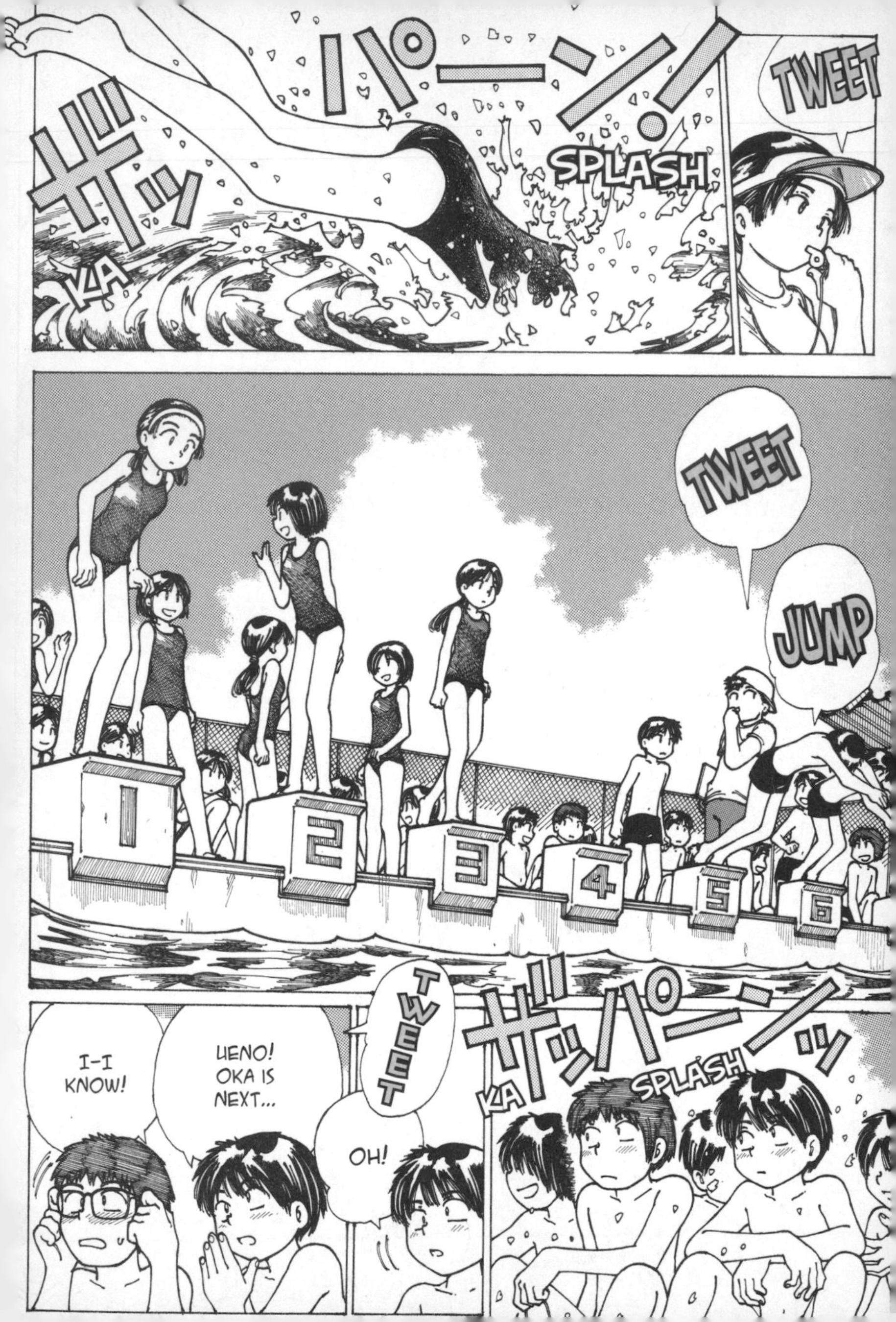
TWEET
パーン！
SPLASH
ザッ
KA
TWEET
JUMP
ザッパーンッ
SPLASH
KA
TWEET
OH!
UENO! OKA IS NEXT...
I-I KNOW!

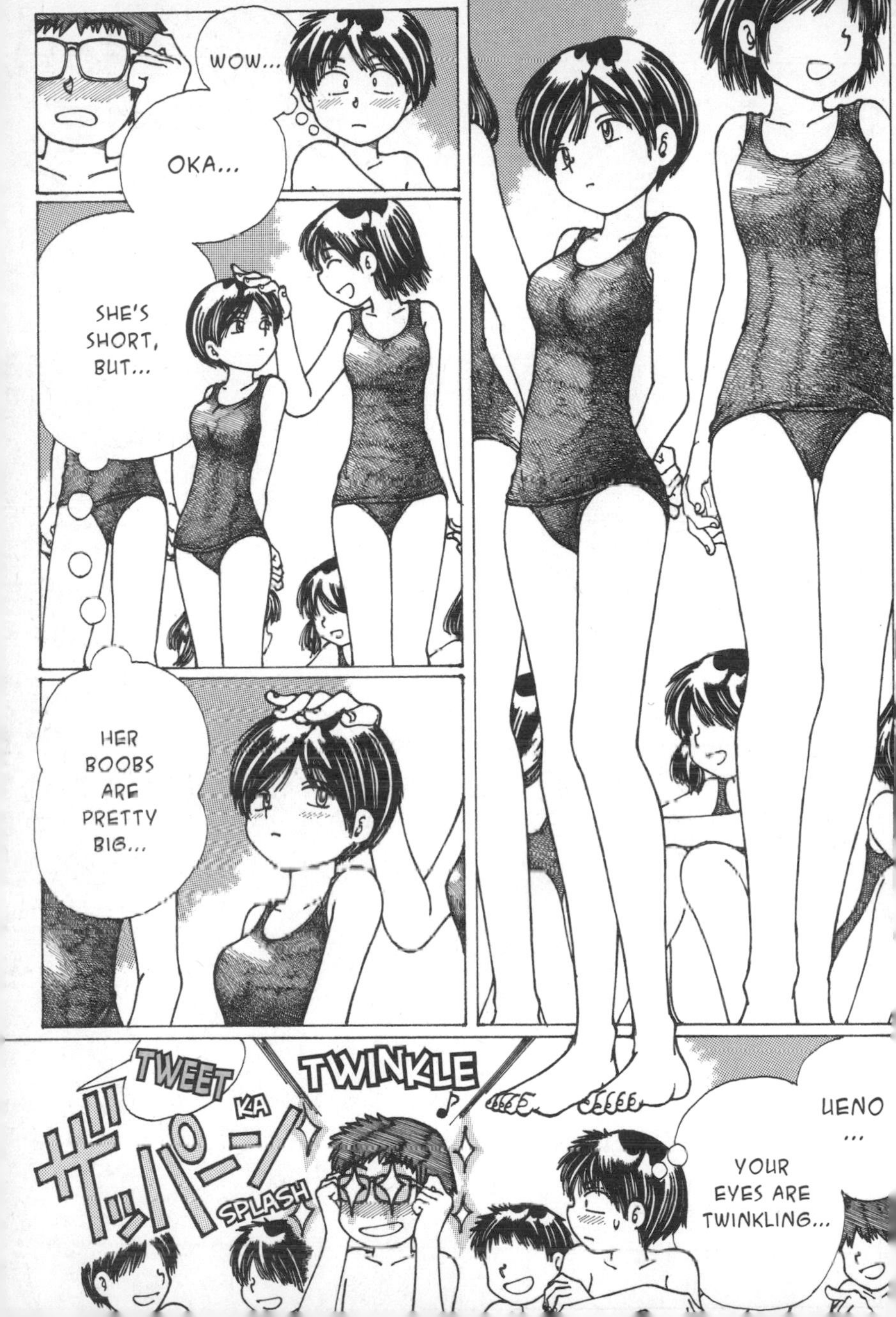
WOW...
OKA...
SHE'S SHORT, BUT...
HER BOOBS ARE PRETTY BIG...
UENO ...
YOUR EYES ARE TWINKLING...
TWINKLE
TWEET
KA
ザッパーン
SPLASH

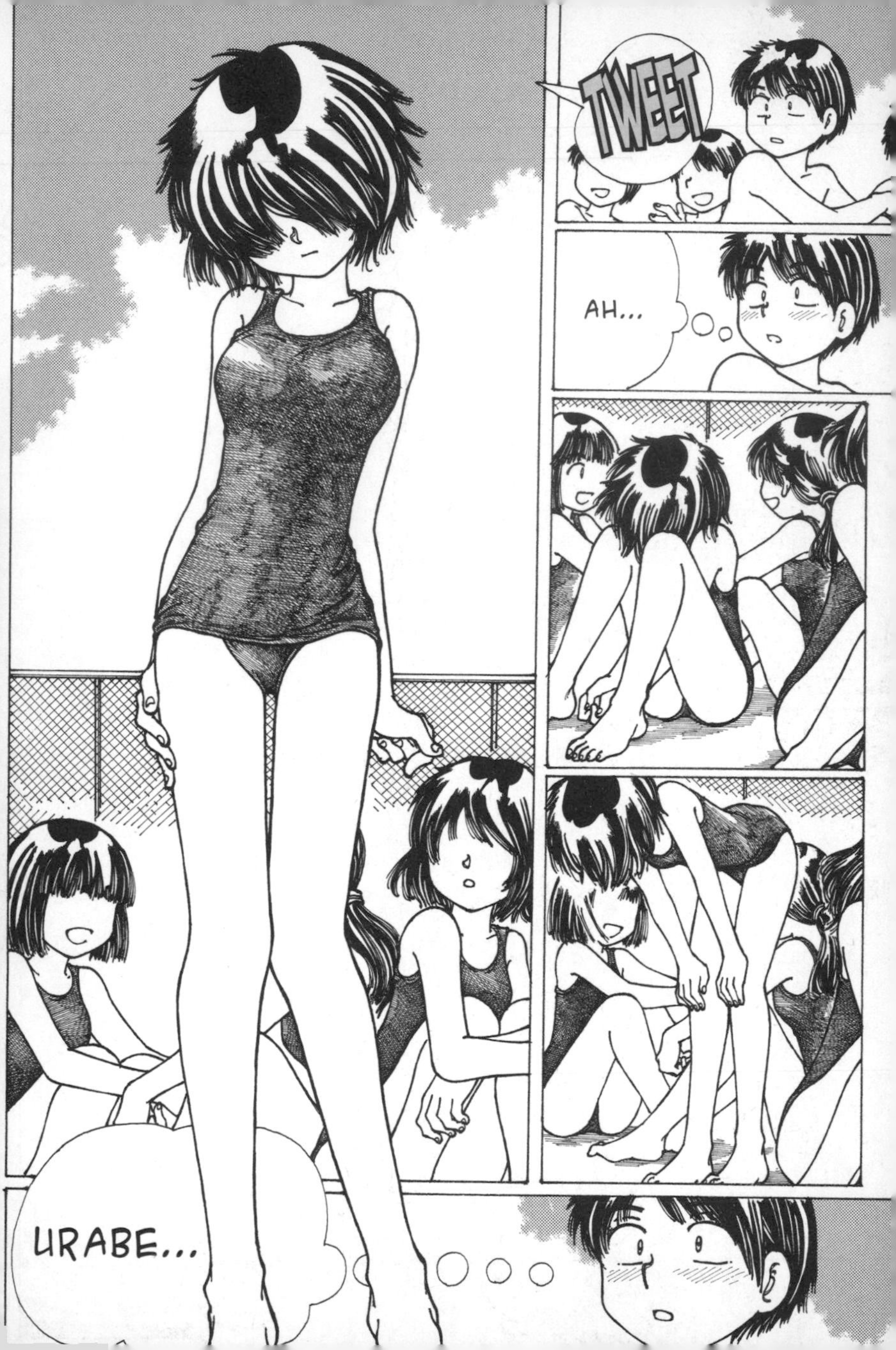
TWEET
AH...
URABE...

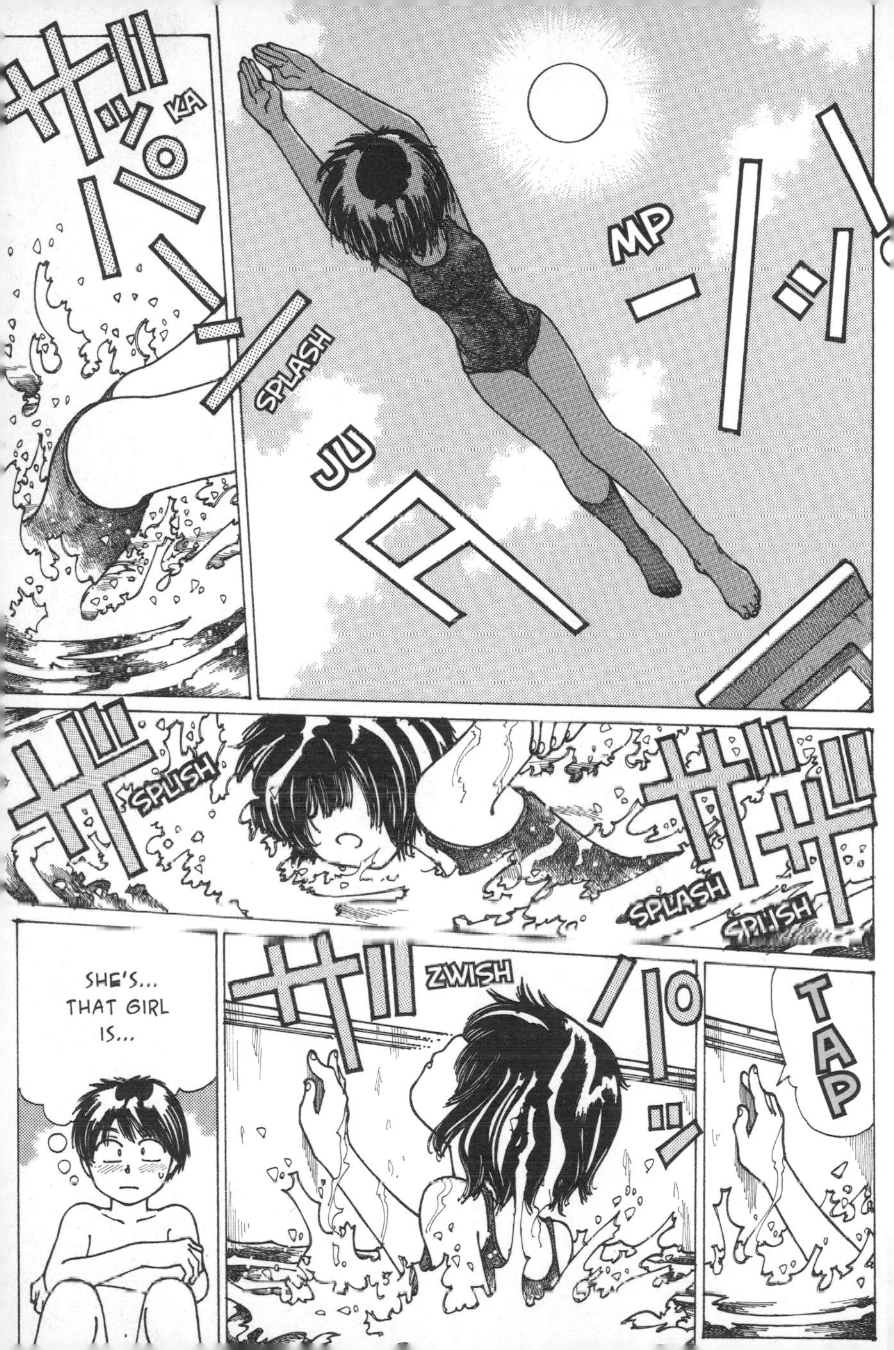
MP
SPLASH
JU
KA
SPLASH
SPLISH
SPLISH
TAP
ZWISH
SHE'S... THAT GIRL IS...

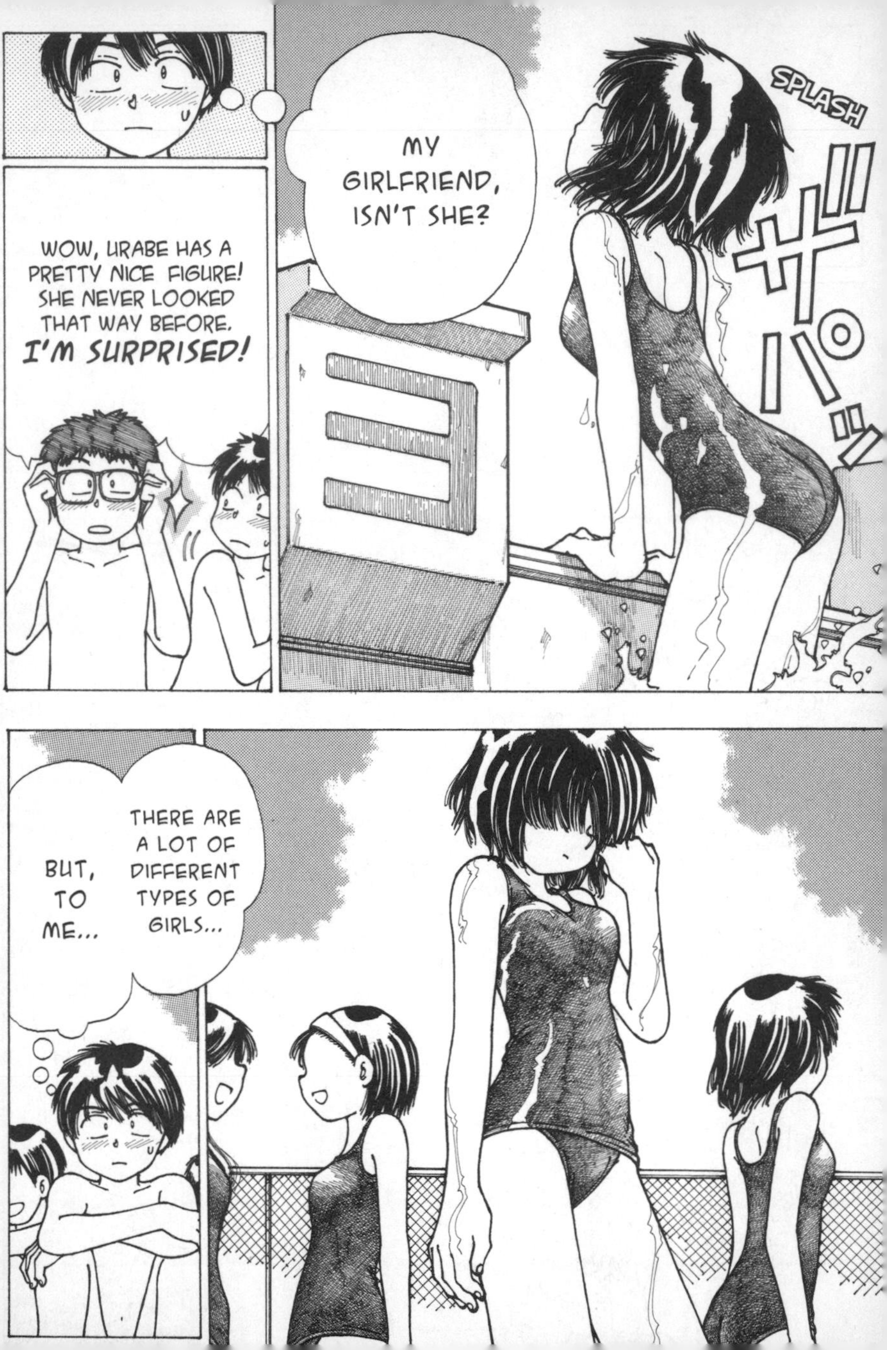
SPLASH
ザパーッ
MY GIRLFRIEND, ISN'T SHE?
WOW, URABE HAS A PRETTY NICE FIGURE! SHE NEVER LOOKED THAT WAY BEFORE. ***I'M SURPRISED!***
THERE ARE A LOT OF DIFFERENT TYPES OF GIRLS...
BUT, TO ME...

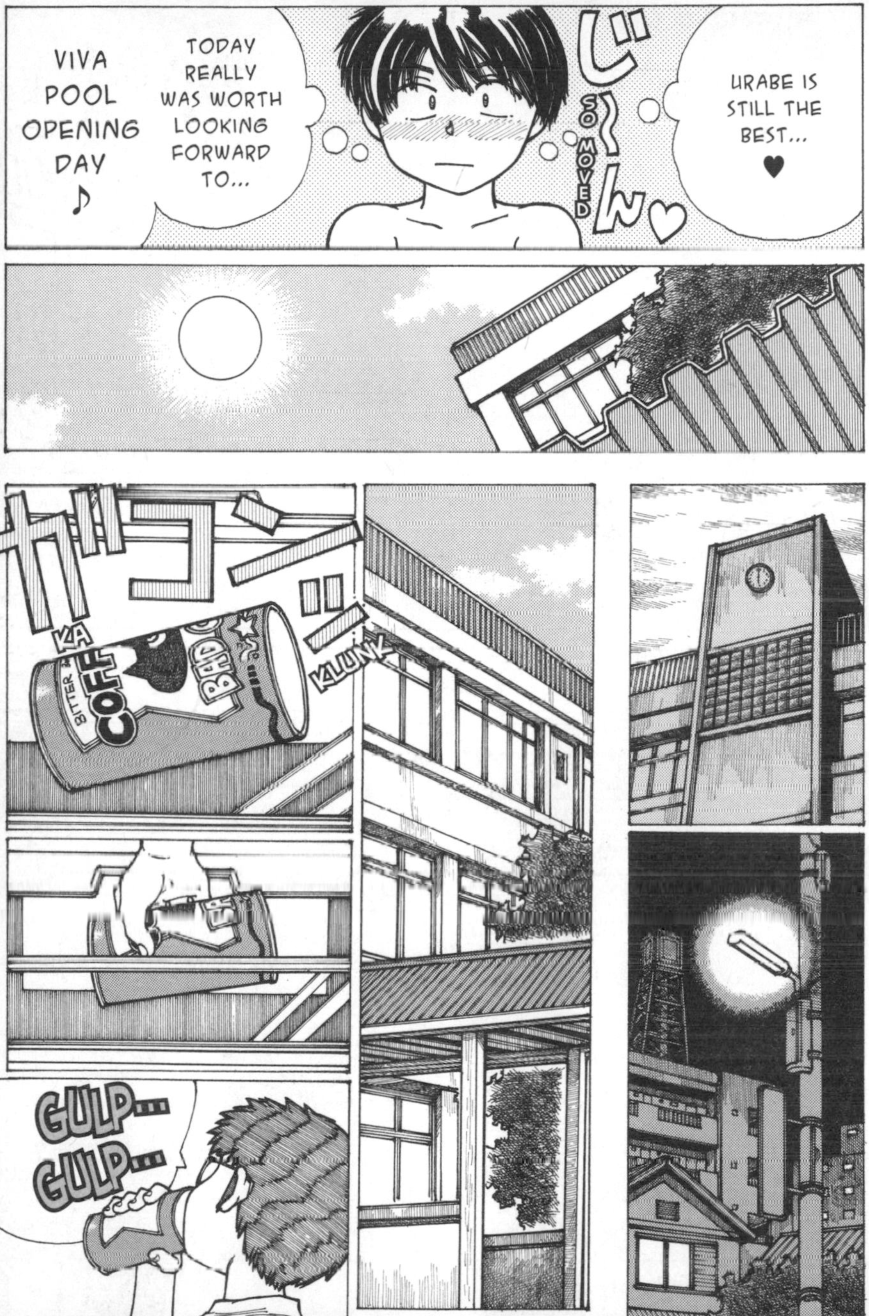
URABE IS STILL THE BEST... ♥
じ～ん
SO MOVED
TODAY REALLY WAS WORTH LOOKING FORWARD TO...
VIVA POOL OPENING DAY ♪
KA
KLUNK
GULP... GULP...

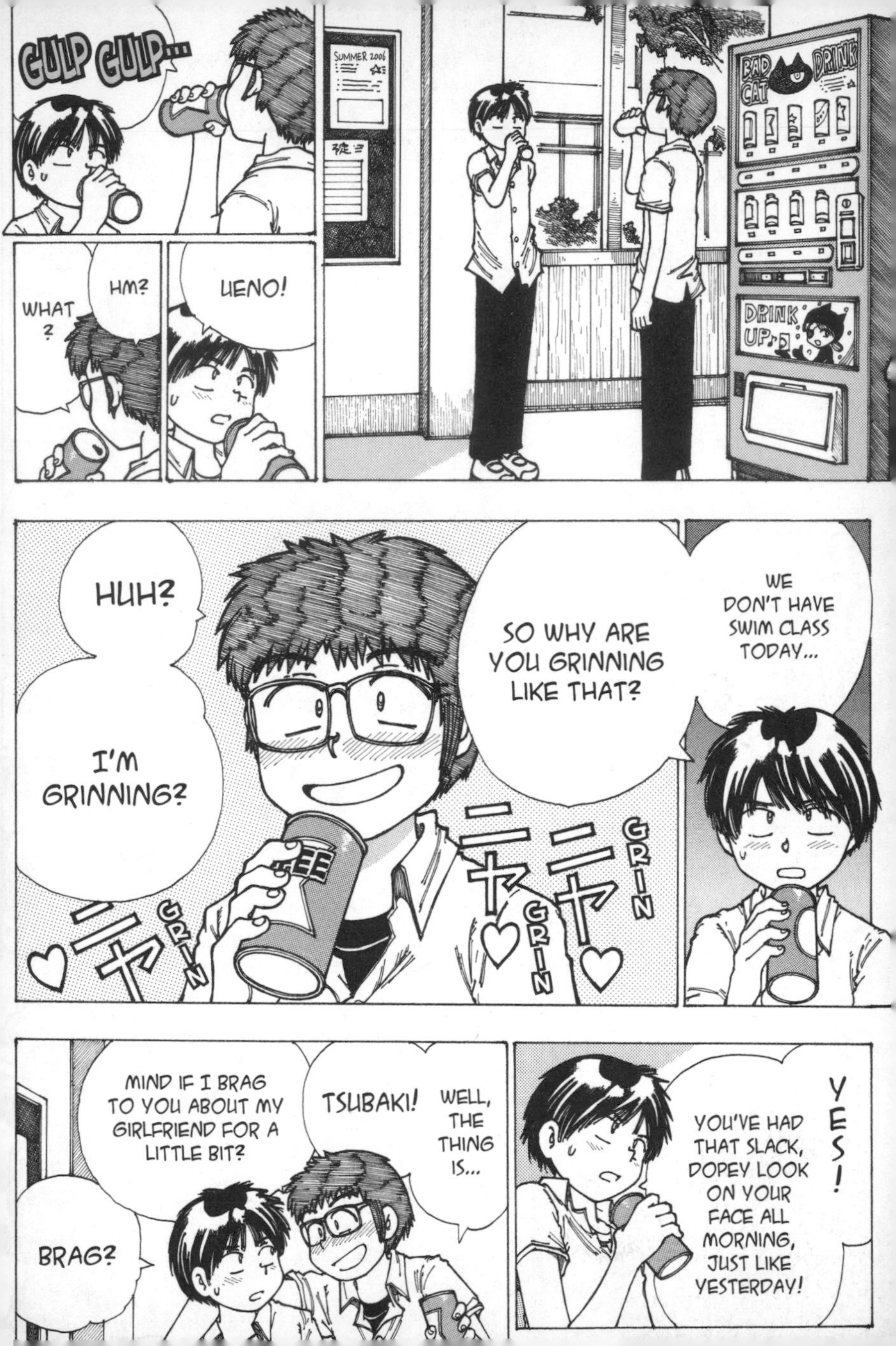
SUMMER 2006
BAD CAT
DRINK
DRINK UP
GULP GULP...
UENO!
HM?
WHAT ?
WE DON'T HAVE SWIM CLASS TODAY...
SO WHY ARE YOU GRINNING LIKE THAT?
HUH?
I'M GRINNING?
GRIN
GRIN
GRIN
YES!
YOU'VE HAD THAT SLACK, DOPEY LOOK ON YOUR FACE ALL MORNING, JUST LIKE YESTERDAY!
WELL, THE THING IS...
TSUBAKI!
MIND IF I BRAG TO YOU ABOUT MY GIRLFRIEND FOR A LITTLE BIT?
BRAG?

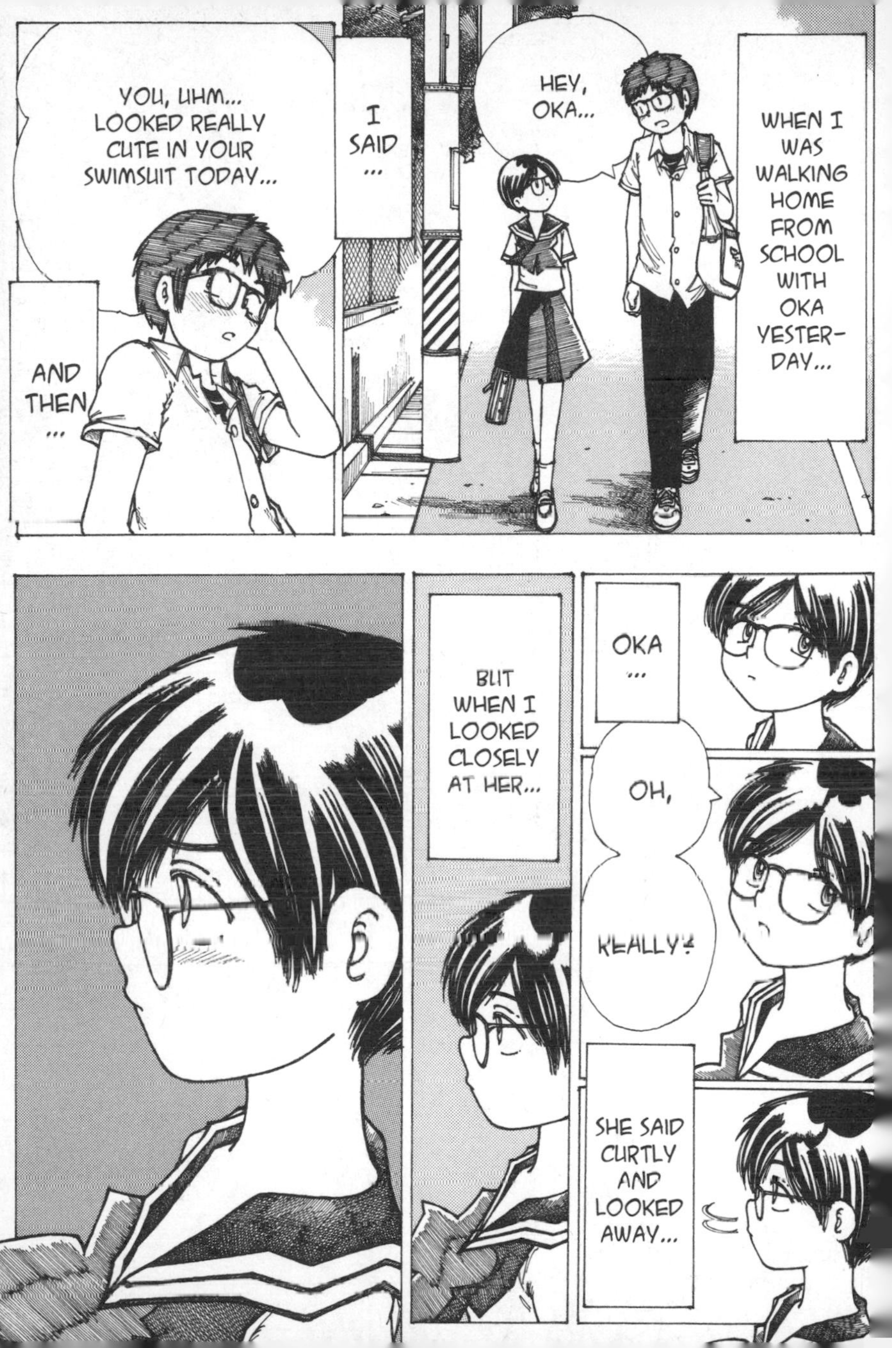
WHEN I WAS WALKING HOME FROM SCHOOL WITH OKA YESTER-DAY...
HEY, OKA...
I SAID ...
YOU, UHM... LOOKED REALLY CUTE IN YOUR SWIMSUIT TODAY...
AND THEN ...
OKA ...
OH,
REALLY?
SHE SAID CURTLY AND LOOKED AWAY...
BUT WHEN I LOOKED CLOSELY AT HER...

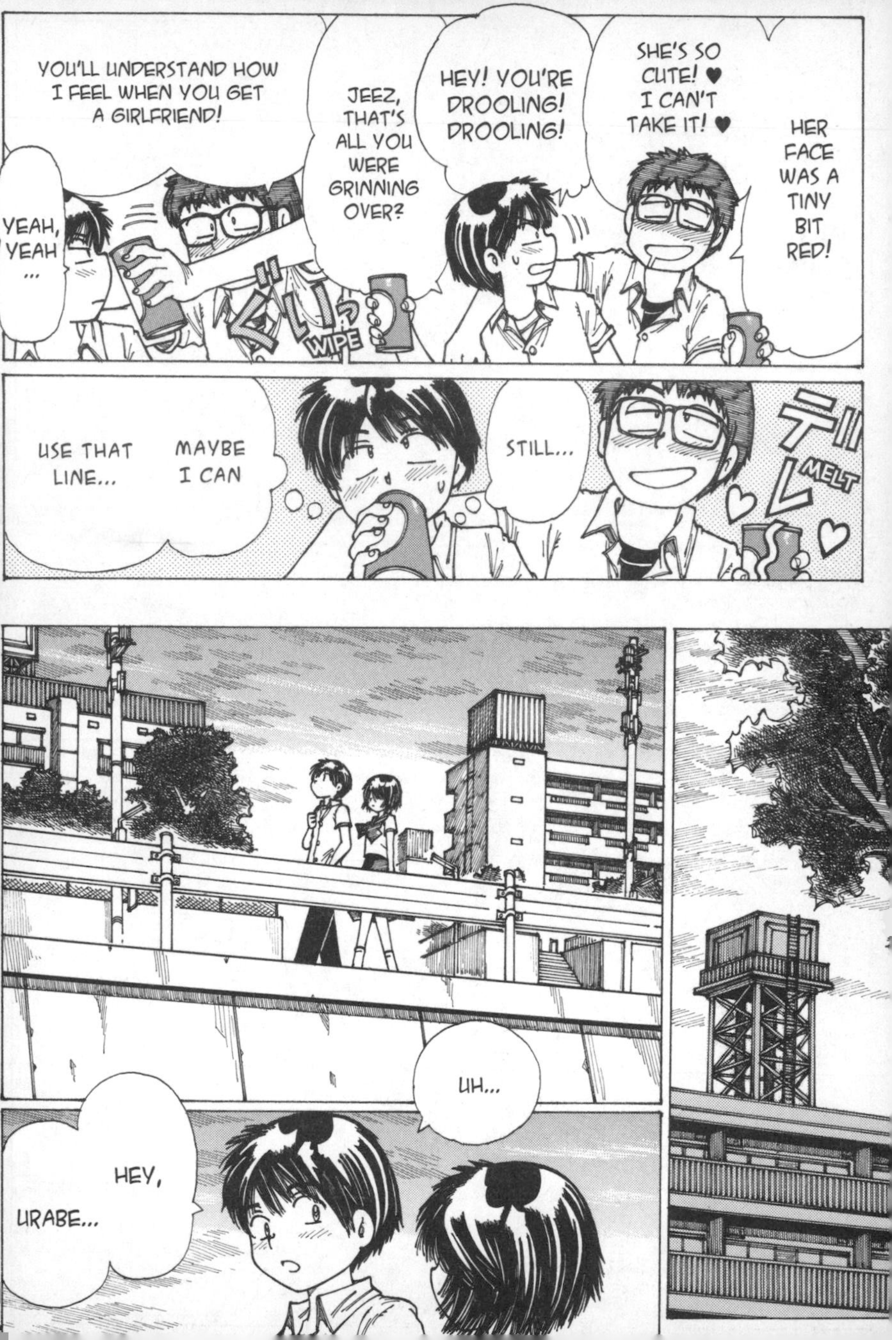
SHE'S SO CUTE! ♥ I CAN'T TAKE IT! ♥
HER FACE WAS A TINY BIT RED!
HEY! YOU'RE DROOLING! DROOLING!
JEEZ, THAT'S ALL YOU WERE GRINNING OVER?
YOU'LL UNDERSTAND HOW I FEEL WHEN YOU GET A GIRLFRIEND!
ぐいっ
WIPE
YEAH, YEAH ...
MELT
STILL...
MAYBE I CAN USE THAT LINE...
UH...
HEY, URABE...

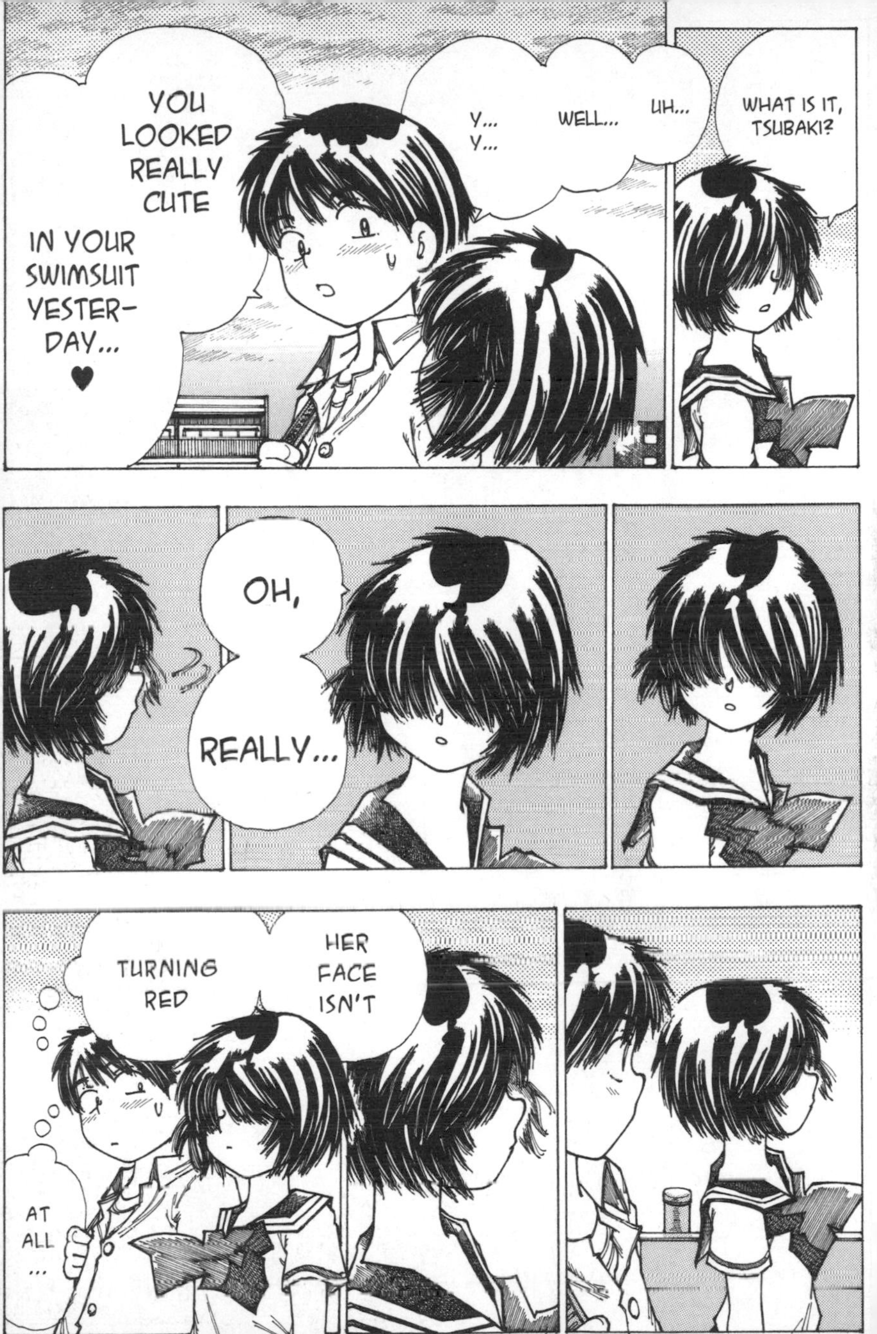
WHAT IS IT, TSUBAKI?
UH...
WELL...
Y... Y...
YOU LOOKED REALLY CUTE IN YOUR SWIMSUIT YESTER-DAY... ♥
OH, REALLY...
HER FACE ISN'T
TURNING RED
AT ALL ...

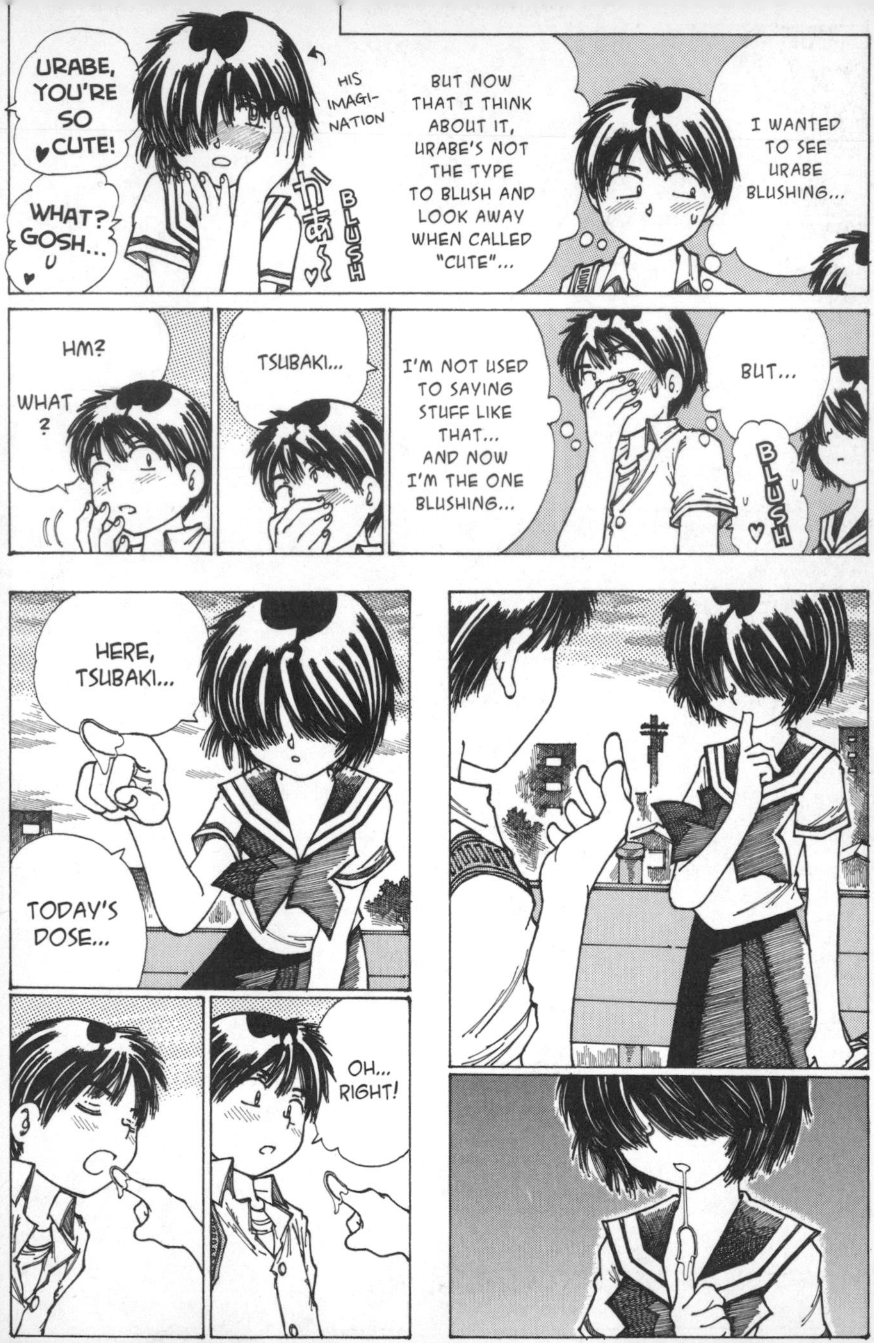
I WANTED TO SEE URABE BLUSHING...
BUT NOW THAT I THINK ABOUT IT, URABE'S NOT THE TYPE TO BLUSH AND LOOK AWAY WHEN CALLED "CUTE"...
HIS IMAGINATION
URABE, YOU'RE SO CUTE!
かぁ~
BLUSH
WHAT? GOSH...
BUT...
BLUSH
I'M NOT USED TO SAYING STUFF LIKE THAT... AND NOW I'M THE ONE BLUSHING...
TSUBAKI...
HM?
WHAT?
HERE, TSUBAKI...
TODAY'S DOSE...
OH... RIGHT!

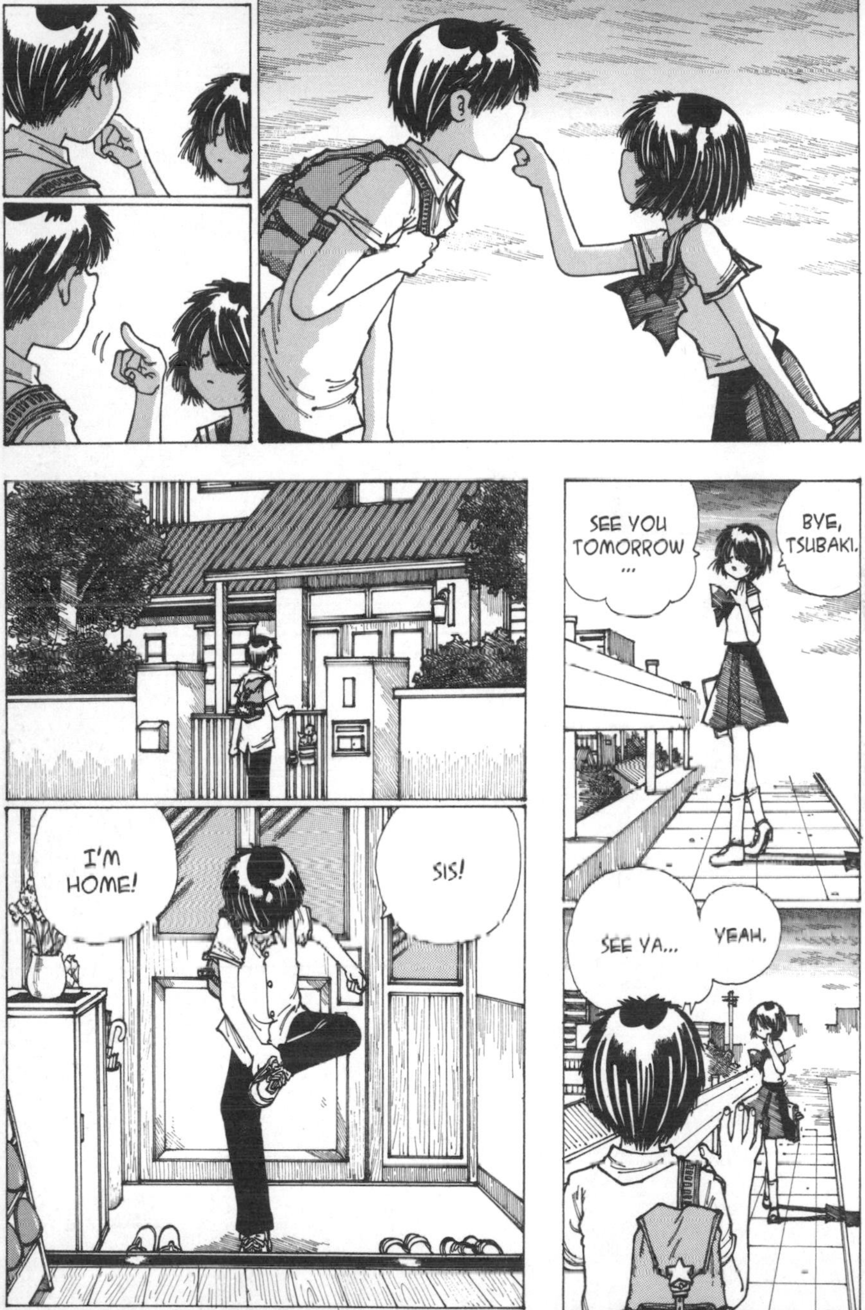
BYE, TSUBAKI.
SEE YOU TOMORROW ...
YEAH.
SEE YA...
SIS!
I'M HOME!

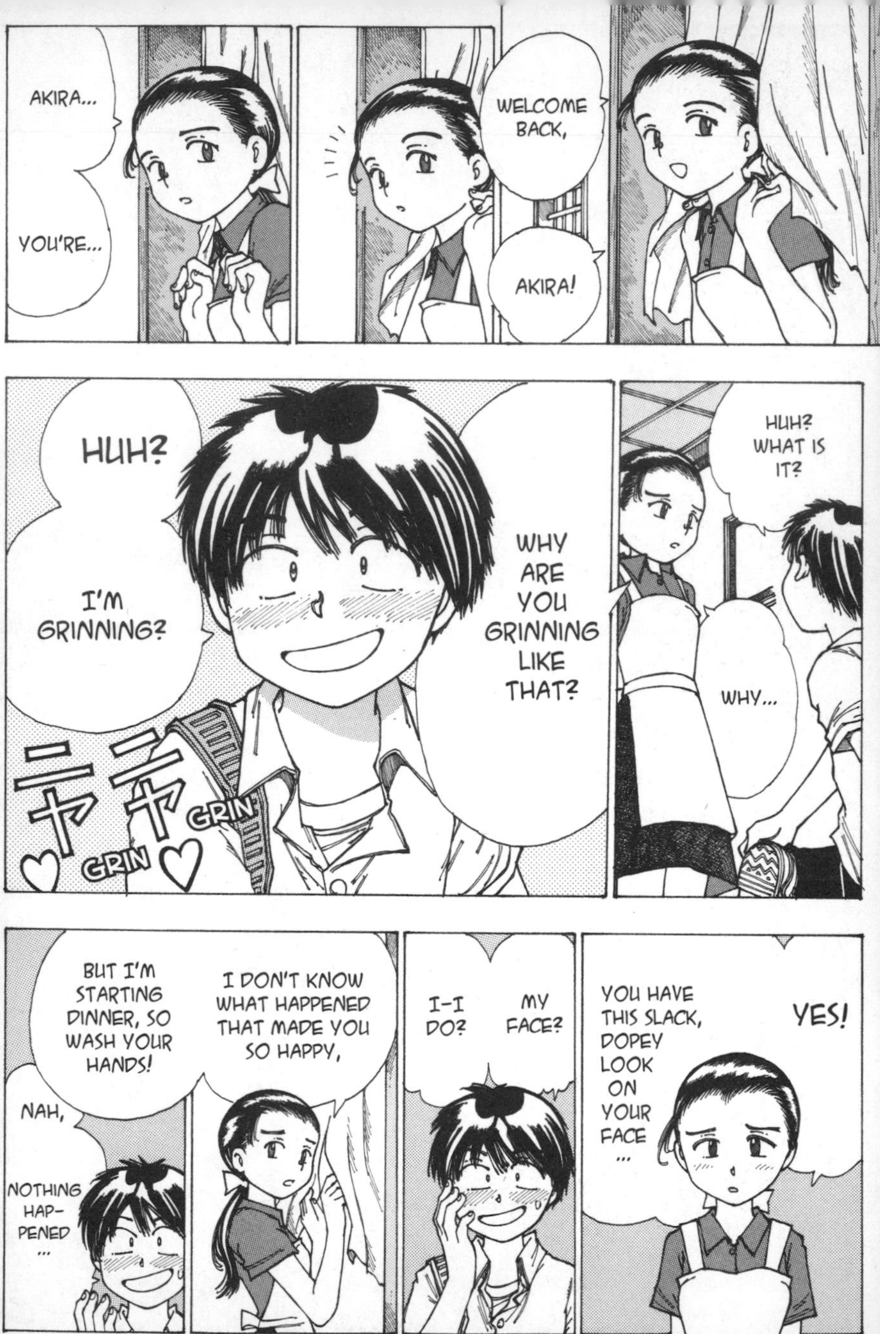
WELCOME BACK,
AKIRA!
AKIRA...
YOU'RE...
HUH? WHAT IS IT?
WHY...
WHY ARE YOU GRINNING LIKE THAT?
HUH?
I'M GRINNING?
GRIN
GRIN
YES!
YOU HAVE THIS SLACK, DOPEY LOOK ON YOUR FACE ...
MY FACE?
I-I DO?
I DON'T KNOW WHAT HAPPENED THAT MADE YOU SO HAPPY,
BUT I'M STARTING DINNER, SO WASH YOUR HANDS!
NAH,
NOTHING HAP-PENED ...

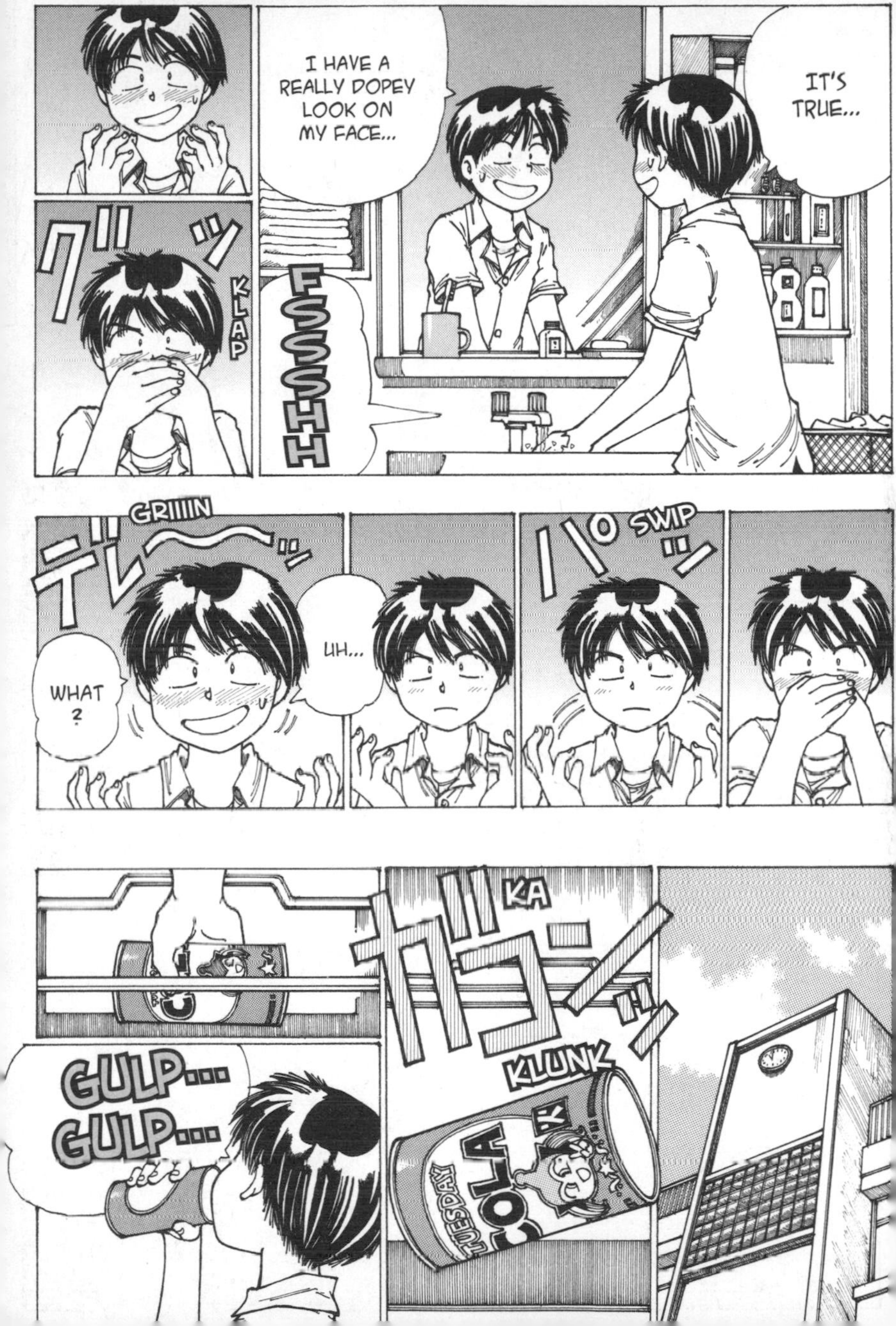
IT'S TRUE...
I HAVE A REALLY DOPEY LOOK ON MY FACE...
FSSSHHH
KLAP
SWIP
UH...
GRIIIIN
WHAT?
KA
KLUNK
TUESDAY COLA
GULP... GULP...

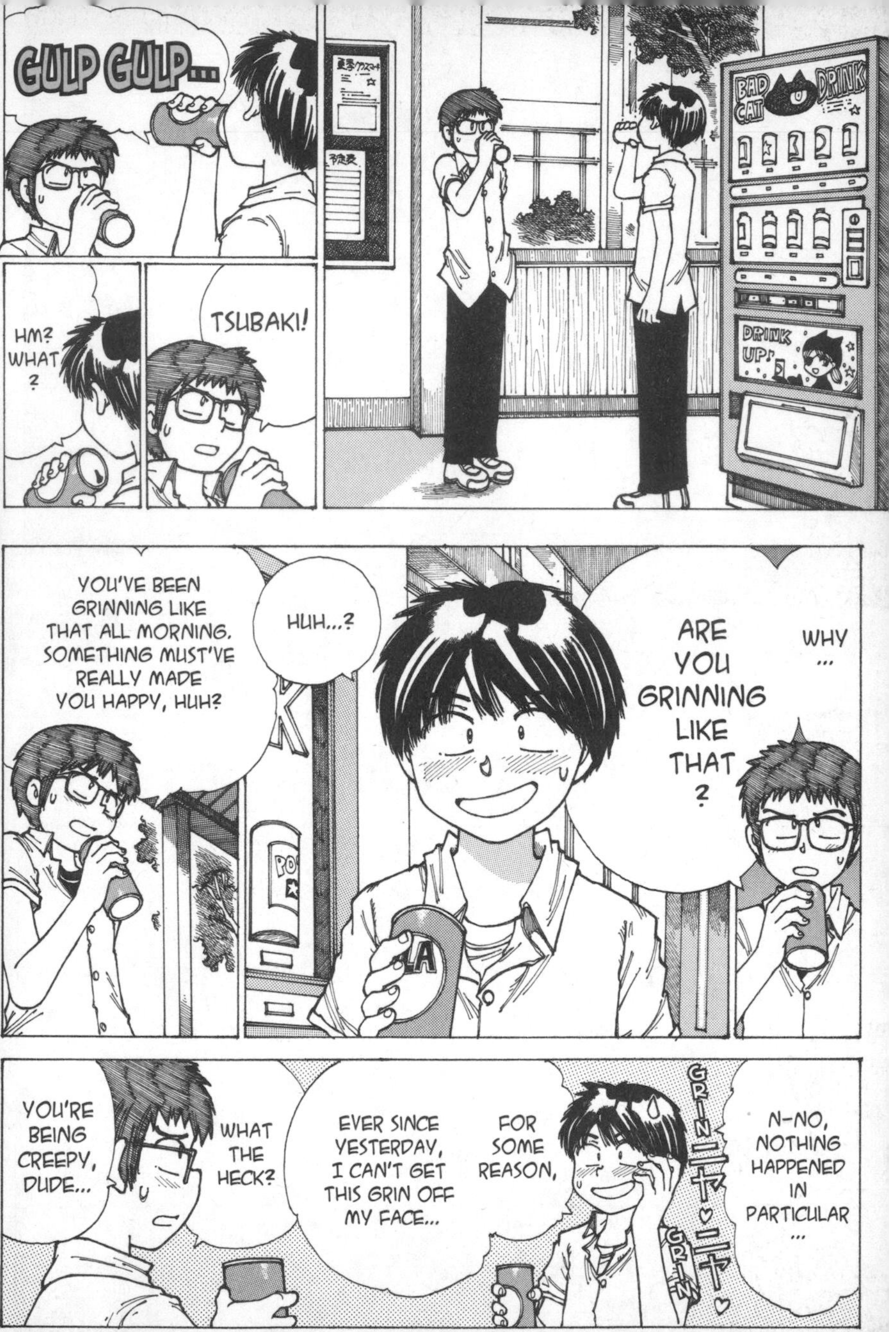
BAD CAT DRINK
DRINK UP♪
GULP GULP...
TSUBAKI!
HM? WHAT?
WHY...
ARE YOU GRINNING LIKE THAT?
HUH...?
YOU'VE BEEN GRINNING LIKE THAT ALL MORNING. SOMETHING MUST'VE REALLY MADE YOU HAPPY, HUH?
N-NO, NOTHING HAPPENED IN PARTICULAR...
GRIN ニヤ ニヤ
GRIN ニヤ ニヤ
FOR SOME REASON,
EVER SINCE YESTERDAY, I CAN'T GET THIS GRIN OFF MY FACE...
WHAT THE HECK?
YOU'RE BEING CREEPY, DUDE...

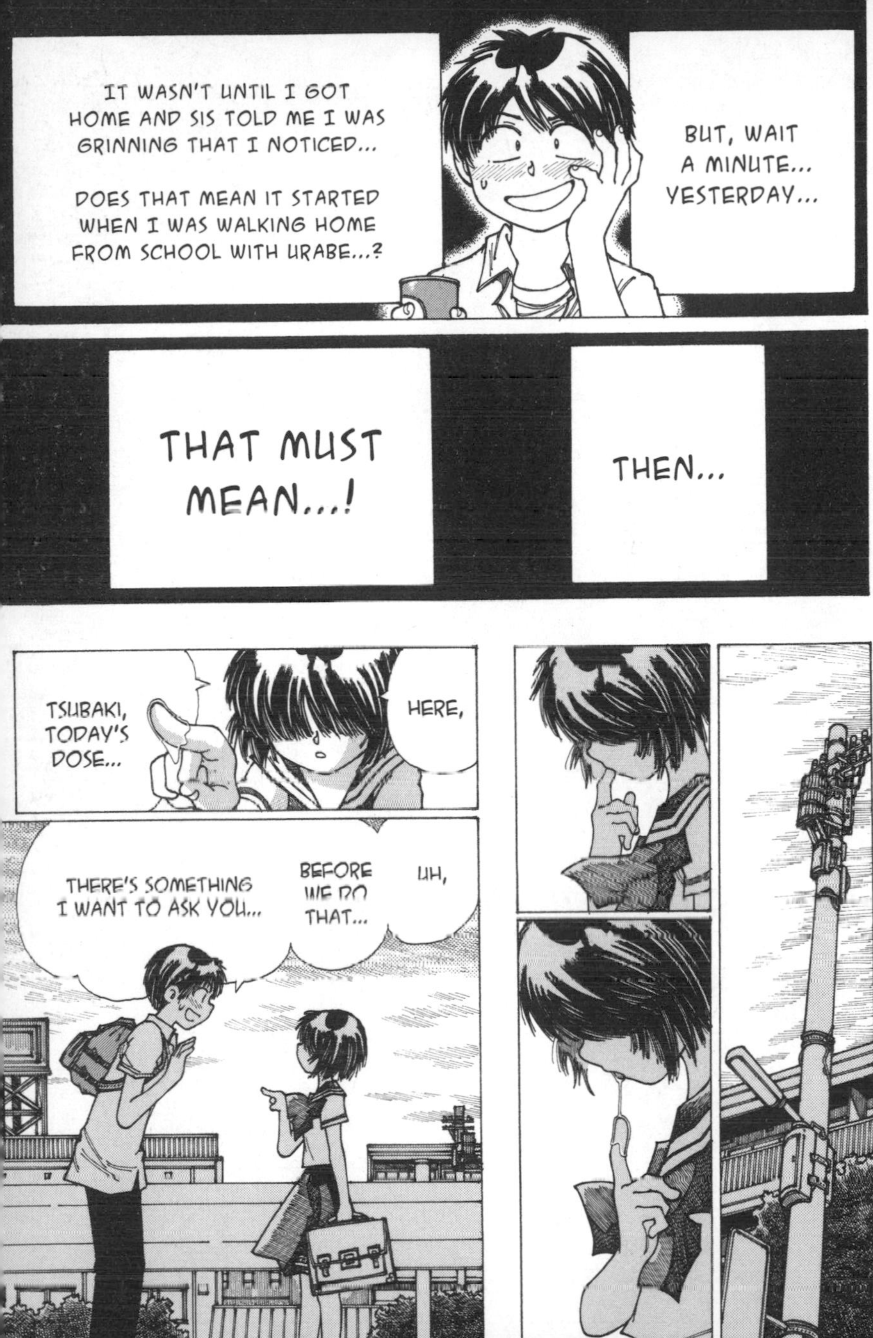
BUT, WAIT A MINUTE... YESTERDAY...
IT WASN'T UNTIL I GOT HOME AND SIS TOLD ME I WAS GRINNING THAT I NOTICED...
DOES THAT MEAN IT STARTED WHEN I WAS WALKING HOME FROM SCHOOL WITH URABE...?
THEN...
THAT MUST MEAN...!
HERE,
TSUBAKI, TODAY'S DOSE...
UH,
BEFORE WE DO THAT...
THERE'S SOMETHING I WANT TO ASK YOU...

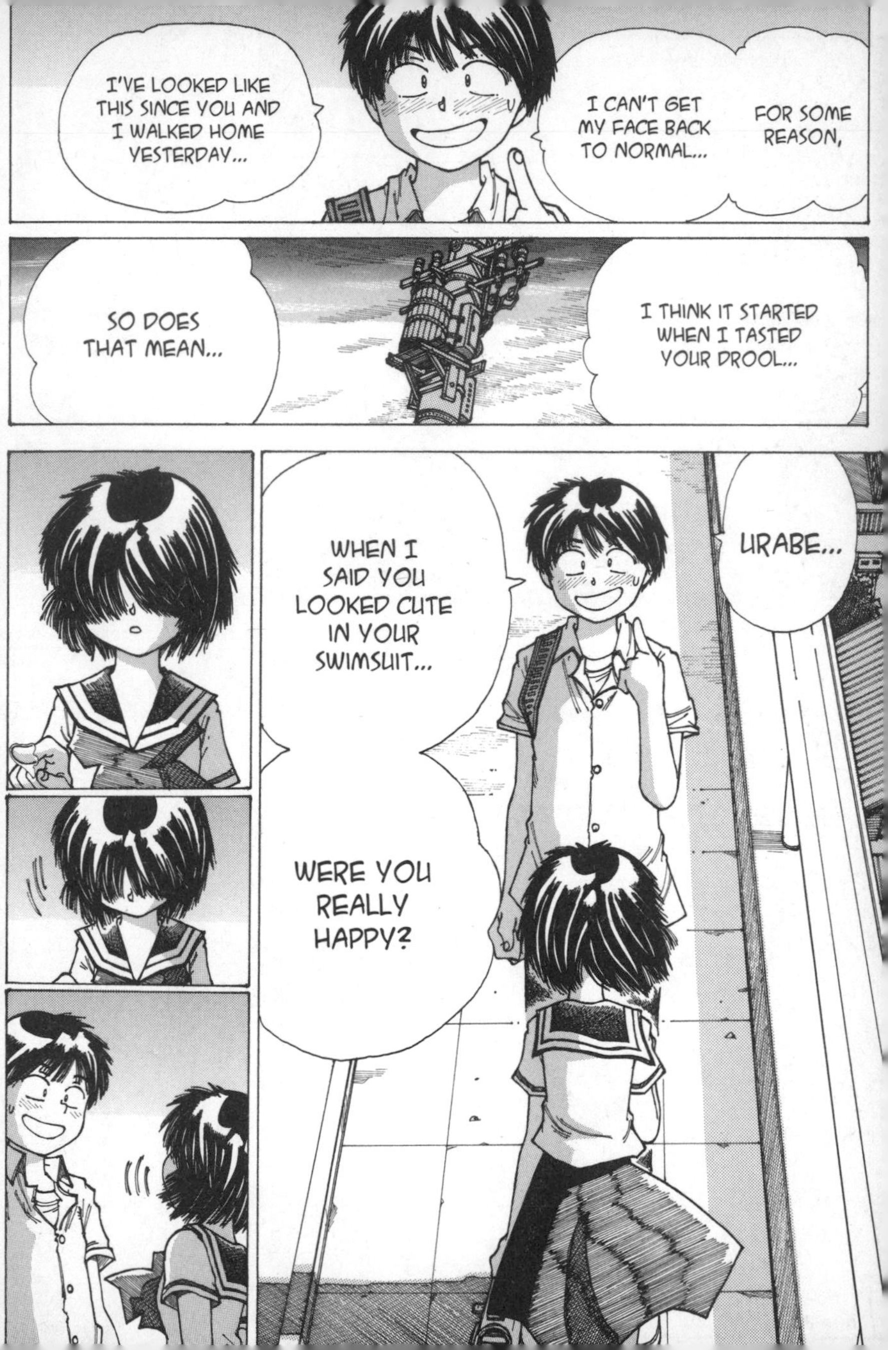
FOR SOME REASON,
I CAN'T GET MY FACE BACK TO NORMAL...
I'VE LOOKED LIKE THIS SINCE YOU AND I WALKED HOME YESTERDAY...
I THINK IT STARTED WHEN I TASTED YOUR DROOL...
SO DOES THAT MEAN...
URABE...
WHEN I SAID YOU LOOKED CUTE IN YOUR SWIMSUIT...
WERE YOU REALLY HAPPY?

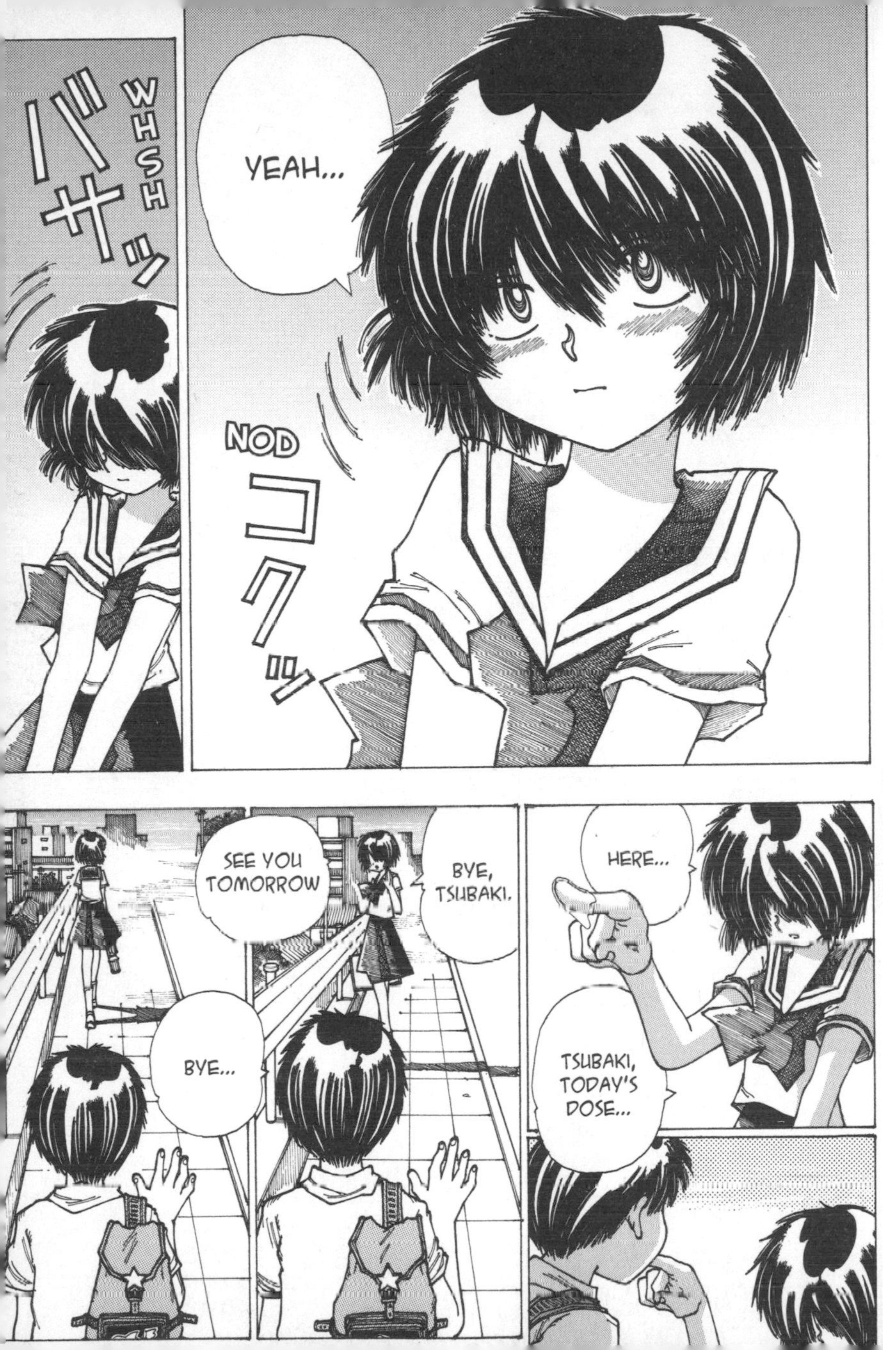
YEAH...
NOD
コクッ
WHSH
バサッ
HERE...
TSUBAKI, TODAY'S DOSE...
BYE, TSUBAKI.
SEE YOU TOMORROW
BYE...

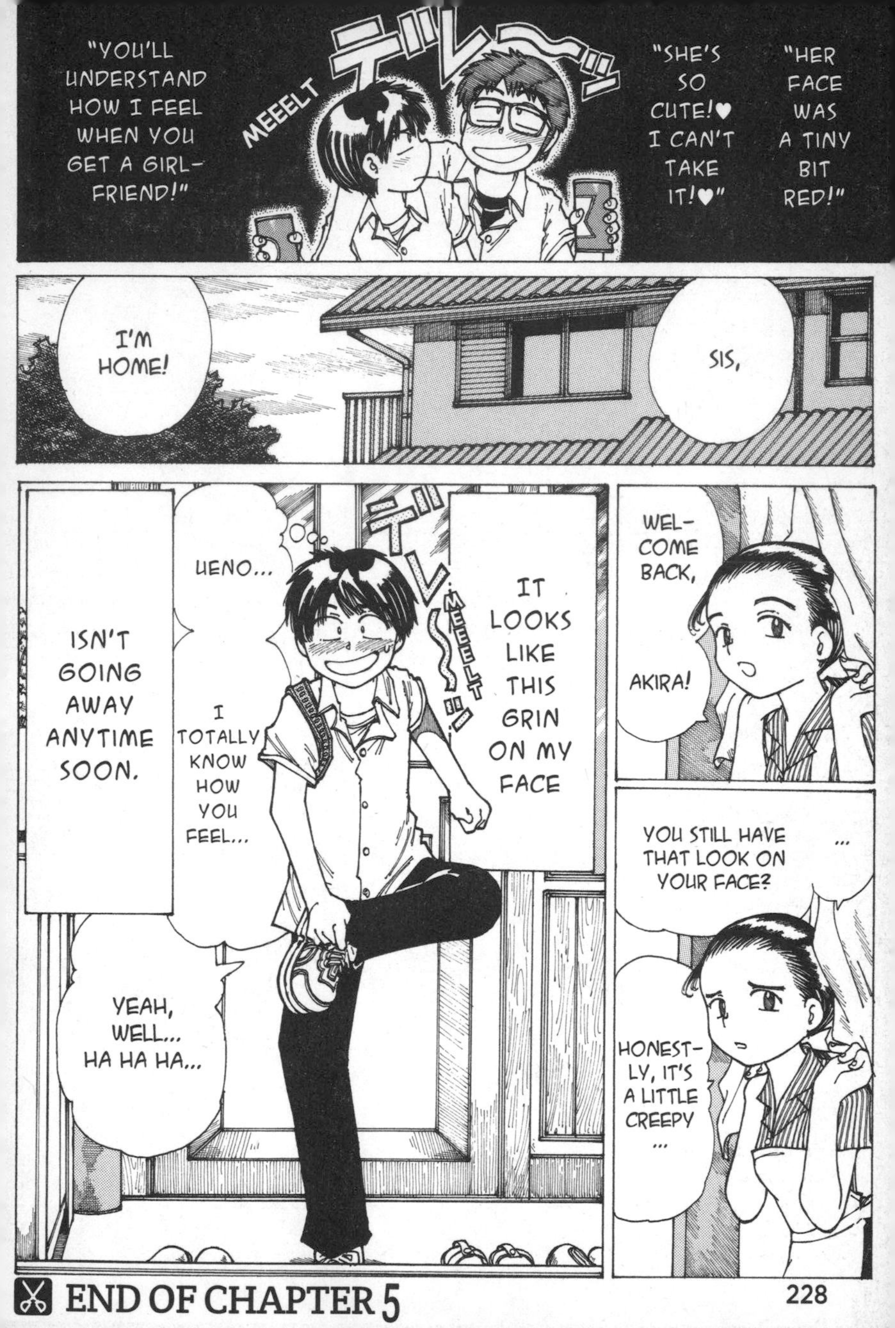
"HER FACE WAS A TINY BIT RED!"
"SHE'S SO CUTE!♥ I CAN'T TAKE IT!♥"
MEEELT
"YOU'LL UNDERSTAND HOW I FEEL WHEN YOU GET A GIRL-FRIEND!"
SIS,
I'M HOME!
WEL-COME BACK,
AKIRA!
YOU STILL HAVE THAT LOOK ON YOUR FACE?
...
HONEST-LY, IT'S A LITTLE CREEPY ...
IT LOOKS LIKE THIS GRIN ON MY FACE
MEEELT
UENO...
I TOTALLY KNOW HOW YOU FEEL...
ISN'T GOING AWAY ANYTIME SOON.
YEAH, WELL... HA HA HA...

END OF CHAPTER 5

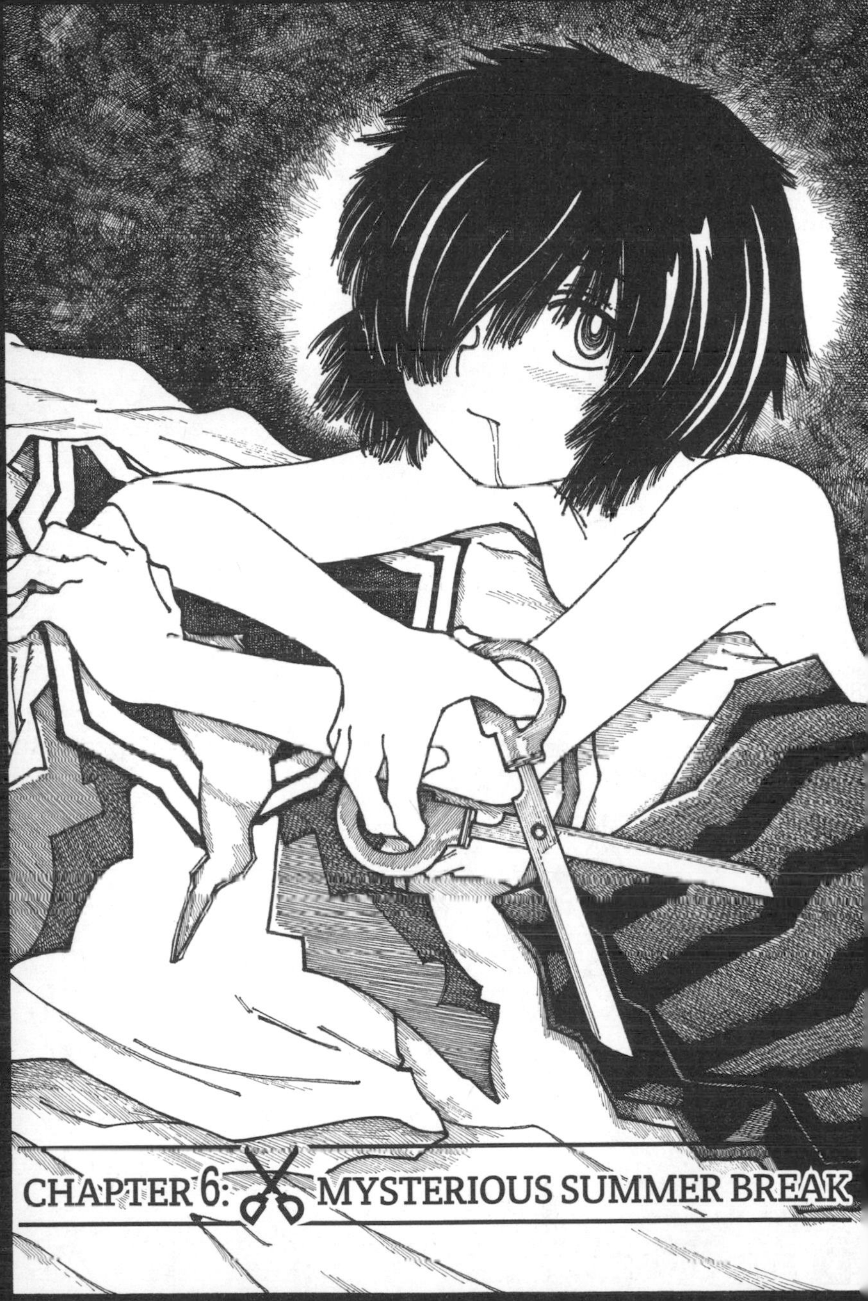

CHAPTER 6: MYSTERIOUS SUMMER BREAK

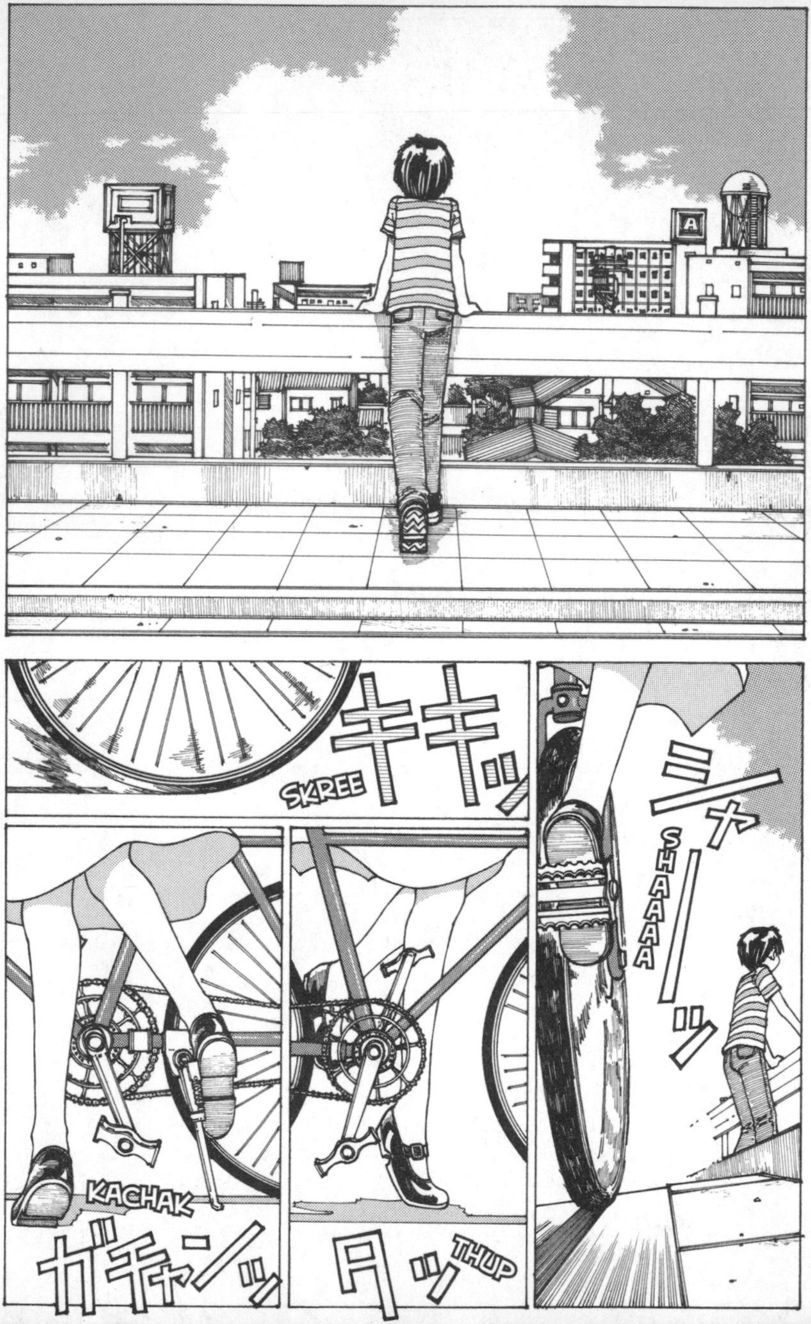
シャーーッ
SHAAAAA
キキッ
SKREE
THUP
KACHAK
ガチャンッ

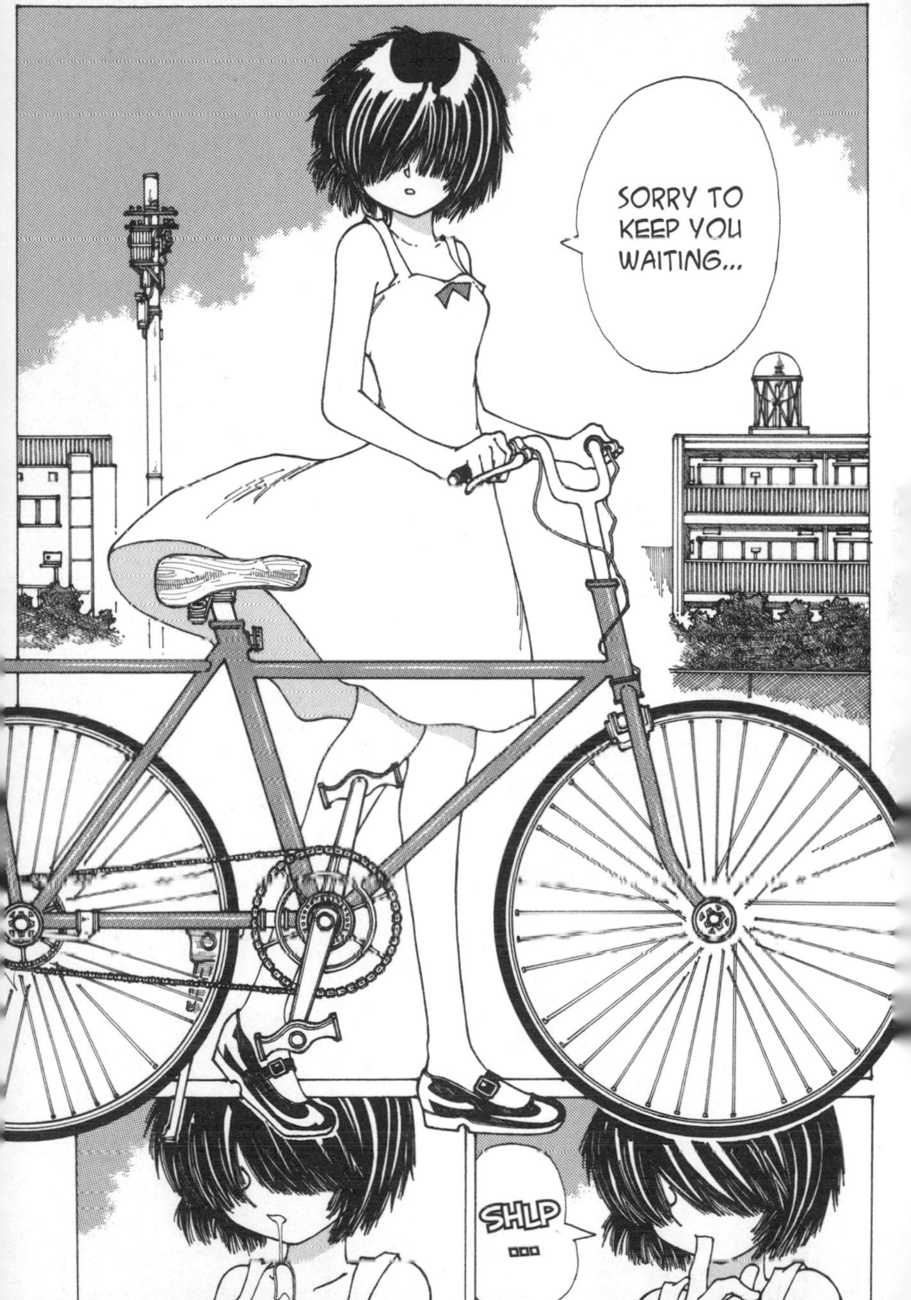
SORRY TO KEEP YOU WAITING...
SHLP
...

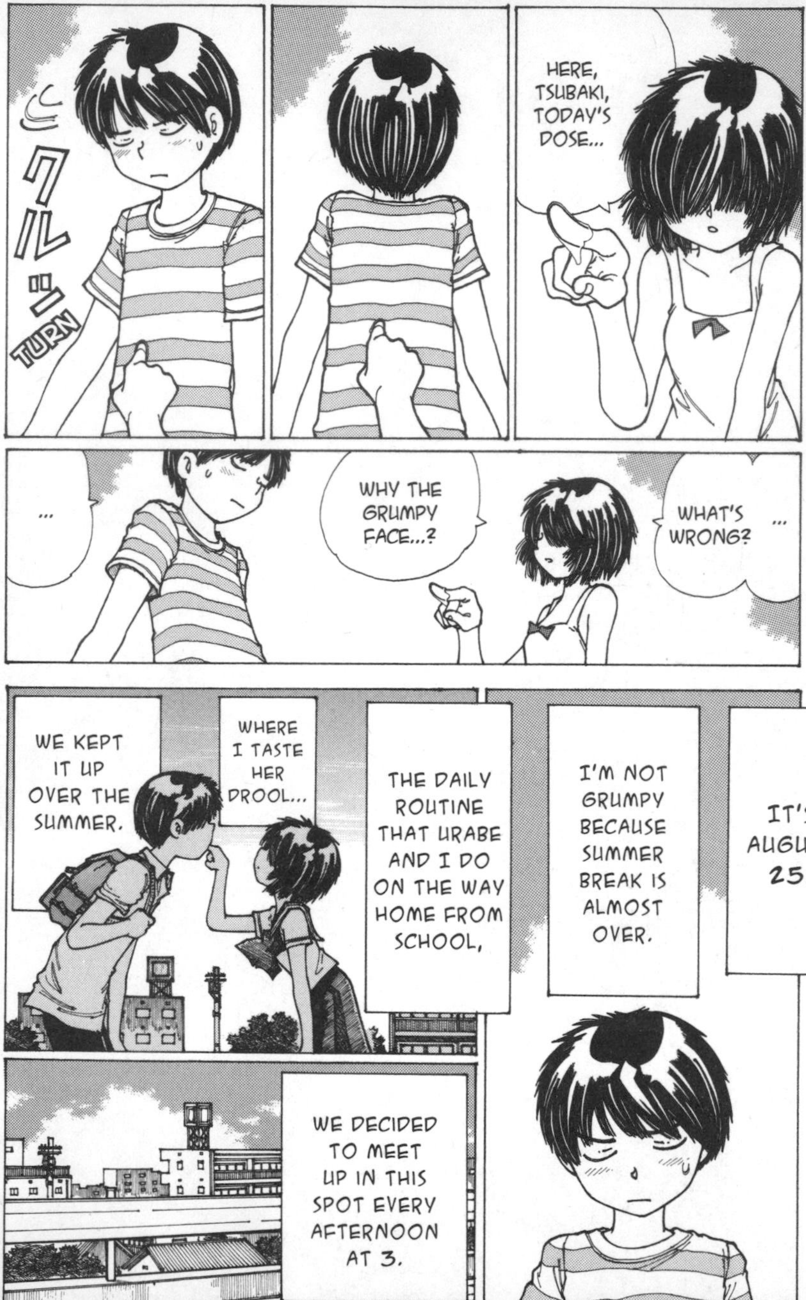
HERE, TSUBAKI, TODAY'S DOSE...
クルッ
TURN
WHAT'S WRONG? ...
WHY THE GRUMPY FACE...?
...
IT'S AUGUST 25.
I'M NOT GRUMPY BECAUSE SUMMER BREAK IS ALMOST OVER.
THE DAILY ROUTINE THAT URABE AND I DO ON THE WAY HOME FROM SCHOOL,
WHERE I TASTE HER DROOL...
WE KEPT IT UP OVER THE SUMMER.
WE DECIDED TO MEET UP IN THIS SPOT EVERY AFTERNOON AT 3.

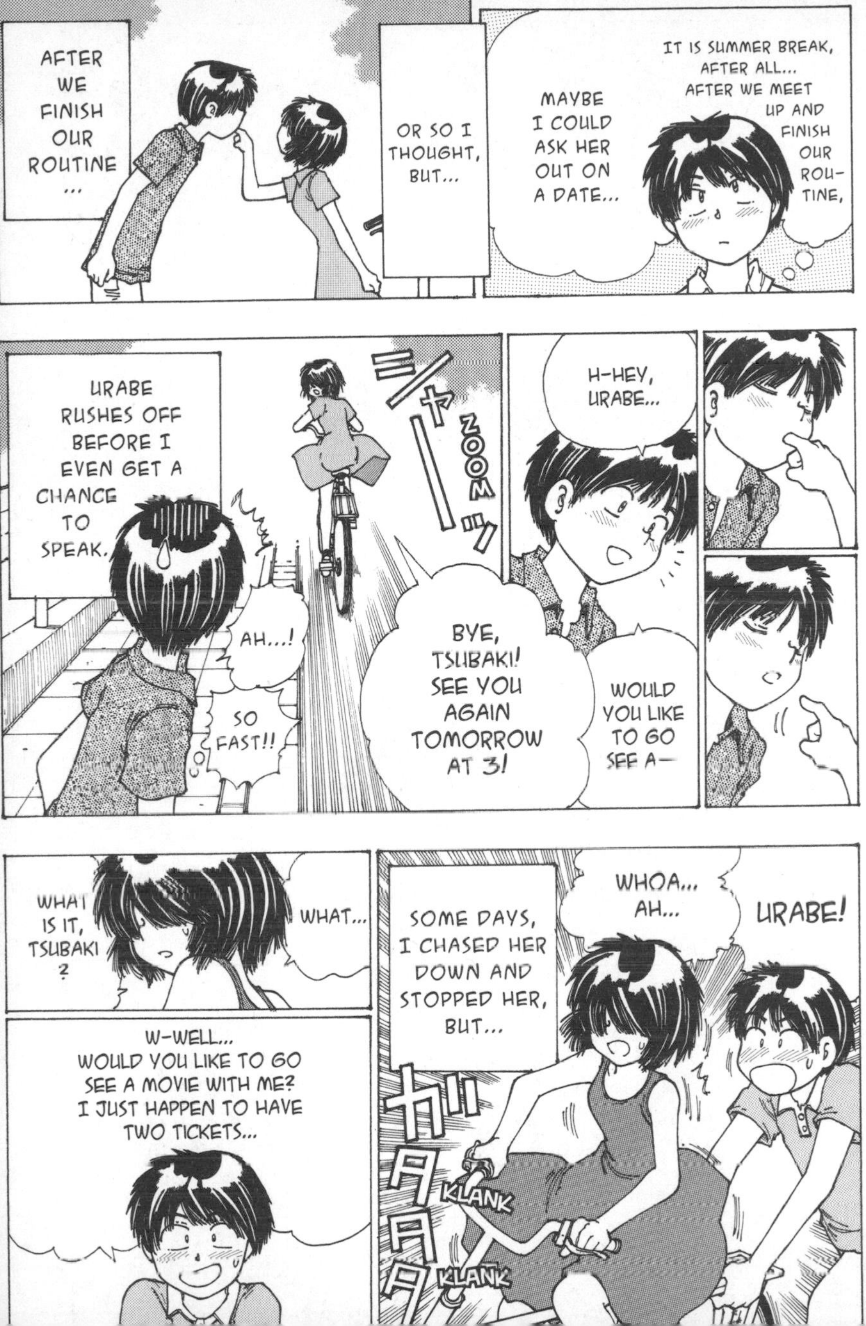
IT IS SUMMER BREAK, AFTER ALL... AFTER WE MEET UP AND FINISH OUR ROU-TINE,
MAYBE I COULD ASK HER OUT ON A DATE...
OR SO I THOUGHT, BUT...
AFTER WE FINISH OUR ROUTINE...
H-HEY, URABE...
WOULD YOU LIKE TO GO SEE A—
BYE, TSUBAKI! SEE YOU AGAIN TOMORROW AT 3!
URABE RUSHES OFF BEFORE I EVEN GET A CHANCE TO SPEAK.
ZOOM
AH...!
SO FAST!!
URABE!
WHOA... AH...
SOME DAYS, I CHASED HER DOWN AND STOPPED HER, BUT...
KLANK
KLANK
WHAT...
WHAT IS IT, TSUBAKI?
W-WELL... WOULD YOU LIKE TO GO SEE A MOVIE WITH ME? I JUST HAPPEN TO HAVE TWO TICKETS...

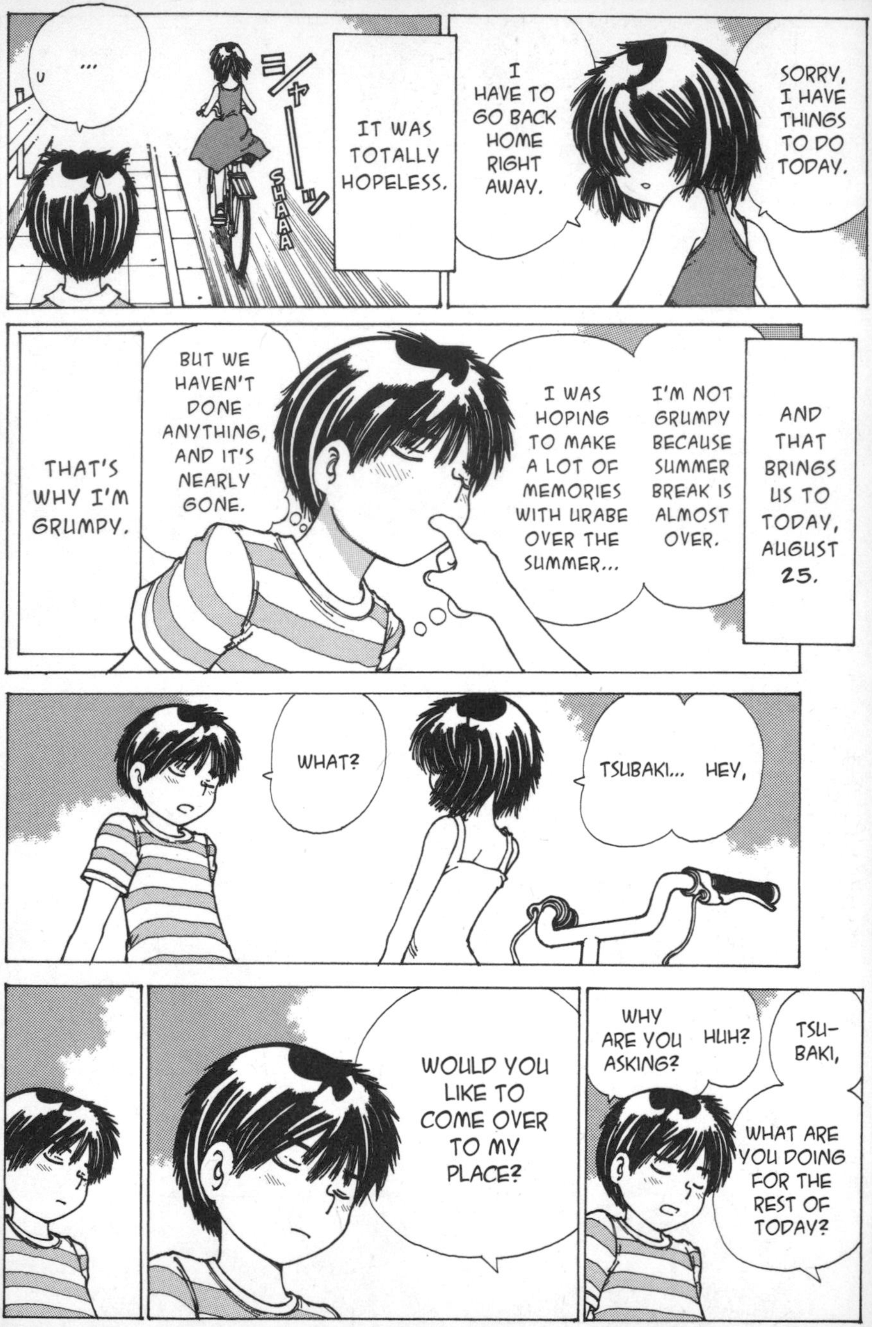
SORRY, I HAVE THINGS TO DO TODAY.
I HAVE TO GO BACK HOME RIGHT AWAY.
IT WAS TOTALLY HOPELESS.
SHAAAA
...
AND THAT BRINGS US TO TODAY, AUGUST 25.
I'M NOT GRUMPY BECAUSE SUMMER BREAK IS ALMOST OVER.
I WAS HOPING TO MAKE A LOT OF MEMORIES WITH URABE OVER THE SUMMER...
BUT WE HAVEN'T DONE ANYTHING, AND IT'S NEARLY GONE.
THAT'S WHY I'M GRUMPY.
TSUBAKI... HEY,
WHAT?
TSU-BAKI,
WHAT ARE YOU DOING FOR THE REST OF TODAY?
HUH?
WHY ARE YOU ASKING?
WOULD YOU LIKE TO COME OVER TO MY PLACE?

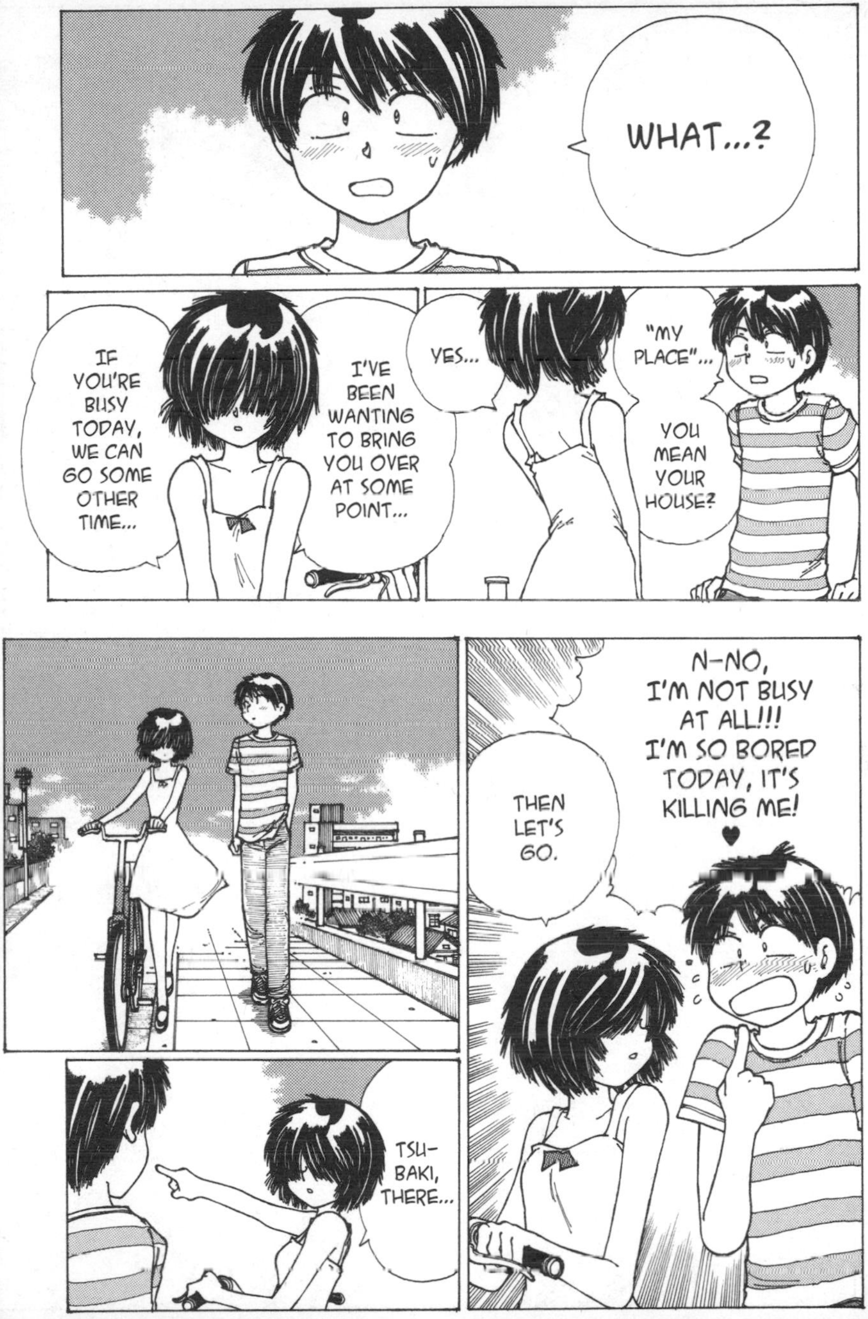
WHAT...?
"MY PLACE"...
YOU MEAN YOUR HOUSE?
YES...
I'VE BEEN WANTING TO BRING YOU OVER AT SOME POINT...
IF YOU'RE BUSY TODAY, WE CAN GO SOME OTHER TIME...
N-NO, I'M NOT BUSY AT ALL!!! I'M SO BORED TODAY, IT'S KILLING ME! ♥
THEN LET'S GO.
TSU-BAKI, THERE...

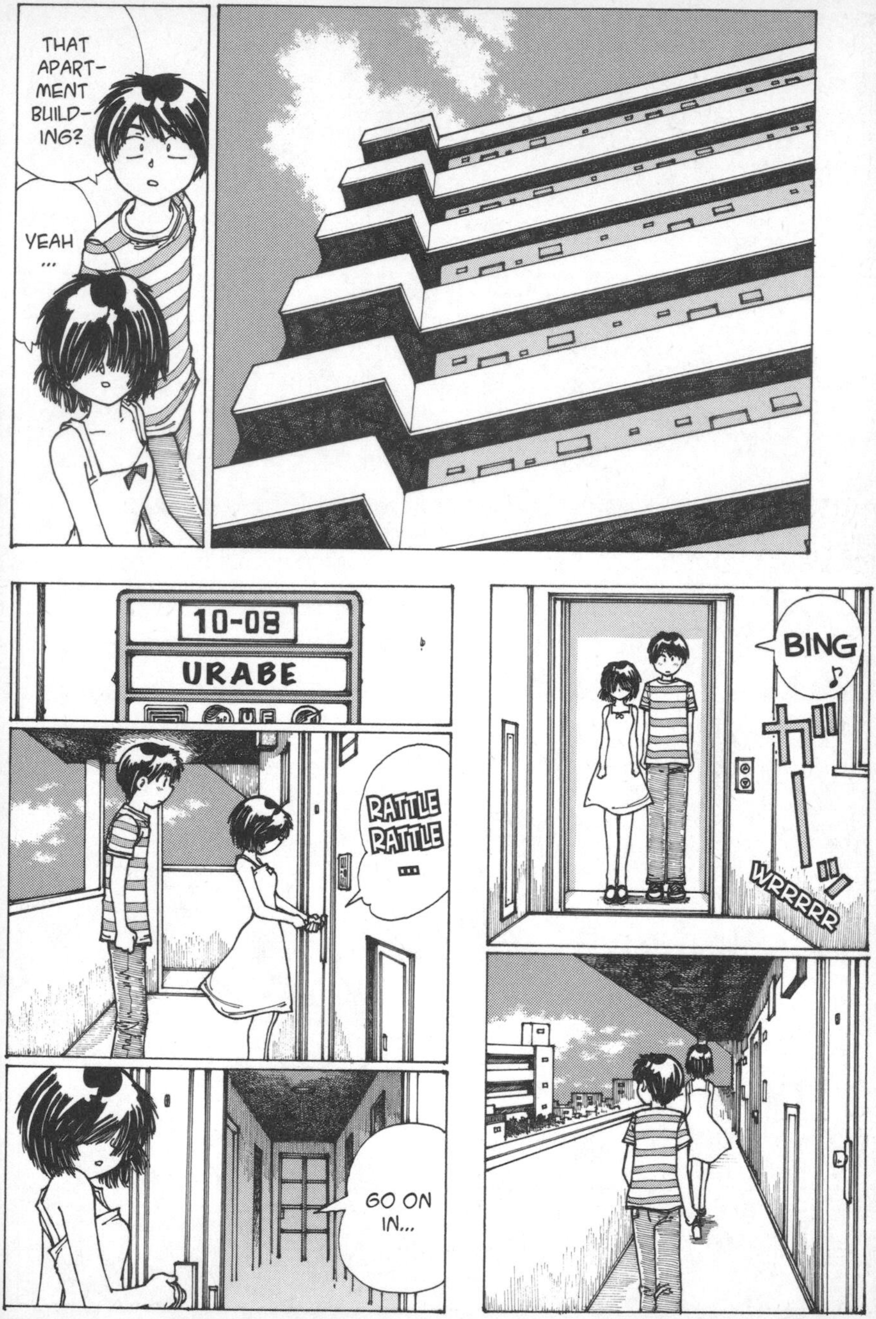
THAT APARTMENT BUILDING?
YEAH ...
BING ♪
ガーッ
WRRRRR
10-08
URABE
RATTLE RATTLE ...
GO ON IN...

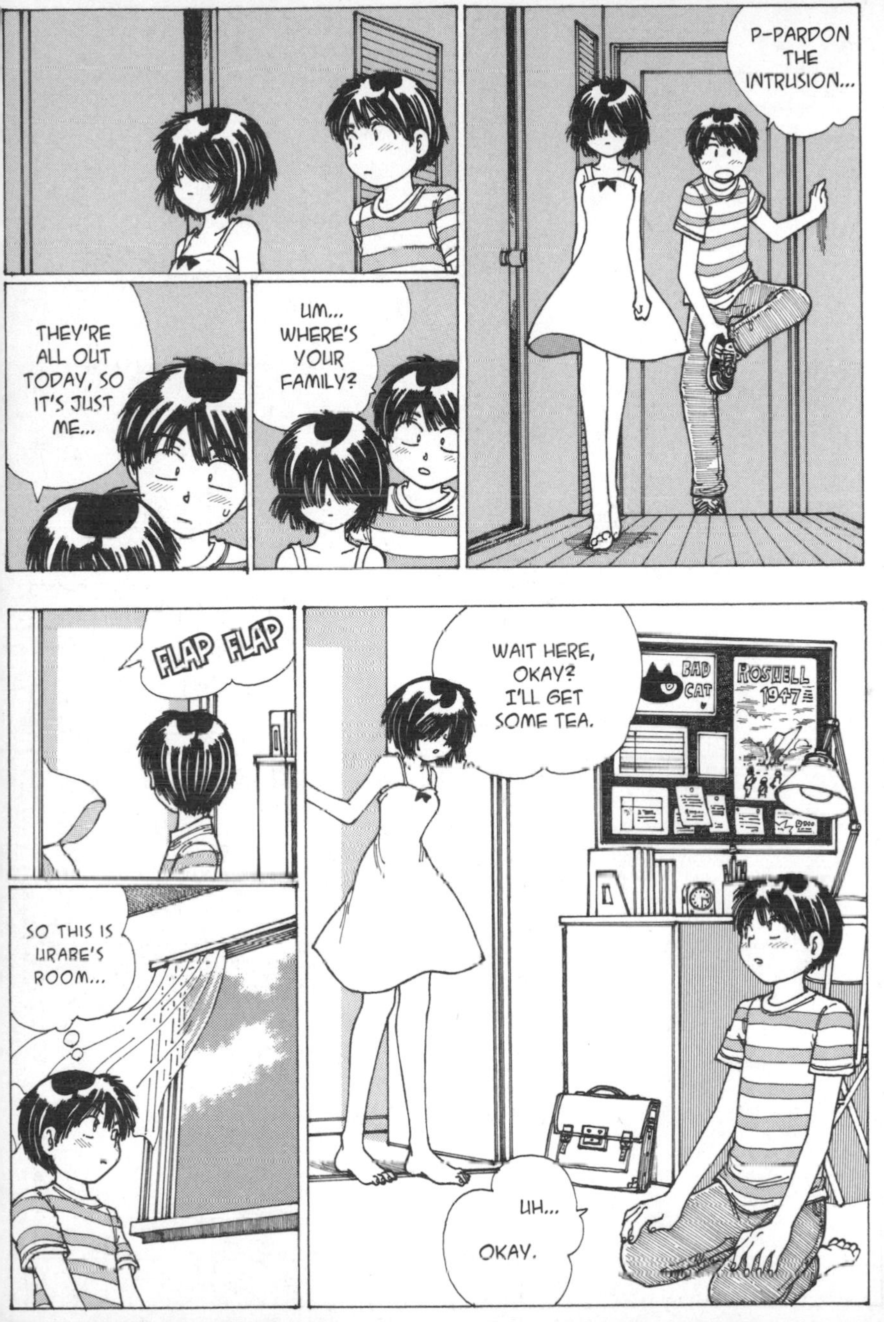
P-PARDON THE INTRUSION...
UM... WHERE'S YOUR FAMILY?
THEY'RE ALL OUT TODAY, SO IT'S JUST ME...
WAIT HERE, OKAY? I'LL GET SOME TEA.
BAD CAT
ROSWELL 1947
UH...
OKAY.
FLAP FLAP
SO THIS IS URABE'S ROOM...

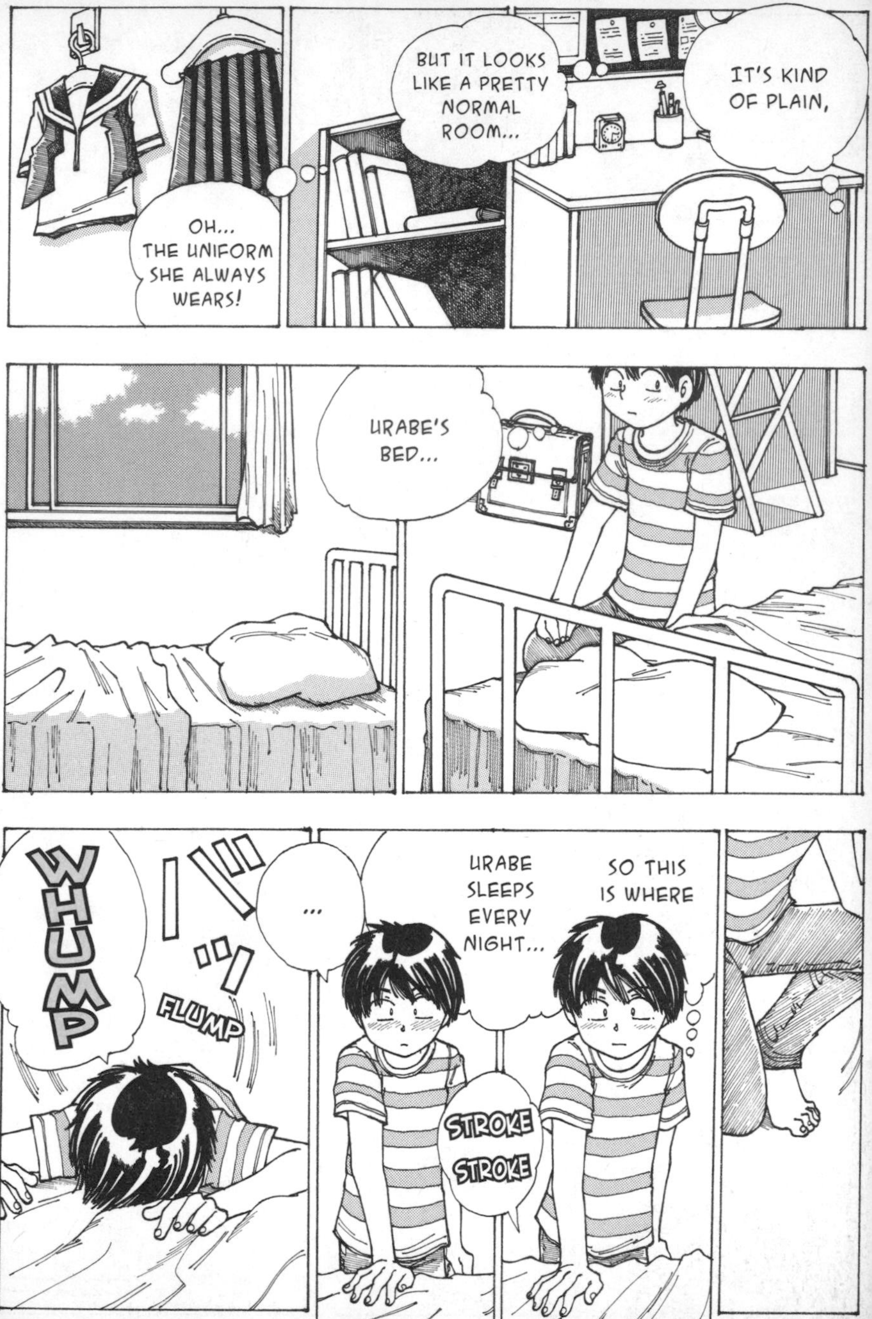

IT'S KIND OF PLAIN,
BUT IT LOOKS LIKE A PRETTY NORMAL ROOM...
OH... THE UNIFORM SHE ALWAYS WEARS!
URABE'S BED...
SO THIS IS WHERE
URABE SLEEPS EVERY NIGHT...
STROKE
STROKE
...
WHUMP
FLUMP

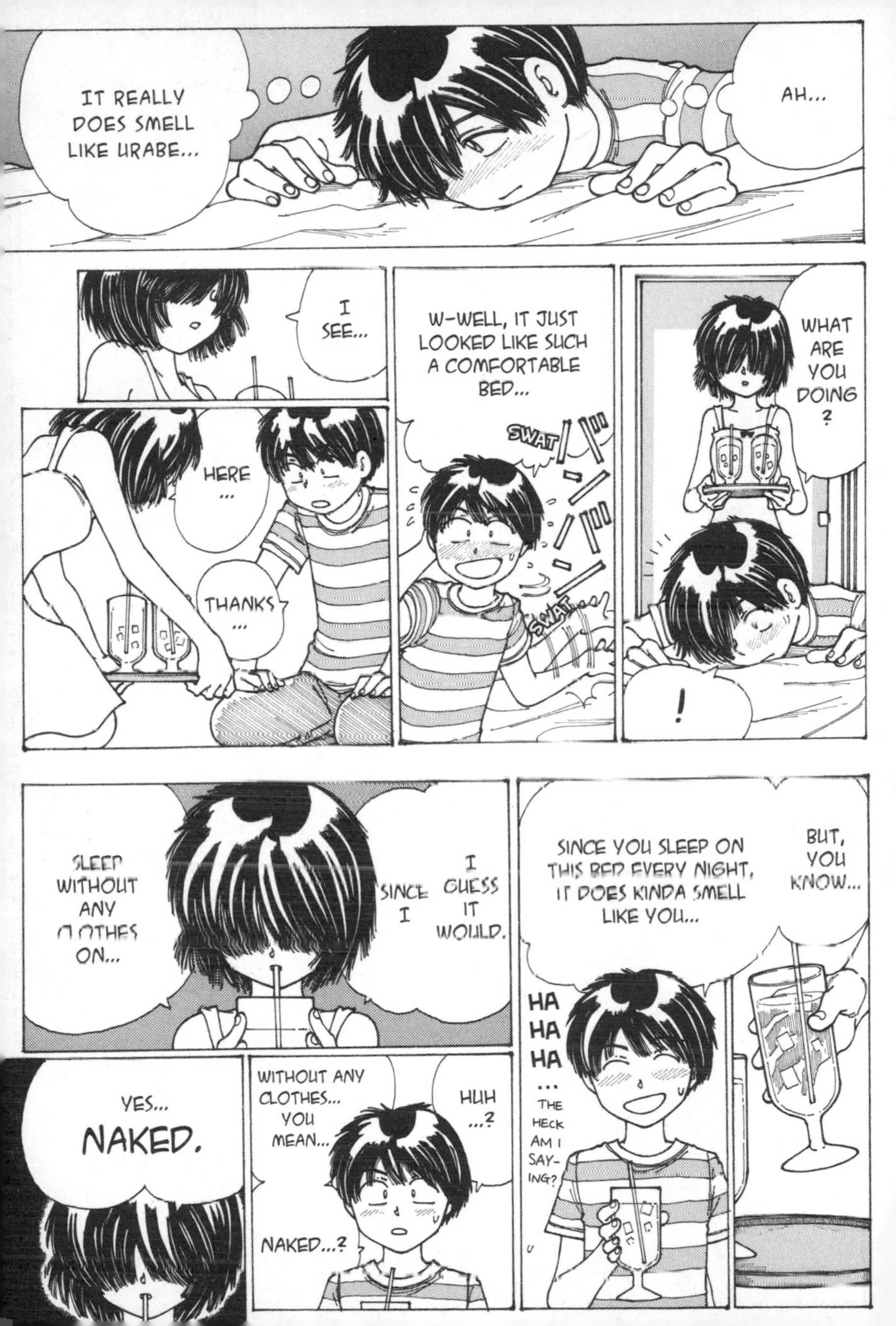

AH...
IT REALLY DOES SMELL LIKE URABE...
WHAT ARE YOU DOING?
!
W-WELL, IT JUST LOOKED LIKE SUCH A COMFORTABLE BED...
SWAT
SWAT
I SEE...
HERE...
THANKS...
BUT, YOU KNOW...
SINCE YOU SLEEP ON THIS BED EVERY NIGHT, IT DOES KINDA SMELL LIKE YOU...
HA HA HA...
THE HECK AM I SAYING?
I GUESS IT WOULD.
SINCE I
SLEEP WITHOUT ANY CLOTHES ON...
HUH...?
WITHOUT ANY CLOTHES... YOU MEAN...
NAKED...?
YES...
NAKED.

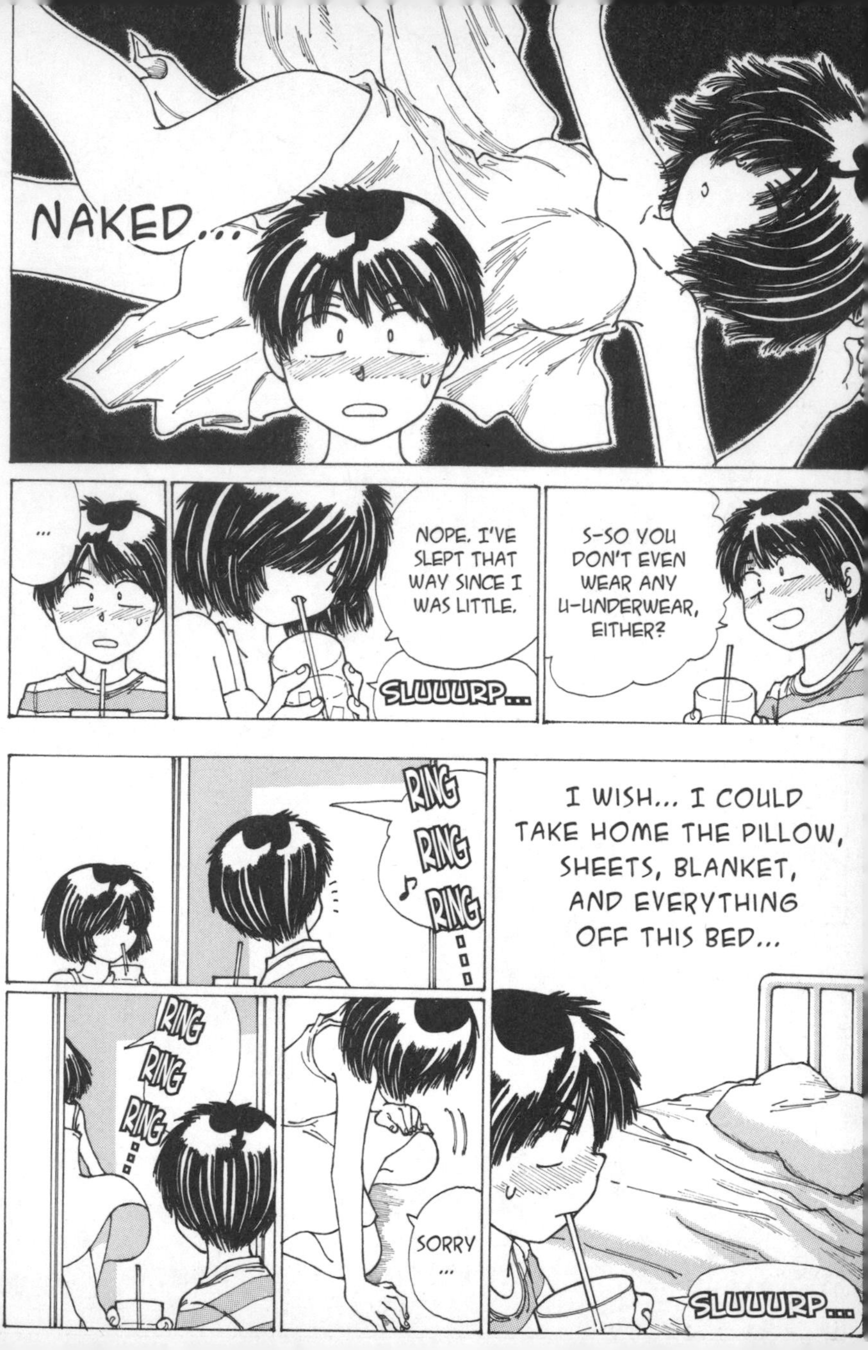
NAKED....
S-SO YOU DON'T EVEN WEAR ANY U-UNDERWEAR, EITHER?
NOPE. I'VE SLEPT THAT WAY SINCE I WAS LITTLE.
SLUUURP...
...
I WISH... I COULD TAKE HOME THE PILLOW, SHEETS, BLANKET, AND EVERYTHING OFF THIS BED...
RING RING RING...
SLUUURP...
SORRY ...
RING RING RING...

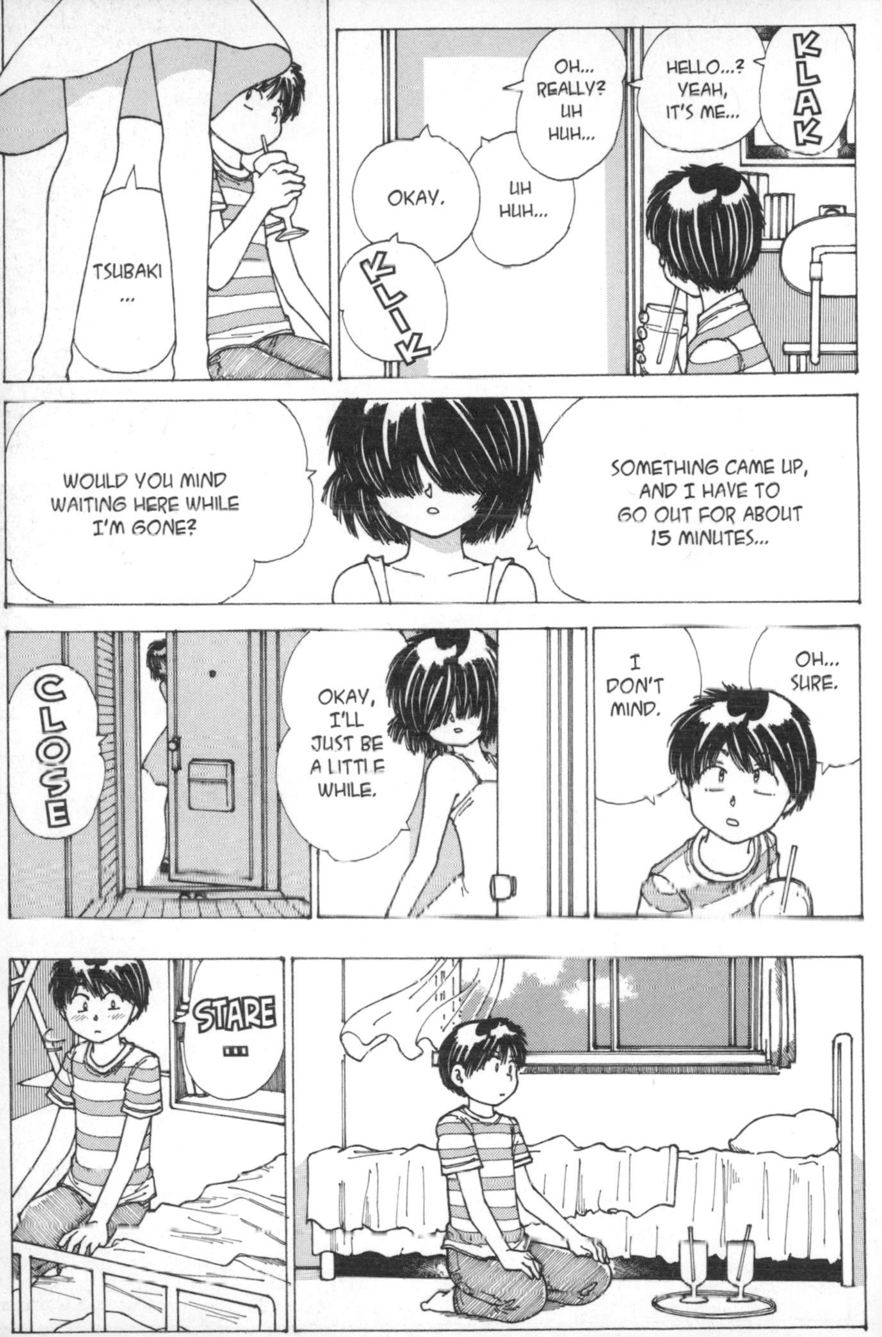

KLAK
HELLO...? YEAH, IT'S ME...
OH... REALLY? UH HUH...
UH HUH...
OKAY.
KLIK
TSUBAKI ...
SOMETHING CAME UP, AND I HAVE TO GO OUT FOR ABOUT 15 MINUTES...
WOULD YOU MIND WAITING HERE WHILE I'M GONE?
OH... SURE.
I DON'T MIND.
OKAY, I'LL JUST BE A LITTLE WHILE.
CLOSE
STARE ...

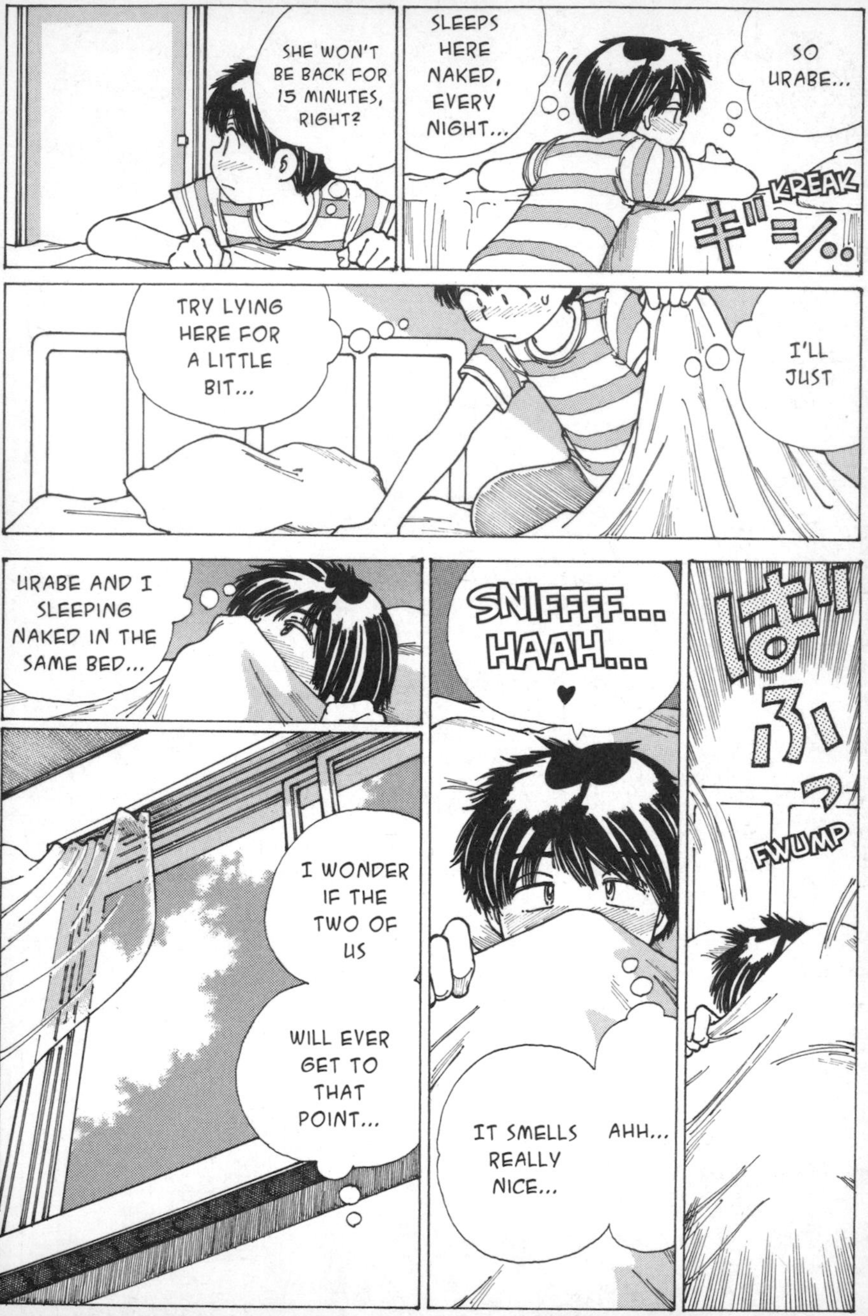
SO URABE...
SLEEPS HERE NAKED, EVERY NIGHT...
KREAK
SHE WON'T BE BACK FOR 15 MINUTES, RIGHT?
I'LL JUST
TRY LYING HERE FOR A LITTLE BIT...
ばふっ
FWUMP
SNIFFFF... HAAH... ♥
AHH...
IT SMELLS REALLY NICE...
URABE AND I SLEEPING NAKED IN THE SAME BED...
I WONDER IF THE TWO OF US
WILL EVER GET TO THAT POINT...

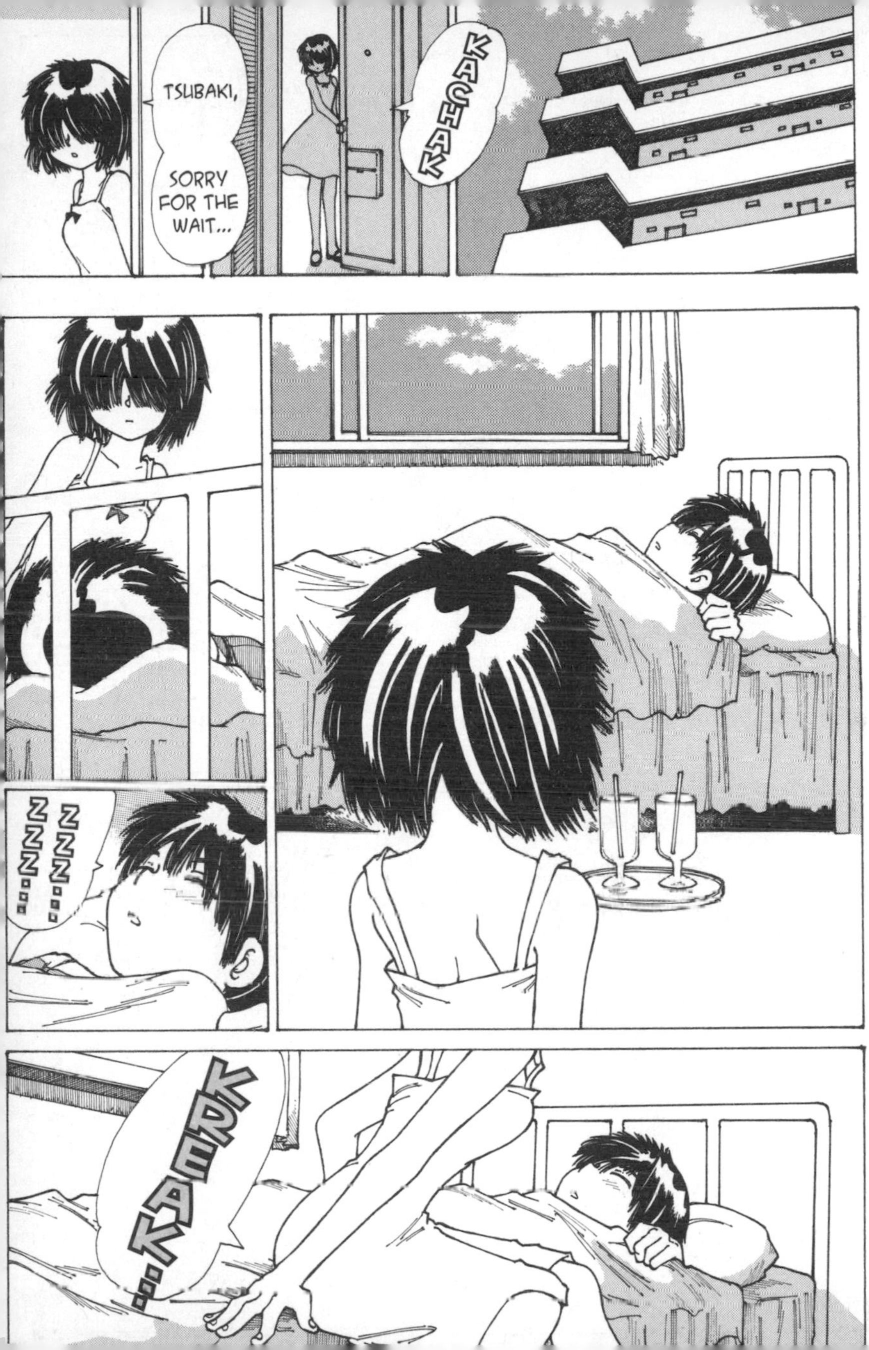
KACHAK
TSUBAKI,
SORRY FOR THE WAIT...
ZZZ... ZZZ...
KREAK...

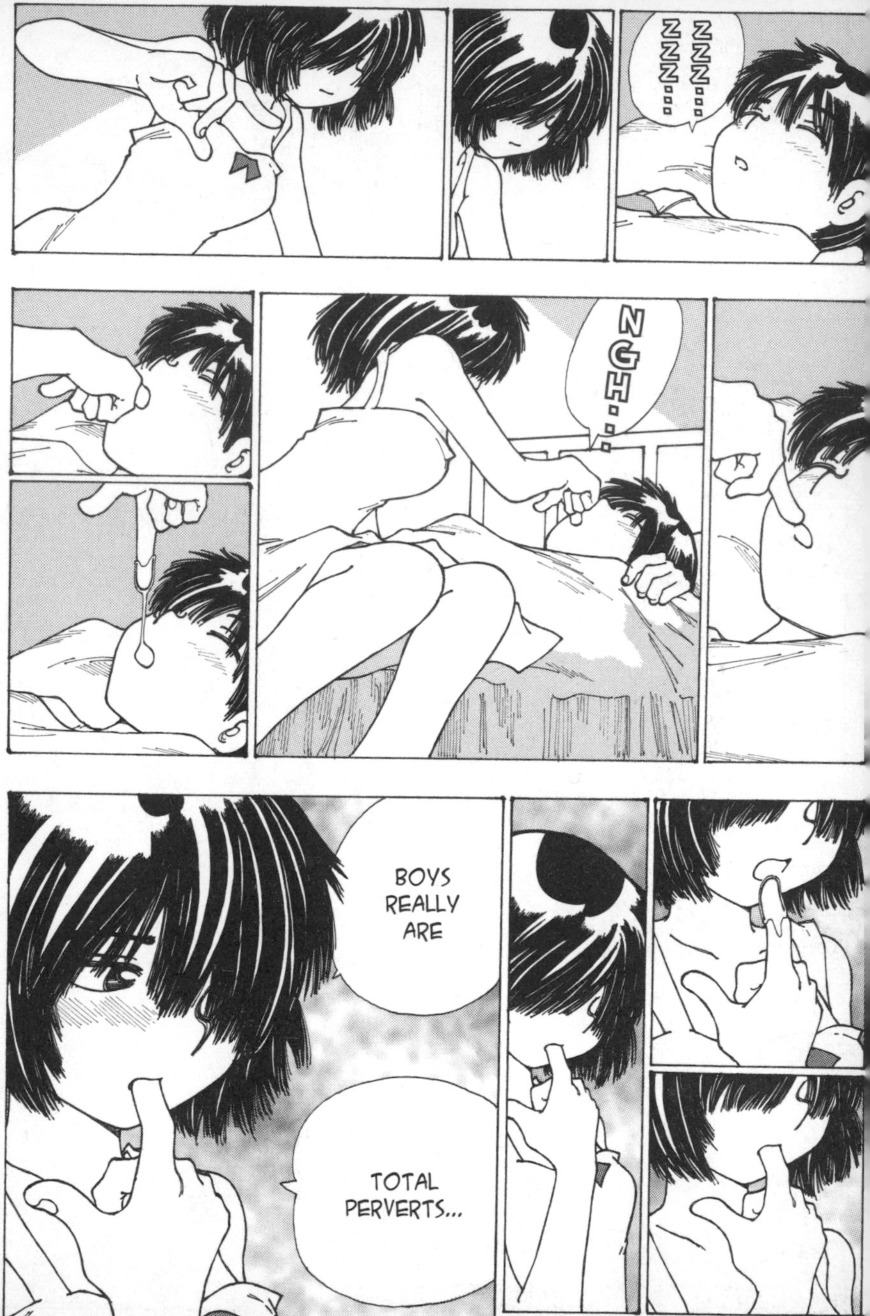
ZZZ...
ZZZ...
NGH...
BOYS REALLY ARE
TOTAL PERVERTS...

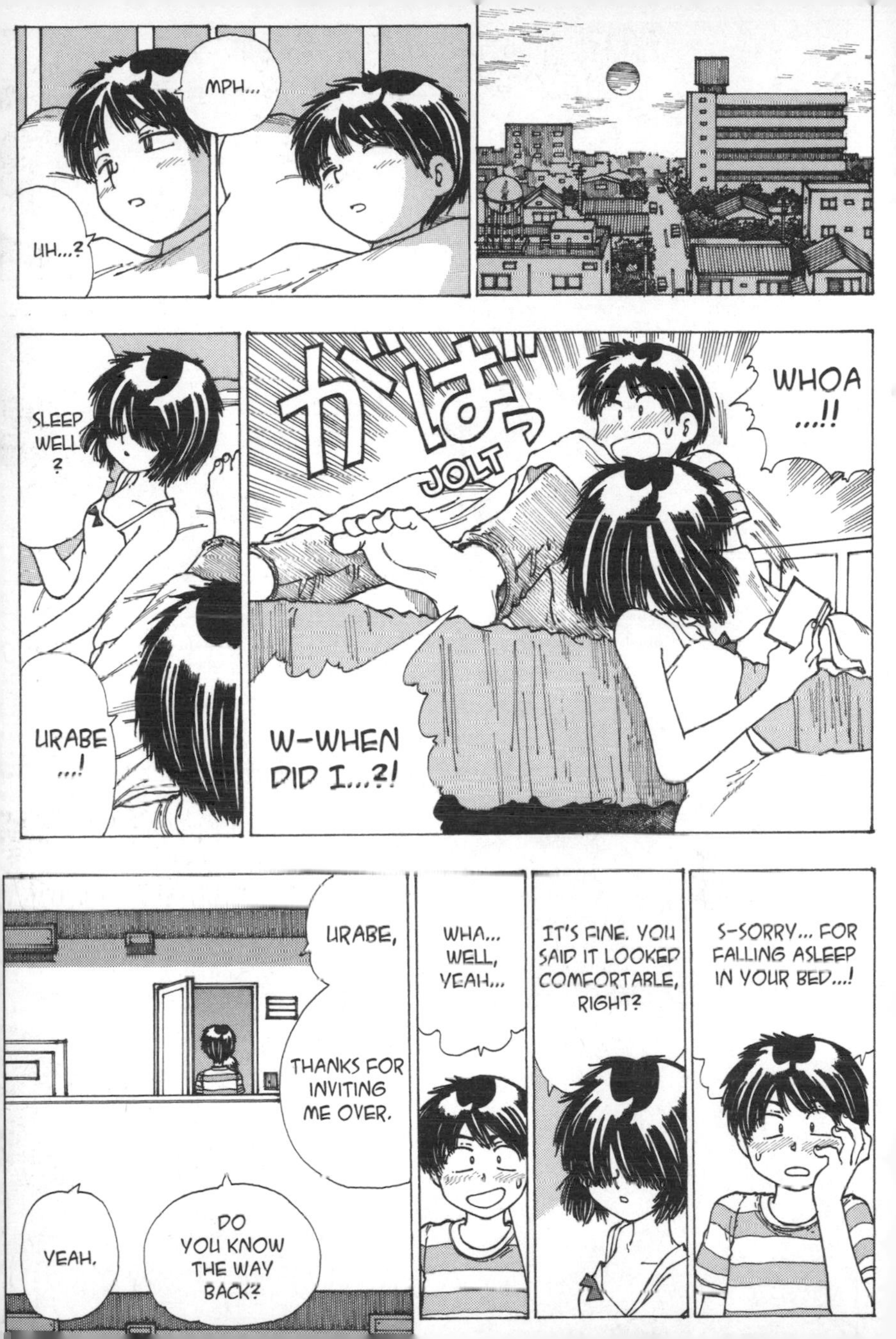
MPH...
UH...?
WHOA ...!!
かばっ
JOLT
W-WHEN DID I...?!
SLEEP WELL ?
URABE ...!
S-SORRY... FOR FALLING ASLEEP IN YOUR BED...!
IT'S FINE. YOU SAID IT LOOKED COMFORTARLE, RIGHT?
WHA... WELL, YEAH...
URABE,
THANKS FOR INVITING ME OVER.
DO YOU KNOW THE WAY BACK?
YEAH.

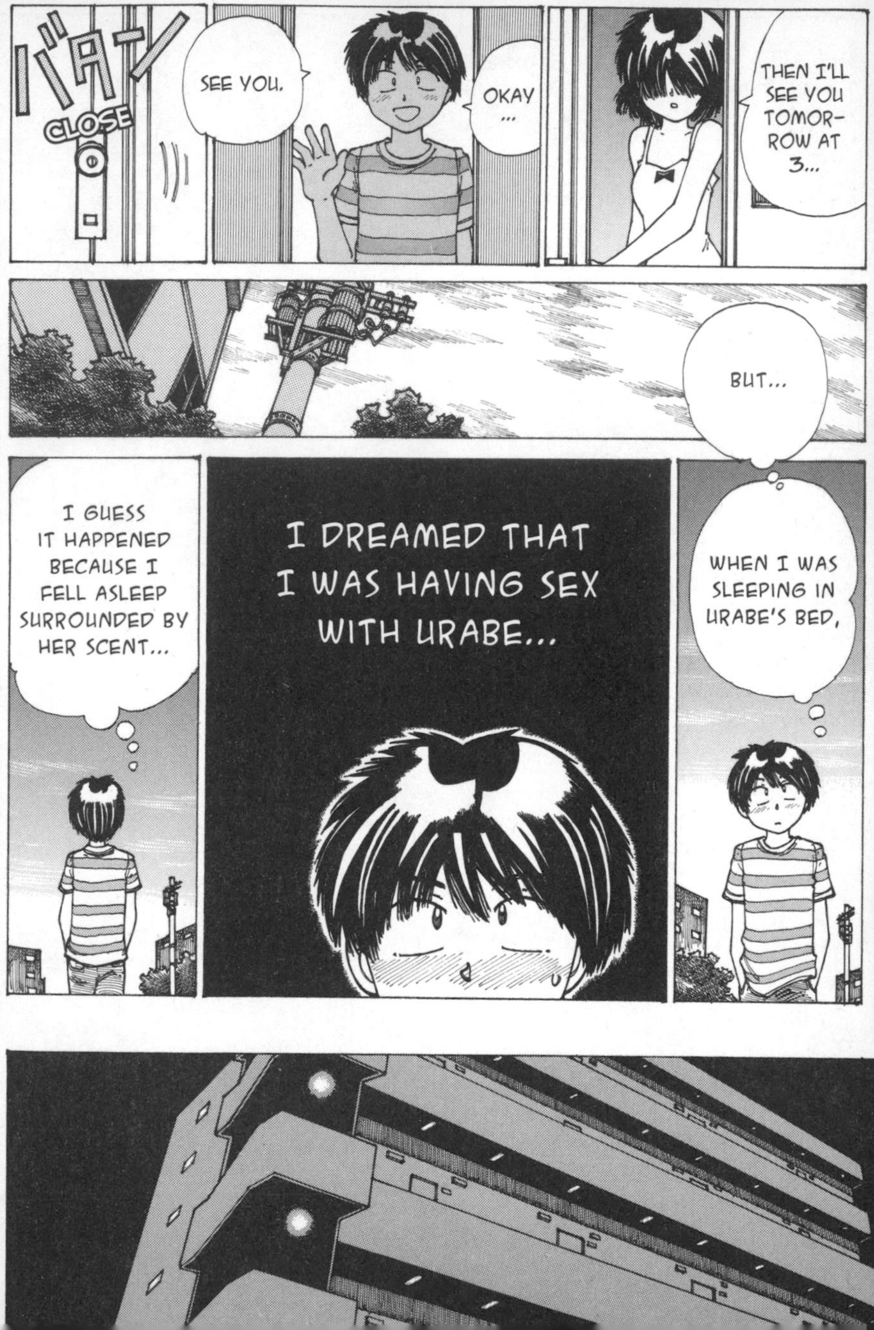
THEN I'LL SEE YOU TOMOR-ROW AT 3...
OKAY ...
SEE YOU.
バタン
CLOSE
BUT...
WHEN I WAS SLEEPING IN URABE'S BED,
I DREAMED THAT I WAS HAVING SEX WITH URABE...
I GUESS IT HAPPENED BECAUSE I FELL ASLEEP SURROUNDED BY HER SCENT...

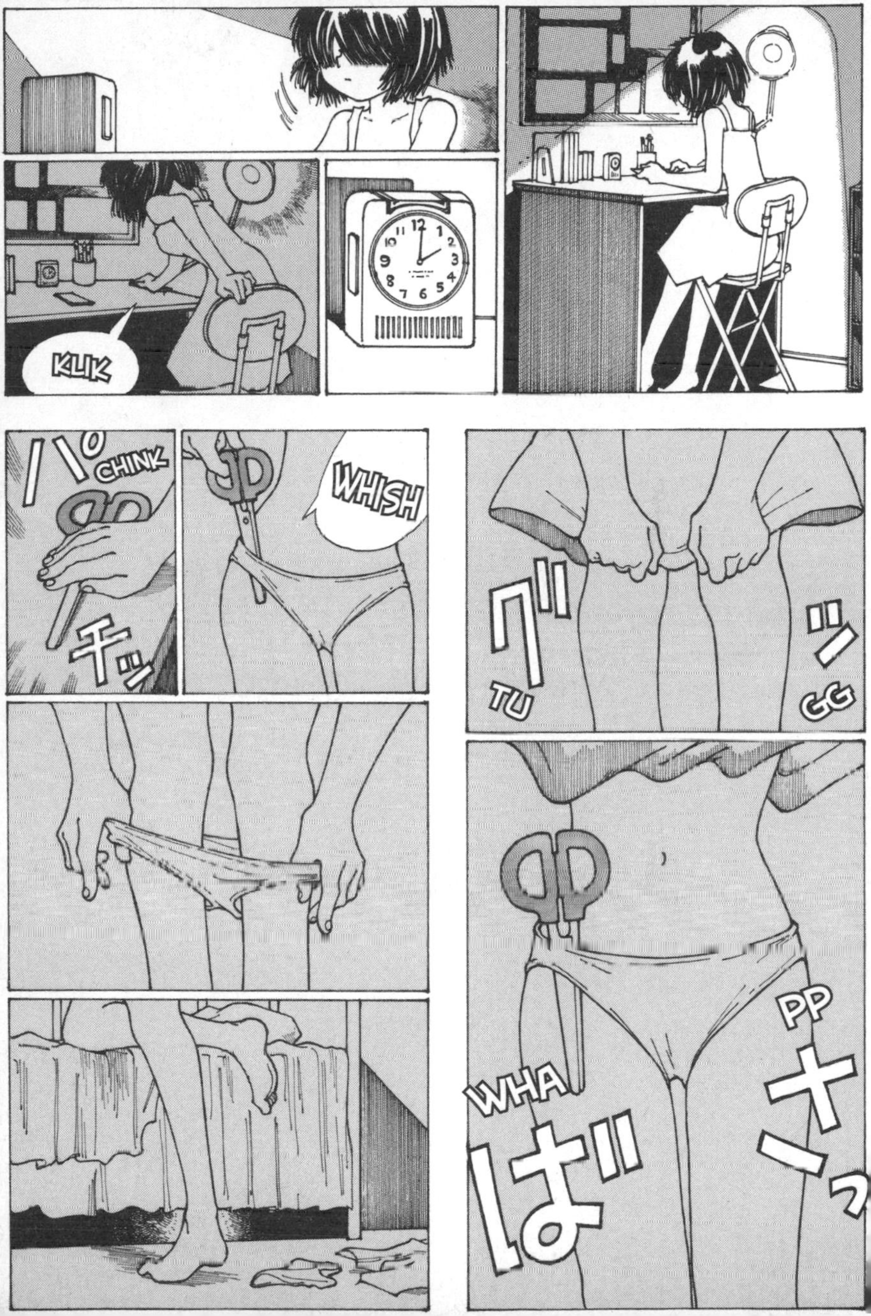
KLIK
TU
GG
WHA
PP
WHISH
CHINK

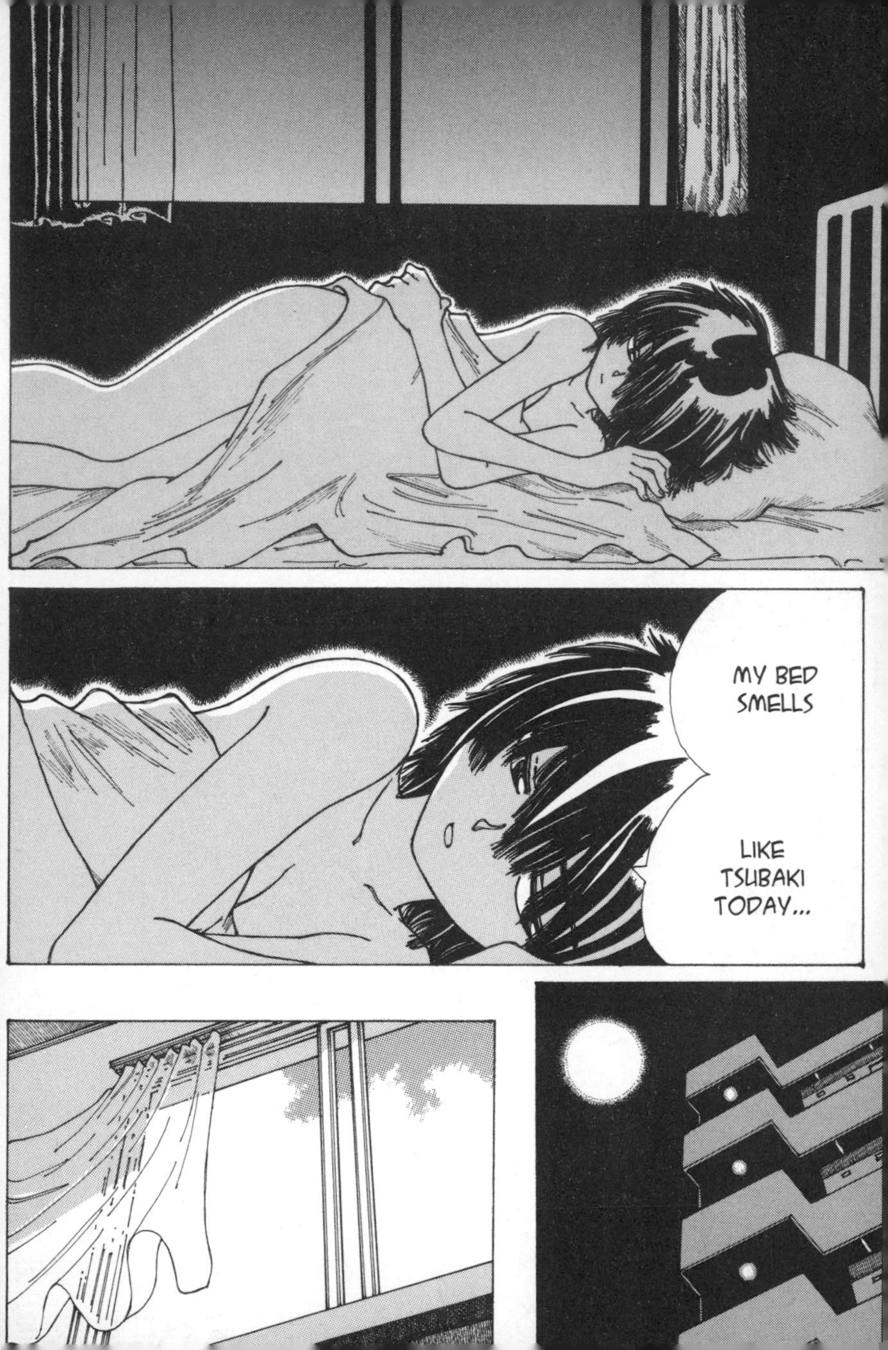
MY BED SMELLS
LIKE TSUBAKI TODAY...

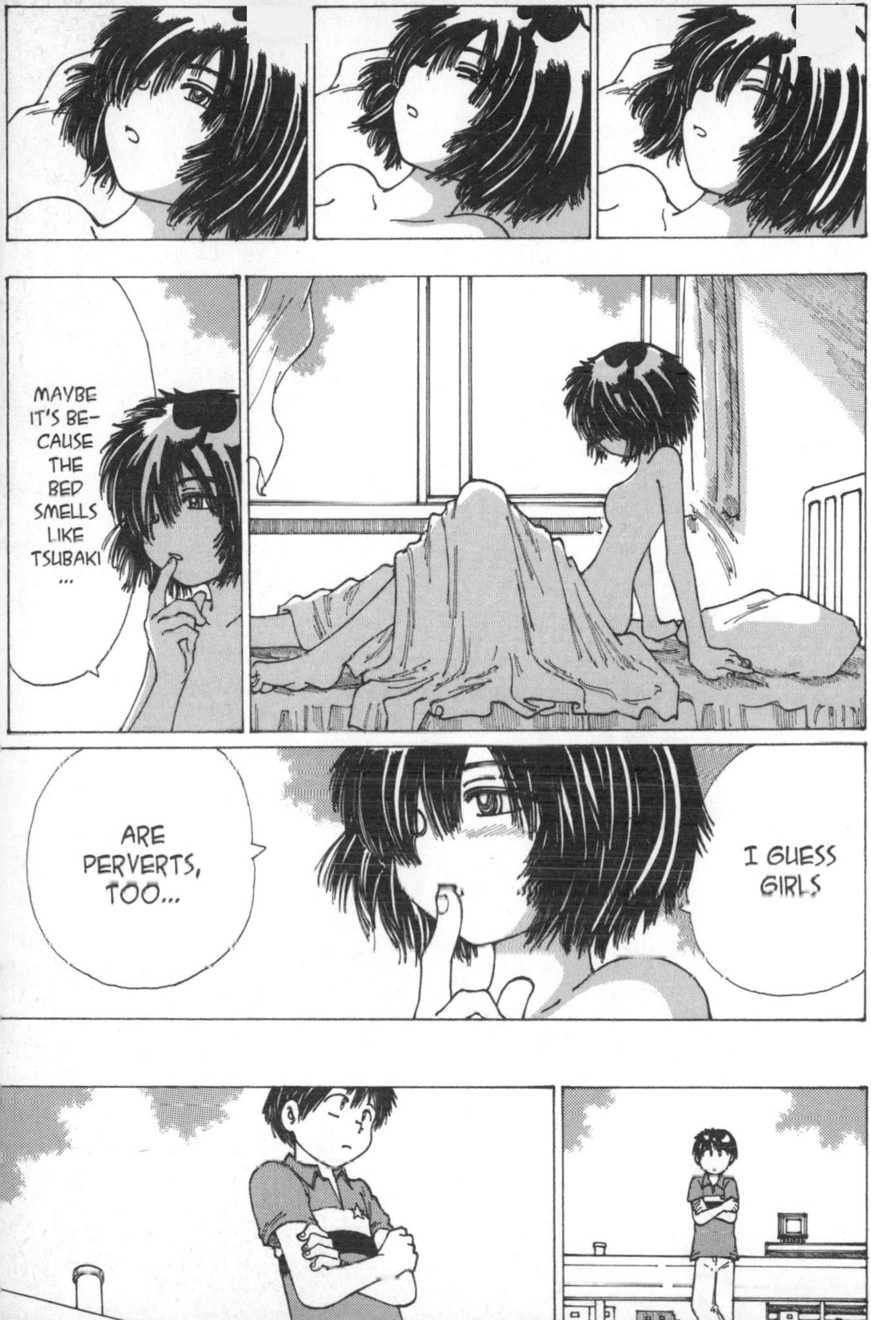
MAYBE IT'S BE-CAUSE THE BED SMELLS LIKE TSUBAKI ...
I GUESS GIRLS
ARE PERVERTS, TOO...

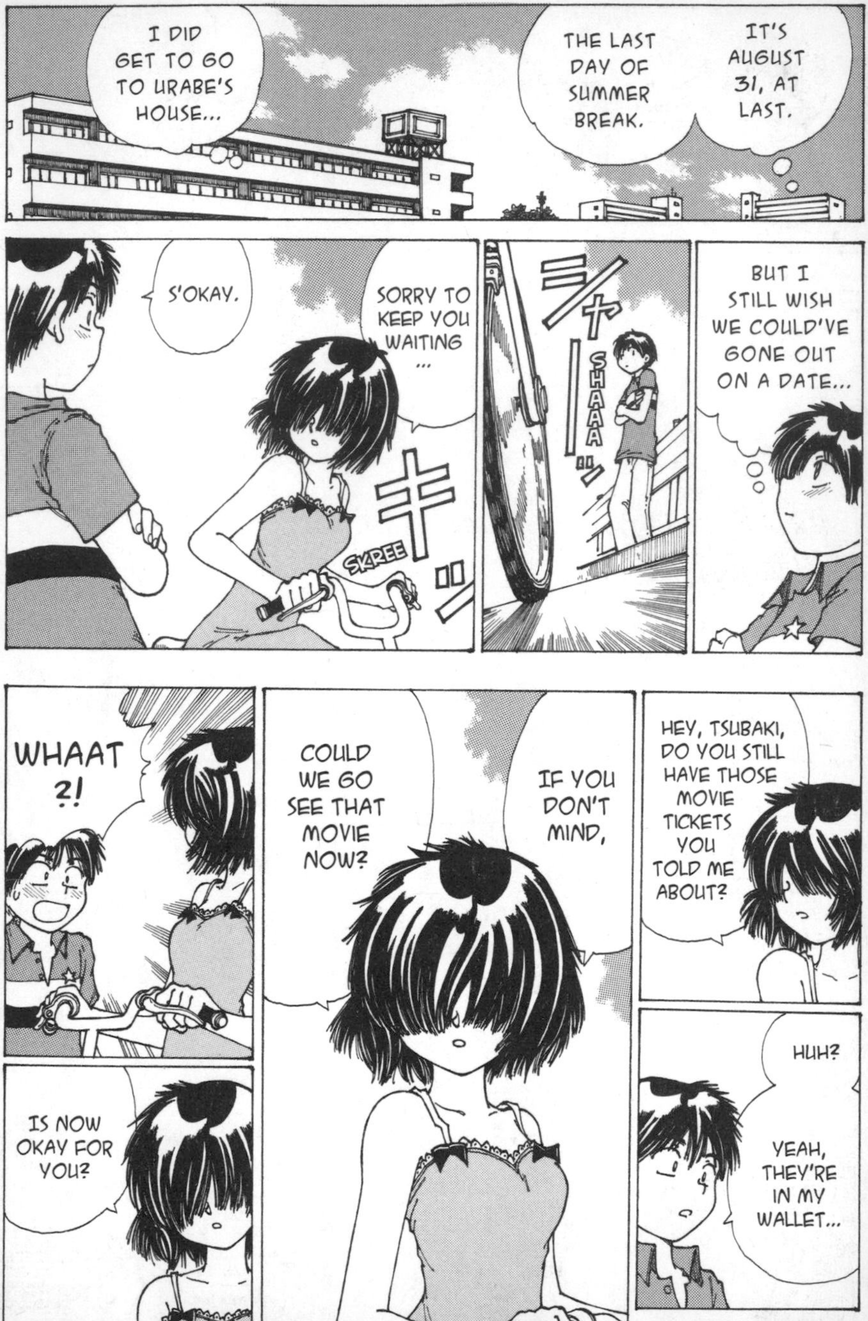
IT'S AUGUST 31, AT LAST.
THE LAST DAY OF SUMMER BREAK.
I DID GET TO GO TO URABE'S HOUSE...
BUT I STILL WISH WE COULD'VE GONE OUT ON A DATE...
SHAAA
SORRY TO KEEP YOU WAITING...
S'OKAY.
SKREE
HEY, TSUBAKI, DO YOU STILL HAVE THOSE MOVIE TICKETS YOU TOLD ME ABOUT?
HUH?
YEAH, THEY'RE IN MY WALLET...
IF YOU DON'T MIND,
COULD WE GO SEE THAT MOVIE NOW?
WHAAT ?!
IS NOW OKAY FOR YOU?

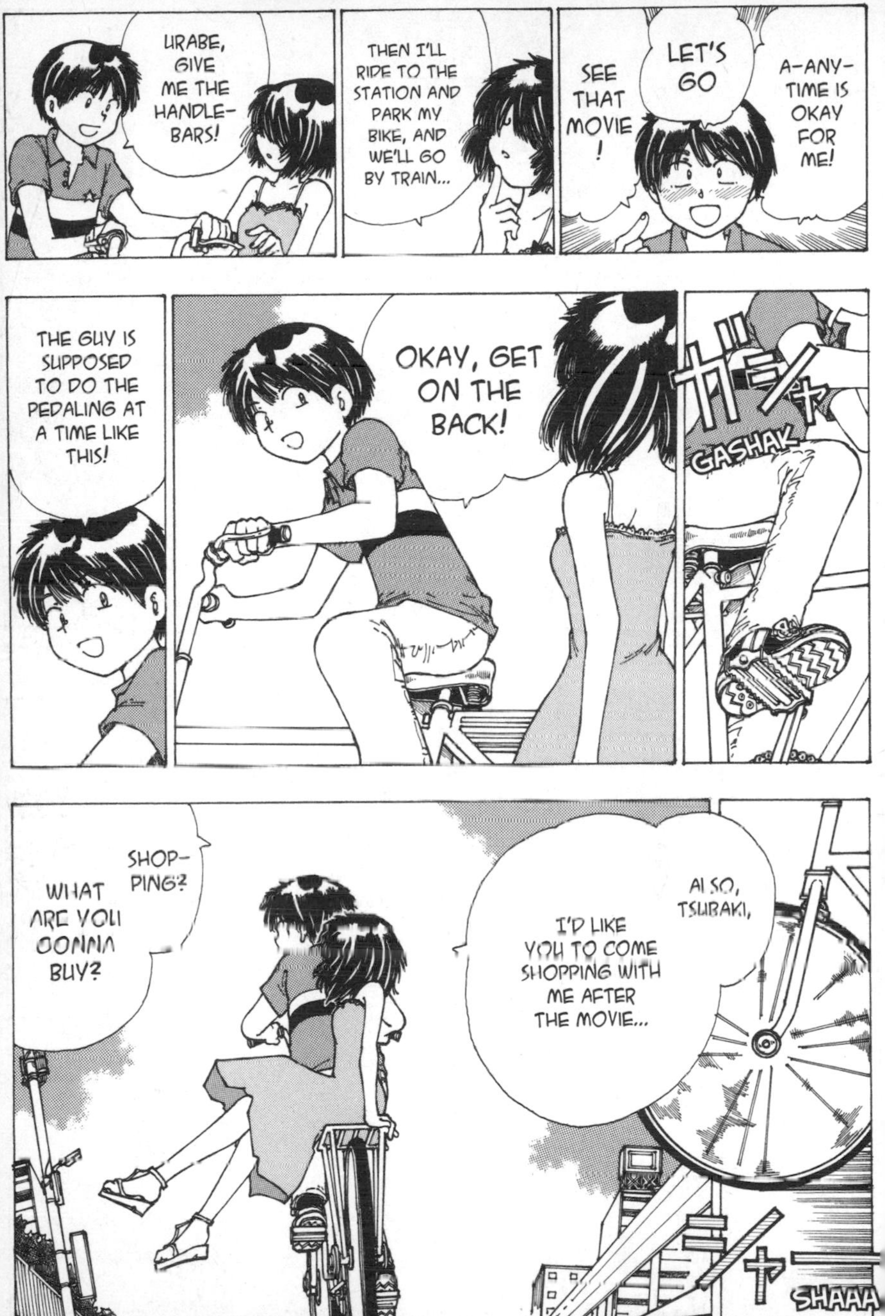
A-ANY-TIME IS OKAY FOR ME!
LET'S GO
SEE THAT MOVIE!
THEN I'LL RIDE TO THE STATION AND PARK MY BIKE, AND WE'LL GO BY TRAIN...
URABE, GIVE ME THE HANDLE-BARS!
GASHAK
OKAY, GET ON THE BACK!
THE GUY IS SUPPOSED TO DO THE PEDALING AT A TIME LIKE THIS!
SHAAA
ALSO, TSUBAKI,
I'D LIKE YOU TO COME SHOPPING WITH ME AFTER THE MOVIE...
SHOP-PING?
WHAT ARE YOU GONNA BUY?

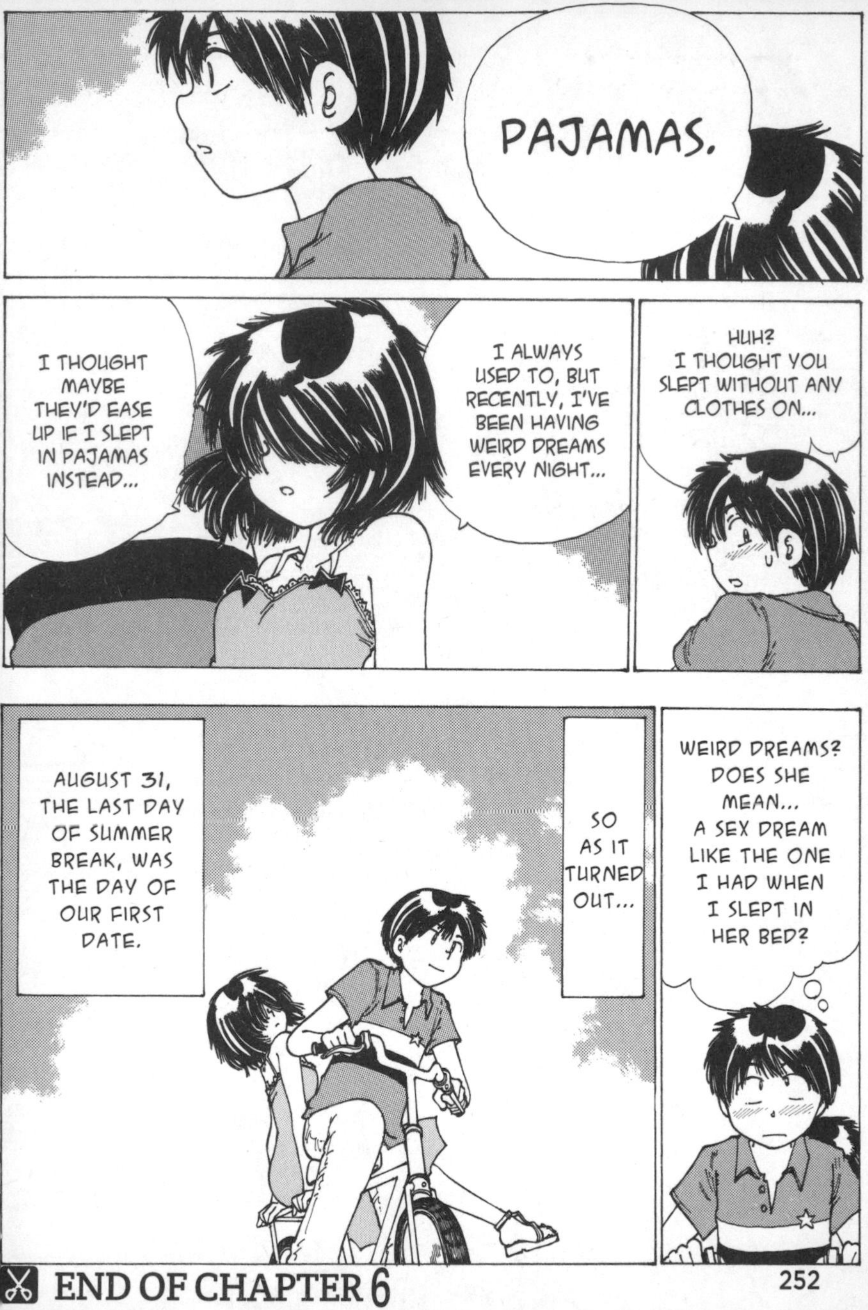
PAJAMAS.
HUH? I THOUGHT YOU SLEPT WITHOUT ANY CLOTHES ON...
I ALWAYS USED TO, BUT RECENTLY, I'VE BEEN HAVING WEIRD DREAMS EVERY NIGHT...
I THOUGHT MAYBE THEY'D EASE UP IF I SLEPT IN PAJAMAS INSTEAD...
WEIRD DREAMS? DOES SHE MEAN... A SEX DREAM LIKE THE ONE I HAD WHEN I SLEPT IN HER BED?
SO AS IT TURNED OUT...
AUGUST 31, THE LAST DAY OF SUMMER BREAK, WAS THE DAY OF OUR FIRST DATE.

END OF CHAPTER 6

CHAPTER 7: MYSTERIOUS GIRL MEETS GIRL

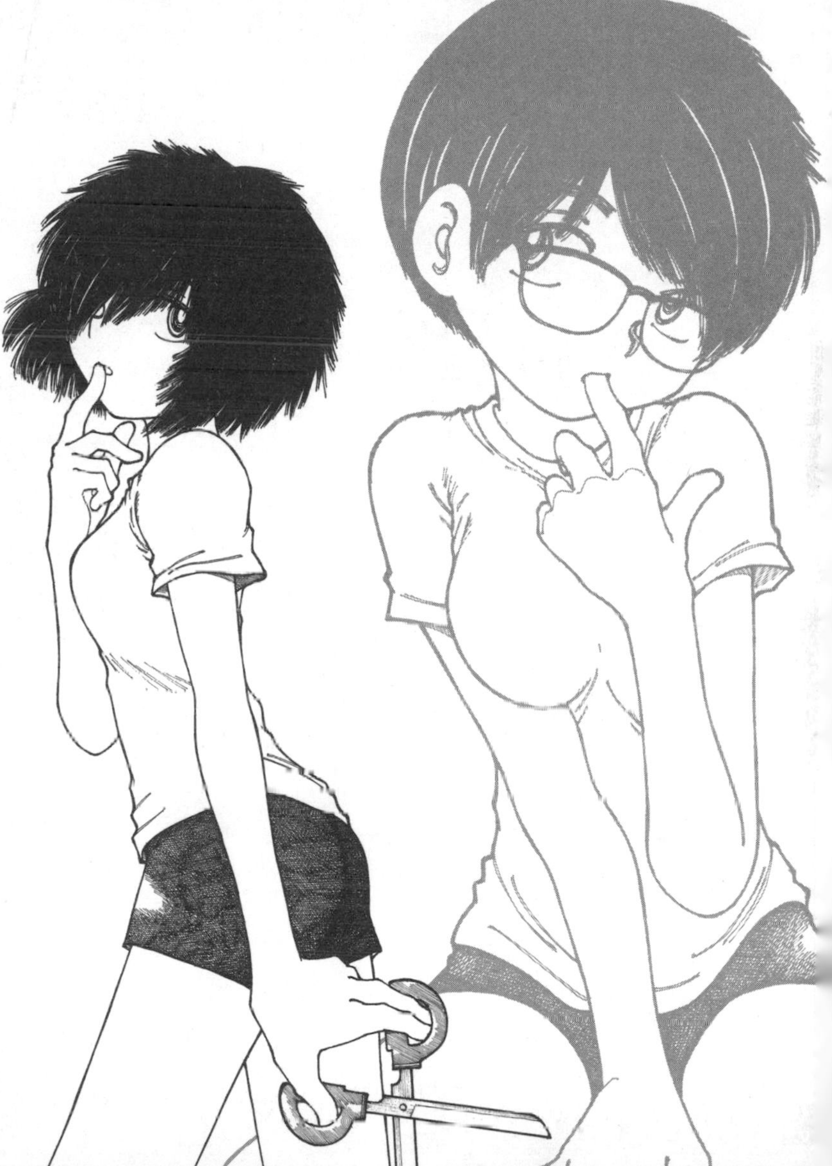

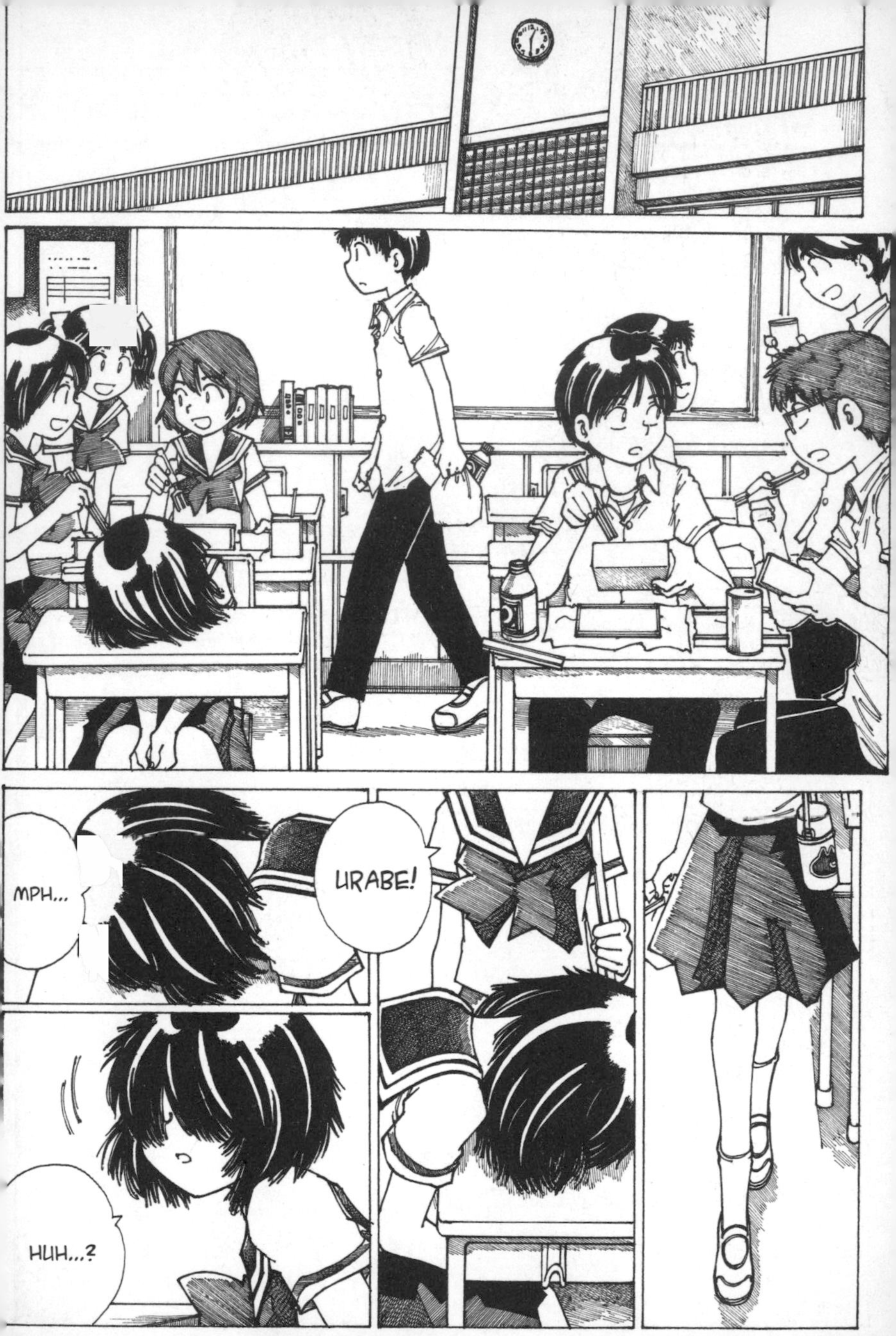
URABE!
MPH...
HUH...?

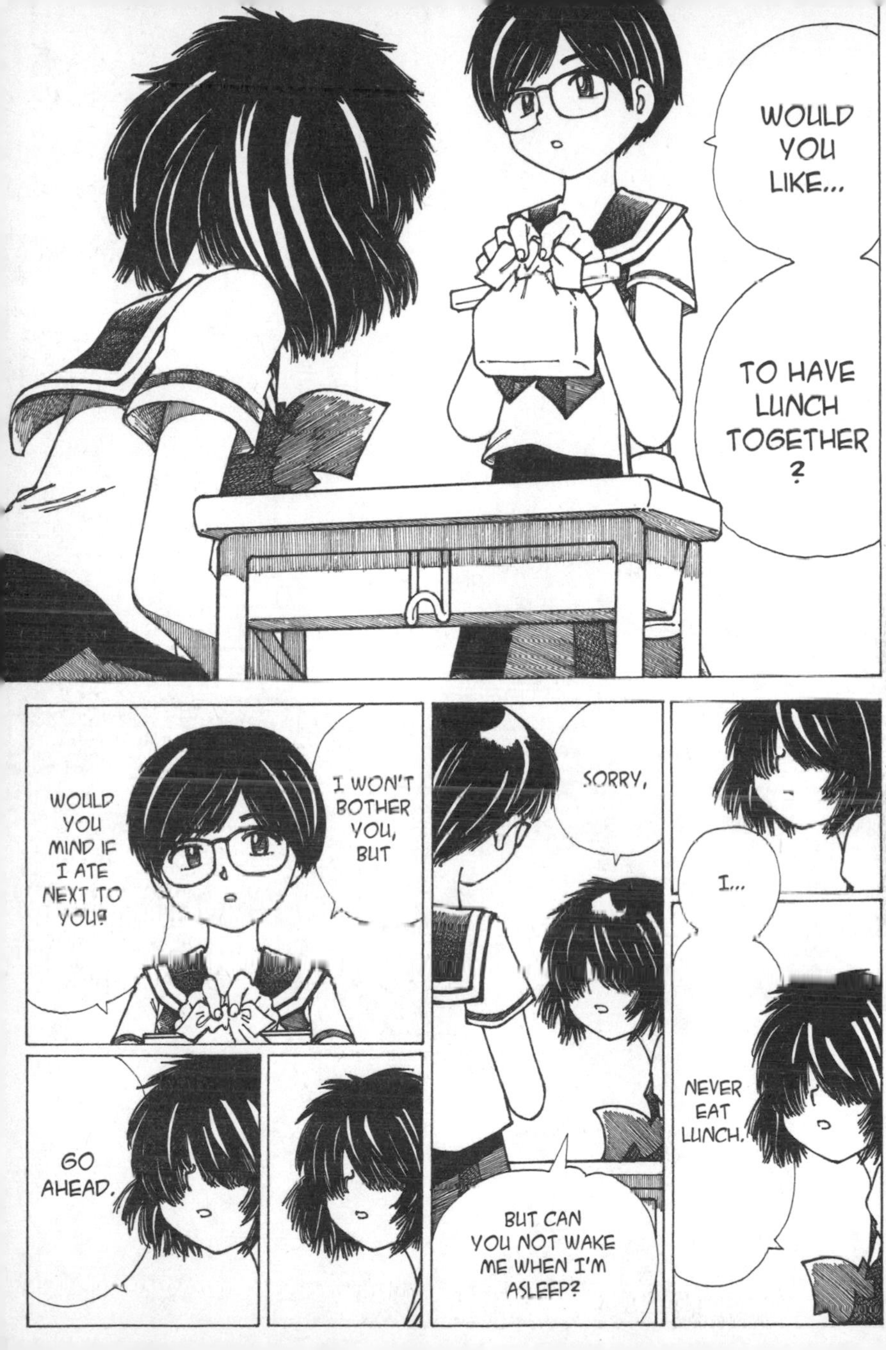
WOULD YOU LIKE...
TO HAVE LUNCH TOGETHER?
I...
NEVER EAT LUNCH.
SORRY,
BUT CAN YOU NOT WAKE ME WHEN I'M ASLEEP?
I WON'T BOTHER YOU, BUT
WOULD YOU MIND IF I ATE NEXT TO YOU?
GO AHEAD.

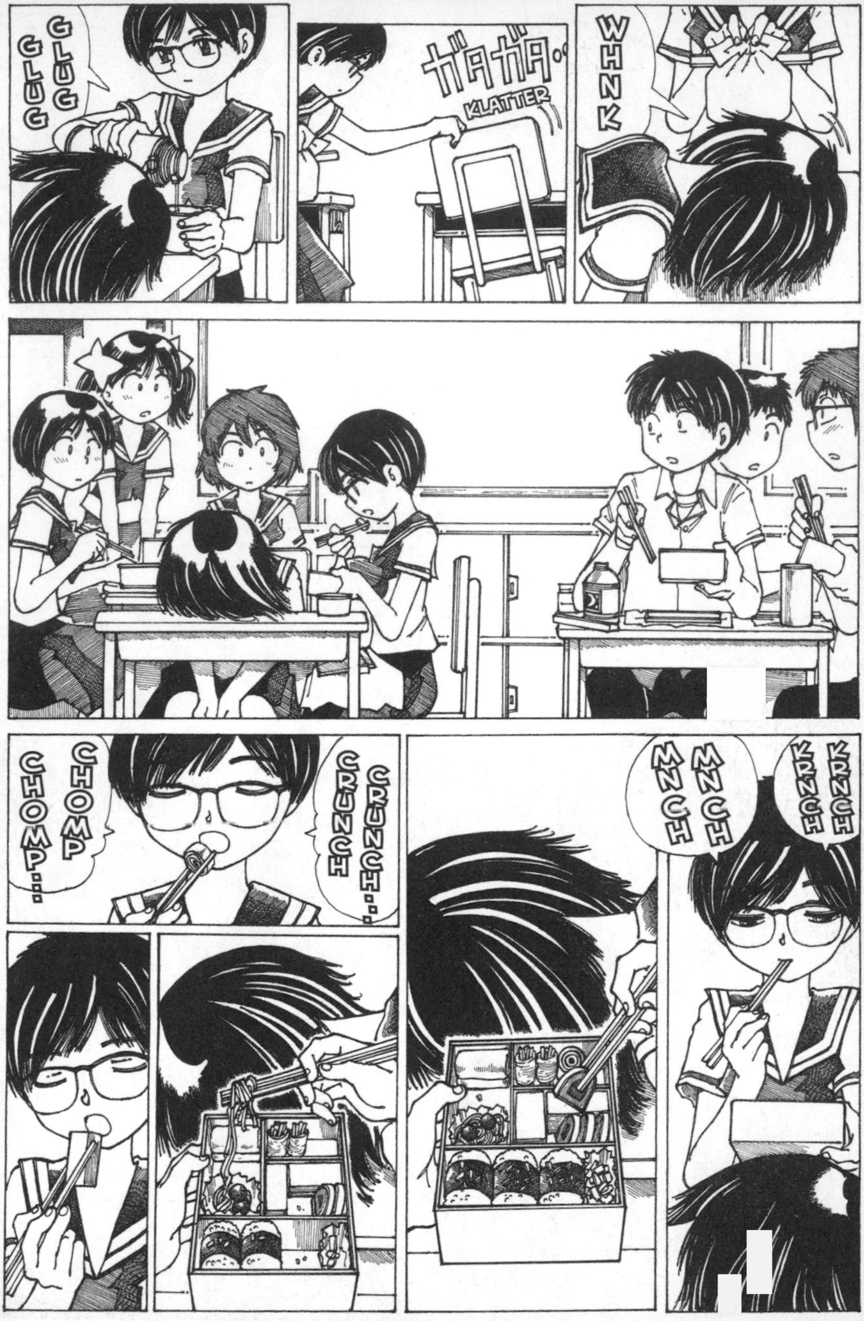
WHNK
ガタガタ
KLATTER
GLUG GLUG GLUG
KRNCH KRNCH
MNCH MNCH
CRUNCH CRUNCH..
CHOMP CHOMP..

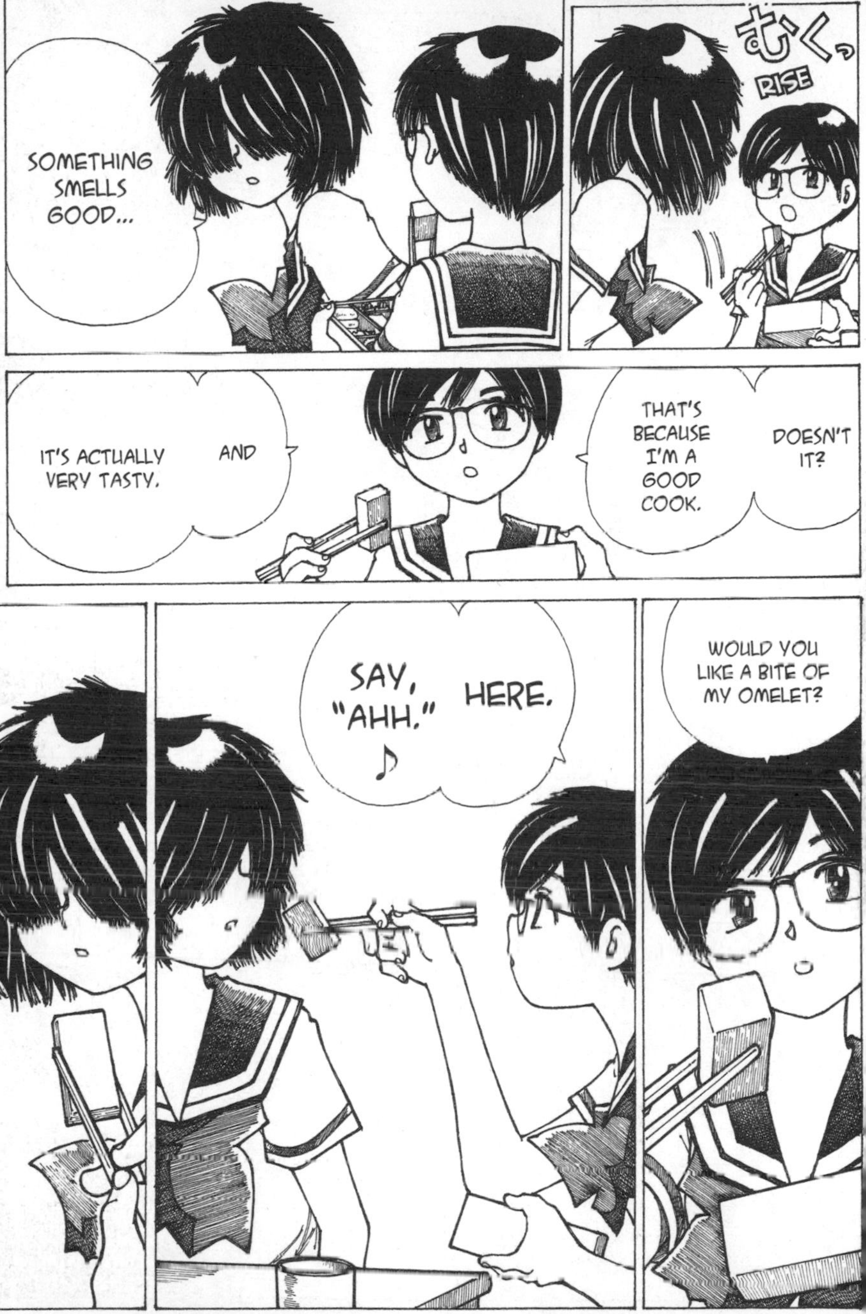
むくっ
RISE
SOMETHING SMELLS GOOD...
DOESN'T IT? THAT'S BECAUSE I'M A GOOD COOK.
AND IT'S ACTUALLY VERY TASTY.
WOULD YOU LIKE A BITE OF MY OMELET?
HERE. SAY, "AHH." ♪

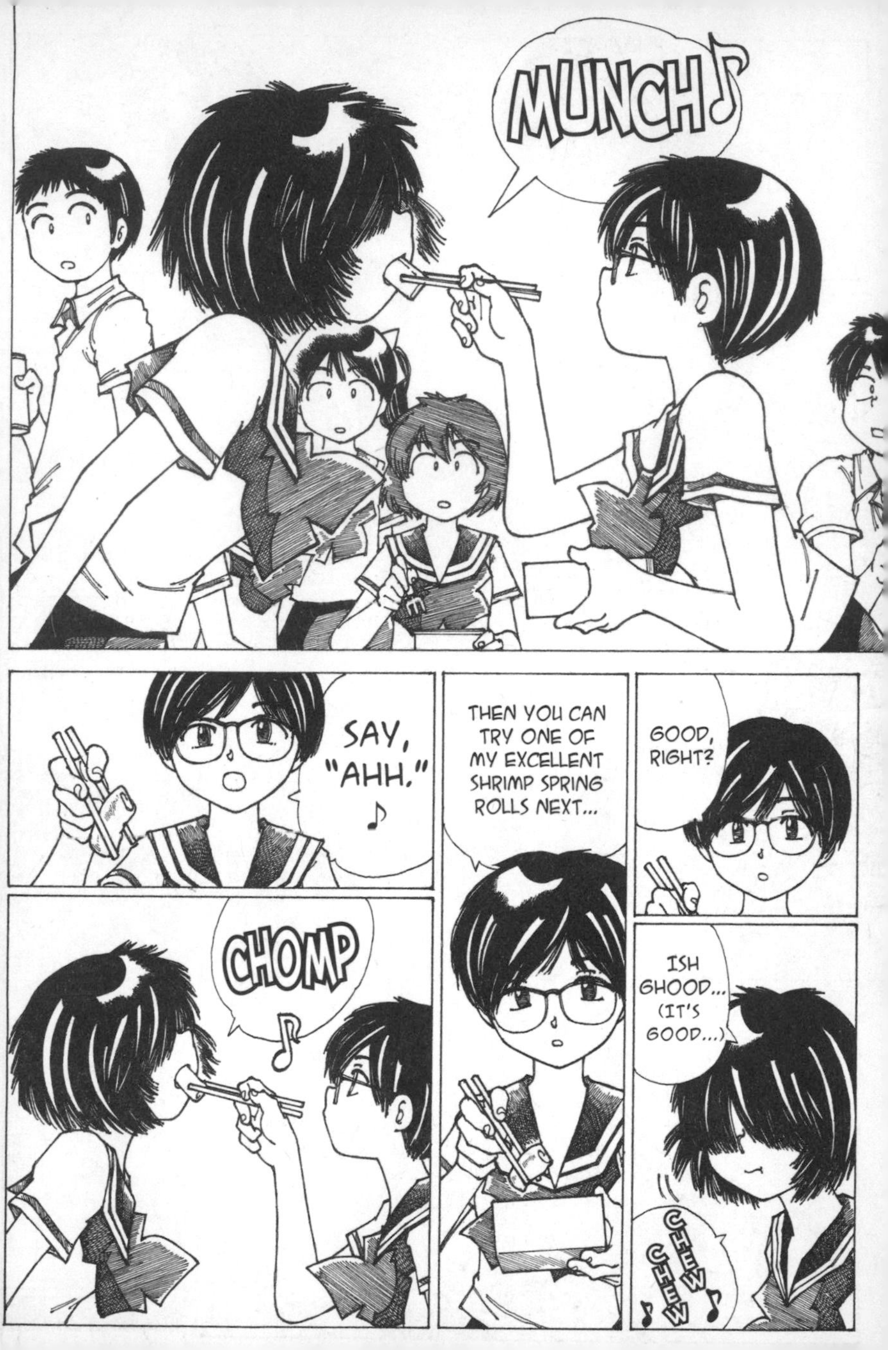
MUNCH♪
GOOD, RIGHT?
ISH GHOOD... (IT'S GOOD...)
CHEW CHEW♪
THEN YOU CAN TRY ONE OF MY EXCELLENT SHRIMP SPRING ROLLS NEXT...
SAY, "AHH."♪
CHOMP♪

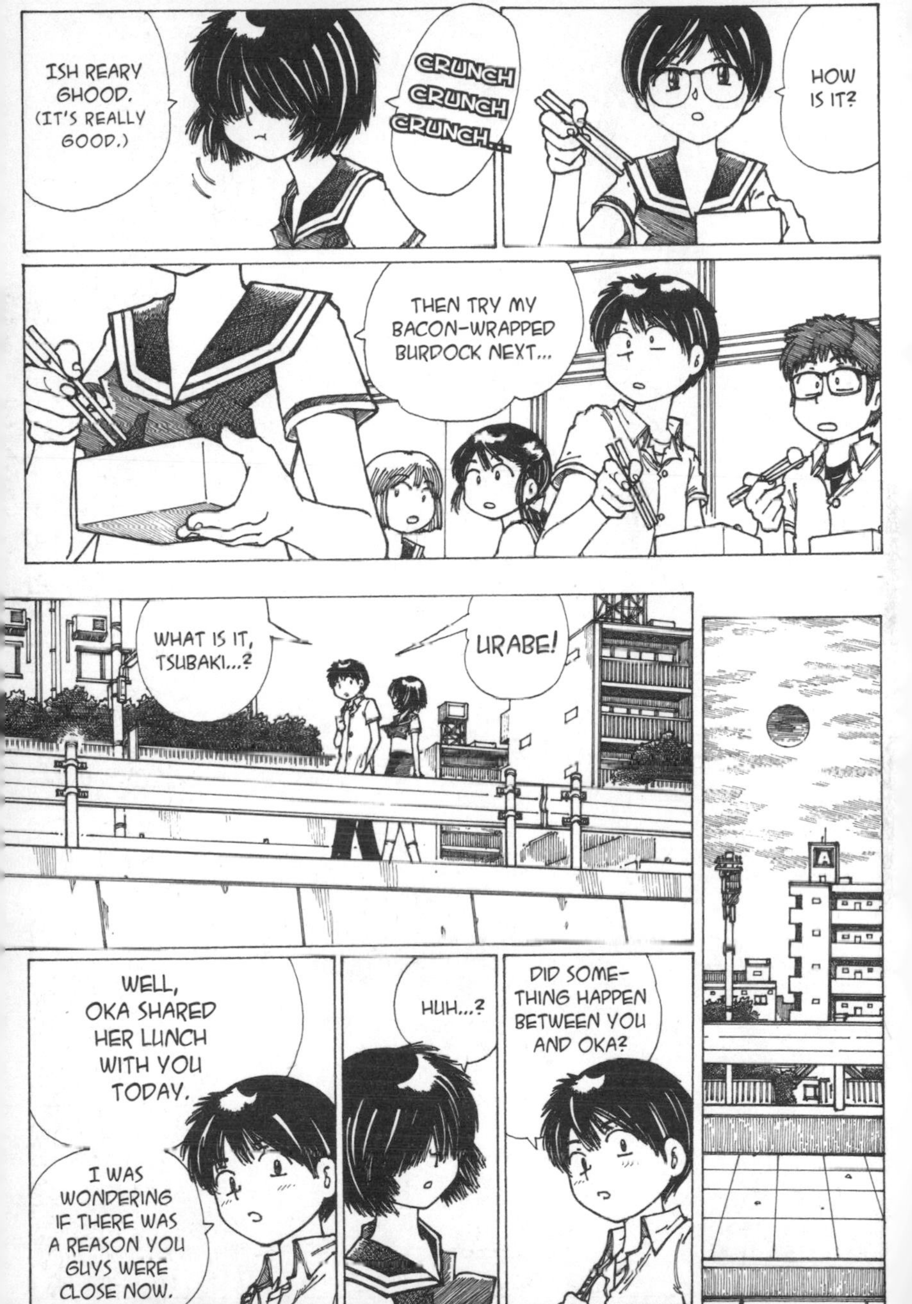
HOW IS IT?
CRUNCH CRUNCH CRUNCH...
ISH REARY GHOOD. (IT'S REALLY GOOD.)
THEN TRY MY BACON-WRAPPED BURDOCK NEXT...
URABE!
WHAT IS IT, TSUBAKI...?
DID SOME-THING HAPPEN BETWEEN YOU AND OKA?
HUH...?
WELL, OKA SHARED HER LUNCH WITH YOU TODAY.
I WAS WONDERING IF THERE WAS A REASON YOU GUYS WERE CLOSE NOW.

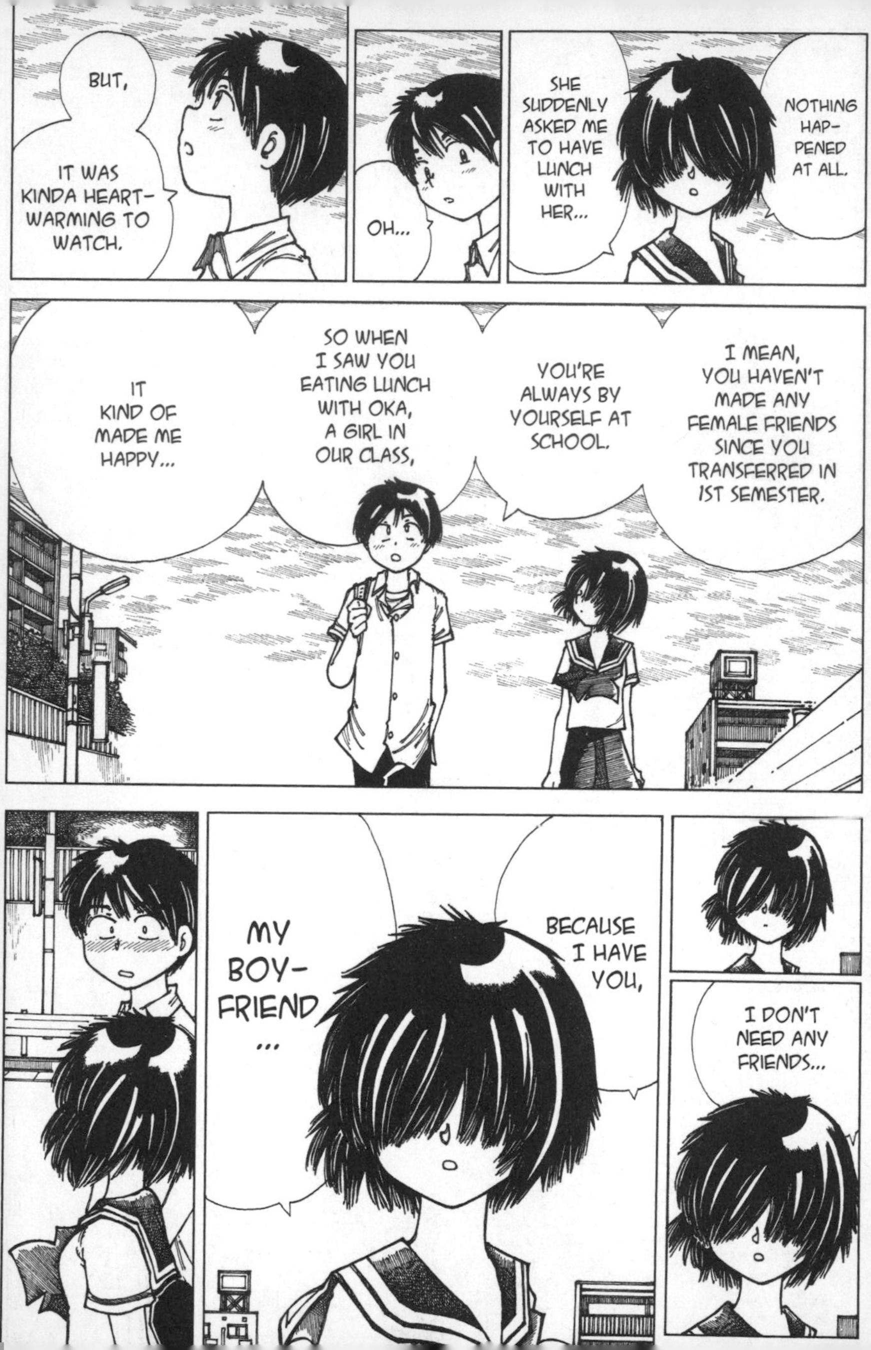
NOTHING HAP-PENED AT ALL.
SHE SUDDENLY ASKED ME TO HAVE LUNCH WITH HER...
OH...
BUT,
IT WAS KINDA HEART-WARMING TO WATCH.
I MEAN, YOU HAVEN'T MADE ANY FEMALE FRIENDS SINCE YOU TRANSFERRED IN 1ST SEMESTER.
YOU'RE ALWAYS BY YOURSELF AT SCHOOL.
SO WHEN I SAW YOU EATING LUNCH WITH OKA, A GIRL IN OUR CLASS,
IT KIND OF MADE ME HAPPY...
I DON'T NEED ANY FRIENDS...
BECAUSE I HAVE YOU,
MY BOY-FRIEND...

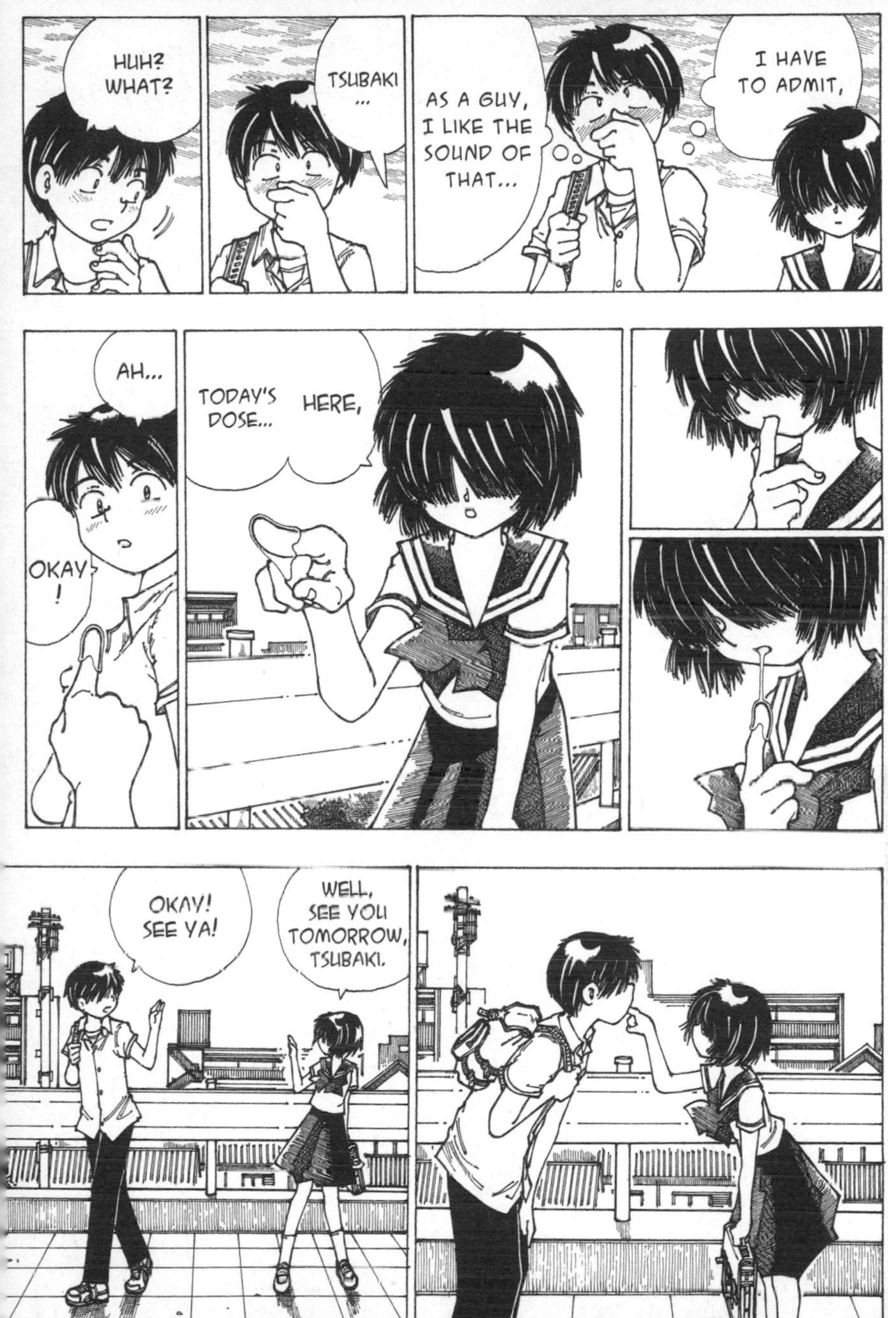
I HAVE TO ADMIT,
AS A GUY, I LIKE THE SOUND OF THAT...
TSUBAKI ...
HUH? WHAT?
HERE,
TODAY'S DOSE...
AH...
OKAY!
WELL, SEE YOU TOMORROW, TSUBAKI.
OKAY! SEE YA!

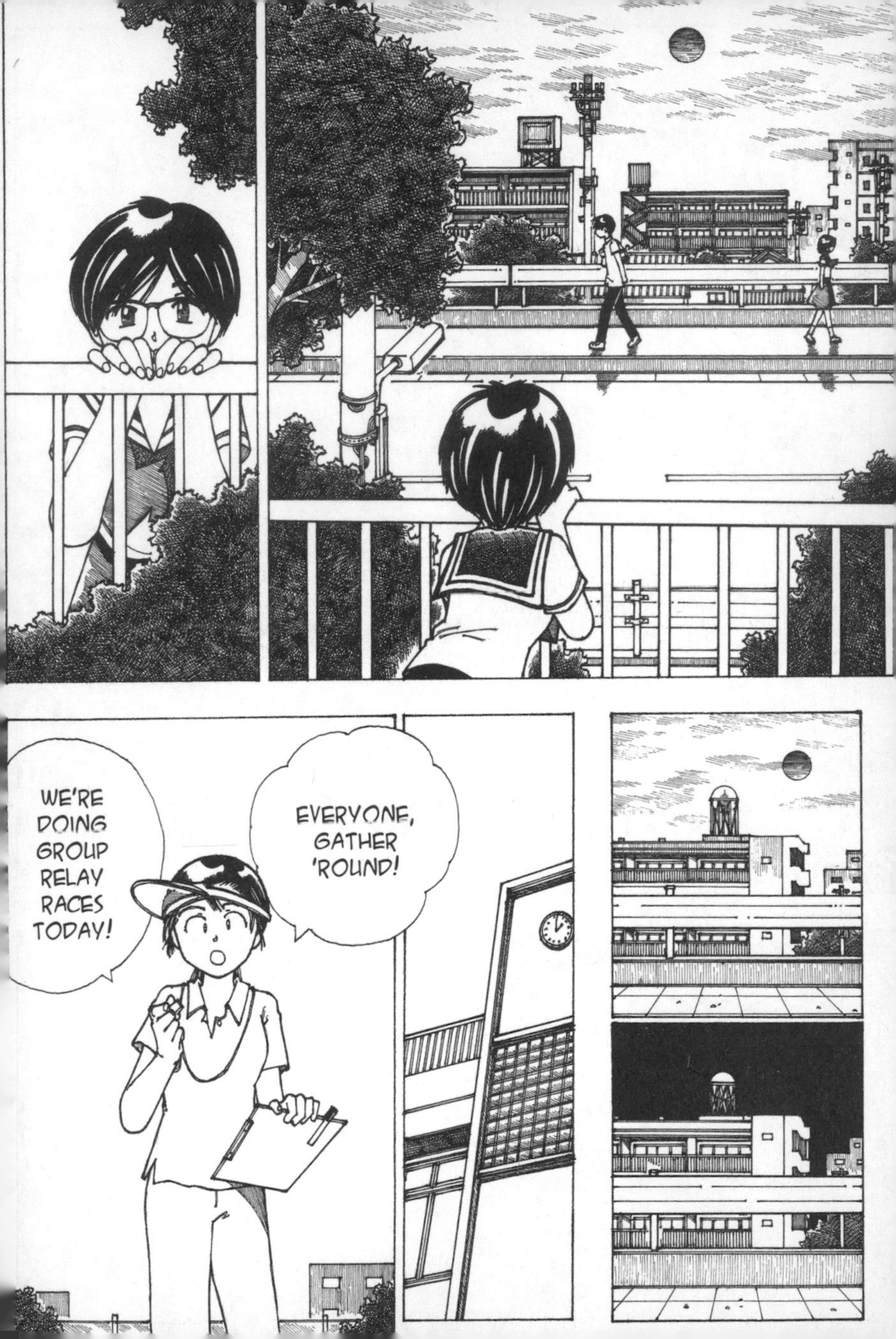
EVERYONE, GATHER 'ROUND!
WE'RE DOING GROUP RELAY RACES TODAY!

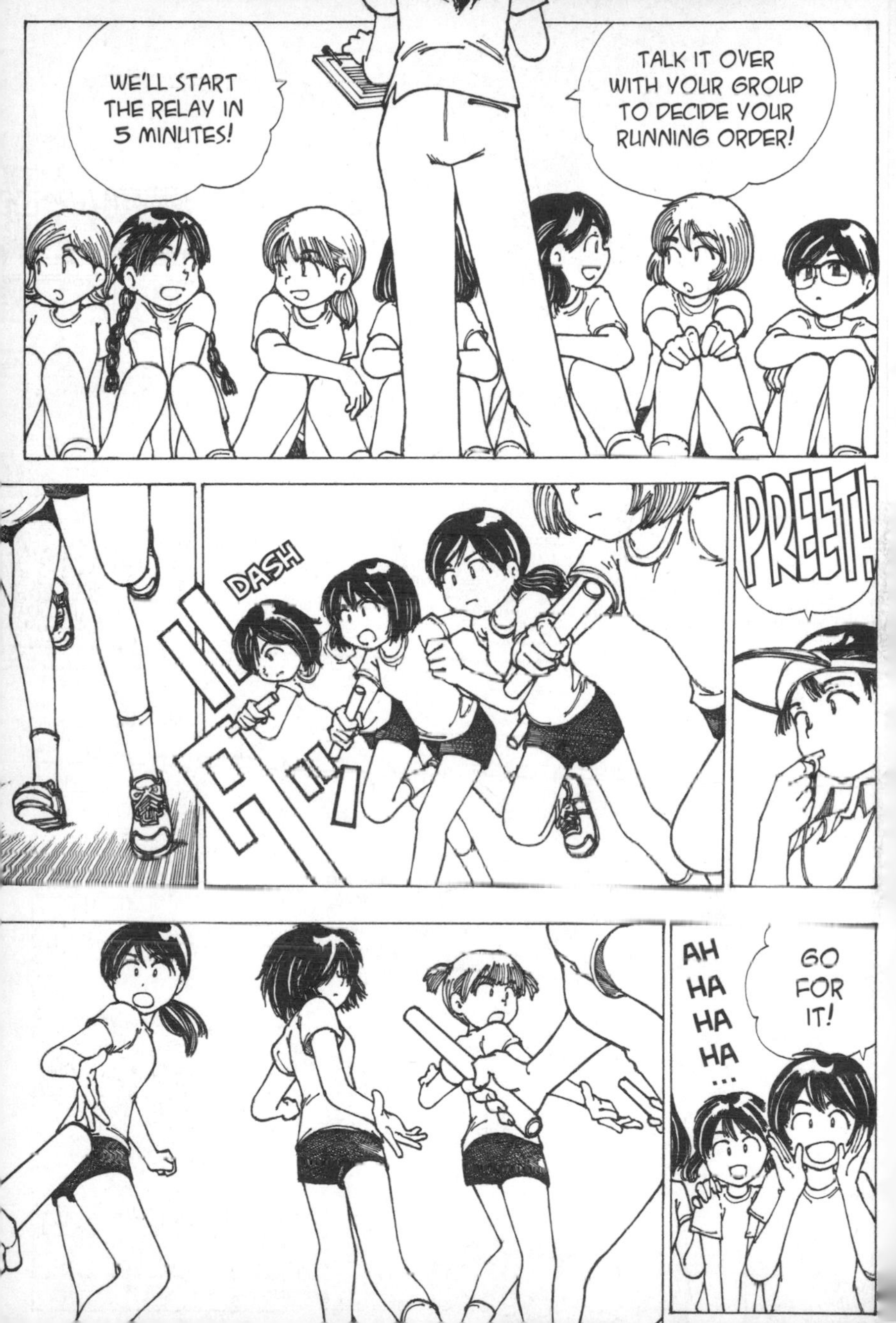
TALK IT OVER WITH YOUR GROUP TO DECIDE YOUR RUNNING ORDER!
WE'LL START THE RELAY IN 5 MINUTES!
PREETH!
DASH
GO FOR IT!
AH HA HA HA...

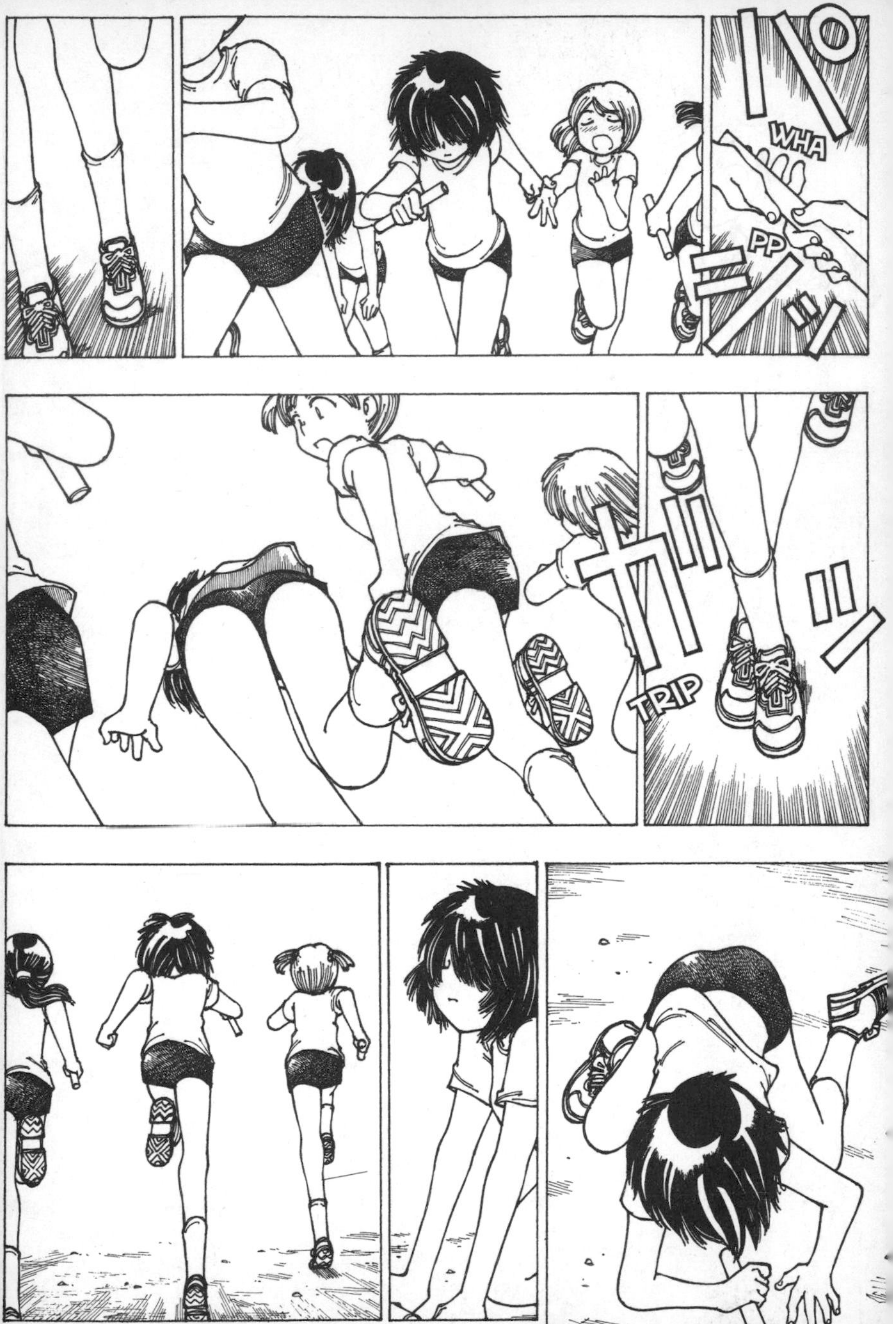
WHA
PP
TRIP

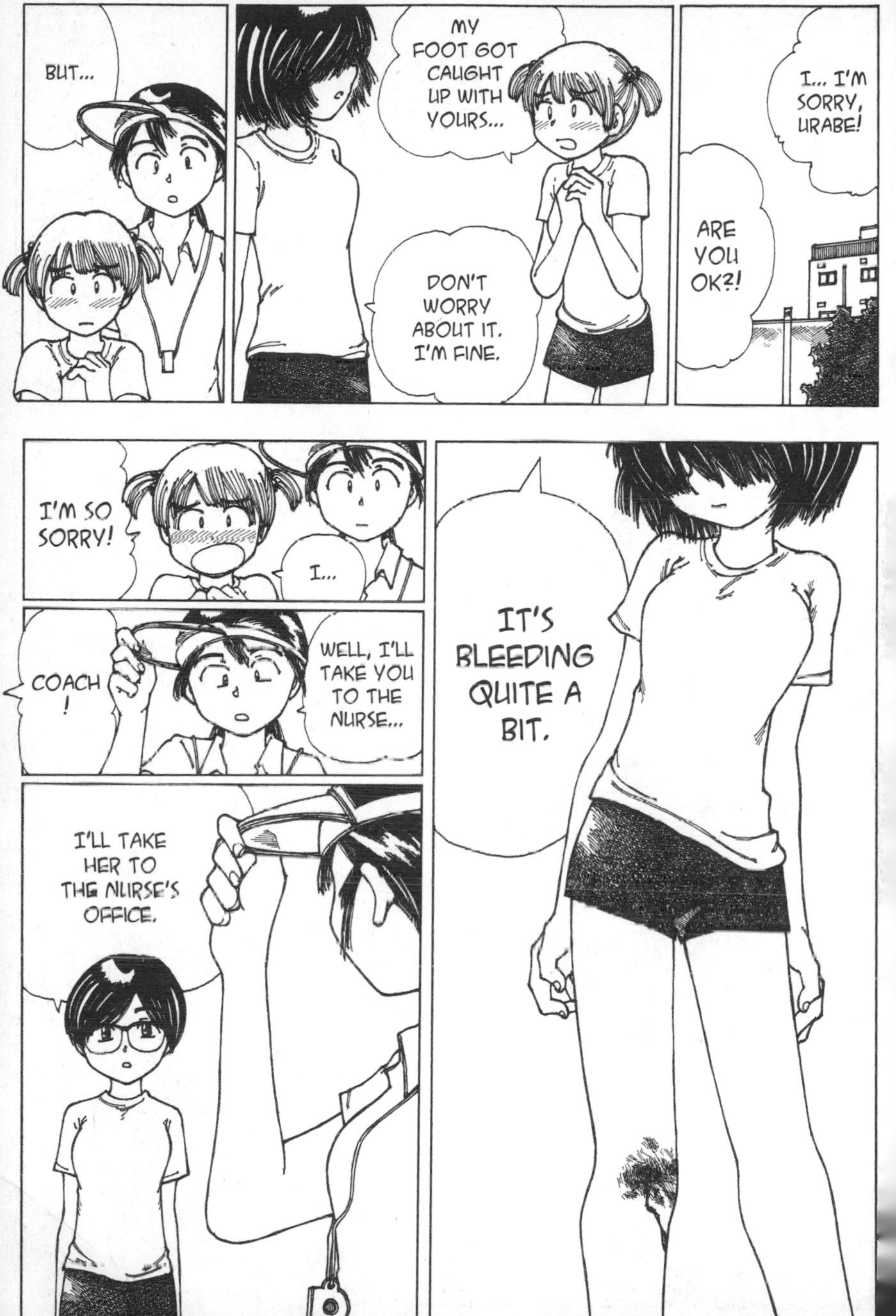
I... I'M SORRY, URABE!
ARE YOU OK?!
MY FOOT GOT CAUGHT UP WITH YOURS...
DON'T WORRY ABOUT IT. I'M FINE.
BUT...
IT'S BLEEDING QUITE A BIT.
I'M SO SORRY!
I...
WELL, I'LL TAKE YOU TO THE NURSE...
COACH!
I'LL TAKE HER TO THE NURSE'S OFFICE.

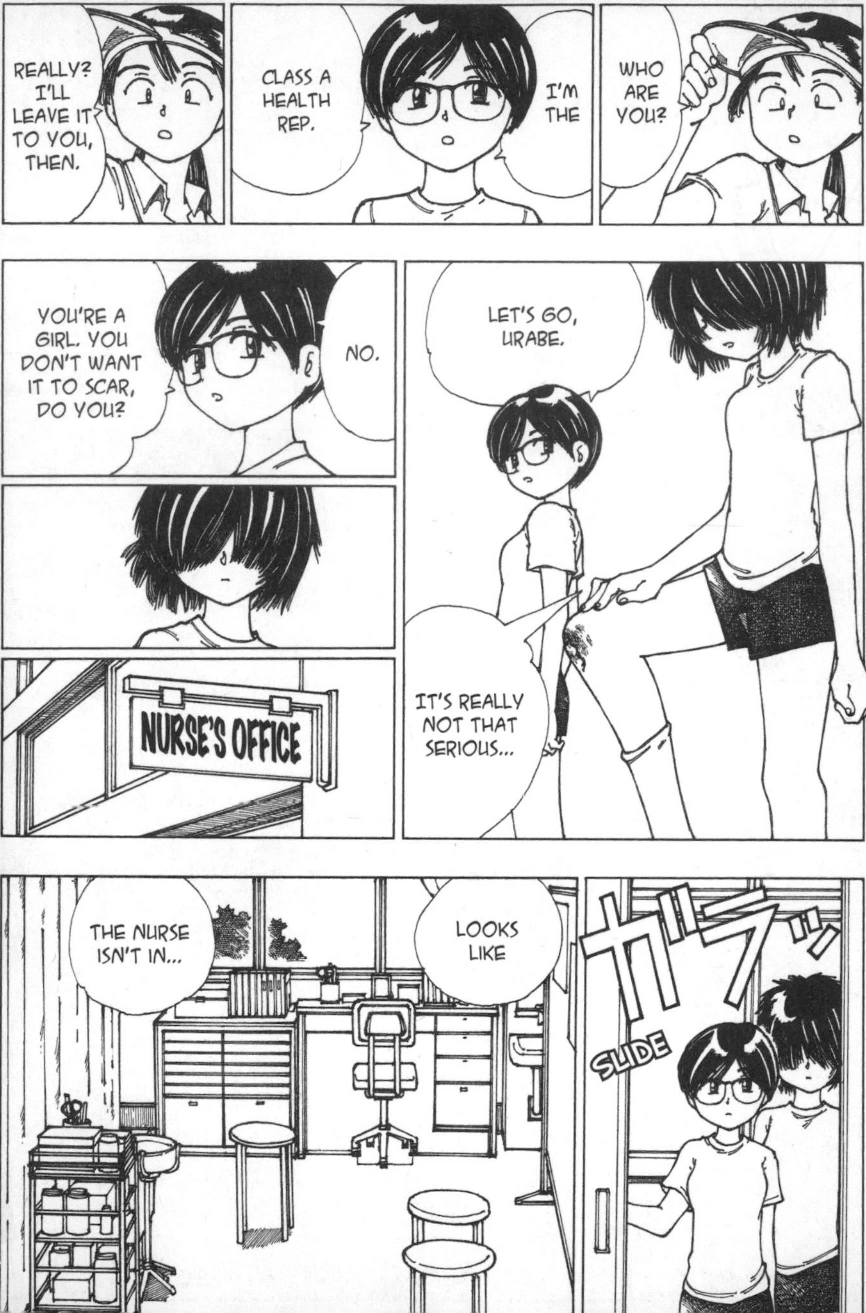
WHO ARE YOU?
I'M THE
CLASS A HEALTH REP.
REALLY? I'LL LEAVE IT TO YOU, THEN.
LET'S GO, URABE.
IT'S REALLY NOT THAT SERIOUS...
NO.
YOU'RE A GIRL. YOU DON'T WANT IT TO SCAR, DO YOU?
NURSE'S OFFICE
ガラッ
SLIDE
LOOKS LIKE
THE NURSE ISN'T IN...

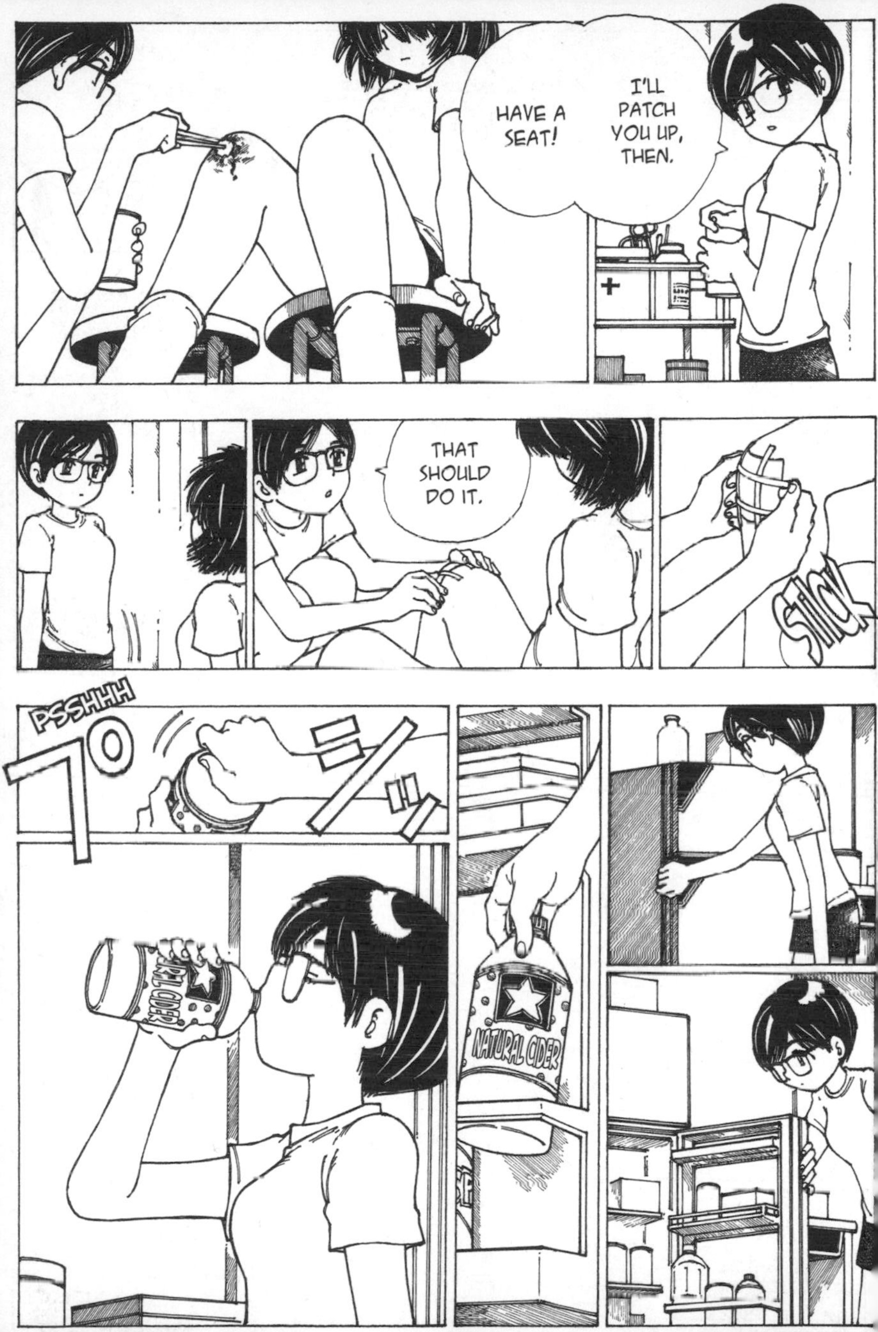
I'LL PATCH YOU UP, THEN.
HAVE A SEAT!
STICK
THAT SHOULD DO IT.
NATURAL CIDER
PSSHHH

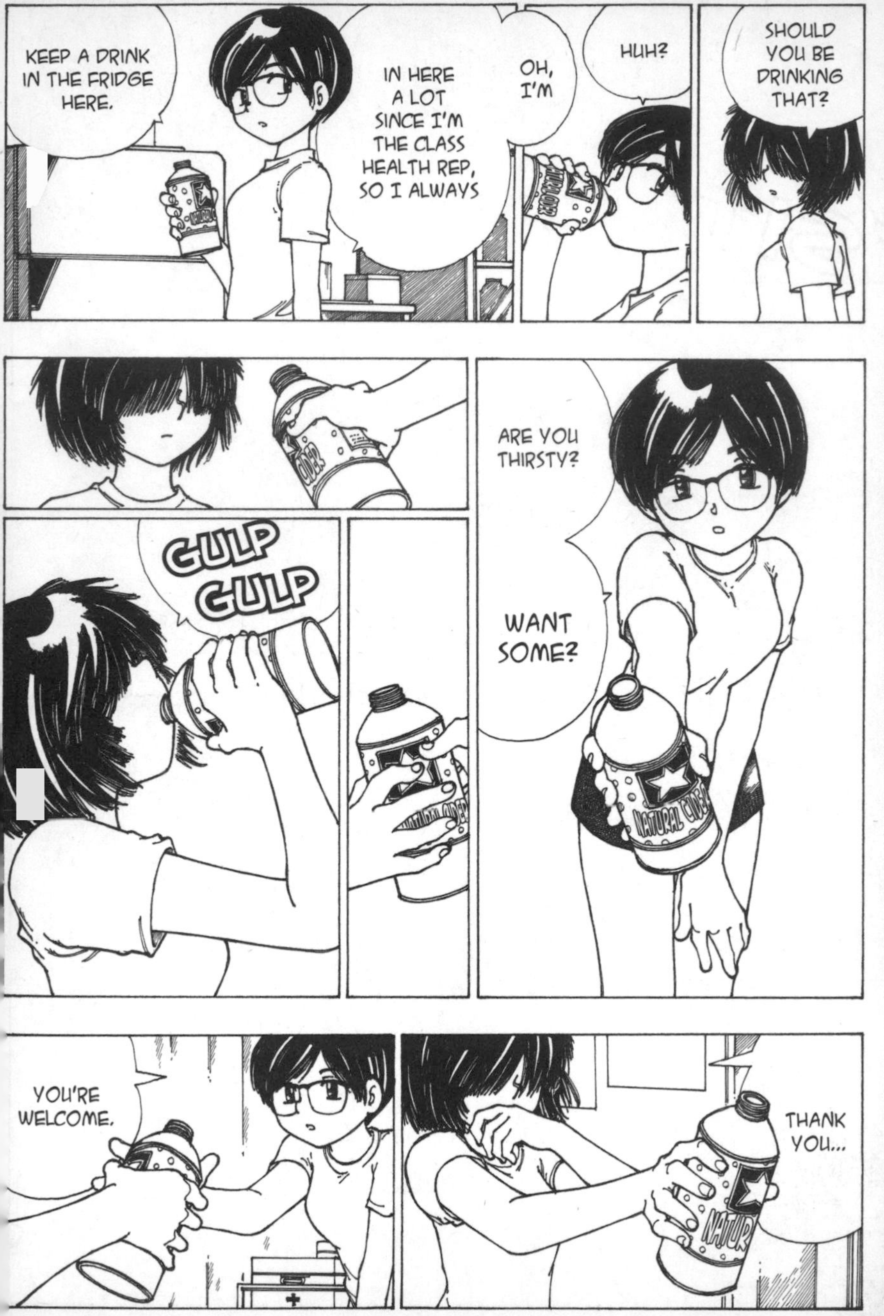
SHOULD YOU BE DRINKING THAT?
HUH?
OH, I'M
IN HERE A LOT SINCE I'M THE CLASS HEALTH REP, SO I ALWAYS
KEEP A DRINK IN THE FRIDGE HERE.
ARE YOU THIRSTY?
WANT SOME?
NATURAL CIDER
GULP GULP
THANK YOU...
YOU'RE WELCOME.

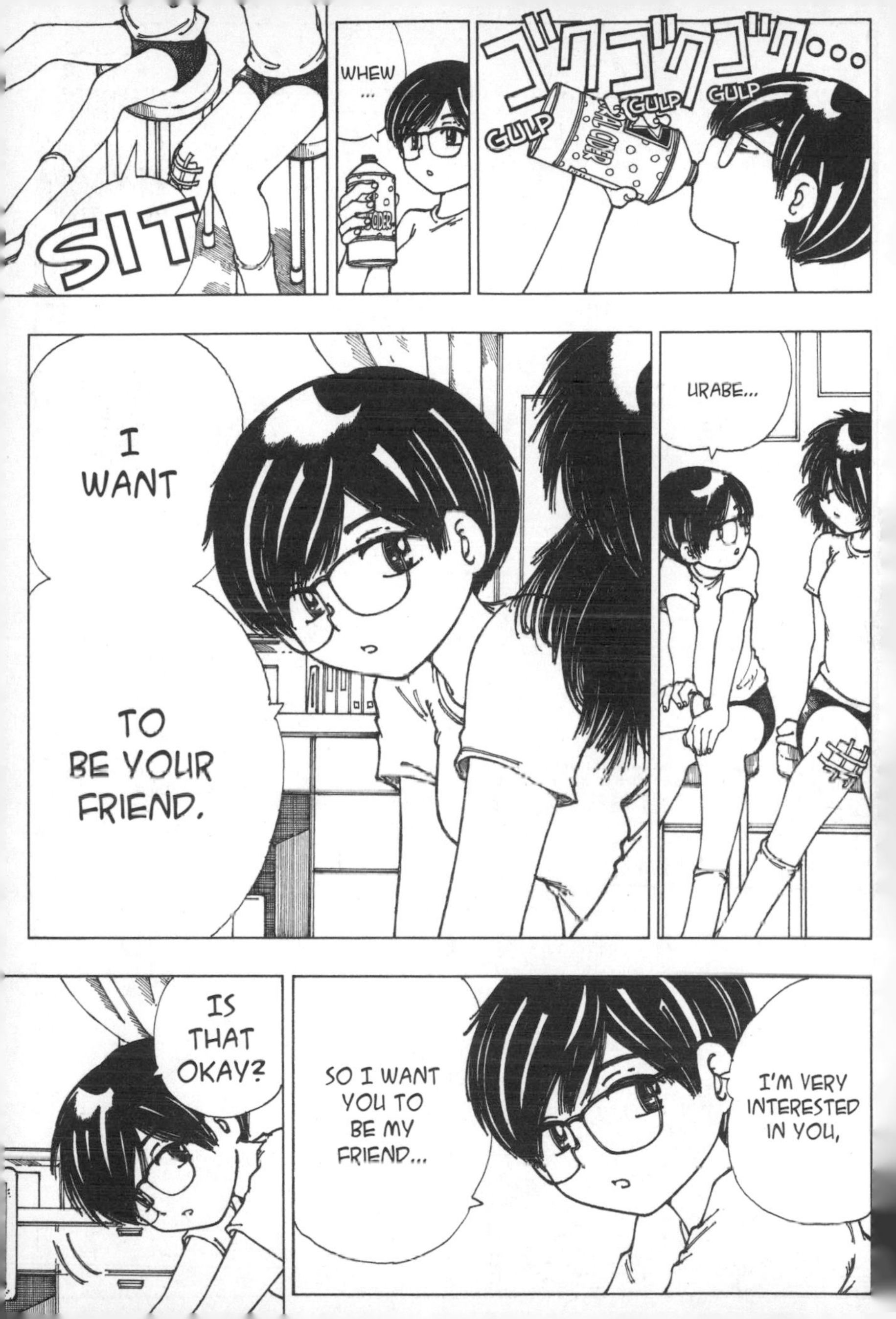
ゴクゴクゴク。。。
GULP GULP GULP
WHEW ...
SIT
URABE...
I WANT TO BE YOUR FRIEND.
I'M VERY INTERESTED IN YOU,
SO I WANT YOU TO BE MY FRIEND...
IS THAT OKAY?

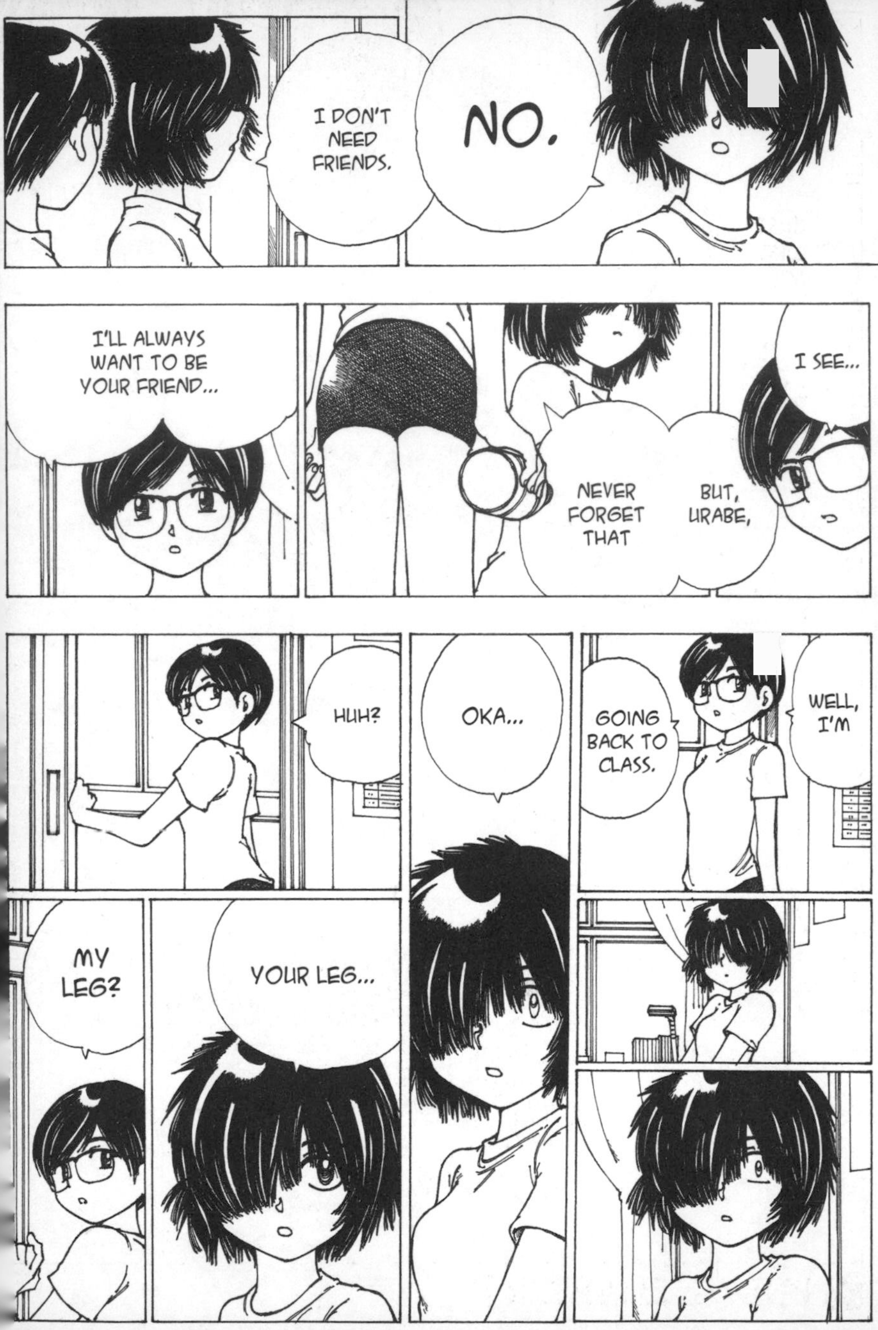
NO.
I DON'T NEED FRIENDS.
I SEE...
BUT, URABE,
NEVER FORGET THAT
I'LL ALWAYS WANT TO BE YOUR FRIEND...
WELL, I'M
GOING BACK TO CLASS.
OKA...
HUH?
YOUR LEG...
MY LEG?

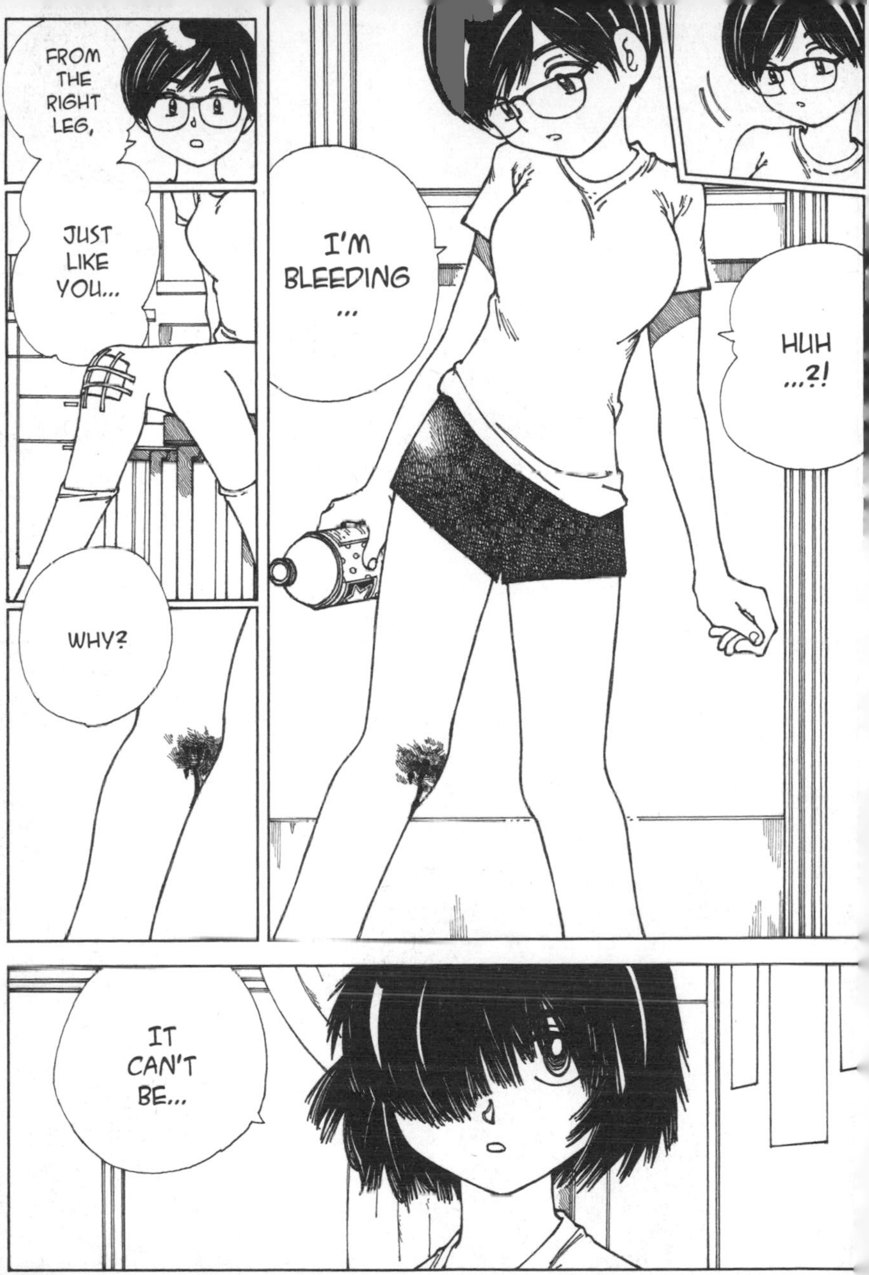
HUH ...?!
I'M BLEEDING ...
FROM THE RIGHT LEG,
JUST LIKE YOU...
WHY?
IT CAN'T BE...

END OF CHAPTER 7

CHAPTER 8: MYSTERIOUS GIRL MEETS GIRL, CONTINUED

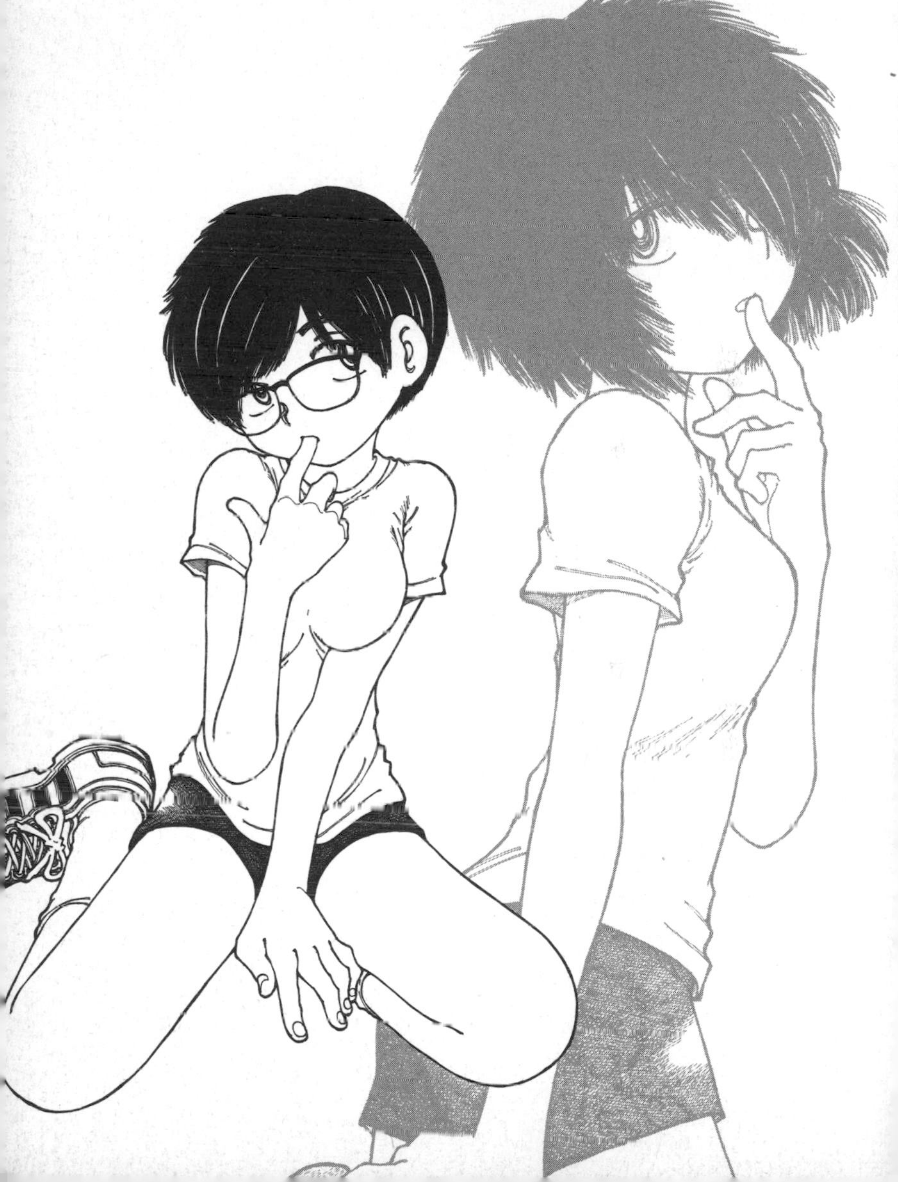

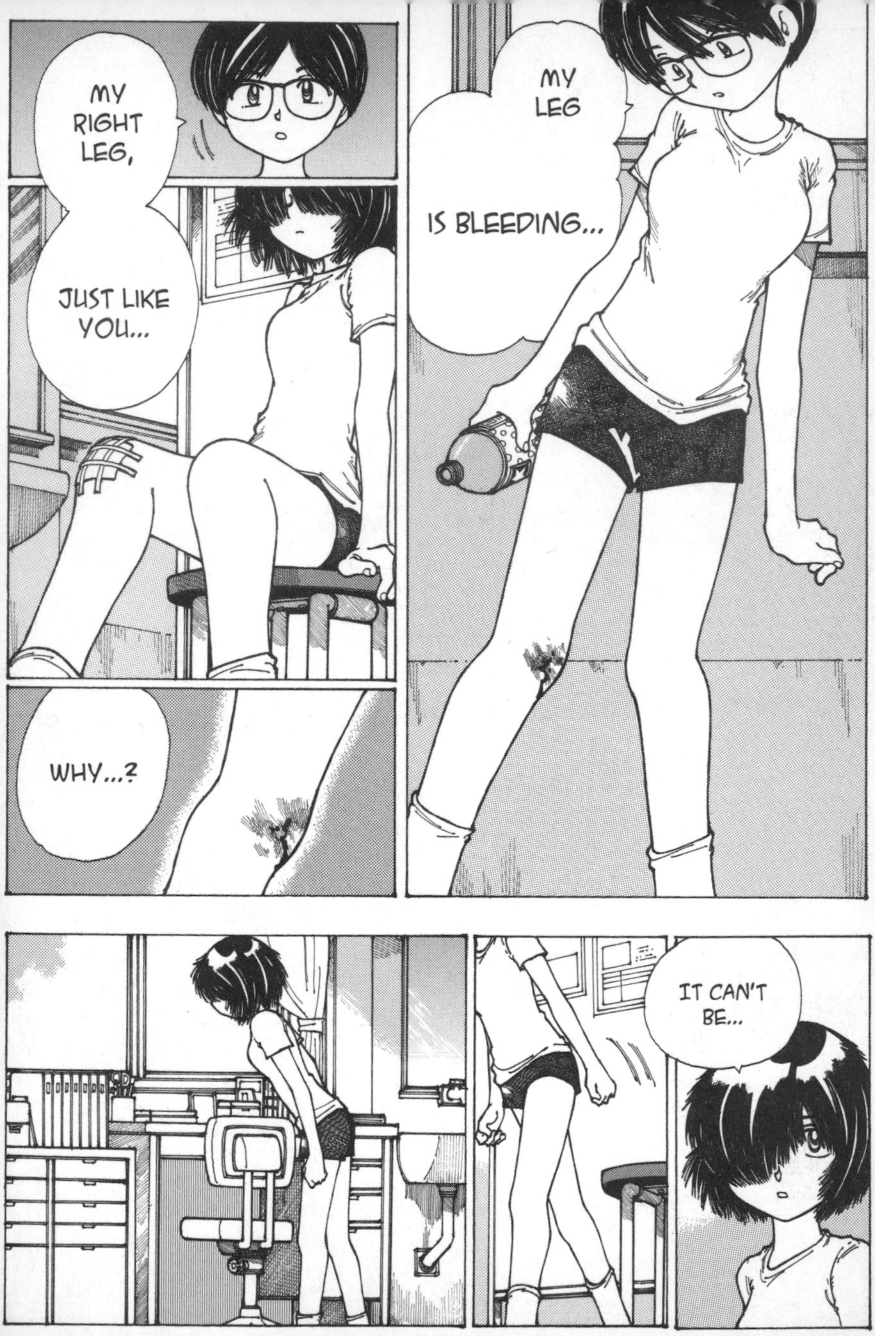
MY LEG
IS BLEEDING...
MY RIGHT LEG,
JUST LIKE YOU...
WHY...?
IT CAN'T BE...

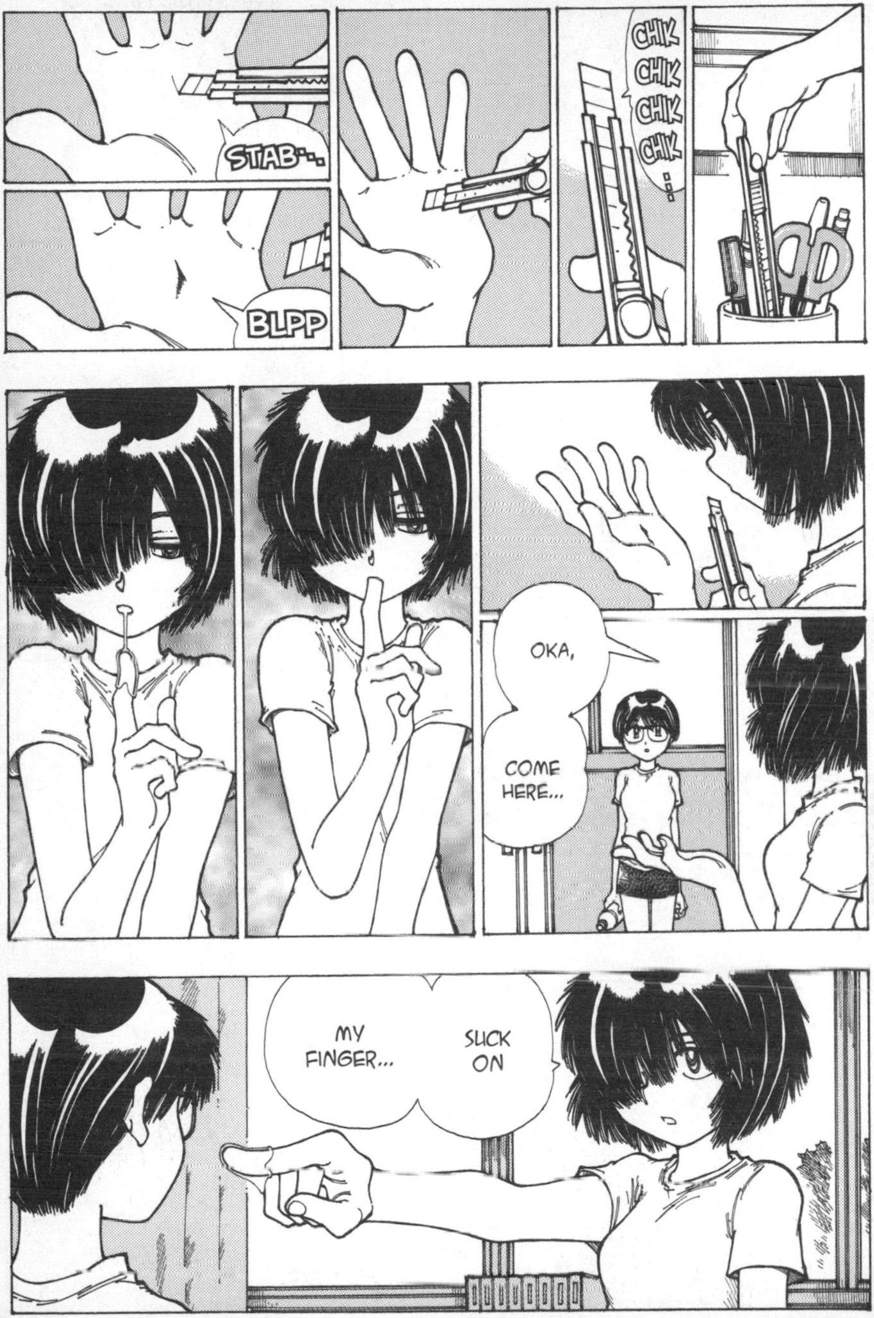
CHIK CHIK CHIK CHIK ...
STAB...
BLPP
OKA,
COME HERE...
SUCK ON
MY FINGER...

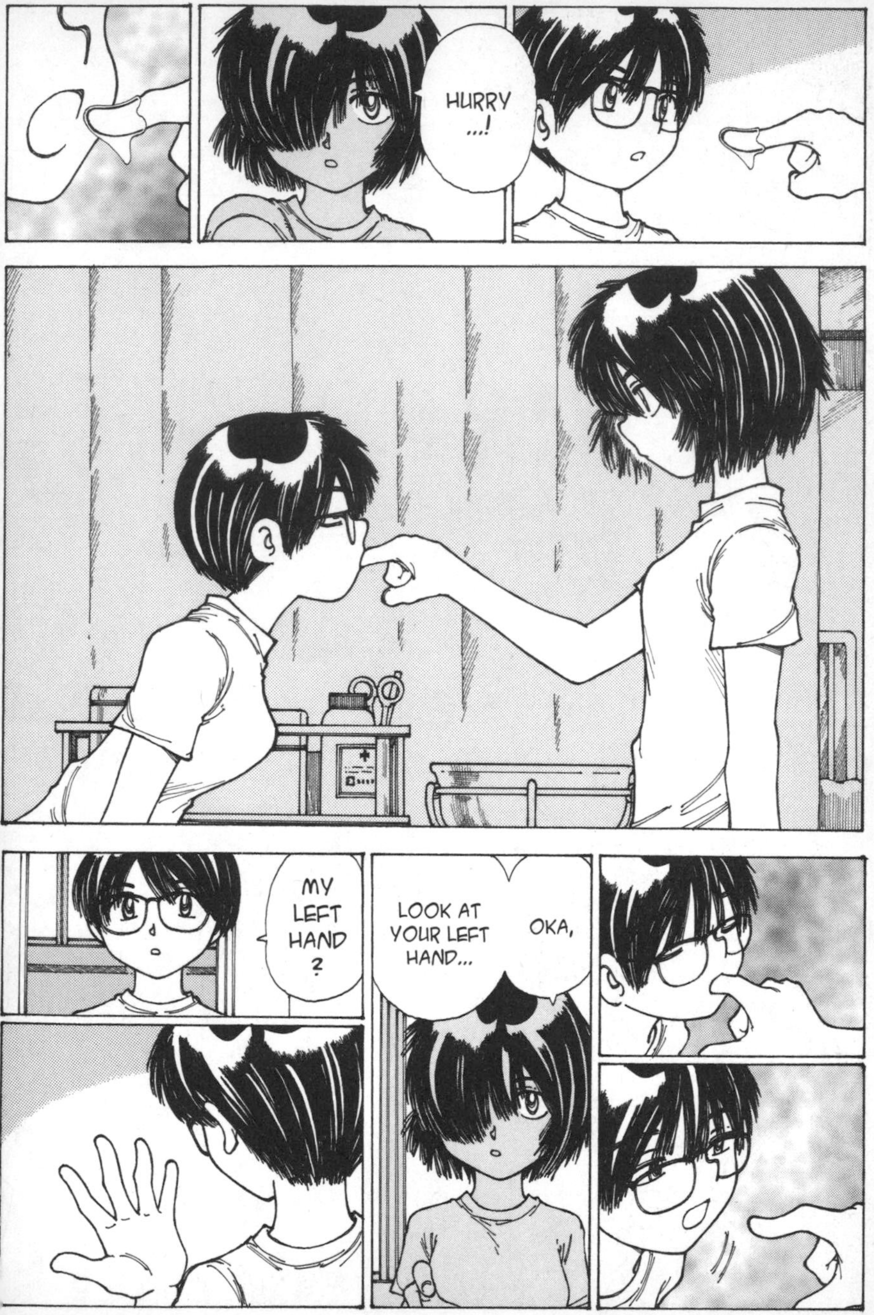
HURRY ...!
OKA,
LOOK AT YOUR LEFT HAND...
MY LEFT HAND ?

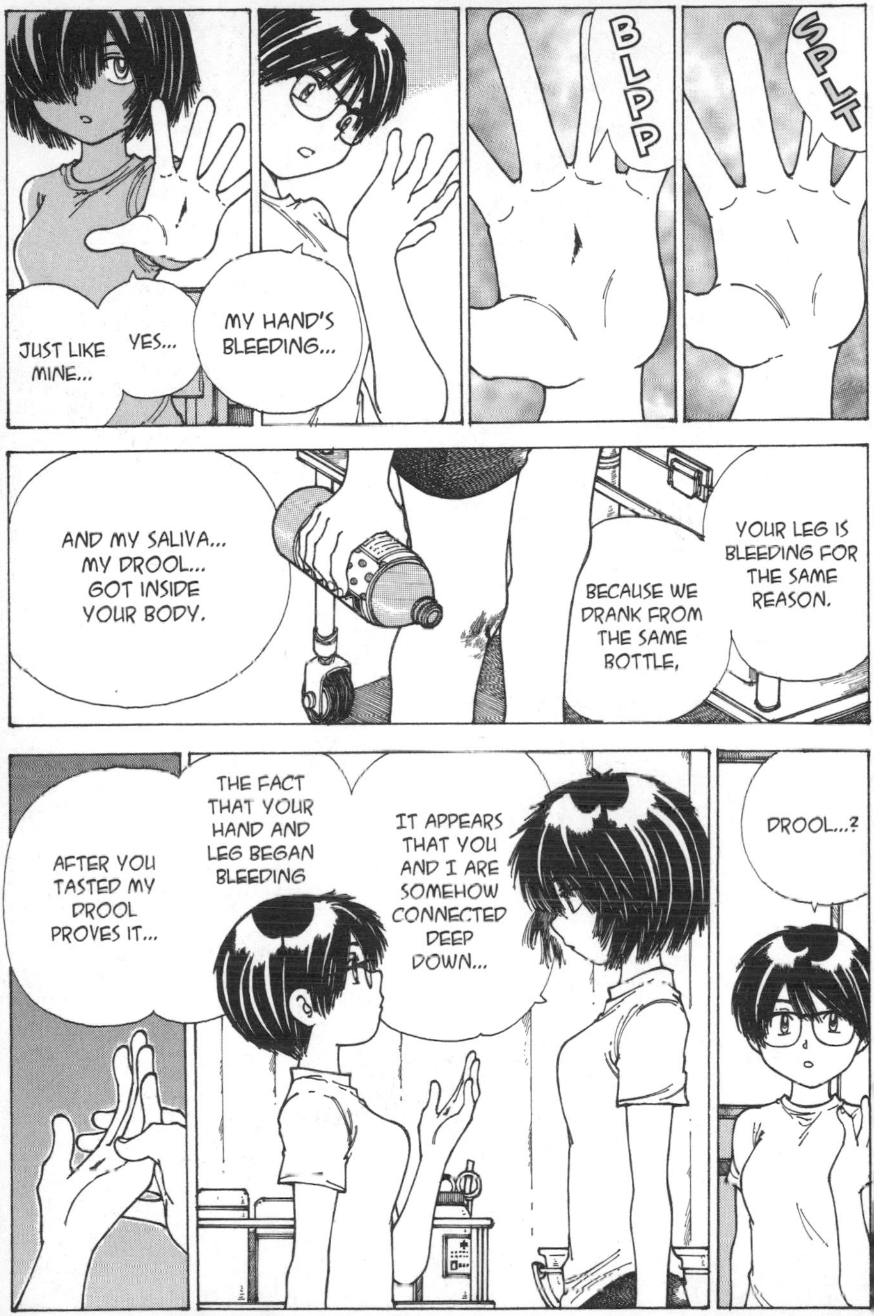
SPLT
BLPP
MY HAND'S BLEEDING...
YES...
JUST LIKE MINE...
YOUR LEG IS BLEEDING FOR THE SAME REASON.
BECAUSE WE DRANK FROM THE SAME BOTTLE,
AND MY SALIVA... MY DROOL... GOT INSIDE YOUR BODY.
DROOL...?
IT APPEARS THAT YOU AND I ARE SOMEHOW CONNECTED DEEP DOWN...
THE FACT THAT YOUR HAND AND LEG BEGAN BLEEDING
AFTER YOU TASTED MY DROOL PROVES IT...

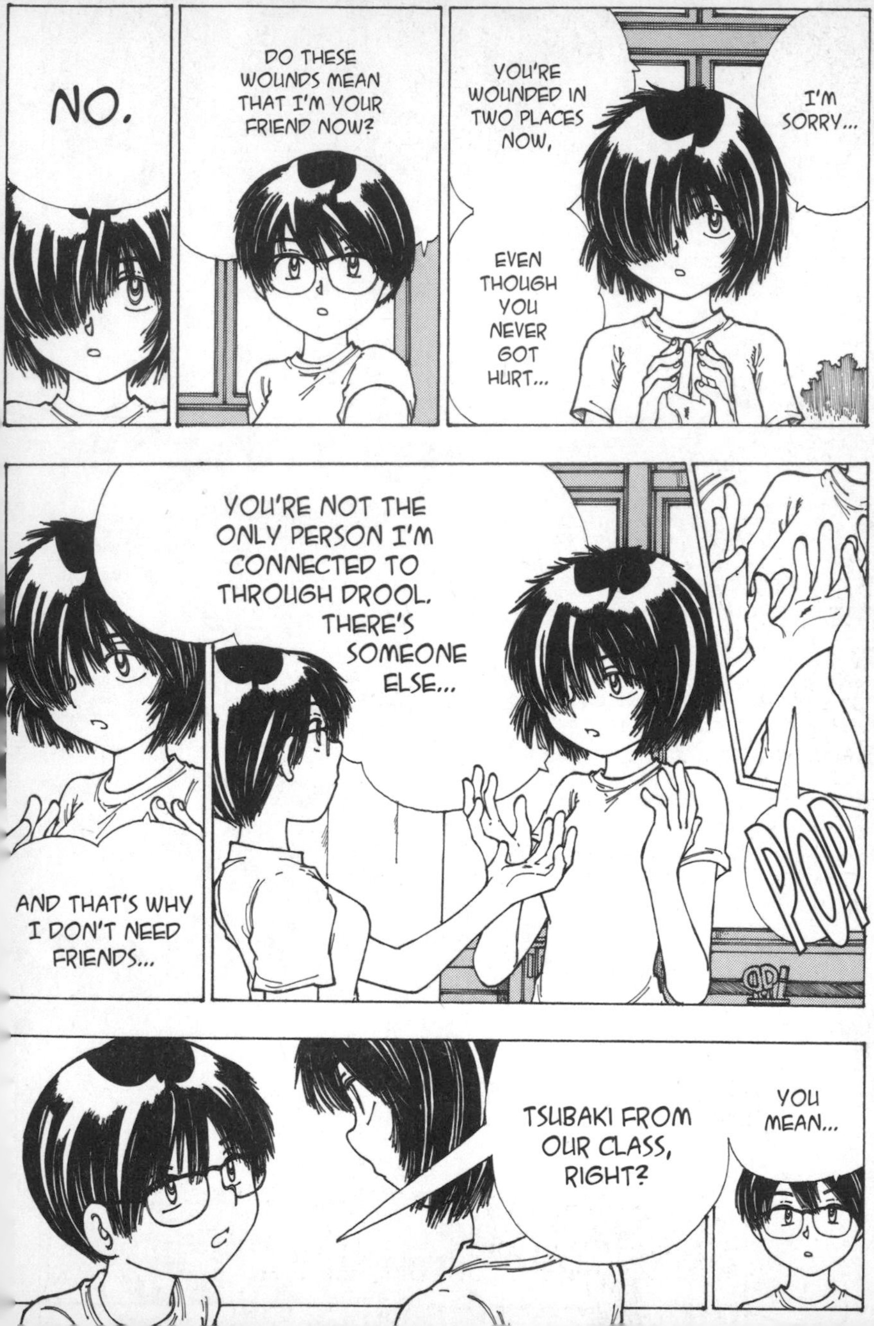
I'M SORRY...
YOU'RE WOUNDED IN TWO PLACES NOW,
EVEN THOUGH YOU NEVER GOT HURT...
DO THESE WOUNDS MEAN THAT I'M YOUR FRIEND NOW?
NO.
POP
YOU'RE NOT THE ONLY PERSON I'M CONNECTED TO THROUGH DROOL. THERE'S SOMEONE ELSE...
AND THAT'S WHY I DON'T NEED FRIENDS...
YOU MEAN...
TSUBAKI FROM OUR CLASS, RIGHT?

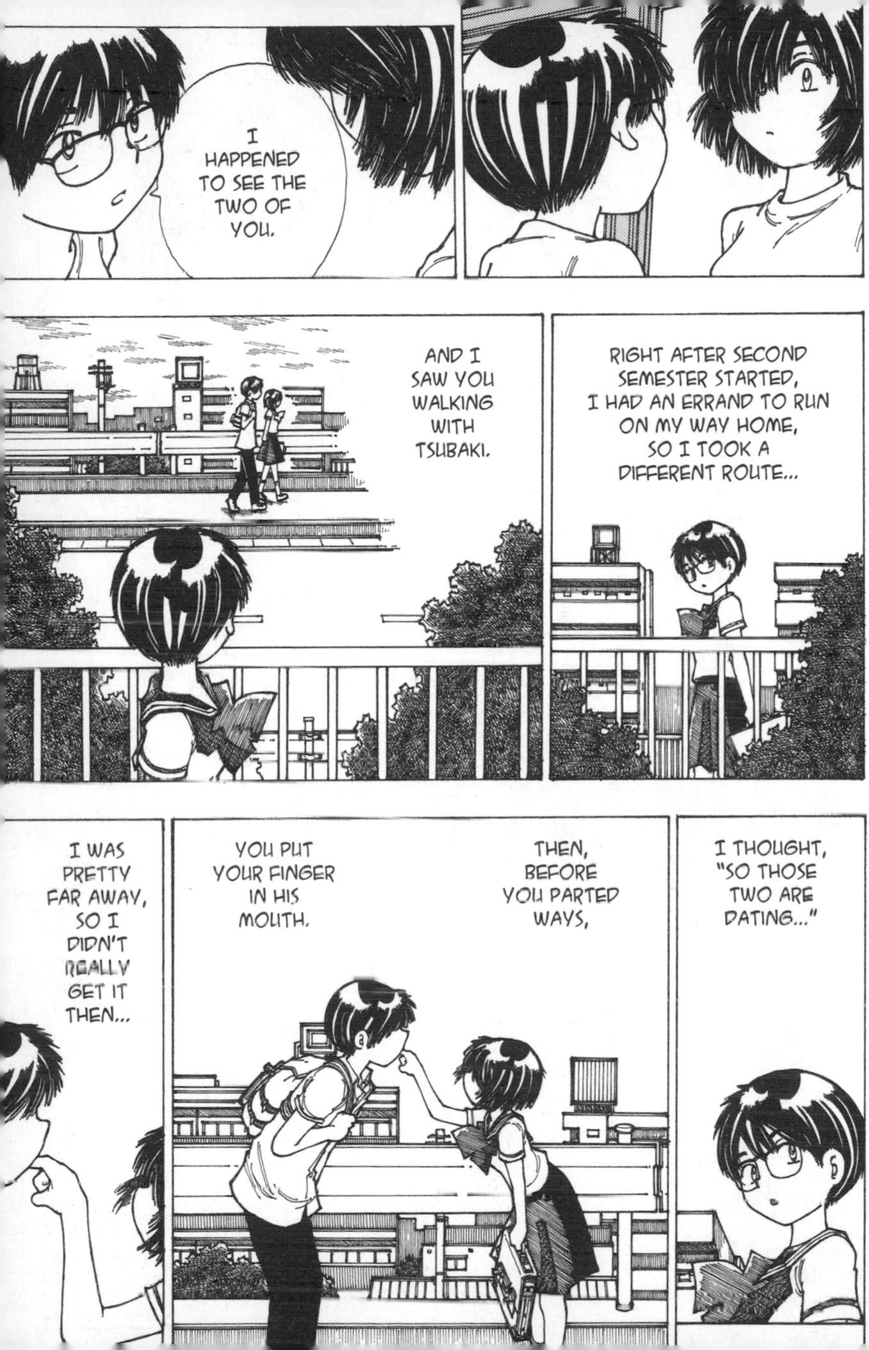
I HAPPENED TO SEE THE TWO OF YOU.
RIGHT AFTER SECOND SEMESTER STARTED, I HAD AN ERRAND TO RUN ON MY WAY HOME, SO I TOOK A DIFFERENT ROUTE...
AND I SAW YOU WALKING WITH TSUBAKI.
I THOUGHT, "SO THOSE TWO ARE DATING..."
THEN, BEFORE YOU PARTED WAYS,
YOU PUT YOUR FINGER IN HIS MOUTH.
I WAS PRETTY FAR AWAY, SO I DIDN'T REALLY GET IT THEN...

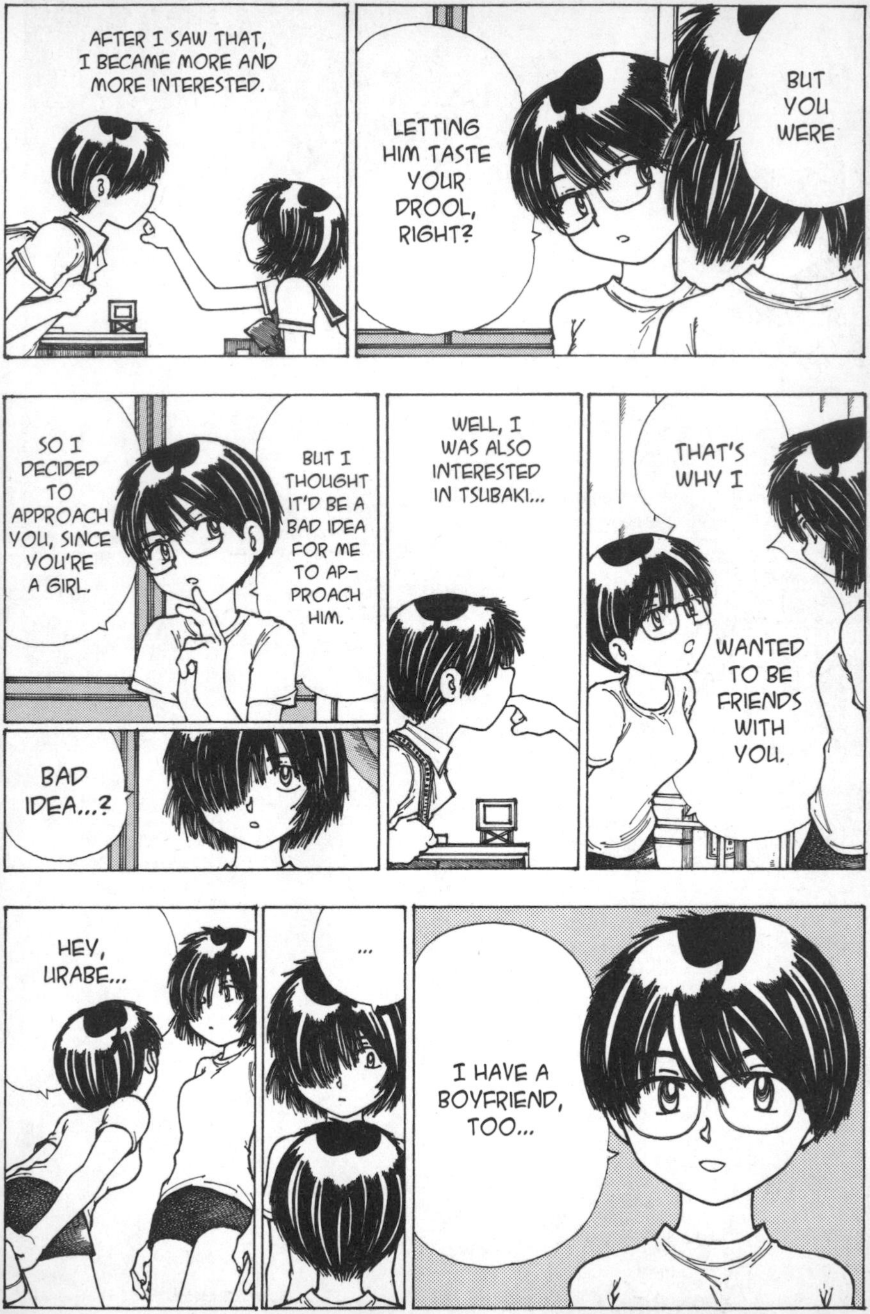
BUT YOU WERE
LETTING HIM TASTE YOUR DROOL, RIGHT?
AFTER I SAW THAT, I BECAME MORE AND MORE INTERESTED.
THAT'S WHY I
WANTED TO BE FRIENDS WITH YOU.
WELL, I WAS ALSO INTERESTED IN TSUBAKI...
BUT I THOUGHT IT'D BE A BAD IDEA FOR ME TO AP- PROACH HIM.
SO I DECIDED TO APPROACH YOU, SINCE YOU'RE A GIRL.
BAD IDEA...?
I HAVE A BOYFRIEND, TOO...
...
HEY, URABE...

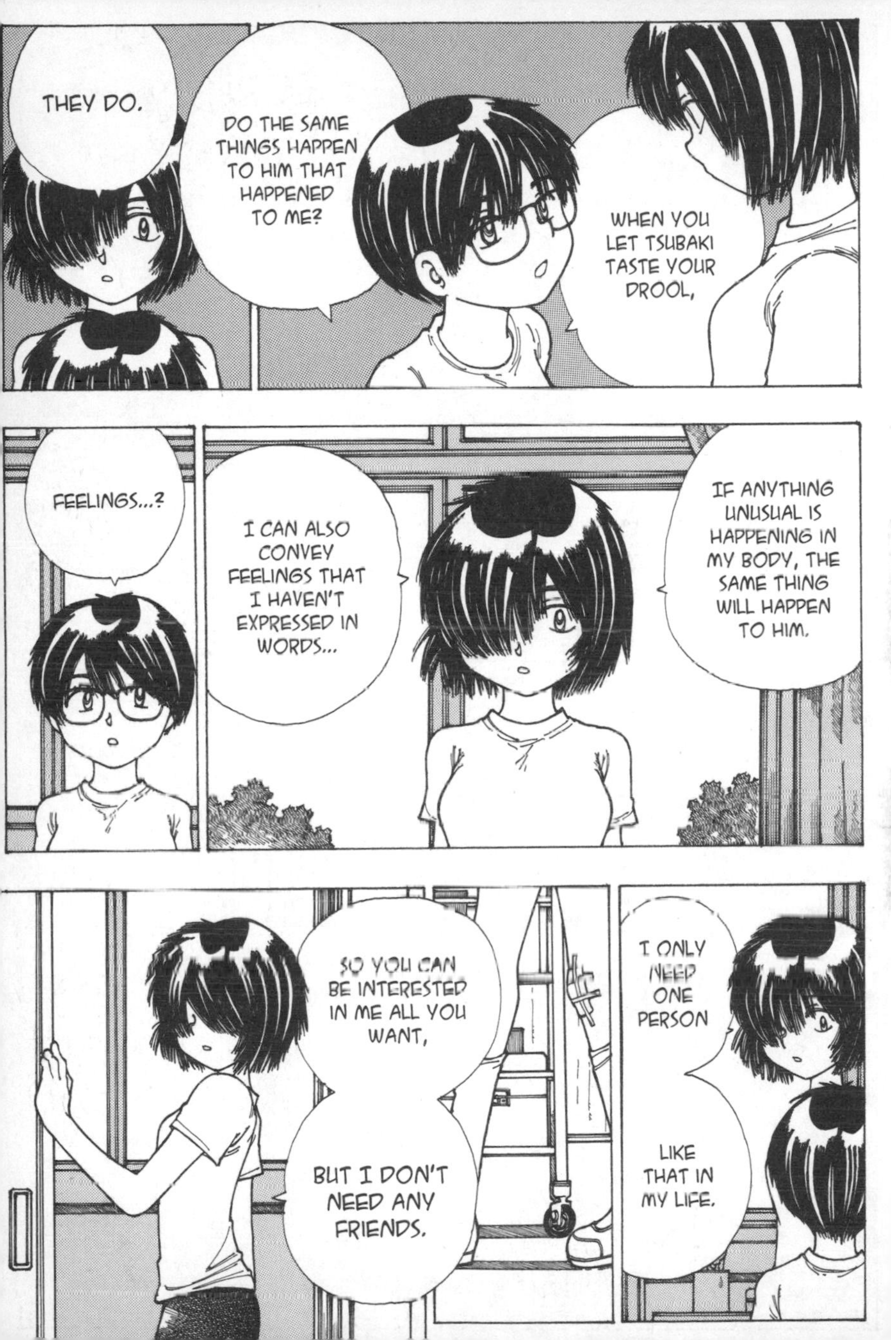
WHEN YOU LET TSUBAKI TASTE YOUR DROOL,
DO THE SAME THINGS HAPPEN TO HIM THAT HAPPENED TO ME?
THEY DO.
IF ANYTHING UNUSUAL IS HAPPENING IN MY BODY, THE SAME THING WILL HAPPEN TO HIM.
I CAN ALSO CONVEY FEELINGS THAT I HAVEN'T EXPRESSED IN WORDS...
FEELINGS...?
I ONLY NEED ONE PERSON
LIKE THAT IN MY LIFE.
SO YOU CAN BE INTERESTED IN ME ALL YOU WANT,
BUT I DON'T NEED ANY FRIENDS.

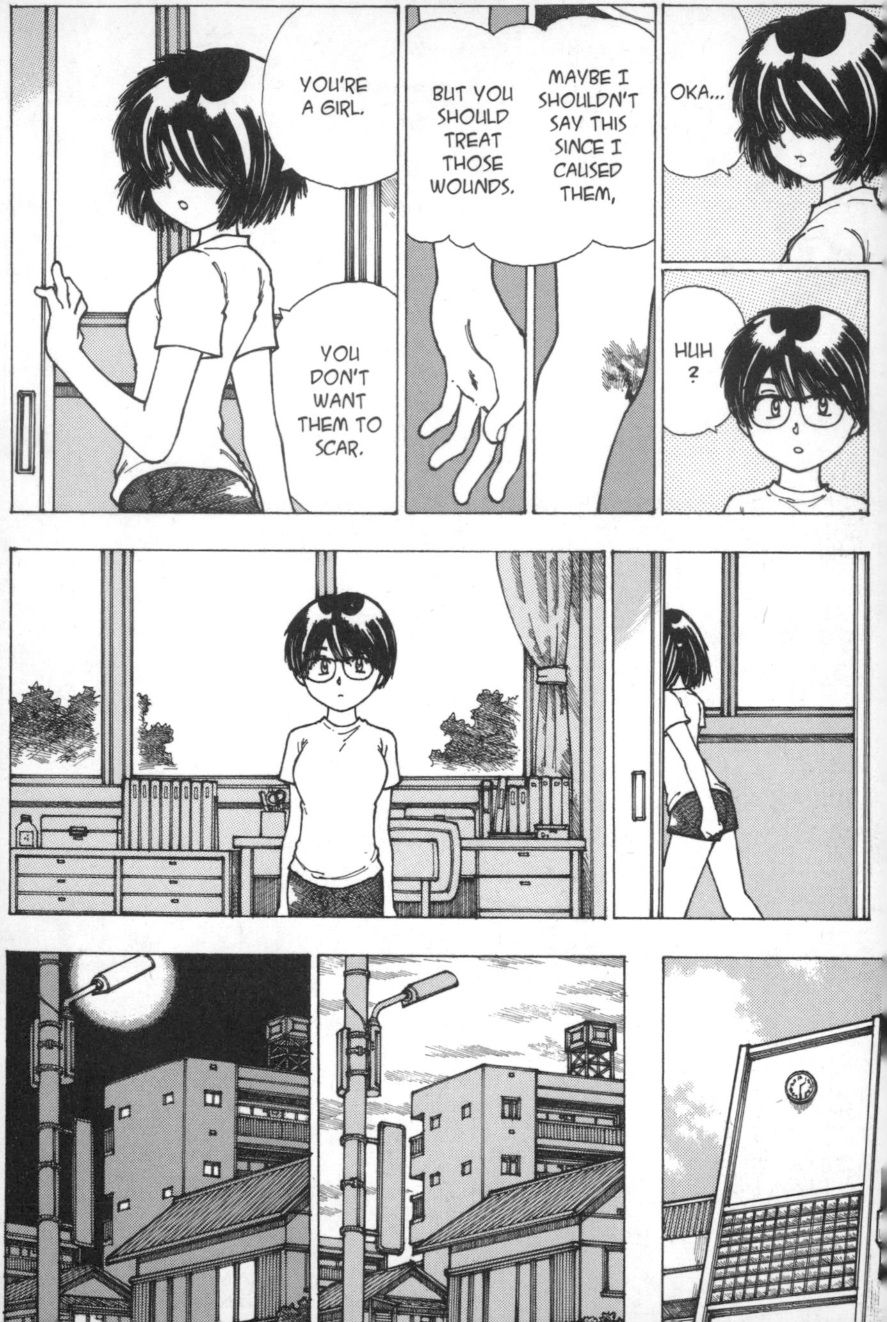
OKA...
HUH ?
MAYBE I SHOULDN'T SAY THIS SINCE I CAUSED THEM,
BUT YOU SHOULD TREAT THOSE WOUNDS.
YOU'RE A GIRL.
YOU DON'T WANT THEM TO SCAR.

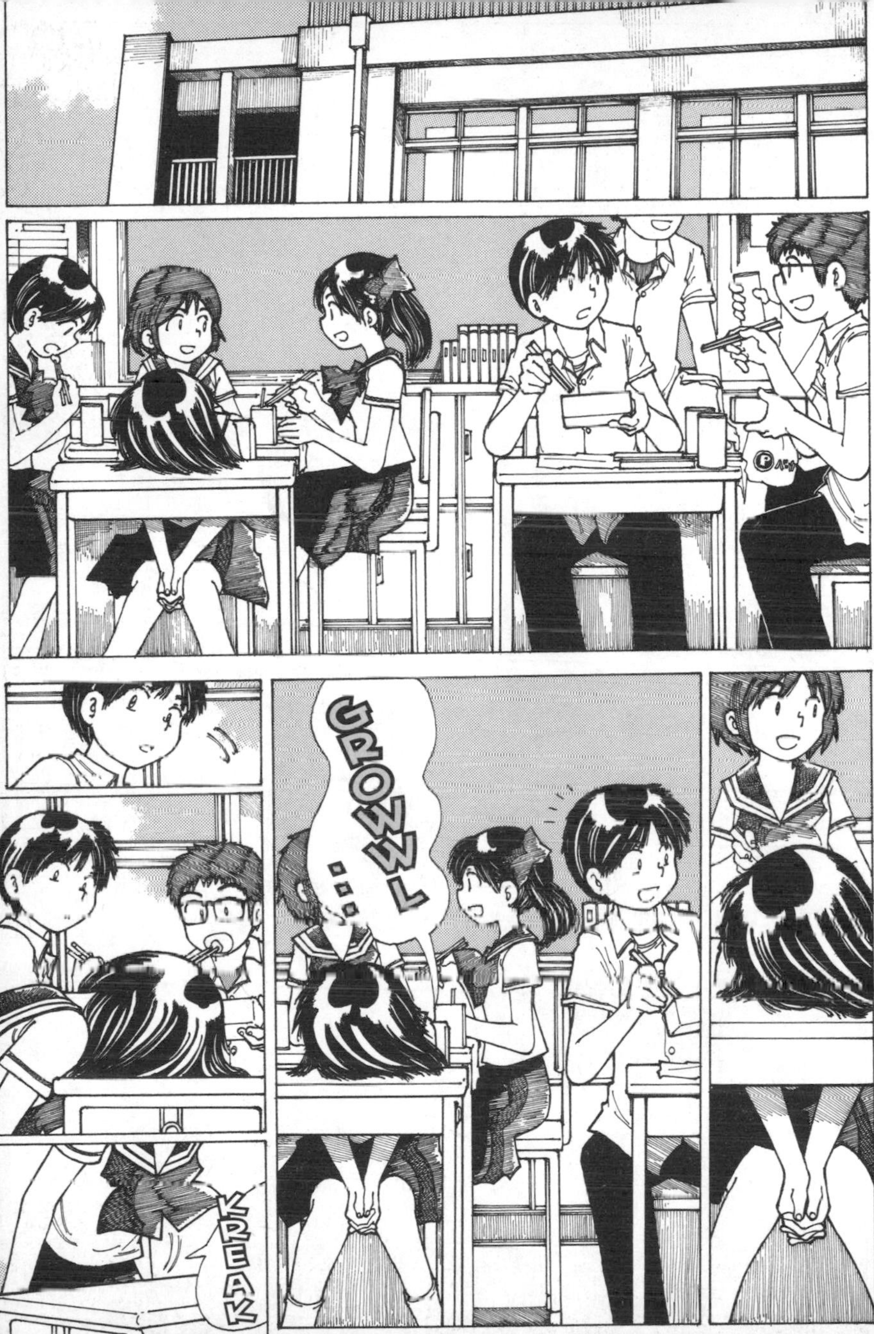
GROWL...
KREAK

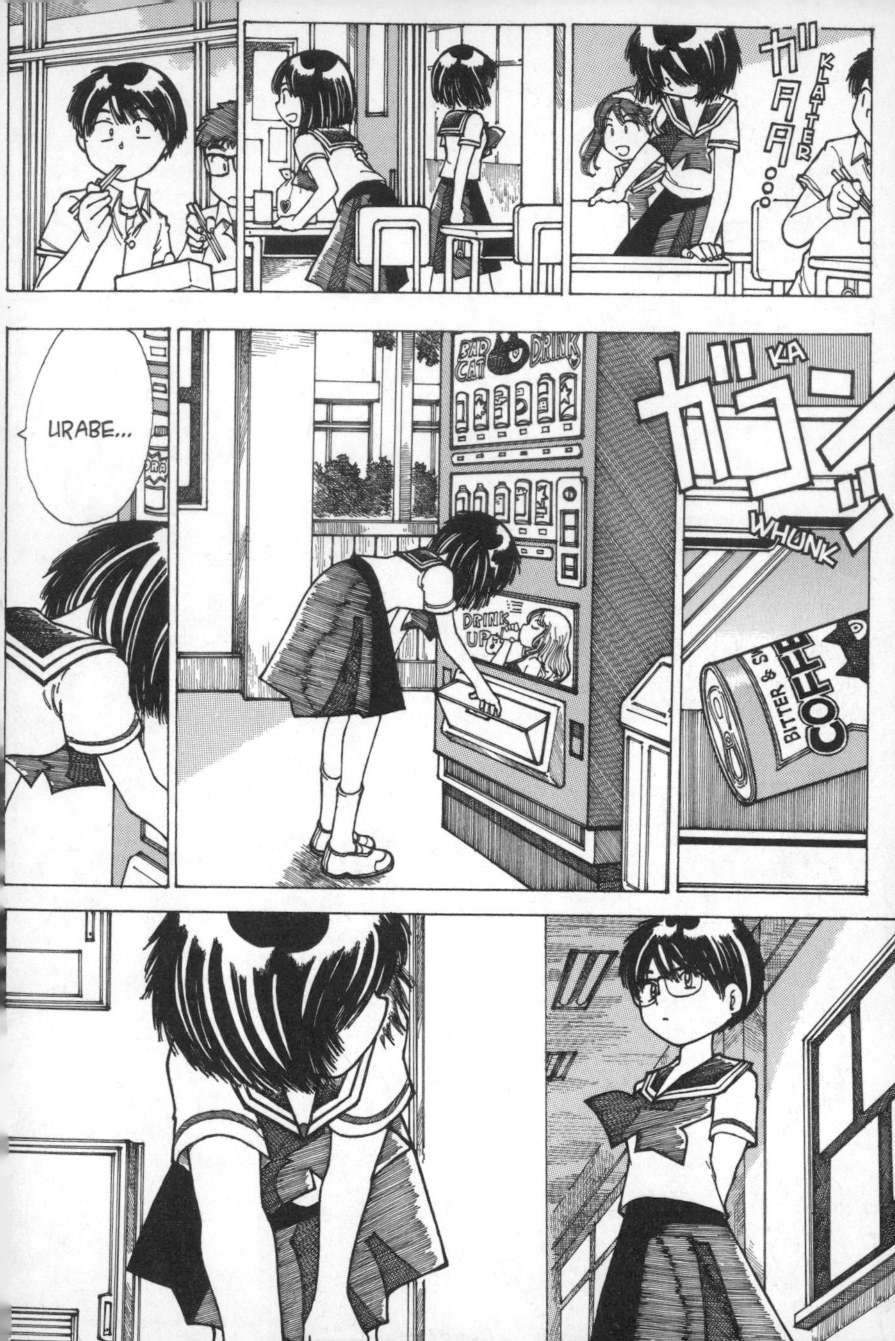
KLATTER
KA
WHUNK
BAD CAT DRINK
DRINK UP
URABE...

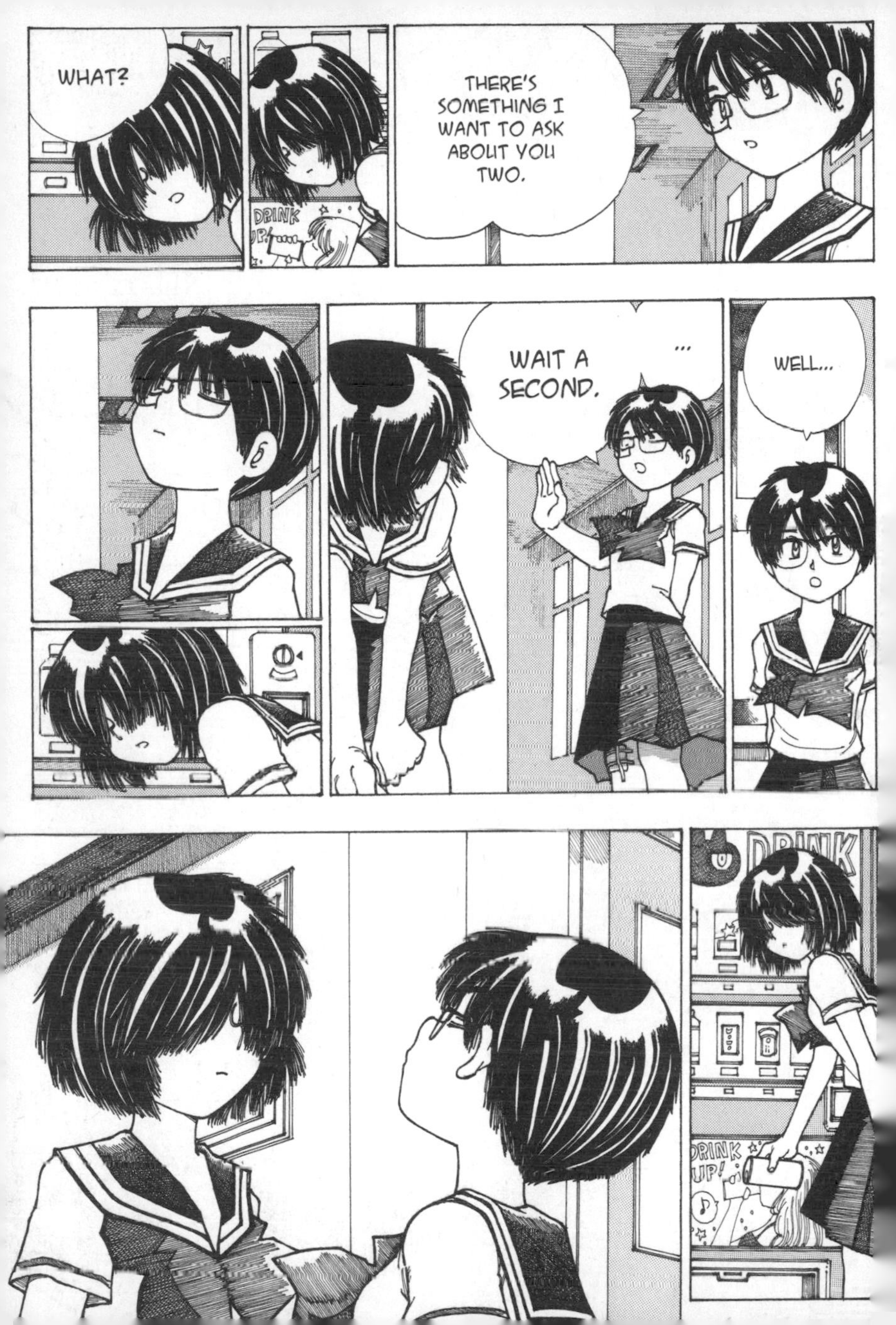
THERE'S SOMETHING I WANT TO ASK ABOUT YOU TWO.
DRINK UP!
WHAT?
WELL...
...
WAIT A SECOND.
DRINK
DRINK UP!

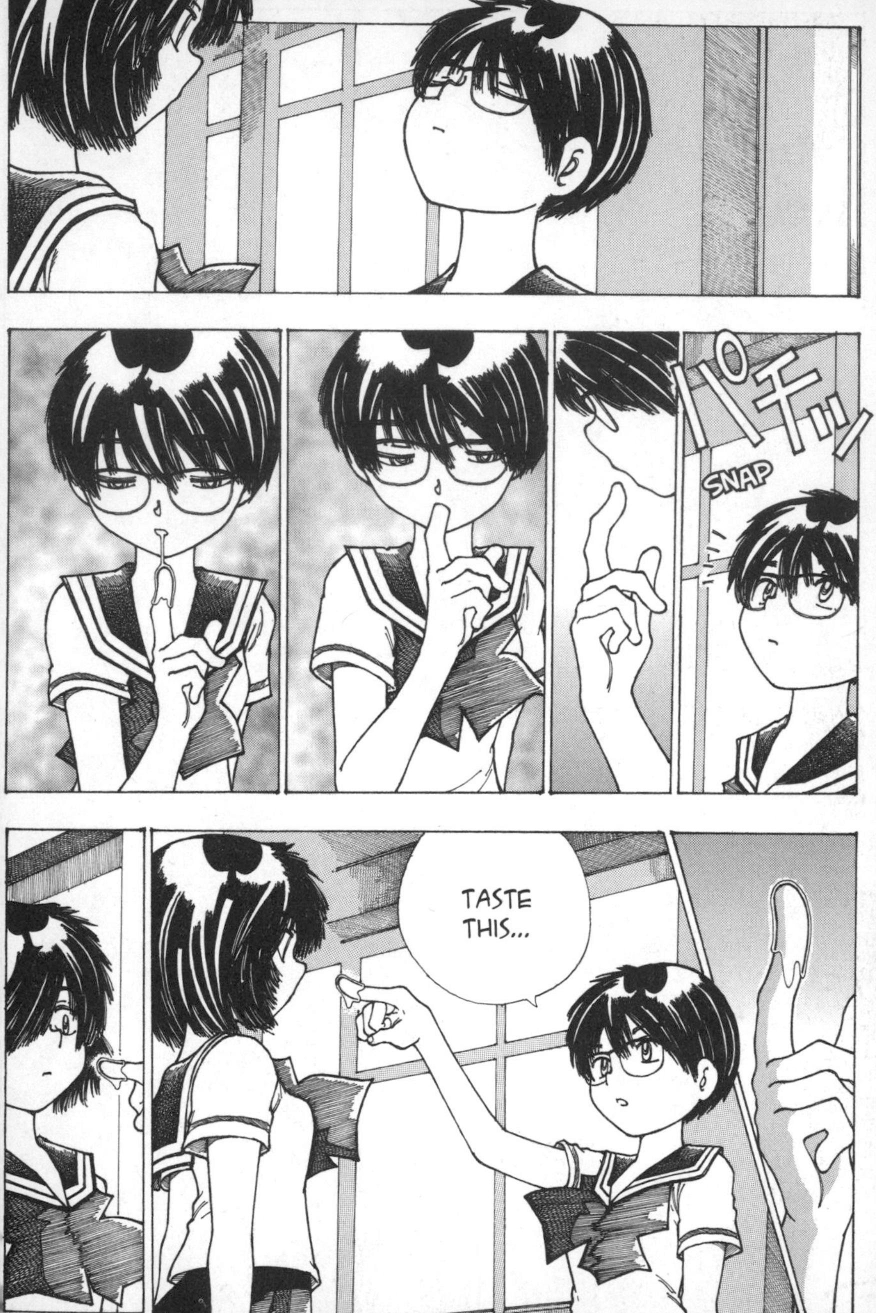
パチッ
SNAP
TASTE THIS...

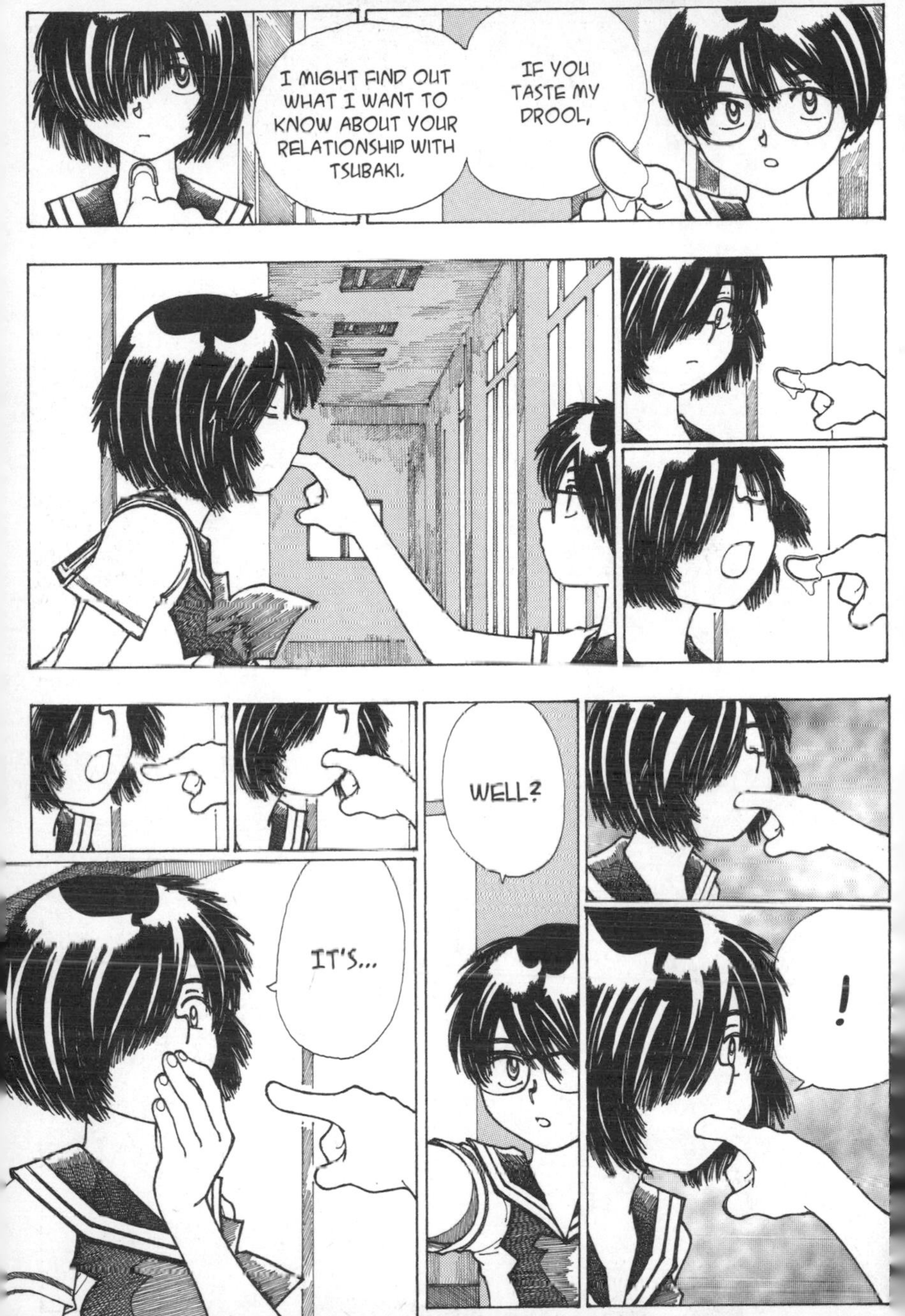
IF YOU TASTE MY DROOL,
I MIGHT FIND OUT WHAT I WANT TO KNOW ABOUT YOUR RELATIONSHIP WITH TSUBAKI.
WELL?
IT'S...
!

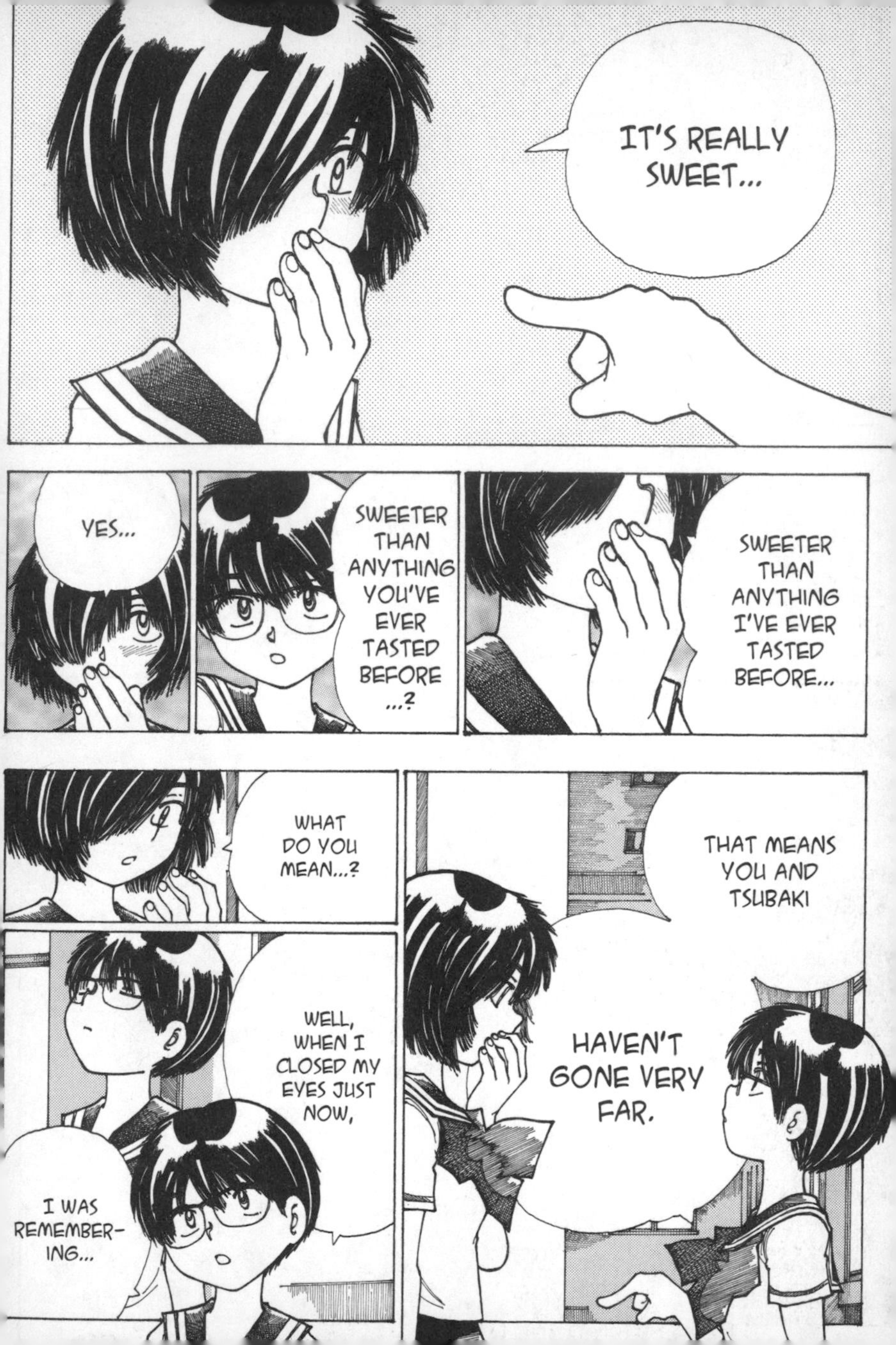
IT'S REALLY SWEET...
SWEETER THAN ANYTHING I'VE EVER TASTED BEFORE...
SWEETER THAN ANYTHING YOU'VE EVER TASTED BEFORE ...?
YES...
THAT MEANS YOU AND TSUBAKI
HAVEN'T GONE VERY FAR.
WHAT DO YOU MEAN...?
WELL, WHEN I CLOSED MY EYES JUST NOW,
I WAS REMEMBER-ING...

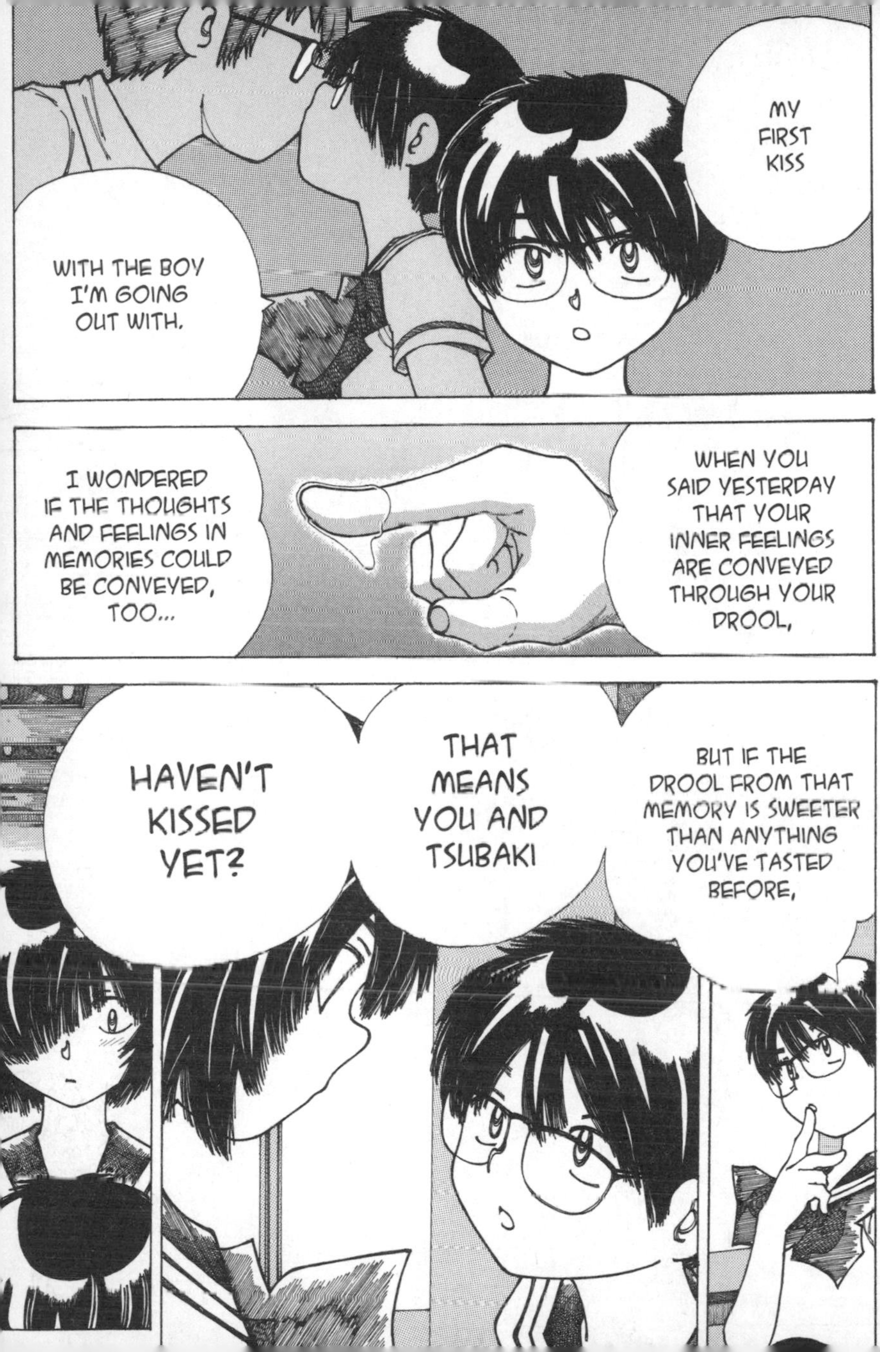
MY FIRST KISS
WITH THE BOY I'M GOING OUT WITH.
WHEN YOU SAID YESTERDAY THAT YOUR INNER FEELINGS ARE CONVEYED THROUGH YOUR DROOL,
I WONDERED IF THE THOUGHTS AND FEELINGS IN MEMORIES COULD BE CONVEYED, TOO...
BUT IF THE DROOL FROM THAT MEMORY IS SWEETER THAN ANYTHING YOU'VE TASTED BEFORE,
THAT MEANS YOU AND TSUBAKI
HAVEN'T KISSED YET?

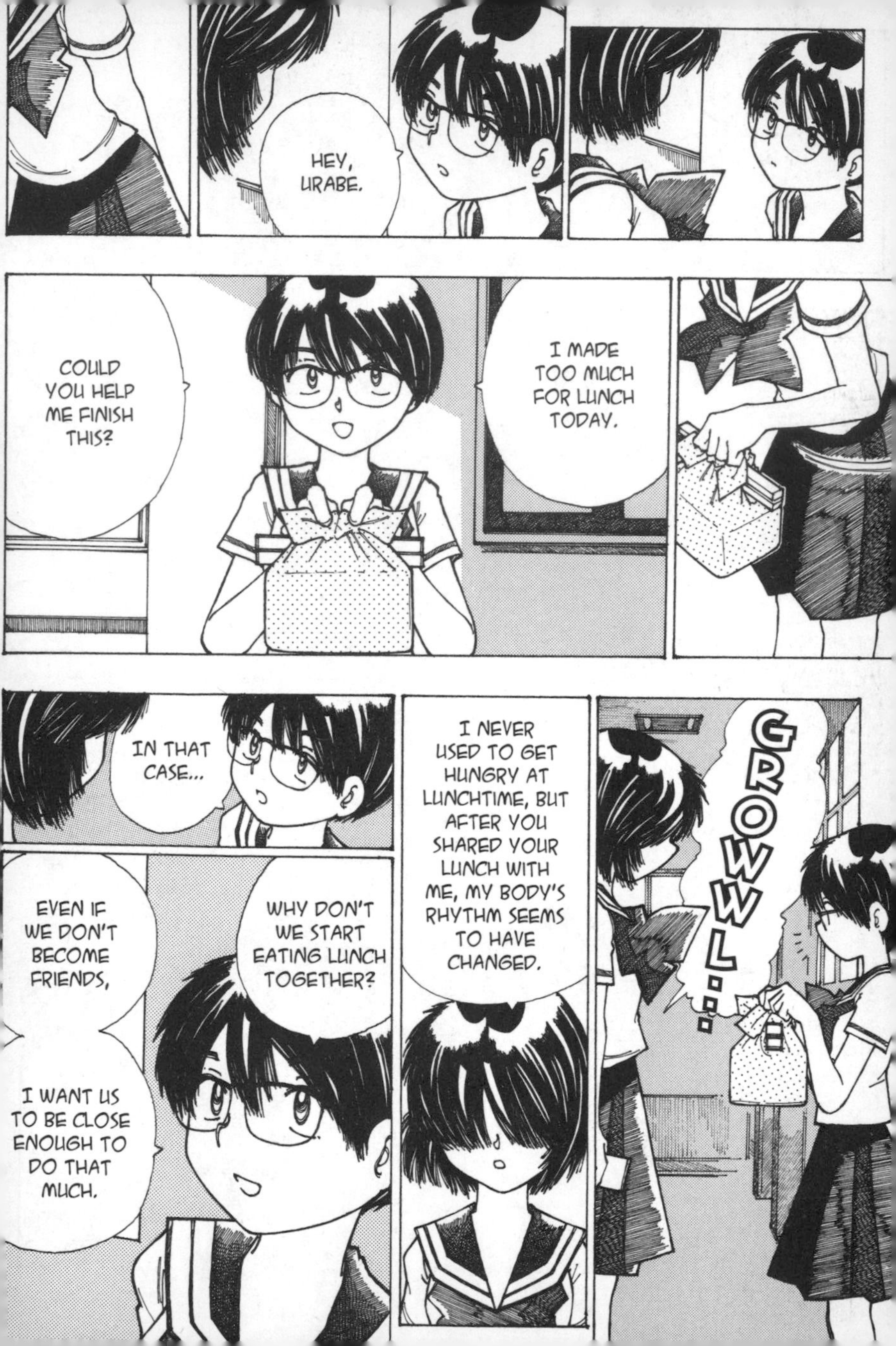
HEY, URABE.
I MADE TOO MUCH FOR LUNCH TODAY.
COULD YOU HELP ME FINISH THIS?
GROWL...
I NEVER USED TO GET HUNGRY AT LUNCHTIME, BUT AFTER YOU SHARED YOUR LUNCH WITH ME, MY BODY'S RHYTHM SEEMS TO HAVE CHANGED.
IN THAT CASE...
WHY DON'T WE START EATING LUNCH TOGETHER?
EVEN IF WE DON'T BECOME FRIENDS,
I WANT US TO BE CLOSE ENOUGH TO DO THAT MUCH.

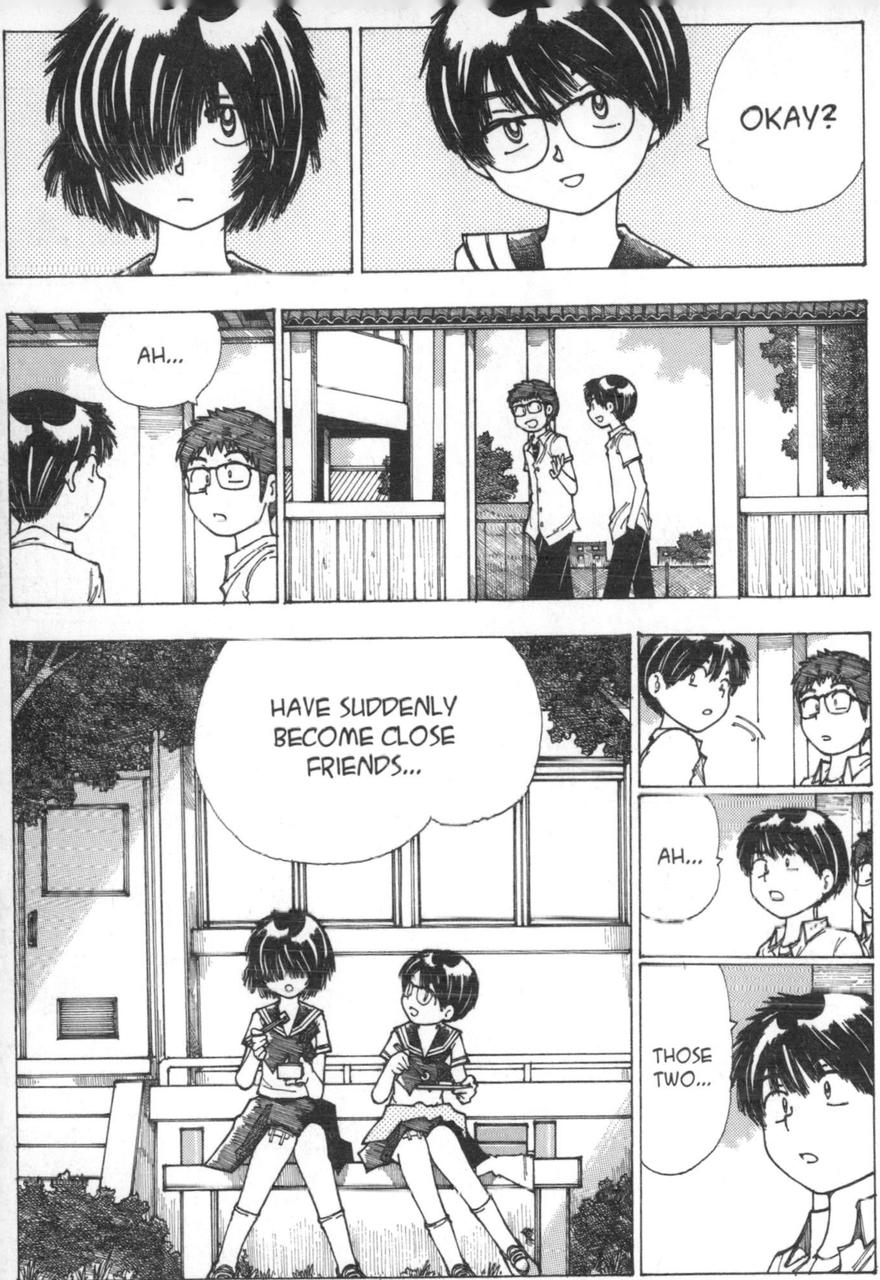
OKAY?
AH...
AH...
THOSE TWO...
HAVE SUDDENLY BECOME CLOSE FRIENDS...

END OF CHAPTER 8

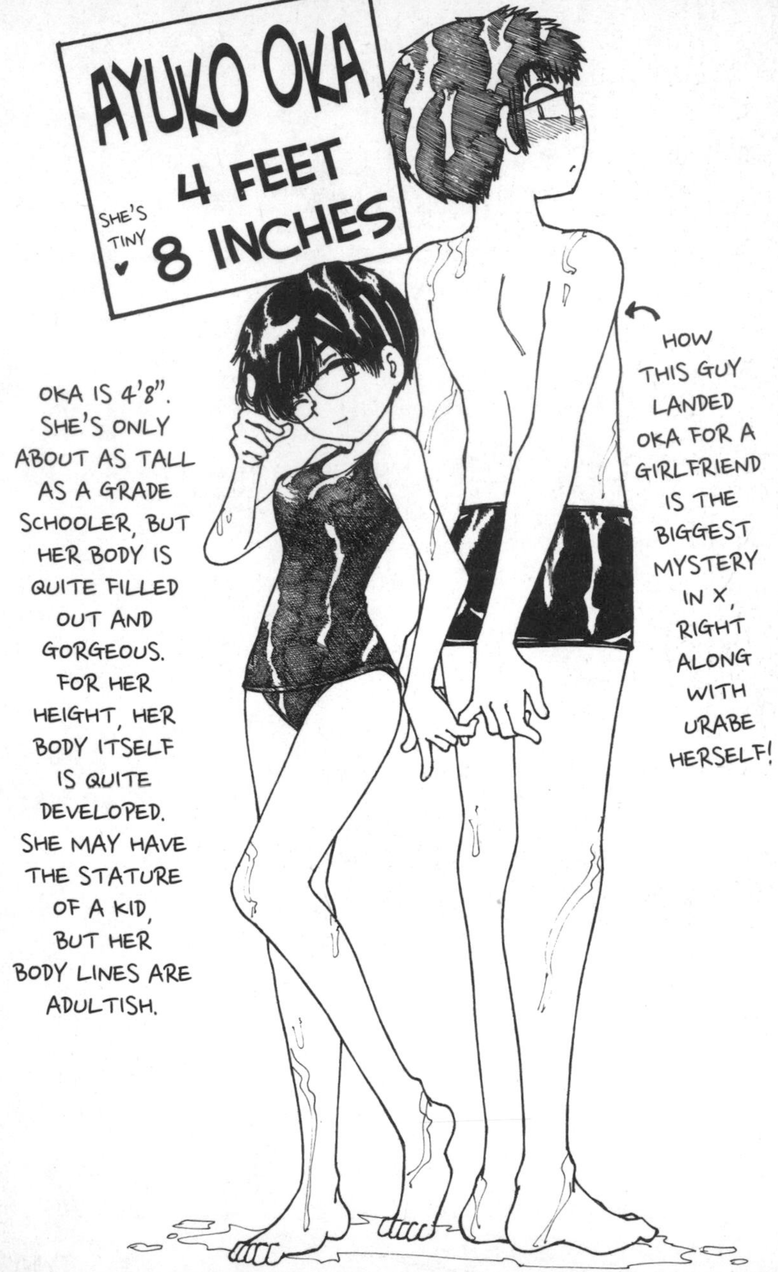
AYUKO OKA
4 FEET
SHE'S TINY ♥
8 INCHES
HOW THIS GUY LANDED OKA FOR A GIRLFRIEND IS THE BIGGEST MYSTERY IN X, RIGHT ALONG WITH URABE HERSELF!
OKA IS 4'8". SHE'S ONLY ABOUT AS TALL AS A GRADE SCHOOLER, BUT HER BODY IS QUITE FILLED OUT AND GORGEOUS. FOR HER HEIGHT, HER BODY ITSELF IS QUITE DEVELOPED. SHE MAY HAVE THE STATURE OF A KID, BUT HER BODY LINES ARE ADULTISH.

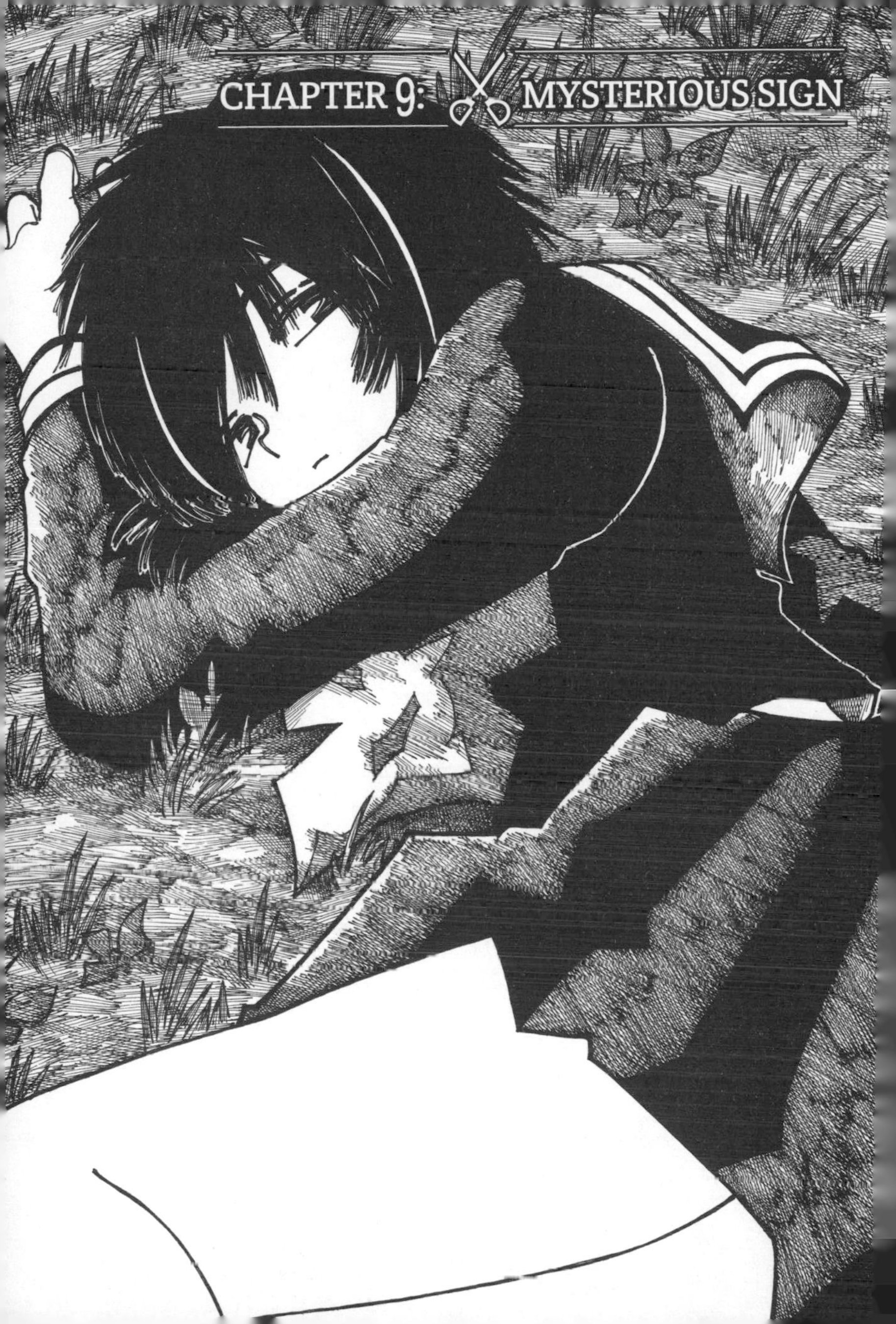
CHAPTER 9: MYSTERIOUS SIGN

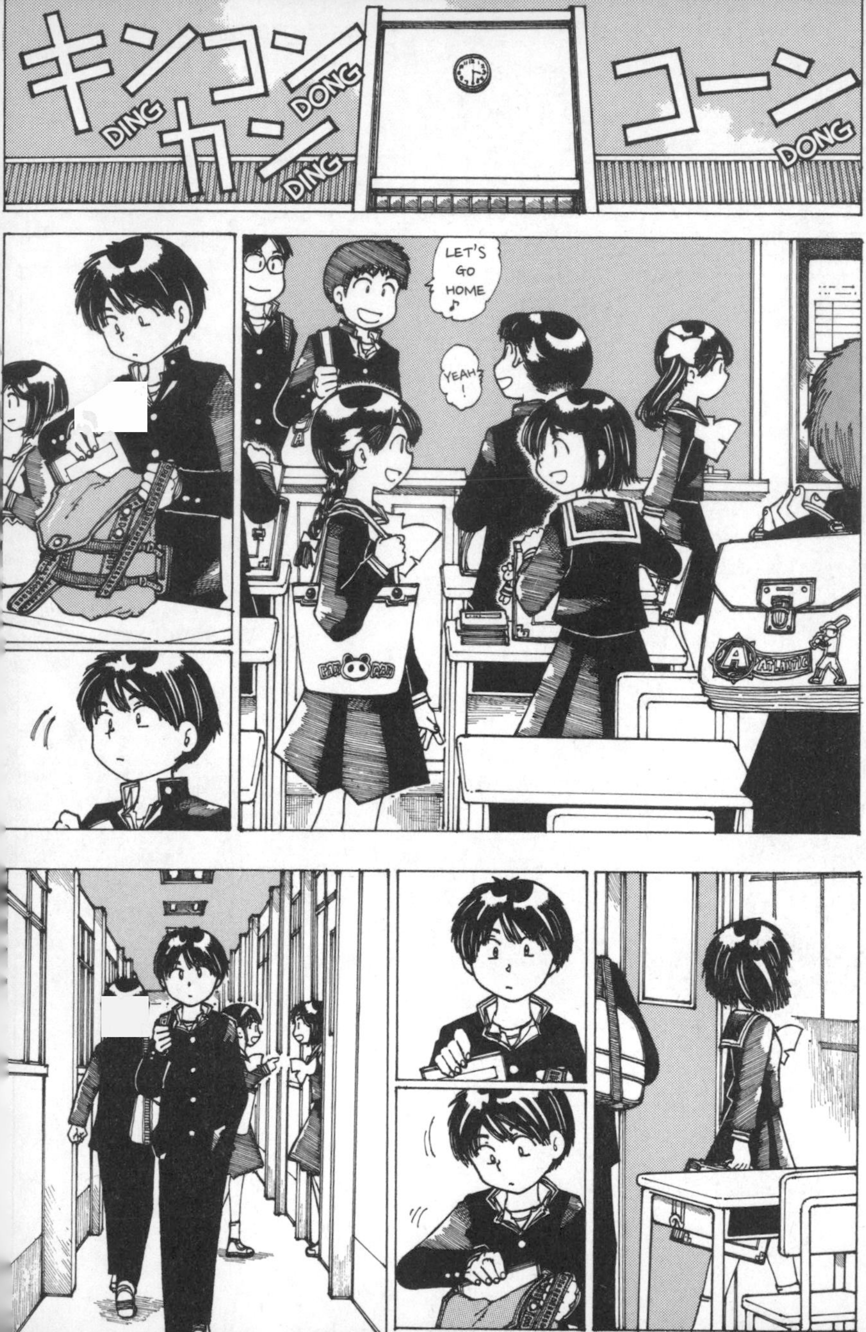
キンコーン
DING
DONG
カーン
DING
コーン
DONG
LET'S GO HOME ♪
YEAH!
ATLANTIC

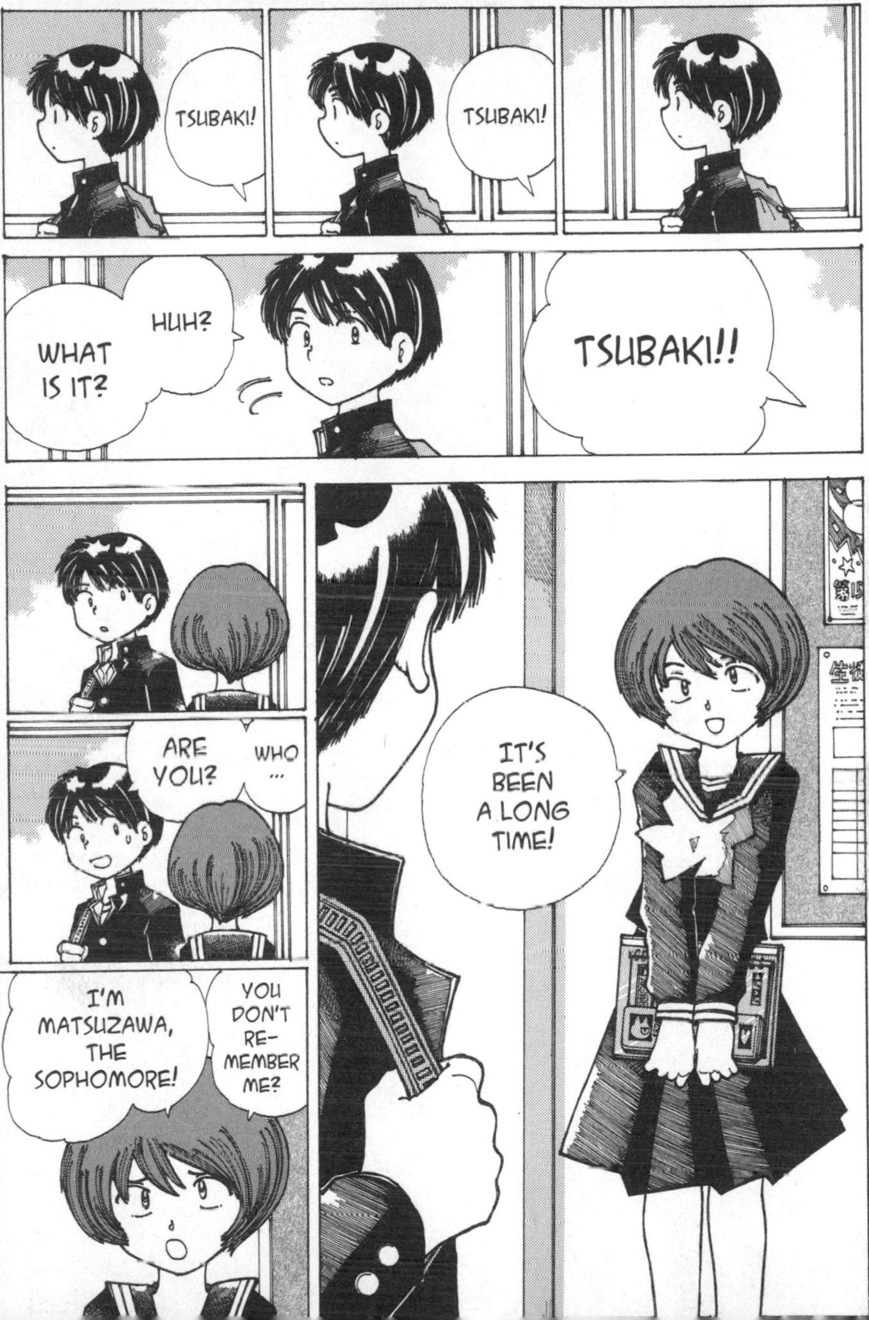
TSUBAKI!
TSUBAKI!
TSUBAKI!!
HUH? WHAT IS IT?
IT'S BEEN A LONG TIME!
WHO ... ARE YOU?
YOU DON'T RE-MEMBER ME?
I'M MATSUZAWA, THE SOPHOMORE!

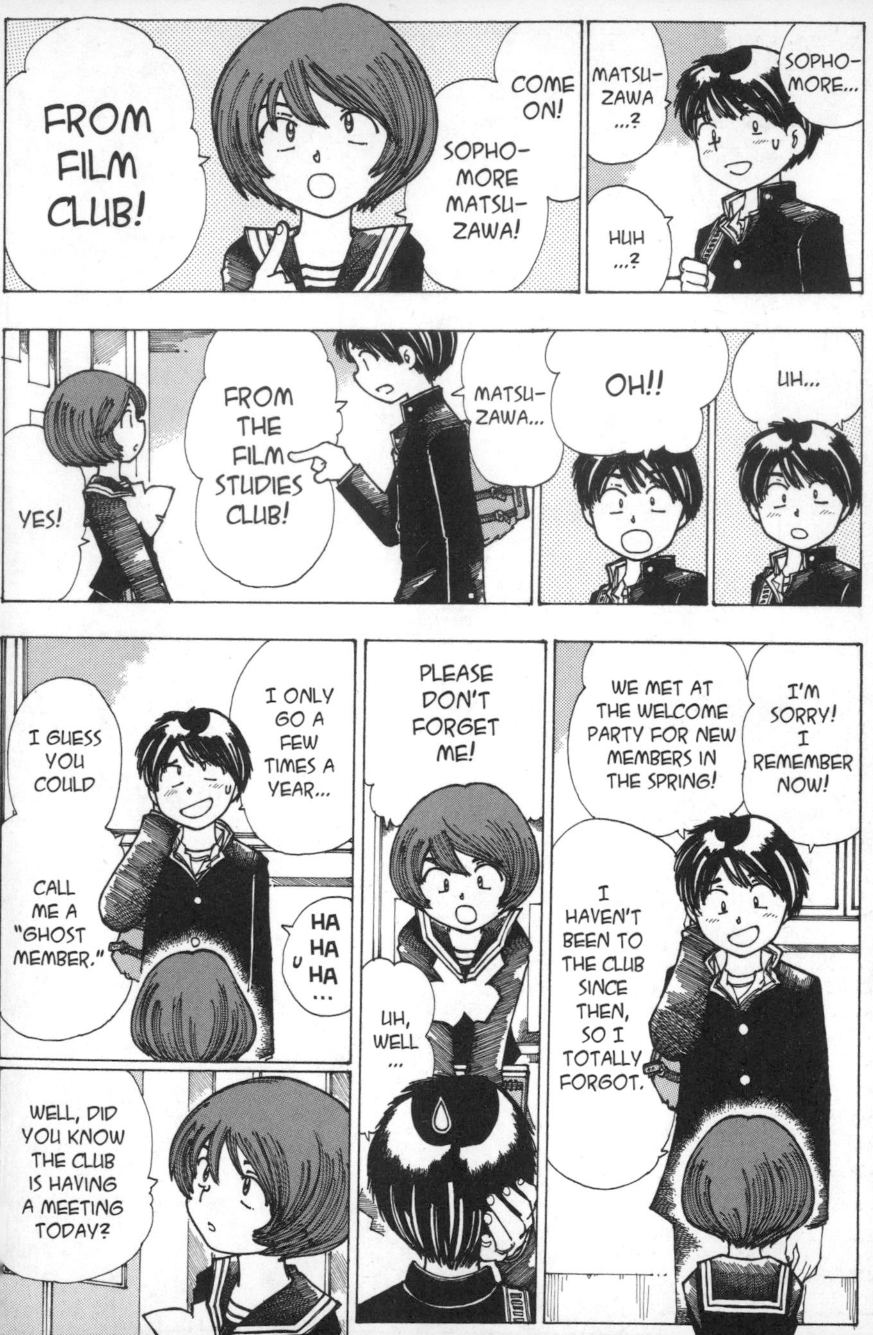
SOPHO-MORE...
MATSU-ZAWA ...?
HUH ...?
COME ON!
SOPHO-MORE MATSU-ZAWA!
FROM FILM CLUB!
UH...
OH!!
MATSU-ZAWA...
FROM THE FILM STUDIES CLUB!
YES!
I'M SORRY! I REMEMBER NOW!
WE MET AT THE WELCOME PARTY FOR NEW MEMBERS IN THE SPRING!
I HAVEN'T BEEN TO THE CLUB SINCE THEN, SO I TOTALLY FORGOT.
PLEASE DON'T FORGET ME!
UH, WELL ...
I ONLY GO A FEW TIMES A YEAR...
I GUESS YOU COULD
CALL ME A "GHOST MEMBER."
HA HA HA ...
WELL, DID YOU KNOW THE CLUB IS HAVING A MEETING TODAY?

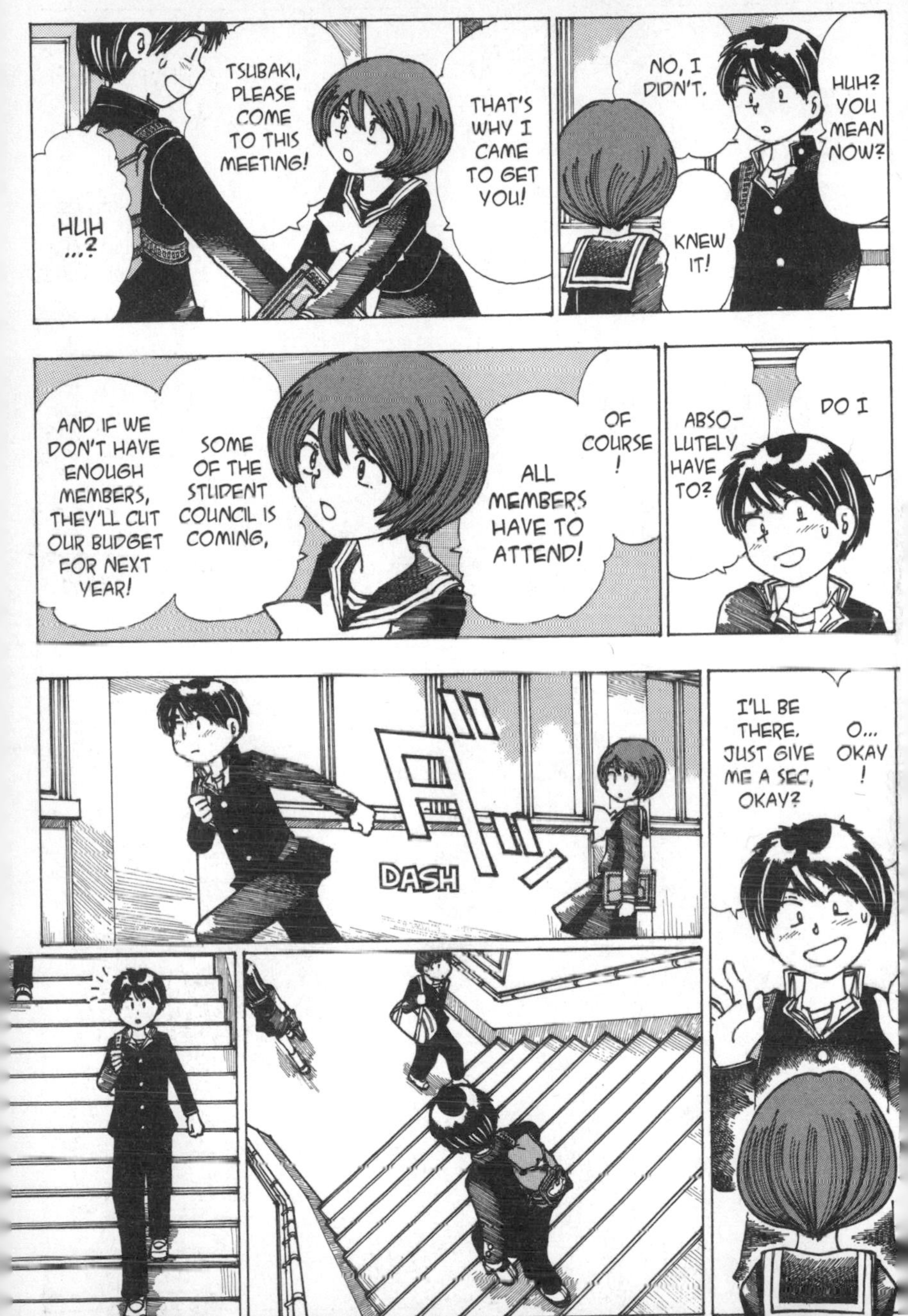

HUH? YOU MEAN NOW?
NO, I DIDN'T.
KNEW IT!
THAT'S WHY I CAME TO GET YOU!
TSUBAKI, PLEASE COME TO THIS MEETING!
HUH ...?
DO I
ABSO-LUTELY HAVE TO?
OF COURSE!
ALL MEMBERS HAVE TO ATTEND!
SOME OF THE STUDENT COUNCIL IS COMING,
AND IF WE DON'T HAVE ENOUGH MEMBERS, THEY'LL CUT OUR BUDGET FOR NEXT YEAR!
I'LL BE THERE. JUST GIVE ME A SEC, OKAY?
O... OKAY!
DASH

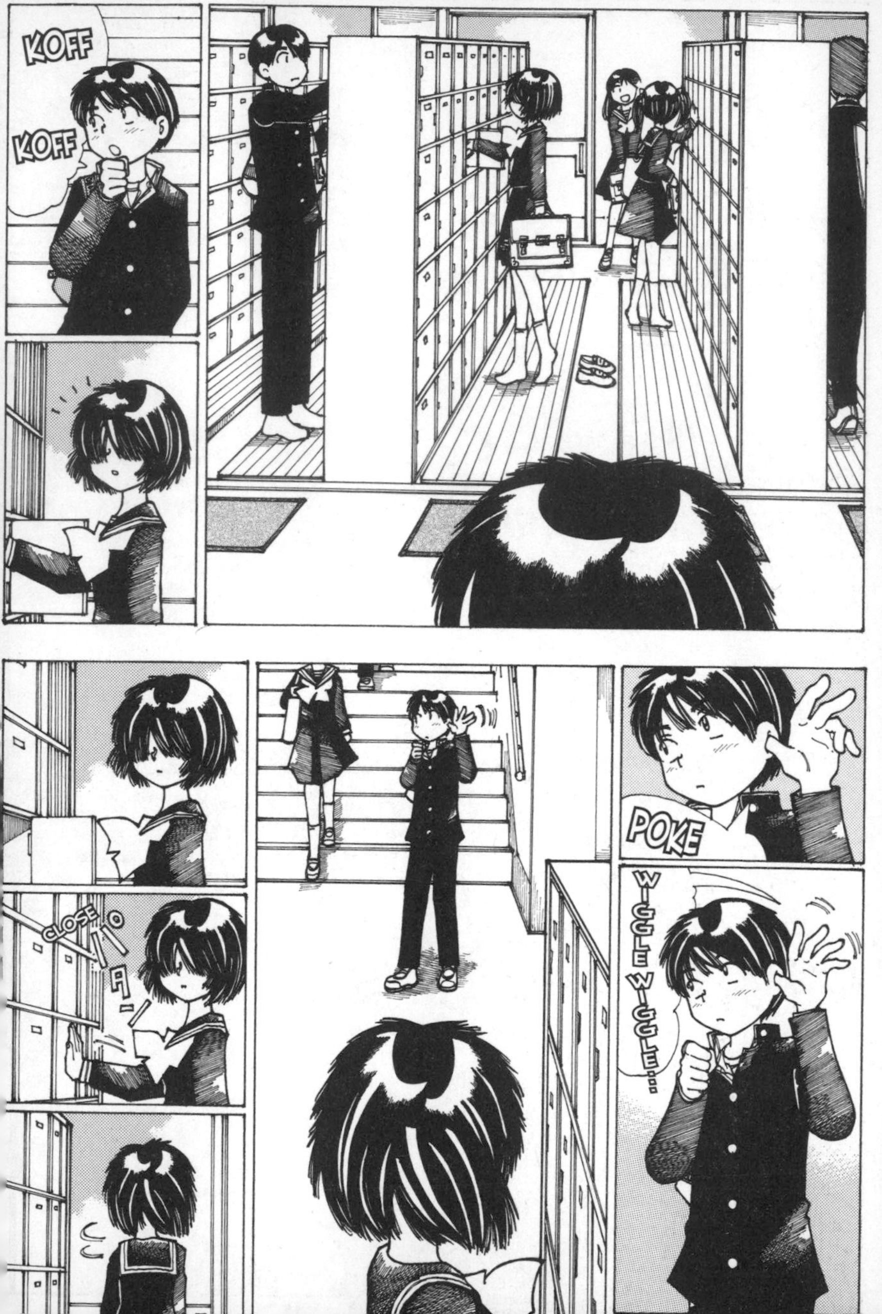
KOFF
KOFF
POKE
WIGGLE WIGGLE...
CLOSE

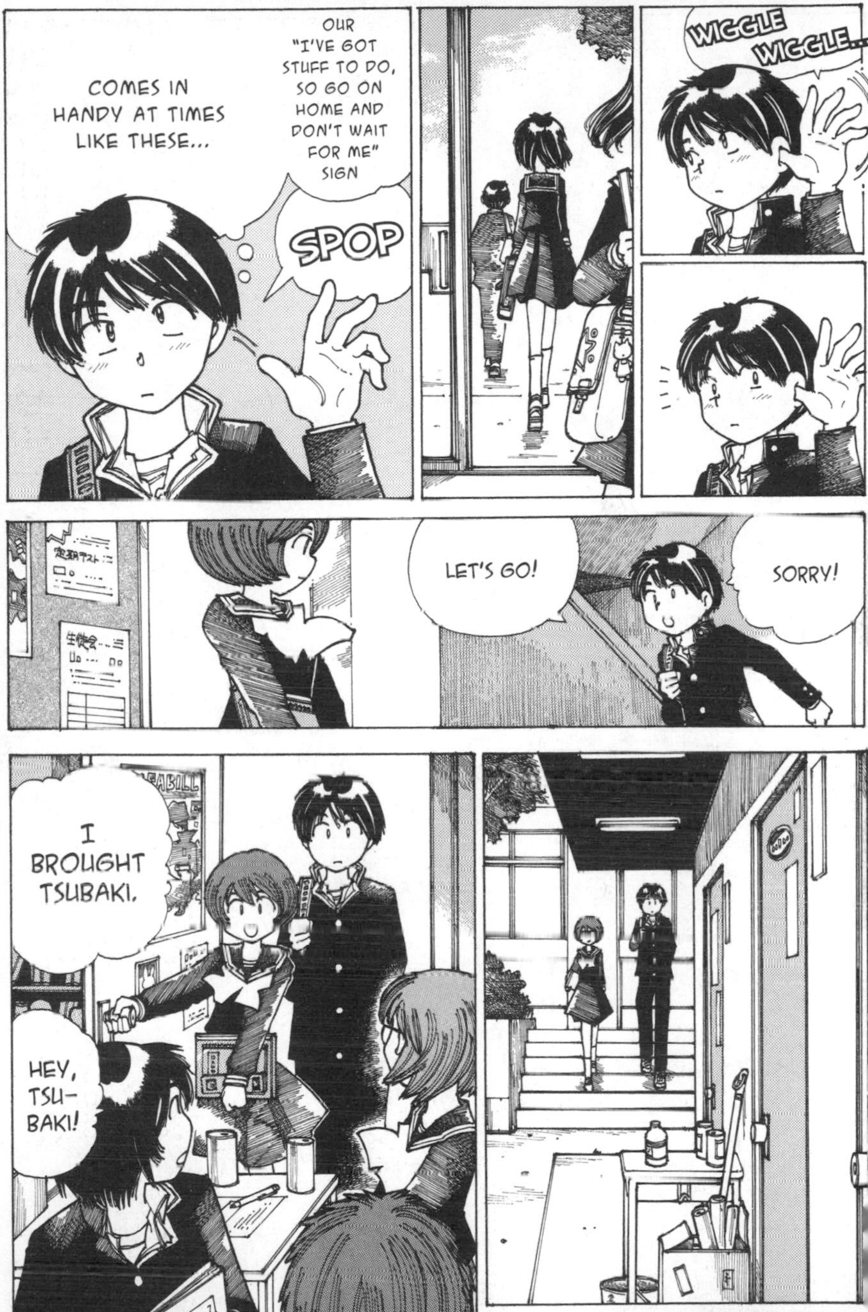
WIGGLE WIGGLE...
OUR "I'VE GOT STUFF TO DO, SO GO ON HOME AND DON'T WAIT FOR ME" SIGN
COMES IN HANDY AT TIMES LIKE THESE...
SPOP
SORRY!
LET'S GO!
I BROUGHT TSUBAKI.
HEY, TSU-BAKI!

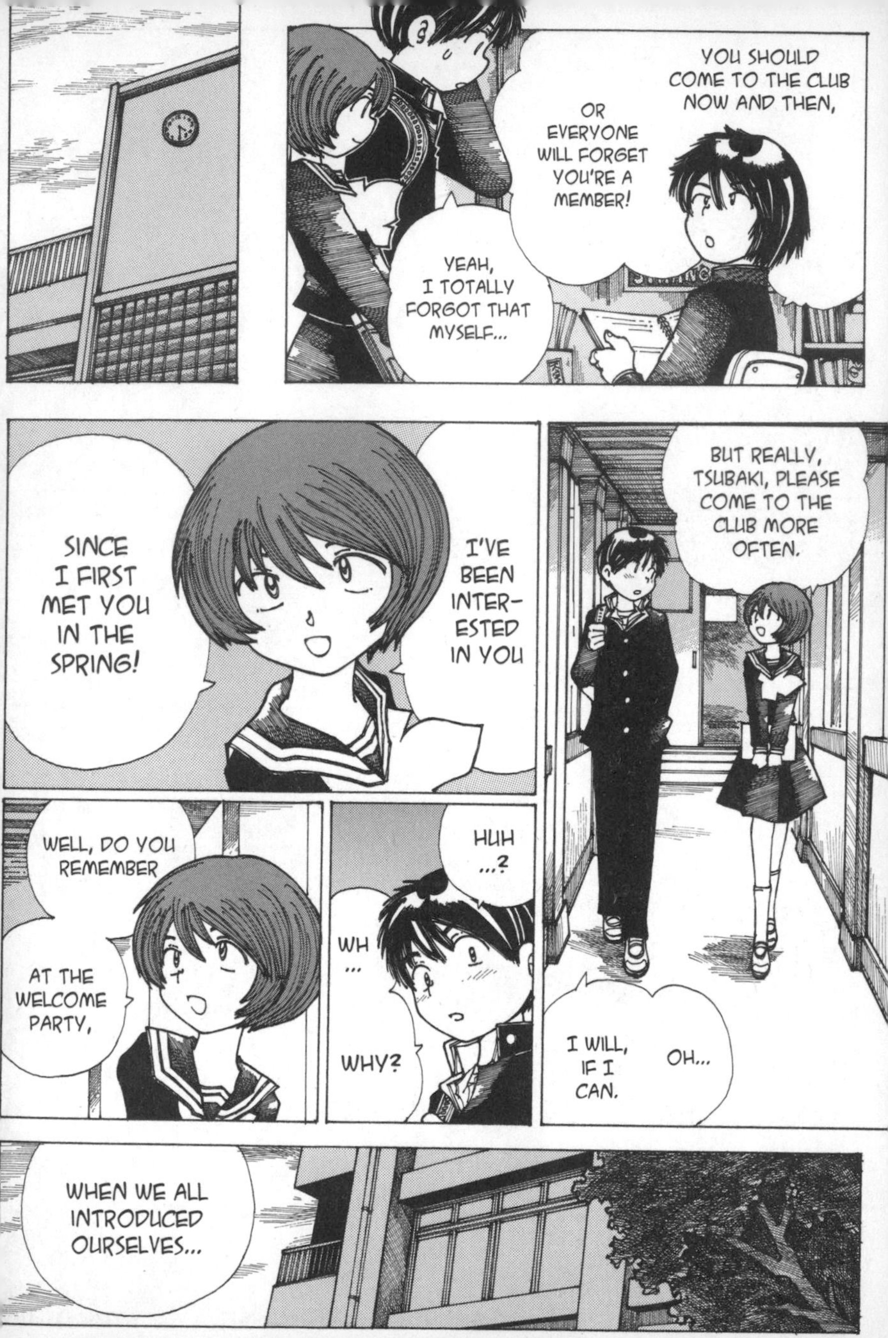
YOU SHOULD COME TO THE CLUB NOW AND THEN,
OR EVERYONE WILL FORGET YOU'RE A MEMBER!
YEAH, I TOTALLY FORGOT THAT MYSELF...
BUT REALLY, TSUBAKI, PLEASE COME TO THE CLUB MORE OFTEN.
OH...
I WILL, IF I CAN.
I'VE BEEN INTERESTED IN YOU
SINCE I FIRST MET YOU IN THE SPRING!
HUH ...?
WH ...
WHY?
WELL, DO YOU REMEMBER
AT THE WELCOME PARTY,
WHEN WE ALL INTRODUCED OURSELVES...

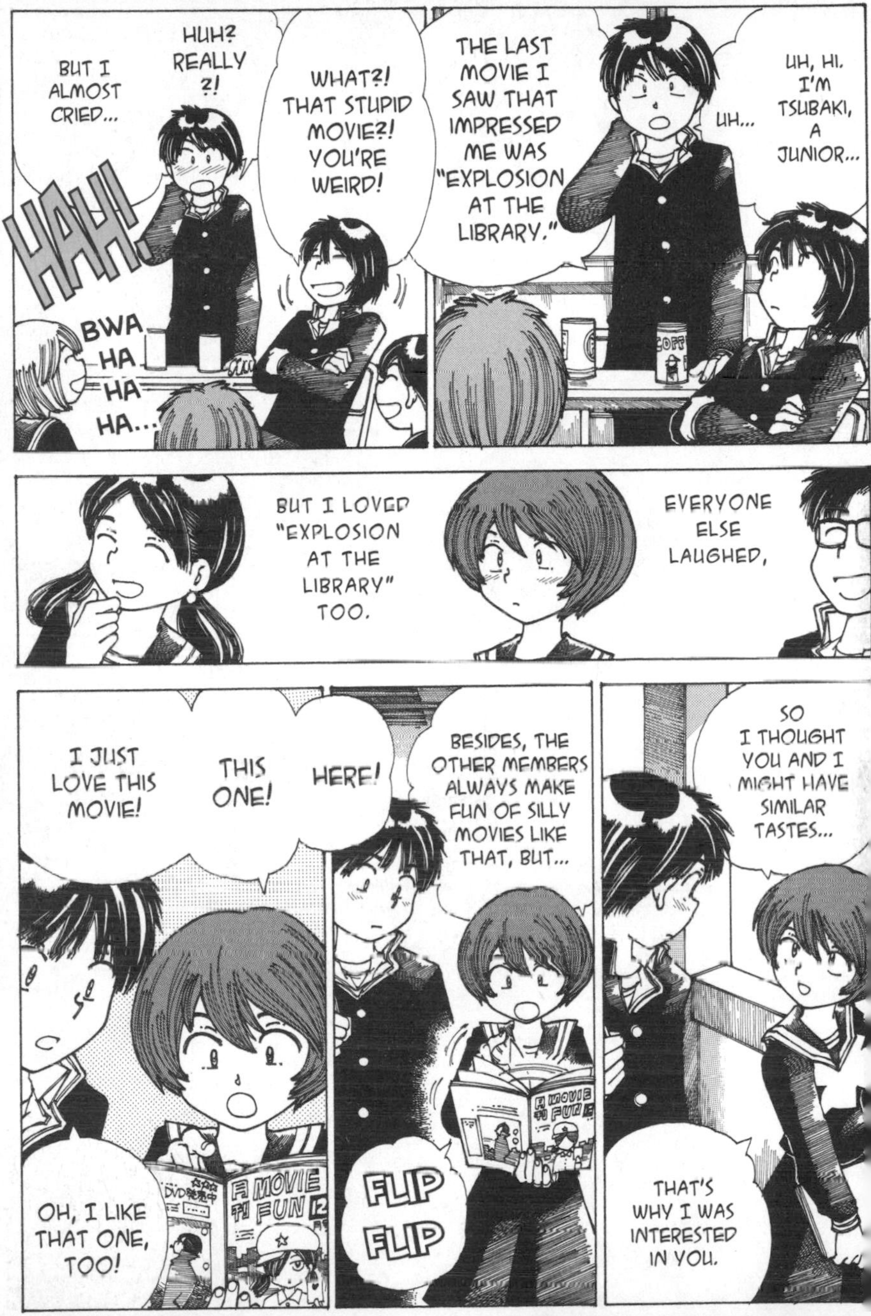
UH, HI. I'M TSUBAKI, A JUNIOR...
UH...
THE LAST MOVIE I SAW THAT IMPRESSED ME WAS "EXPLOSION AT THE LIBRARY."
WHAT?! THAT STUPID MOVIE?! YOU'RE WEIRD!
HUH? REALLY?!
BUT I ALMOST CRIED...
HAH!
BWA HA HA HA...
EVERYONE ELSE LAUGHED,
BUT I LOVED "EXPLOSION AT THE LIBRARY" TOO.
SO I THOUGHT YOU AND I MIGHT HAVE SIMILAR TASTES...
THAT'S WHY I WAS INTERESTED IN YOU.
BESIDES, THE OTHER MEMBERS ALWAYS MAKE FUN OF SILLY MOVIES LIKE THAT, BUT...
FLIP FLIP
HERE!
THIS ONE!
I JUST LOVE THIS MOVIE!
OH, I LIKE THAT ONE, TOO!

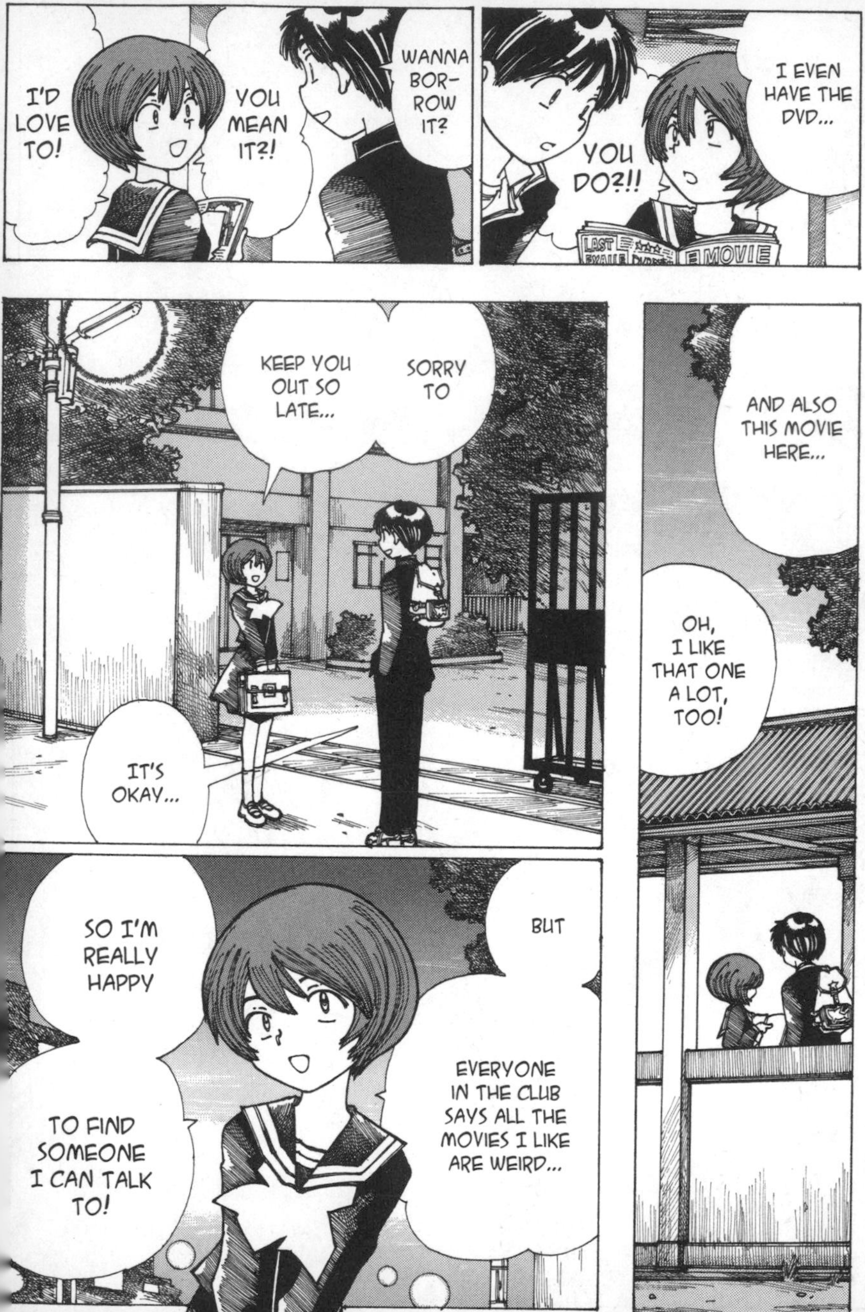
I EVEN HAVE THE DVD...
YOU DO?!!
MOVIE
WANNA BOR-ROW IT?
YOU MEAN IT?!
I'D LOVE TO!
AND ALSO THIS MOVIE HERE...
OH, I LIKE THAT ONE A LOT, TOO!
SORRY TO
KEEP YOU OUT SO LATE...
IT'S OKAY...
BUT
EVERYONE IN THE CLUB SAYS ALL THE MOVIES I LIKE ARE WEIRD...
SO I'M REALLY HAPPY
TO FIND SOMEONE I CAN TALK TO!

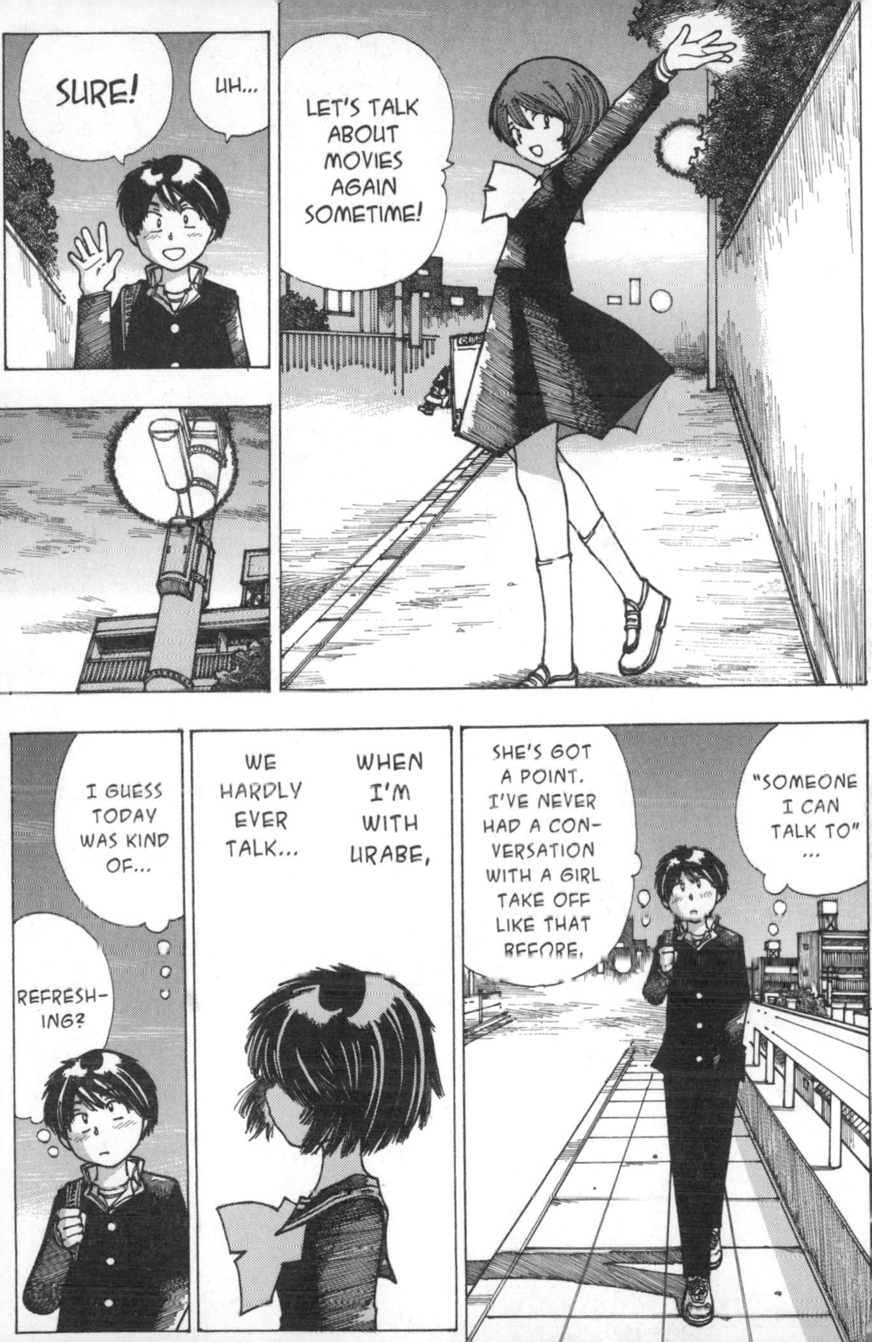
LET'S TALK ABOUT MOVIES AGAIN SOMETIME!
UH...
SURE!
"SOMEONE I CAN TALK TO" ...
SHE'S GOT A POINT. I'VE NEVER HAD A CON-VERSATION WITH A GIRL TAKE OFF LIKE THAT BEFORE.
WHEN I'M WITH URABE,
WE HARDLY EVER TALK...
I GUESS TODAY WAS KIND OF...
REFRESH-ING?

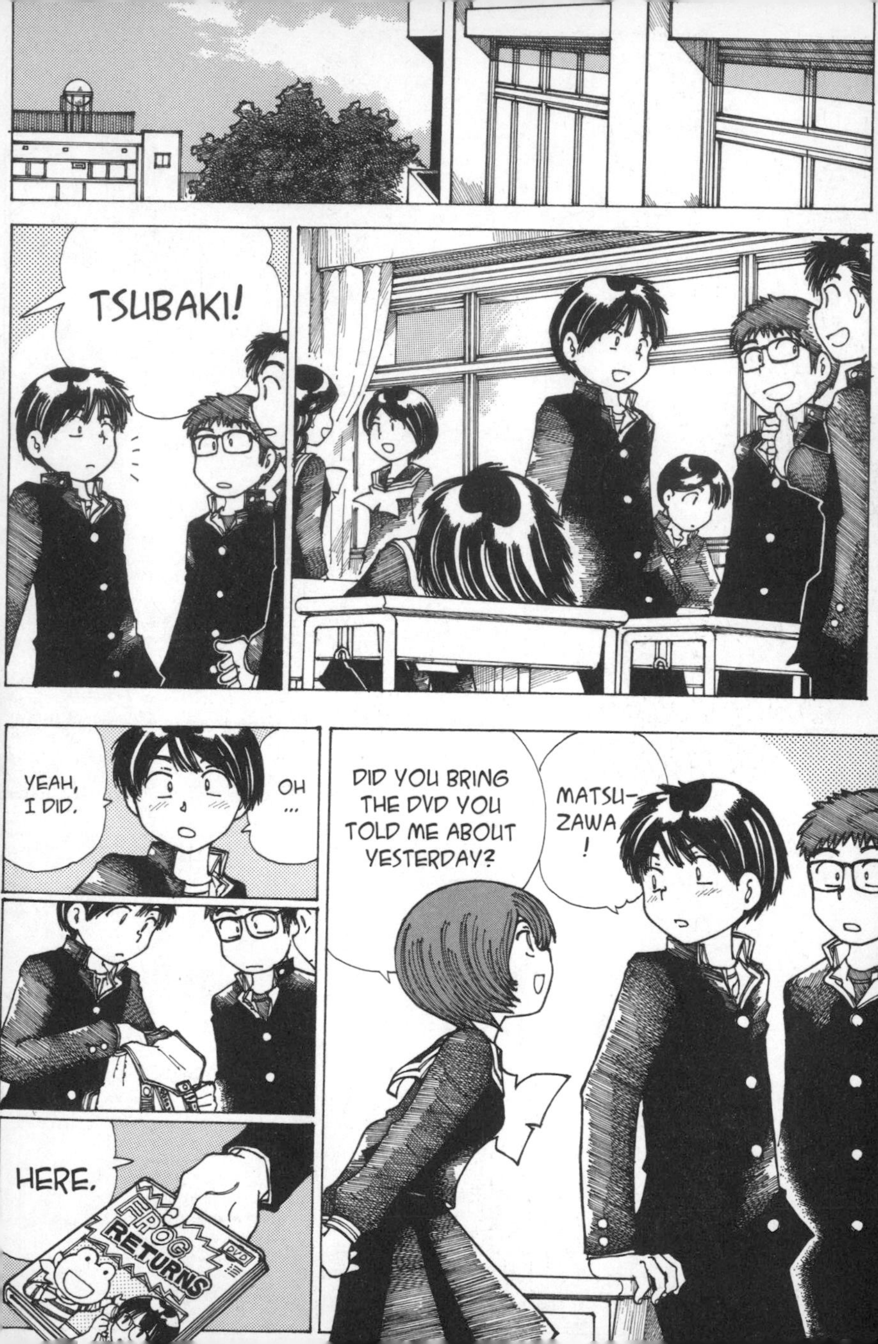
TSUBAKI!
MATSU-ZAWA!
DID YOU BRING THE DVD YOU TOLD ME ABOUT YESTERDAY?
OH ...
YEAH, I DID.
HERE.
FROG RETURNS
DVD

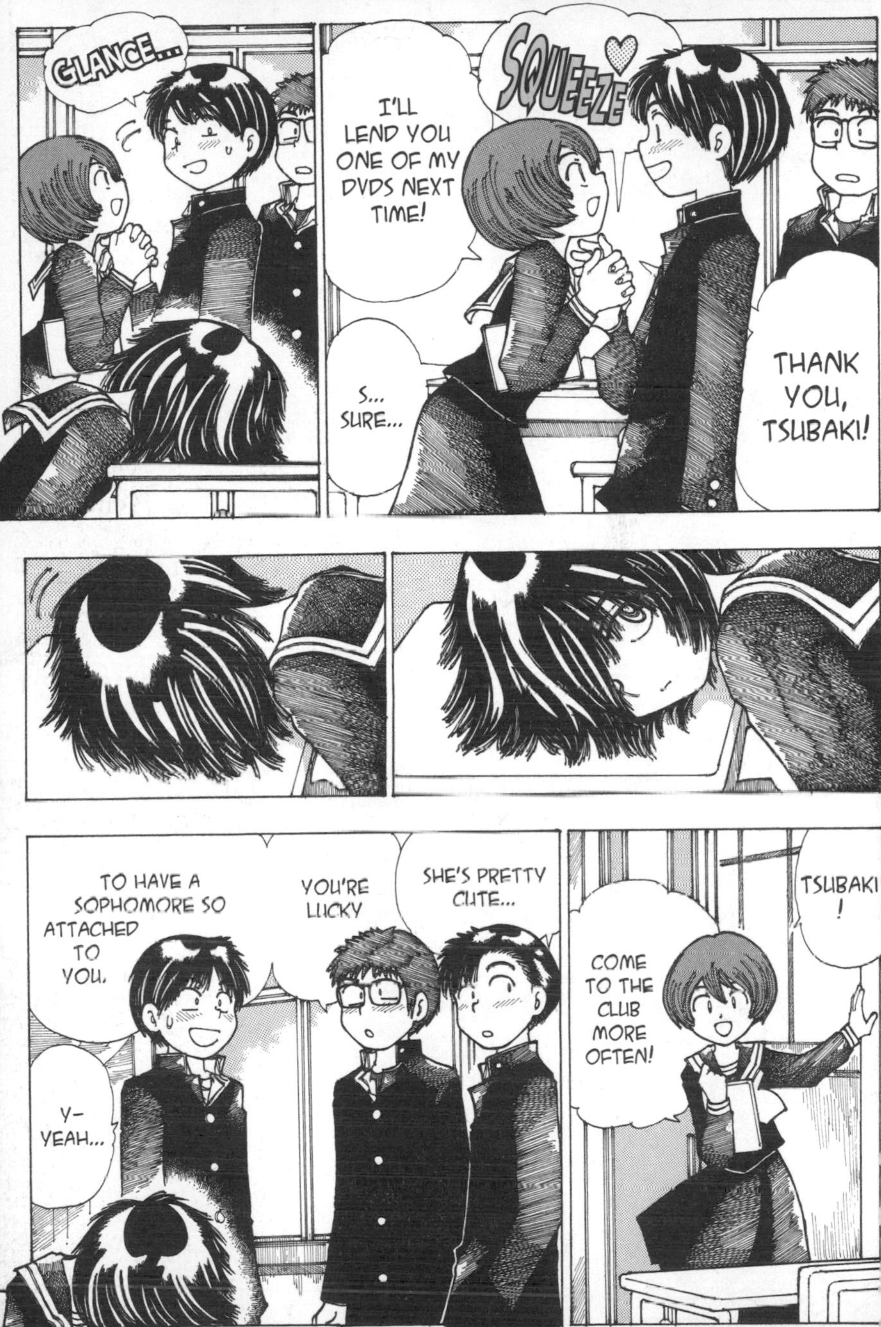
SQUEEZE
THANK YOU, TSUBAKI!
I'LL LEND YOU ONE OF MY DVDS NEXT TIME!
S... SURE...
GLANCE...
TSUBAKI!
COME TO THE CLUB MORE OFTEN!
SHE'S PRETTY CUTE...
YOU'RE LUCKY
TO HAVE A SOPHOMORE SO ATTACHED TO YOU.
Y-YEAH...

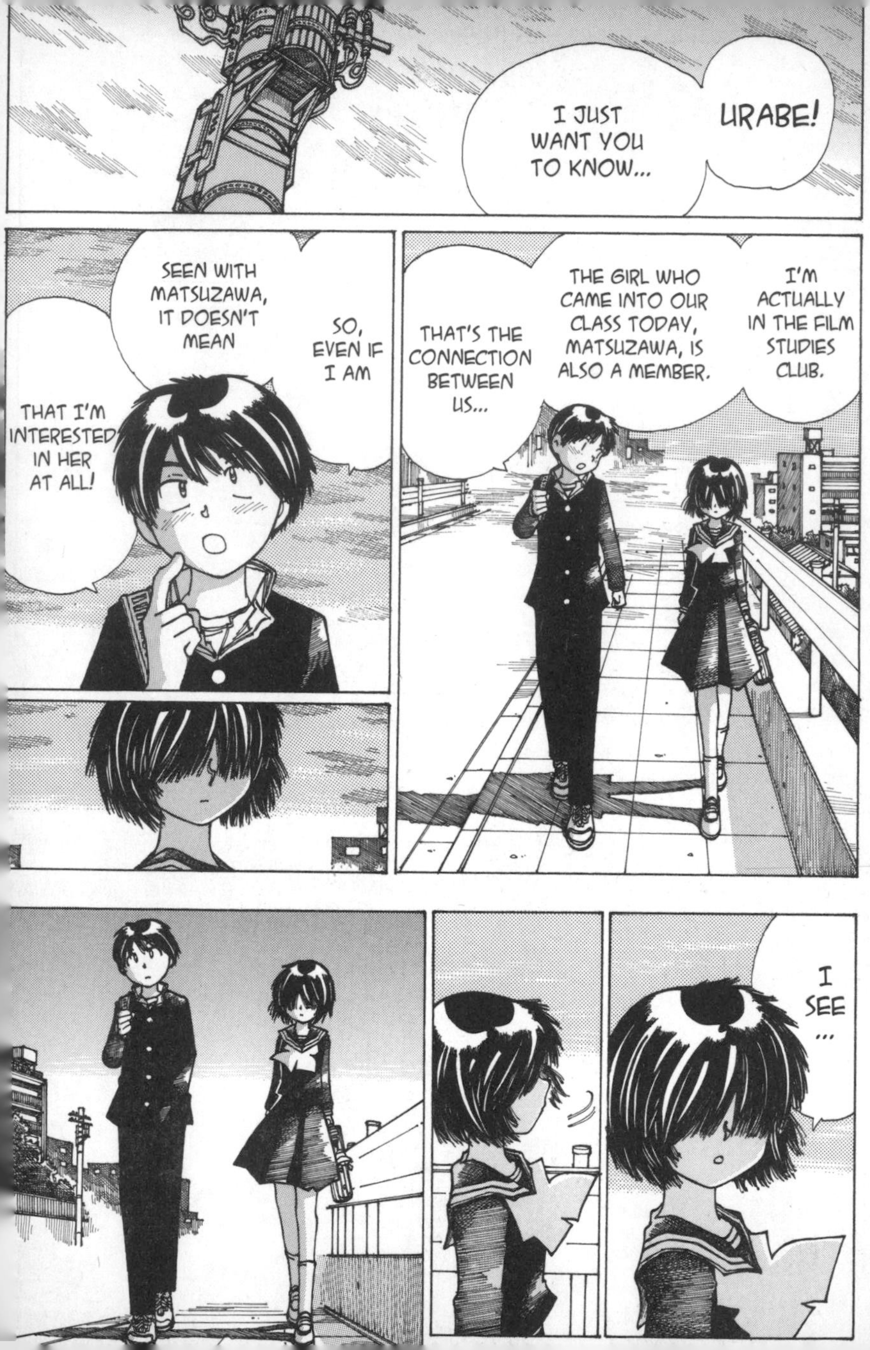
URABE!
I JUST WANT YOU TO KNOW...
I'M ACTUALLY IN THE FILM STUDIES CLUB.
THE GIRL WHO CAME INTO OUR CLASS TODAY, MATSUZAWA, IS ALSO A MEMBER.
THAT'S THE CONNECTION BETWEEN US...
SO, EVEN IF I AM
SEEN WITH MATSUZAWA, IT DOESN'T MEAN
THAT I'M INTERESTED IN HER AT ALL!
I SEE ...

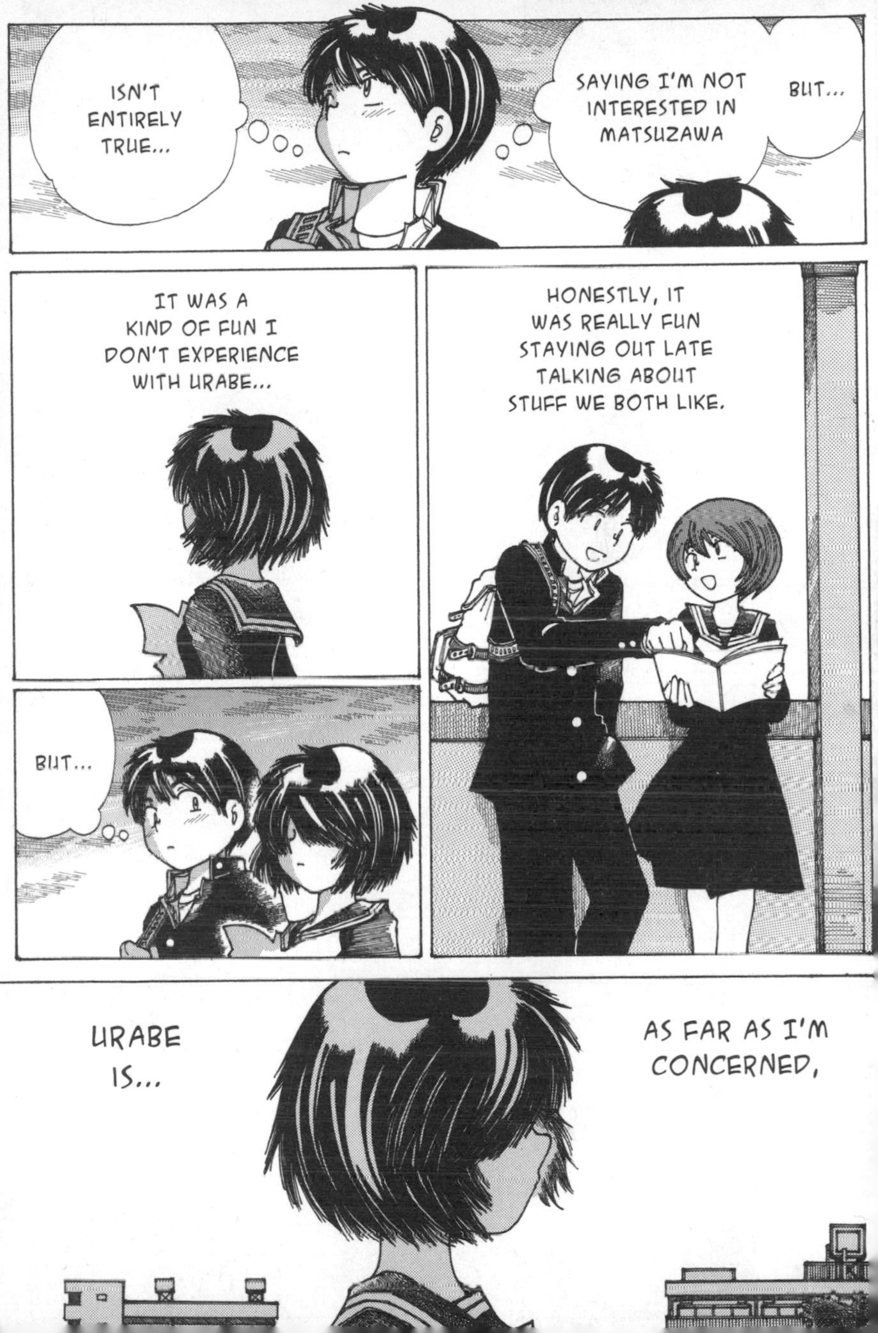
SAYING I'M NOT INTERESTED IN MATSUZAWA
ISN'T ENTIRELY TRUE...
BUT...
HONESTLY, IT WAS REALLY FUN STAYING OUT LATE TALKING ABOUT STUFF WE BOTH LIKE.
IT WAS A KIND OF FUN I DON'T EXPERIENCE WITH URABE...
BUT...
AS FAR AS I'M CONCERNED,
URABE IS...

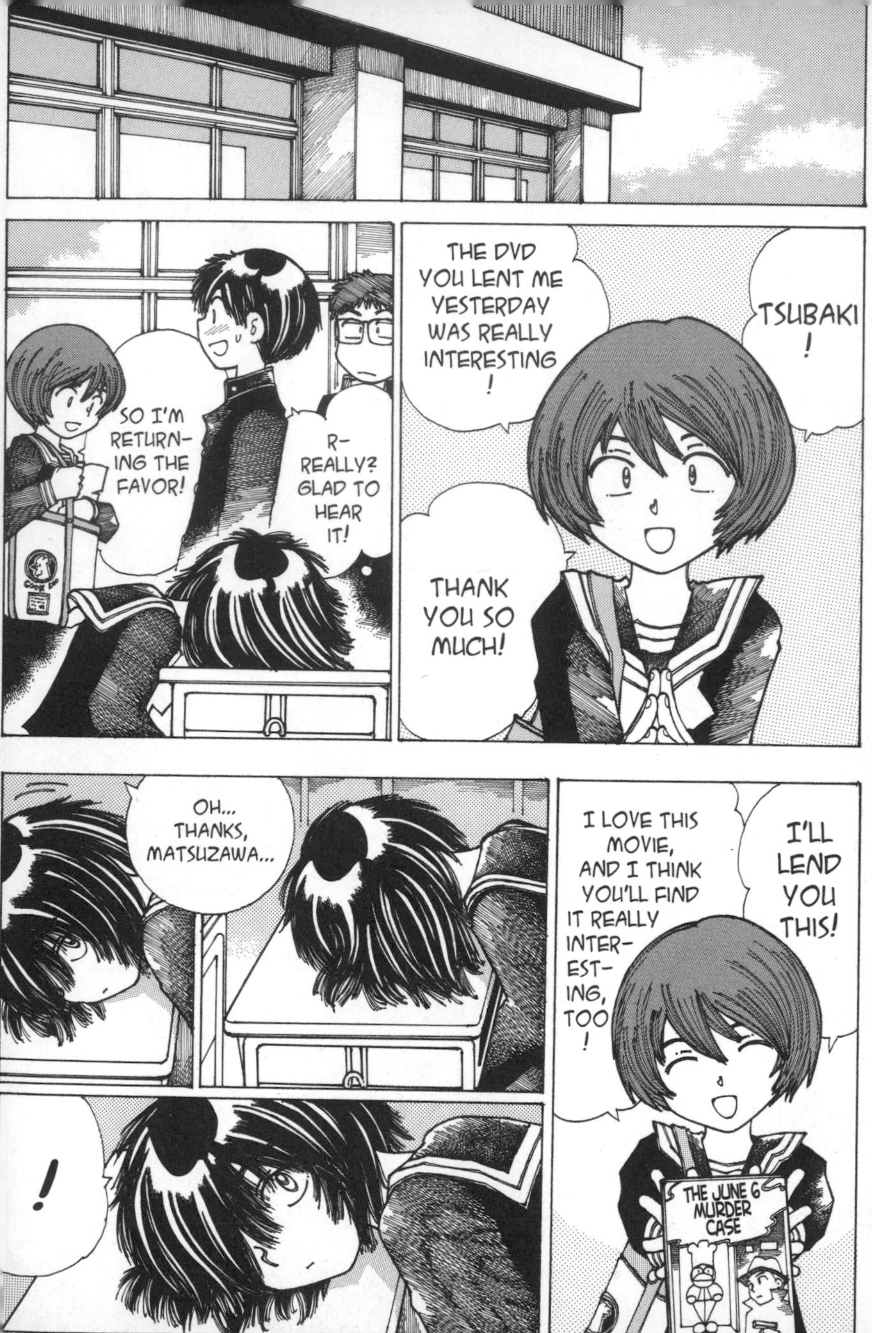
TSUBAKI!
THE DVD YOU LENT ME YESTERDAY WAS REALLY INTERESTING!
THANK YOU SO MUCH!
R-REALLY? GLAD TO HEAR IT!
SO I'M RETURNING THE FAVOR!
I'LL LEND YOU THIS!
I LOVE THIS MOVIE, AND I THINK YOU'LL FIND IT REALLY INTER-EST-ING, TOO!
THE JUNE 6 MURDER CASE
OH... THANKS, MATSUZAWA...
!

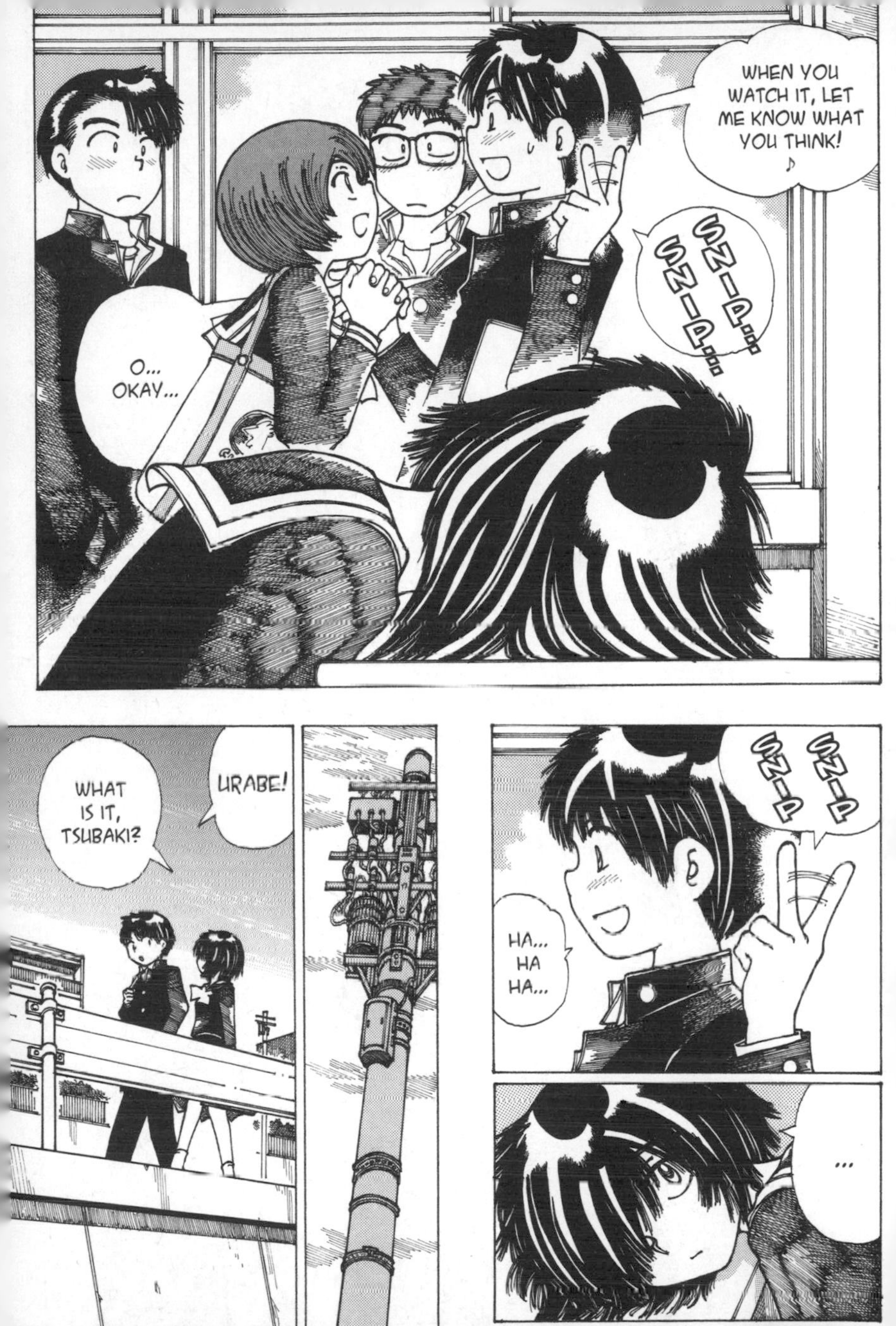
WHEN YOU WATCH IT, LET ME KNOW WHAT YOU THINK! ♪
SNIP... SNIP...
O... OKAY...
SNIP SNIP
HA... HA HA...
...
URABE!
WHAT IS IT, TSUBAKI?

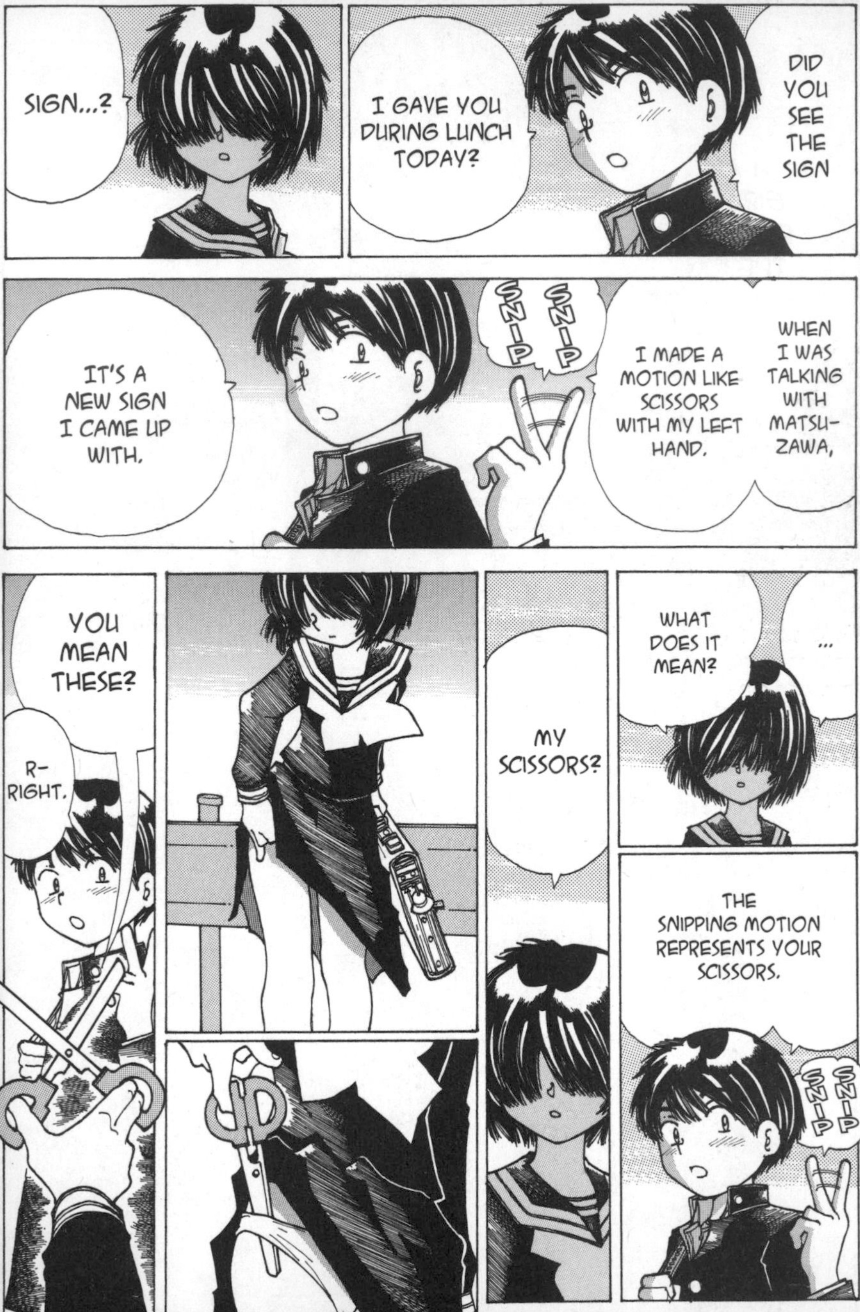
DID YOU SEE THE SIGN
I GAVE YOU DURING LUNCH TODAY?
SIGN...?
WHEN I WAS TALKING WITH MATSU-ZAWA,
I MADE A MOTION LIKE SCISSORS WITH MY LEFT HAND.
SNIP SNIP
IT'S A NEW SIGN I CAME UP WITH.
...
WHAT DOES IT MEAN?
THE SNIPPING MOTION REPRESENTS YOUR SCISSORS.
SNIP SNIP
MY SCISSORS?
YOU MEAN THESE?
R-RIGHT.

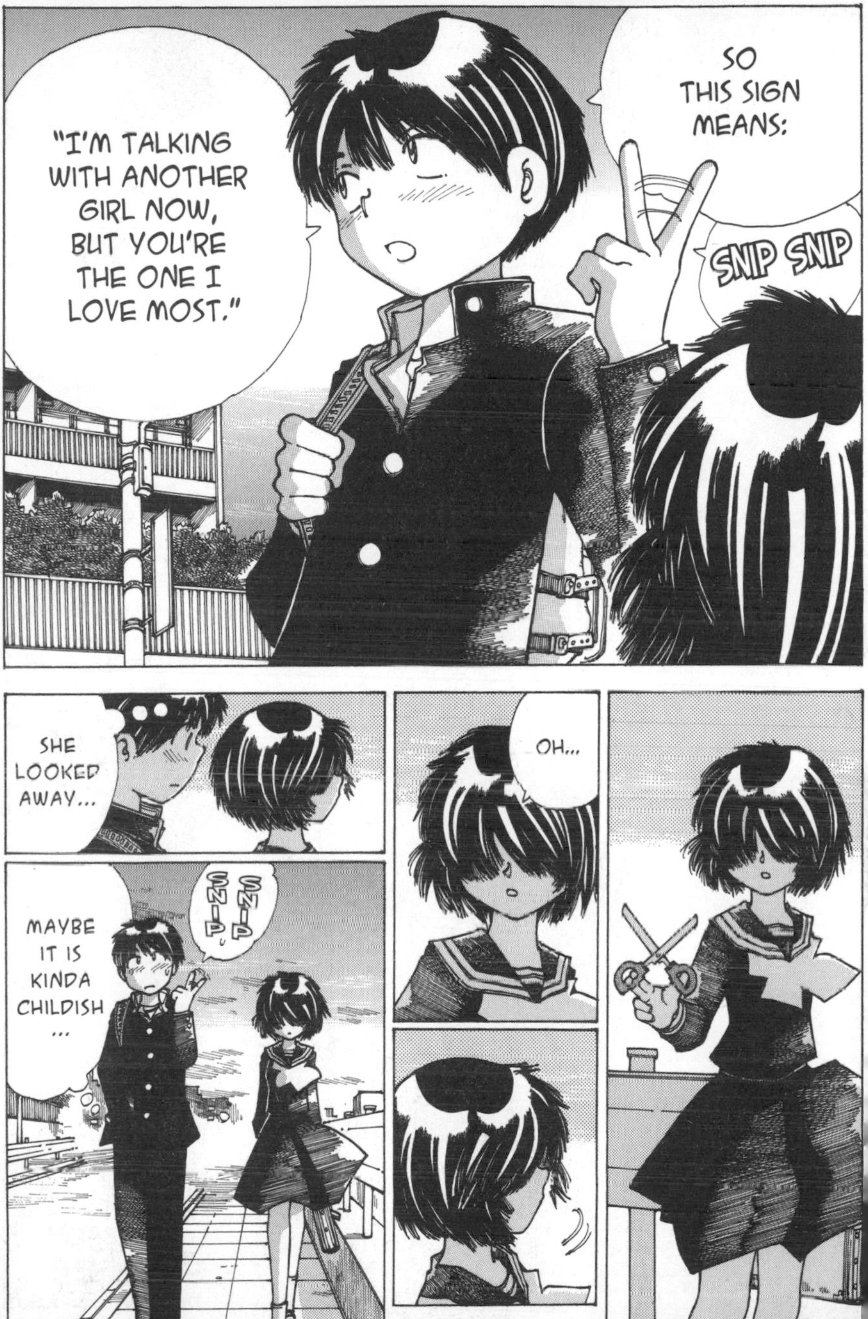
SO THIS SIGN MEANS:
"I'M TALKING WITH ANOTHER GIRL NOW, BUT YOU'RE THE ONE I LOVE MOST."
SNIP SNIP
OH...
SHE LOOKED AWAY...
SNIP SNIP
MAYBE IT IS KINDA CHILDISH ...

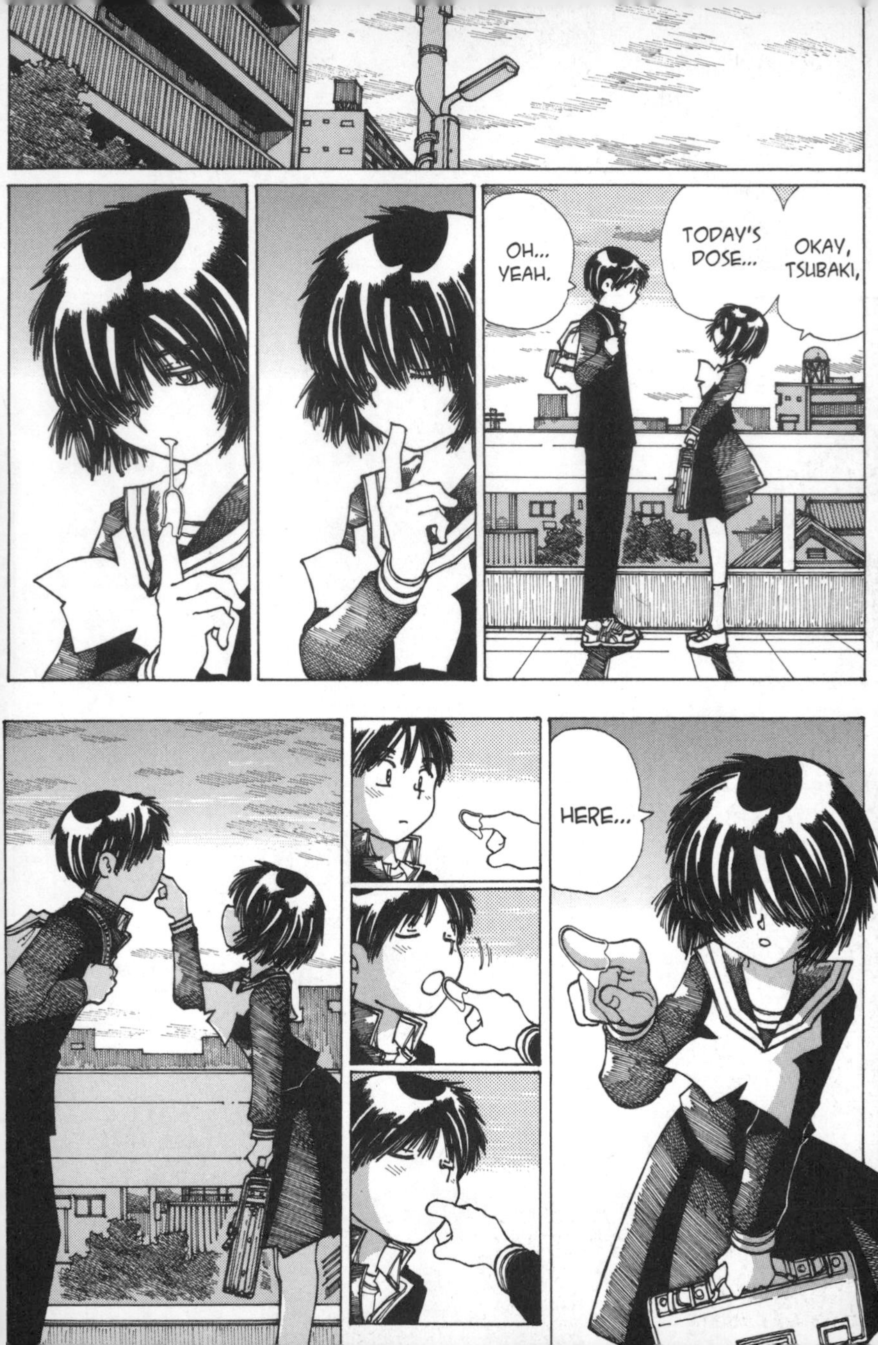
OKAY, TSUBAKI,
TODAY'S DOSE...
OH... YEAH.
HERE...

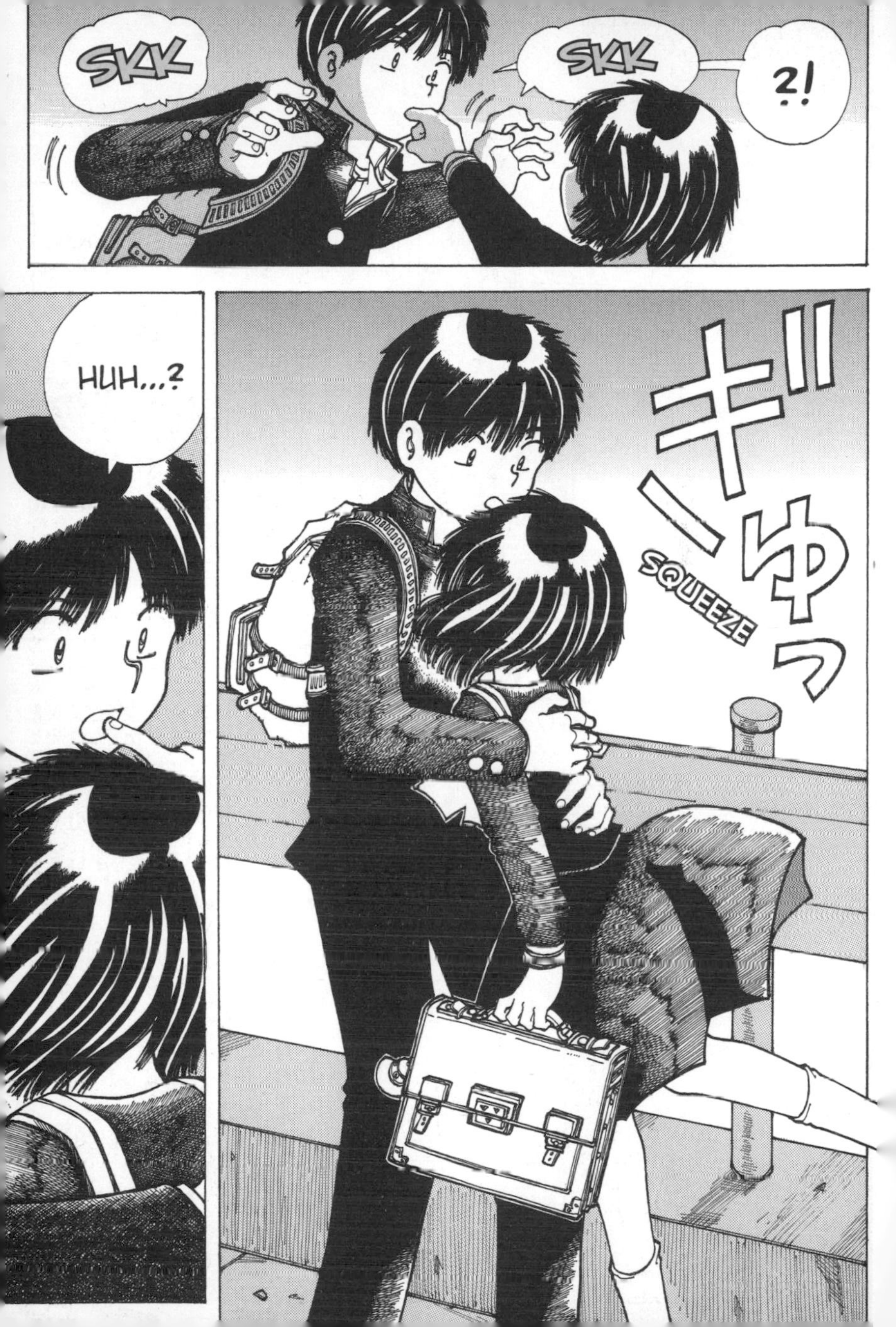
?!
SKK
SKK
ギゅーっ
SQUEEZE
HUH...?

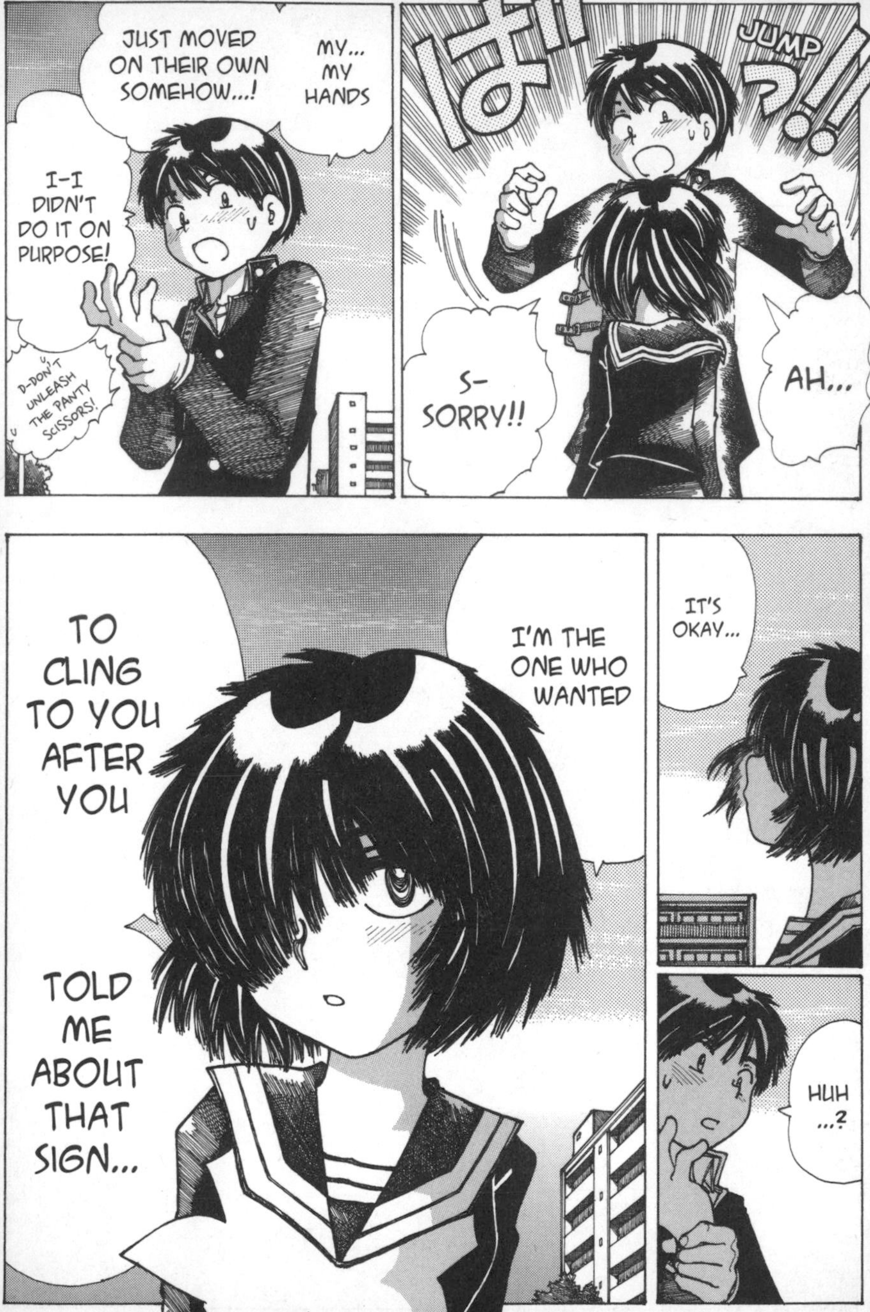

ぱっ!!
JUMP
AH...
S-SORRY!!
MY... MY HANDS
JUST MOVED ON THEIR OWN SOMEHOW...!
I-I DIDN'T DO IT ON PURPOSE!
D-DON'T UNLEASH THE PANTY SCISSORS!
IT'S OKAY...
HUH ...?
I'M THE ONE WHO WANTED
TO CLING TO YOU AFTER YOU
TOLD ME ABOUT THAT SIGN...

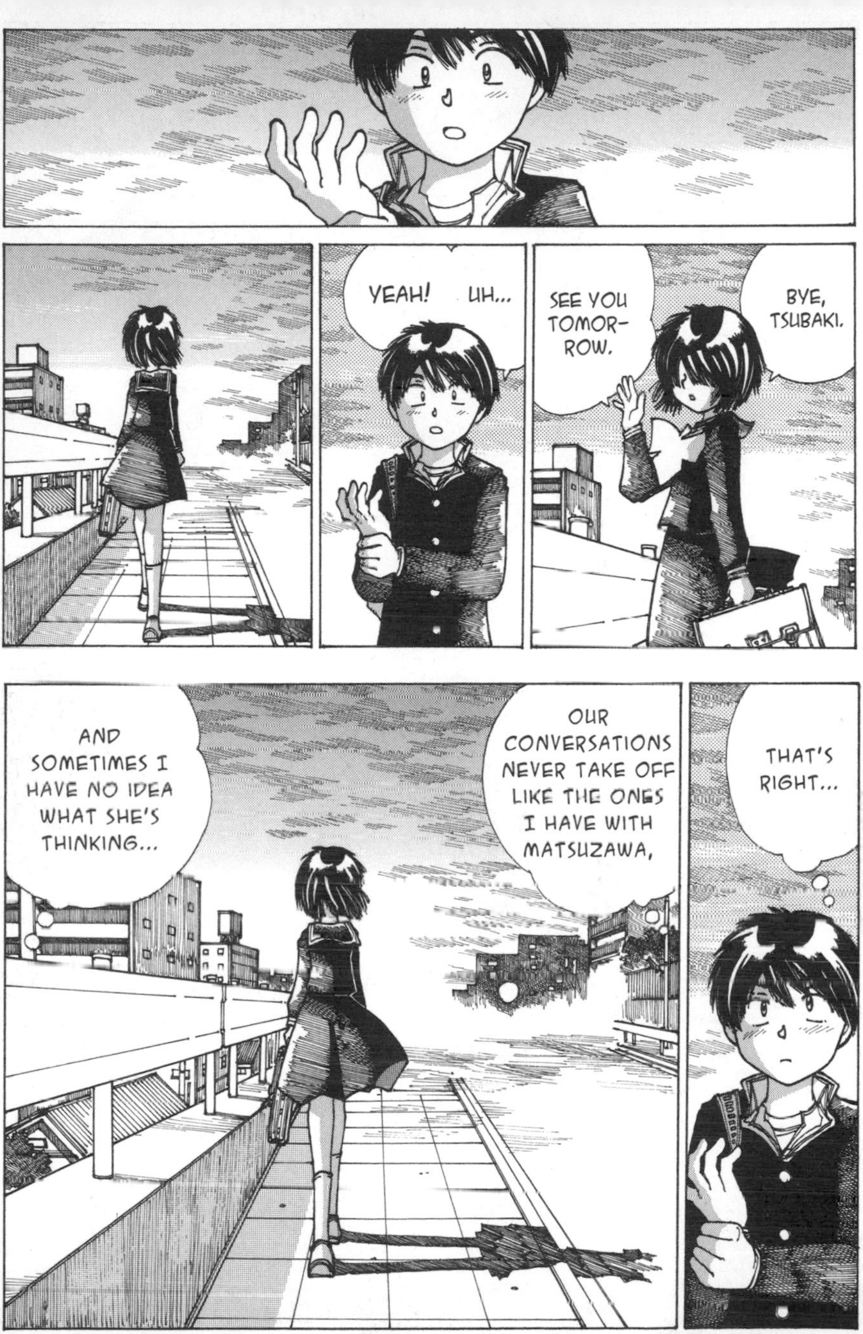
BYE, TSUBAKI.
SEE YOU TOMORROW.
YEAH! UH...
THAT'S RIGHT...
OUR CONVERSATIONS NEVER TAKE OFF LIKE THE ONES I HAVE WITH MATSUZAWA,
AND SOMETIMES I HAVE NO IDEA WHAT SHE'S THINKING...

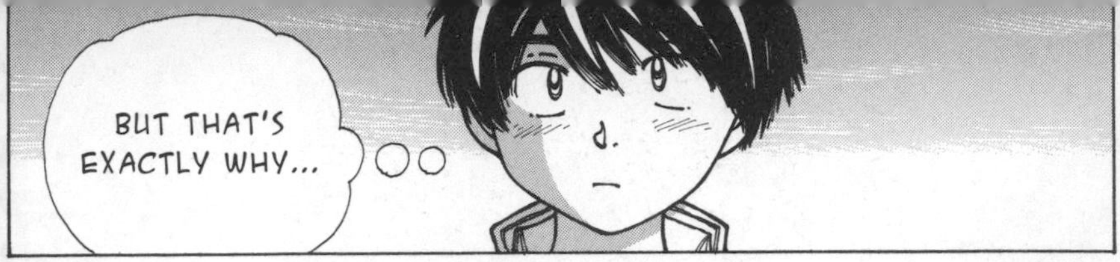
BUT THAT'S EXACTLY WHY...

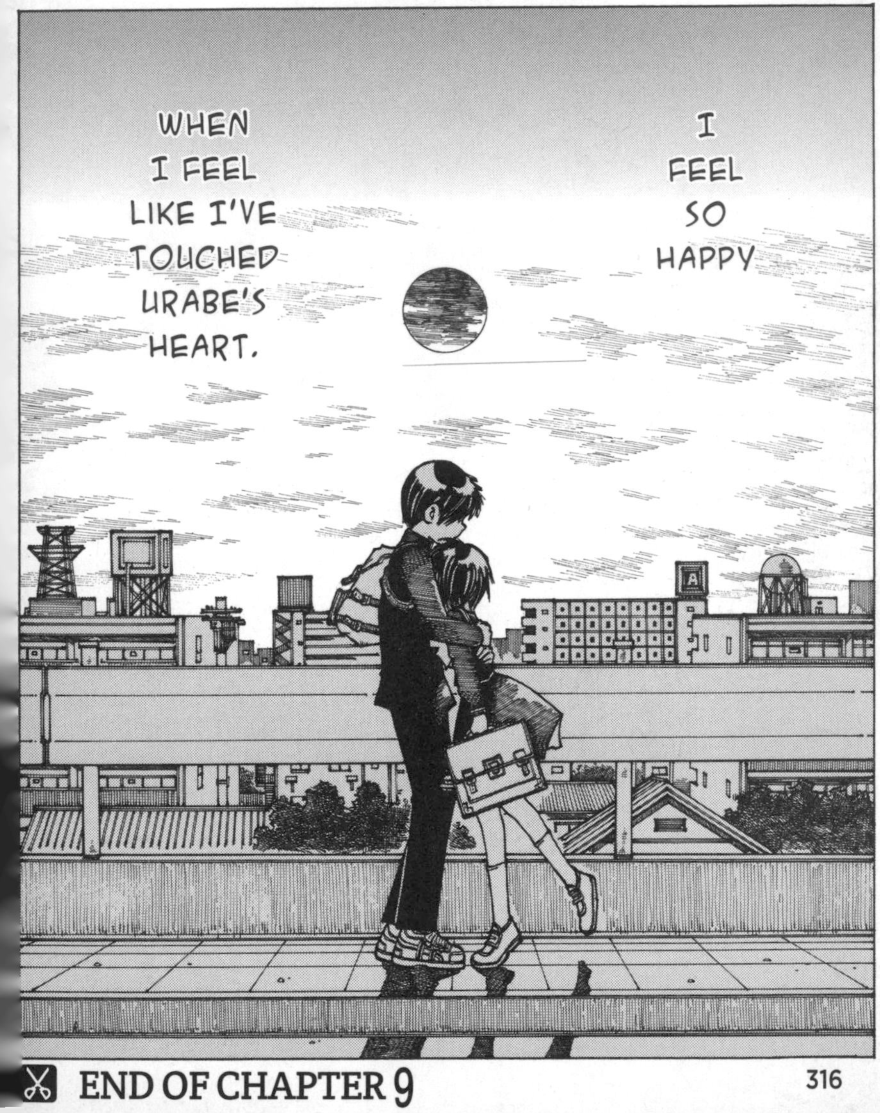
WHEN I FEEL LIKE I'VE TOUCHED URABE'S HEART.
I FEEL SO HAPPY

END OF CHAPTER 9

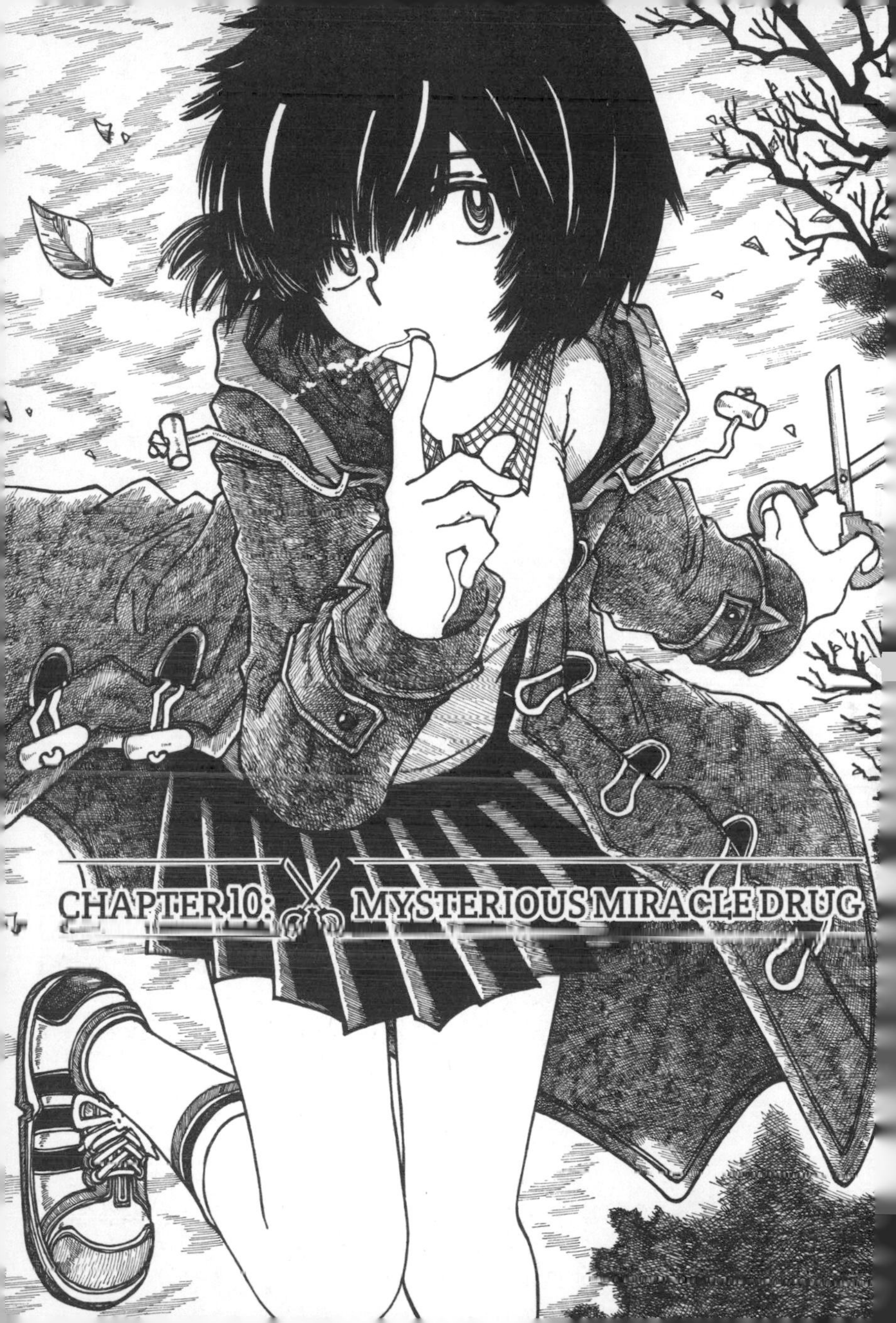
CHAPTER 10: MYSTERIOUS MIRACLE DRUG

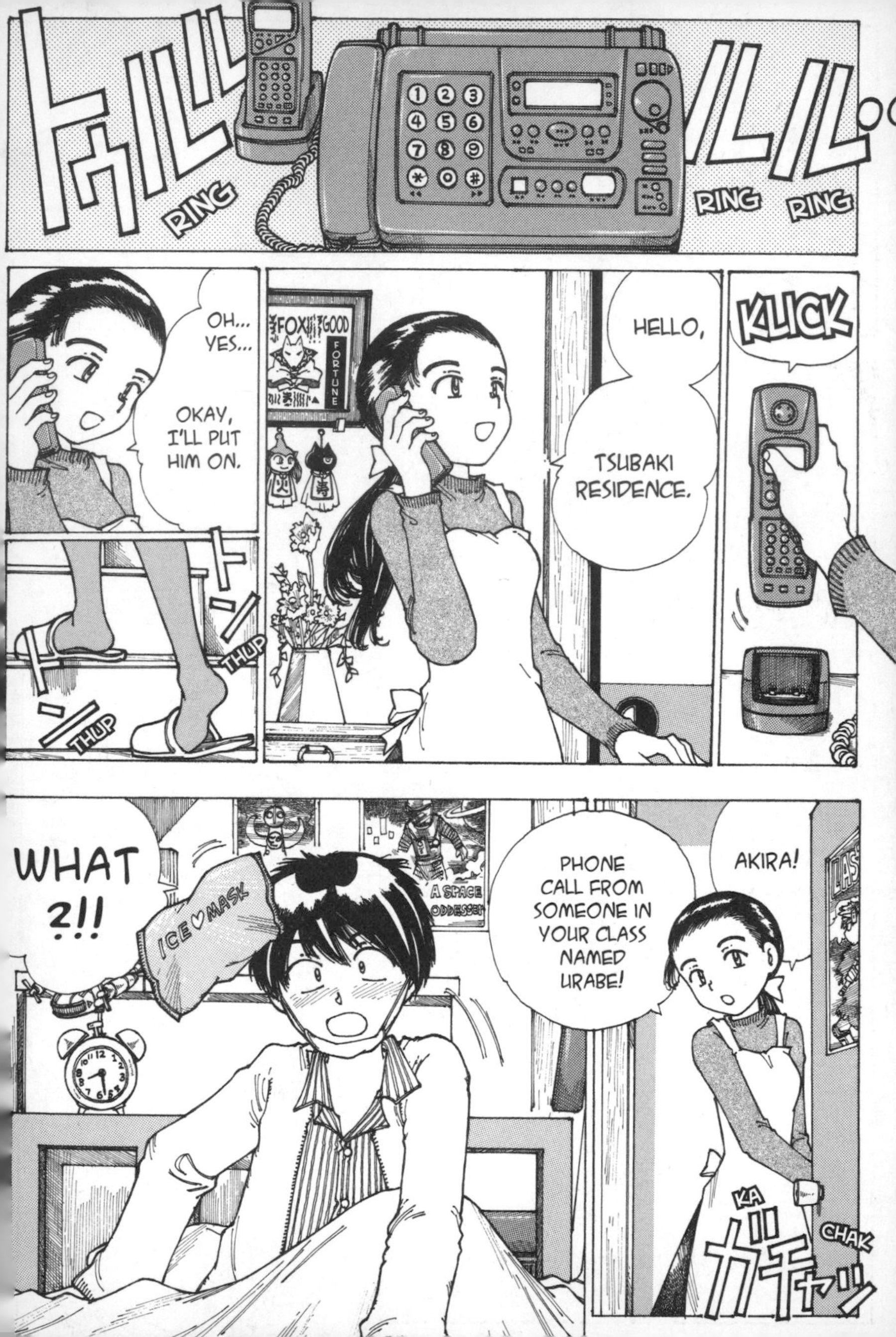

トゥルル
ルル‥
RING
RING RING
KLICK
HELLO,
TSUBAKI RESIDENCE.
FOX GOOD FORTUNE
OH... YES...
OKAY, I'LL PUT HIM ON.
トン
THUP
トン
THUP
AKIRA!
PHONE CALL FROM SOMEONE IN YOUR CLASS NAMED URABE!
KA
CHAK
ガチャッ
A SPACE ODDESSEY
WHAT ?!!
ICE♥MASK

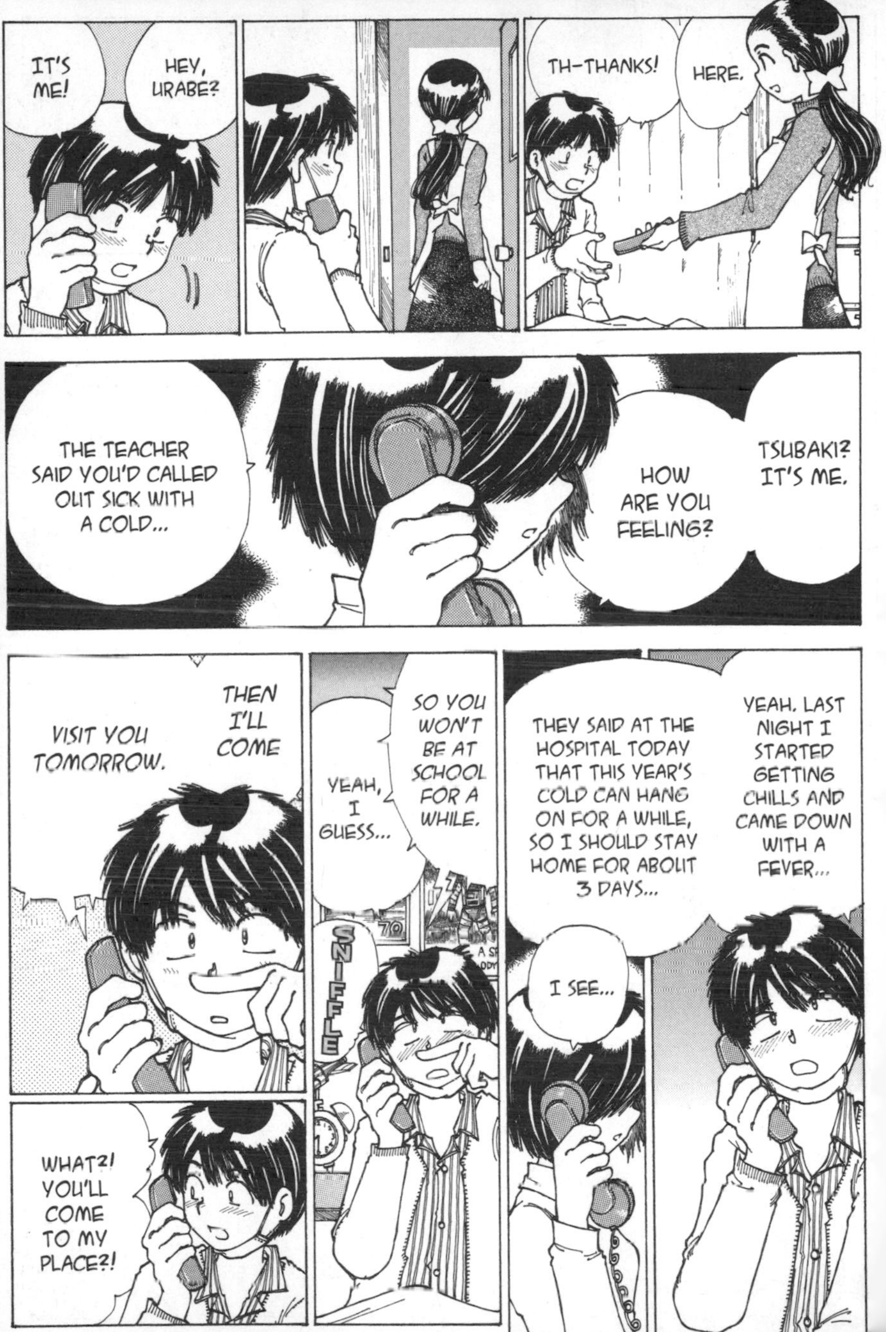
HERE.
TH-THANKS!
HEY, URABE?
IT'S ME!
TSUBAKI? IT'S ME.
HOW ARE YOU FEELING?
THE TEACHER SAID YOU'D CALLED OUT SICK WITH A COLD...
YEAH. LAST NIGHT I STARTED GETTING CHILLS AND CAME DOWN WITH A FEVER...
THEY SAID AT THE HOSPITAL TODAY THAT THIS YEAR'S COLD CAN HANG ON FOR A WHILE, SO I SHOULD STAY HOME FOR ABOUT 3 DAYS...
I SEE...
SO YOU WON'T BE AT SCHOOL FOR A WHILE.
YEAH, I GUESS...
SNIFFLE
THEN I'LL COME VISIT YOU TOMORROW.
WHAT?! YOU'LL COME TO MY PLACE?!

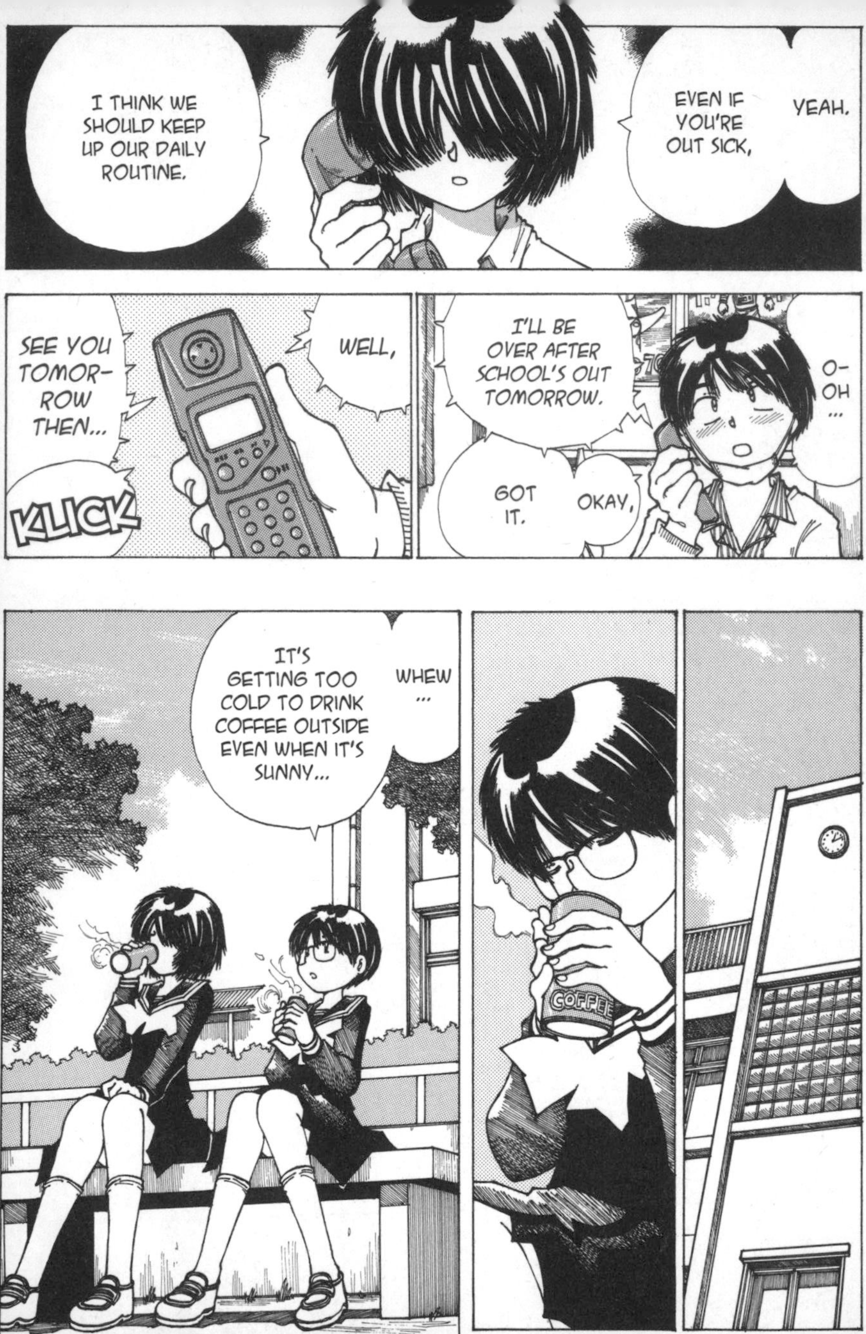
YEAH.
EVEN IF YOU'RE OUT SICK,
I THINK WE SHOULD KEEP UP OUR DAILY ROUTINE.
O-OH ...
I'LL BE OVER AFTER SCHOOL'S OUT TOMORROW.
OKAY,
GOT IT.
WELL,
SEE YOU TOMORROW THEN...
KLICK
COFFEE
WHEW ...
IT'S GETTING TOO COLD TO DRINK COFFEE OUTSIDE EVEN WHEN IT'S SUNNY...

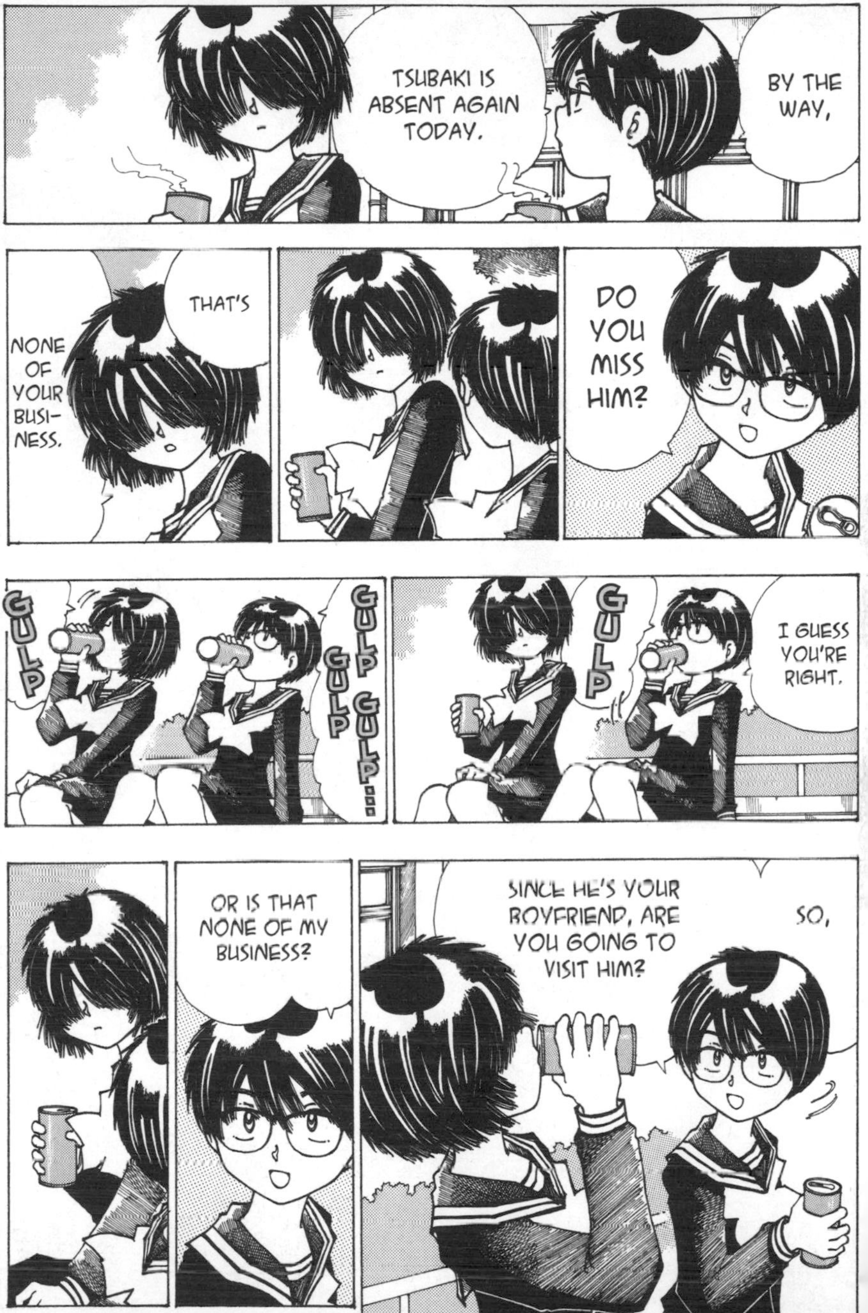
BY THE WAY,
TSUBAKI IS ABSENT AGAIN TODAY.
DO YOU MISS HIM?
THAT'S
NONE OF YOUR BUSI-NESS.
I GUESS YOU'RE RIGHT.
GULP
GULP GULP...
GULP
GULP
SO,
SINCE HE'S YOUR BOYFRIEND, ARE YOU GOING TO VISIT HIM?
OR IS THAT NONE OF MY BUSINESS?

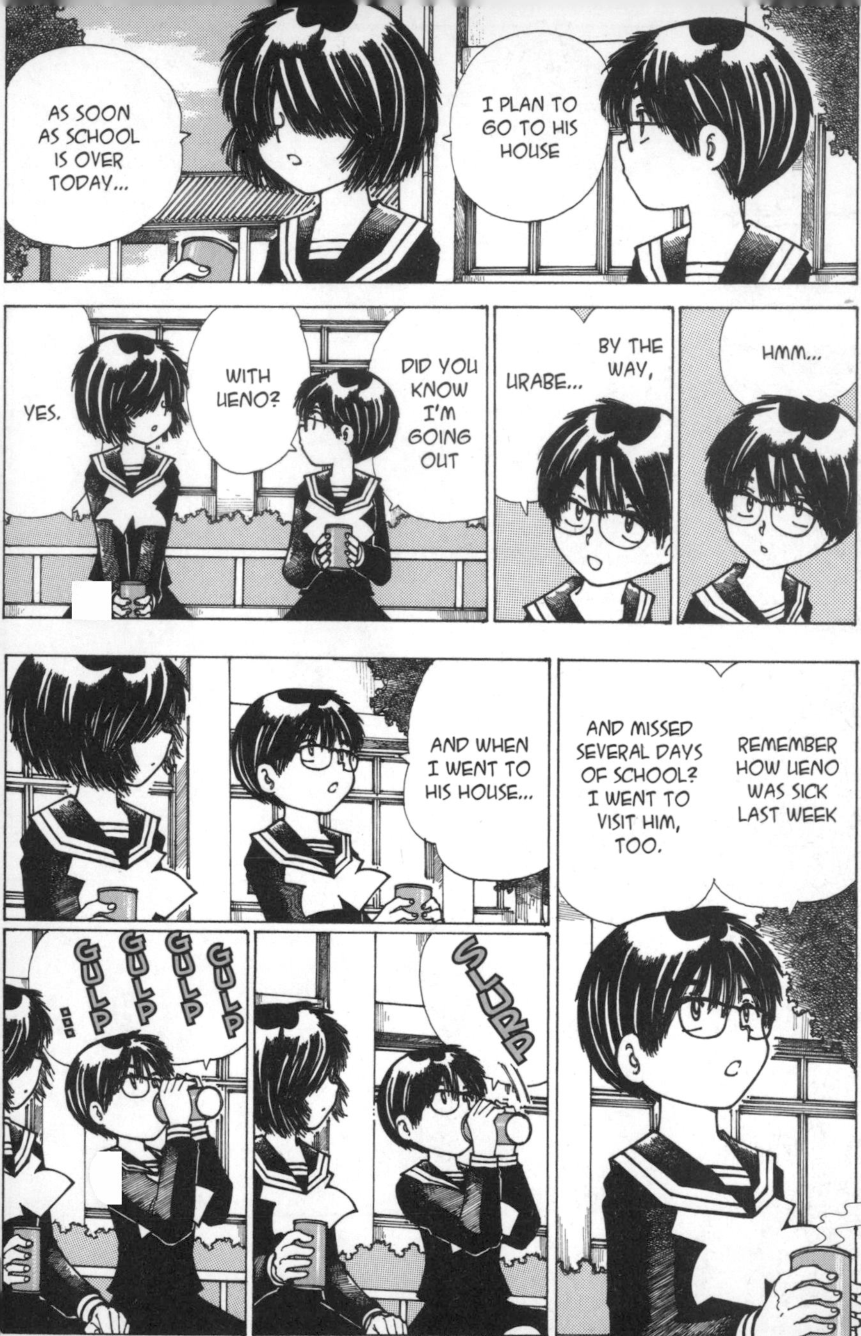
I PLAN TO GO TO HIS HOUSE
AS SOON AS SCHOOL IS OVER TODAY...
HMM...
BY THE WAY, URABE...
DID YOU KNOW I'M GOING OUT
WITH UENO?
YES.
REMEMBER HOW UENO WAS SICK LAST WEEK
AND MISSED SEVERAL DAYS OF SCHOOL? I WENT TO VISIT HIM, TOO.
AND WHEN I WENT TO HIS HOUSE...
SLURP
GULP GULP GULP GULP
...

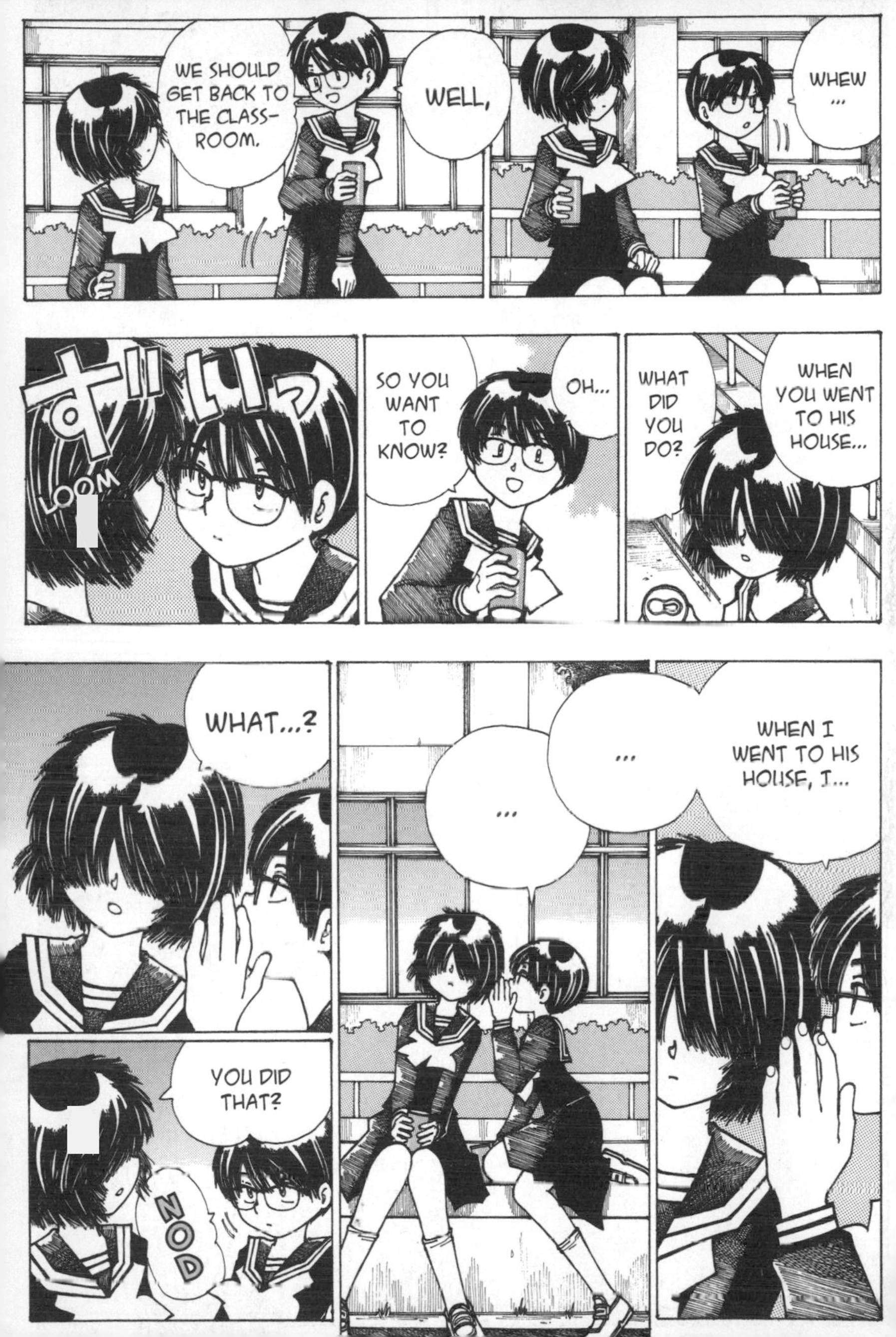
WHEW ...
WELL,
WE SHOULD GET BACK TO THE CLASS-ROOM.
WHEN YOU WENT TO HIS HOUSE...
WHAT DID YOU DO?
OH...
SO YOU WANT TO KNOW?
ずいっ
LOOM
WHEN I WENT TO HIS HOUSE, I...
...
...
WHAT...?
YOU DID THAT?
NOD

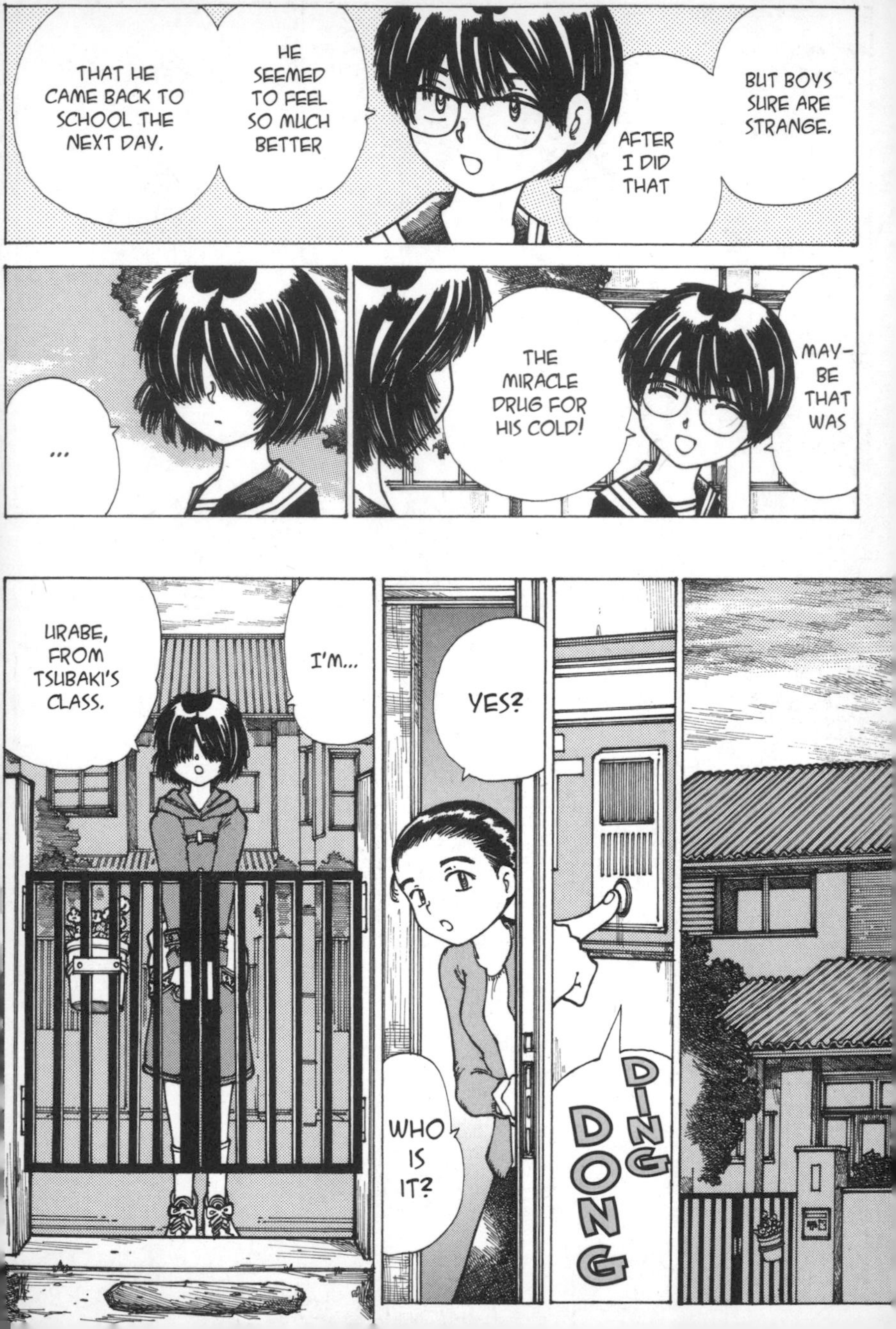
BUT BOYS SURE ARE STRANGE.
AFTER I DID THAT
HE SEEMED TO FEEL SO MUCH BETTER
THAT HE CAME BACK TO SCHOOL THE NEXT DAY.
MAY-BE THAT WAS
THE MIRACLE DRUG FOR HIS COLD!
...
DING DONG
YES?
WHO IS IT?
I'M...
URABE, FROM TSUBAKI'S CLASS.

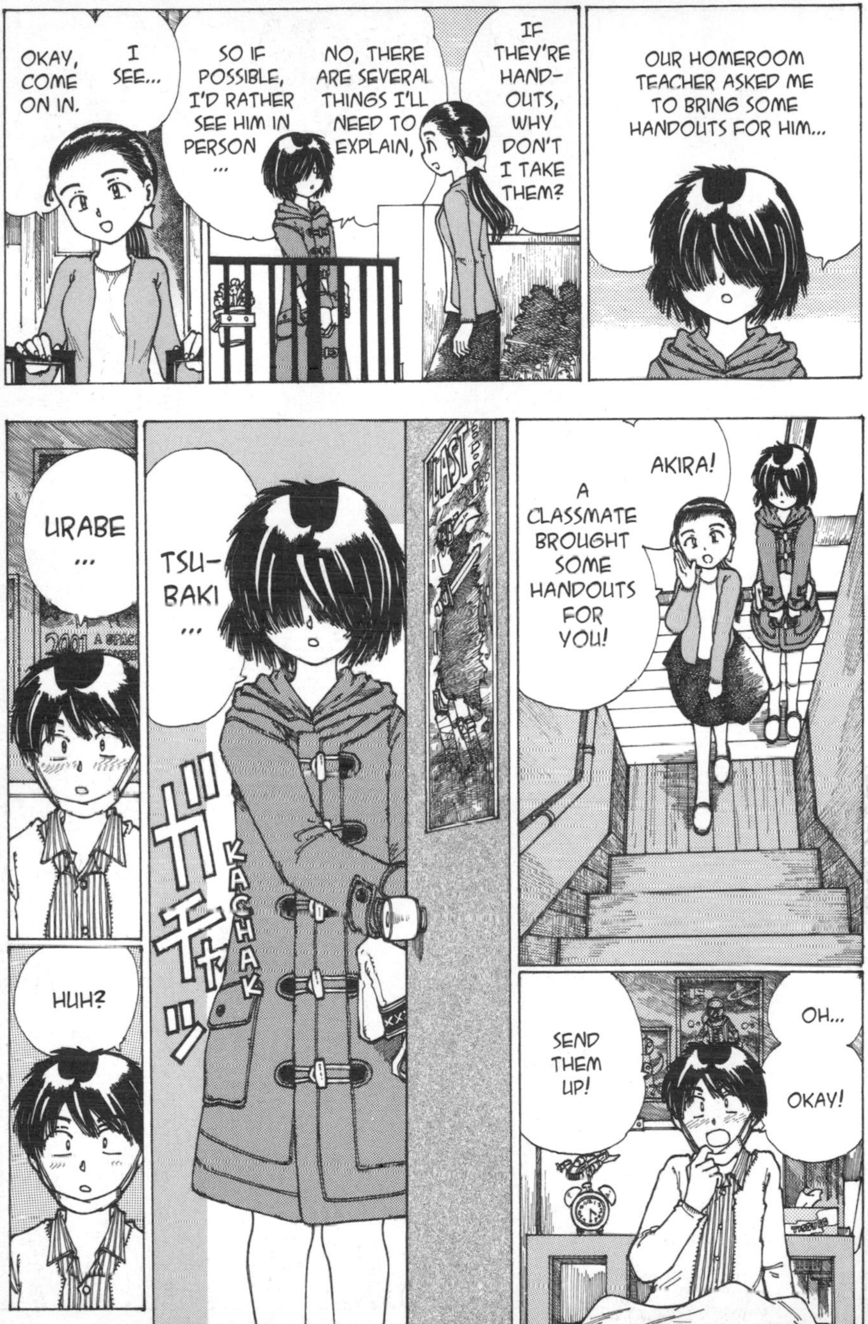
OUR HOMEROOM TEACHER ASKED ME TO BRING SOME HANDOUTS FOR HIM...
IF THEY'RE HAND-OUTS, WHY DON'T I TAKE THEM?
NO, THERE ARE SEVERAL THINGS I'LL NEED TO EXPLAIN,
SO IF POSSIBLE, I'D RATHER SEE HIM IN PERSON ...
I SEE...
OKAY, COME ON IN.
AKIRA!
A CLASSMATE BROUGHT SOME HANDOUTS FOR YOU!
OH... OKAY!
SEND THEM UP!
TSU-BAKI ...
ガチャッ
KACHAK
URABE ...
HUH?

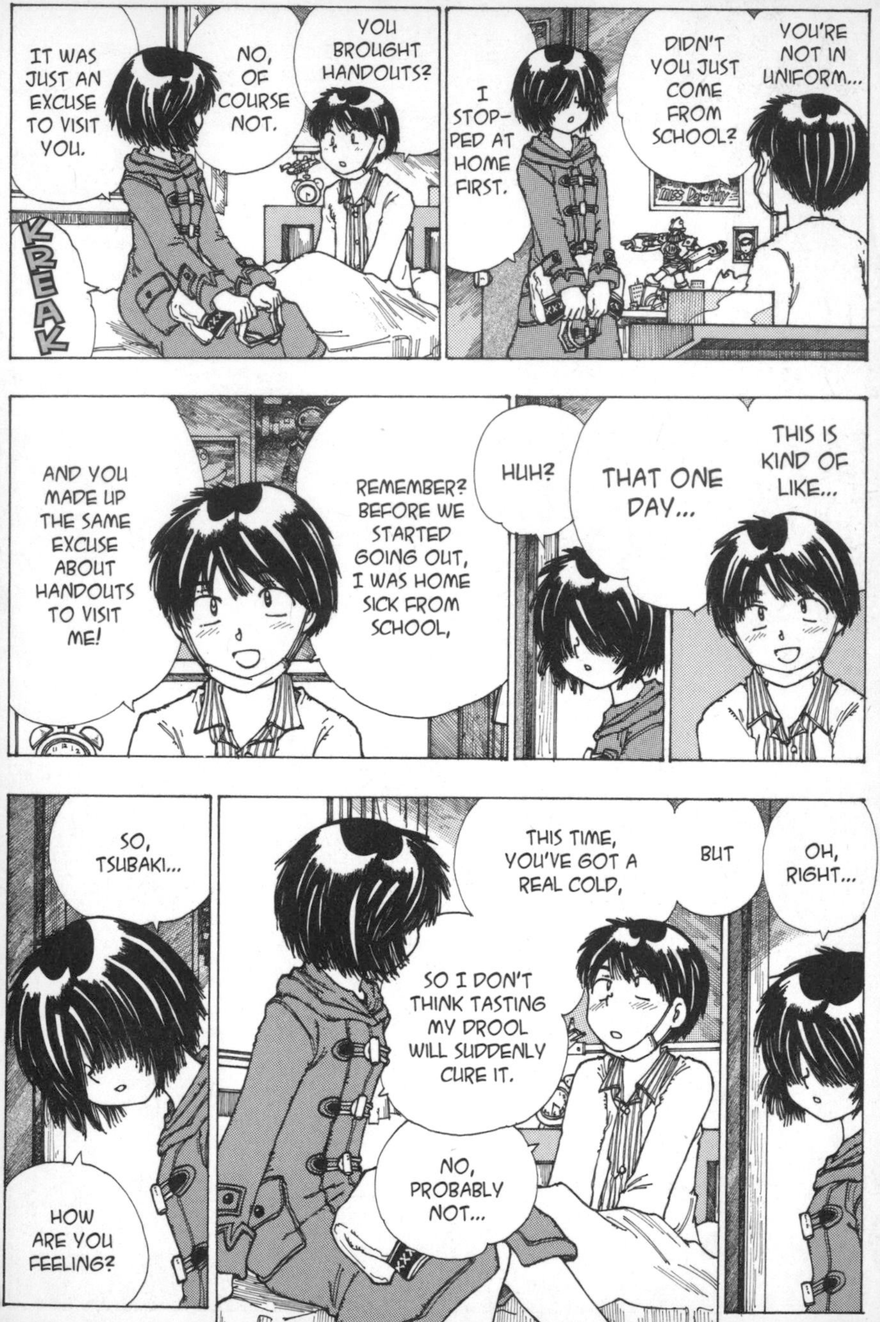
YOU'RE NOT IN UNIFORM...
DIDN'T YOU JUST COME FROM SCHOOL?
I STOP-PED AT HOME FIRST.
YOU BROUGHT HANDOUTS?
NO, OF COURSE NOT.
IT WAS JUST AN EXCUSE TO VISIT YOU.
KREAK
THIS IS KIND OF LIKE...
THAT ONE DAY...
HUH?
REMEMBER? BEFORE WE STARTED GOING OUT, I WAS HOME SICK FROM SCHOOL,
AND YOU MADE UP THE SAME EXCUSE ABOUT HANDOUTS TO VISIT ME!
OH, RIGHT...
BUT
THIS TIME, YOU'VE GOT A REAL COLD,
SO I DON'T THINK TASTING MY DROOL WILL SUDDENLY CURE IT.
NO, PROBABLY NOT...
SO, TSUBAKI...
HOW ARE YOU FEELING?

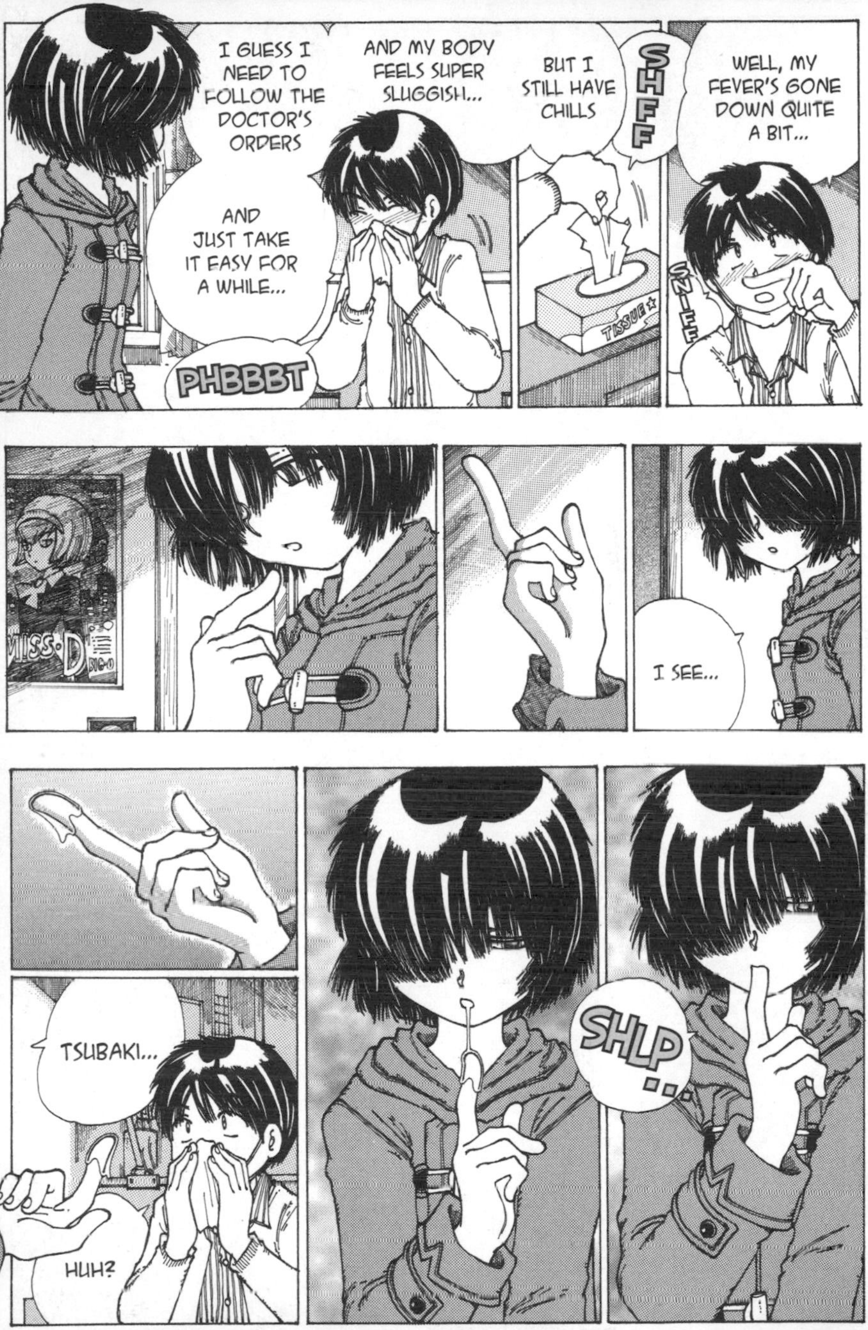
WELL, MY FEVER'S GONE DOWN QUITE A BIT...
SNIFF
SHFF
BUT I STILL HAVE CHILLS
AND MY BODY FEELS SUPER SLUGGISH...
I GUESS I NEED TO FOLLOW THE DOCTOR'S ORDERS
AND JUST TAKE IT EASY FOR A WHILE...
PHBBBT
TISSUE
I SEE...
MISS·D
SHLP...
TSUBAKI...
HUH?

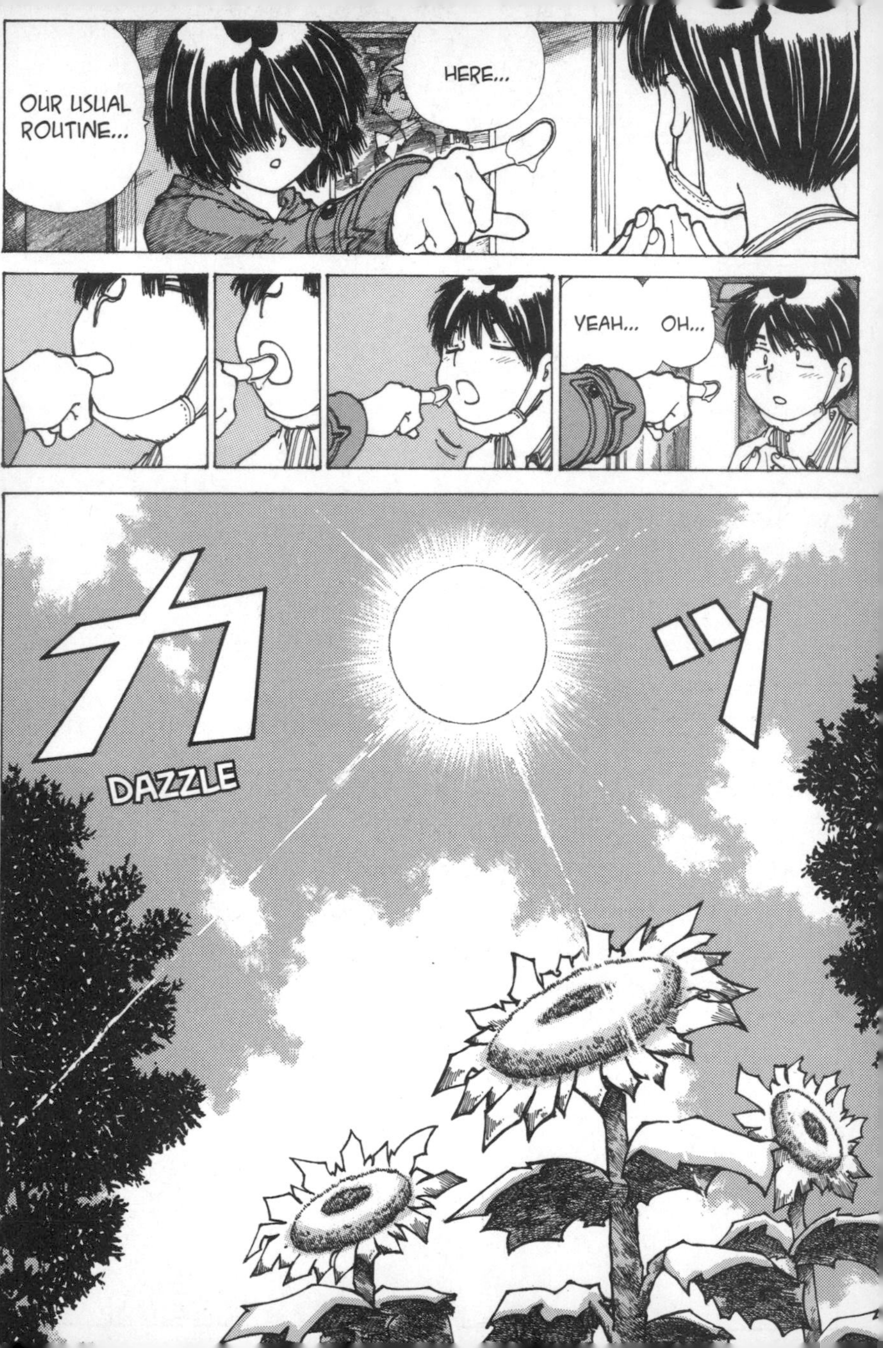
HERE...
OUR USUAL ROUTINE...
YEAH... OH...
カッ
DAZZLE

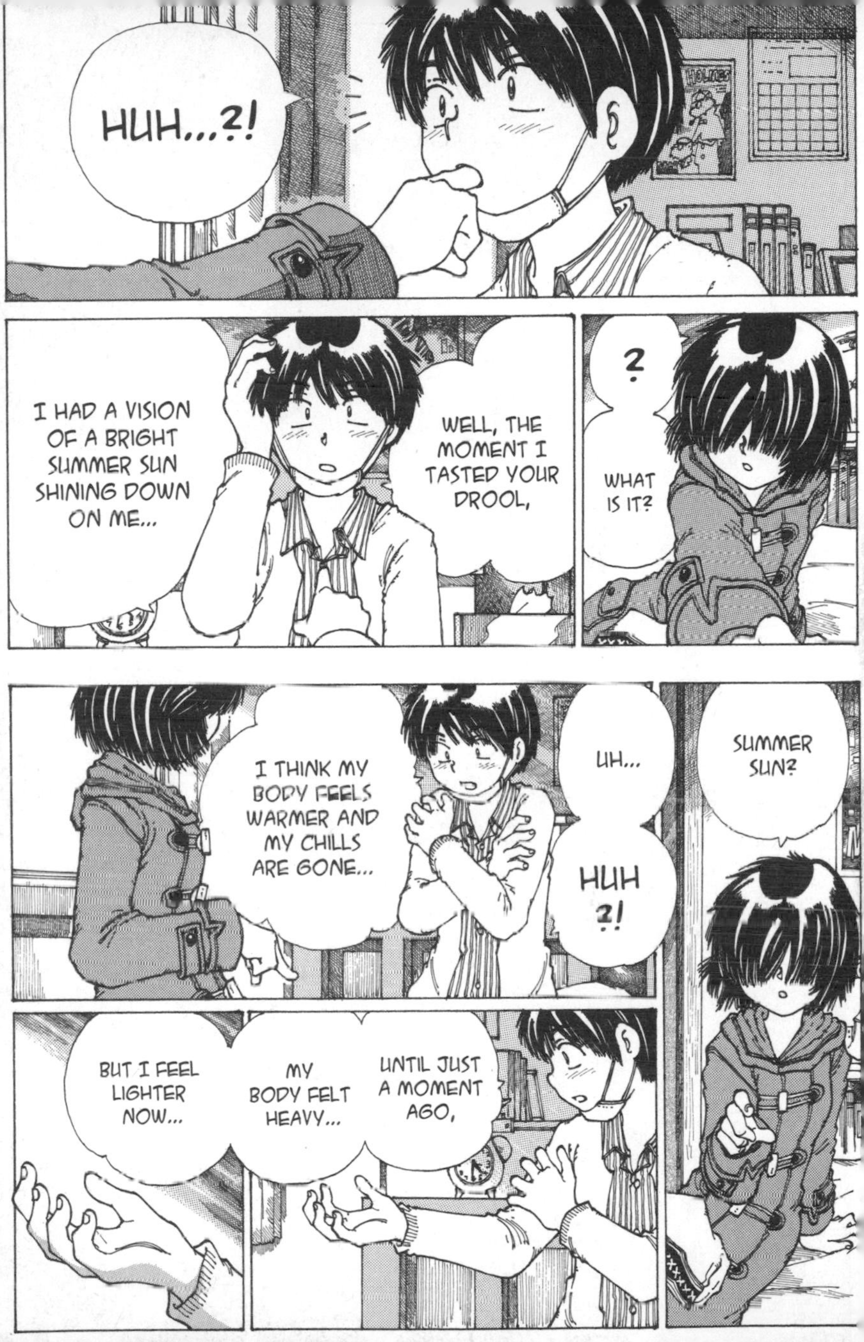
HUH...?!
?
WHAT IS IT?
WELL, THE MOMENT I TASTED YOUR DROOL,
I HAD A VISION OF A BRIGHT SUMMER SUN SHINING DOWN ON ME...
SUMMER SUN?
UH...
HUH ?!
I THINK MY BODY FEELS WARMER AND MY CHILLS ARE GONE...
UNTIL JUST A MOMENT AGO,
MY BODY FELT HEAVY...
BUT I FEEL LIGHTER NOW...

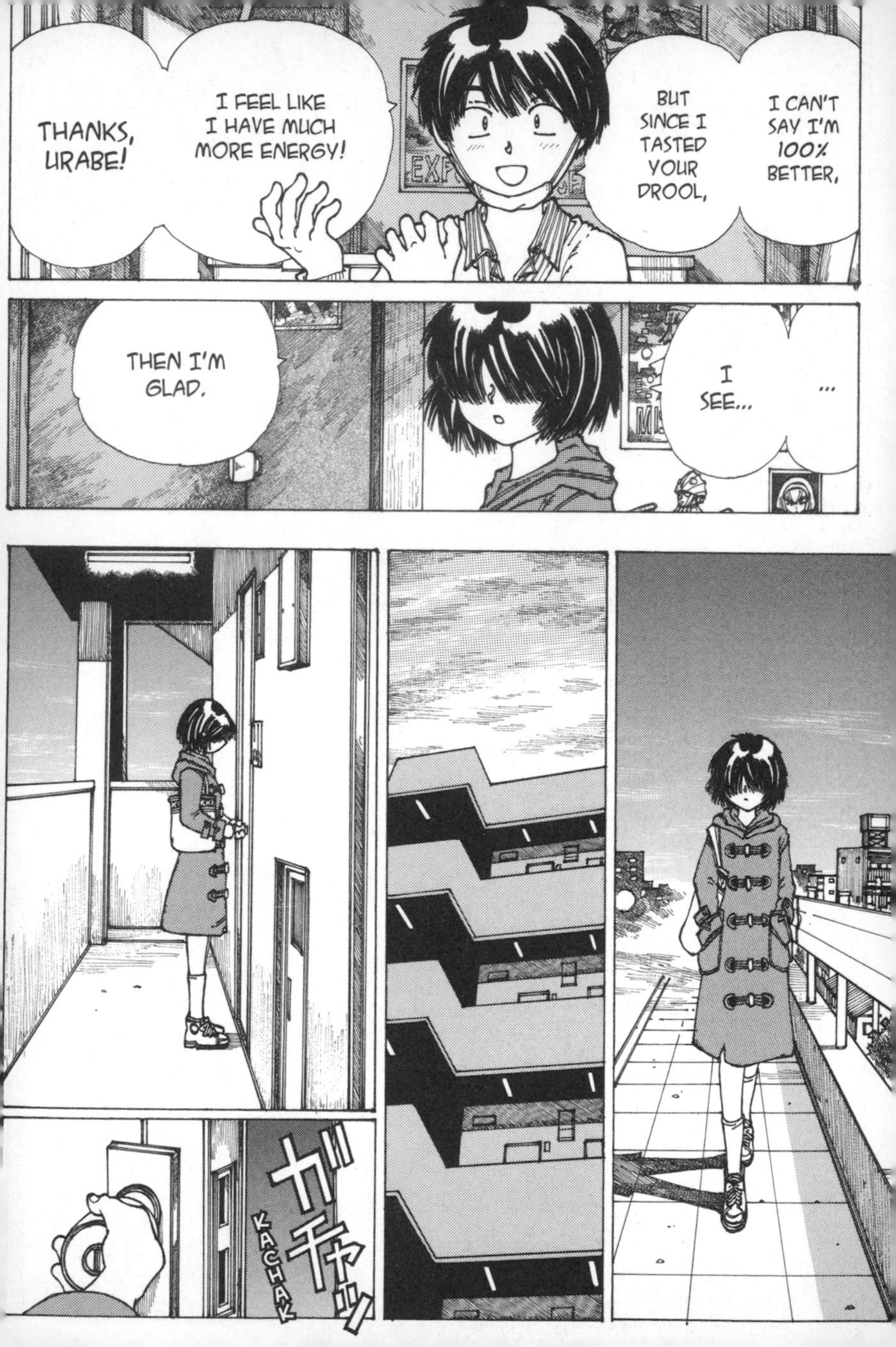
I CAN'T SAY I'M 100% BETTER,
BUT SINCE I TASTED YOUR DROOL,
I FEEL LIKE I HAVE MUCH MORE ENERGY!
THANKS, URABE!
...
I SEE...
THEN I'M GLAD.
ガチャッ
KACHAK

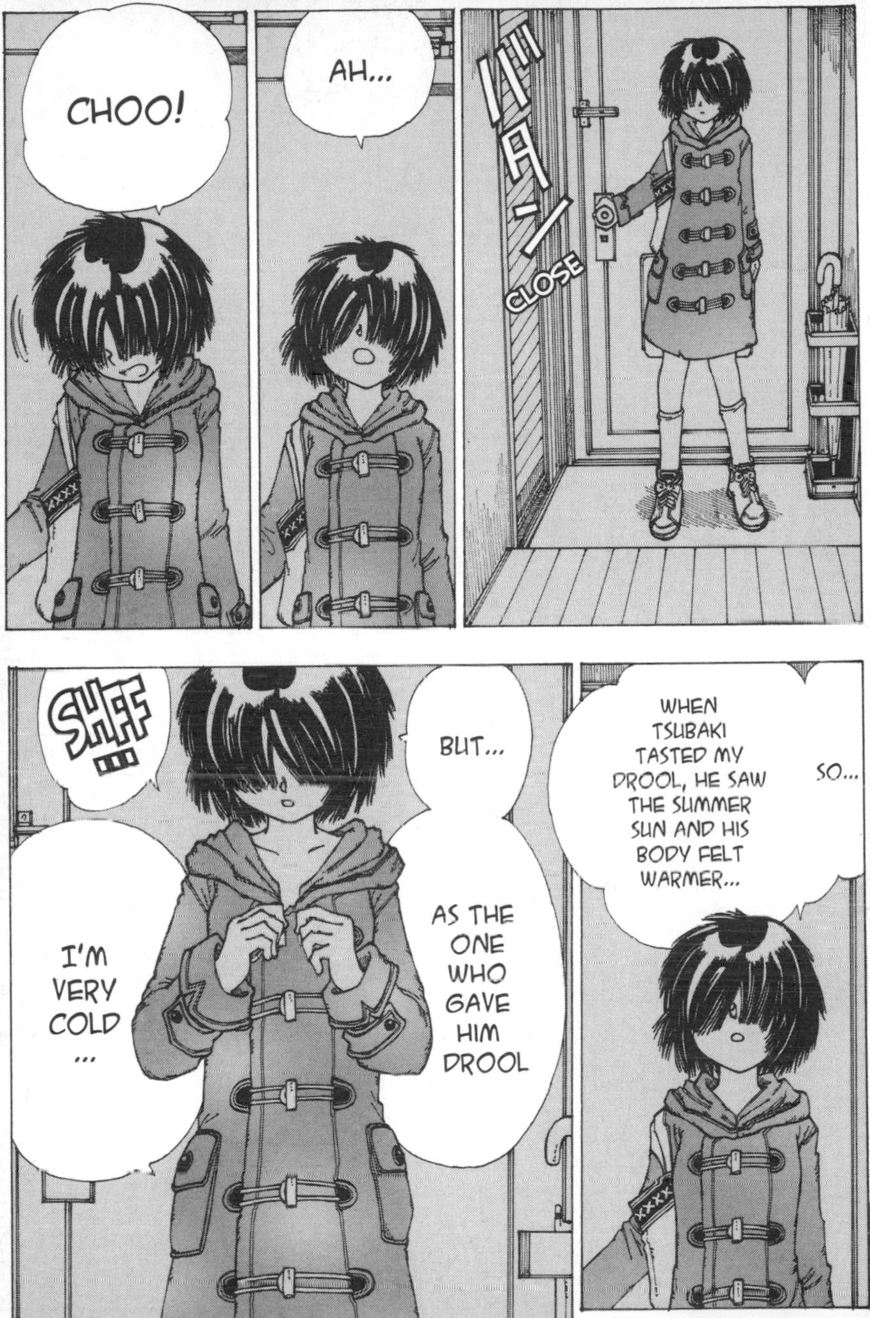
CLOSE
AH...
CHOO!
WHEN TSUBAKI TASTED MY DROOL, HE SAW THE SUMMER SUN AND HIS BODY FELT WARMER...
SO...
BUT...
SNIFF...
AS THE ONE WHO GAVE HIM DROOL
I'M VERY COLD...

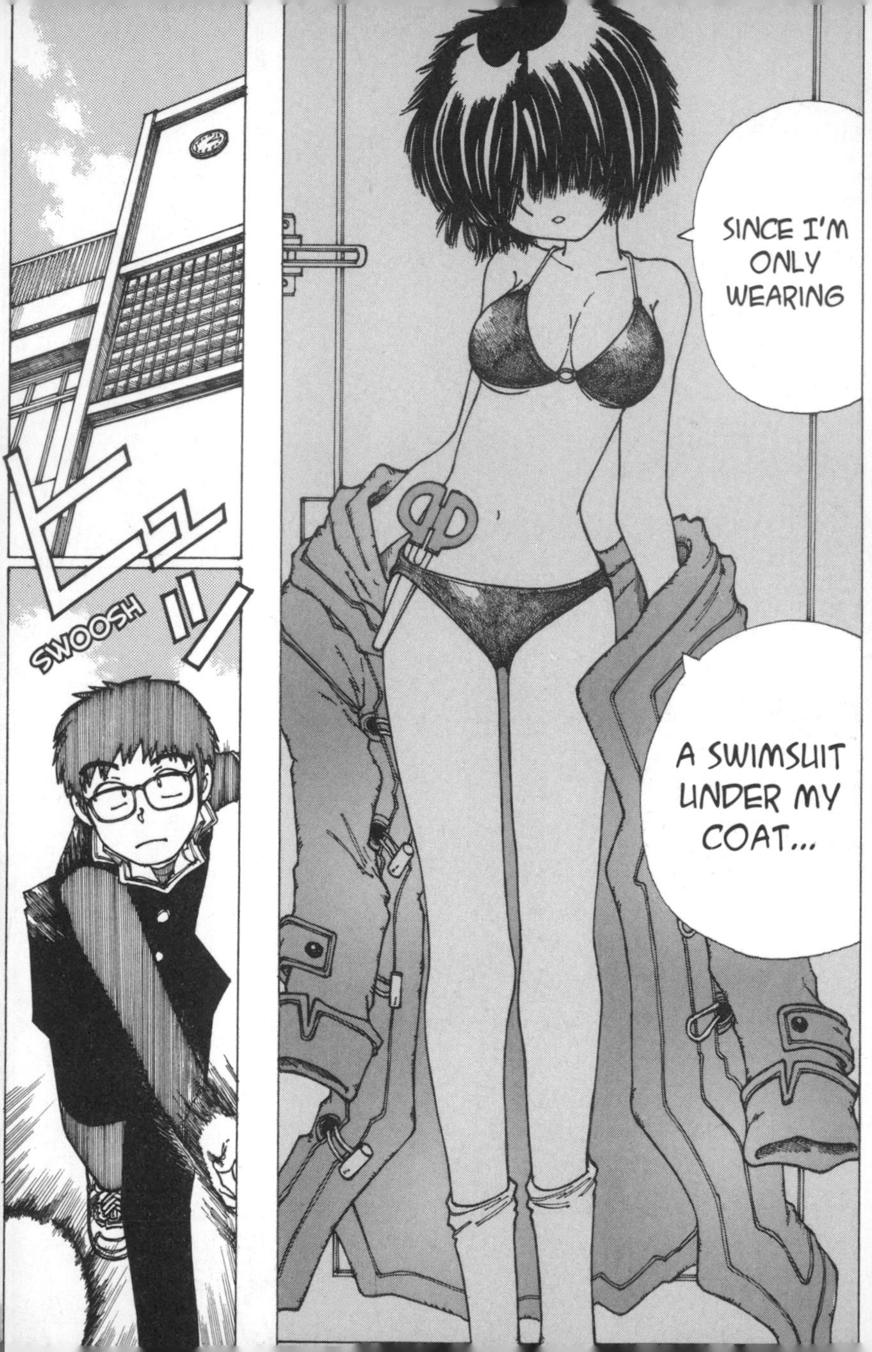
SINCE I'M ONLY WEARING
A SWIMSUIT UNDER MY COAT...
SWOOSH

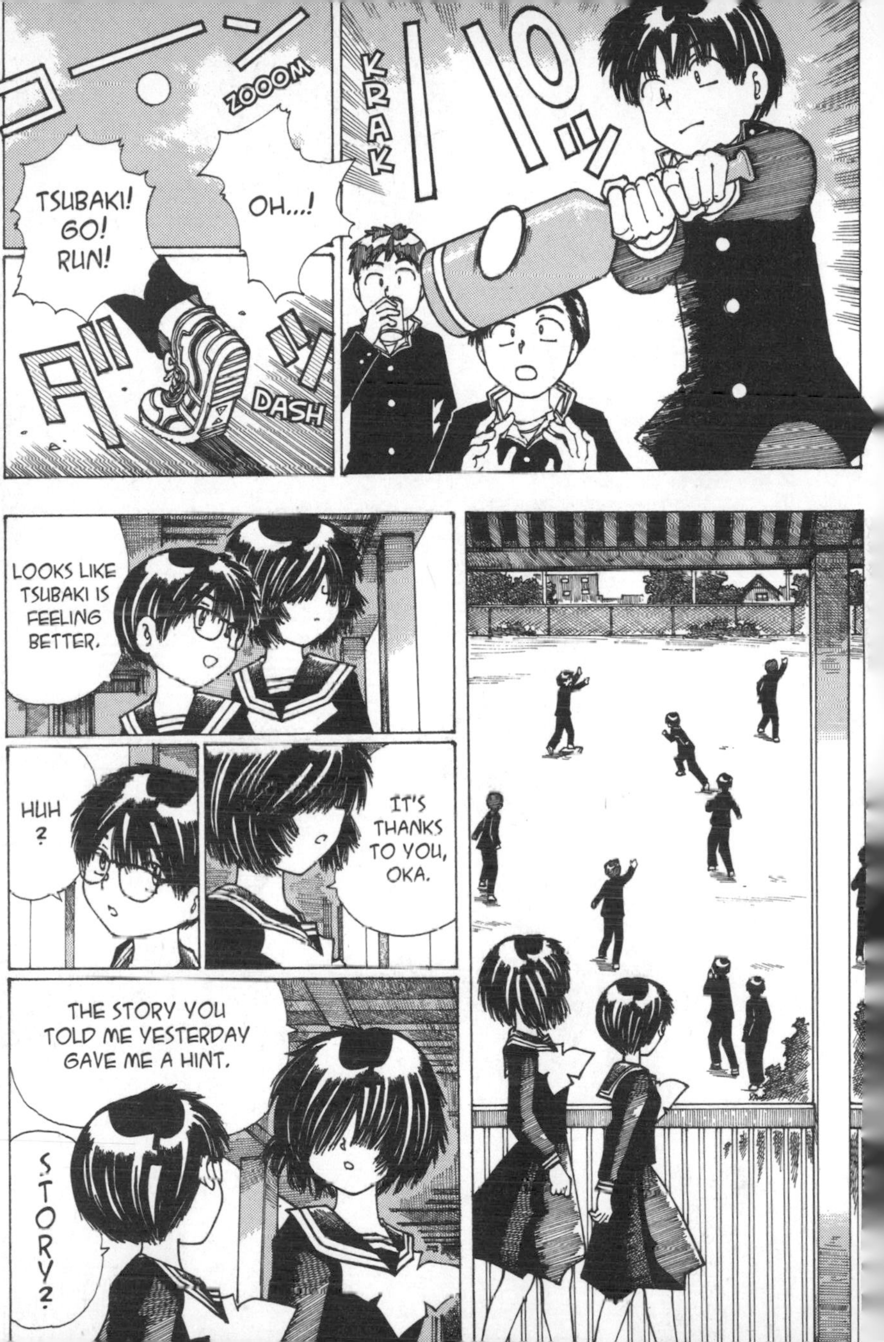
KRAK
OH...!
ZOOOM
TSUBAKI! GO! RUN!
DASH
LOOKS LIKE TSUBAKI IS FEELING BETTER.
IT'S THANKS TO YOU, OKA.
HUH?
THE STORY YOU TOLD ME YESTERDAY GAVE ME A HINT.
STORY?

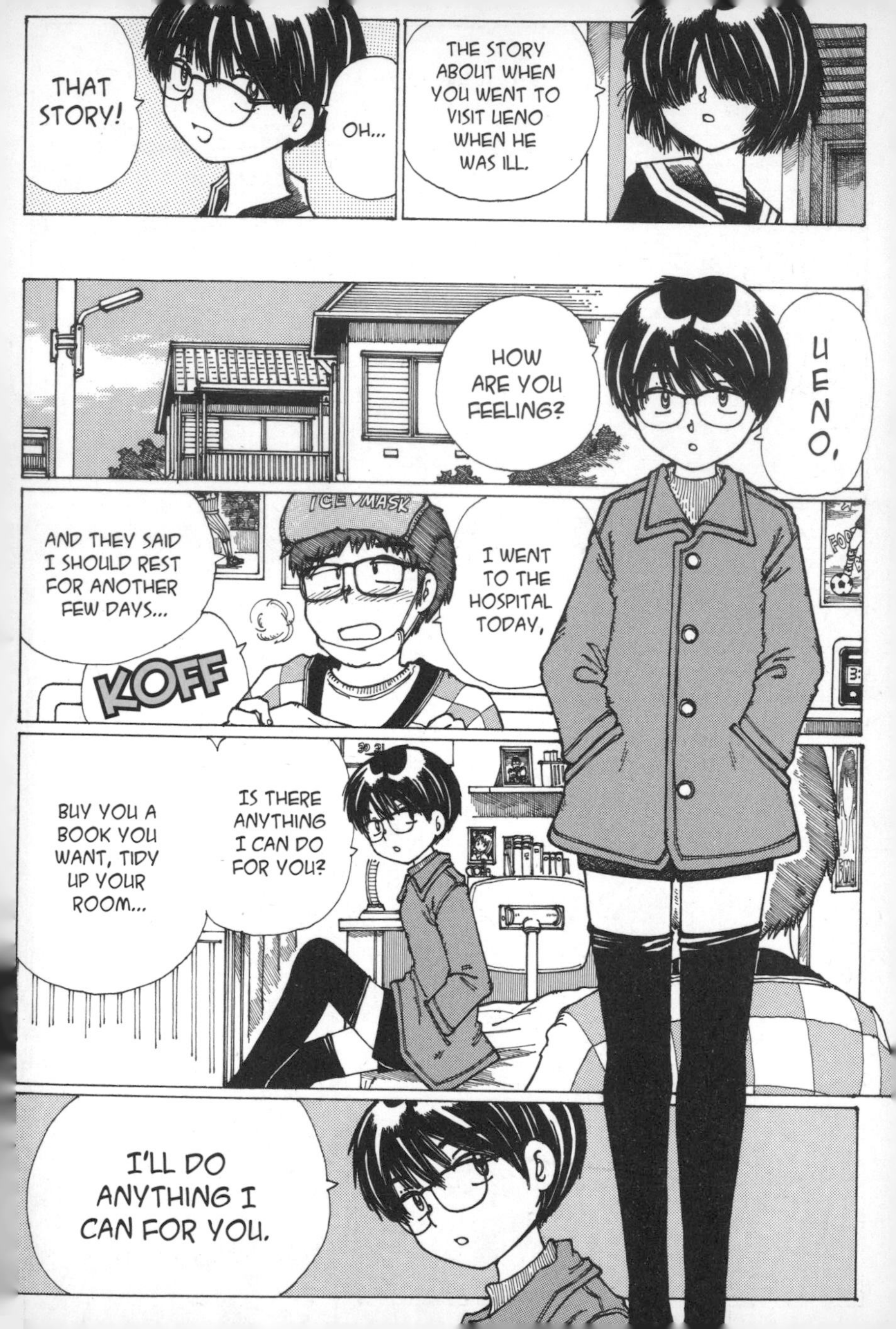
THE STORY ABOUT WHEN YOU WENT TO VISIT UENO WHEN HE WAS ILL.
OH...
THAT STORY!
UENO,
HOW ARE YOU FEELING?
I WENT TO THE HOSPITAL TODAY,
ICE MASK
AND THEY SAID I SHOULD REST FOR ANOTHER FEW DAYS...
KOFF
IS THERE ANYTHING I CAN DO FOR YOU?
BUY YOU A BOOK YOU WANT, TIDY UP YOUR ROOM...
I'LL DO ANYTHING I CAN FOR YOU.

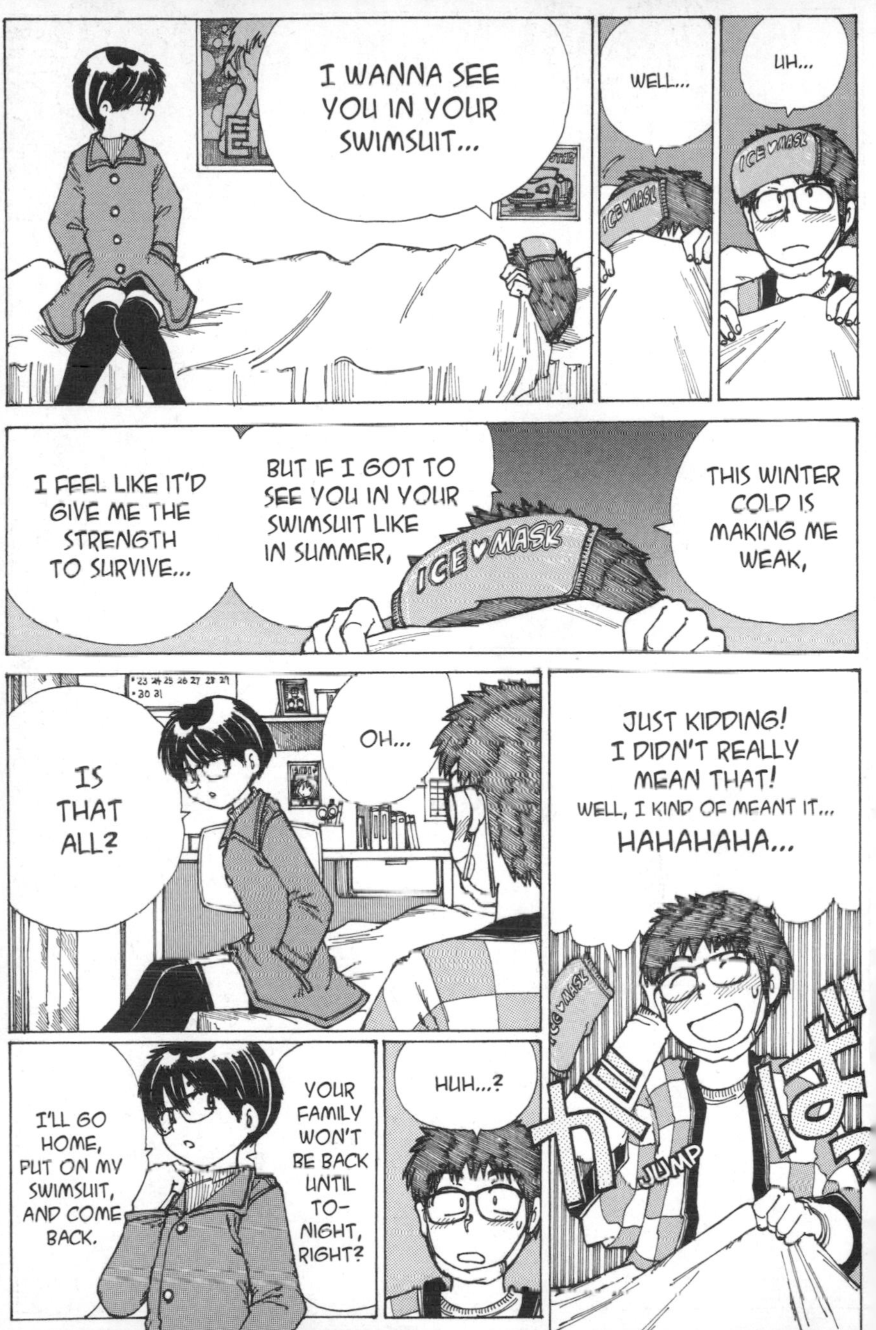
UH...
WELL...
I WANNA SEE YOU IN YOUR SWIMSUIT...
THIS WINTER COLD IS MAKING ME WEAK,
BUT IF I GOT TO SEE YOU IN YOUR SWIMSUIT LIKE IN SUMMER,
I FEEL LIKE IT'D GIVE ME THE STRENGTH TO SURVIVE...
ICE ♥ MASK
JUST KIDDING! I DIDN'T REALLY MEAN THAT!
WELL, I KIND OF MEANT IT...
HAHAHAHA...
がばっ
JUMP
OH...
IS THAT ALL?
HUH...?
YOUR FAMILY WON'T BE BACK UNTIL TO-NIGHT, RIGHT?
I'LL GO HOME, PUT ON MY SWIMSUIT, AND COME BACK.

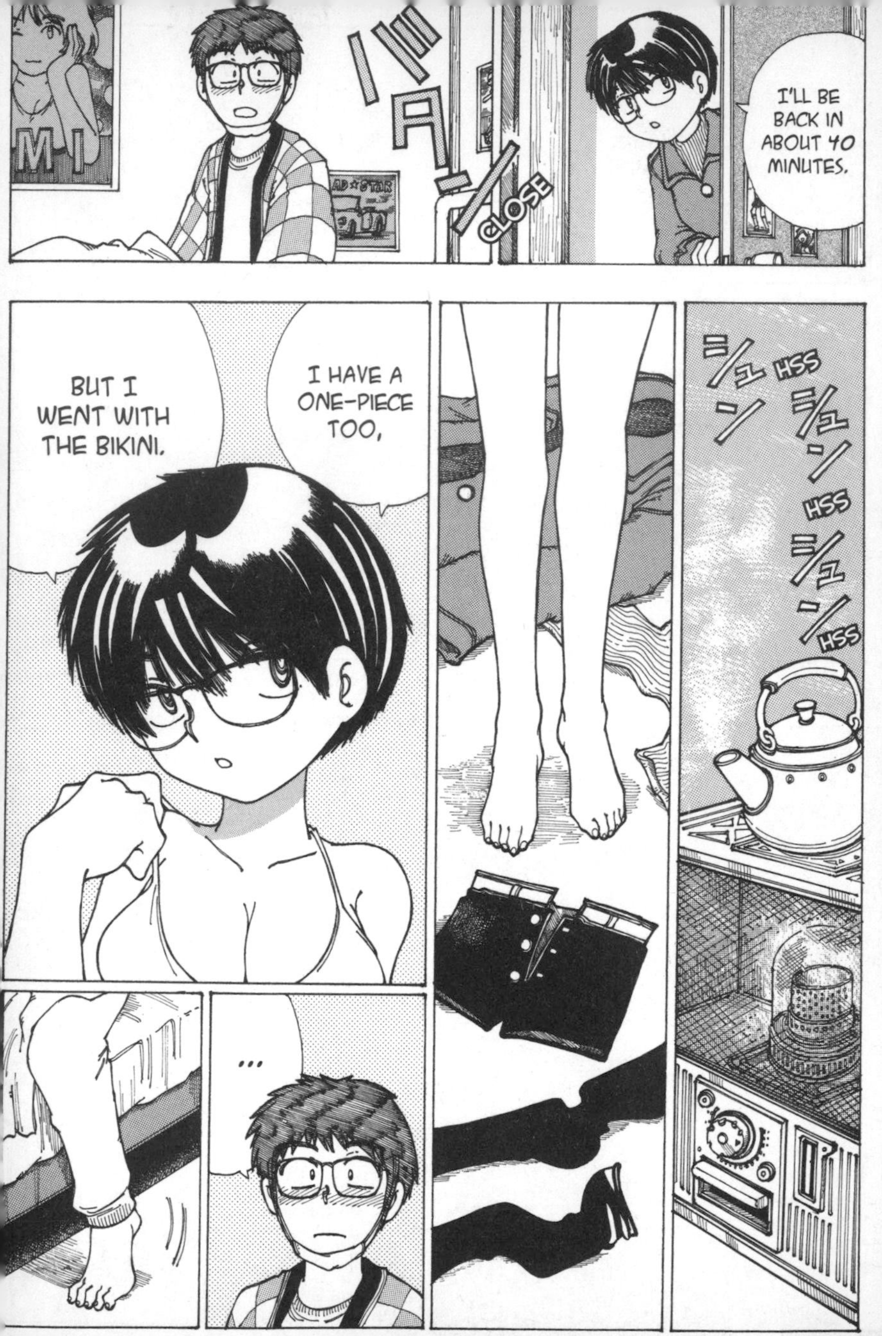
I'LL BE BACK IN ABOUT 40 MINUTES.
CLOSE
シュン
HSS
シュン
HSS
シュン
HSS
I HAVE A ONE-PIECE TOO,
BUT I WENT WITH THE BIKINI.
...

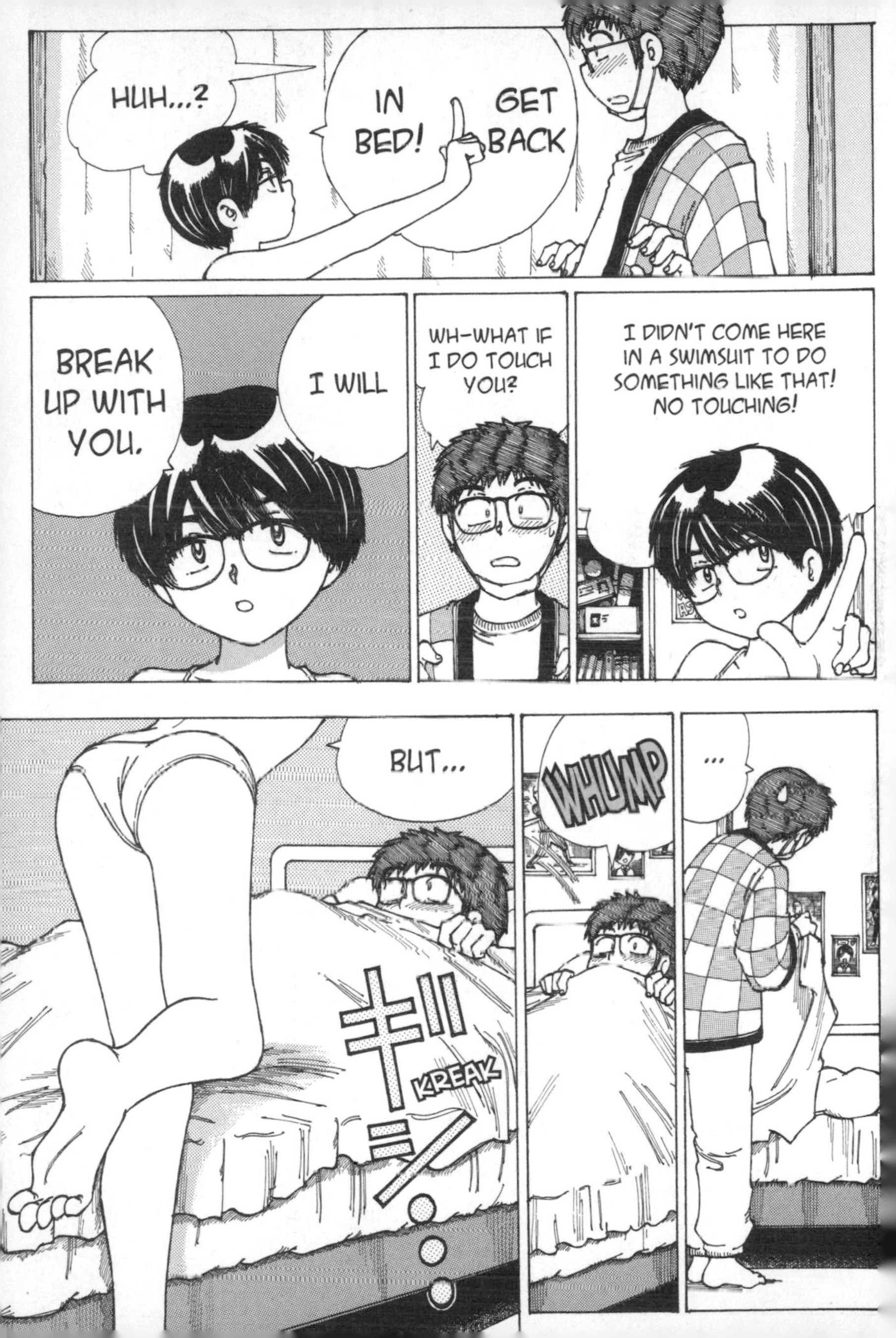
GET BACK IN BED!
HUH...?
I DIDN'T COME HERE IN A SWIMSUIT TO DO SOMETHING LIKE THAT! NO TOUCHING!
WH-WHAT IF I DO TOUCH YOU?
I WILL
BREAK UP WITH YOU.
...
WHUMP
BUT...
KREAK

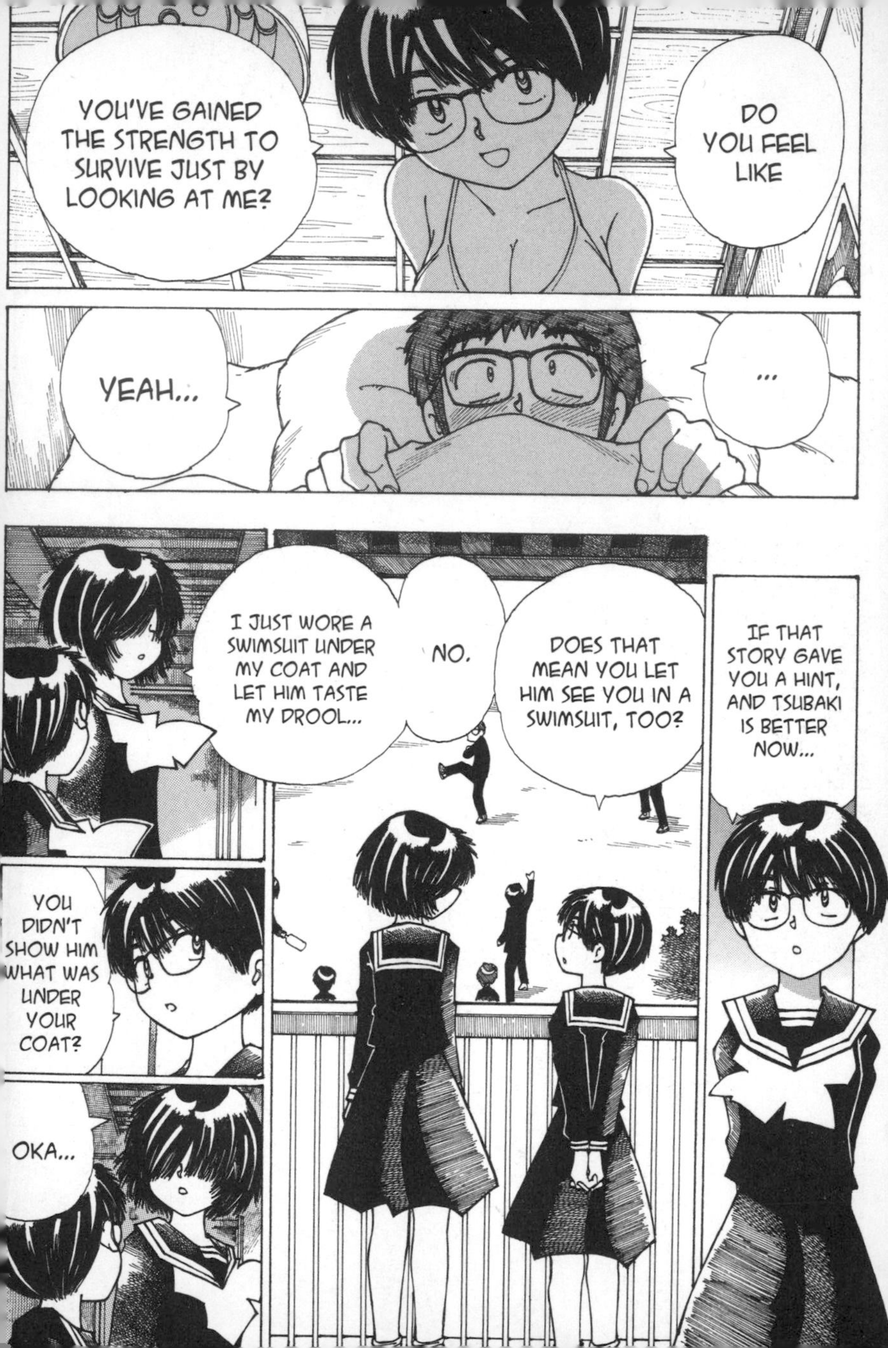
DO YOU FEEL LIKE
YOU'VE GAINED THE STRENGTH TO SURVIVE JUST BY LOOKING AT ME?
...
YEAH...
IF THAT STORY GAVE YOU A HINT, AND TSUBAKI IS BETTER NOW...
DOES THAT MEAN YOU LET HIM SEE YOU IN A SWIMSUIT, TOO?
NO.
I JUST WORE A SWIMSUIT UNDER MY COAT AND LET HIM TASTE MY DROOL...
YOU DIDN'T SHOW HIM WHAT WAS UNDER YOUR COAT?
OKA...

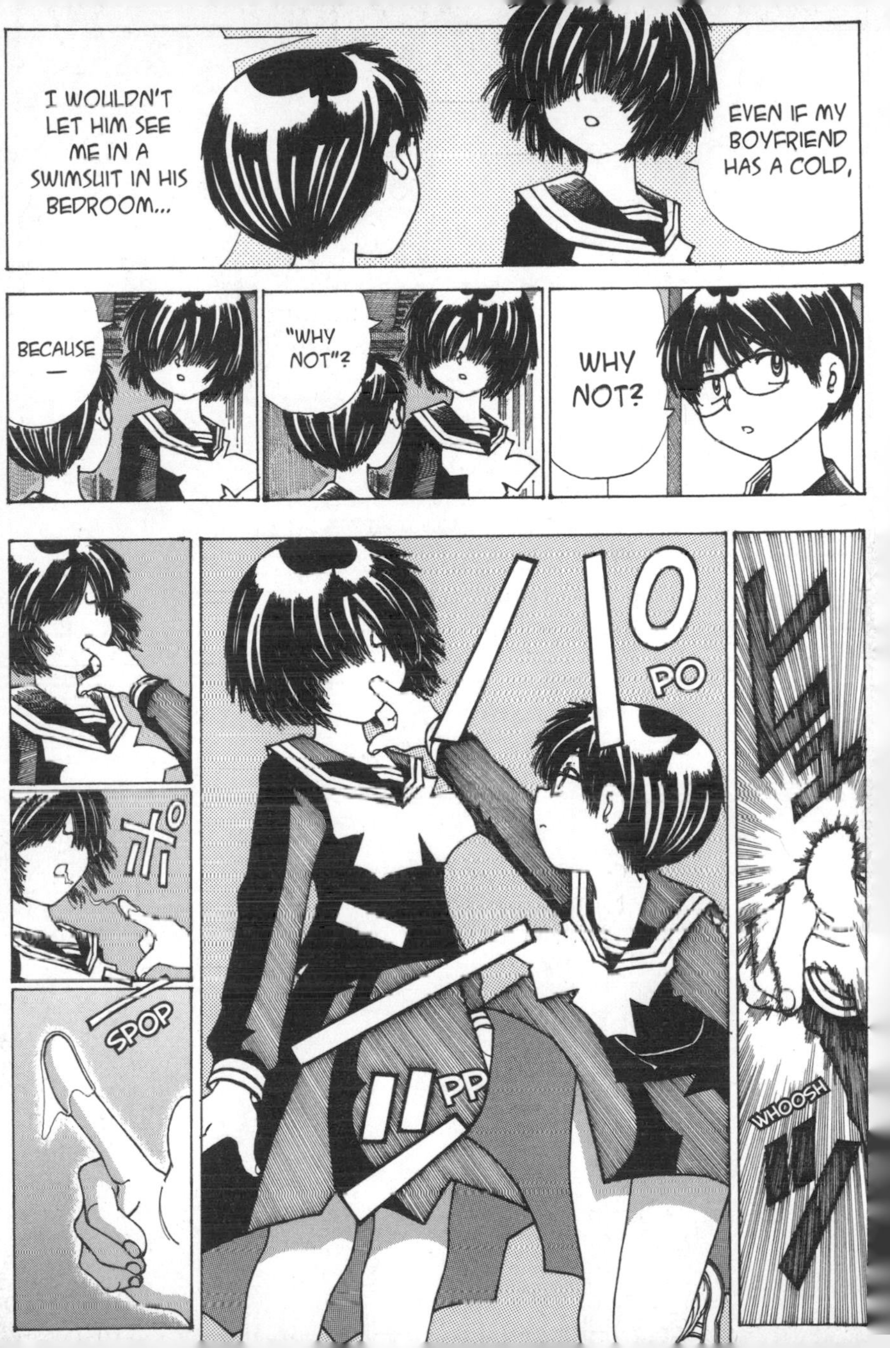
EVEN IF MY BOYFRIEND HAS A COLD,
I WOULDN'T LET HIM SEE ME IN A SWIMSUIT IN HIS BEDROOM...
WHY NOT?
"WHY NOT"?
BECAUSE —
WHOOSH
PO
PP
SPOP

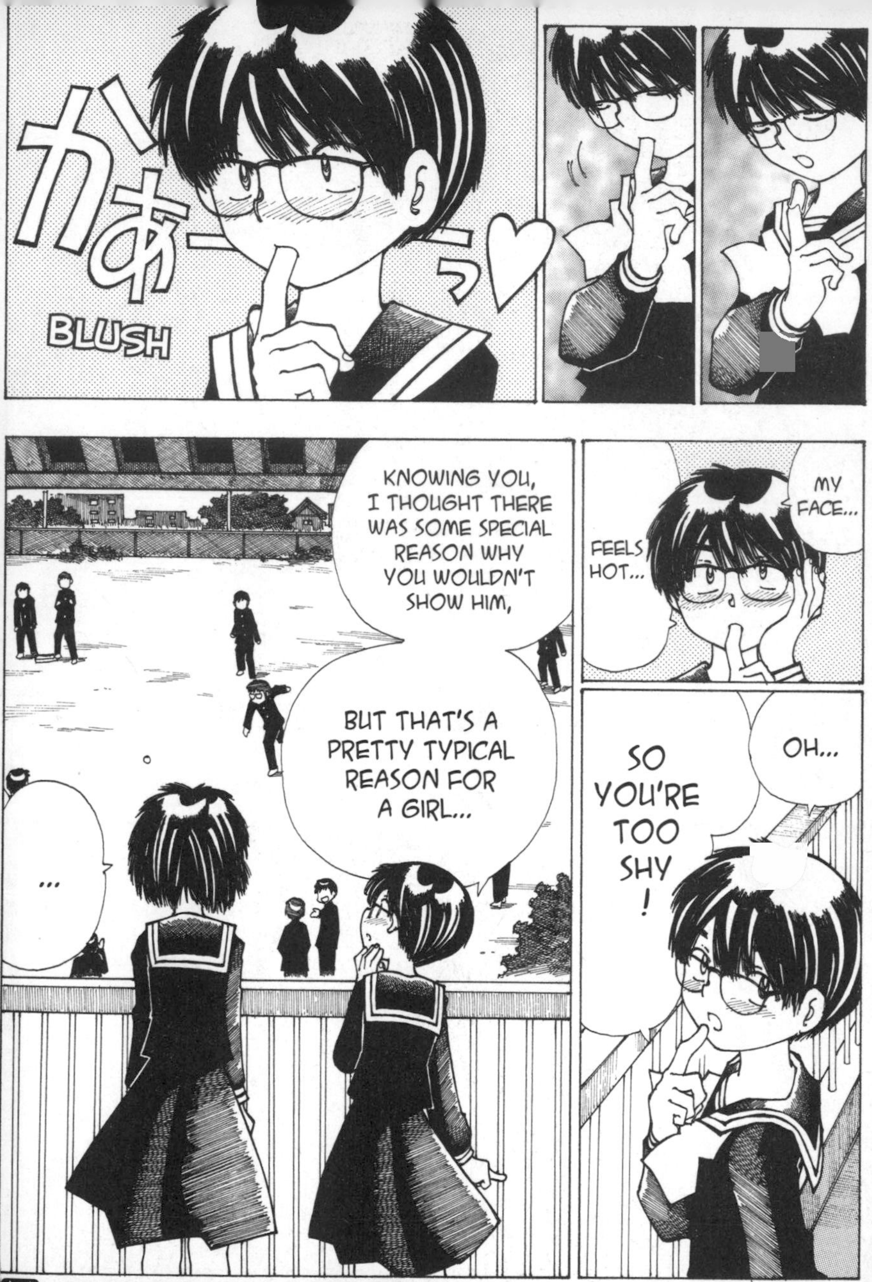

かぁーっ♥
BLUSH
MY FACE...
FEELS HOT...
OH...
SO YOU'RE TOO SHY!
KNOWING YOU, I THOUGHT THERE WAS SOME SPECIAL REASON WHY YOU WOULDN'T SHOW HIM,
BUT THAT'S A PRETTY TYPICAL REASON FOR A GIRL...
...

END OF CHAPTER 10

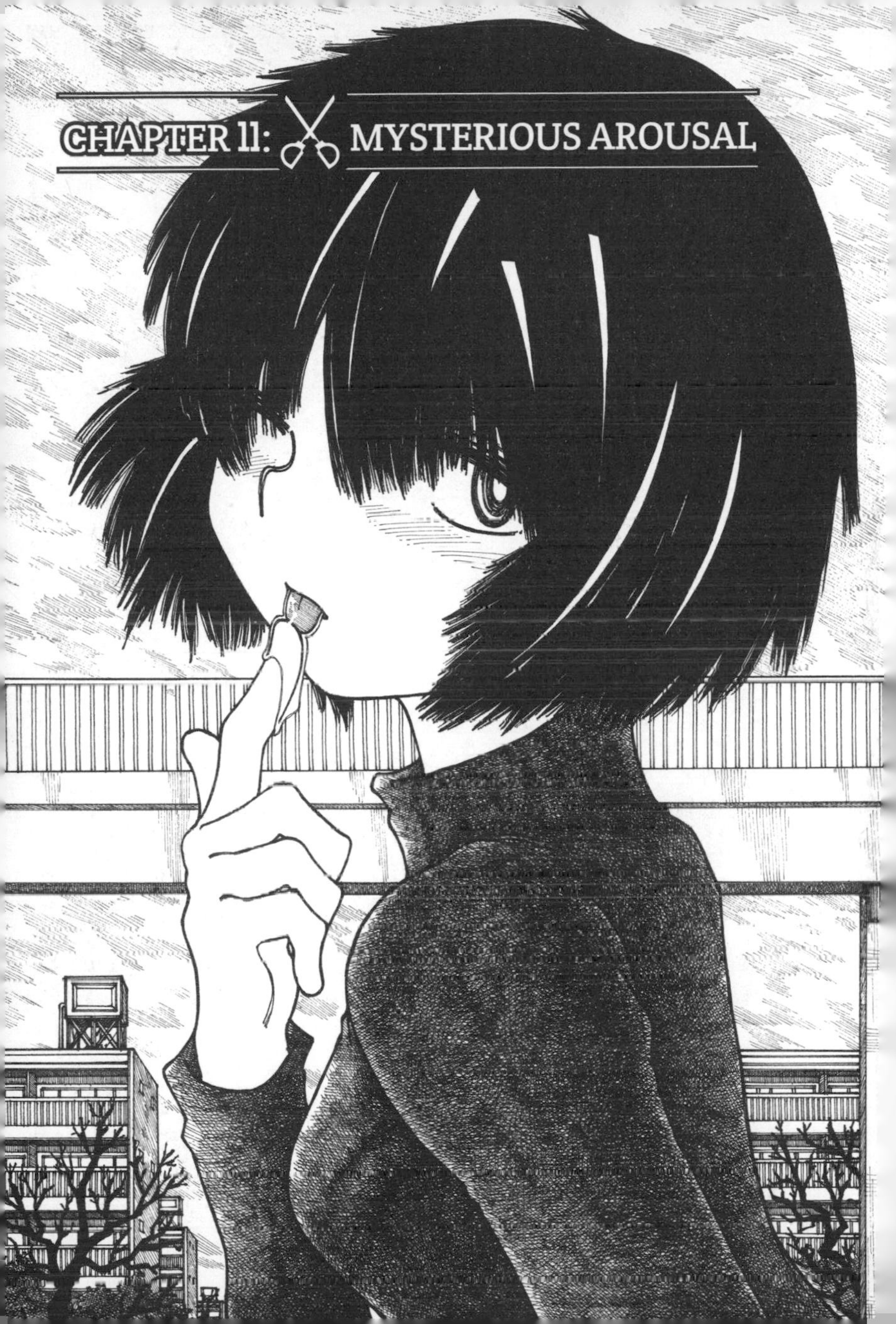
CHAPTER 11: MYSTERIOUS AROUSAL

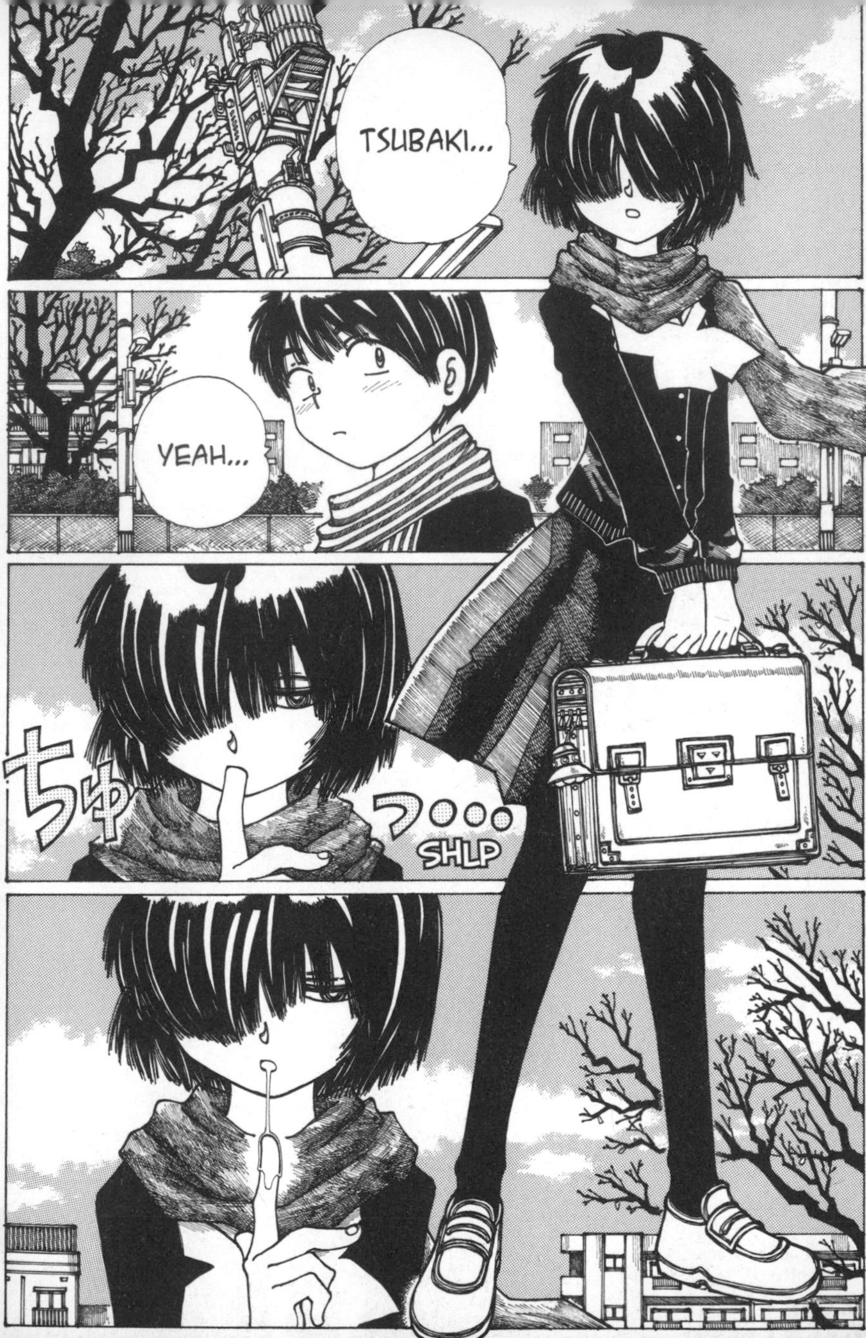
TSUBAKI...
YEAH...
ちゅっ...
SHLP

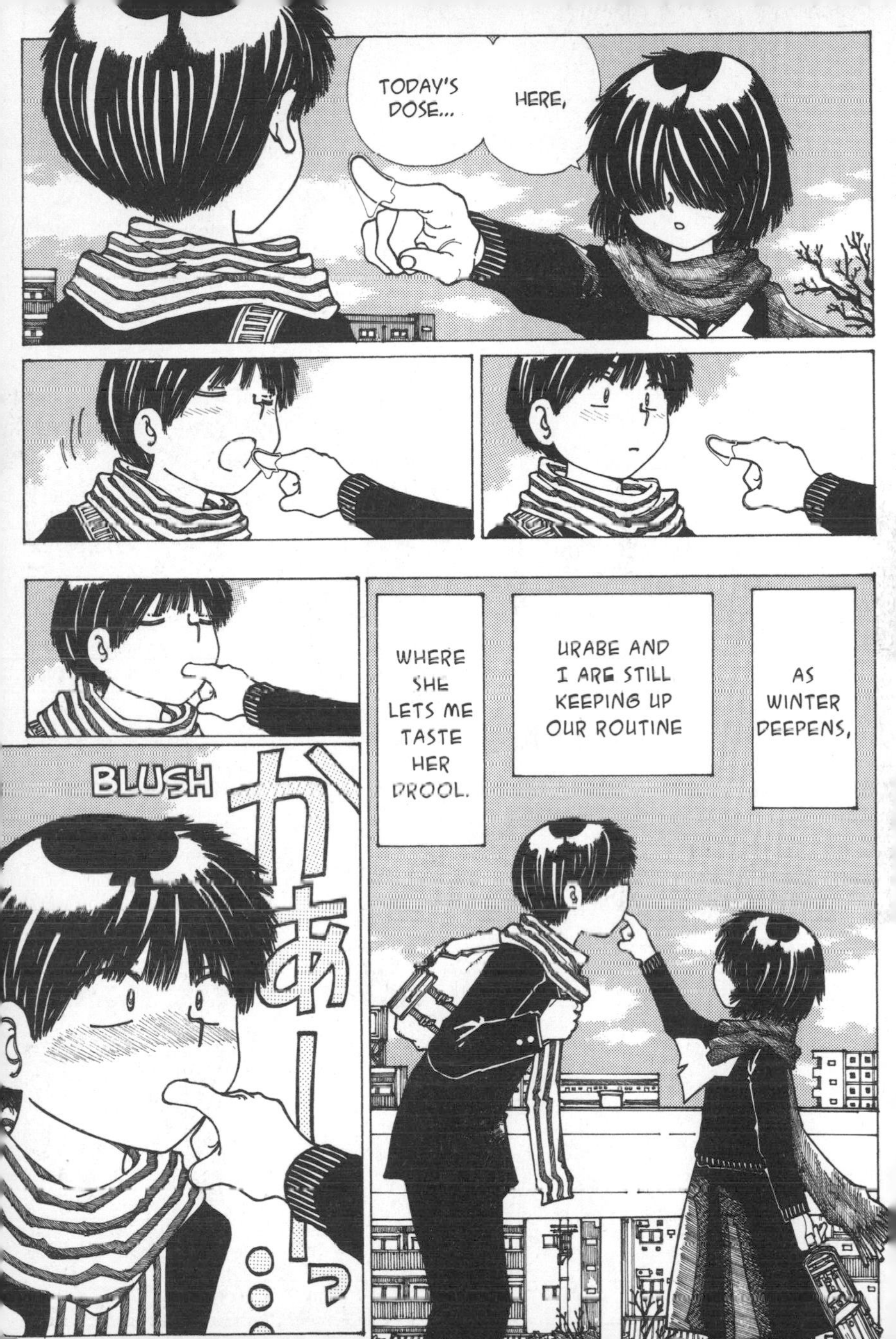
HERE,
TODAY'S DOSE...
AS WINTER DEEPENS,
URABE AND I ARE STILL KEEPING UP OUR ROUTINE
WHERE SHE LETS ME TASTE HER DROOL.
BLUSH
かぁーっ
…

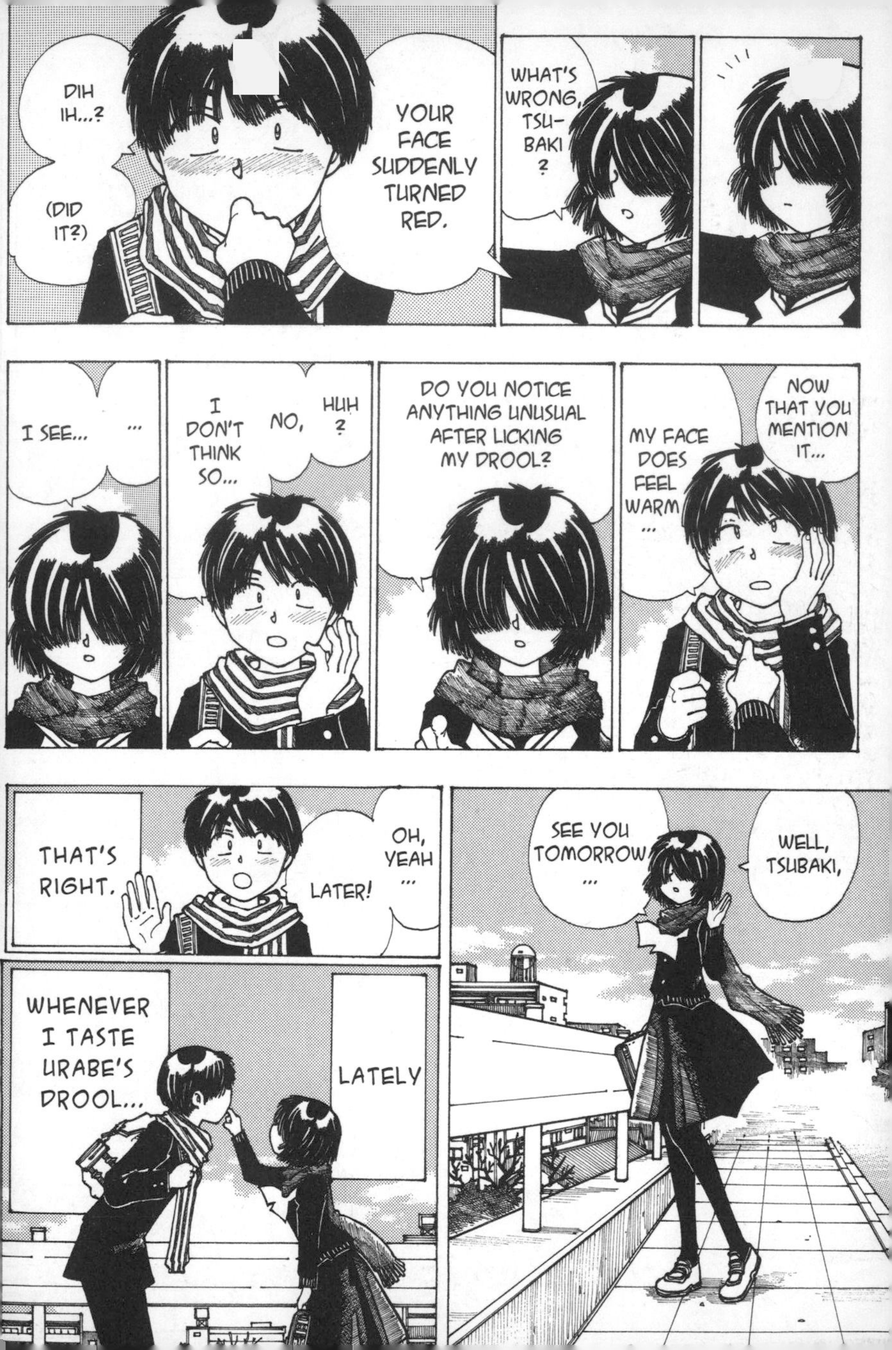
WHAT'S WRONG, TSUBAKI?
YOUR FACE SUDDENLY TURNED RED.
DIH IH...?
(DID IT?)
NOW THAT YOU MENTION IT...
MY FACE DOES FEEL WARM...
DO YOU NOTICE ANYTHING UNUSUAL AFTER LICKING MY DROOL?
HUH?
NO,
I DON'T THINK SO...
...
I SEE...
WELL, TSUBAKI,
SEE YOU TOMORROW...
OH, YEAH...
LATER!
THAT'S RIGHT.
LATELY
WHENEVER I TASTE URABE'S DROOL...

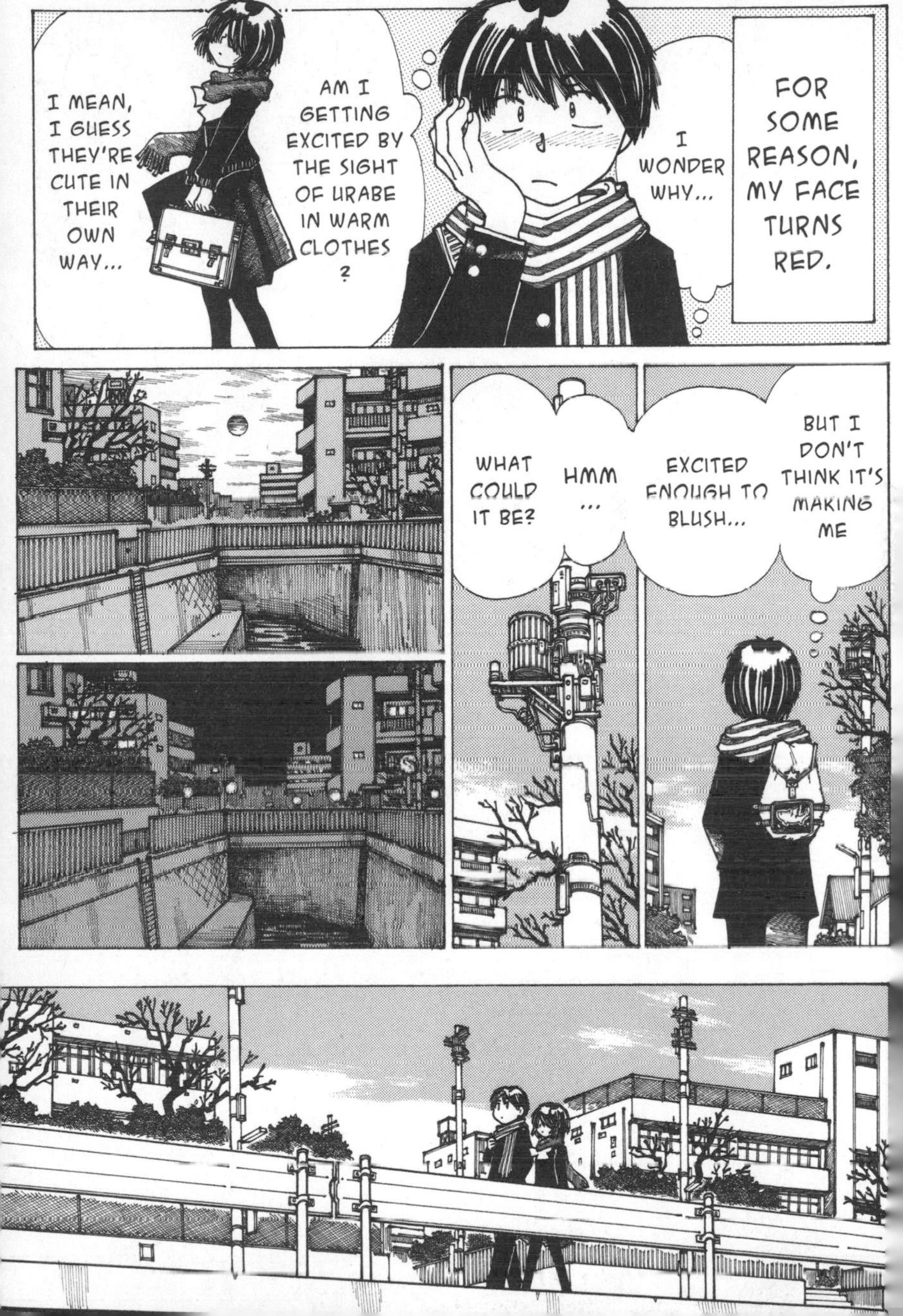
FOR SOME REASON, MY FACE TURNS RED.
I WONDER WHY...
AM I GETTING EXCITED BY THE SIGHT OF URABE IN WARM CLOTHES?
I MEAN, I GUESS THEY'RE CUTE IN THEIR OWN WAY...
BUT I DON'T THINK IT'S MAKING ME
EXCITED ENOUGH TO BLUSH...
HMM ...
WHAT COULD IT BE?

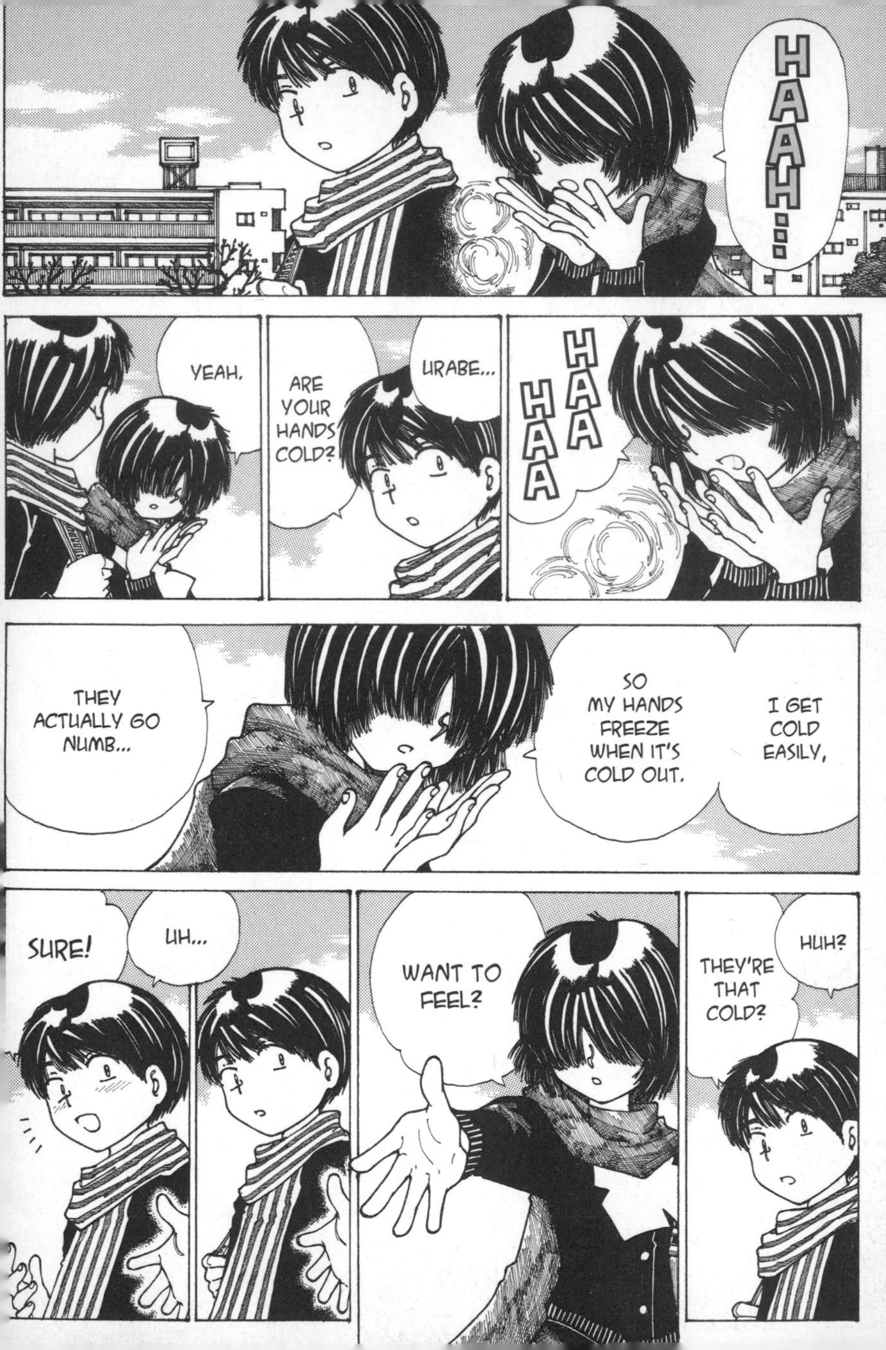
HAAAH...
HAA
HAA
URABE...
ARE YOUR HANDS COLD?
YEAH.
I GET COLD EASILY,
SO MY HANDS FREEZE WHEN IT'S COLD OUT.
THEY ACTUALLY GO NUMB...
HUH?
THEY'RE THAT COLD?
WANT TO FEEL?
UH...
SURE!

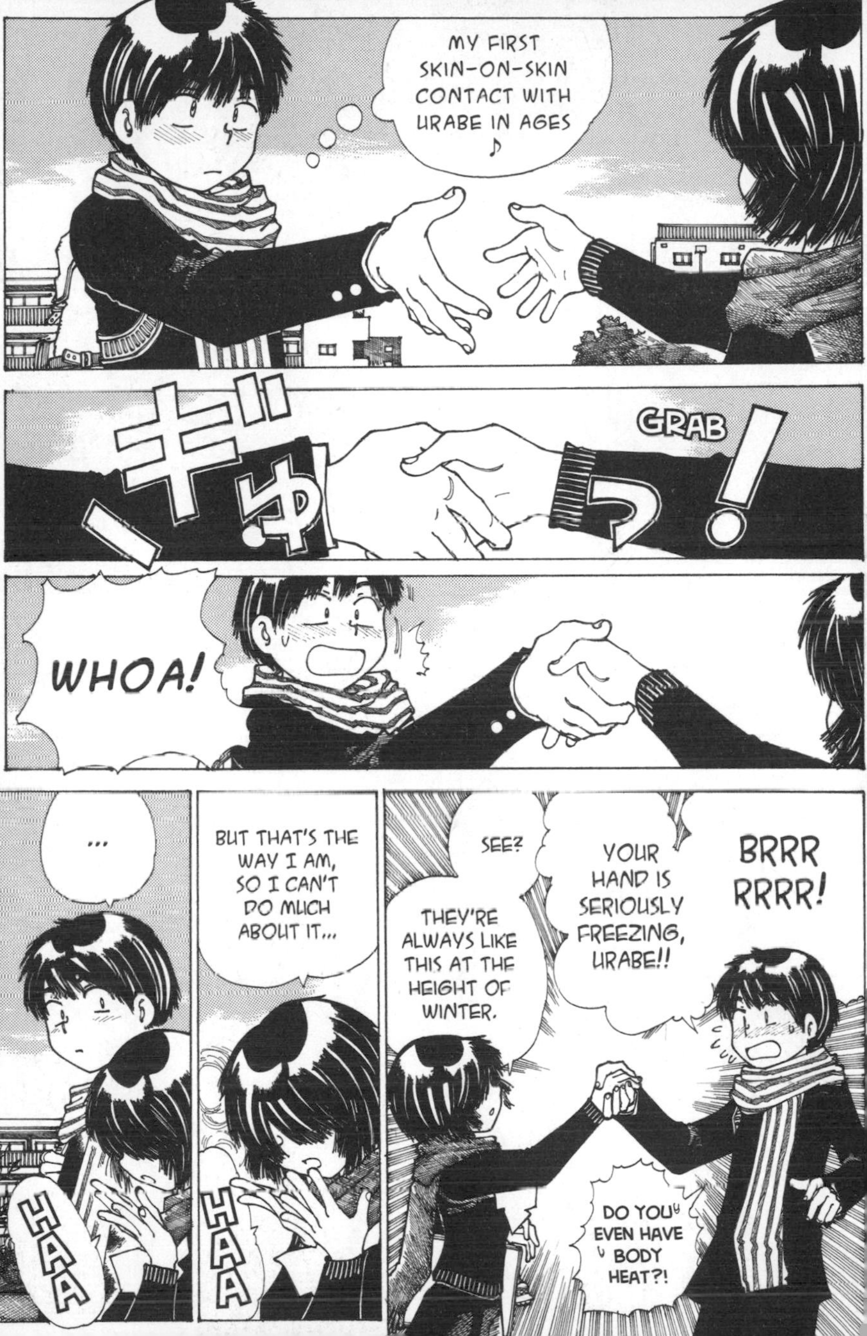
MY FIRST SKIN-ON-SKIN CONTACT WITH URABE IN AGES ♪
ぎゅっ!
GRAB
WHOA!
BRRR RRRR!
YOUR HAND IS SERIOUSLY FREEZING, URABE!!
SEE?
THEY'RE ALWAYS LIKE THIS AT THE HEIGHT OF WINTER.
DO YOU EVEN HAVE BODY HEAT?!
BUT THAT'S THE WAY I AM, SO I CAN'T DO MUCH ABOUT IT...
HAA
...
HAA

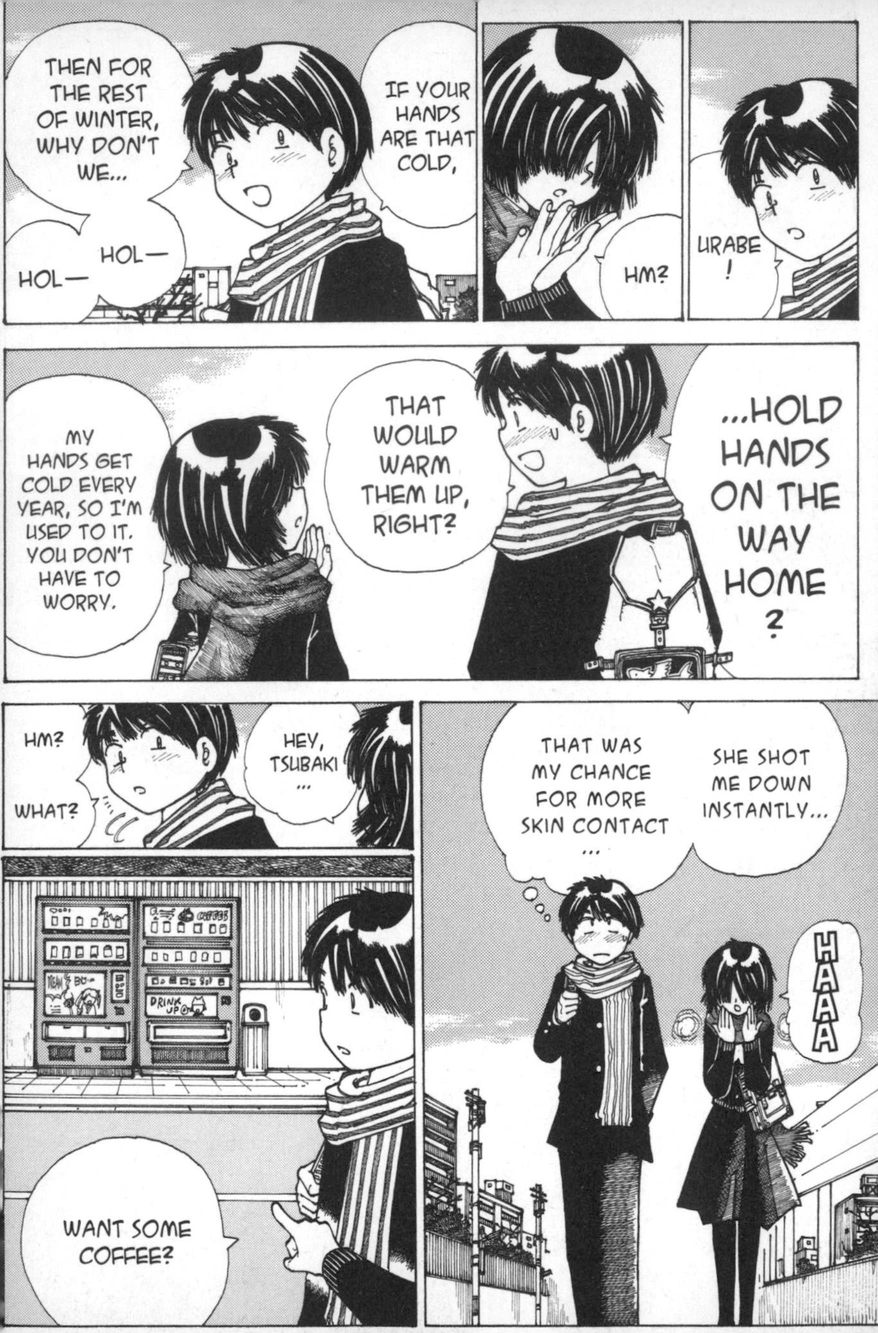
URABE !
HM?
IF YOUR HANDS ARE THAT COLD,
THEN FOR THE REST OF WINTER, WHY DON'T WE...
HOL—
HOL—
...HOLD HANDS ON THE WAY HOME?
THAT WOULD WARM THEM UP, RIGHT?
MY HANDS GET COLD EVERY YEAR, SO I'M USED TO IT. YOU DON'T HAVE TO WORRY.
SHE SHOT ME DOWN INSTANTLY...
THAT WAS MY CHANCE FOR MORE SKIN CONTACT ...
HAAAA
HEY, TSUBAKI ...
HM?
WHAT?
DRINK UP
WANT SOME COFFEE?

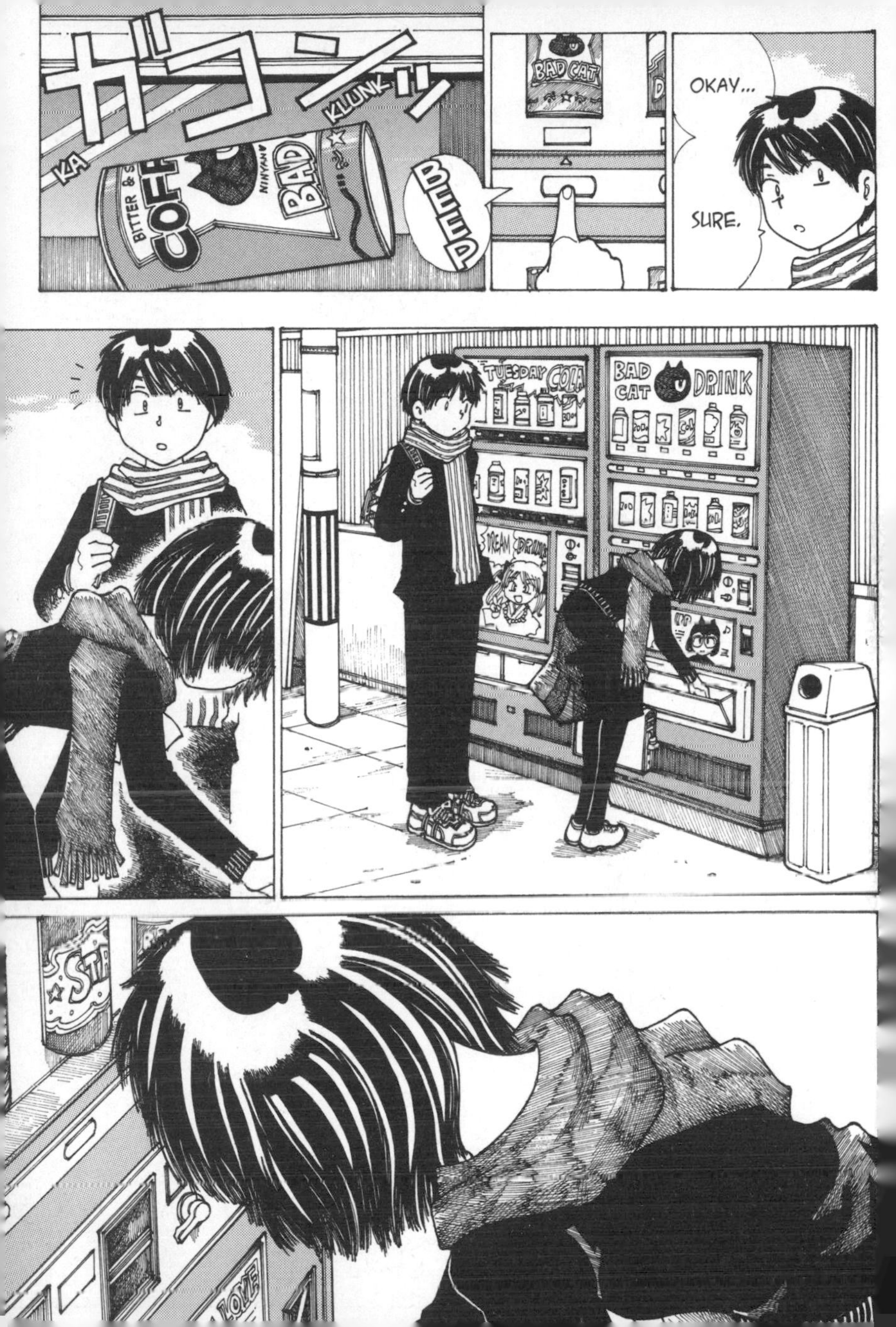
OKAY...
SURE.
BAD CAT
BEEP
ガコーン
KA KLUNK!!
BITTER & S
COFF
NINYAN♥
BAD
BAD CAT DRINK
TUESDAY COLA
DREAM DRINK
STR
LOVE

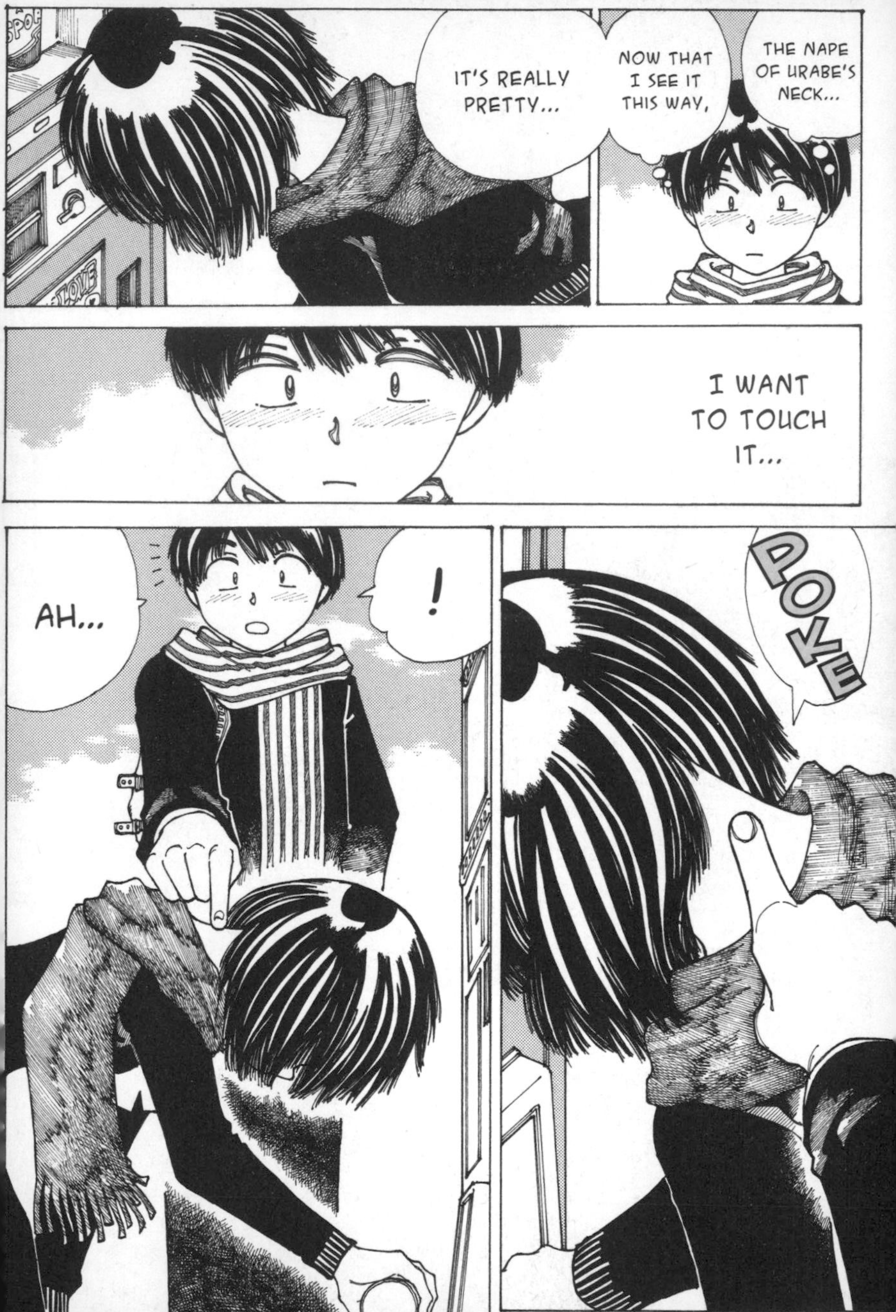
THE NAPE OF URABE'S NECK...
NOW THAT I SEE IT THIS WAY,
IT'S REALLY PRETTY...
I WANT TO TOUCH IT...
POKE
!
AH...

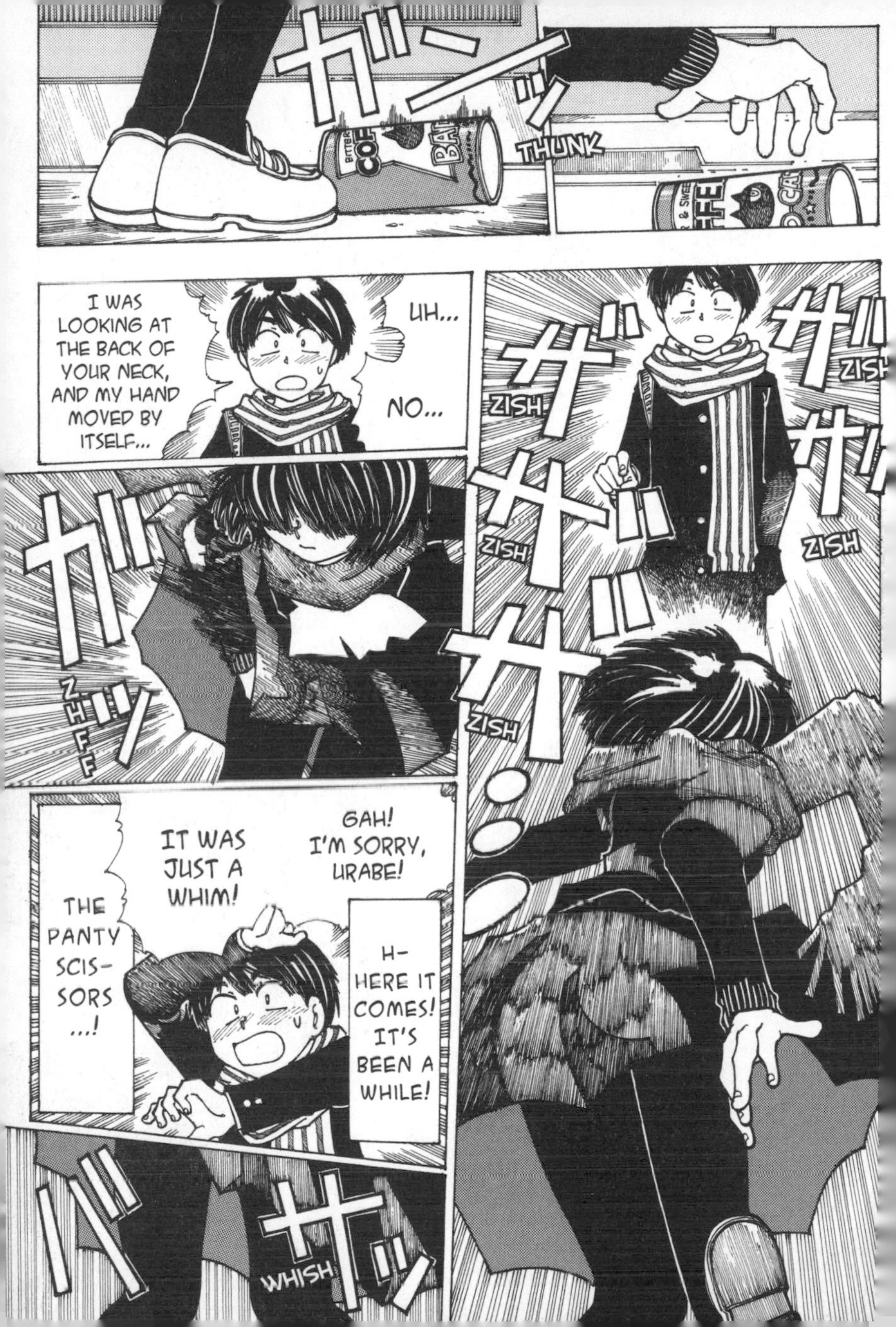
THUNK
ZISH
ZISH
ZISH
ZISH
ZISH
UH...
NO...
I WAS LOOKING AT THE BACK OF YOUR NECK, AND MY HAND MOVED BY ITSELF...
ZHFFF
GAH! I'M SORRY, URABE!
IT WAS JUST A WHIM!
H-HERE IT COMES! IT'S BEEN A WHILE!
THE PANTY SCISSORS ...!
WHISH

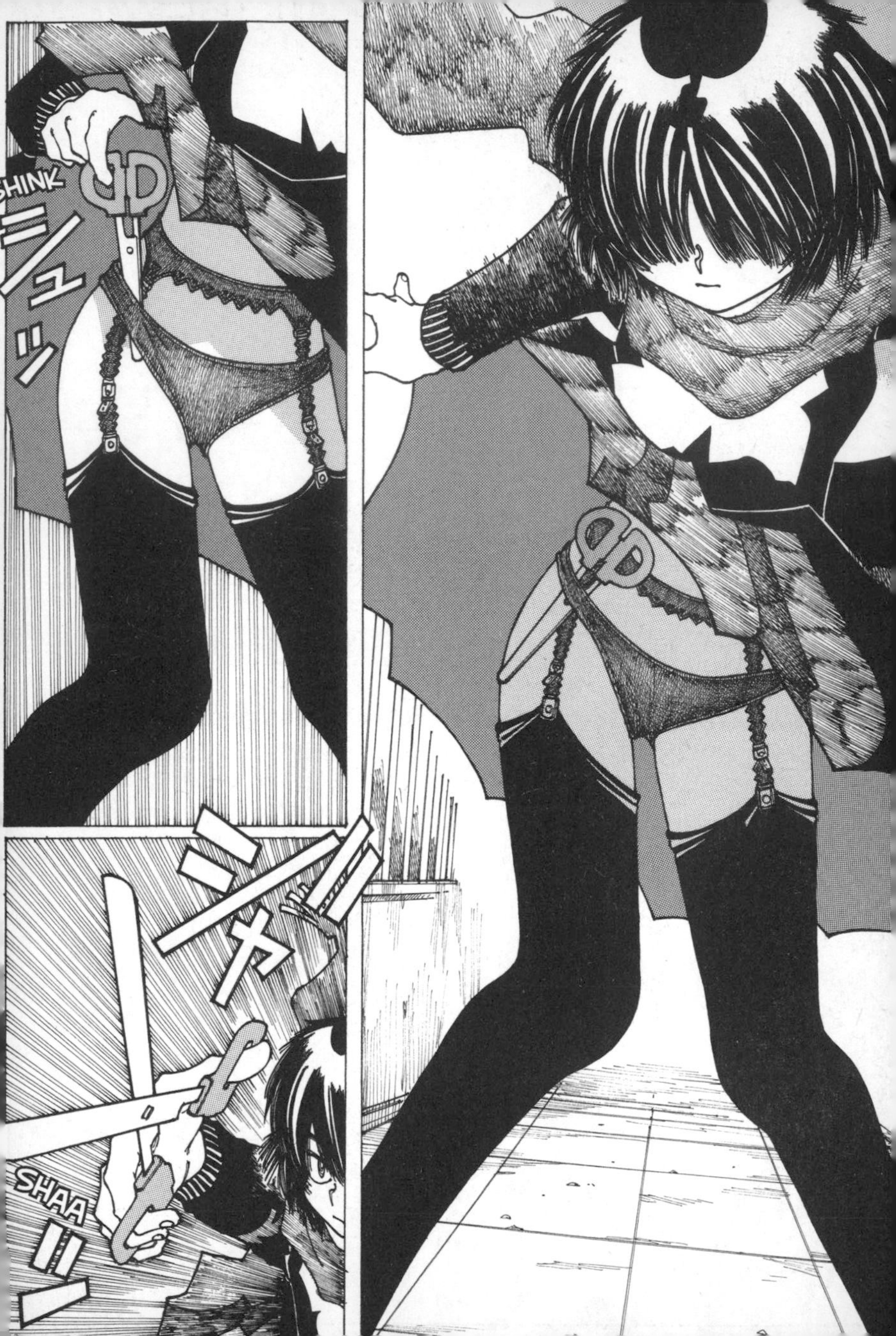
SHINK
シュッ
シャ
SHAA

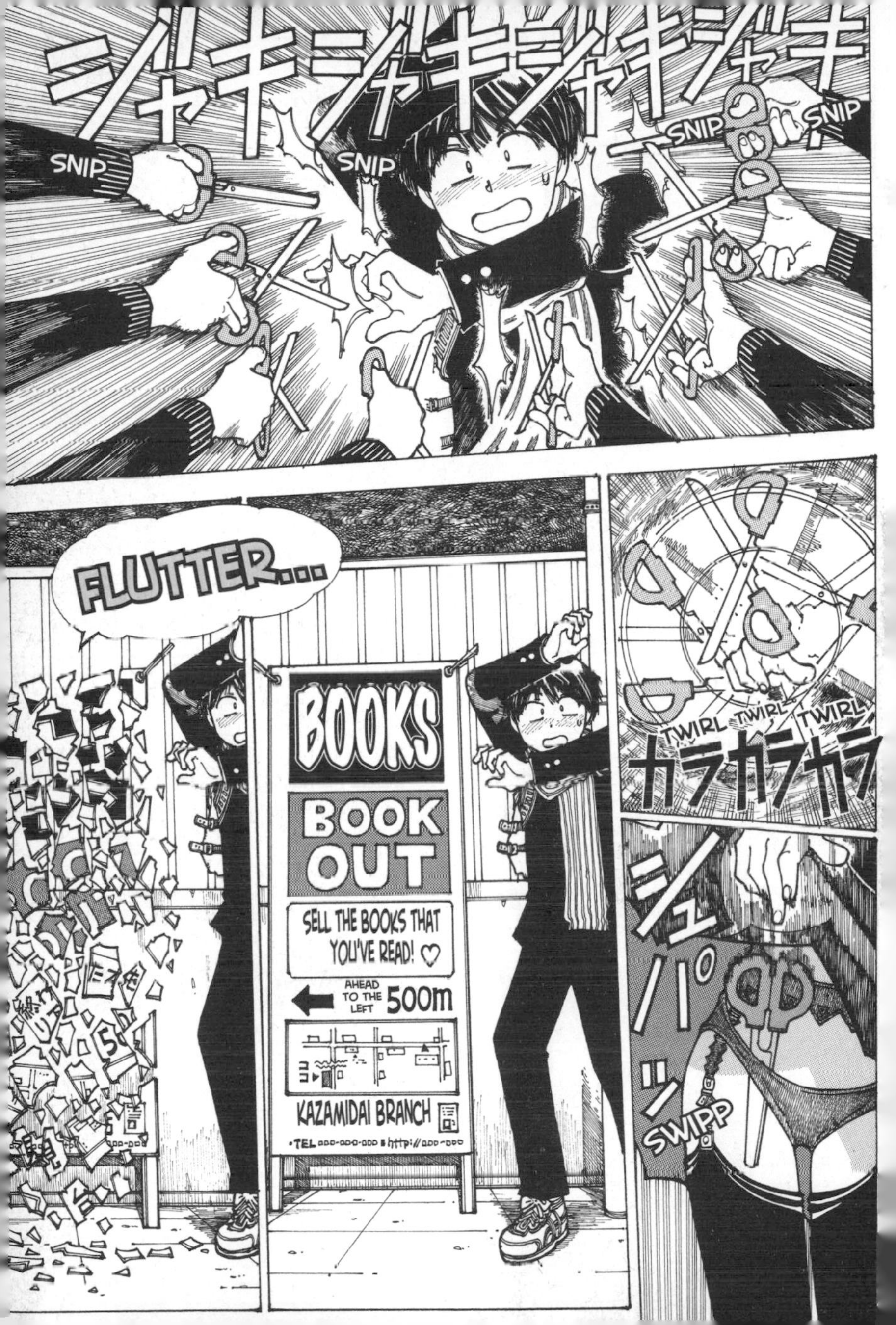
ジャキジャキジャキジャキ
SNIP
SNIP
SNIP
SNIP
SNIP
TWIRL TWIRL TWIRL
カラカラカラ
シュパッ
SWIPP
FLUTTER...
BOOKS
BOOK OUT
SELL THE BOOKS THAT YOU'VE READ! ♡
AHEAD TO THE LEFT 500m
KAZAMIDAI BRANCH
•TEL ▫▫▫-▫▫-▫-▫▫▫ ■ http://▫▫▫-▫▫▫

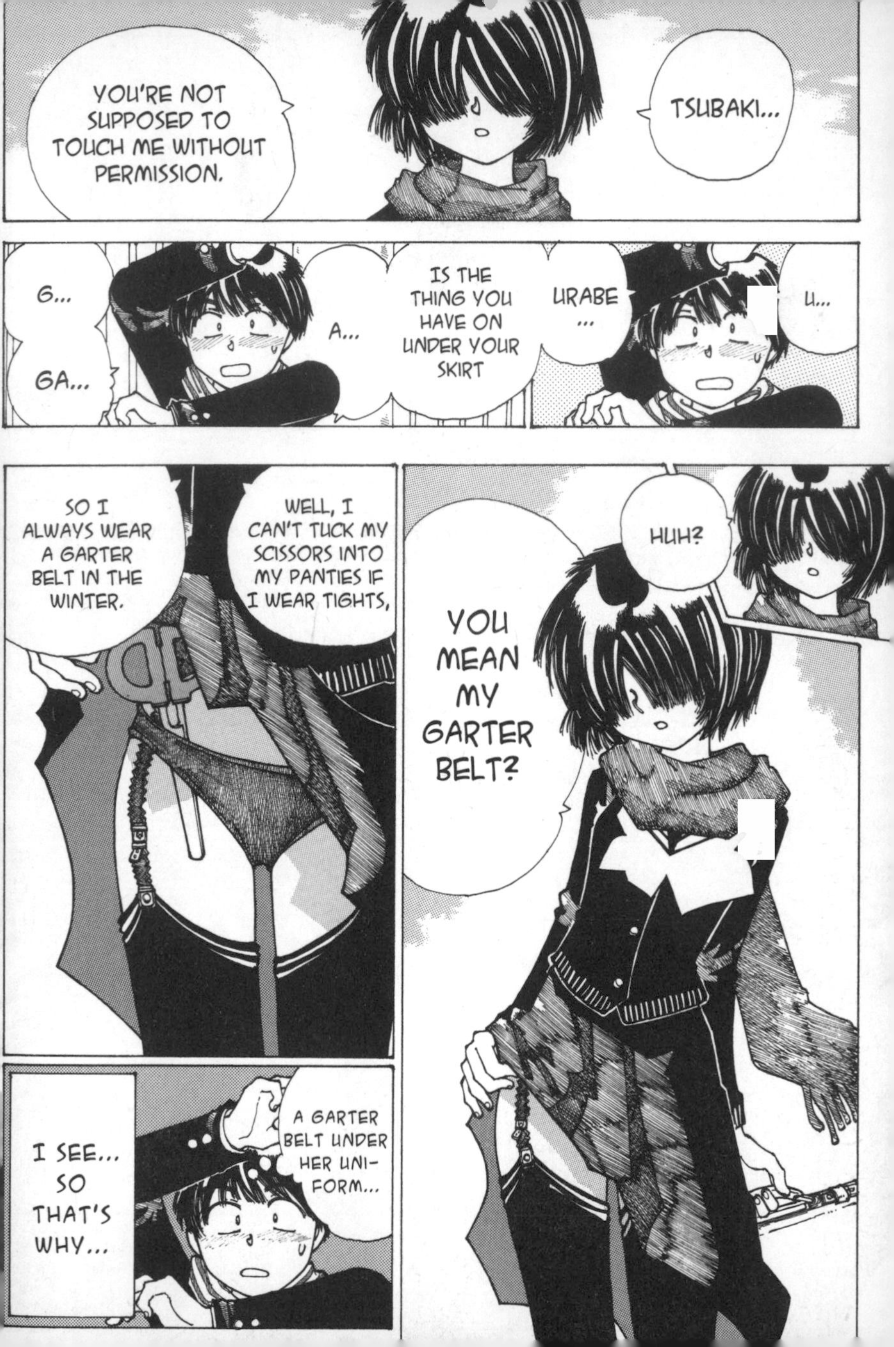
TSUBAKI...
YOU'RE NOT SUPPOSED TO TOUCH ME WITHOUT PERMISSION.
U...
URABE ...
IS THE THING YOU HAVE ON UNDER YOUR SKIRT
A...
G...
GA...
HUH?
YOU MEAN MY GARTER BELT?
WELL, I CAN'T TUCK MY SCISSORS INTO MY PANTIES IF I WEAR TIGHTS,
SO I ALWAYS WEAR A GARTER BELT IN THE WINTER.
A GARTER BELT UNDER HER UNI-FORM...
I SEE... SO THAT'S WHY...

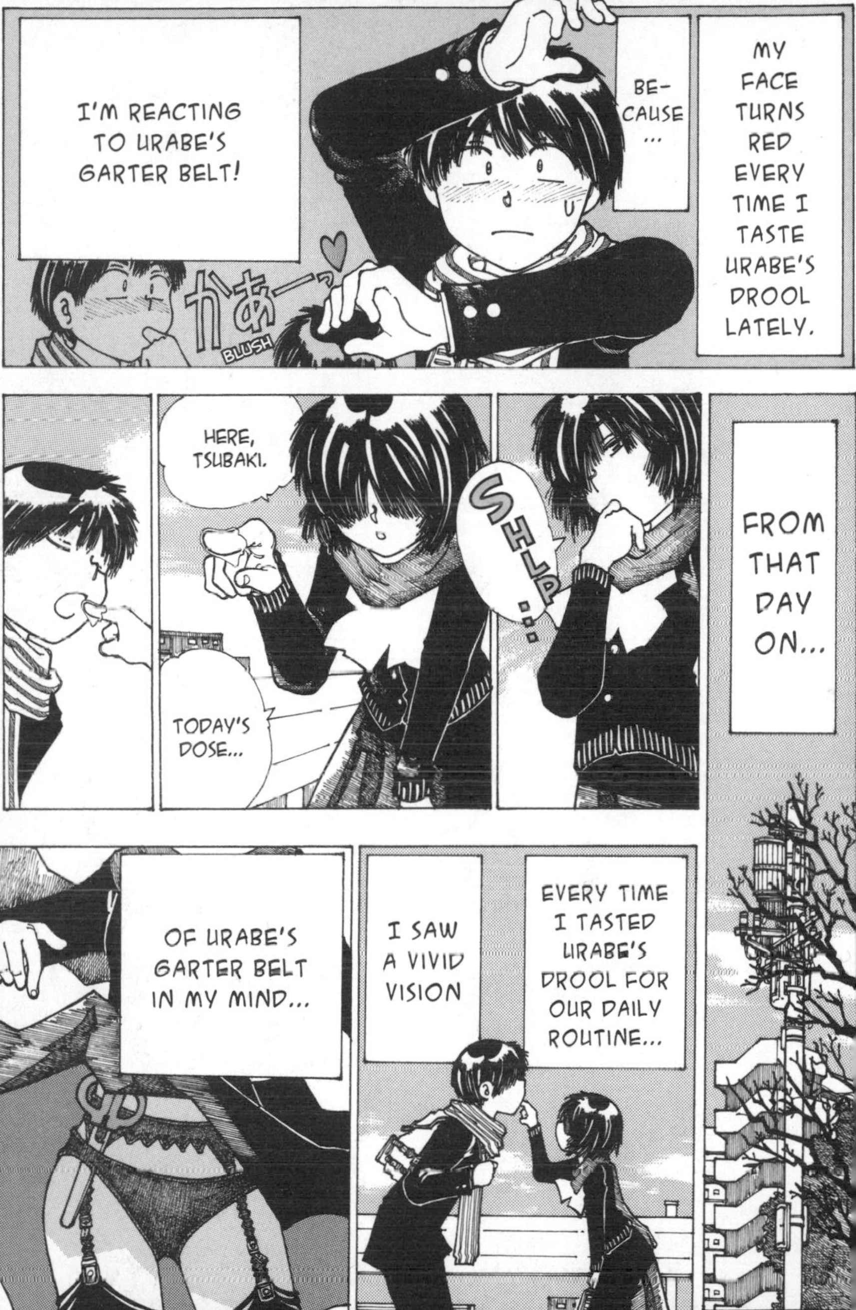
MY FACE TURNS RED EVERY TIME I TASTE URABE'S DROOL LATELY.
BE-CAUSE ...
I'M REACTING TO URABE'S GARTER BELT!
かあーっ
BLUSH
FROM THAT DAY ON...
SHLP..
HERE, TSUBAKI.
TODAY'S DOSE...
EVERY TIME I TASTED URABE'S DROOL FOR OUR DAILY ROUTINE...
I SAW A VIVID VISION
OF URABE'S GARTER BELT IN MY MIND...

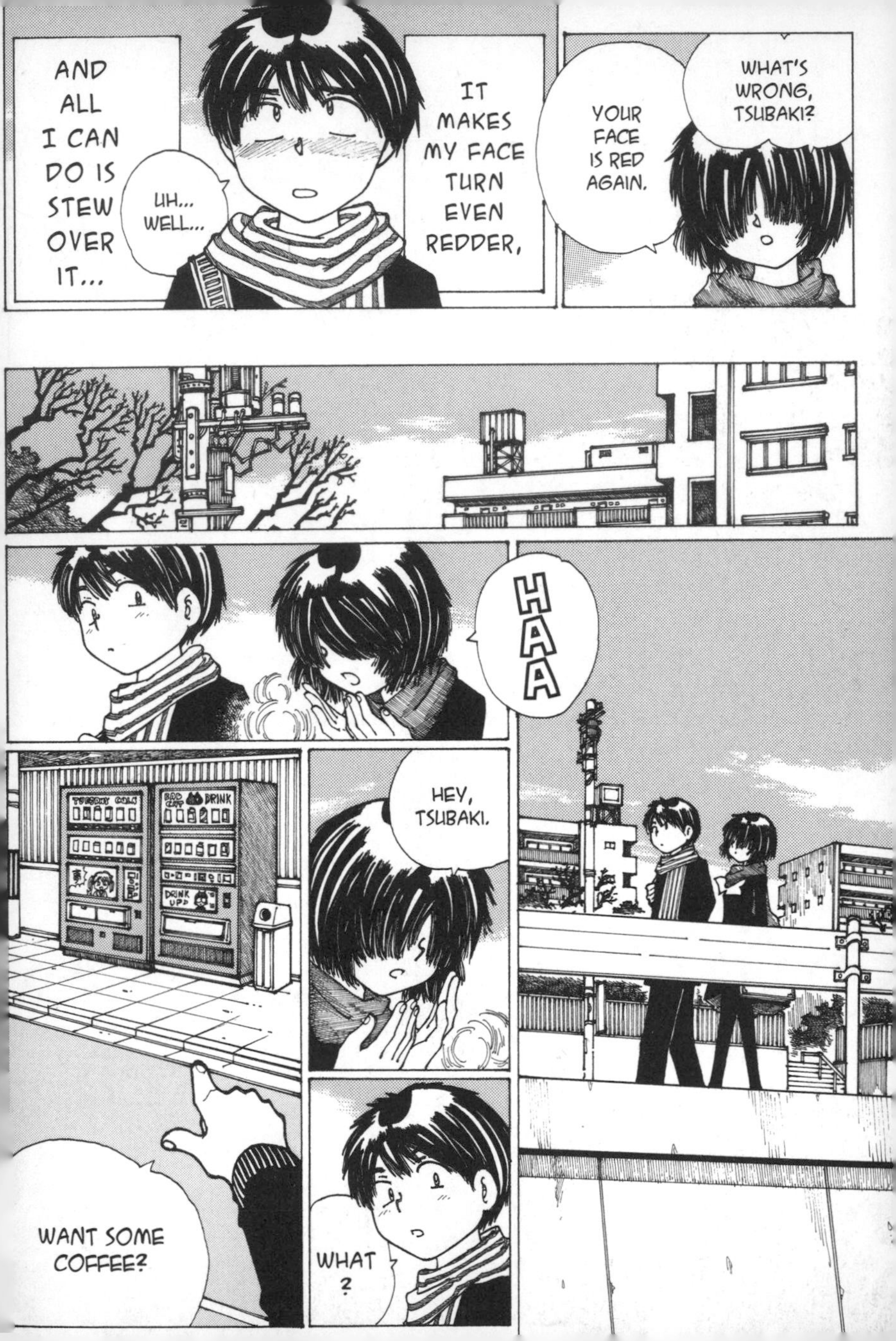
WHAT'S WRONG, TSUBAKI?
YOUR FACE IS RED AGAIN.
IT MAKES MY FACE TURN EVEN REDDER,
UH... WELL...
AND ALL I CAN DO IS STEW OVER IT...
HAA
HEY, TSUBAKI.
WHAT?
DRINK
WANT SOME COFFEE?

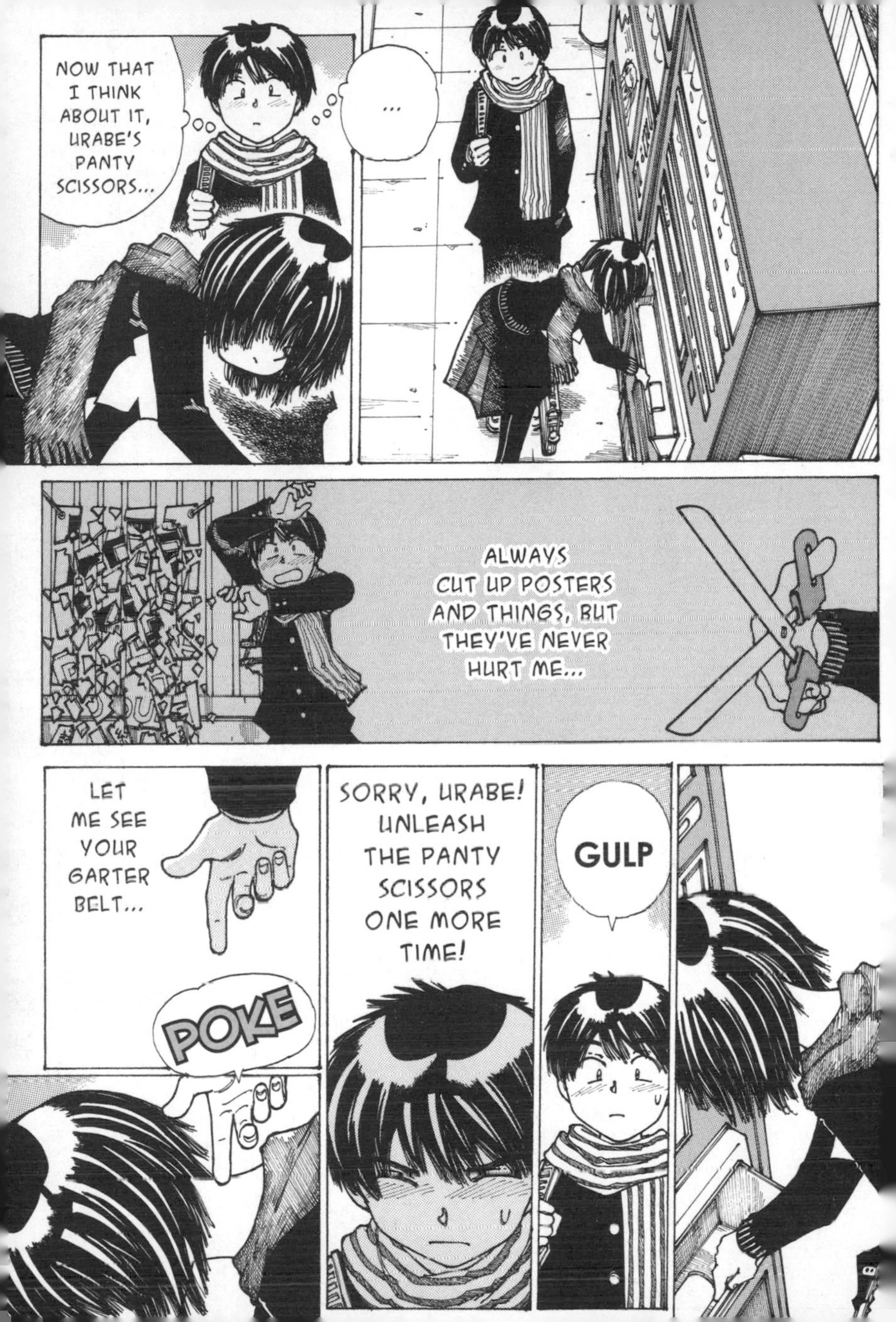
...
NOW THAT I THINK ABOUT IT, URABE'S PANTY SCISSORS...
ALWAYS CUT UP POSTERS AND THINGS, BUT THEY'VE NEVER HURT ME...
GULP
SORRY, URABE! UNLEASH THE PANTY SCISSORS ONE MORE TIME!
LET ME SEE YOUR GARTER BELT...
POKE

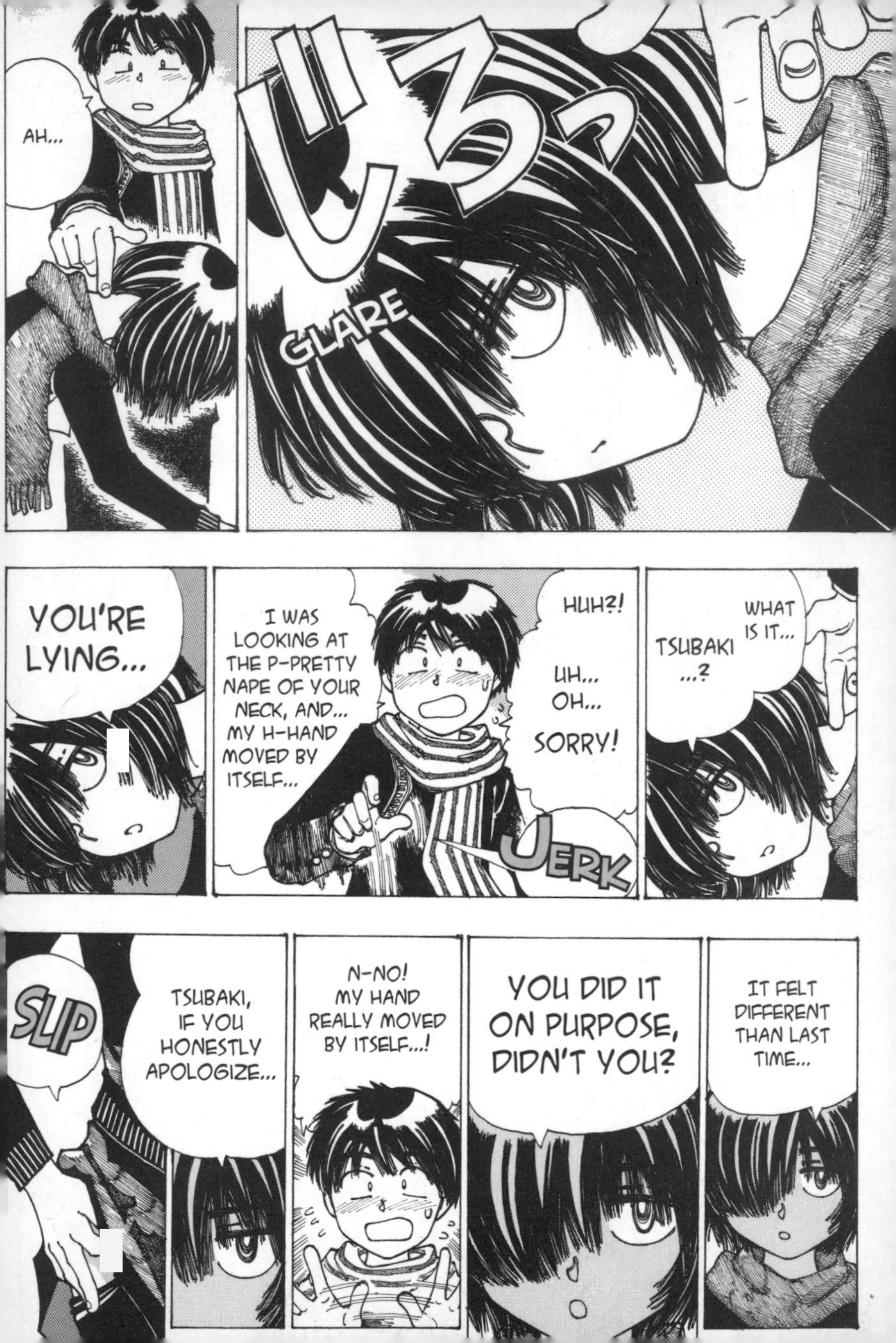
じろっ
GLARE
AH...
WHAT IS IT...
TSUBAKI ...?
HUH?!
UH... OH...
SORRY!
I WAS LOOKING AT THE P-PRETTY NAPE OF YOUR NECK, AND... MY H-HAND MOVED BY ITSELF...
JERK
YOU'RE LYING...
IT FELT DIFFERENT THAN LAST TIME...
YOU DID IT ON PURPOSE, DIDN'T YOU?
N-NO! MY HAND REALLY MOVED BY ITSELF...!
TSUBAKI, IF YOU HONESTLY APOLOGIZE...
SLIP

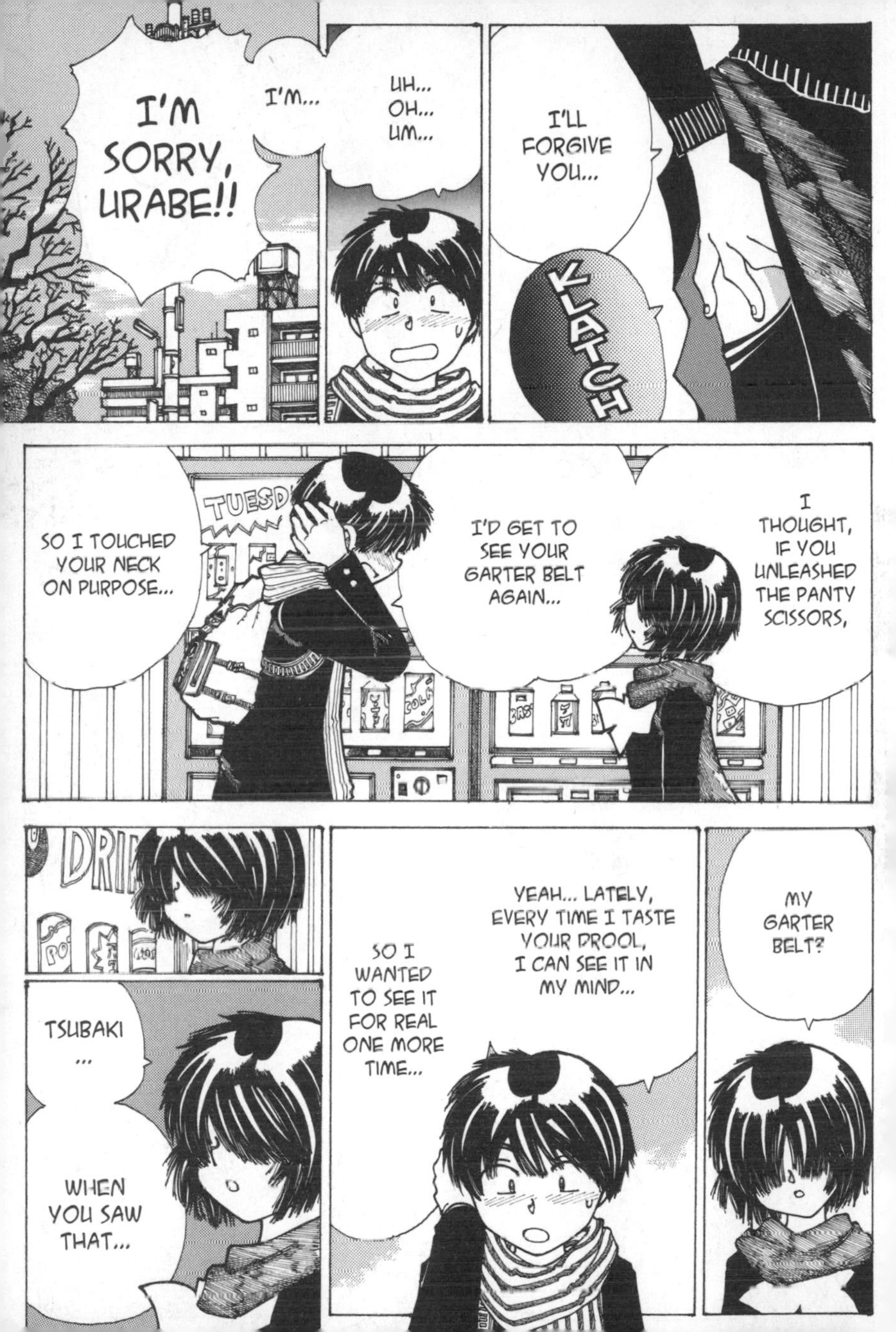
I'LL FORGIVE YOU...
KLATCH
UH... OH... UM...
I'M...
I'M SORRY, URABE!!
I THOUGHT, IF YOU UNLEASHED THE PANTY SCISSORS,
I'D GET TO SEE YOUR GARTER BELT AGAIN...
SO I TOUCHED YOUR NECK ON PURPOSE...
MY GARTER BELT?
YEAH... LATELY, EVERY TIME I TASTE YOUR DROOL, I CAN SEE IT IN MY MIND...
SO I WANTED TO SEE IT FOR REAL ONE MORE TIME...
TSUBAKI ...
WHEN YOU SAW THAT...

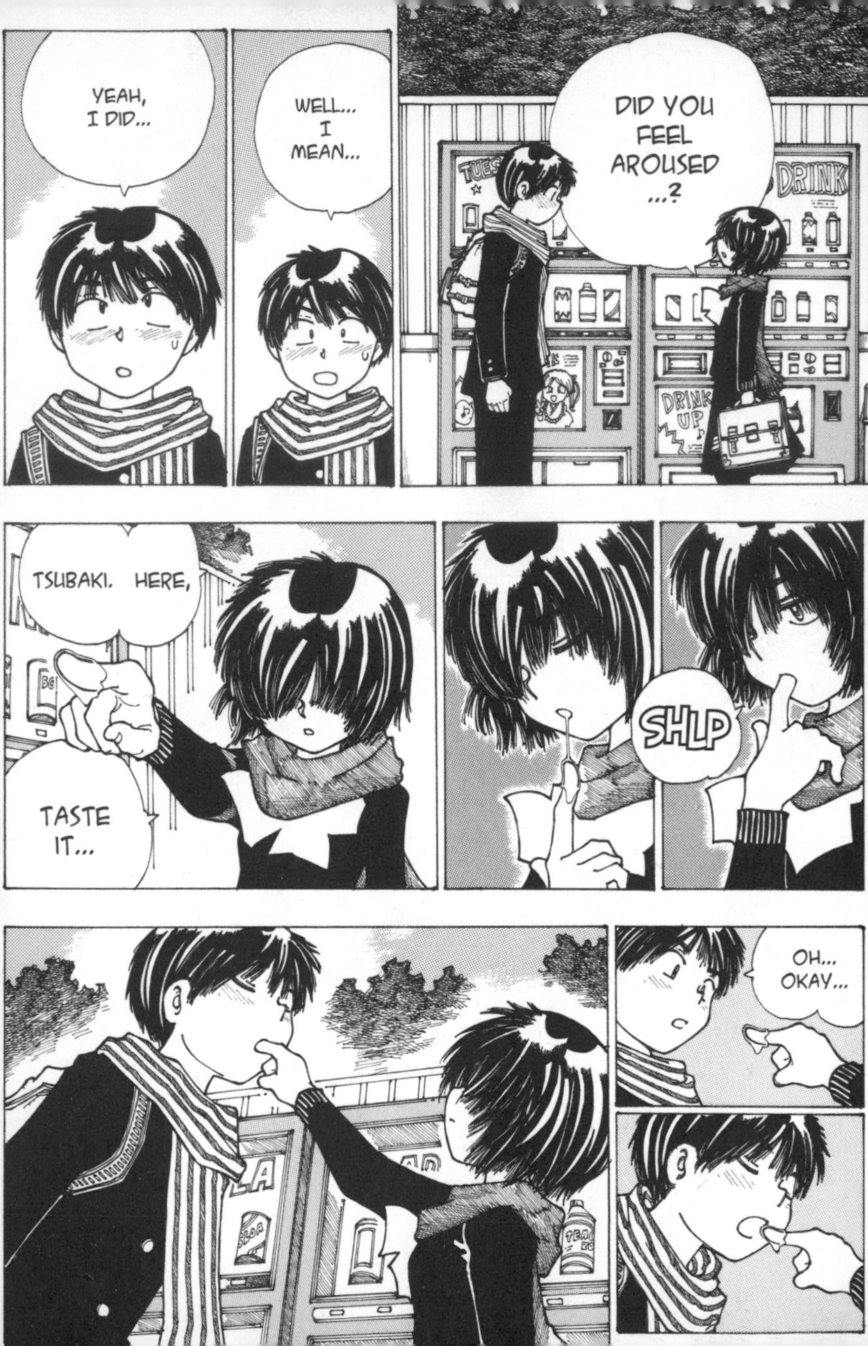
DID YOU FEEL AROUSED ...?
WELL... I MEAN...
YEAH, I DID...
SHLP
TSUBAKI. HERE,
TASTE IT...
OH... OKAY...

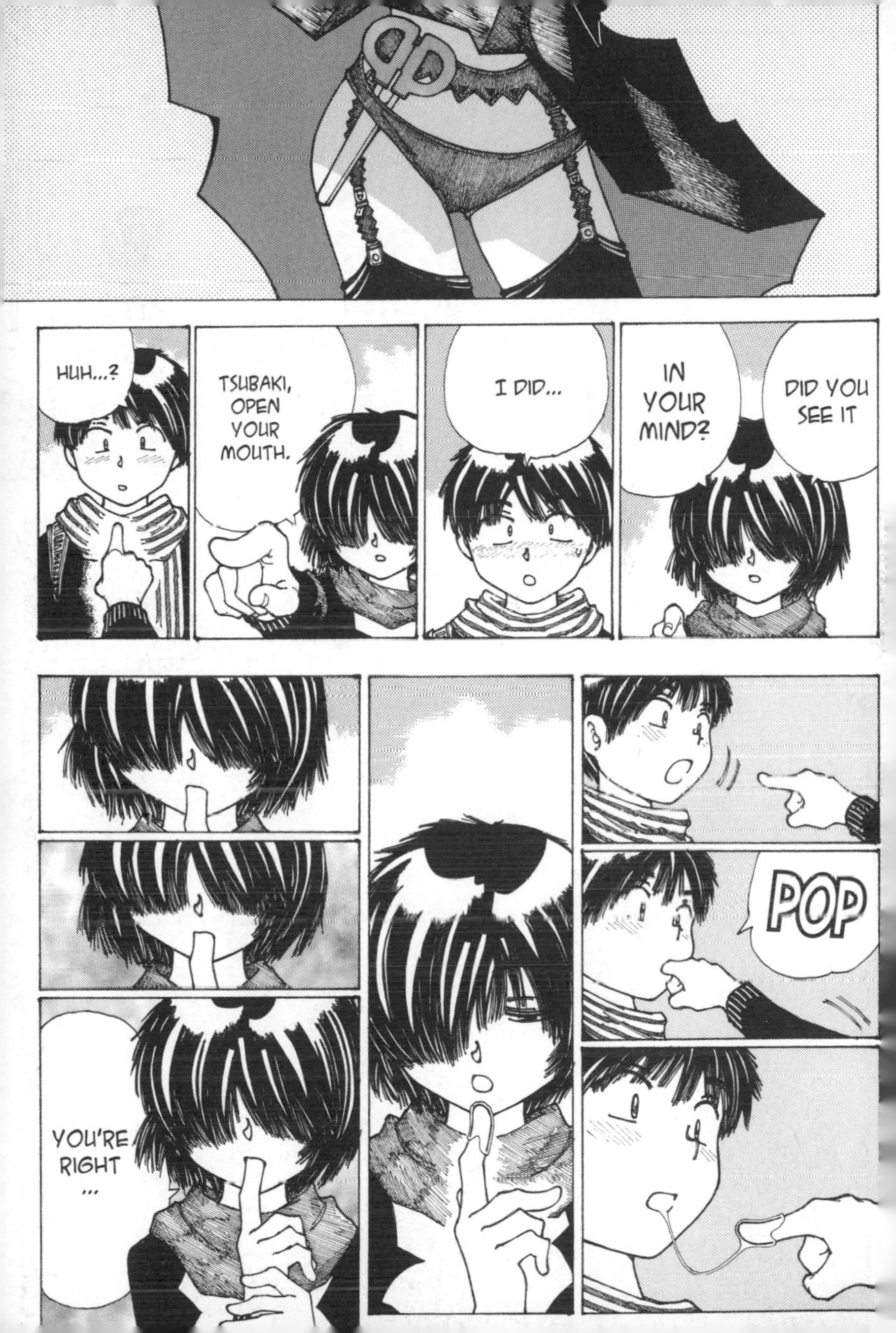
DID YOU SEE IT
IN YOUR MIND?
I DID...
TSUBAKI, OPEN YOUR MOUTH.
HUH...?
POP
YOU'RE RIGHT ...

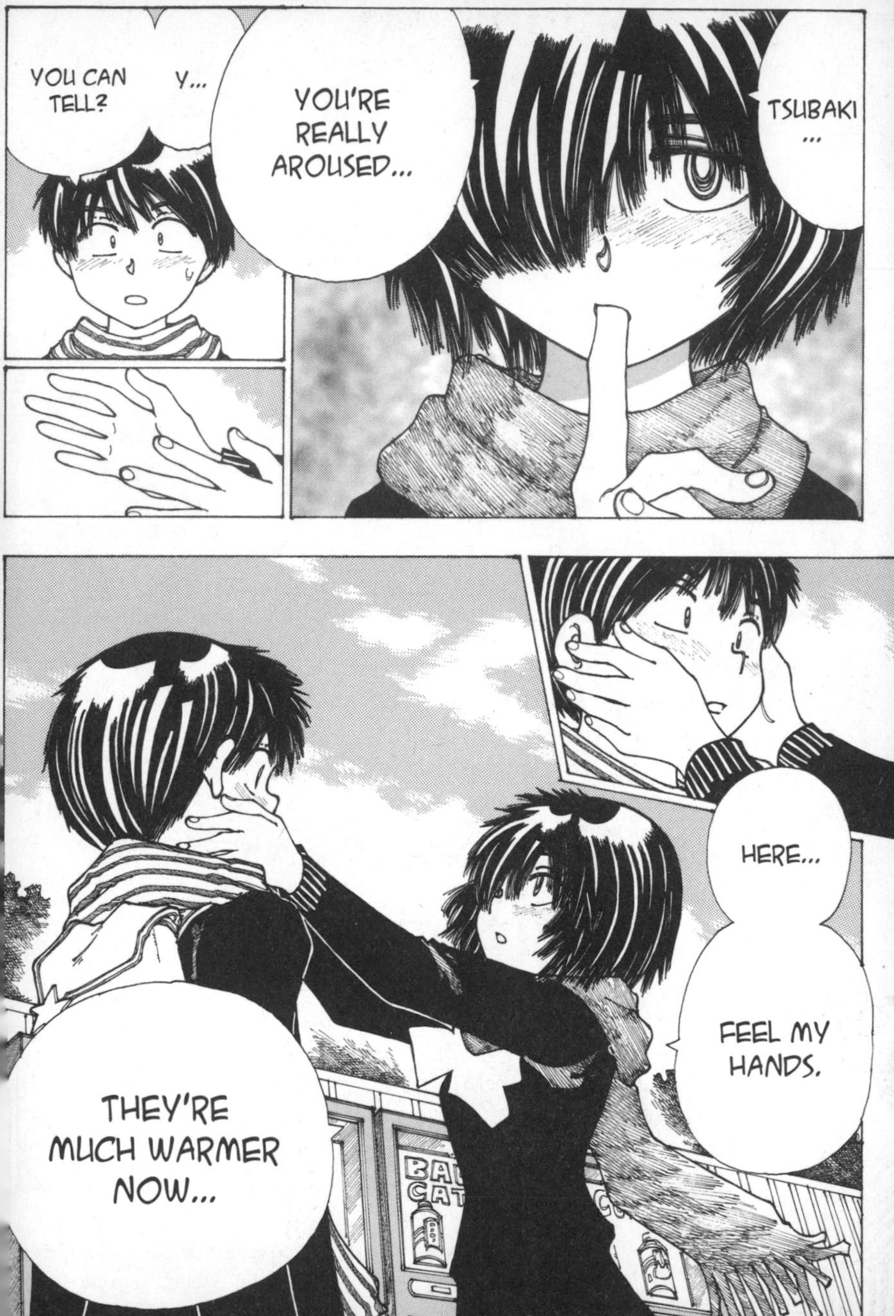
TSUBAKI ...
YOU'RE REALLY AROUSED...
Y...
YOU CAN TELL?
HERE...
FEEL MY HANDS.
THEY'RE MUCH WARMER NOW...

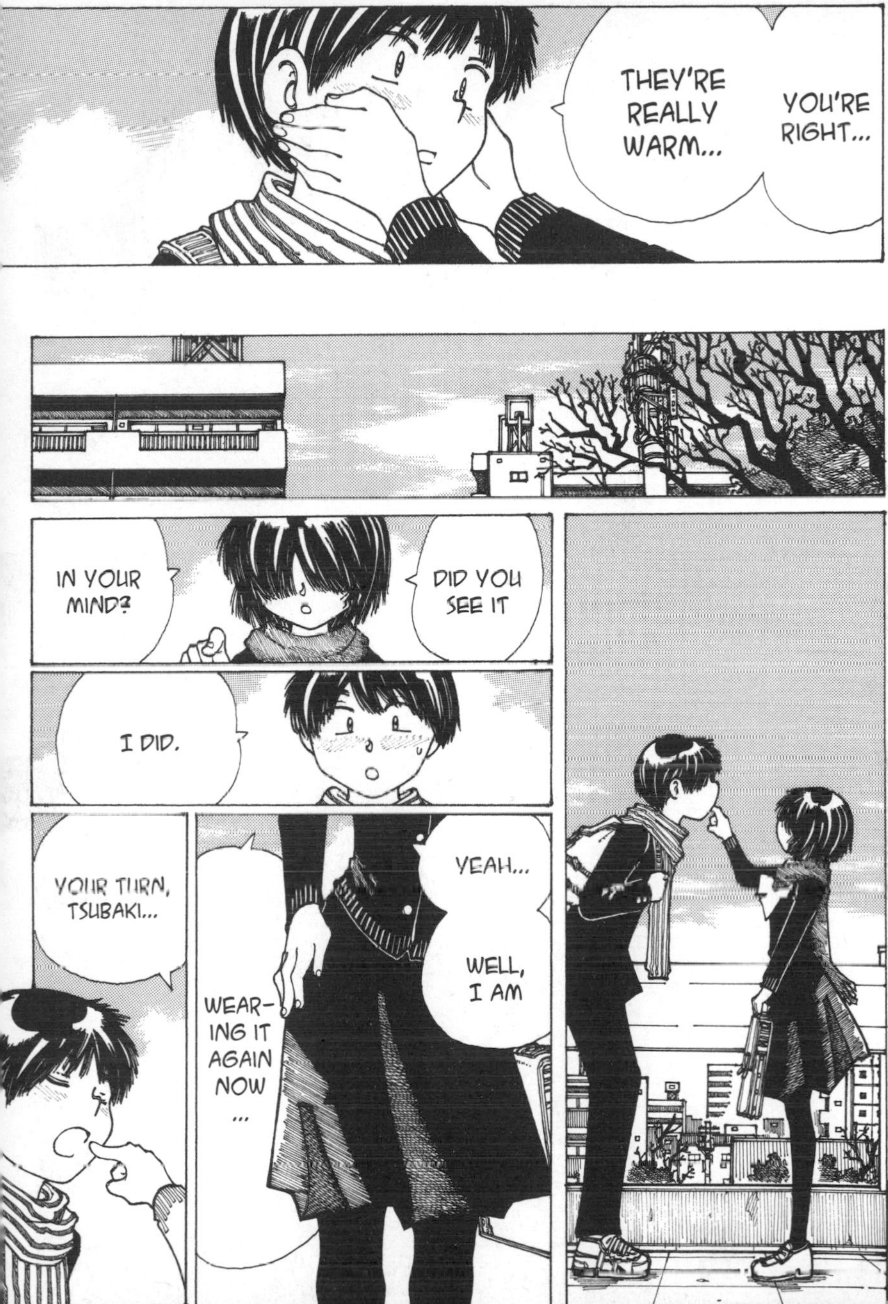
YOU'RE RIGHT...
THEY'RE REALLY WARM...
DID YOU SEE IT
IN YOUR MIND?
I DID.
YEAH...
WELL, I AM
WEAR-ING IT AGAIN NOW ...
YOUR TURN, TSUBAKI...

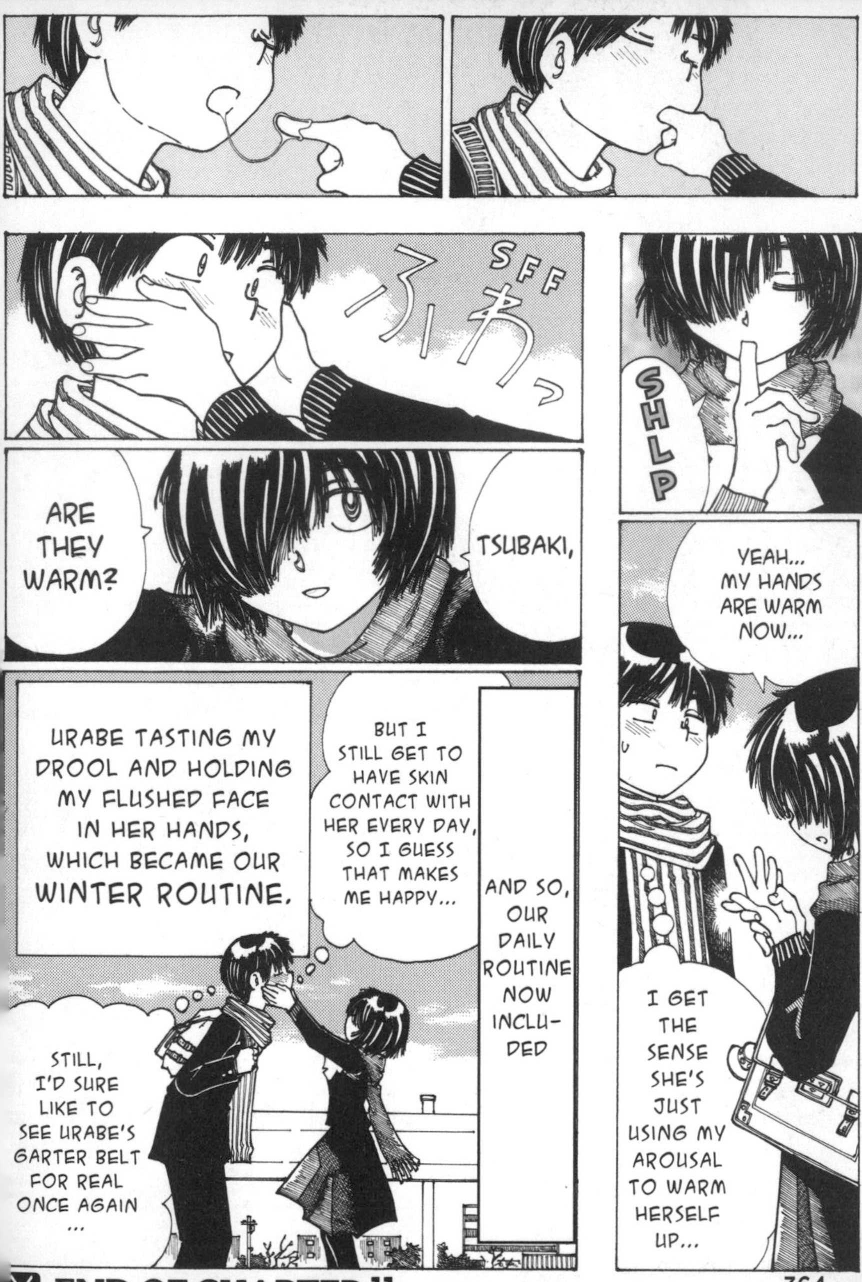
SHLP
SFF
ふあっ
TSUBAKI,
ARE THEY WARM?
YEAH... MY HANDS ARE WARM NOW...
I GET THE SENSE SHE'S JUST USING MY AROUSAL TO WARM HERSELF UP...
AND SO, OUR DAILY ROUTINE NOW INCLU-DED
BUT I STILL GET TO HAVE SKIN CONTACT WITH HER EVERY DAY, SO I GUESS THAT MAKES ME HAPPY...
URABE TASTING MY DROOL AND HOLDING MY FLUSHED FACE IN HER HANDS, WHICH BECAME OUR WINTER ROUTINE.
STILL, I'D SURE LIKE TO SEE URABE'S GARTER BELT FOR REAL ONCE AGAIN ...

END OF CHAPTER 11

CHAPTER 12: MYSTERIOUS MEMORY

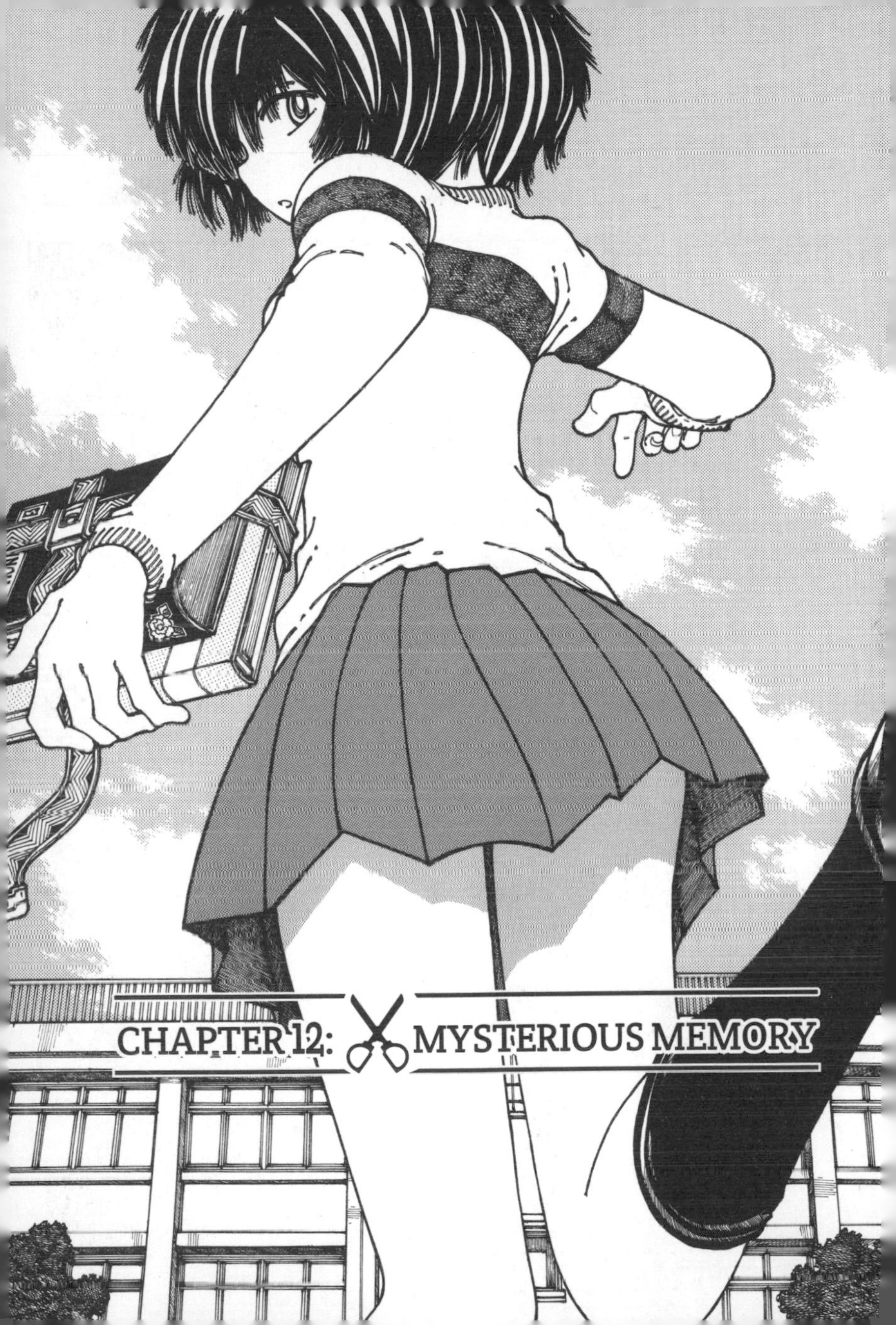

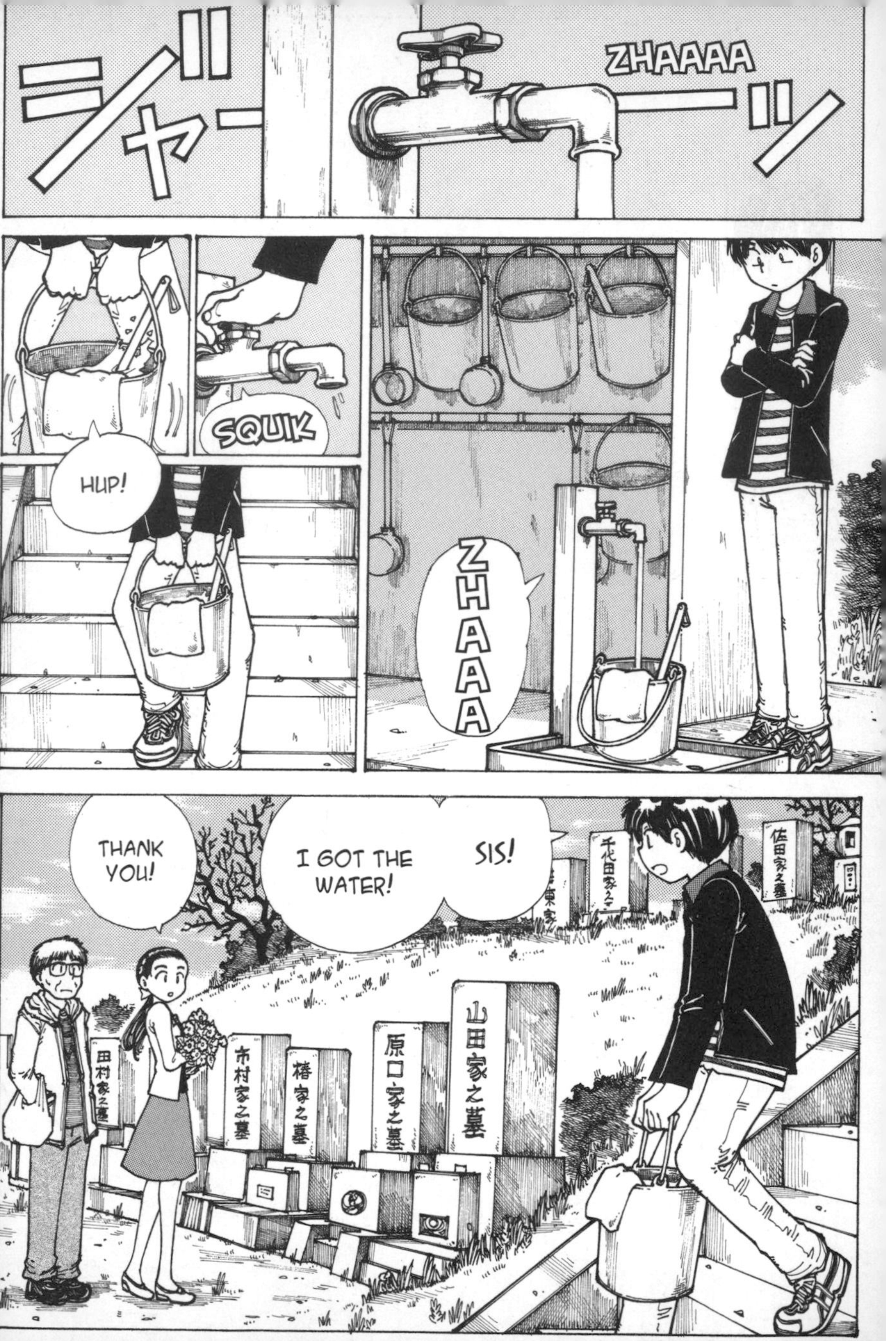

シャー
ーッ
ZHAAAA
ZHAAAA
SQUIK
HUP!
SIS!
I GOT THE WATER!
THANK YOU!
佐田家之墓
千代田家之墓
山田家之墓
原口家之墓
椿家之墓
市村家之墓
田村家之墓

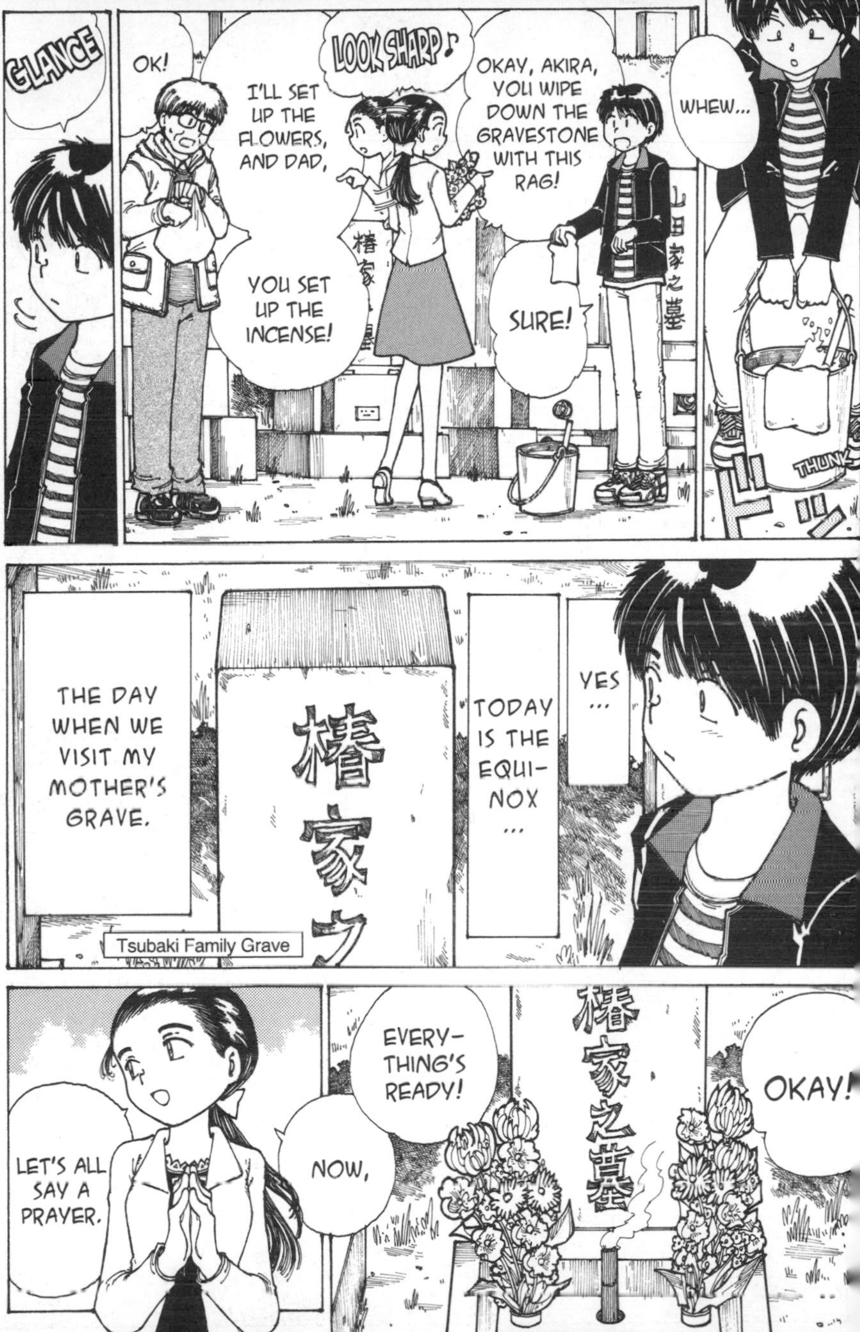
WHEW...
THUNK
OKAY, AKIRA, YOU WIPE DOWN THE GRAVESTONE WITH THIS RAG!
SURE!
山田家之墓
LOOK SHARP♪
I'LL SET UP THE FLOWERS, AND DAD,
YOU SET UP THE INCENSE!
OK!
GLANCE
YES ...
TODAY IS THE EQUI-NOX ...
THE DAY WHEN WE VISIT MY MOTHER'S GRAVE.
Tsubaki Family Grave
OKAY!
椿家之墓
EVERY-THING'S READY!
NOW,
LET'S ALL SAY A PRAYER.

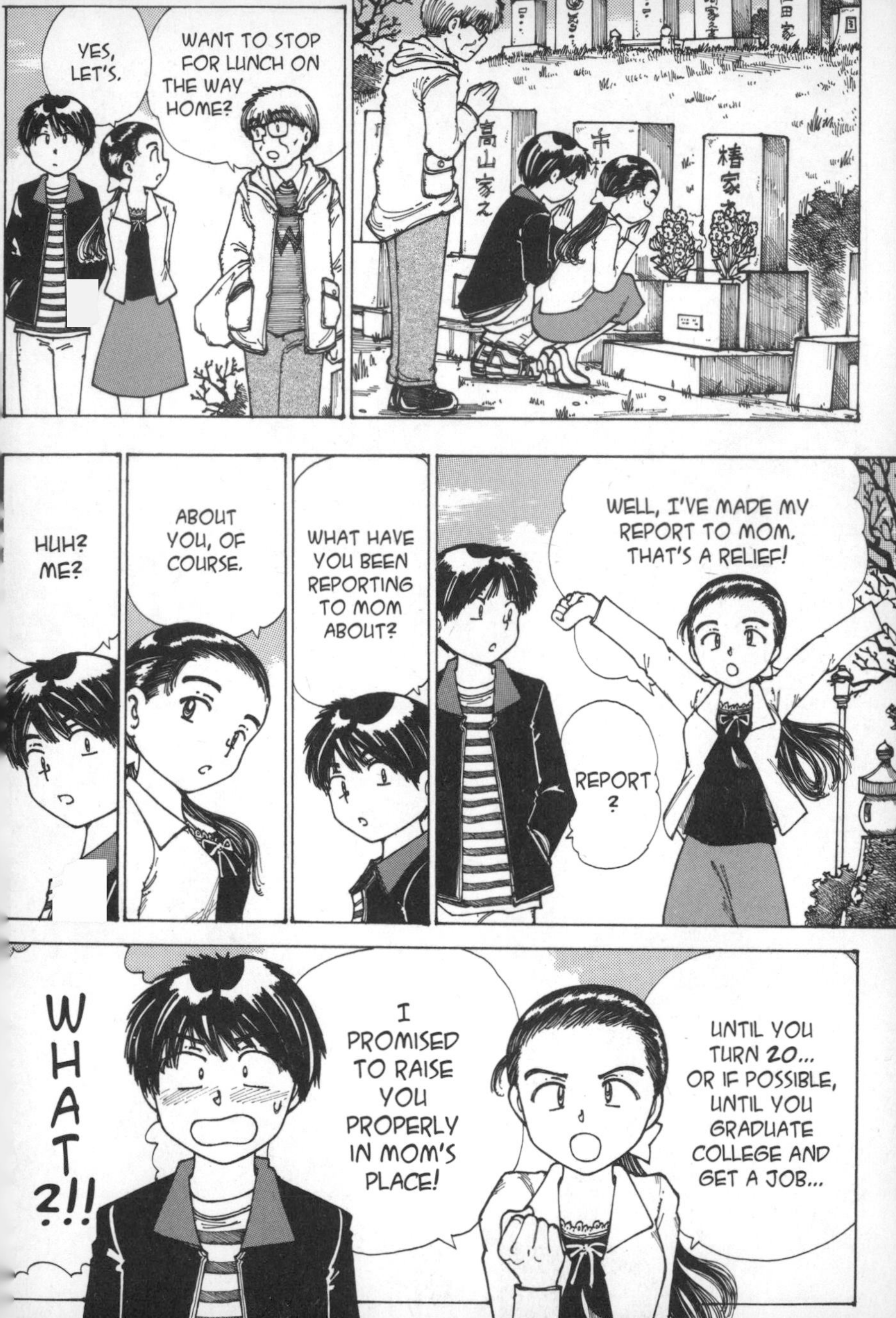
WANT TO STOP FOR LUNCH ON THE WAY HOME?
YES, LET'S.
WELL, I'VE MADE MY REPORT TO MOM. THAT'S A RELIEF!
REPORT?
WHAT HAVE YOU BEEN REPORTING TO MOM ABOUT?
ABOUT YOU, OF COURSE.
HUH? ME?
UNTIL YOU TURN 20... OR IF POSSIBLE, UNTIL YOU GRADUATE COLLEGE AND GET A JOB...
I PROMISED TO RAISE YOU PROPERLY IN MOM'S PLACE!
WHAT?!!

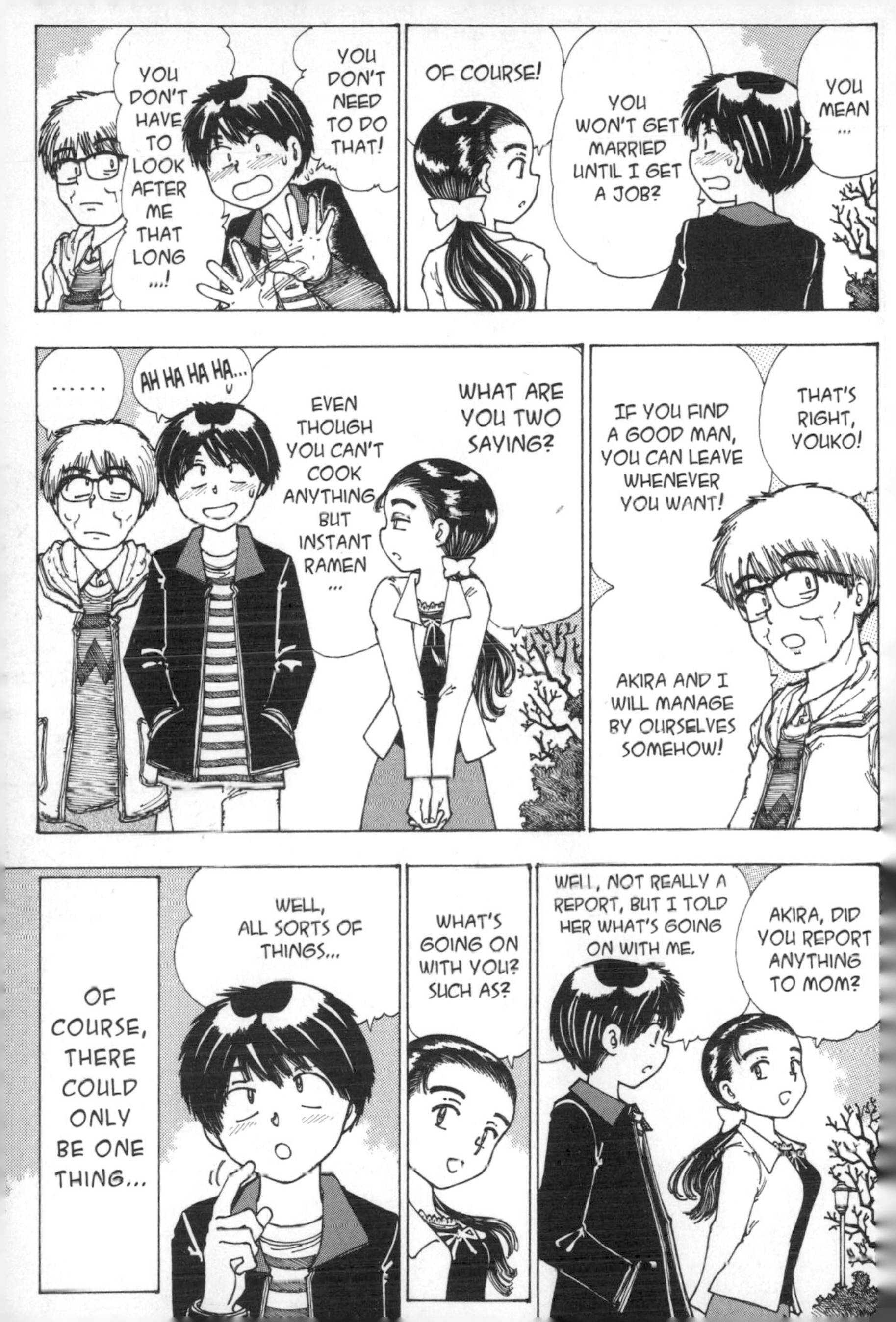
YOU MEAN ...
YOU WON'T GET MARRIED UNTIL I GET A JOB?
OF COURSE!
YOU DON'T NEED TO DO THAT!
YOU DON'T HAVE TO LOOK AFTER ME THAT LONG ...!
THAT'S RIGHT, YOUKO!
IF YOU FIND A GOOD MAN, YOU CAN LEAVE WHENEVER YOU WANT!
AKIRA AND I WILL MANAGE BY OURSELVES SOMEHOW!
WHAT ARE YOU TWO SAYING?
EVEN THOUGH YOU CAN'T COOK ANYTHING BUT INSTANT RAMEN ...
AH HA HA HA...
......
AKIRA, DID YOU REPORT ANYTHING TO MOM?
WELL, NOT REALLY A REPORT, BUT I TOLD HER WHAT'S GOING ON WITH ME.
WHAT'S GOING ON WITH YOU? SUCH AS?
WELL, ALL SORTS OF THINGS...
OF COURSE, THERE COULD ONLY BE ONE THING...

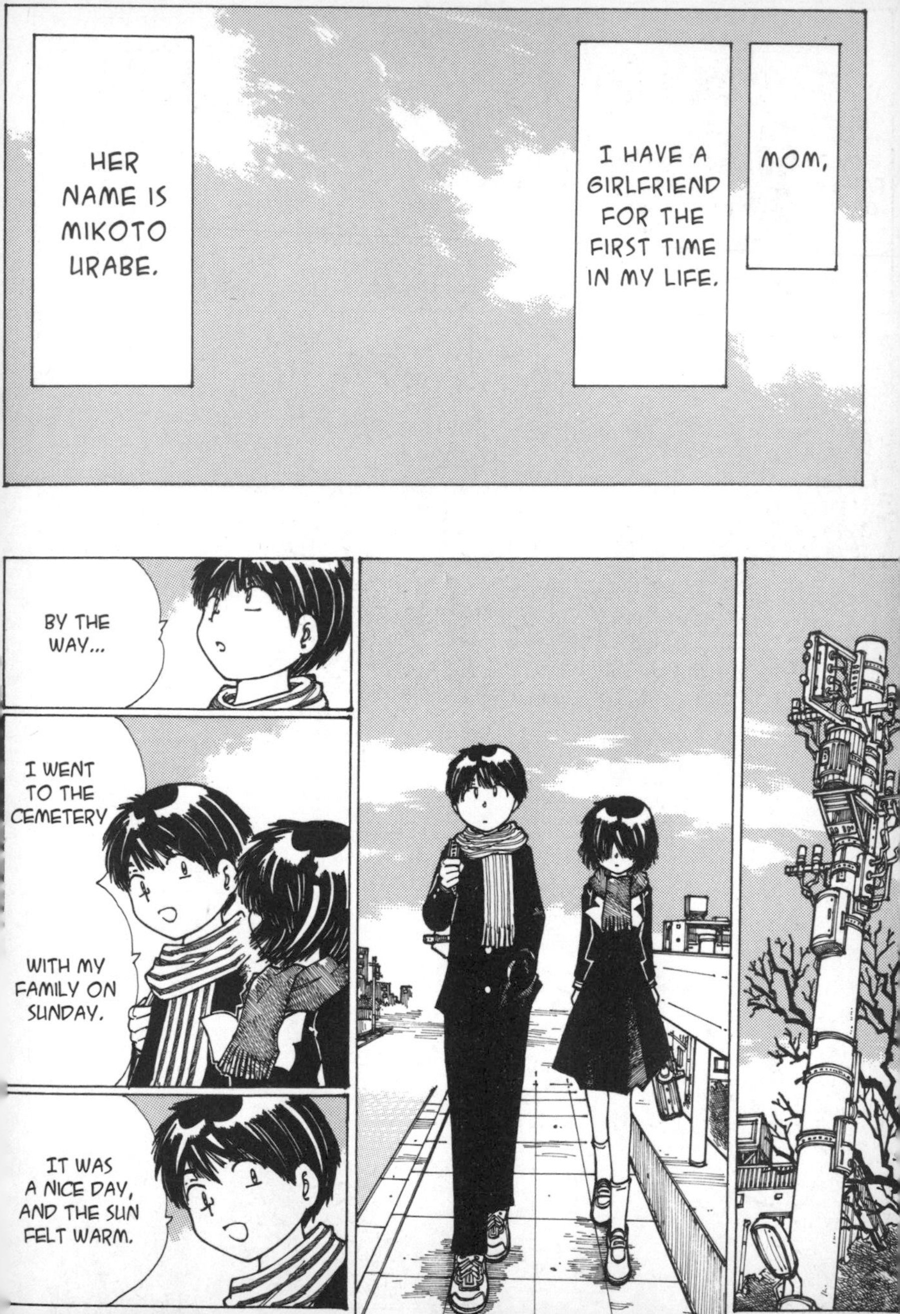
MOM,
I HAVE A GIRLFRIEND FOR THE FIRST TIME IN MY LIFE.
HER NAME IS MIKOTO URABE.
BY THE WAY...
I WENT TO THE CEMETERY
WITH MY FAMILY ON SUNDAY.
IT WAS A NICE DAY, AND THE SUN FELT WARM.

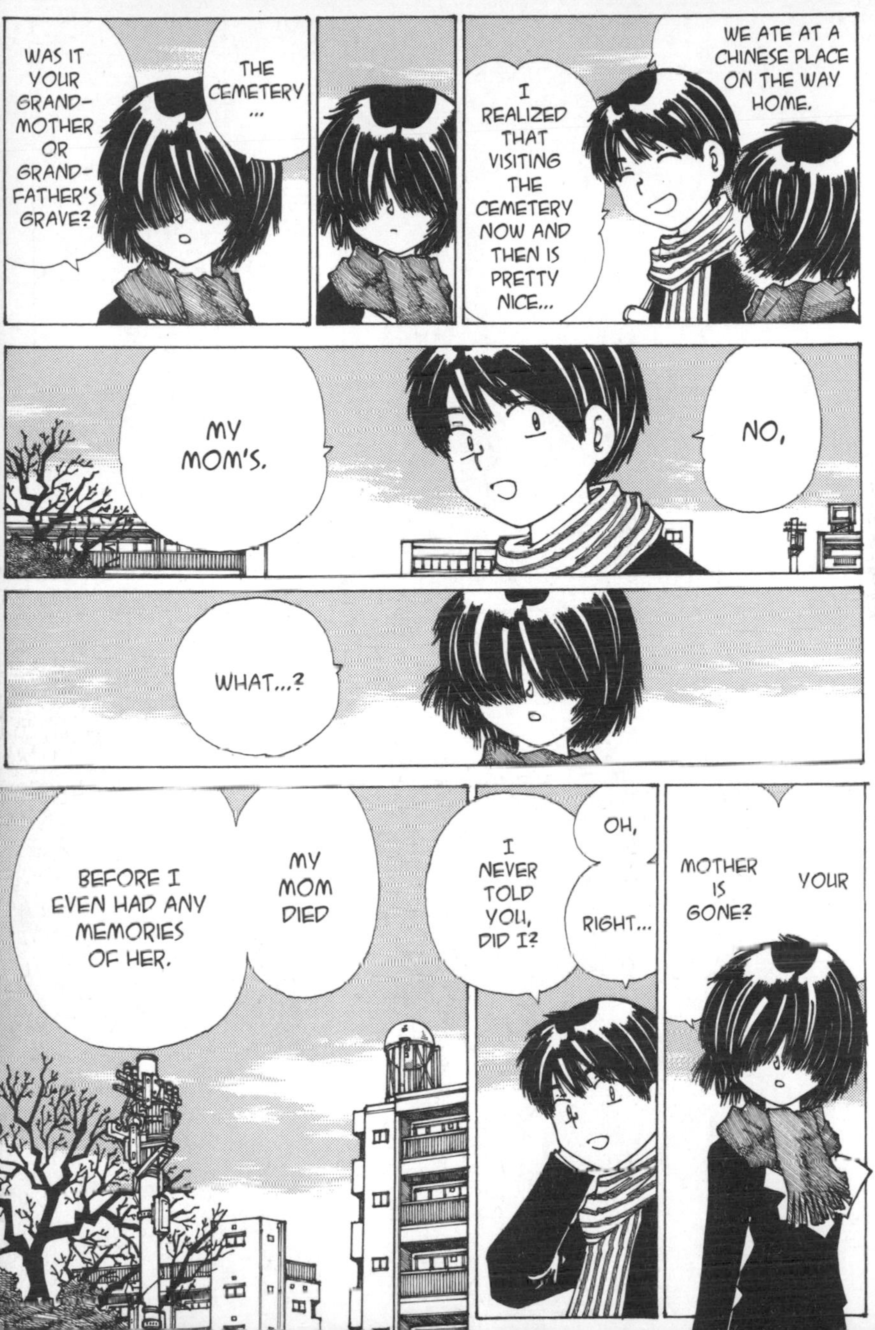
WE ATE AT A CHINESE PLACE ON THE WAY HOME.
I REALIZED THAT VISITING THE CEMETERY NOW AND THEN IS PRETTY NICE...
THE CEMETERY ...
WAS IT YOUR GRANDMOTHER OR GRANDFATHER'S GRAVE?
NO,
MY MOM'S.
WHAT...?
YOUR
MOTHER IS GONE?
OH,
RIGHT...
I NEVER TOLD YOU, DID I?
MY MOM DIED
BEFORE I EVEN HAD ANY MEMORIES OF HER.

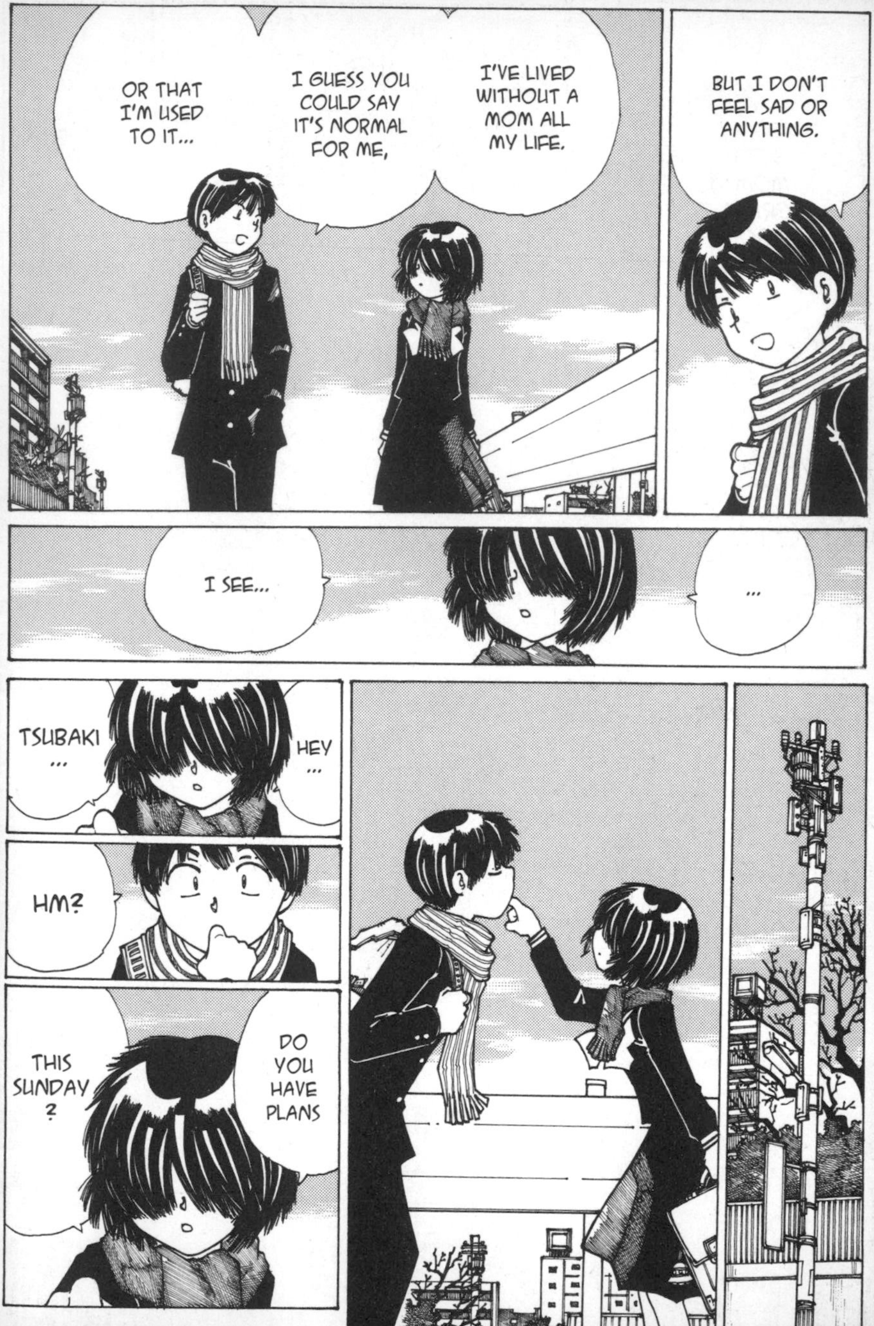
BUT I DON'T FEEL SAD OR ANYTHING.
I'VE LIVED WITHOUT A MOM ALL MY LIFE.
I GUESS YOU COULD SAY IT'S NORMAL FOR ME,
OR THAT I'M USED TO IT...
...
I SEE...
HEY ...
TSUBAKI ...
HM?
DO YOU HAVE PLANS
THIS SUNDAY ?

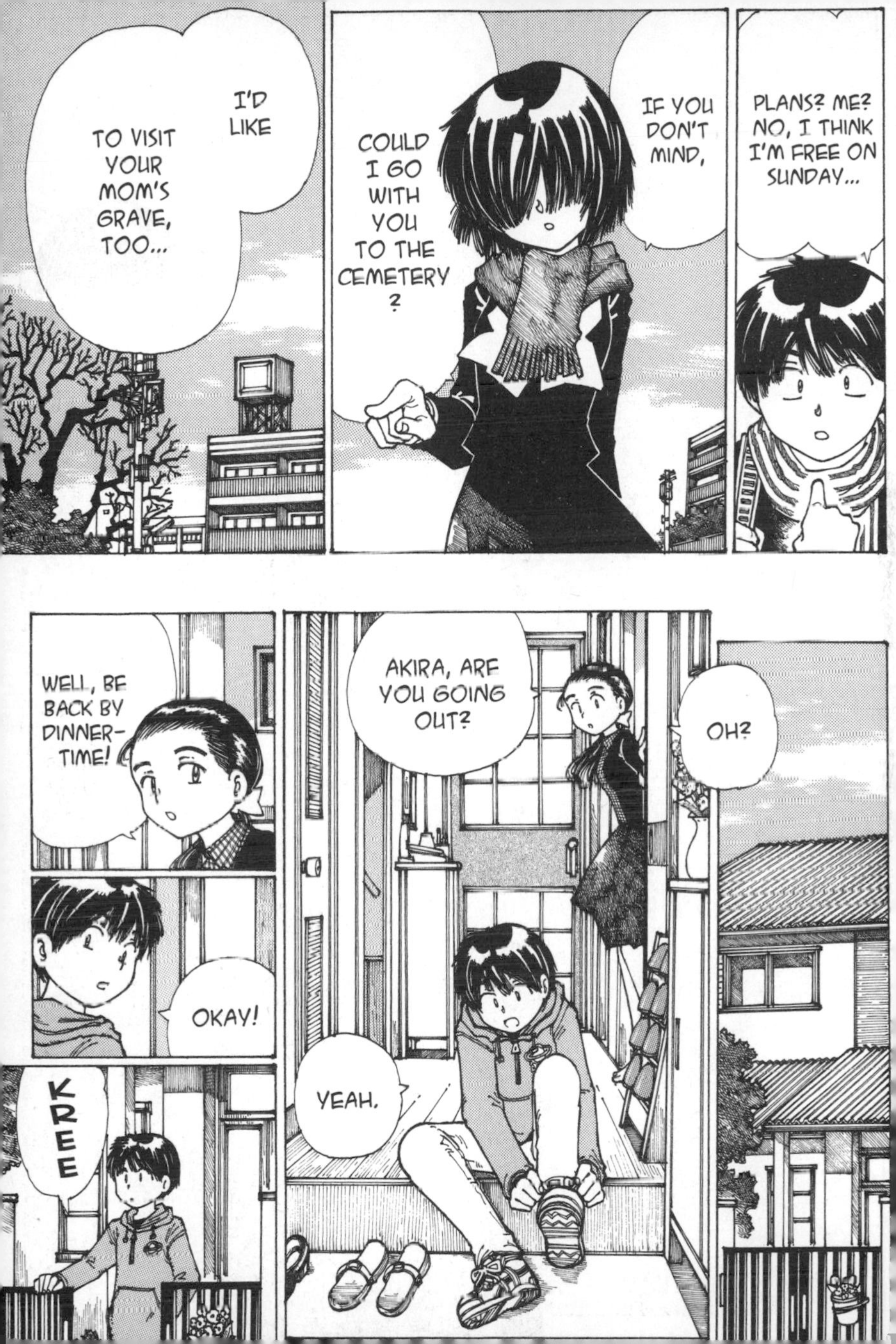
PLANS? ME? NO, I THINK I'M FREE ON SUNDAY...
IF YOU DON'T MIND,
COULD I GO WITH YOU TO THE CEMETERY?
I'D LIKE
TO VISIT YOUR MOM'S GRAVE, TOO...
OH?
AKIRA, ARE YOU GOING OUT?
YEAH.
WELL, BE BACK BY DINNER-TIME!
OKAY!
KREE

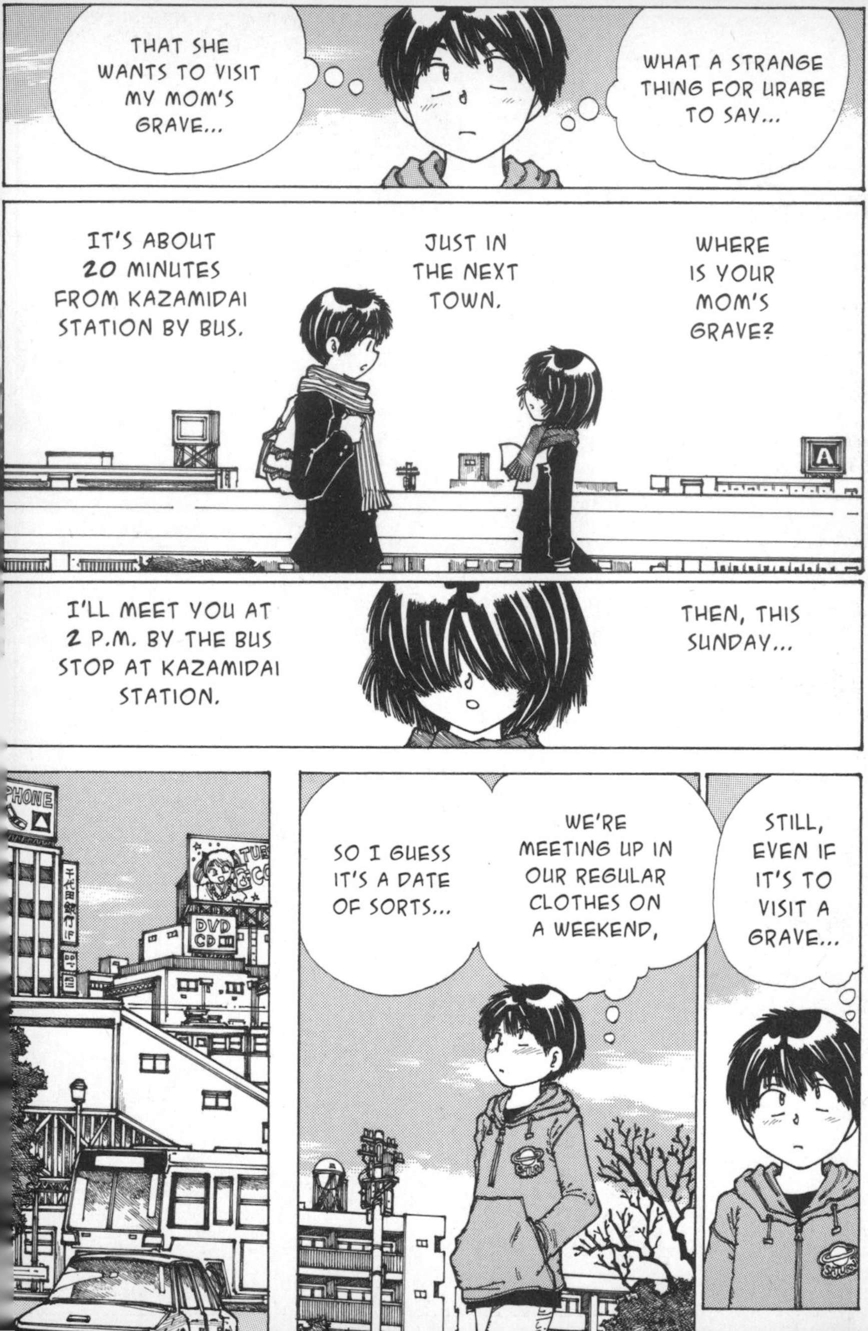
WHAT A STRANGE THING FOR URABE TO SAY...
THAT SHE WANTS TO VISIT MY MOM'S GRAVE...
WHERE IS YOUR MOM'S GRAVE?
JUST IN THE NEXT TOWN.
IT'S ABOUT 20 MINUTES FROM KAZAMIDAI STATION BY BUS.
THEN, THIS SUNDAY...
I'LL MEET YOU AT 2 P.M. BY THE BUS STOP AT KAZAMIDAI STATION.
STILL, EVEN IF IT'S TO VISIT A GRAVE...
WE'RE MEETING UP IN OUR REGULAR CLOTHES ON A WEEKEND,
SO I GUESS IT'S A DATE OF SORTS...
PHONE
DVD CD

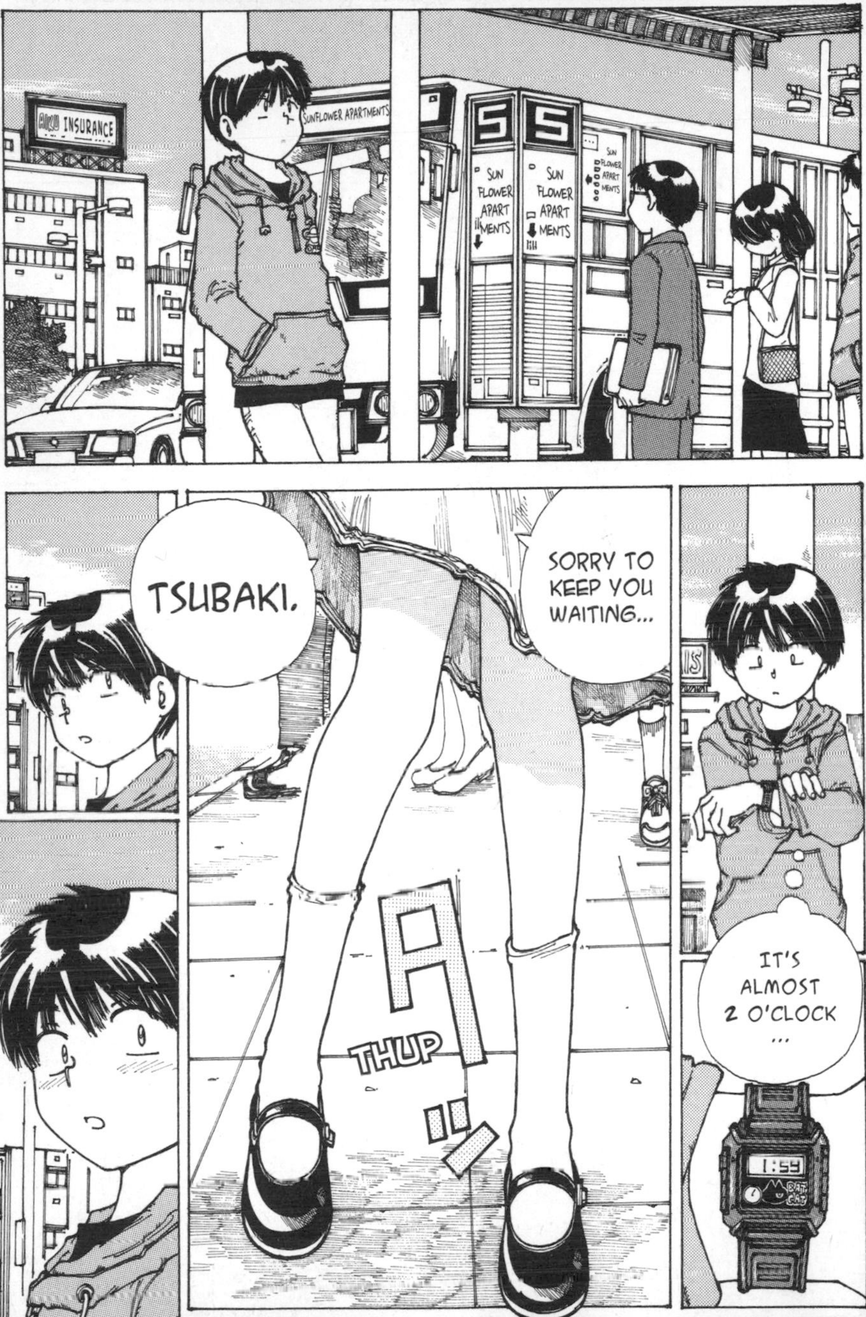
INSURANCE
SUNFLOWER APARTMENTS
SUN FLOWER APART MENTS
SUN FLOWER APART MENTS
SUN FLOWER APART MENTS
IT'S ALMOST 2 O'CLOCK ...
1:59
BAT CAT
SORRY TO KEEP YOU WAITING...
THUP
TSUBAKI.

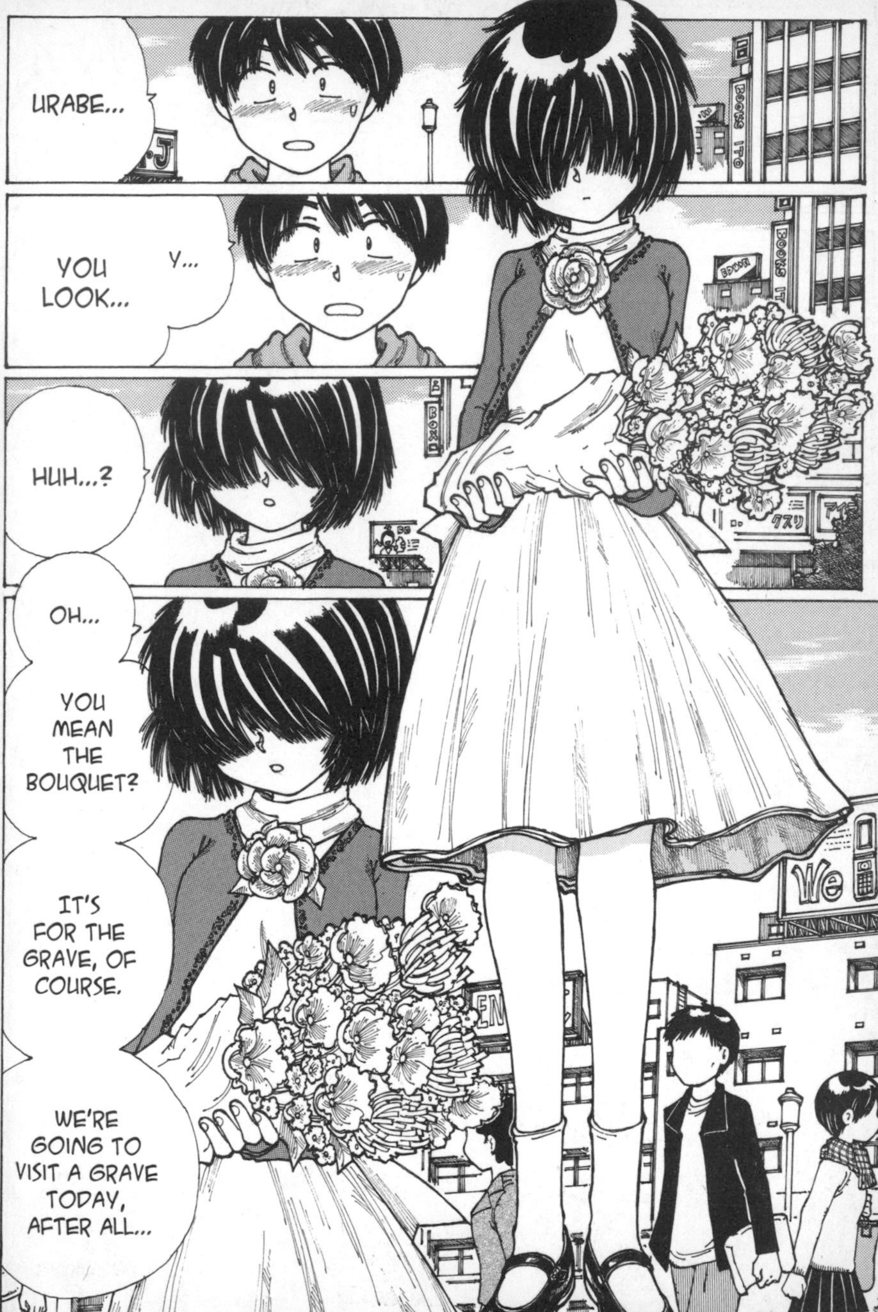
URABE...
YOU LOOK... Y...
HUH...?
OH...
YOU MEAN THE BOUQUET?
IT'S FOR THE GRAVE, OF COURSE.
WE'RE GOING TO VISIT A GRAVE TODAY, AFTER ALL...

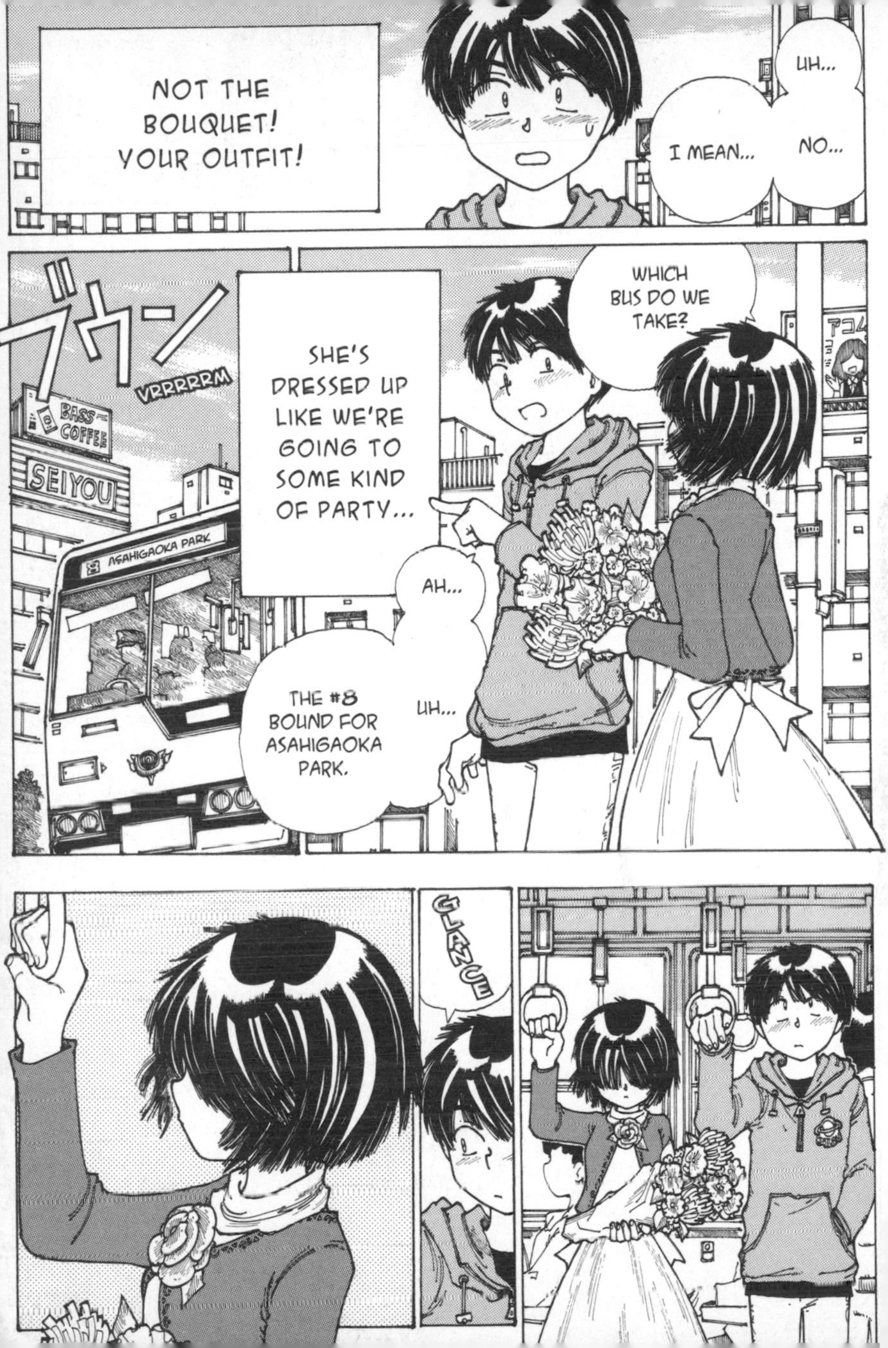
UH...
NO...
I MEAN...
NOT THE BOUQUET! YOUR OUTFIT!
WHICH BUS DO WE TAKE?
アコム
SHE'S DRESSED UP LIKE WE'RE GOING TO SOME KIND OF PARTY...
ブウーン
VRRRRRM
BASS COFFEE
SEIYOU
8 ASAHIGAOKA PARK
AH...
UH...
THE #8 BOUND FOR ASAHIGAOKA PARK.
GLANCE

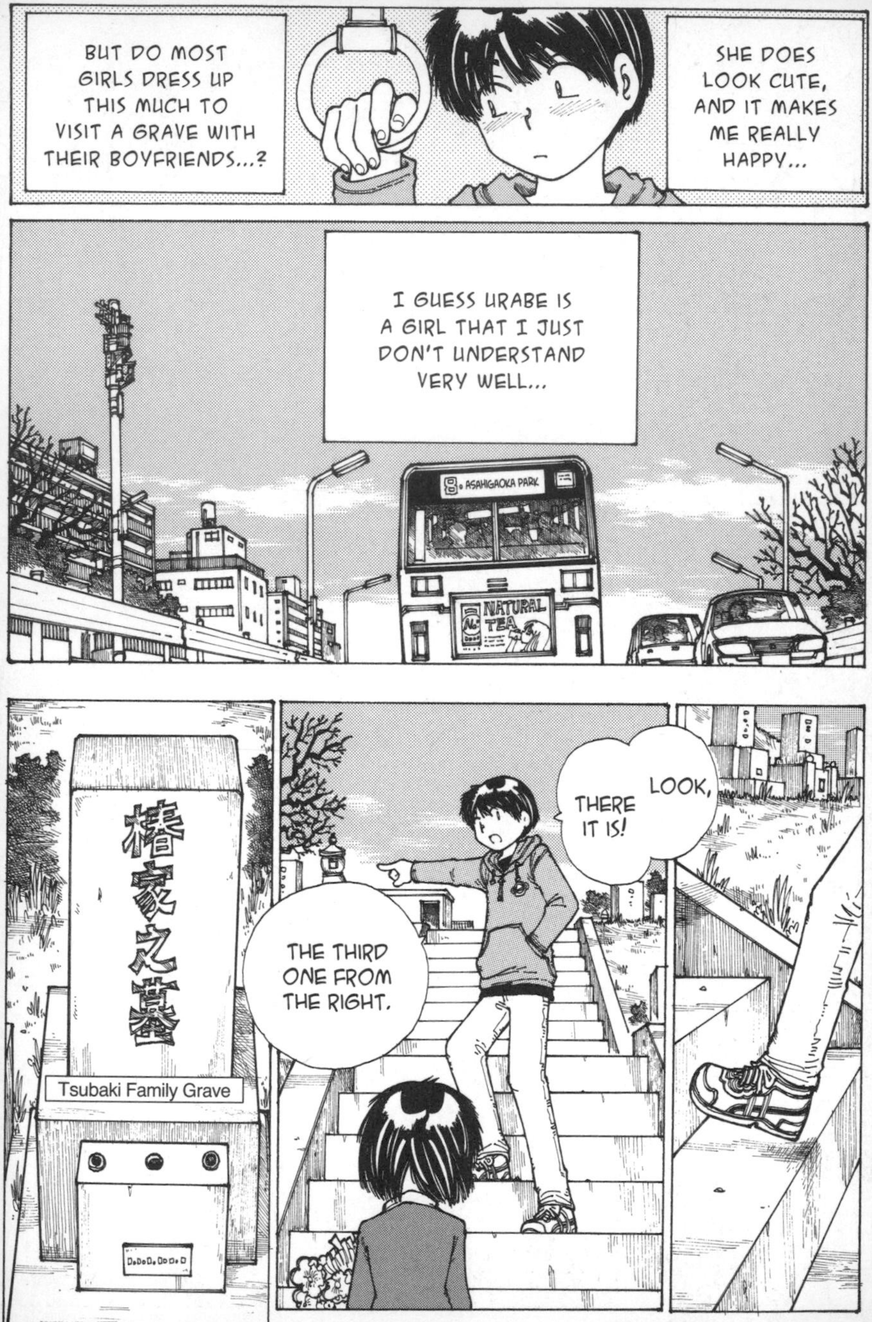
SHE DOES LOOK CUTE, AND IT MAKES ME REALLY HAPPY...
BUT DO MOST GIRLS DRESS UP THIS MUCH TO VISIT A GRAVE WITH THEIR BOYFRIENDS...?
I GUESS URABE IS A GIRL THAT I JUST DON'T UNDERSTAND VERY WELL...
ASAHIGAOKA PARK
NATURAL TEA
LOOK, THERE IT IS!
THE THIRD ONE FROM THE RIGHT.
椿家之墓
Tsubaki Family Grave

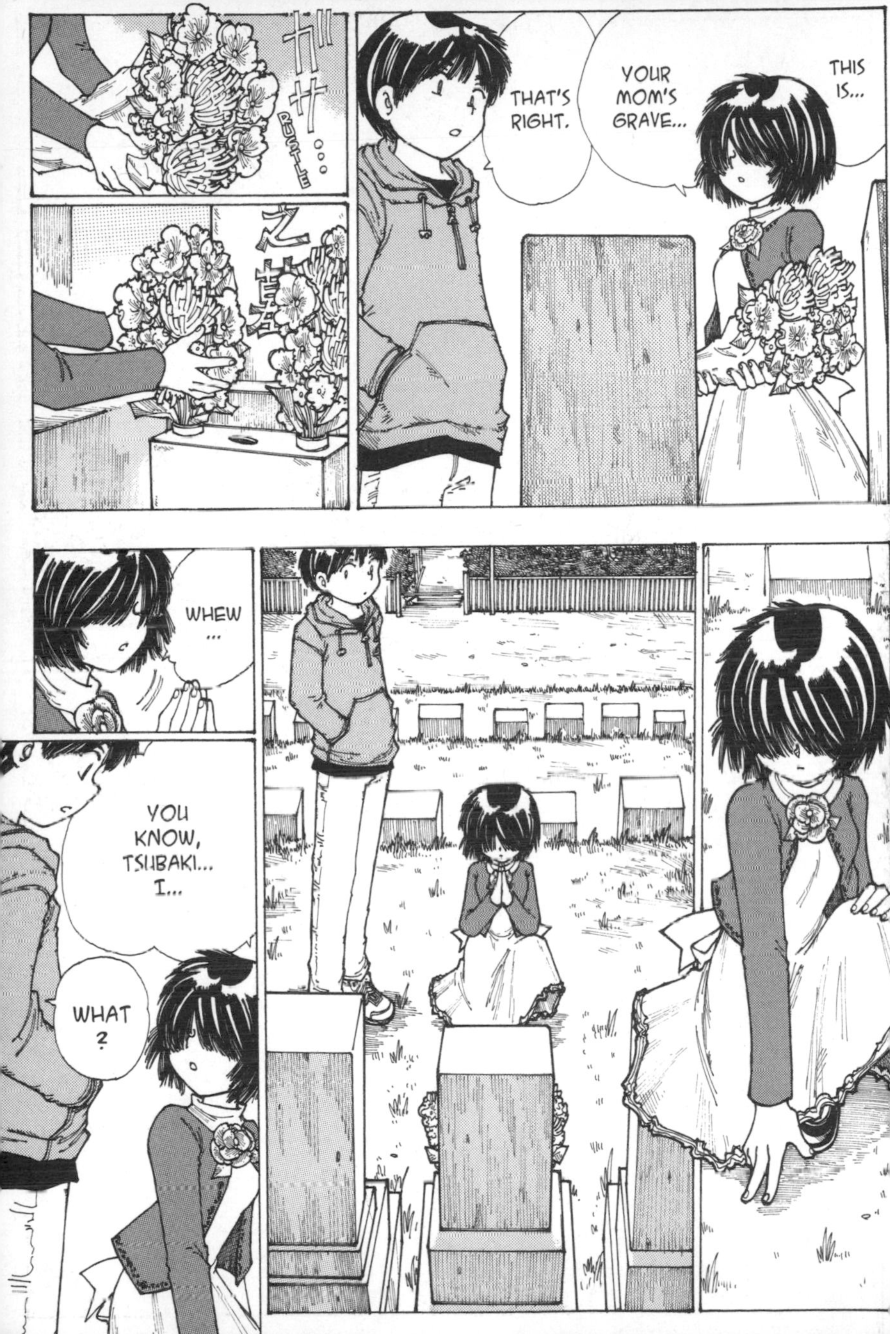
THIS IS...
YOUR MOM'S GRAVE...
THAT'S RIGHT.
ガサ
RUSTLE
之墓
WHEW ...
YOU KNOW, TSUBAKI... I...
WHAT ?

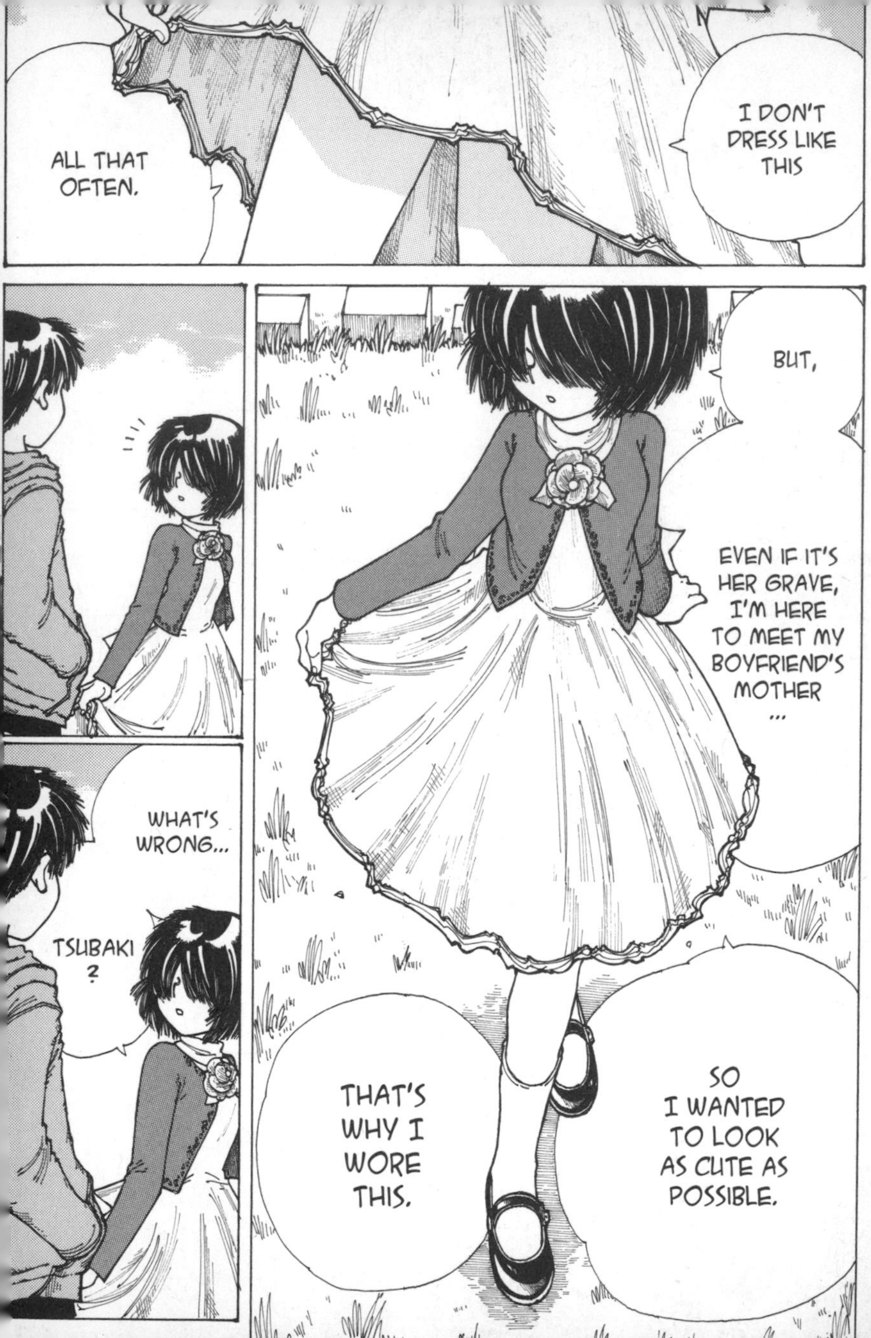
I DON'T DRESS LIKE THIS
ALL THAT OFTEN.
BUT,
EVEN IF IT'S HER GRAVE, I'M HERE TO MEET MY BOYFRIEND'S MOTHER ...
SO I WANTED TO LOOK AS CUTE AS POSSIBLE.
THAT'S WHY I WORE THIS.
WHAT'S WRONG...
TSUBAKI ?

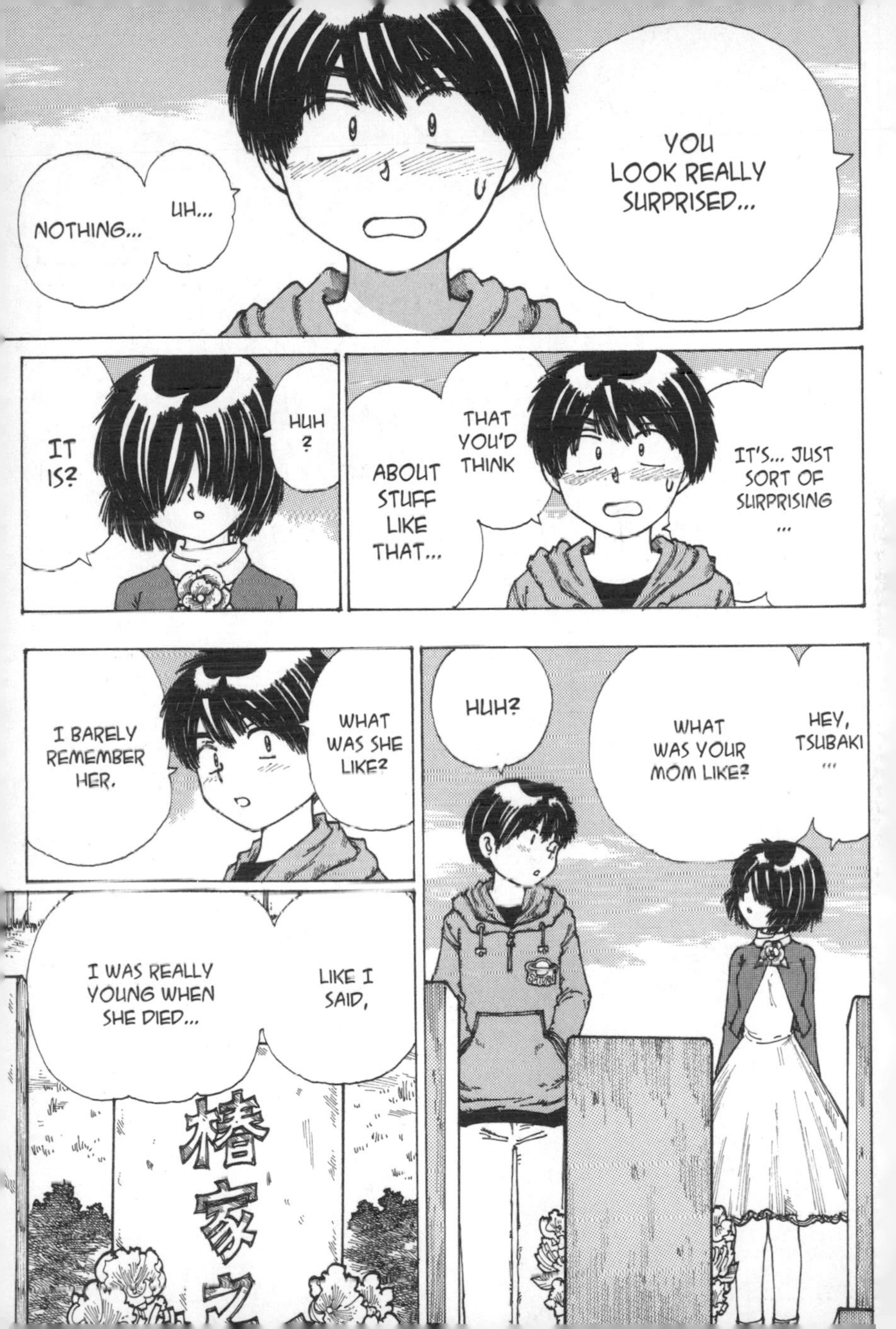
YOU LOOK REALLY SURPRISED...
UH...
NOTHING...
IT'S... JUST SORT OF SURPRISING ...
THAT YOU'D THINK
ABOUT STUFF LIKE THAT...
HUH?
IT IS?
HEY, TSUBAKI ...
WHAT WAS YOUR MOM LIKE?
HUH?
WHAT WAS SHE LIKE?
I BARELY REMEMBER HER.
LIKE I SAID,
I WAS REALLY YOUNG WHEN SHE DIED...
椿家

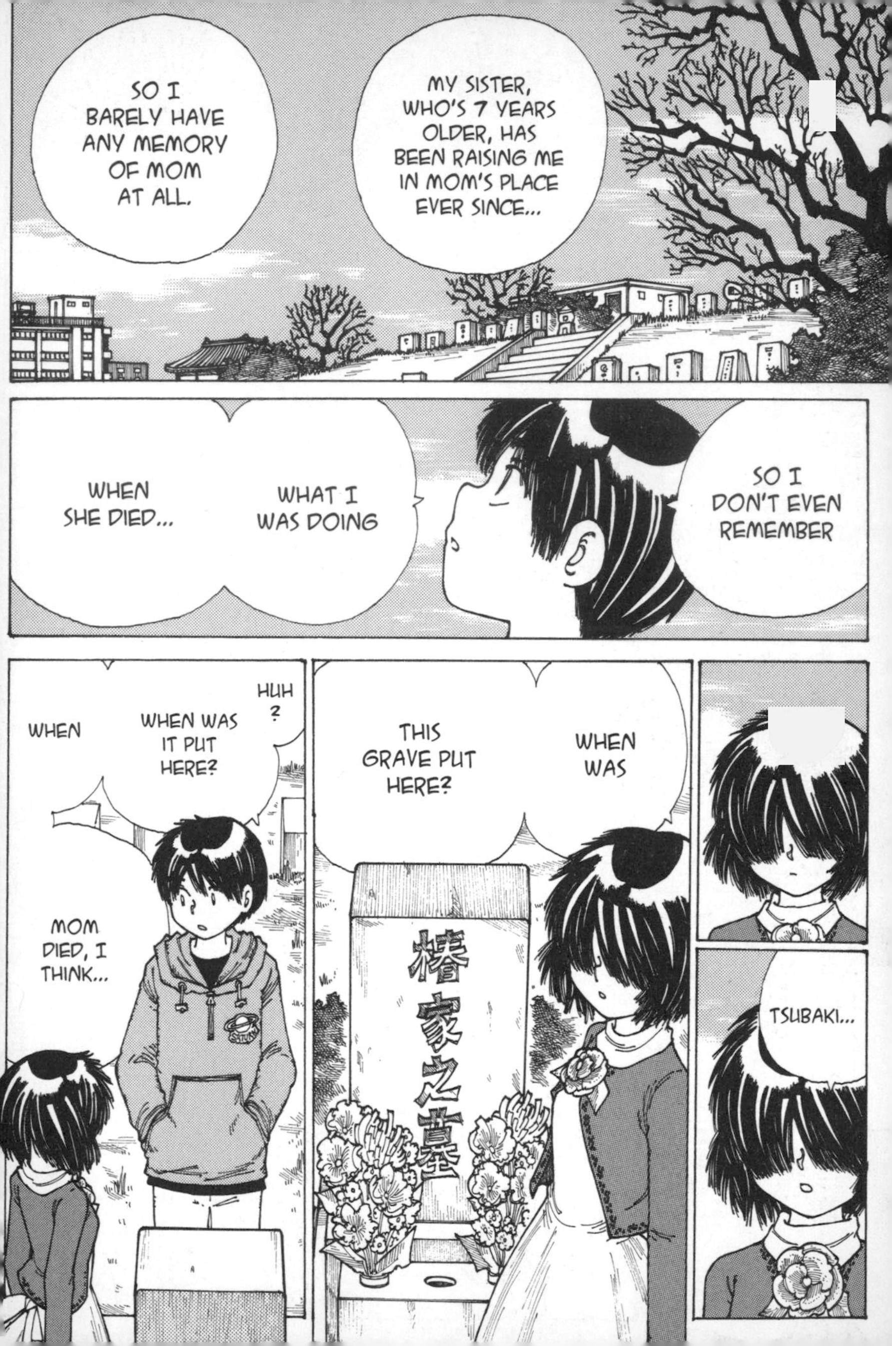
MY SISTER, WHO'S 7 YEARS OLDER, HAS BEEN RAISING ME IN MOM'S PLACE EVER SINCE...
SO I BARELY HAVE ANY MEMORY OF MOM AT ALL.
SO I DON'T EVEN REMEMBER
WHAT I WAS DOING
WHEN SHE DIED...
TSUBAKI...
WHEN WAS
THIS GRAVE PUT HERE?
椿家之墓
HUH?
WHEN WAS IT PUT HERE?
WHEN
MOM DIED, I THINK...

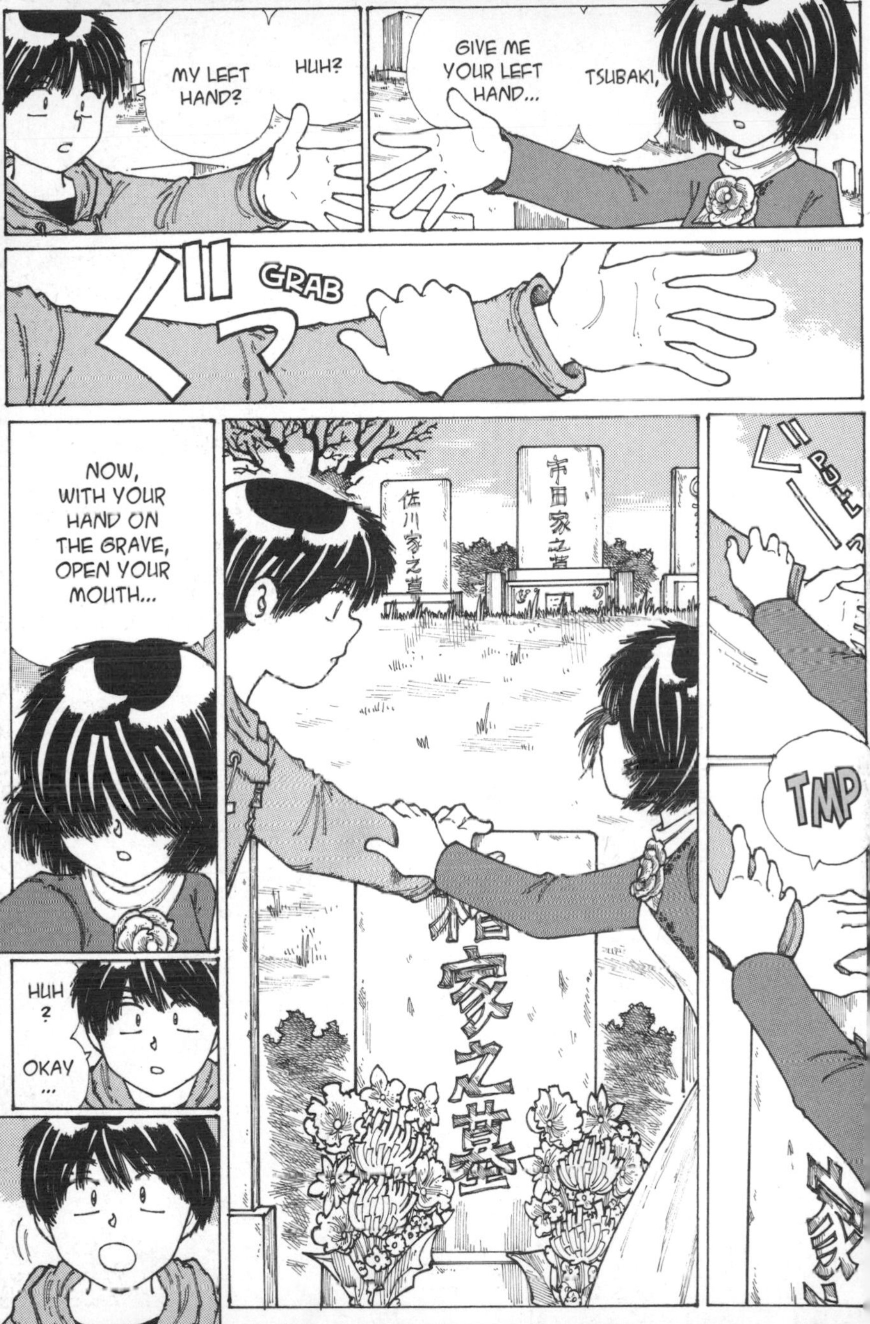
TSUBAKI,
GIVE ME YOUR LEFT HAND...
HUH?
MY LEFT HAND?
ぐっ
GRAB
PULL
TMP
NOW, WITH YOUR HAND ON THE GRAVE, OPEN YOUR MOUTH...
HUH?
OKAY...

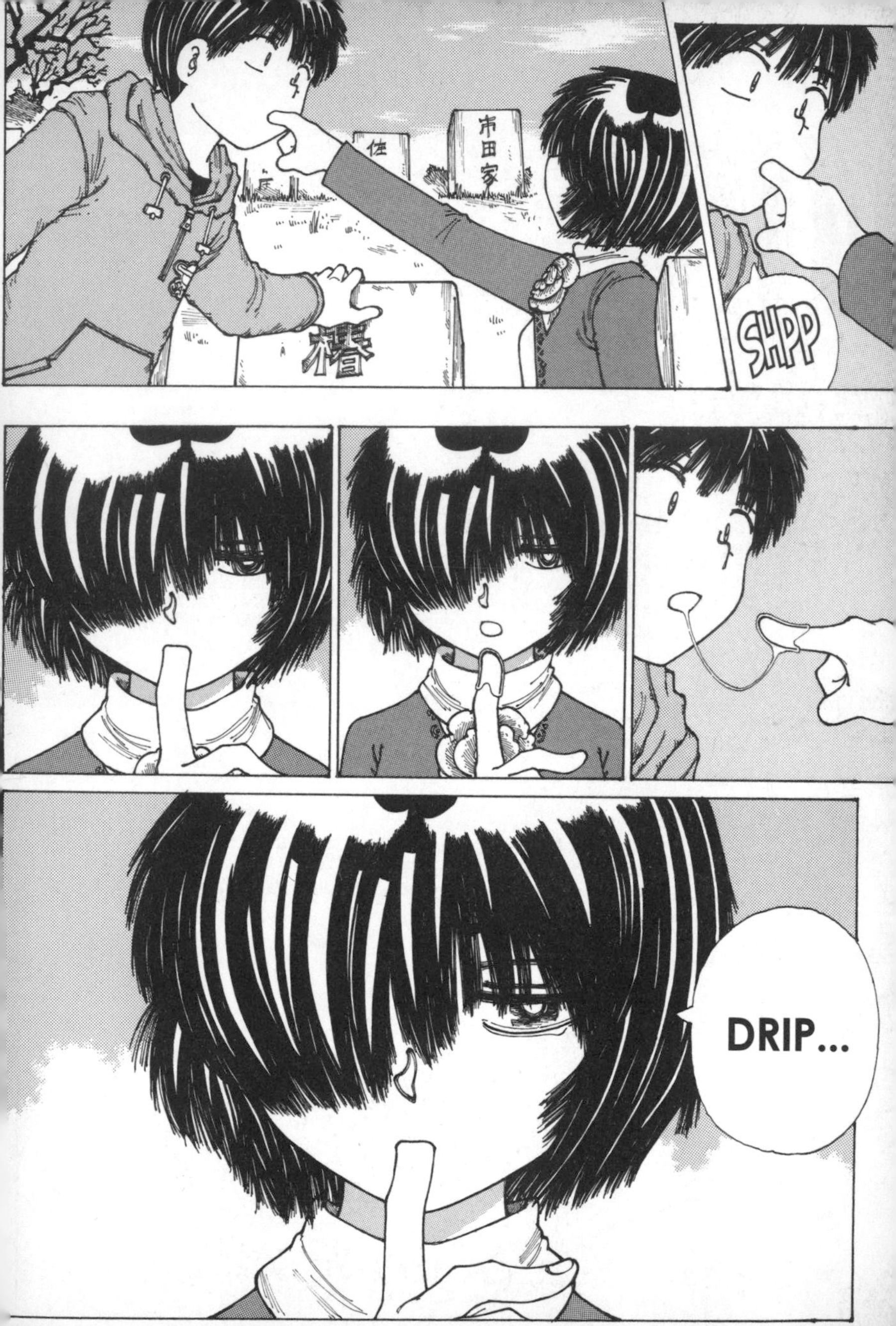
SHPP
DRIP...

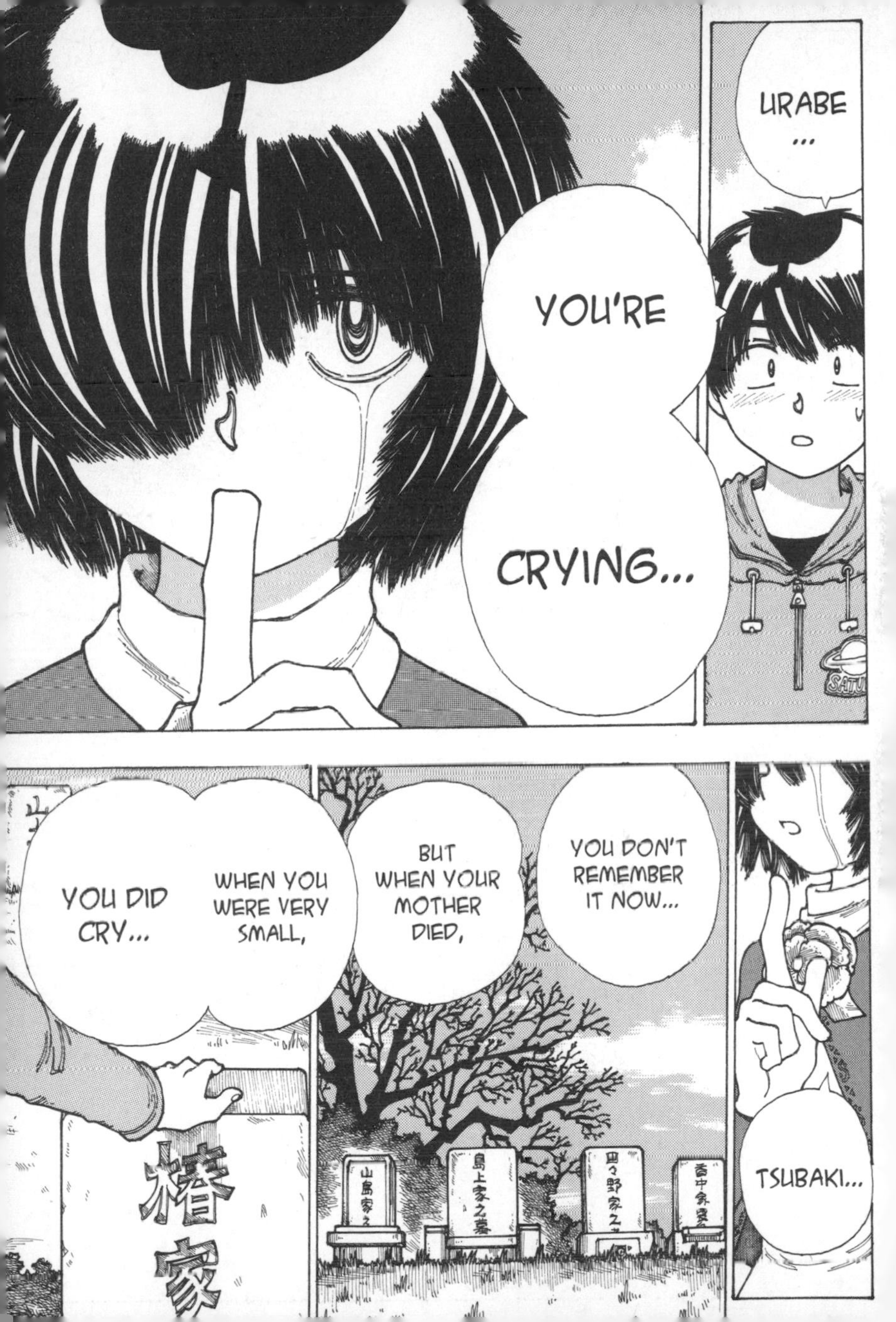
URABE ...
YOU'RE CRYING...
TSUBAKI...
YOU DON'T REMEMBER IT NOW...
BUT WHEN YOUR MOTHER DIED,
WHEN YOU WERE VERY SMALL,
YOU DID CRY...
島上家之墓
椿家

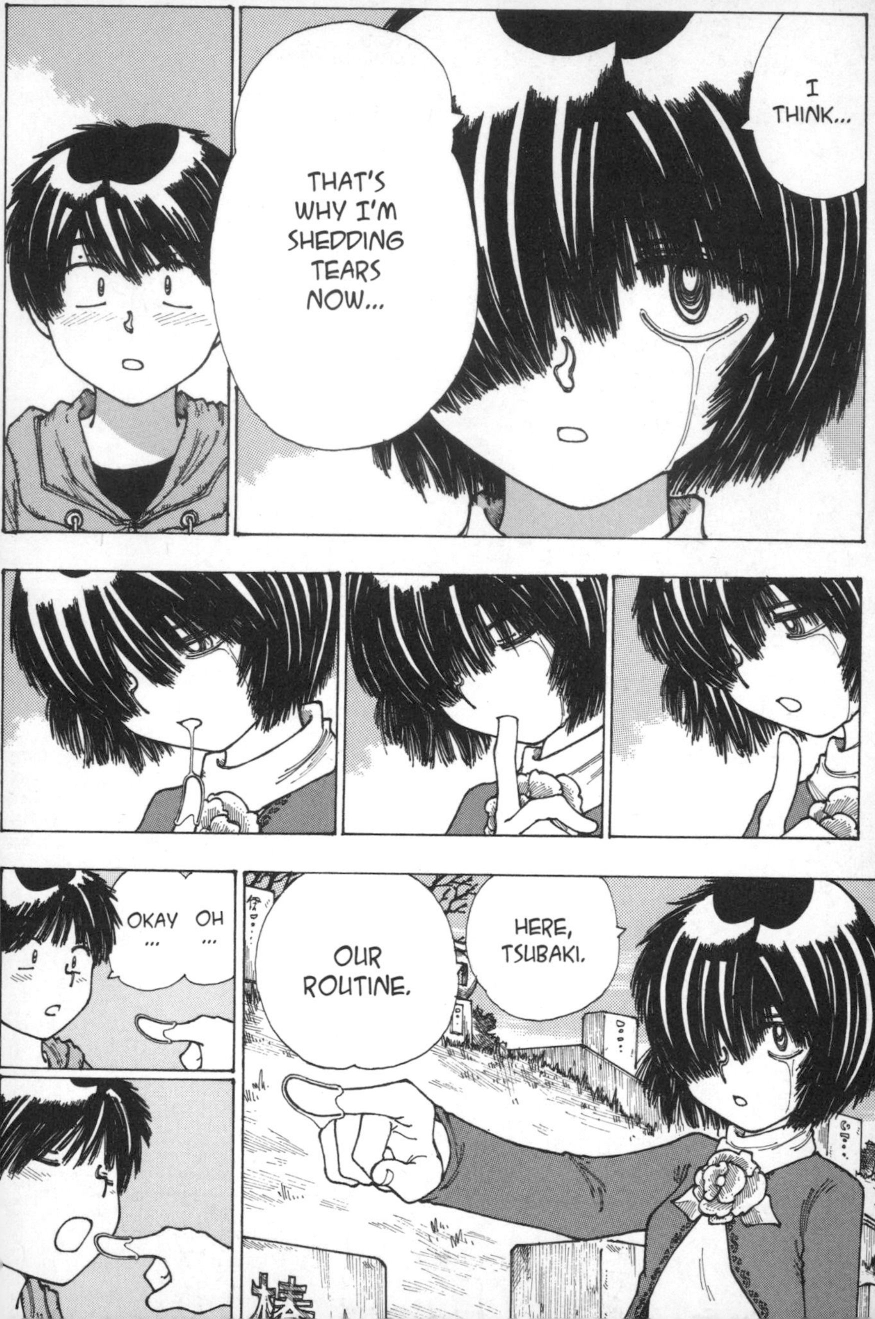
I THINK...
THAT'S WHY I'M SHEDDING TEARS NOW...
HERE, TSUBAKI.
OUR ROUTINE.
OH ...
OKAY ...

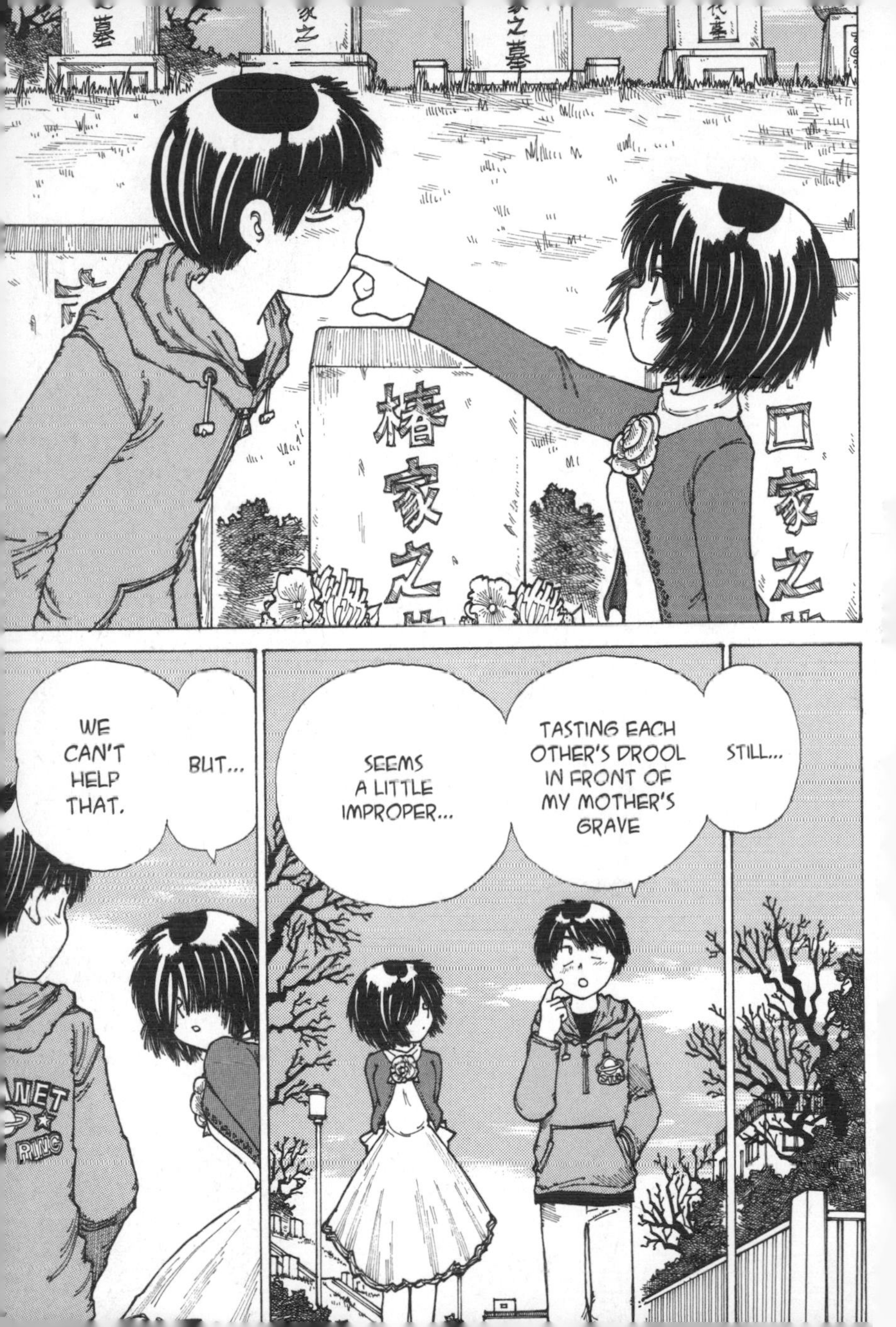
椿家之
STILL...
TASTING EACH OTHER'S DROOL IN FRONT OF MY MOTHER'S GRAVE
SEEMS A LITTLE IMPROPER...
BUT...
WE CAN'T HELP THAT.

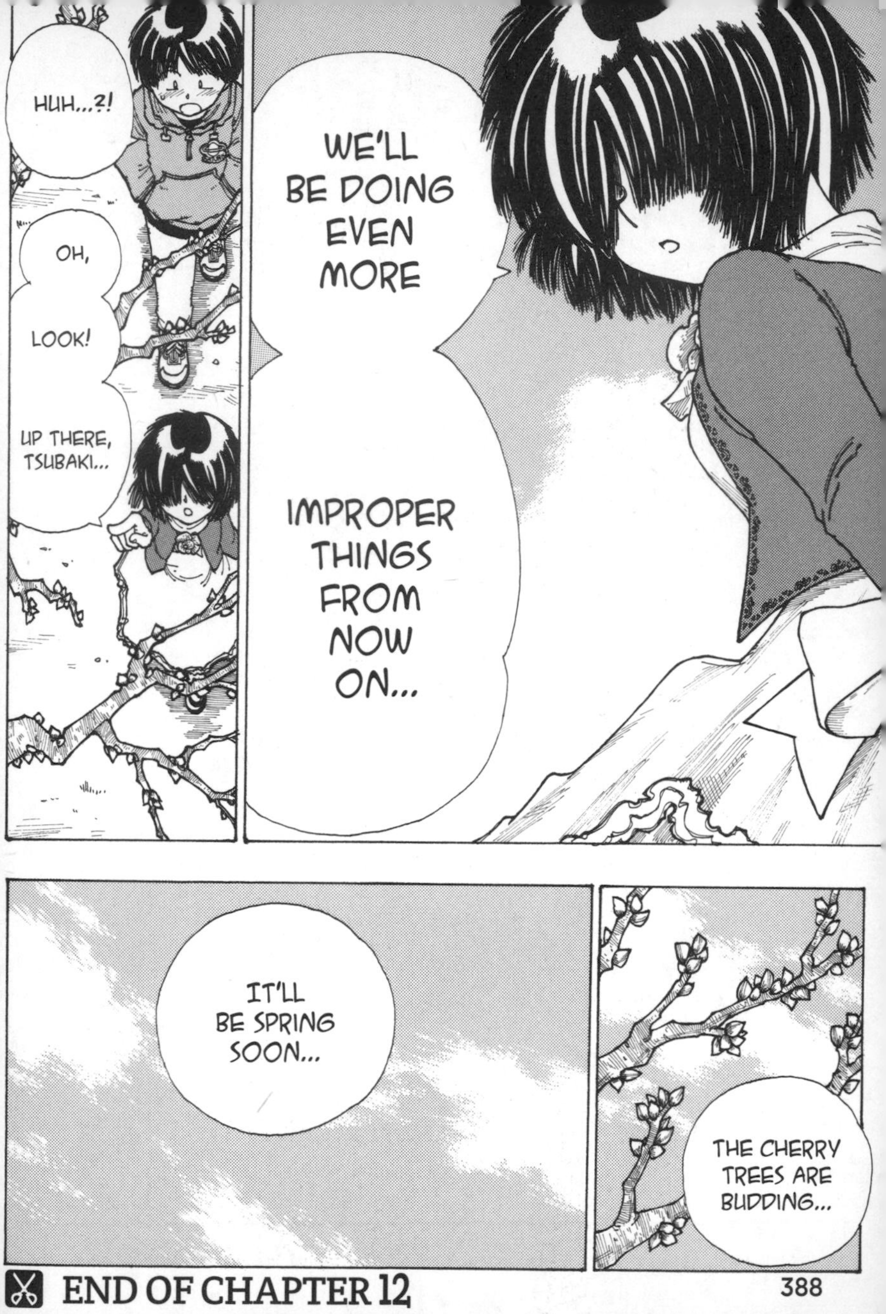
WE'LL BE DOING EVEN MORE IMPROPER THINGS FROM NOW ON...
HUH...?!
N...
OH, LOOK! UP THERE, TSUBAKI...
THE CHERRY TREES ARE BUDDING...
IT'LL BE SPRING SOON...

END OF CHAPTER 12

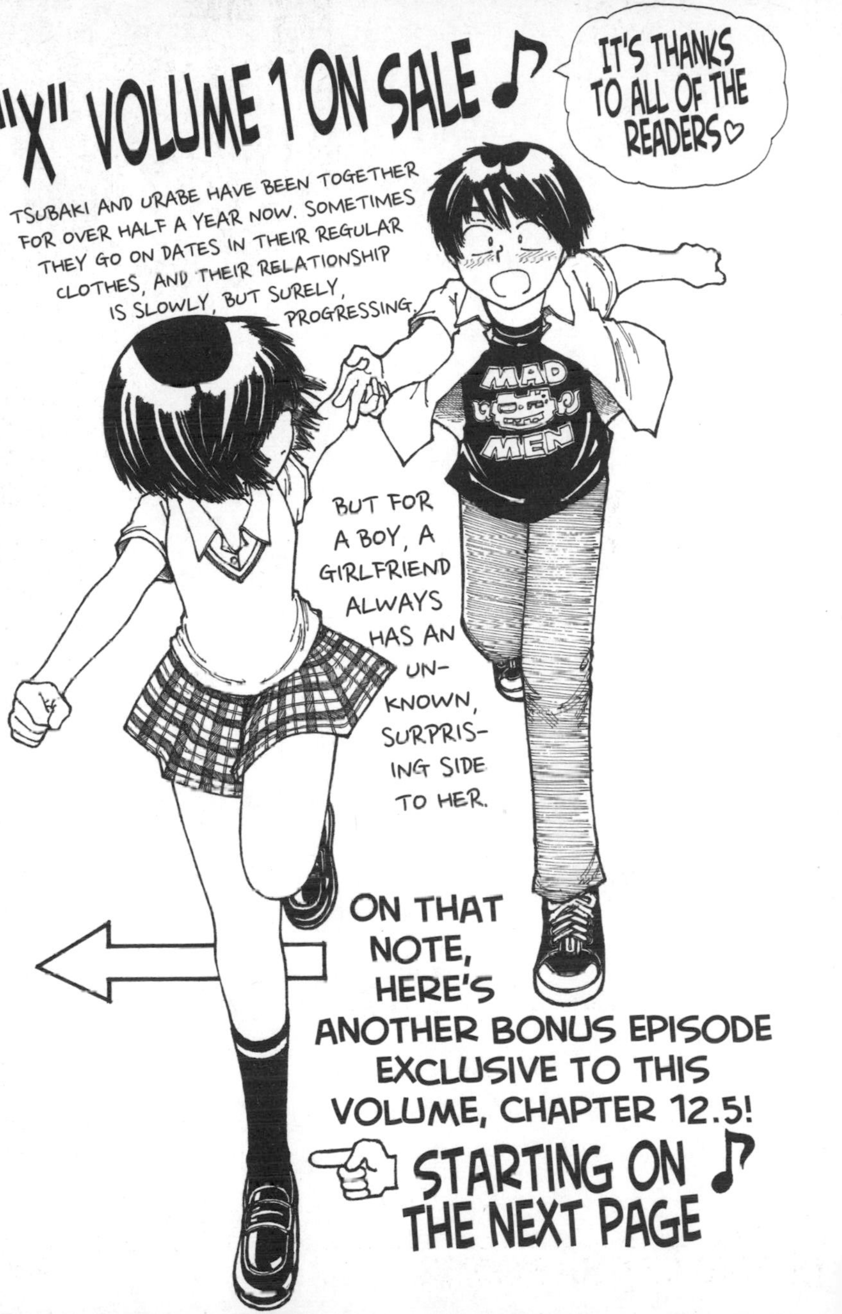
"X" VOLUME 1 ON SALE ♪
IT'S THANKS TO ALL OF THE READERS ♡
TSUBAKI AND URABE HAVE BEEN TOGETHER FOR OVER HALF A YEAR NOW. SOMETIMES THEY GO ON DATES IN THEIR REGULAR CLOTHES, AND THEIR RELATIONSHIP IS SLOWLY, BUT SURELY, PROGRESSING.
MAD MEN
BUT FOR A BOY, A GIRLFRIEND ALWAYS HAS AN UN-KNOWN, SURPRIS-ING SIDE TO HER.
ON THAT NOTE, HERE'S ANOTHER BONUS EPISODE EXCLUSIVE TO THIS VOLUME, CHAPTER 12.5!
STARTING ON THE NEXT PAGE ♪

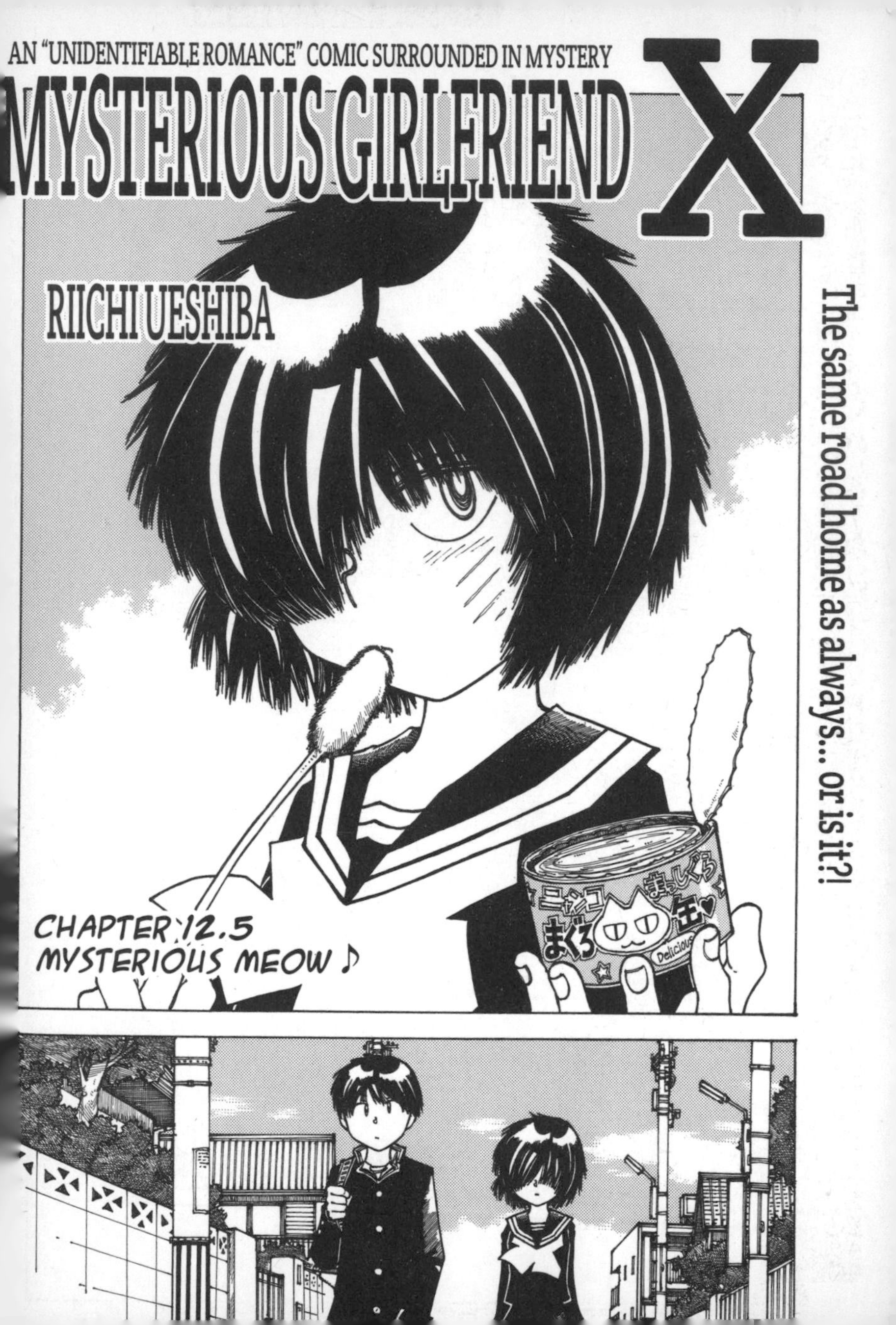
AN "UNIDENTIFIABLE ROMANCE" COMIC SURROUNDED IN MYSTERY
MYSTERIOUS GIRLFRIEND X
RIICHI UESHIBA
The same road home as always... or is it?!
CHAPTER 12.5
MYSTERIOUS MEOW ♪
ニャンコ まっしぐら
まぐろ 缶♥
Delicious

About This Chapter

AKIRA TSUBAKI AND MIKOTO URABE ARE A COUPLE. BUT THEY DO HARDLY ANY OF THE THINGS THAT COUPLES DO. THE ONLY THING THAT COMES CLOSE IS WHEN TSUBAKI TASTES URABE'S DROOL AS THEY WALK HOME FROM SCHOOL TOGETHER. TSUBAKI IS AT THE MERCY OF THE STRANGE URABE EVERY DAY, BUT THE DISTANCE BETWEEN THEM SEEMS TO BE GRADUALLY GETTING SHORTER... WHAT EXCITING MOMENTS AWAIT THEM FROM NOW ON?

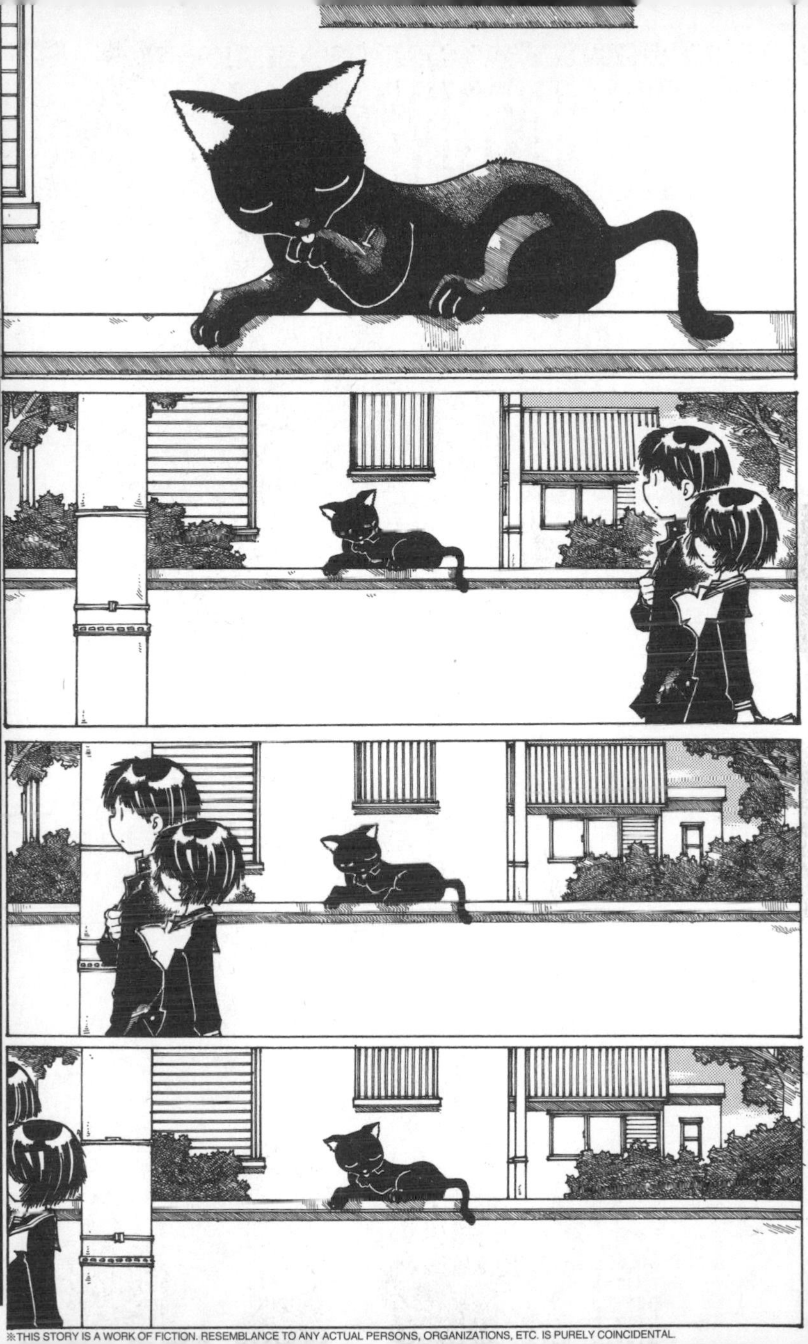

※THIS STORY IS A WORK OF FICTION. RESEMBLANCE TO ANY ACTUAL PERSONS, ORGANIZATIONS, ETC. IS PURELY COINCIDENTAL.

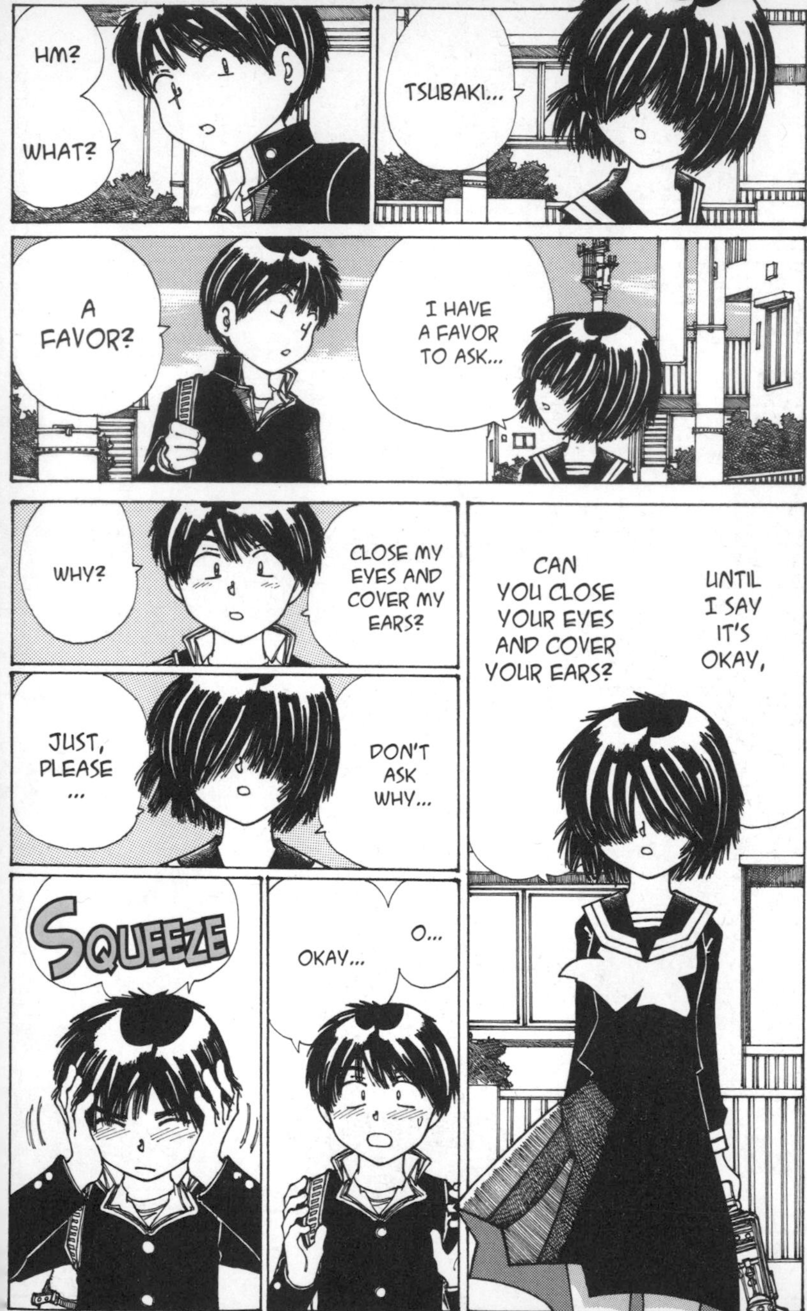
TSUBAKI...
HM?
WHAT?
I HAVE A FAVOR TO ASK...
A FAVOR?
UNTIL I SAY IT'S OKAY,
CAN YOU CLOSE YOUR EYES AND COVER YOUR EARS?
CLOSE MY EYES AND COVER MY EARS?
WHY?
DON'T ASK WHY...
JUST, PLEASE ...
O...
OKAY...
SQUEEZE

MYSTERIOUS GIRLFRIEND X

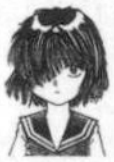

RIICHI UESHIBA

THE BOND BETWEEN TSUBAKI AND URABE IS HER... AN "UNIDENTIFIABLE ROMANCE" COMIC SURROUNDED IN MYSTERY!!

The Latest from the Author

Riichi Ueshiba

RECENTLY, I'VE BEEN GETTING INTO "T.P. BON (TIME PATROL BON)" BY FUJIO F. FUJIKO. I SPENT A LOT OF TIME ABSORBED IN THE COMIC WHEN I WAS IN 5TH AND 6TH GRADE, BUT I READ IT AGAIN NOT LONG AGO AND FELT MY FASCINATION COME BACK TO LIFE. BOTH OF BON'S FEMALE PARTNERS, REAM IN PART 1 AND YUMIKO IN PART 2, WERE CHARMING IN THEIR OWN WAYS. I REALLY LIKE IT.

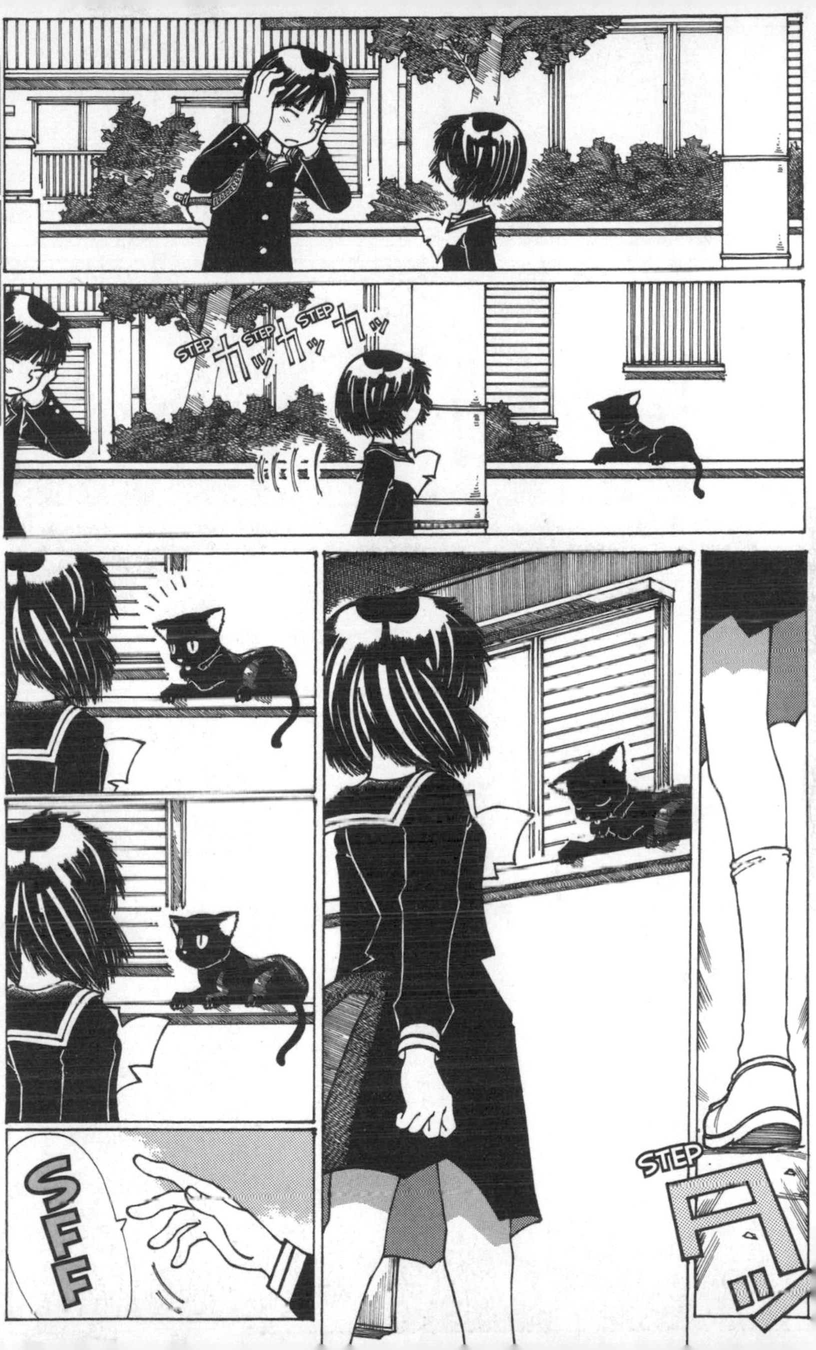
STEP
STEP
STEP
STEP
SFF

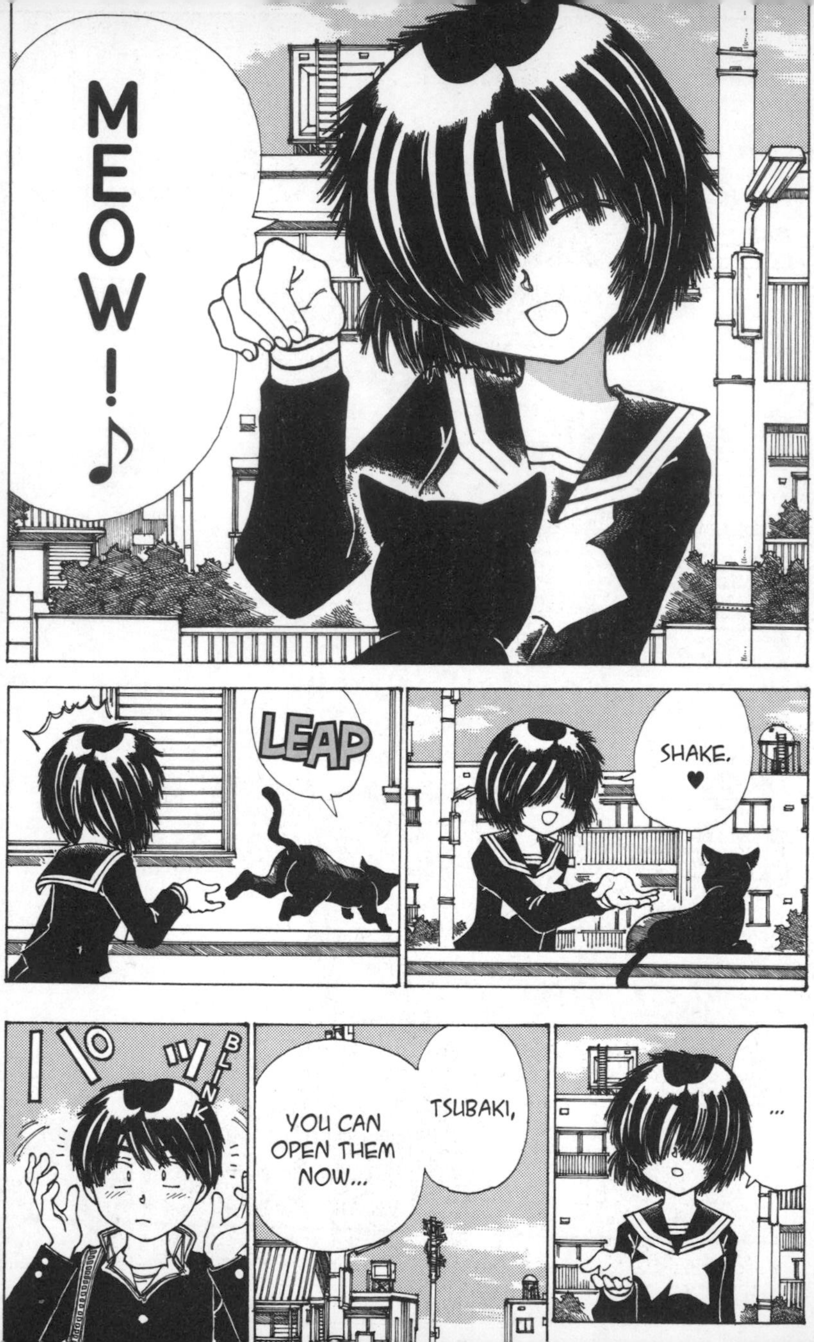
MEOW!♪
SHAKE. ♥
LEAP
...
TSUBAKI,
YOU CAN OPEN THEM NOW...
BLINK

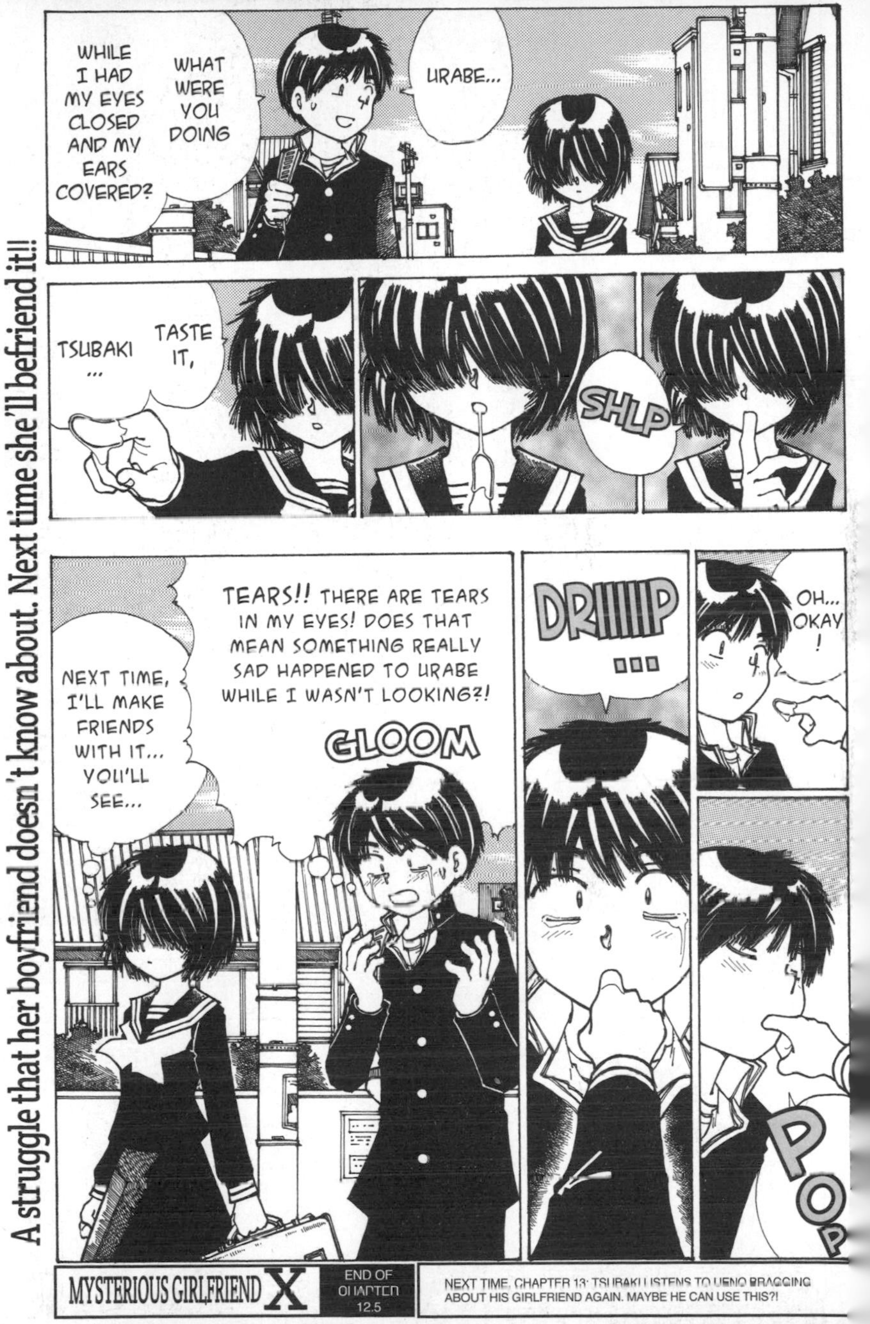
URABE...
WHAT WERE YOU DOING
WHILE I HAD MY EYES CLOSED AND MY EARS COVERED?
SHLP
TASTE IT,
TSUBAKI...
OH... OKAY!
POP
DRIIIIP
...
TEARS!! THERE ARE TEARS IN MY EYES! DOES THAT MEAN SOMETHING REALLY SAD HAPPENED TO URABE WHILE I WASN'T LOOKING?!
NEXT TIME, I'LL MAKE FRIENDS WITH IT... YOU'LL SEE...
GLOOM

A struggle that her boyfriend doesn't know about. Next time she'll befriend it!!

MYSTERIOUS GIRLFRIEND X

END OF CHAPTER 12.5

NEXT TIME, CHAPTER 13: TSUBAKI LISTENS TO UENO BRAGGING ABOUT HIS GIRLFRIEND AGAIN. MAYBE HE CAN USE THIS?!

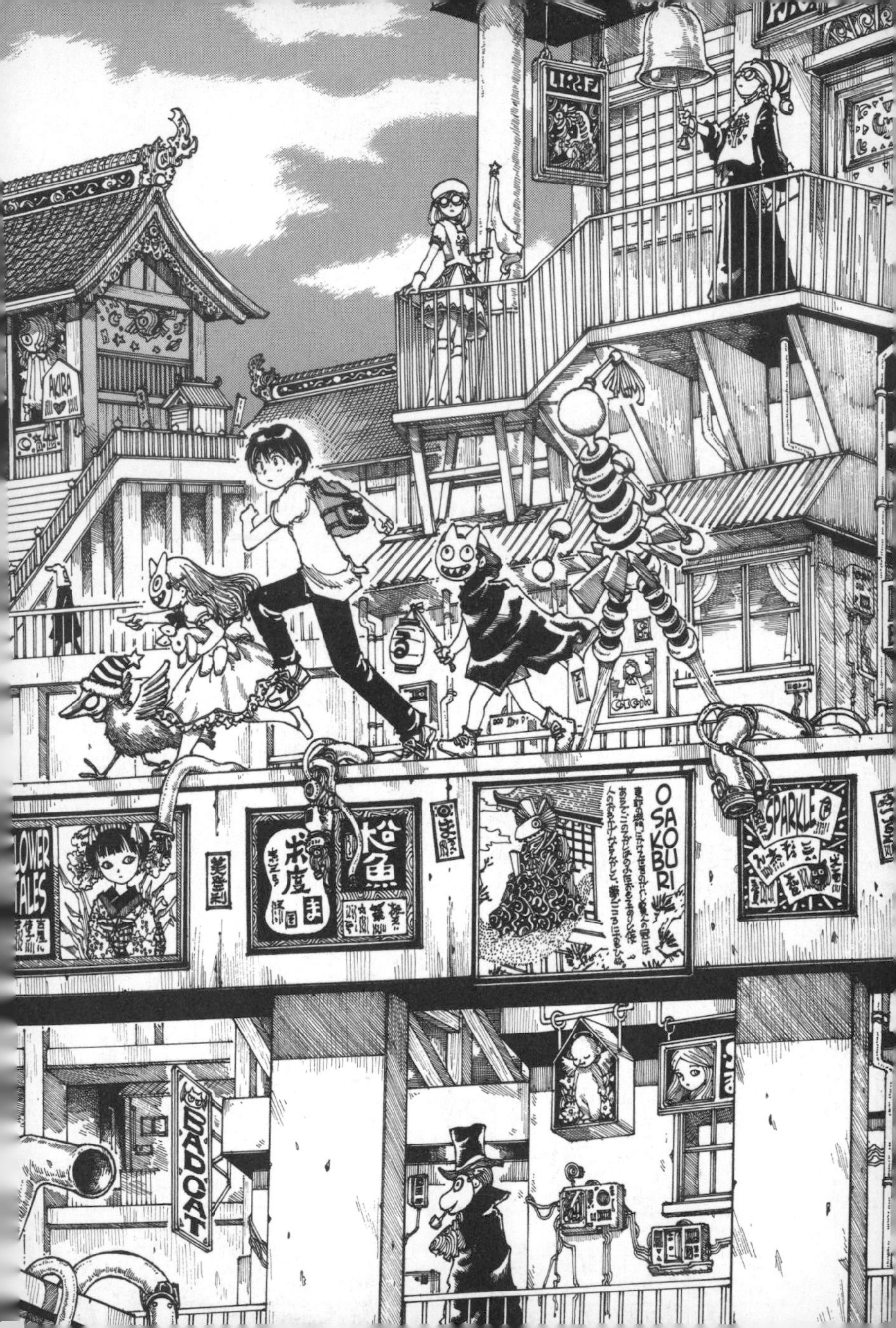
AKIRA
LOWER
TALES
る
O SAKOBURI
SPARKLE
BAD CAT

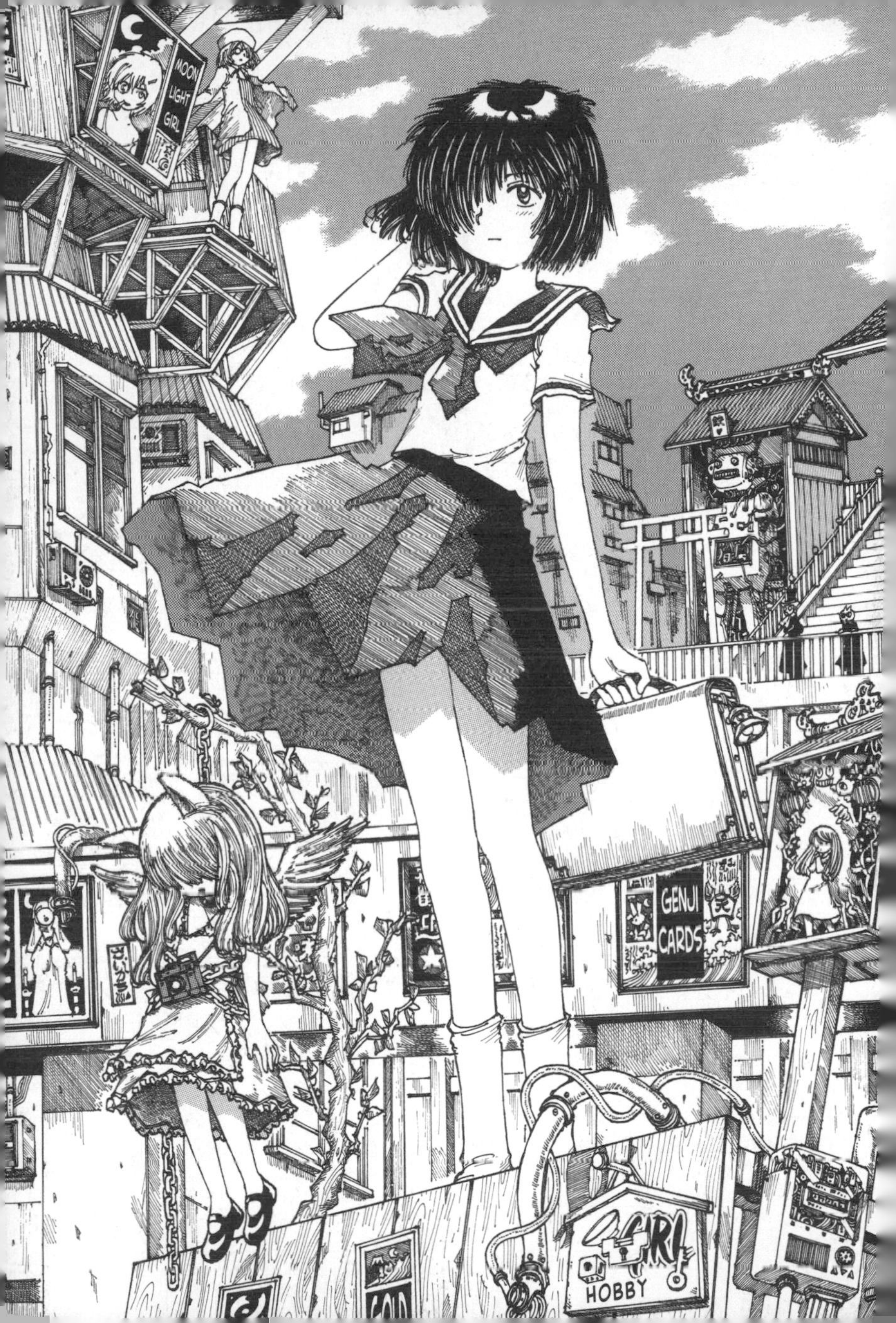
MOON LIGHT GIRL
GENJI CARDS
HOBBY

The protagonist of "Mysterious Girlfriend X," Akira Tsubaki, is a 17-year-old boy. He has a girlfriend named Mikoto Urabe, but I'm sure there are more 17-year-old boys in this world without girlfriends than there are 17-year-old boys with girlfriends. Naturally, I didn't have a girlfriend when I was 17, either. To a boy of 17, at the height of adolescence, girlfriends are strange and mysterious beings that can be overwhelming in many ways. If I'd had a girlfriend when I was 17, of course I would've been happy, but now, as an adult, I think I would have been just as much bewildered, if not more. And when I think of it that way, I can't help thinking that a boy of 17 getting a girlfriend is actually quite similar to a "robot anime" scenario. When a boy becomes the pilot of a giant, overwhelming robot, every day is filled with both joy and fear. And when a boy starts a relationship with the overwhelming presence that is a girl, every day is filled with joy and bewilderment. In the sense that both involve a boy encountering a new, unknown entity and running helter-skelter in the new world that opens up to him, I think the two scenarios are very similar.

Well, that may be a rather forced interpretation, but I did have that in mind when I gave the catch copy of "an unidentifiable romance comic" to this story when serialization began. But I personally work under the complacent conviction that the comic known as "Mysterious Girlfriend X" is actually my first attempt at a robot anime. What do you think?

NE DAY, UGUST 2006 RIICHI ESHIBA

AD CAT

POP
I-I DON'T KNOW WHY... BUT AFTER TASTING URABE'S DROOL TODAY, MY HEART IS POUNDING...
BA-DUM
BA-DUM
SEE YOU TOMORROW, URABE!
THAT'S SURPRISING...
I DIDN'T KNOW TSUBAKI HAD A TASTE FOR THIS KIND OF THING...
BA-DUM
BA-DUM
BA-DUM
SHE'S ACTUALLY BEEN WEARING GLASSES ALL DAY.
SNUG
BA-DUM

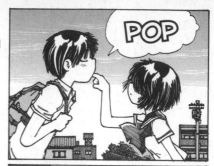

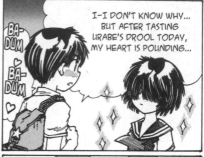

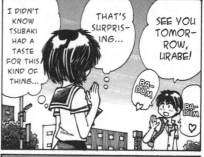

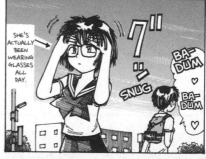

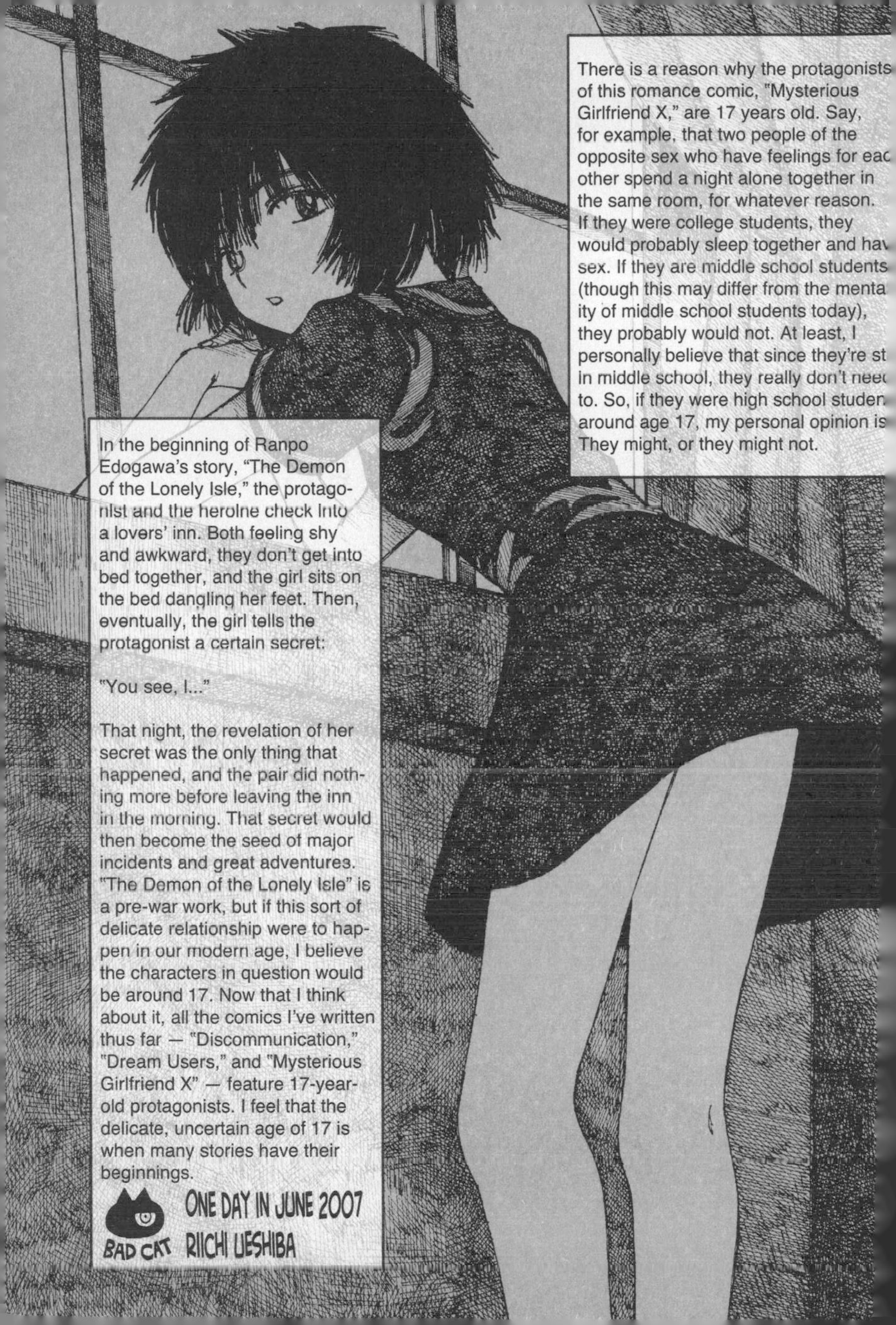

There is a reason why the protagonists of this romance comic, "Mysterious Girlfriend X," are 17 years old. Say, for example, that two people of the opposite sex who have feelings for eac other spend a night alone together in the same room, for whatever reason. If they were college students, they would probably sleep together and hav sex. If they are middle school students (though this may differ from the menta ity of middle school students today), they probably would not. At least, I personally believe that since they're st in middle school, they really don't neec to. So, if they were high school studen around age 17, my personal opinion is They might, or they might not.

In the beginning of Ranpo Edogawa's story, "The Demon of the Lonely Isle," the protagonist and the heroine check into a lovers' inn. Both feeling shy and awkward, they don't get into bed together, and the girl sits on the bed dangling her feet. Then, eventually, the girl tells the protagonist a certain secret:

"You see, I..."

That night, the revelation of her secret was the only thing that happened, and the pair did nothing more before leaving the inn in the morning. That secret would then become the seed of major incidents and great adventures. "The Demon of the Lonely Isle" is a pre-war work, but if this sort of delicate relationship were to happen in our modern age, I believe the characters in question would be around 17. Now that I think about it, all the comics I've written thus far — "Discommunication," "Dream Users," and "Mysterious Girlfriend X" — feature 17-year-old protagonists. I feel that the delicate, uncertain age of 17 is when many stories have their beginnings.

BAD CAT

ONE DAY IN JUNE 2007
RIICHI UESHIBA

SHE'S A MYSTERY, SHE'S ALL MYSTERY BUT I STILL LOVE HER!!

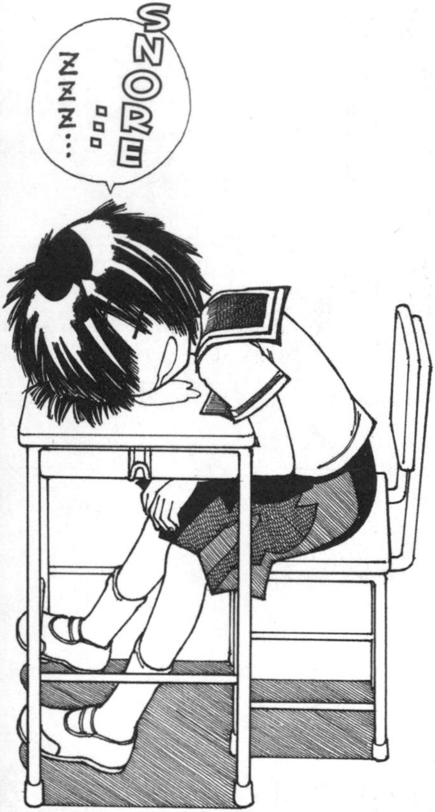
SNORE...
ZZZ...

DON'T YOU THINK A GIRL WHO DROOLS WHEN SHE FALLS ASLEEP IS CUTE? WELL, THIS IS A COMIC ABOUT THAT SORT OF GIRL.

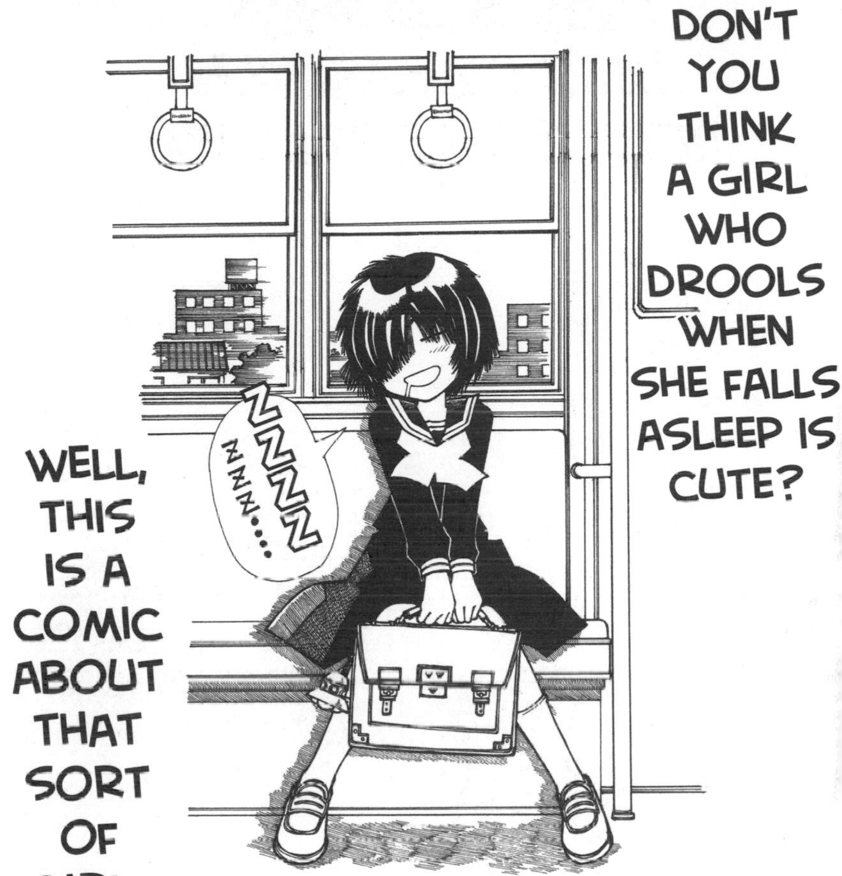
DON'T YOU THINK A GIRL WHO DROOLS WHEN SHE FALLS ASLEEP IS CUTE?
ZZZZ ZZZZ....
WELL, THIS IS A COMIC ABOUT THAT SORT OF GIRL.

PLEASE LOOK FORWARD TO VOLUME 2.

MYSTERIOUS GIRLFRIEND X, VOLUME 1

A Vertical Comics Edition

Translation: Rebecca Cottrill
Production: Risa Cho
          Anthony Quintessenza

© 2016 Riichi Ueshiba. All rights reserved.
First published in Japan in 2006-07 by Kodansha, Ltd., Tokyo
Publication rights for this English edition arranged through Kodansha, Ltd., Tokyo
English language version produced by Vertical, Inc., New York

Published by Vertical, Inc., New York

Originally published in Japanese as *Nazo no Kanojo X 1 & 2* by Kodansha, Ltd., 2006-07
Nazo no Kanojo X first serialized in *Afternoon*, Kodansha, Ltd., 2004, 2006-2014

This is a work of fiction.

ISBN: 978-1-942993-45-2

Manufactured in Canada

First Edition

Vertical, Inc.
451 Park Avenue South
7th Floor
New York, NY 10016
www.vertical-comics.com

Vertical books are distributed through Penguin-Random House Publisher Services.